BASIC STATICS
AND
STRESS
ANALYSIS

SI METRIC

BASIC
STATICS
AND
STRESS
ANALYSIS

SI METRIC

G. WAYNE BROWN

Cambrian College
Sudbury, Ontario

McGraw-Hill Ryerson Limited

Toronto Montréal New York Auckland Bogotá Cairo Guatemala
Hamburg Johannesburg Lisbon London Madrid Mexico New Delhi
Panama Paris San Juan São Paulo Singapore Sydney Tokyo

BASIC STATICS AND STRESS ANALYSIS

ISBN 0-07-092374-4

1 2 3 4 5 6 7 8 9 0 D 4 3 2 1 0 9 8 7 6 5

Printed and bound in Canada by John Deyell Company

Care has been taken to trace ownership of copyright material
contained in this text. The publishers will gladly take any
information that will enable them to rectify any reference or credit in
subsequent editions.

Canadian Cataloguing in Publication Data

Brown, G. Wayne
    Basic statics and stress analysis

Includes index.
ISBN 0-07-092374-4

1. Statics. 2. Strains and stresses. 3. Strength of materials.
I. Title.

TA351.B76 1985   620.1'03 C85-098400-9

CONTENTS

PREFACE

There is an old Chinese proverb that says
> I hear and I forget
> I see and I remember
> I do and I understand

In many years of teaching mechanics, the truth of this proverb has been very apparent. Even as a student, when I had the good fortune to have some of the best mechanics teachers, I found that the only method for really understanding mechanics was "doing."

The organization of this book is based on the Chinese proverb. The text material itself is an overview giving the basic information necessary to describe the concept being discussed. This is the equivalent of the "hear" part of the proverb, and regrettably, also the "forget."

Accompanying each concept discussion is a variety of example problems ranging from simple to moderately complex. The simple problems help students sort out such things as terminology, symbols and units, and are part of the process of walking before running. The more complex problems show applications and provide the student with guidance in solving problems with multiple steps. This is the "see" part.

Students learn by doing problems. A large number of problems have been included, ranging from very easy to moderately difficult. If a student has trouble with one problem, there will usually be another one of a similar form which can be tackled after obtaining assistance with the first one. This permits the student to build confidence. The eager and ambitious student will find that there are sufficient problems to obtain plenty of practice without recourse to other texts. Many students have found the material in its draft form to be exceedingly useful for self-study. The problems are obviously the "do."

As implied by the title, the emphasis is on the development of expertise in working with basic concepts in statics and stress analysis, on the premise that faster progress will be made in the design subjects if the basic concepts have been thoroughly mastered. Practical applications are illustrated where possible in the text, but it does not claim to be a design text.

In an attempt to make things simpler for students, one type of problem frequently found in similar texts has been virtually eliminated. This is the problem that refers the student to a series of previous problems to collect the necessary information for the problem at hand. It is not practical to eliminate reference to various tables, but wherever possible, all the basic problem information is contained in the problem statement.

The introduction of the SI system of measurement provides everyone with an excellent opportunity to do some housecleaning on symbols, definitions and style. With this objective in mind, a concerted effort has been made to have the style, symbols and definitions used follow those set out in recognized sources such as are prepared by the Canadian Standards Association and the American Society for Testing and Materials.

Over the lengthy period of time that this project has taken, a number of people have provided assistance. Many of my students have used a draft version of this text, and the constructive criticism and positive comments have been very helpful. Several of my colleagues have provided encouragement, and the critical review of several chapters of the stress analysis section by W. A. Este was particularly useful. My wife, Professor Christine Maxwell, reviewed the manuscript and checked example problem calculations. The various editors and staff at McGraw-Hill Ryerson whom I have outlasted must be thanked for their patience. Even more important, I appreciate the fact that they allowed me to have much influence on the format of the finished text.

Although I have tried very hard to make the text error-free, I am fallible. It would be very much appreciated if users of the text would contact me through the publisher to advise me of any errors.

G. Wayne Brown

BASIC
STATICS
AND
STRESS
ANALYSIS

SI METRIC

1 INTRODUCTION

1-1 WHAT IS STATICS?

Statics is the study of bodies in *equilibrium*. Equilibrium is defined as the condition of a body when it is at rest or when it is in uniform motion in a straight line. The study of bodies that are not in equilibrium is called *dynamics*. The combined study of statics and dynamics is called *mechanics*, which is really a branch of physics, the study of which dates back to the ancient Greek, Archimedes. The emphasis in this book will be on the application of mechanics to real problems. This study is based on the work of Isaac Newton, who is responsible for developing mechanics in its present form.

It will be assumed that all bodies dealt with in the study of mechanics are rigid bodies. No body is perfectly rigid, but this premise will not introduce significant errors in calculations. When the deformation of bodies is considered, *stress analysis*, or strength of materials, is being studied. The study of stress analysis is an application of the principles of statics.

1-2 APPLICATIONS OF STATICS

In many technical areas, statics is the basic building block for a very large number of other subjects, all of which depend on an understanding of statics to develop their concepts. Figure 1-1 is a flow chart of subjects that depend directly or indirectly on a good understanding of statics for their development. Normally, no one student would take all of the subjects shown. However, depending on whether the student is studying civil, mechanical, electronics, electrical, architectural, mining or aeronautical technology, the student will study many of the subjects shown in the figure.

Figure 1-2 further illustrates places where the principles of mechanics are applied. The design of the crane boom, the cable mechanism and the engine all depend on a knowledge of statics as well as dynamics and stress analysis and fluid mechanics. The latter subjects can be mastered successfully only with a thorough understanding of statics. The strength of the soil on which the

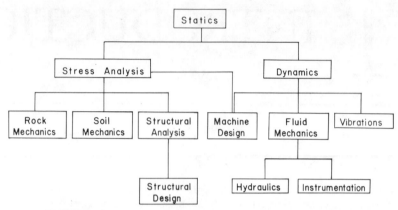

FIGURE 1-1

FIGURE 1-2 Both the crane and the building illustrate a multitude of areas of application of the principles of statics. *Photo courtesy of Northwest Engineering.*

crane rests can be analyzed using the principles of soil mechanics, which is based on the principles of statics. The design of the building frame depends on a combination of structural analysis and stress analysis, both of which are based on statics.

1-3 PROBLEM SOLUTIONS

There are basically two ways in which problems in statics may be solved. The analytical method depends on using the principles of mathematics to describe relationships between forces, usually by setting up one or more equations to be solved. In the graphical method, a drawing is made to scale to represent the forces, and from this drawing other forces can be determined. The approach that will be used here is the analytical method. However, where practical, the graphical method will also be described. It is recommended that both methods be used, with the one being a check on the other.

Regardless of which method is chosen for solving a problem, the importance of neat, well-organized calculations cannot be overemphasized. Whether in the classroom or industry, someone is likely to check most calculations, because mistakes cost time and money. Although one should check one's own work, one should also make certain that it is in such a form that someone else may quickly and easily check the work as well. Remember that whether you are talking about an impression created by a person or the quality of work that one does, it is appearance that creates the first impression. Good appearance, whether in a person or a set of notes, never goes out of style.

Throughout this text you will find a large number of example problems. The solution to each problem is written in regular type and contains the minimum information that should be included in a problem solution. Since a few words of explanation are often helpful in an example problem, these comments, which should aid in your understanding of the solution, are printed in *italics*. These italicized comments do not normally form part of the solution.

In following the advice previously given, many example problems will contain a graphical check, so that the student may become familiar with both the graphical and analytical procedures, as well as the example of performing the check on one's own work.

1-4 SYSTEME INTERNATIONAL

As far as possible, this text will conform to the *Système international d'unités*, commonly known as the SI system of units. The SI-base units that will be used are the metre (m) as the unit of length, the kilogram (kg) as the unit of mass, and the second (s) as the unit of time. Other units that will be used are derived from these three. In mechanics, which deals with forces, the unit for force is the newton (N), which is the force that, when applied to a body having a mass of one kilogram, gives the body an acceleration of one metre per second squared. In terms of base units, the newton has units of kg·m/s². Additional units will be ex plained as they are introduced.

The SI system includes a number of prefixes that reduce the quantity of digits required to express very large or very small quantities. Those prefixes that will be of use in mechanics are given in Table 1-1. Although the system contains many other prefixes, the ones in the table are the ones that will be utilized in this text.

TABLE 1-1   COMMON SI PREFIXES

Name	Symbol	Meaning	Multiplier
giga	G	one thousand million	1 000 000 000
mega	M	one million	1 000 000
kilo	k	one thousand	1 000
milli	m	one thousandth	0.001
micro	μ	one millionth	0.000 001

Generally, the standard engineering practice is to dimension drawings using millimetres (mm) as the units. If units other than mm are used, the unit should be shown along with the dimension. Thus, drawings where no units are shown are dimensioned in mm.

One other important aspect of SI is that much of the notation is standardized to minimize confusion. For instance, the upper-case M means mega, and never milli, which is represented by the lowercase m. In writing numbers there are several simple rules that should also be observed. If the number being written is less than one, there should always be a zero placed to the left of the decimal marker; for example 0.315 is correct, but .315 is poor form. Another format rule is that groups of three digits to the left or right of the decimal marker are to be separated by a space. For example, 57 832 is preferred to 57832 or 57,832, and 8.707 36 is the correct form while 8.70736 and 8.707,36 are poor form. In the case of four digits to the left or right of the decimal marker, the use of the space is optional, unless the number is in a column, in which case the digit spacing should be consistent within the column.

1-5   CHECKING WITH UNITS

Ultimately, the principles of statics will be used on the job by most people who study statics, and since errors cost money, and may even cost an employee a job, it is important to develop the practice of checking your own work to minimize errors. One method of checking is to make certain that the units in a problem solution are compatible with the given information and the equations used in the solution.

For instance, in a calculation for moment the units would usually be N·m (newton metres). As will be studied in Chap. 2, the moment can be obtained from

$$M_A = Fd$$

where M_A is the moment in N·m about an axis through A,
    F is the force causing the moment, and
    d is the perpendicular distance from the axis of rotation A
        to the line of action of the force.

If, in the given information, the moment was caused by the effect of gravity on a mass of 25 kg at a perpendicular distance of 75 mm from the axis of rotation, the units obtained would be:

$$N·m = kg × mm$$

This is certainly not a valid equation, and one should check the units being used. For instance, kg is not a force unit, and if the units of moment are N·m, then the distance units should be m. To make the conversion from mass to force, the mass must be multiplied by g, the acceleration due to gravity, which has units of m/s^2. The distance must be converted from mm to m. The unit equation then becomes

$$N·m = (kg·m/s^2) \left(mm × \frac{m}{mm} \right)$$

The newton, N, is a derived unit, which has units of $kg·m/s^2$. Thus, N may be substituted for $kg·m/s^2$ and the equation becomes

$$N·m = N·m$$

which is a valid unit equation.

Whenever there is any element of doubt about the suitability of units being used in a solution, the units should be checked to determine that they are the same on both sides of the equation. If they are not the same, there is an error either in the choice of units or in the equation being used. If the units on both sides of the equation are the same, the setup for the solution may be correct, but unfortunately, this does not guarantee the correctness of the solution.

1-6 ACCURACY AND SIGNIFICANT FIGURES

Mathematical calculations can be made with precision. However, in many instances, the information available on which to base engineering calculations is not precise. For instance, the loads that might be applied to a bridge over its lifetime are not precisely known, and the designer will not know the number or mass of vehicles that are likely to be on the bridge at any one time. Thus, in many design situations, the designer must make the best possible estimate of the loads that will be applied to have a basis for analyzing the structure. In some instances, there will be a code that will govern the loads to be used for design purposes. In either instance, the information will not be precise, and the lack of precision will be indicated by the use of only one, two or three significant figures in presenting the information. For instance, the mass of a truck, with its load, is likely to be given as 30 000 kg rather than as 29 876.4 kg.

Scientific and mathematical practice demands that calculations be carried out with no more precision in the final value than existed in the least precise value in the original data. In other words, the quantity of significant figures in the final answer should be the same as the smallest quantity of significant figures in any of the values in the original information. Engineering practice is somewhat different, in that there is a long tradition of giving final values with three significant figures, even if the original information tends not to justify such accuracy. The tradition comes, in part, from the use of the slide rule for making engineering calculations. This tool was used for many generations, and generally provides only three-figure accuracy. In addition, many engineering calculations are part of a long series, and premature rounding off can lead to results that would be misleading in some instances. It will be the practice here to use four or more significant figures for most intermediate calculations, and to round off final values to three significant figures. There is some problem with angles and significant figures. The practice in this text will be to give all final values of angles to two places of decimal.

When rounding off values, there are some fairly simple, but exact, rules to be followed:

1) If the first discarded digit is smaller than five, the retained digits are unchanged; for example, 578 341 becomes 578 300 for four significant figures.

2) If the first digit to be discarded is greater than five, or five followed by any other digits, the last retained digit should be increased by one; for example, 468.53 would become 469 for three significant figures.

3) If the first digit to be discarded is either five with nothing following, or five followed by zeros: when the last retained digit is even, it is unchanged; when it is odd, it is increased by one.

For example, 0.0345 becomes 0.034 for two significant figures, and 1.715 00 becomes 1.72 for three significant figures.

1-7 LOADS ON MEMBERS

There are several different types of loads or forces that may be applied to a body. They are shown in Fig. 1-3.

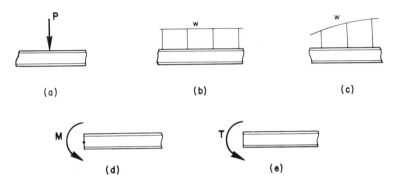

FIGURE 1-3

The concentrated load (sometimes called a point load) is shown in Fig. 1-3(a) and occurs wherever a force is applied over a very small area relative to the total area being considered. For instance, a filing cabinet on a floor may be considered to be a concentrated load on a floor for purposes of designing the beams supporting the floor. Figure 1-3(b) represents a uniformly distributed load, as might occur on the beams of a warehouse floor on which all the material has about the same density and is uniformly distributed over the floor. In Fig. 1-3(c) is shown a nonuniform load, which would occur on a roof truss that carried a snow load where the snow did not have a uniform depth.

Figures 1-3(d) and (e) show a moment and a couple, both of which are measures of the tendency to cause rotation. A moment about the support of a diving board would be caused by the diver standing at the end of the board. A couple can be applied by a lug wrench, or by the drive shaft of an automobile. Both of these topics will be discussed in detail in Chap. 2.

1-8 TYPES OF SUPPORTS

Most structural elements that will be dealt with will be supported by one of three types of support. Figure 1-4 illustrates the various supports. The roller, as shown in Fig. 1-4(a), would permit a member to move along its axis and to rotate about the

(a)

FIGURE 1-4

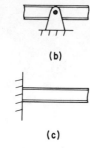

(b)

(c)

FIGURE 1-4 cont'd

roller. As a matter of interest, a roller can easily be designed to resist an uplift force. The pin shown in Fig. 1-4(b) will not permit translation of the member, but will permit the member to rotate about the pin. In three dimensions, a ball-and-socket connection is somewhat similar to a pin, except that a ball and socket permits rotation in all directions, while restricting translation. Figure 1-4(c) shows a fixed support, which permits neither translation nor rotation. This type of support would occur with a member built into or bolted to a wall.

1-9 CLASSES OF MEMBERS

Every structure, whether it is a machine, a building or any other load-carrying device, can be considered to be made up of a number of structural elements that have well-defined names. Figure 1-5 shows the most common types of members or structural elements.

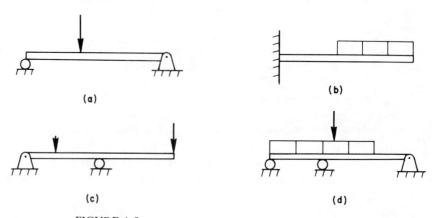

(a)

(b)

(c)

(d)

FIGURE 1-5

The beam may be defined as a member that carries loads perpendicular to its longitudinal axis. The simple beam, as shown in Fig. 1-5(a), is supported at each end, usually by one roller and one pin. As will be discovered later, such a support system is necessary to provide stability; it also provides a system that can be analyzed. The cantilever beam is supported at one end by a fixed support, as shown in Fig. 1-5(b). The simple beam with overhang, as shown in Fig. 1-5(c), is self-explanatory. The continuous beam shown in Fig. 1-5(d) has three or more supports, and, as a result, the forces acting on it cannot be analyzed using the methods of statics.

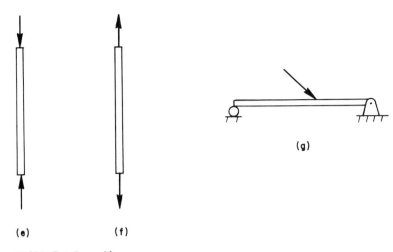

(e)   (f)

(g)

FIGURE 1-5 cont'd

Members with loads parallel to the longitudinal axis are either columns, struts, cables or tie-bars. A column has its load in compression (a push) as show in Fig. 1-5(e). A strut is similar to a column, except that it is relatively short. A member in tension (a pull) may be either a cable or some other flexible member, or a solid member, such as a tie-bar, as shown in Fig. 1-5(f).

The beam-column is a member that has part of its load parallel to the longitudinal axis and part of the load perpendicular to the longitudinal axis, as shown in Fig. 1-5(g). It is often called simply a beam.

1-10   TRIGONOMETRY

The study of the relationships between angles and the lengths of sides in triangles is called trigonometry. It is a branch of mathematics that is very useful in any technical application where measurements of length or angle must be made.

Trigonometric relationships are based on the proportions of right-angle triangles and the relationships are called *trigonometric functions*, or trig functions. Relationships between angles and side lengths for other than right-angle triangles are based on the *sine law* and *cosine law*.

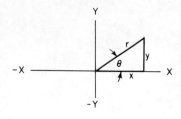

(a)

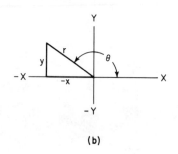

(b)

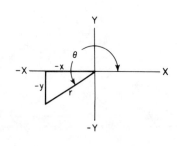

(c)

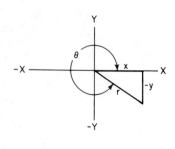

(d)

FIGURE 1-6

1-11   TRIGONOMETRIC FUNCTIONS

The basic trig functions are definitions based on the right-angle triangle shown in Fig. 1-6(a). The definitions are as follows:

$$\text{sine } \theta = \frac{\text{opposite}}{\text{hypotenuse}} \qquad \sin \theta = \frac{y}{r} \qquad (1\text{-}1)$$

$$\text{cosine } \theta = \frac{\text{adjacent}}{\text{hypotenuse}} \qquad \cos \theta = \frac{x}{r} \qquad (1\text{-}2)$$

$$\text{tangent } \theta = \frac{\text{opposite}}{\text{adjacent}} \qquad \tan \theta = \frac{y}{x} \qquad (1\text{-}3)$$

$$\text{cosecant } \theta = \frac{\text{hypotenuse}}{\text{opposite}} \qquad \csc \theta = \frac{r}{y} \qquad (1\text{-}4)$$

$$\text{secant } \theta = \frac{\text{hypotenuse}}{\text{adjacent}} \qquad \sec \theta = \frac{r}{x} \qquad (1\text{-}5)$$

$$\text{cotangent } \theta = \frac{\text{adjacent}}{\text{opposite}} \qquad \cot \theta = \frac{x}{y} \qquad (1\text{-}6)$$

where opposite refers to the length of the side opposite the angle θ,

adjacent refers to the length of the side adjacent to the angle θ, and

hypotenuse is the hypotenuse of the right-angle triangle.

The same trig functions apply to angles larger than 90°, as shown in Figs. 1-6(b), (c) and (d). Note that in different quadrants, the values for x and y may be either positive or negative, but the value for the hypotenuse, r, is always positive. As a result, the various trig functions will have different signs, depending on the size of the angle. All the trig functions are positive in the first quadrant.

It might be noted that, with the widespread use of the electronic calculator, the cosecant, secant and cotangent are receiving much less use.

A convention used in trigonometry is that angles that are measured counterclockwise are considered to be positive angles, and angles that are measured clockwise are negative. This convention is illlustrated in Fig. 1-7. Normally, angles are measured from the positive x axis. By using this convention, many diagrams can be avoided, for everyone should have the same understanding of the statement "at an angle of 47.3°." It means an

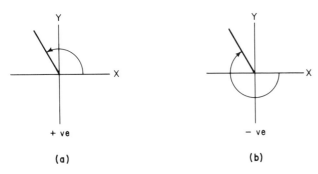

FIGURE 1-7

angle of 47.3° measured counterclockwise from the positive x axis, as shown in Fig. 1-8(a). Similarly, "at an angle of −225°" means an angle of 225° measured clockwise from the positive x axis, as shown in Fig. 1-8(b).

For angles in the second quadrant, there are three relationships that have been developed to relate the trig functions of the first quadrant to second-quadrant angles. They are as follows:

$$\sin \theta = \sin (180° - \theta) = -\cos (90° + \theta) \qquad (1\text{-}7)$$

$$\cos \theta = -\cos (180° - \theta) = \sin (90° + \theta) \qquad (1\text{-}8)$$

$$\tan \theta = -\tan (180° - \theta) = -\cot (90° + \theta) \qquad (1\text{-}9)$$

It is very important to keep in mind that all of the above definitions are based on the use of right-angle triangles. There are no corresponding definitions for triangles that are not right-angle triangles.

Although not a trigonometric definition, the Pythagorean theorem applies only to right-angle triangles, and may be noted here. The Pythagorean theorem states that the square of the hypotenuse of a right-angle triangle is equal to the sum of the squares of the other two sides of the triangle. It may be written as

$$r^2 = x^2 + y^2 \qquad (1\text{-}10)$$

and is often written as

$$r = (x^2 + y^2)^{1/2} \qquad (1\text{-}11)$$

It is frequently necessary to use an expression such as "the angle whose sine is . . . ." Two notations have been developed, as follows:

$$\theta = \sin^{-1} m = \arcsin m$$

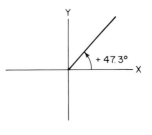

(a)

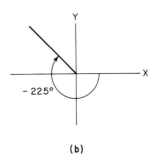

(b)

FIGURE 1-8

This means that θ = the angle whose sine is m, and similarly,

$$\theta = \cos^{-1} m = \text{arccos } m$$

means that θ = the angle whose cosine is m, and

$$\theta = \tan^{-1} m = \text{arctan } m$$

means that θ = the angle whose tangent is m.

EXAMPLE 1-1

Determine the sin, cos and tan for an angle of 53.16°.

SOLUTION

This information can be obtained using an electronic calculator, math tables or a scale drawing of a right-angle triangle containing an angle of 53.16°.

From the calculator:

$$\sin 53.16° = 0.800\ 31$$
$$\cos 53.16° = 0.599\ 58$$
$$\tan 53.16° = 1.3348$$

From five-place math tables

$$\sin 53.16° = 0.800\ 31$$
$$\cos 53.16° = 0.599\ 58$$
$$\tan 53.16° = 1.3348$$

If a protractor and scale are used to draw a right-angle triangle with one angle of 53.16°, as shown in Fig. 1-9, *the dimensions may be used to calculate the trig functions required.*

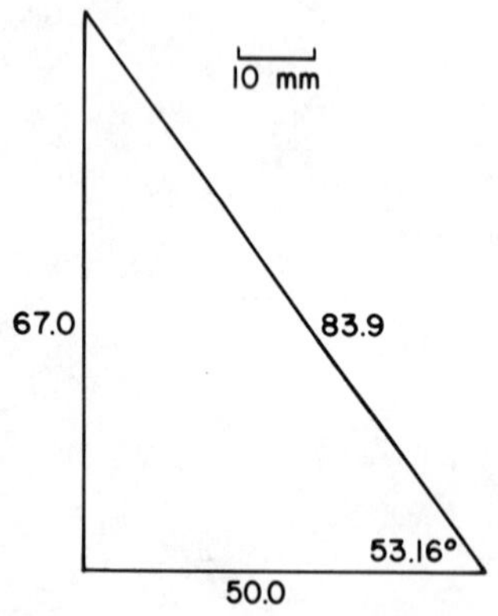

$$\sin 53.16° = \frac{67.0}{83.9} = 0.7986$$

$$\cos 53.16° = \frac{50.0}{83.9} = 0.5959$$

$$\tan 53.16° = \frac{67.0}{50.0} = 1.340$$

FIGURE 1-9

Since it is not possible, using an ordinary protractor, to draw angles with high precision, the small error obtained from the graphical solution can be expected. In spite of this error, the procedure does provide a back-up process in case the electronic calculator breaks down. It is also strongly recommended that a neat summary of the answer should accompany each solution.

$$\sin 53.16° = 0.800$$
$$\cos 53.16° = 0.600$$
$$\tan 53.16° = 1.34$$

EXAMPLE 1-2

For an angle of 167.2°, find the sin, cos and tan.

SOLUTION

The problem may be solved using an electronic calculator, a set of math tables, or a scale drawing of a right-angle triangle containing the given angle.

From the calculator:

$$\sin 167.2° = 0.2215$$

$$\cos 167.2° = -0.9751$$

$$\tan 167.2° = -0.2272$$

Some calculations do not give trig functions for angles greater than 90°. In this case, Eq. (1-7), (1-8) *and* (1-9) *must be used.*

$$\sin 167.2° = \sin (180° - 167.2°)$$
$$= \sin 12.8°$$
$$= 0.2215$$
$$\cos 167.2° = -\cos (180° - 167.2°)$$
$$= -\cos 12.8°$$
$$= -0.9751$$
$$\tan 167.2° = -\tan (180° - 167.2°)$$
$$= -\tan 12.8°$$
$$= -0.2272$$

From five-place math tables:

$$\sin 167.2° = 0.221\ 55$$

$$\cos 167.2° = -0.975\ 15$$

$$\tan 167.2° = -0.227\ 19$$

An accurate drawing made with protractor and scale, as shown in Fig. 1-10, will also provide a method of calculating the trig functions.

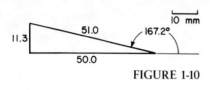

FIGURE 1-10

$$\sin 167.2° = \frac{11.3}{51.0}$$

$$= 0.2216$$

$$\cos 167.2° = \frac{-50.0}{51.0}$$

$$= -0.9804$$

$$\tan 167.2° = \frac{11.3}{-50.0}$$

$$= -0.2260$$

Due to limitations in the accuracy of the drawing, there is a small error in the graphical solution, which shows in the third significant figure. The problem solution should end with a concise summary of the answers.

$$\sin 167.2° = \;\;0.222$$
$$\cos 167.2° = -0.975$$
$$\tan 167.2° = -0.227$$

EXAMPLE 1-3

A 10 m utility pole, on level ground, is to be supported by a guy wire from the top of the pole to the ground. If the guy makes an angle of 25° with the top of the pole, determine the length of the guy and the distance from the base of the pole to the anchor point on the ground.

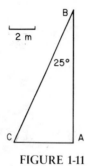

FIGURE 1-11

SOLUTION

Although the problem can be solved without a drawing, it is recommended that a scale drawing be prepared, both as an aid to the problem solution, and as a check on the accuracy of the solution. Figure 1-11 is a scale drawing of the pole and guy.

Guy length:

$$\frac{AB}{BC} = \cos 25°$$

$$BC = \frac{10}{\cos 25°}$$

$$= 11.03 \text{ m}$$

Distance to anchor:

$$\frac{AC}{AB} = \tan 25°$$

$$AC = 10 \tan 25°$$

$$= 4.663 \text{ m}$$

The Pythagorean theorem will provide a check on the work.

Check:

$$BC = (AB^2 + AC^2)^{1/2}$$

$$= (10^2 + 4.663^2)^{1/2}$$

$$= (100.00 + 21.74)^{1/2}$$

$$= 121.74^{1/2}$$

$$= 11.03 \text{ m}$$

> Guy length = 11.0 m
> Distance to anchor = 4.66 m

Scaling the lengths from Fig. 1-11 *also provides a useful check.*

By scale:

Guy length = 11.0 m

Anchor distance = 4.6 m

PROBLEMS

1-1 Find the sine, cosine and tangent for an angle of 30°.

1-2 For an angle of 50°, find the sine, cosine and tangent.

1-3 Determine the sine, cosine and tangent for an angle of 75.3°.

1-4 Find the sine, cosine and tangent for an angle of 41.6°.

1-5 Determine the sine, cosine and tangent for an angle of 98°.

1-6 For an angle of 135°, find the sine, cosine and tangent.

1-7 Find the sine, cosine and tangent for an angle of 171.4°.

1-8 Determine the sine, cosine and tangent for an angle of 147.1°.

1-9 A right-angle triangle has sides of 4 m and 7 m. Determine the sine, cosine and tangent of the smallest angle.

1-10 If the sides of a right-angle triangle are 9 mm and 15 mm, find the tangent of the angle opposite the 15 mm side, and find the sine and cosine of the same angle.

1-11 A right-angle triangle has sides of 20 mm and 48 mm. Determine the length of the hypotenuse and the sizes of the other two angles.

1-12 Determine the magnitudes of the interior angles for a right-angle triangle with sides of 5 m and 12 m. Also determine the hypotenuse.

1-13 Find the hypotenuse and the two interior angles for a right-angle triangle with sides of 60 m and 80 m.

1-14 For a right-angle triangle with sides of 3 m and 4 m, determine the sizes of the other two angles, and the length of the hypotenuse.

1-15 A roof truss for a house spans a distance of 8 m, and at the peak (at mid-span) must have a height of 2 m. Determine the length of the rafter (the top member) and the angle between the rafter and the joist (the bottom member).

1-16 A guy for a 20 m TV-antenna tower is to be fastened from the top of the tower to a point 4 m horizontally from the base of the tower. Determine the length of guy required and the angle the guy will form with the tower.

1-17 A roof overhang is to be supported by a brace, as shown in Fig. P1-17. Determine the length of brace *AB* and the angle the brace makes with the wall.

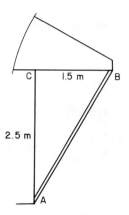

FIGURE P1-17

1-18 A corner lot is a rectangle 15 by 25 m. Determine the distance saved by taking a short-cut along the diagonal of the lot, compared with walking along the two sides.

1-12 SINE AND COSINE LAWS

For the case of triangles that are not right-angled, two laws have been developed for determining angles and the lengths of sides in the triangles. They are the sine law and the cosine law. The sine law is

$$\frac{A}{\sin \alpha} = \frac{B}{\sin \beta} = \frac{C}{\sin \gamma} \tag{1-12}$$

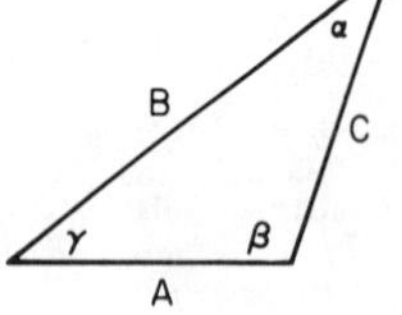

Referring to Fig. 1-12, it is seen that the sine law is a statement of ratios, where the length of a side divided by the sine of the angle opposite is equal to the length of any other side in the triangle divided by the sine of its opposite angle. The equation may be rewritten in several different forms, depending on the given information and the information being sought.

FIGURE 1-12

The cosine law is

$$A^2 = B^2 + C^2 - 2BC \cos \alpha \qquad (1\text{-}13)$$

Again referring to Fig. 1-12, it is seen that the cosine law indicates that the square of the length of one side of a triangle is equal to the sum of the squares of the lengths of the other two sides, minus twice the product of the lengths of the two sides and the cosine of the angle contained by the two sides. From the above statement, it should be apparent that the cosine law can be rewritten in other forms, so that either of the other two sides or the contained angles could also be obtained.

EXAMPLE 1-4

In a triangle, the length of side A is 50 mm and side C is 18 mm. The angle γ, opposite C, is 20°. Determine the size of angle α, which is opposite side A.

SOLUTION

This would appear to be an application of the sine law. An accurate scale drawing, such as Fig. 1-13, *is an aid to using the sine law.*

$$\frac{\sin \alpha}{A} = \frac{\sin \gamma}{C}$$

$$\sin \alpha = \frac{50 \sin 20°}{18}$$

$$= 0.9501$$

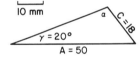

FIGURE 1-13

In this instance, it is clear from the accurate scale drawing of Fig. 1-13 *that α is greater than 90°. Using* Eq. (1-7), *it is found that*

$$\alpha = 180.00° - 71.82°$$

$$= 108.18°$$

$$\boxed{\alpha = 108.18°}$$

EXAMPLE 1-5

A triangle has sides of 90 mm and 120 mm, and an angle of 27° contained between the two given sides. Determine the length of the third side.

SOLUTION

Since the given information includes two sides and the contained angle, the cosine law should be used, along with an accurate scale drawing, such as Fig. 1-14, *which serves as an aid to setting up the equation, as well as a check on the accuracy of the calculations.*

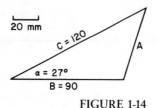

FIGURE 1-14

$$A^2 = B^2 + C^2 - 2BC \cos \alpha$$
$$= 90^2 + 120^2 - 2 \times 90 \times 120 \cos 27°$$
$$= 8100.0 + 14\ 400.0 - 19\ 245.7$$
$$= 3254.3$$
$$A = 57.046 \text{ mm}$$

$$\boxed{A = 57.0 \text{ mm}}$$

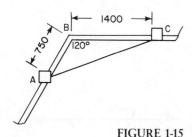

FIGURE 1-15

EXAMPLE 1-6

A control cable must connect two mechanisms on a machine at points *A* and *C*, as shown in Fig. 1-15. Determine the length of the cable *AC* and the angle the cable makes with part *AB* of the frame and part *BC* of the frame.

SOLUTION

Length AC may be obtained using the cosine law and the drawing with critical dimensions, as shown in Fig. 1-16. *If the drawing is to scale, it will also serve as a check on the accuracy of the calculations.*

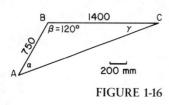

FIGURE 1-16

$$(AC)^2 = (AB)^2 + (BC)^2 - 2(AB)(BC) \cos \beta$$
$$= 750^2 + 1400^2 - 2 \times 750 \times 1400 \cos 120°$$
$$= 562\ 500 + 1\ 960\ 000 + 1\ 050\ 000$$
$$= 3\ 572\ 500$$
$$AC = 1890.1 \text{ mm}$$

Note that since β was greater than 90°, cos β was negative, giving the third term a positive sign.

The angle α may be obtained by using the sine law.

$$\frac{\sin \alpha}{BC} = \frac{\sin \beta}{AC}$$

$$\sin \alpha = \frac{1400 \sin 120°}{1890.1}$$

$$= 0.641\ 46$$

$$\alpha = 39.90°$$

$$\gamma = 180.00° - 120.00° - 39.90°$$

$$= 20.10°$$

> AC = 1890 mm
> Angle with AB = 39.90°
> Angle with BC = 20.10°

PROBLEMS

1-19 A triangle contains angles of 27.3° and 63.9°. If the side opposite the 27.3° angle is 4.6 m, determine the length of the other two sides.

1-20 Calculate the lengths of the other two sides in a triangle if one side is 47 mm and is opposite an angle of 76.1°. A second angle in the triangle is 48.9°.

1-21 A triangle has sides of 50 mm and 55 mm, and the angle opposite the 50 mm side is 63°. Determine the magnitudes of the other two angles. (There are two possible solutions to this problem.)

1-22 An angle of 41.3° is opposite a side of 14.3 m. If the length of the second side is 20.2 m, determine the sizes of the other two angles. (There are two possible sets of answers to this question.)

1-23 A survey crew has to find the distance *AB*, as shown in Fig. P1-23, but is unable to walk on water. They measure the length of *AC*, the angle α, which is found to be 28.6°, and γ, which is found to be 98.6°. Calculate *AB*.

1-24 A ship's navigator determines the ship's distance from the coast by taking bearings on a smoke stack, *S*, and a church steeple, *C*, as

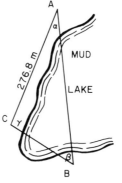

FIGURE P1-23

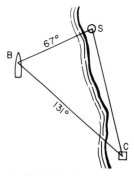

FIGURE P1-24

shown in Fig. P1-24. From the chart the navigator determines that the distance from the steeple to the stack is 1460 m and that the bearing is 346°. Calculate the distance from the vessel *B* to the stack. (Navigational bearings are measured clockwise from zero at north.)

1-25 A jet aircraft normally covers a distance of about 7 km in 30 s at normal cruising speed. A surveyor measures the vertical angle to the aircraft's flight path at 62.5° at the start of a 30 s interval, and 39.2° at the end of the interval. Based on this information, what is the approximate height of the aircraft if the flight path is in the plane of the vertical angles the surveyor measures?

1-26 The 100 m transmission tower is supported by guy wires as shown in Fig. P1-26. If the slope of the ground is 1:7, calculate the length of guy *BC* and guy *BD*.

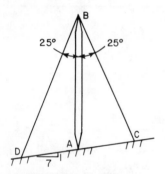

FIGURE P1-26

1-27 For the truss shown in Fig. P1-27, determine the length of members *CD* and *DG* and the three interior angles in *CDG*.

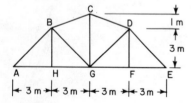

FIGURE P1-27

1-28 The altitude of a kite may be determined reasonably accurately by positioning two surveyor's transits a known distance apart directly upwind of the kite, as shown in Fig. P1-28, and measuring the vertical angles to the kite. For the values shown, determine the altitude *h* of the kite. Assume that each transit is 1.50 m above the ground.

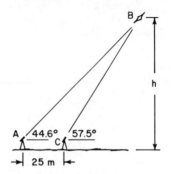

FIGURE P1-28

1-29 A triangle has sides of $A = 120$ mm and $B = 200$ mm, with a contained angle of $\gamma = 17°$. Determine the length of the third side, *C*.

1-30 Determine the length of side *B* of a triangle if it is opposite the angle $\beta = 50°$ contained between sides $A = 1$ m and $C = 2$ m.

1-31 A survey crew must obtain the distance between points *B* and *C*. The line of sight is obstructed by a building, as shown in Fig. P1-31. By measuring the angle at *A* and the distances *AB* and *AC*, distance *BC* can be measured. What is distance *BC*?

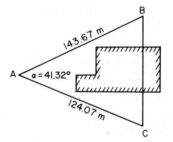

FIGURE P1-31

1-32 A derrick boom, as shown in Fig. P1-32, is to operate at 30° from the vertical. What is the length of the tie-back *AC*?

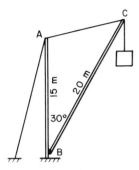

FIGURE P1-32

1-33 The chair shown in Fig. P1-33 has a leg brace, *BC*. If *AB* is 200 mm and *AC* is 350 mm, and the angle at *A* is 115°, determine the length of the brace *BC*.

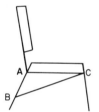

FIGURE P1-33

1-34 Determine the length of side *A* and the size of the angle γ for the triangle shown in Fig. P1-34.

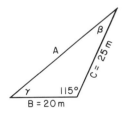

FIGURE P1-34

1-35 Determine the size of the angle α for the triangle shown in Fig. P1-35.

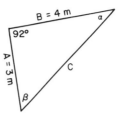

FIGURE P1-35

1-36 For the triangle shown in Fig. P1-36, calculate the size of the angle β.

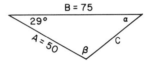

FIGURE P1-36

1-37 A triangle has sides of 5, 7 and 9 m. Determine each of the angles in the triangle.

1-38 Find the angles in a triangle if the lengths of the sides are 190, 260 and 300 mm.

1-39 Determine the angles in a triangle if the lengths of the sides are 15, 40 and 50 mm.

1-40 If a triangle has sides with lengths of 8, 12 and 17 m, determine the angles in the triangle.

2 FORCES

2-1 FORCE DEFINED

A force may be defined as the action of one body on another. This action can take place by means of direct contact or by gravitational, magnetic or electrical attraction between bodies.

A *contact* force exists because the two bodies involved are touching each other, as in the case of a book on a desk or feet on the floor. It is one of the most common types of force. The *gravitational* force exists because of the mutual attraction that exists between any two bodies. The best recognized gravitational force is that which is present between the earth and any body on the earth. This is the force that many measuring devices provide when *weight* is measured, since weight is a measure of the gravitational force acting on a body on the earth's surface. The gravitational force acting on a one kg mass on the earth's surface is about 9.807 N. Although this gravitational attraction exists between any two bodies, the magnitude tends to be very small unless one of the bodies has a very large mass, such as the earth or the moon.

Magnetic forces exist between a magnet and certain types of materials, while *electrical* forces exist between charged particles. In some areas of specialty, such as electrical or electronics technology, these will be the forces that will be dealt with most frequently.

Regardless of what causes the force, the characteristics of the force and the method of making calculations with the force will not be affected.

The most significant characteristic of a force is that both its magnitude and its direction must be given in order to completely describe the force. A quantity that has both magnitude and direction is called a *vector*. As a result, mathematical calculations with forces must be treated differently than most other mathematical calculations that have been done with quantities that are not vectors.

Figure 2-1 should help to illustrate the significance of providing information on the direction of a force as well as its magnitude. Although all the tugs shown may exert a force of

FIGURE 2-1 Forces of a similar size applied in different directions on a body will have different effects on the body, as illustrated by the tugs docking the cruise ships. *Photo courtesy Home Lines.*

approximately the same magnitude, it is fairly obvious from the location of the tugs that some tend to turn one ship, while others tend to pull a second ship. From this it can be seen that the direction of a force has considerable influence on the effect of the force on the body on which it acts.

2-2 VECTORS AND SCALARS

A *vector* is a mathematical quantity that must be described by both a magnitude and a direction. A *scalar* is a mathematical quantity that is described by its magnitude only. Some of the more common scalar quantities are age, area, length and volume. These are all concepts that do not include any direction in the description. Some of the more common vector concepts are force, velocity and displacement, all of which must be described by both a magnitude and a direction.

One way to better visualize the difference is to look in detail at the difference between two concepts that do have some relationship, displacement and length.

Figure 2-2(a) shows two points, *A* and *B*. The line with the arrowhead in Fig. 2-2(b) represents the displacement vector *AB*. It has a magnitude and a very definite direction. The distance between *A* and *B* is the length *AB*. In other words, length is the magnitude of a displacement vector. The displacement vector, however, must be described by both its length and its direction. If the vector *CD* is drawn the same length as *AB*, as shown in Fig. 2-2(c), it is a different vector, even though the lengths of lines *AB* and *CD* are the same.

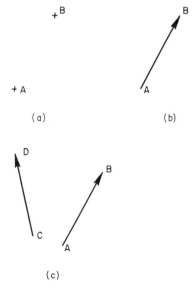

FIGURE 2-2

The displacement vector is probably the vector that is most easy to visualize, and it is often helpful to think in terms of the displacement vector if difficulty is encountered with visualizing some of the vector operations to be discussed later.

Since vectors are a different type of mathematical quantity than scalars, it may be expected that they will be shown in a different form of notation. In printed material, vectors are usually shown by using boldface type, such as **B**, as compared with the regular type, B. In written work, it is necessary to use a different method to distinguish between vectors and scalars. Usually, in written work, a line or an arrow is drawn over the vector quantity, as $\overline{B}$ or $\vec{B}$, to distinguish the vector from the scalar. It is generally understood that the scalar symbol refers to the magnitude of the same vector quantity. In other words, **F** would represent the force vector, while *F* would be the magnitude of the force. All vectors can be shown graphically by drawing a line, to scale, with an arrow in the direction of the vector. Thus, all vectors can be shown in a manner similar to that used in Fig. 2-2.

2-3   VECTOR ADDITION

Several methods of adding vectors will be described. Each has an application in different situations, so each method is important. The basic rule is the *triangle rule* for vector addition, which states that the sum of two vectors may be obtained by drawing the vectors to scale, tip to tail. The sum of the two vectors is that vector from the tail of the first vector to the tip of the second vector. The concept is illustrated in Fig. 2-3, where Fig. 2-3(a) shows two vectors, **A** and **B**, and the two vectors are shown tip to tail in Fig. 2-3(b). The vector **R** is the sum of vectors **A** and **B** as shown in Fig. 2-3(b). The mathematical statement for the sum of two vectors may be written as:

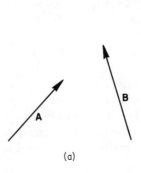

(a)

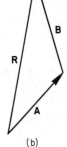

(b)

FIGURE 2-3

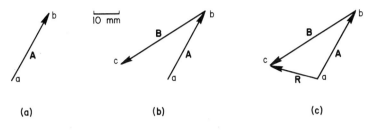

FIGURE 2-4

$$R = A + B \qquad (2\text{-}1)$$

The idea of vector addition can be further illustrated by means of Fig. 2-4, which shows the path of a gnat across the page from *a* to *b*. This is displacement vector **A**. The gnat then travels from *b* to *c*, which is another displacement vector, **B**. The sum of these two vectors is the vector from *a* to *c*, which is shown as vector **R**. The final displacement for the gnat, measured from its initial starting point, *a*, is described by the vector **R**. Note that each of these vectors has both a magnitude and a direction. Also note that if **A** has a magnitude of 30 mm and **B** has a magnitude of 40 mm, the magnitude of **R** is *not* 70 mm, but, according to the scale, is 20 mm. This helps to illustrate the difference between algebraic addition, in which 30 + 40 = 70, and vector addition, in which the sum of the vectors of 30 and 40 units is not necessarily 70, because of the influence of direction.

The *parallelogram rule* for vector addition is related to the triangle rule. In the parallelogram rule, the two vectors are drawn with their tails at a common point, and a parallelogram is formed using the vectors as two sides. The diagonal of the parallelogram, drawn from the common tails of the two vectors, is the sum of the two vectors. The parallelogram rule is illustrated in Fig. 2-5. Note that by inspecting Fig. 2-5(c) it is seen that the triangle rule can be considered as a special case of the parallelogram rule, for the parallelogram is really made up of two triangles with sides of vectors **A** and **B**. It should also be noted that it

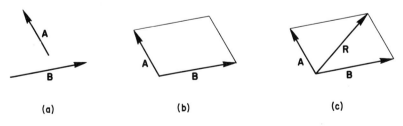

FIGURE 2-5

makes no difference to the sum whether it is **A** + **B** or **B** + **A** that is added. In both cases, the same sum is obtained:

$$\mathbf{A} + \mathbf{B} = \mathbf{R}$$

$$\mathbf{B} + \mathbf{A} = \mathbf{R}$$

The actual value for the sum of two vectors can be obtained either by drawing the vectors accurately to scale and obtaining the sum from the scale drawing, or by using trigonometry to solve the triangle for the unknown side and angle. In either case, the value for the sum *must* include both a magnitude and a direction. It is recommended that the scale drawing be done at all times, for it provides a quick and convenient check on the accuracy of the trigonometric calculations.

EXAMPLE 2-1

Find the sum of the two vectors shown in Fig. 2-6.

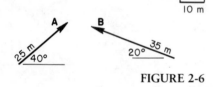

FIGURE 2-6

SOLUTION

The recommended first step is to draw the vector triangle to scale, as shown in Fig. 2-7(a), *or the vector parallelogram, as shown in* Fig. 2-7(b). *In either case, there is a triangle with given information on two sides and the contained angle, and thus the cosine law is used to find the length R. Note that the same triangle is repeated as part of the parallelogram in* Fig. 2-7(b).

$$\phi = 20° + 40°$$

$$= 60°$$

$$R^2 = A^2 + B^2 - 2AB \cos \phi$$

$$= 25^2 + 35^2 - 2 \times 25 \times 35 \cos 60°$$

$$= 975.00$$

$$R = 31.22 \text{ m}$$

To find the direction, find the angle β using the sine law.

$$\frac{\sin \beta}{B} = \frac{\sin \phi}{R}$$

$$\sin \beta = \frac{35 \sin 60°}{31.22}$$

$$= 0.9709$$

$$\beta = 76.14°$$

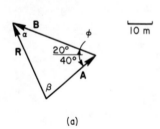

(a)

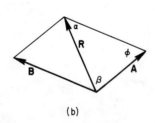

(b)

FIGURE 2-7

Direction of $\vec{R}$ = 40.00° + 76.14°

= 116.14°

$$\vec{R} = 31.2 \text{ m at } 116.14°$$

By scaling from Fig. 2-7(a) or Fig. 2-7(b):

$\vec{R}$ = 31.2 m at 116°

EXAMPLE 2-2

For two velocity vectors, **A** = 75 km/h at 27° and **B** = 125 km/h at 300°, determine their sum.

SOLUTION

The first step is to draw the vector triangle or parallelogram to scale, as shown in Fig. 2-8. *Note that the triangle shown in Fig. 2-8(a) is repeated as part of the parallelogram. The triangle, which has two sides and the contained angle given, may be solved for R using the cosine law.*

$\phi = 180° - 27° - 60°$

$= 93°$

$R^2 = A^2 + B^2 - 2AB \cos \phi$

$= 75^2 + 125^2 - 2 \times 75 \times 125 \cos 93°$

$= 22\ 231.3$

$R = 149.10 \text{ km/h}$

To find the direction of **R**, *first find the angle* β, *using the sine law.*

$\dfrac{\sin \beta}{B} = \dfrac{\sin \phi}{R}$

$\sin \beta = \dfrac{125 \sin 93°}{149.10}$

$= 0.837\ 20$

$\beta = 56.85°$

Direction of $\vec{R}$ = 27.00° − 56.85°

= −29.85°

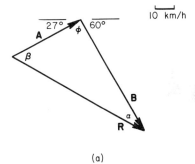

(a)

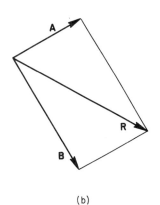

(b)

FIGURE 2-8

or Direction of $\vec{R}$ = 360.00° − 29.85°

= 330.15°

$$\boxed{\vec{R} = 149 \text{ km/h at } 330.15°}$$

From the scale drawing of Fig. 2-8, ***R*** *can be obtained:*

$\vec{R}$ = 149 km/h at 330°

PROBLEMS

2-1 A force vector of 75 N points horizontally to the right, and a second force vector of 100 N points vertically up. Determine the sum of the two vectors.

2-2 A 3 MN force points vertically upwards and a second vector of 4 MN points horizontally to the right. Calculate the sum of the two vectors.

2-3 A 50 m displacement vector points vertically up. A second vector of 120 m points horizontally to the right. Find the sum of the two vectors.

2-4 A displacement vector of 480 m is directed vertically up and a second one of 200 m is directed horizontally to the right. Evaluate the sum of the two vectors.

2-5 A velocity vector of 50 m/s points horizontally to the left and a second vector of 25 m/s points vertically up. Determine the sum of the two vectors.

2-6 Determine the sum of two velocity vectors, one of which is 90 km/s horizontally to the left, and the second of which is 110 km/s vertically up.

2-7 Determine the sum of the two acceleration vectors, **A** = 250 m/s² at 290° and **B** = 160 m/s² at 70°.

2-8 Determine the sum of the two vectors shown in Fig. P2-8.

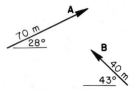

FIGURE P2-8

2-9 Displacement vector **A** is 40 m at 35° and displacement vector **B** is 50 m at 110°. Determine **A** + **B**.

2-10 Find the sum of velocity vectors **A** = 45 km/h at 90° and **B** = 75 km/h at 15°.

2-11 Find the sum of the two forces shown in Fig. P2-11.

FIGURE P2-11

2-12 Linear impulse vector **A** = 5000 N·s at 175° is to be added to vector **B** = 7000 N·s at 25°. Determine the sum of the two vectors.

2-4 VECTOR SUBTRACTION

The process for vector subtraction is very similar to that for vector addition. A negative vector is the same as a positive one, except that it is opposite in direction. The vector **A** is shown in Fig. 2-9(a) and the vector −**A** is shown in Figure 2-9(b). Mathematically, it is said that −**A** = −(**A**).

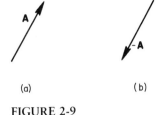

(a)   (b)

FIGURE 2-9

The vector difference may be written as

$$R = A - B$$

$$= A + (-B)$$

The last part of the expression is recognized as a vector sum, which has already been studied. Two vectors are shown in Fig. 2-10(a). The difference **R** = **A** − **B**, obtained by the triangle rule, is shown in Fig. 2-10(b); obtained by the parallelogram rule, it is shown in Fig. 2-10(c). When subtracting a vector, the negative vector is added to the first vector, so that the process is the same as either the triangle or the parallelogram rule for vector addition.

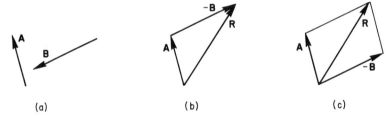

(a)   (b)   (c)

FIGURE 2-10

Once again, actual values for **R** may be obtained by either an accurate scale drawing of the vector triangle or parallelogram, or by using the principles of trigonometry to solve for the unknown side and angle in the triangle which is formed.

It should be noted that **A** − **B** ≠ **B** − **A**, so in vector subtraction, the sequence is important.

EXAMPLE 2-3

Find **A** − **B** for the two vectors shown in Fig. 2-11.

SOLUTION

The recommended first step is to draw the vector triangle to scale, as shown in Fig. 2-12(a), keeping in mind that −B has the same magnitude as B but is opposite in direction. The vector

FIGURE 2-11

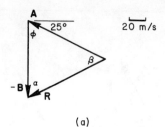

(a)

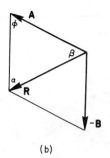

(b)

FIGURE 2-12

parallelogram could also be drawn, as shown in Fig. 2-12(b). *Note that the triangle is repeated as part of the parallelogram. From the triangle we observe that there are two known sides and the contained angle. The third side may be obtained using the cosine law.*

$$\phi = 90° - 25°$$

$$= 65°$$

$$R^2 = A^2 + B^2 - 2AB \cos \phi$$

$$= 200^2 + 175^2 - 2 \times 200 \times 175 \cos 65°$$

$$= 41\ 041.7$$

$$R = 202.59 \text{ m/s}$$

The direction of **R** *may be obtained by using the sine law to calculate the angle β.*

$$\frac{\sin \beta}{B} = \frac{\sin \phi}{R}$$

$$\sin \beta = \frac{175 \sin 65°}{202.59}$$

$$= 0.782\ 89$$

$$\beta = 51.52°$$

$$\text{Direction of } \vec{R} = 180.00° - 25.00° + 51.52°$$

$$= 206.52°$$

$$\boxed{\vec{R} = 203 \text{ m/s at } 206.52°}$$

By using the scale drawing of Fig. 2-12, *the value of* **R** *may be checked by scaling.*

$$\vec{R} = 203 \text{ m/s at } 207°$$

EXAMPLE 2-4

Determine **A** – **B** for the two displacement vectors **A** = 25 m at 120° and **B** = 35 m at 340°.

SOLUTION

First the vector triangle, as shown in Fig. 2-13(a), *or the vector parallelogram, as shown in* Fig. 2-13(b), *should be drawn to*

FIGURE 2-13

scale. *From the drawing it is observed that the triangle has two known sides and the contained angle, so that the cosine law can be used to solve for the length of the third side.*

$$\phi = 20° + 120°$$

$$= 140°$$

$$R^2 = A^2 + B^2 - 2AB \cos \phi$$

$$= 25^2 + 35^2 - 2 \times 25 \times 35 \cos 140°$$

$$= 625.00 + 1225.00 + 1340.58$$

$$= 3190.58$$

$$R = 56.49 \text{ m}$$

To find the direction of **R**, *first find the angle* β, *using the sine law.*

$$\frac{\sin \beta}{B} = \frac{\sin \phi}{R}$$

$$\sin \beta = \frac{35 \sin 140°}{56.49}$$

$$= 0.398\ 29$$

$$\beta = 23.47°$$

Direction of $\vec{R} = 120.00° + 23.47°$

$$= 143.47°$$

$$\boxed{\vec{R} = 56.5 \text{ m at } 143.47°}$$

From the scale drawing of Fig. 2-13, *the value of* **R** *can be obtained using a scale and protractor.*

$$\vec{R} = 56.5 \text{ m at } 143°$$

PROBLEMS

2-13 Determine **A** − **B** for the two vectors **A** = 100 m at 0° and **B** = 75 m at 90°.

2-14 For the vectors **A** = 30 m/s at 90° and **B** = 40 m/s at 180°, determine **A** − **B**.

2-15 Determine **A** − **B** for the two linear impulse vectors **A** = 50 N·s at 40° and **B** = 120 N·s at 130°.

2-16 Find the difference **A** − **B** for the two displacement vectors **A** = 24 mm at 160° and **B** = 10 mm at 70°.

2-17 Find **A** − **B** for the two moment vectors **A** = 150 N·m at 47° and **B** = 150 N·m at 12°.

2-18 Determine **A** − **B** for **A** = 200 N at 60° and **B** = 100 N at 30°.

2-19 For the acceleration vectors **A** = 80 m/s² at 315° and **B** = 95 m/s² at 265°, calculate **A** − **B**.

2-20 Find **A** − **B** for the displacement vectors shown in Fig. P2-20.

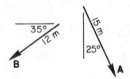

FIGURE P2-20

2-21 For the vectors shown in Fig. P2-21, calculate **A** − **B**.

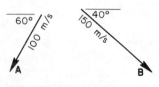

FIGURE P2-21

2-22 Acceleration vector **A** is 250 m/s² at 65° and **B** is 150 m/s² at 300°. Determine **A** − **B**.

2-23 For the two velocity vectors shown in Fig. P2-23, find **B** − **A**.

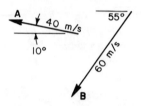

FIGURE P2-23

2-24 Determine **B** − **A** for the two moment vectors shown in Fig. P2-24.

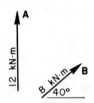

FIGURE P2-24

2-5   VECTOR COMPONENTS

Vectors can be broken up into components or parts just as they can be added. In fact, the components of a vector are defined as those vectors which, when added together, give the original vector. Two vectors, **A** and **B**, are shown in Fig. 2-14(a). When added together, they form **R**, as shown in Fig. 2-14(b). **A** and **B** are vector components of the vector **R**. **C** and **D**, as shown in Fig. 2-14(c), are also components of the vector **R**, for they also meet the requirement that **C** + **D** = **R**.

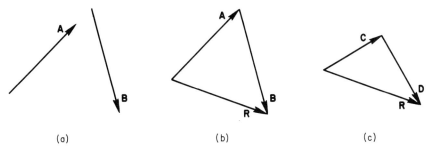

(a)   (b)   (c)

FIGURE 2-14

Figure 2-14(c) further illustrates the special case of rectangular components, or components that are perpendicular to each other. The rectangular components are the components that are used most frequently. Those that are parallel to the x and y axes will be used regularly in the solution of many problems in all areas of mechanics.

In the special case of rectangular components parallel to the x and y axes, a triangle is formed, as shown in Fig. 2-15. From the right-angle triangle and the trigonometric definitions, it is seen that

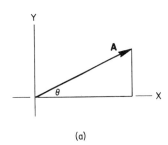

(a)

$$\frac{A_x}{A} = \cos \theta$$

or $A_x = A \cos \theta$ (2-2)

and $\frac{A_y}{A} = \sin \theta$

or $A_y = A \sin \theta$ (2-3)

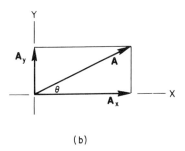

(b)

FIGURE 2-15

There is a sign convention for the x and y components, which eliminates the need to indicate whether the component points up

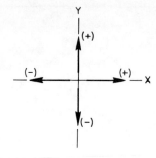

FIGURE 2-16

or down, left or right. The convention is illustrated in Fig. 2-16. A component parallel to the x axis is positive if it is directed to the positive end of the x axis and negative if it is directed to the negative end of the x axis. Similarly, a component parallel to the y axis is positive if it is directed to the positive end of the y axis and negative if it is directed to the negative end of the y axis.

In the general case, to determine the components, some information on the magnitude or direction of the components must be given, in order that a triangle can be formed, as shown in Fig. 2-17(a). Depending on the available information, the sine law or the cosine law can be used to obtain the missing information, so that the components can be fully determined, as shown in Fig. 2-17(b).

(a)   (b)

FIGURE 2-17

For reasons that will not become apparent until later, it is important that the components of a vector be concurrent at a point on the line of action of the vector, as shown in Fig. 2-18(a) or Fig. 2-18(b). The arrangement shown in Fig. 2-18(c) is not acceptable.

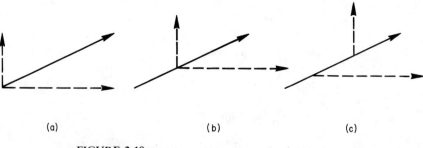

(a)   (b)   (c)

FIGURE 2-18

EXAMPLE 2-5

Calculate the x and y components for the displacement vector shown in Fig. 2-19.

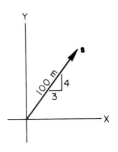

FIGURE 2-19

SOLUTION

It is possible to use the angle formed by the vector and the x axis, and Eq. (2-2) and Eq. (2-3). However, this is one case where it is more efficient to use similar triangles, as shown in Fig. 2-20. *(Note that the usual symbol for the displacement vector is s.) If* Fig. 2-20 *is drawn to scale, then the values for s_x and s_y can be checked by scaling.*

From similar triangles:

$$\frac{s_x}{s} = \frac{3}{5}$$

$$s_x = \frac{3}{5} \times 100$$

$$= 60.00 \text{ m}$$

$$\frac{s_y}{s} = \frac{4}{5}$$

$$s_y = \frac{4}{5} \times 100$$

$$= 80.00 \text{ m}$$

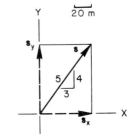

FIGURE 2-20

$$\boxed{\begin{array}{l} s_x = 60.0 \text{ m} \\ s_y = 80.0 \text{ m} \end{array}}$$

The signs for both components are positive since the x component is directed to the positive end of the x axis and the y component is directed to the positive end of the y axis.

By scaling from Fig. 2-20, *the following values are obtained:*

$$s_x = 60 \text{ m}$$

$$s_y = 80 \text{ m}$$

EXAMPLE 2-6

For a force vector of 15 MN at an angle of $215°$, determine the x and y components.

SOLUTION

The recommended procedure is to make a scale drawing, as shown in Fig. 2-21, *and determine the angle* ϕ. *It is then possible to use Eqs.* (2-2) *and* (2-3) *to determine the values for* F_x *and* F_y. *In each case, the correct sign, based on the sign convention illustrated in* Fig. 2-16, *must be chosen, and given to the values.*

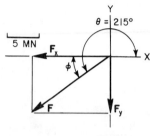

FIGURE 2-21

$$\phi = 215° - 180°$$
$$= 35°$$
$$F_x = F \cos \phi$$
$$= -15 \cos 35°$$
$$= -12.287 \text{ MN}$$
$$F_y = F \sin \phi$$
$$= -15 \sin 35°$$
$$= -8.604 \text{ MN}$$

$$\boxed{\begin{array}{l} F_x = -12.3 \text{ MN} \\ F_y = -8.60 \text{ MN} \end{array}}$$

Note that since the x component points to the left, it has been given a negative sign, and since the y component points down, it also has been given a negative sign.

(It is possible to solve for F_x *and* F_y *directly using Eqs.* (2-2) *and* (2-3), *provided the calculator in use can handle functions for angles greater than* 90°. *However, using angles greater than* 90° *is likely to lead to problems with signs when the study of moments is undertaken, and is therefore not recommended.)*

From the scale drawing of Fig. 2-21, *the following values for the components are obtained:*

$$F_x = -12.3 \text{ MN}$$
$$F_y = -8.60 \text{ MN}$$

EXAMPLE 2-7

A velocity vector is 275 m/s at 87°. Determine the two components of the vector at 0° and 130°.

SOLUTION

The first step is to draw a vector triangle, preferably to scale, as shown in Fig. 2-22, *showing the vectors* **v**, **v**₁ *and* **v**₂ *where* **v**₁ *is the vector at* 0° *and* **v**₂ *is the vector at* 130°. *From the vector triangle, the sine law can be used to obtain the lengths of* **v**₁ *and* **v**₂.

$$\beta = 180° - 130°$$

$$= 50°$$

$$\phi = 180° - 87° - 50°$$

$$= 43°$$

$$\frac{v_1}{\sin \phi} = \frac{v}{\sin \beta}$$

$$v_1 = \frac{275 \sin 43°}{\sin 50°}$$

$$= 244.8 \text{ m/s}$$

$$\frac{v_2}{\sin \alpha} = \frac{v}{\sin \beta}$$

$$v_2 = \frac{275 \sin 87°}{\sin 50°}$$

$$= 358.5 \text{ m/s}$$

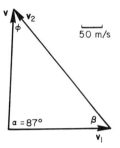

FIGURE 2-22

$$\boxed{\begin{array}{l} v_1 = 245 \text{ m/s} \\ v_2 = 358 \text{ m/s} \end{array}}$$

From the scale drawing, Fig. 2-22, *the following is obtained:*

$$v_1 = 245 \text{ m/s}$$
$$v_2 = 360 \text{ m/s}$$

PROBLEMS

2-25 Calculate the x and y components of the vector shown in Fig. P2-25.

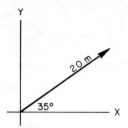

FIGURE P2-25

2-26 For the vector shown in Fig. P2-26, determine the x and y components.

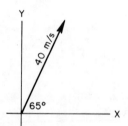

FIGURE P2-26

2-27 Calculate the x and y components of the force shown in Fig. P2-27.

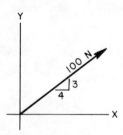

FIGURE P2-27

2-28 For the force shown in Fig. P2-28, determine the x and y components.

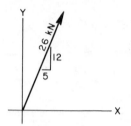

FIGURE P2-28

2-29 For the vector shown in Fig. P2-29, determine the x and y components.

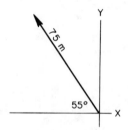

FIGURE P2-29

2-30 Evaluate the x and y components for the acceleration vector shown in Fig. P2-30.

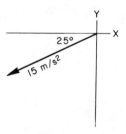

FIGURE P2-30

2-31 For the force shown in Fig. P2-31, calculate the *x* and *y* components.

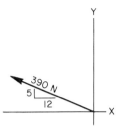

FIGURE P2-31

2-32 Evaluate the *x* and *y* components for the force shown in Fig. P2-32.

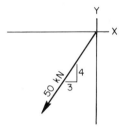

FIGURE P2-32

2-33 Determine the *x* and *y* components for a 200 kN·m moment vector at 265°.

2-34 Find the *x* and *y* components of a 6 MN force vector at 120°.

2-35 A man walks 500 m in a direction 25° west of north. Determine the north and west components of his displacement.

2-36 If an aircraft flies a distance of 200 km in a direction 55° west of south, determine the south and west components of its flight.

2-37 A velocity vector of 400 km/h is directed vertically down. Determine the components of the vector that have directions of 180° and 300°.

2-38 A force of 75 kN is directed horizontally to the left. It is to be replaced by two components, component **B** at 90° and component **C** at 250°. Determine the two components.

2-39 If a vector is 300 kN vertically up, determine the two components at 75° and 200°.

2-40 The direct flight between two points is 500 km at 95°. Because of the topography (a mountain range), the pilot of a light aircraft first flies a course of 37° and then follows a course of 170°. Determine the length of each component of the flight. (Navigational directions are measured clockwise from 0° at north.)

2-41 Much layout work in steel and sheet metal is really an exercise in calculating components of displacement vectors. Determine the lengths of the components at 20° and 250° for a displacement vector of 760 mm at 330°.

2-42 Determine the components at 45° and 80° for a force of 500 N at 60°.

2-43 For a displacement vector of 75 m at 135°, determine the length of the one component at 90° and the direction of the second component, which is 60 m in length. (There are two possible solutions.)

2-44 Determine the components, one of 150 kN and unknown direction, and one of unknown magnitude and at 195°, of a 200 kN force at 155°. (This problem has two possible solutions.)

2-45 A velocity vector of 500 m/s at 37° has components of 600 m/s and 200 m/s. Determine the directions of the two components. (There are two correct solutions to this problem.)

2-46 Find the directions of the two components of a 200 mm displacement vector at 340° if one component is 120 mm and the second is 240 mm. (There are two possible correct solutions.)

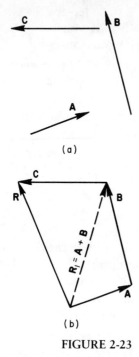

(a)

(b)

FIGURE 2-23

2-6   THE VECTOR POLYGON

In some cases, it is necessary to find the sum of more than two vectors. This could be done by forming a series of vector triangles. Three vectors are shown in Fig. 2-23(a). From Fig. 2-23(b), it is seen that $R_1 = A + B$ and $R = R_1 + C$ or $R = A + B + C$. In the process, a vector polygon has been formed. The *polygon rule* for vector addition states that the sum of several vectors may be obtained by drawing the vectors tip to tail, to scale. The sum is the vector drawn from the tail of the first vector to the tip of the last vector, as shown in Fig. 2-23(b). This provides a very fast method for obtaining accurate graphical values for the sum of any number of vectors. It may also be used if one or more of the vectors is negative, if it is kept in mind that the negative vector is simply opposite in direction to the positive vector.

It might be noted that the triangle rule is actually a special case of the polygon rule, for a triangle is just a three-sided polygon.

The vector polygon is not a direct method for the analytical solution of vector addition problems, so a somewhat modified approach must be used. Three vectors are shown in Fig. 2-24(a), and the vector polygon of $A + B + C$ is shown in Fig. 2-24(b). Also shown in Fig. 2-24(b) are the x components of each of the vectors. From Fig. 2-24(b) it can be seen that

$$R_x = A_x + B_x + C_x \qquad (2\text{-}4)$$

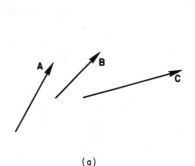

(a)

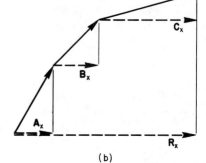

(b)

FIGURE 2-24

Similarly, from Fig. 2-24(c), it can be seen that in the y direction

$$R_y = A_y + B_y + C_y \qquad (2\text{-}5)$$

In the case of the addition of more than three vectors, Eqs. (2-4) and (2-5) can be expanded to take into account any number of vectors. Attention must be paid to the signs of the components to ensure that the proper value for R_x and R_y is obtained.

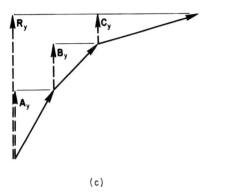

(c)

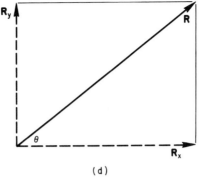

(d)

FIGURE 2-24 cont'd

The magnitude of **R** may be obtained using the Pythagorean theorem:

$$R = (R_x^2 + R_y^2)^{1/2} \qquad (2\text{-}6)$$

The angle θ may be obtained from

$$\frac{R_y}{R_x} = \tan \theta$$

$$\text{or } \theta = \tan^{-1} \frac{R_y}{R_x}$$

In this book θ, as determined by Eq. (2-7), is always the angle between the x component of the resultant and the resultant. When using Eq. (2-7), one is calculating an angle in a right-angled triangle; so R_x and R_y are used without their signs. The same applies to the use of Eq. (2-8), where R_y will always be used without its sign so that the value of R will always be positive.

The magnitude of **R** may be obtained from

$$R = \frac{R_y}{\sin \theta} \qquad (2\text{-}8)$$

Equation (2-8) is more convenient to use on most calculators than Eq. (2-6).

EXAMPLE 2-8

Determine the sum of the three vectors shown in Fig. 2-25.

SOLUTION

The first step is to find the x and y components of the sum, using Eqs. (2-4) and (2-5), along with the procedure for calculating rectangular components outlined in Article 2-5.

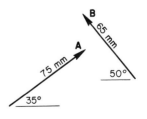

FIGURE 2-25

$$R_x = A_x + B_x + C_x$$
$$= 75 \cos 35° - 65 \cos 50°$$
$$= 61.44 - 41.78$$
$$= 19.66 \text{ mm}$$

*Note that the components, with their correct signs, are added algebraically. Vector **C** has no x component, since it is vertical.*

$$R_y = A_y + B_y + C_y$$
$$= 75 \sin 35° + 65 \sin 50° - 40$$
$$= 43.02 + 49.79 - 40.00$$
$$= 52.81 \text{ mm}$$

*The direction of **R** may be obtained from Eq. (2-7).*

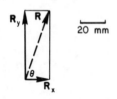

FIGURE 2-26

$$\theta = \tan^{-1} \frac{R_y}{R_x}$$
$$= \tan^{-1} \frac{52.81}{19.66}$$
$$= 69.58°$$

Since both R_x and R_y are positive, θ is a first-quadrant angle. A sketch showing R_x and R_y, as shown in Fig. 2-26, *is recommended as an aid in evaluating the angle θ and determining the direction of **R**.*

*The length of **R** may now be obtained from Eq. (2-8).*

$$R = \frac{R_y}{\sin \theta}$$
$$= \frac{52.81}{\sin 69.58°}$$
$$= 56.351 \text{ mm}$$

$$\boxed{\vec{R} = 56.4 \text{ mm at } 69.58°}$$

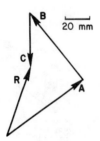

FIGURE 2-27

The vector polygon, drawn to scale, as shown in Fig. 2-27, *provides an independent check, as well as a separate method of evaluating **A** + **B** + **C**.*

EXAMPLE 2-9

For the three force vectors, $\mathbf{A} = 5$ kN at $70°$, $\mathbf{B} = 10$ kN at $200°$ and $\mathbf{C} = 8$ kN at $240°$, determine $\mathbf{A} + \mathbf{B} - \mathbf{C}$.

SOLUTION

As an aid to the analytical solution, it is recommended that the vector polygon, as shown in Fig. 2-28, *be drawn first. Note that* $-\mathbf{C}$ *is the same as* $\mathbf{C}$, *but opposite in direction. In* Fig. 2-28 *the vectors in the polygon cross. This is permissible.*

With the drawing to aid in the calculations, the components of the sum can now be determined using Eq. (2-4) *and* Eq. (2-5).

$$R_x = A_x + B_x - C_x$$
$$= 5 \cos 70° - 10 \cos 20° + 8 \cos 60°$$
$$= 1.710 - 9.397 + 4.000$$
$$= -3.687 \text{ kN}$$

$$R_y = A_y + B_y - C_y$$
$$= 5 \sin 70° - 10 \sin 20° + 8 \sin 60°$$
$$= 4.698 - 3.420 + 6.928$$
$$= 8.206 \text{ kN}$$

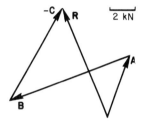

FIGURE 2-28

In the above calculations, each component has been determined by forming a right-angle triangle with the components and assigning the correct sign to the value of each component.

To minimize errors, a drawing of R_x, R_y *and* $\mathbf{R}$, *as shown in* Fig. 2-29, *is recommended. From* Fig. 2-29 *and* Eq. (2-7), *the value for* θ *can be obtained. Since* θ *is an angle less than* $90°$ *in a right-angled triangle, the magnitudes, and not the signs, of* R_x *and* R_y *are used.*

$$\theta = \tan^{-1} \frac{R_y}{R_x}$$
$$= \tan^{-1} \frac{8.206}{3.687}$$
$$= 65.80°$$

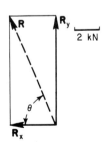

FIGURE 2-29

From this information, the direction of $\mathbf{R}$ *may be obtained.*

$$\text{Direction of } \vec{R} = 180.00° - 65.80°$$
$$= 114.20°$$

The magnitude of $\mathbf{R}$ *is obtained from* Eq. (2-8).

$$R = \frac{R_y}{\sin \theta}$$

$$= \frac{8.206}{\sin 65.80°}$$

$$= 8.996 \text{ kN}$$

$$\boxed{\vec{R} = 9.00 \text{ kN at } 114.20°}$$

The scale drawing of Fig. 2-29 *can also be used to obtain the value for **R**.*

$$\vec{R} = 9.00 \text{ kN at } 114°$$

PROBLEMS

2-47 Determine the sum of the three displacement vectors shown in Fig. P2-47.

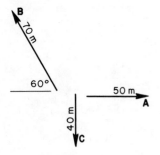

FIGURE P2-47

2-48 For the three vectors shown in Fig. P2-48 obtain their vector sum.

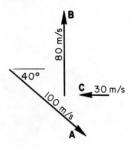

FIGURE P2-48

2-49 Find the sum of the three force vectors shown in Fig. P2-49.

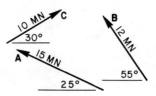

FIGURE P2-49

2-50 For the displacement vectors shown in Fig. P2-50, determine **A** + **B** + **C**.

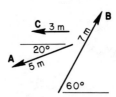

FIGURE P2-50

2-51 Determine the sum of the three velocity vectors, **A** = 200 m/s at 110°, **B** = 150 m/s at 320° and **C** = 175 m/s at 215°

2-52 Find **A** + **B** + **C** for the three vectors **A** = 12 MN at 15°, **B** = 15 MN at 245° and **C** = 10 MN at 160°.

2-53 For the vectors **A** = 25 kN at 40°, **B** = 15 kN at 270°, **C** = 45 kN at 300° and **D** = 20 kN at 215°, determine **A** + **B** + **C** + **D**.

2-54 Evaluate the sum of the four displacement vectors **A** = 140 mm at 250°, **B** = 60 mm at 105°, **C** = 300 mm at 25° and **D** = 100 mm at 260°.

2-55 Determine **A** + **B** - **C** for the three velocity vectors shown in Fig. P2-55.

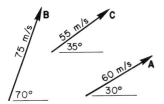

FIGURE P2-55

2-56 Find **A** - **B** + **C** for the three vectors shown in Fig. P2-56.

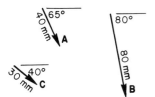

FIGURE P2-56

2-57 For the acceleration vectors shown in Fig. P2-57, determine **A** - **B** + **C**.

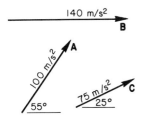

FIGURE P2-57

2-58 Determine **A** + **B** - **C** for the three forces shown in Fig. P2-58.

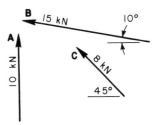

FIGURE P2-58

2-59 Evaluate **A** - **B** + **C** for the three vectors **A** = 100 N at 180°, **B** = 70 N at 60° and **C** = 110 N at 320°.

2-60 For the displacement vectors **A** = 40 m at 30°, **B** = 20 m at 0° and **C** = 30 m at 230°, find **A** - **B** + **C**.

2-61 For the momentum vectors **A** = 200 kg·m/s at 215°, **B** = 170 kg·m/s at 160°, **C** = 225 kg·m/s at 60° and **D** = 250 kg·m/s at 25°, determine **A** - **B** - **C** + **D**.

2-62 Calculate **A** + **B** - **C** - **D** for the four moment vectors **A** = 50 kN·m at 270°, **B** = 200 kN·m at 40°, **C** = 90 kN·m at 55° and **D** = 40 kN·m at 115°.

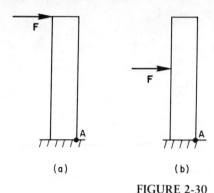

(a)   (b)

FIGURE 2-30

2-7 MOMENT OF A FORCE

The moment of a force may be defined as a measure of the tendency of that force to cause rotation about an axis.

The moment of a force can be visualized by considering the action of a force on a tall bookcase. Figure 2-30 shows an end view of such a bookcase. In Fig. 2-30(a) a force is applied horizontally at the top, and one knows from experience that the bookcase is likely to overturn. However, if the same force is applied at a lower point, as shown in Fig. 2-30(b), the bookcase is less likely to overturn. It can be seen that the farther the force is from the axis of rotation (in the example of the bookcase, the axis of rotation passes through A), the greater the tendency to cause rotation. Note that in statics a moment will tend to cause rotation, whereas in dynamics, where bodies are in motion, the moment may actually cause rotation.

The magnitude of a moment may be calculated from

$$M_A = Fd \qquad (2\text{-}9)$$

where M is the magnitude of the moment,

$\qquad A$ is the axis of rotation with respect to which the moment is measured,

$\qquad F$ is the magnitude of the force, and

$\qquad d$ is the perpendicular distance from the axis of rotation to the line of action of the force. It is sometimes called the *moment arm*.

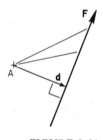

FIGURE 2-31

Some of these quantities are illustrated in Fig. 2-31. Particular emphasis must be placed on d, the *perpendicular* distance. There are an infinite number of distances from A to the line of action of F, but a glance at Fig. 2-31 shows that there is only one perpendicular distance, and hence only one possible value for the magnitude of the moment.

Since the units of force are newtons, and the units of distance are metres, the units of moment are newton-metres, for which N·m is the correct abbreviation. Multiples of the N·m, such as kN·m or MN·m, will also be used.

A moment is a vector quantity because it has both magnitude and direction. The moment vector is perpendicular to the plane that contains the force vector and the perpendicular distance. Strictly speaking, the perpendicular distance is the displacement vector from the axis of rotation to the line of action of the force. The relationship between the force, distance and moment is illustrated in Fig. 2-32. Note that, since the discussion is limited to plane or two-dimensional force systems, usually in the x-y plane, then the moment vectors will be parallel to the z axis.

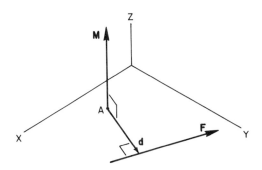

FIGURE 2-32

Thus, as long as the force system being dealt with is a plane system, the moment vectors will all be parallel.

For such plane systems, a sign convention for moments known as the *right-hand rule* has been developed. According to the right-hand rule, if the fingers of the right hand curl in the direction of the potential rotation, and the thumb, placed along the axis of rotation, points to the positive end of the z axis (for the axis system shown in Fig. 2-32), the moment is positive. If the thumb points to the negative end of the axis, the moment is considered to be negative.

Looking at the tendency to cause rotation in a plane, as illustrated in Fig. 2-32, a force that tends to cause counterclockwise rotation about the axis A causes a positive moment, and a force that tends to cause clockwise rotation about the axis causes a negative moment. Note carefully that the sign of the moment does not depend on the sign of the force, but on the direction of rotation that tends to be caused. The forces in both Fig. 2-33(a) and Fig. 2-33(b) are positive, but in Fig. 2-33(a) the force causes a positive moment about the axis A and in Fig. 2-33(b) it causes a negative moment about the axis A.

Since moments are vectors, they can be added using vector procedures. However, since the discussion relates to force systems in a plane, and the moment vectors will therefore all be parallel, for this set of conditions the moment vectors can be added algebraically, simply by paying due attention to their signs.

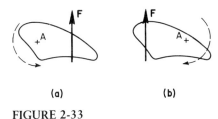

(a)   (b)

FIGURE 2-33

EXAMPLE 2-10

A 65 kg diver stands on the end of a diving board 3 m long. Determine the moment the diver causes about an axis through the support for the board.

SOLUTION

A diagram, such as Fig. 2-34, *showing forces and dimensions may assist in solving the problem. It is necessary to convert the mass of the man to the force, in newtons, that he exerts on the board. The force due to gravity acting on the man is equal to his mass times the gravitational constant g, which is approximately 9.807. The sign of the moment is assigned based on the fact that in* Fig. 2-34 *the force would cause clockwise or negative rotation about an axis through A.*

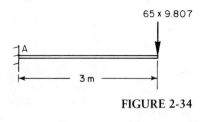

FIGURE 2-34

$$M_A = Fd$$
$$= -(65 \times 9.807 \times 3)$$
$$= -1912 \text{ N·m}$$

$$\boxed{M_A = -1910 \text{ N·m}}$$

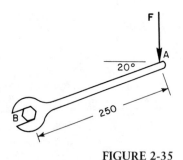

FIGURE 2-35

EXAMPLE 2-11

Determine the moment the 150 N force causes about the bolt *B* shown in Fig. 2-35.

SOLUTION

A drawing with pertinent dimensions, as shown in Fig. 2-36, *would be helpful. The perpendicular distance from the axis of rotation to the line of action of the force can be calculated using trigonometry. Note that the distance should be expressed in metres so that the units of moment will be newton metres. Since the force causes clockwise rotation about the axis through B, the sign of the moment will be negative.*

$$d = 0.250 \cos 20°$$
$$M_B = Fd$$
$$= -(150 \times 0.250 \cos 20°)$$
$$= -35.24 \text{ N·m}$$

$$\boxed{M_B = -35.2 \text{ N·m}}$$

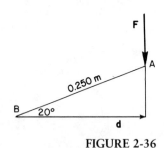

FIGURE 2-36

EXAMPLE 2-12

For the two forces shown in Fig. 2-37, determine the sum of their moments with respect to an axis through the origin.

SOLUTION

A drawing, as shown in Fig. 2-38, *will be an aid in determining the perpendicular distance, d_2, required in calculating the moment of the 150 N force. The sum of the moments will be the algebraic sum of the two moments.*

$$d_2 = 7 \sin 30°$$

$$\Sigma M_o = F_1 d_1 + F_2 d_2$$

$$= -(100 \times 5) + 150 \times 7 \sin 30°$$

$$= -500.0 + 525.0$$

$$= 25.0 \text{ N·m}$$

$$\boxed{M_o = 25.0 \text{ N·m}}$$

FIGURE 2-37

FIGURE 2-38

PROBLEMS

2-63 Determine the moment of the force shown in Fig. P2-63 about an axis through the origin.

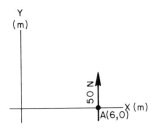

FIGURE P2-63

2-64 For the force shown in Fig. P2-64, calculate the moment about the origin.

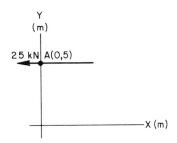

FIGURE P2-64

50 *Forces*

2-65 Find the moment of the force shown in Fig. P2-65 about an axis through point *A*.

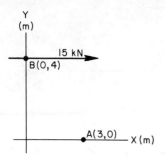

FIGURE P2-65

2-66 Calculate the moment of the force shown in Fig. P2-66 about an axis passing through point *A*.

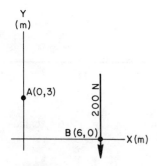

FIGURE P2-66

2-67 Determine the moment of the force shown in Fig. P2-67 about an axis through point *B*.

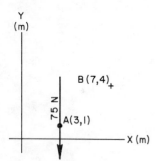

FIGURE P2-67

2-68 For the force shown in Fig. P2-68, determine its moment about an axis passing through point *B*.

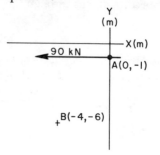

FIGURE P2-68

2-69 The starter cord used on the recoil starter for a small engine as shown in Fig. P2-69 applies a moment about the axis at *A*. If the magnitude of the moment required to start the engine is 10.0 N·m, determine the force that must be applied.

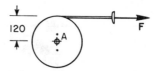

FIGURE P2-69

2-70 The device shown in Fig. P2-70 is a link in a control mechanism. To operate the mechanism, the force F_1 must create a moment with a magnitude of 25.0 N·m about an axis through *A*. Calculate the size of F_1.

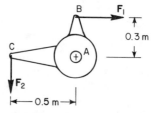

FIGURE P2-70

2-71 Calculate the moment of the force shown in Fig. P2-71 about an axis through *A*.

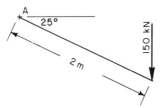

FIGURE P2-71

2-72 Find the moment of the force shown in Fig. P2-72 about an axis through *A*.

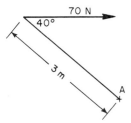

FIGURE P2-72

2-73 For the force shown in Fig. P2-73, determine the moment created about an axis through *A*.

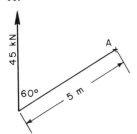

FIGURE P2-73

2-74 Determine the moment about an axis through *A* caused by the force shown in Fig. P2-74.

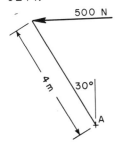

FIGURE P2-74

2-75 To activate the shift lever shown in Fig. P2-75, a moment of −30 N·m must be exerted about the axis at *A*. If the shift lever is 0.50 m long, determine the horizontal force F required to cause this moment.

FIGURE P2-75

2-76 One of the factors that limits the reach of a crane is the moment created by the load, measured with respect to an axis *A* at the base of the front support. If the boom shown in Fig. P2-76 is 30 m long, and at an angle of 25° with the horizontal, determine the moment of the 20 000 kg load about an axis through *A*.

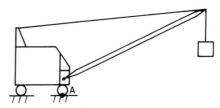

FIGURE P2-76

2-77 For the forces shown in Fig. P2-77, determine the sum of the moments about an axis through *A*.

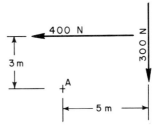

FIGURE P2-77

52 *Forces*

2-78 Determine the sum of the moments with respect to an axis through *A* for the two forces shown in Fig. P2-78.

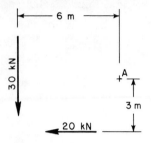

FIGURE P2-78

2-79 Find the sum of the moments about an axis through *A* for the forces shown in Fig. P2-79.

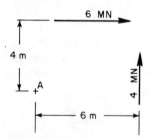

FIGURE P2-79

2-80 Determine the sum of the moments about an axis through *A* for the forces shown in Fig. P2-80.

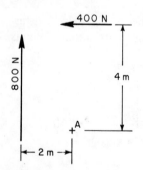

FIGURE P2-80

2-81 For the two forces shown in Fig. P2-81, determine the sum of their moments with respect to an axis through *A*.

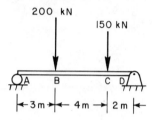

FIGURE P2-81

2-82 Calculate the sum of the moments of the two forces shown in Fig. P2-82 with respect to an axis through *A*.

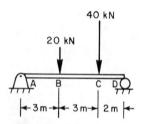

FIGURE P2-82

2-83 For the forces shown in Fig. P2-83, determine the sum of their moments with respect to an axis through *A*.

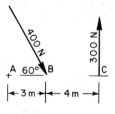

FIGURE P2-83

2-84 Calculate the sum of the moments about an axis through A for the two forces shown in Fig. P2-84.

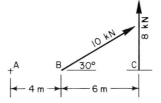

FIGURE P2-84

2-8 VARIGNON'S THEOREM

In some cases, the determination of moments is made difficult because calculating the perpendicular distance from the axis of rotation to the line of action of the force is somewhat complicated and time-consuming. Varignon's theorem provides an approach that will greatly simplify many such calculations. According to Varignon's theorem, the moment of a force about an axis is equal to the sum of the moments of the components of the force about the same axis.

A force $\mathbf{F}$ is shown in Fig. 2-39, and to determine its moment about an axis through A, it would be necessary to first use trigonometry to calculate the perpendicular distance d. Alternatively, the components $\mathbf{F}_x$ and $\mathbf{F}_y$ could be calculated. The perpendicular distances d_x and d_y are usually readily available. The sum of

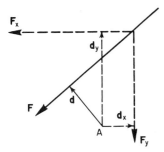

FIGURE 2-39

the moments about A of $\mathbf{F}_x$ and $\mathbf{F}_y$ could then be easily calculated, and the value obtained would be the same as that obtained from Fd. It must be remembered that the components must be concurrent on the line of action of the force.

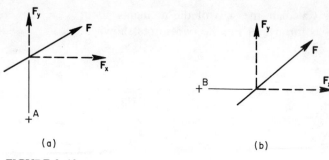

(a)   (b)

FIGURE 2-40

It is often possible to further simplify the calculation of a moment using Varignon's theorem by carefully selecting the location of the point of concurrency of the components, so that one of the components is collinear with the axis of rotation, as shown in Fig. 2-40. In Fig. 2-40(a) the y component is collinear with A, and thus has no moment about A. Similarly, the moment of F about an axis through B in Fig. 2-40(b) could be obtained by using only F_y, since F_x is collinear with B, and would have no moment about B.

EXAMPLE 2-13

Determine the moment of the force shown in Fig. 2-41 with respec· to an axis through A.

SOLUTION

This problem may be solved by using Varignon's theorem. If the components are concurrent at B, then the x component will have no moment about A. Only the moment of the y component will enter into the calculation.

$$M_A = Fd$$
$$= -(250 \sin 50° \times 11)$$
$$= -2106.6 \text{ N·m}$$

$$\boxed{M_A = -2110 \text{ N·m}}$$

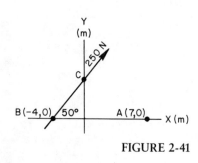

FIGURE 2-41

Note that if the components are concurrent at C, both the x and y components would have a moment about A, but the value for M_A is unchanged.

EXAMPLE 2-14

For the 80 kN force shown in Fig. 2-42, determine the moment with respect to an axis passing through B.

SOLUTION

Varignon's theorem will provide the simplest solution. The point of concurrency for the two components should be A, since it is the only known point on the line of action of the force. Note that the sign of the moment of each component must be determined separately, for the sign is not necessarily the same for both moments.

$$M_B = Fd$$

$$= -(80 \cos 40° \times 3) + 80 \sin 40° \times 7$$

$$= -183.85 + 359.96$$

$$= 176.11 \text{ kN} \cdot \text{m}$$

$$\boxed{M_B = 176 \text{ kN} \cdot \text{m}}$$

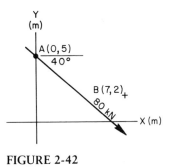

FIGURE 2-42

EXAMPLE 2-15

Determine the sum of the moments of the two forces shown in Fig. 2-43 about an axis through C.

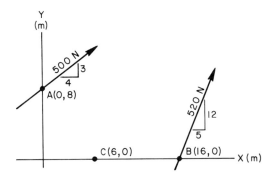

FIGURE 2-43

SOLUTION

The moment of each force can be most readily calculated using Varignon's theorem. In the case of the 500 N force, both components (when concurrent at A) will have a moment about C. For the 520 N force, only the y component (if the components are concurrent at B) will have a moment about C. The sign of the moment due to each component must be individually determined.

$$\Sigma\,M_c = \Sigma\,Fd$$

$$= -\left(\frac{4}{5} \times 500\right) \times 8 - \left(\frac{3}{5} \times 500\right) \times 6$$

$$+ \left(\frac{12}{13} \times 520\right) \times 10$$

$$= -3200.0 - 1800.0 + 4800.0$$

$$= -200.0\ \text{N·m}$$

$$\boxed{M_c = -200\ \text{N·m}}$$

PROBLEMS

2-85 Determine the moment caused by the force shown in Fig P2-85 about an axis through the origin.

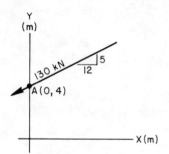

FIGURE P2-85

2-86 Calculate the moment of the force shown in Fig. P2-86 about an axis through the origin.

2-87 Determine the moment about an axis through the origin of the force shown in Fig. P2-87.

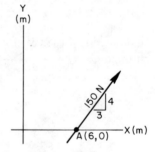

FIGURE P2-86

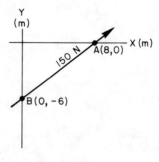

FIGURE P2-87

2-88 For the force shown in Fig. P2-88, calculate its moment about an axis through the origin.

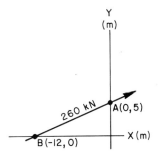

FIGURE P2-88

2-89 For the force shown in Fig. P2-89, find its moment about an axis through *B*.

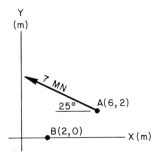

FIGURE P2-89

2-90 Calculate the moment of the force shown in Fig. P2-90 with respect to an axis through *B*.

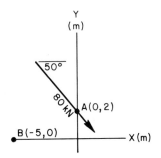

FIGURE P2-90

2-91 Determine the moment of the force shown in Fig. P2-91 about an axis through *B*.

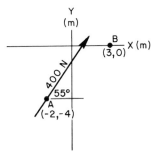

FIGURE P2-91

2-92 For the force shown in Fig. P2-92, find its moment about an axis through *B*.

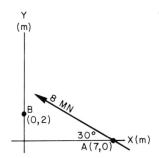

FIGURE P2-92

2-93 For the member shown in Fig. P2-93, calculate the moment of the 500 N force about an axis through point *A*.

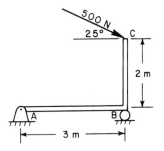

FIGURE P2-93

2-94 Calculate the moment of the 20 kN force with respect to an axis through A as shown in Fig. P2-94.

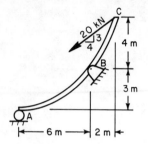

FIGURE P2-94

2-95 For the two forces shown in Fig. P2-95, calculate the sum of their moments about an axis through A.

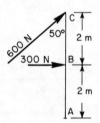

FIGURE P2-95

2-96 Determine the sum of the moments about an axis through A caused by the two forces shown in Fig. P2-96.

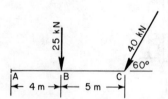

FIGURE P2-96

2-97 For the two forces shown in Fig. P2-97, find the sum of their moments about an axis through A.

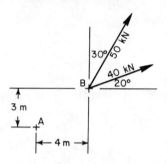

FIGURE P2-97

2-98 Determine the sum of the moments with respect to an axis through A for the two forces shown in Fig. P2-98.

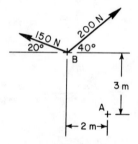

FIGURE P2-98

2-99 For the truss shown in Fig. P2-99, determine the sum of the moments of the two forces with respect to an axis through A.

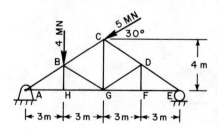

FIGURE P2-99

2-100 Calculate the sum of the moments with respect to an axis through D for the two forces acting on the truss shown in Fig. P2-100.

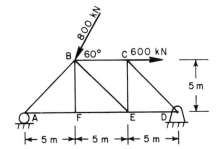

FIGURE P2-100

2-9 COUPLES

A couple is a force system that tends to cause rotation only. It is also known as a *torque*, particularly when the rotation tends to be caused by a shaft. There are many force systems that can cause pure rotation. The simplest system consists of two parallel forces, equal in magnitude and opposite in direction, as shown in Fig. 2-44. Since the two forces are equal in magnitude and opposite in direction, their sum will be zero. However, if moments are taken about an axis through either A or B, the magnitude of the couple can be determined to be

$$T = Fd \qquad (2\text{-}10)$$

where T is the magnitude of the couple,
F is the magnitude of the force, and
d is the perpendicular distance between the two forces.

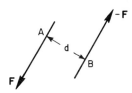

FIGURE 2-44

The sign of the couple is determined by the right-hand rule, and thus a couple tending to cause counterclockwise rotation is positive, and a couple tending to cause clockwise rotation is negative.

The magnitude of a couple is obtained by determining the sum of the moments of the forces about some axis. In the special case of the couple, the location of the axis of rotation makes no difference to the magnitude or sign of the couple, while in the case of the moment of a force, the location of the axis with respect to the force is critical.

Two forces forming a couple are shown in Fig. 2-45. To determine the magnitude of the couple, moments are taken about A, which is a distance e from $-F$.

$$\begin{aligned} T &= -(Fe) + F(e + d) \\ &= -Fe + Fe + Fd \\ &= Fd \end{aligned}$$

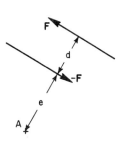

FIGURE 2-45

From the above simple proof, it can be seen that the point chosen for an axis for calculating the tendency to cause rotation has no effect on the magnitude of the couple.

Although the above discussion has been based on a couple consisting of two forces of equal magnitude and opposite direction, any force system whose sum is zero yet that tends to cause rotation is a couple. Figure 2-46 illustrates just two more possible configurations for couples, where the sum of the forces is zero and there is a tendency to cause rotation.

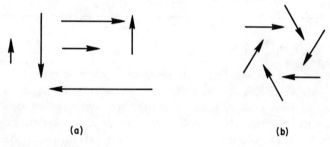

(a)   **(b)**

FIGURE 2-46

EXAMPLE 2-16

Determine the couple caused by the two forces shown in Fig. 2-47.

SOLUTION

Moments of the two forces can be taken about an axis passing through either A or B. The angle shown has no influence on the couple. Since the couple tends to cause clockwise rotation, its sign is negative.

$$T = Fd$$
$$= -(40 \times 0.250)$$
$$= -10.0 \ N \cdot m$$

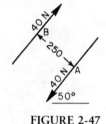

FIGURE 2-47

$$\boxed{T = -10.0 \ N \cdot m}$$

EXAMPLE 2-17

Determine the couple created by the system of forces shown in Fig. 2-48.

SOLUTION

Although the given system of forces may appear complex, it can be quickly noted that the sum of the forces in both the x and y directions is zero, and hence the sum of all the forces will be zero. However, the possibility still exists that the system forms a couple. Since two forces are concurrent at D, it is simplest to take moments about an axis through D. If the forces do create a moment about any point, then the system is a couple.

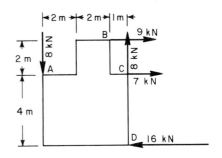

FIGURE 2-48

$$
\begin{aligned}
T &= \Sigma M_D = \Sigma Fd \\
&= 8 \times 5 - (9 \times 6) - (7 \times 4) \\
&= 40.00 - 54.00 - 28.00 \\
&= -42.00 \text{ kN}\cdot\text{m}
\end{aligned}
$$

$$\boxed{T = -42.0 \text{ kN}\cdot\text{m}}$$

EXAMPLE 2-18

The forces exerted by a socket on the head of a bolt being tightened are as shown in Fig. 2-49. If the specifications call for a torque of 250 N·m to be applied to the bolt, determine the magnitude of each of the forces applied to the head of the bolt.

FIGURE 2-49

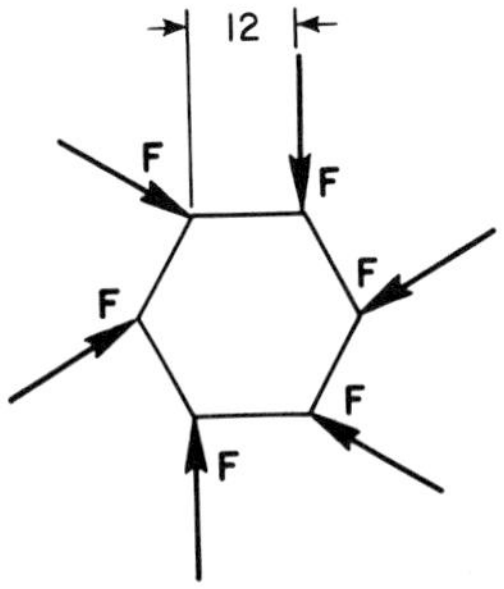

SOLUTION

The force system shown consists of three sets of parallel forces, equal in magnitude and opposite in direction. The calculations will be simplified if the system is treated as three couples. The sign of the couple has been neglected since only the magnitude of the forces is required.

$$
\begin{aligned}
T &= \Sigma Fd \\
250 &= 3(F \times 0.012) \\
F &= \frac{250}{3 \times 0.012} \\
&= 6944 \text{ N}
\end{aligned}
$$

$$\boxed{F = 6940 \text{ N}}$$

PROBLEMS

2-101 Two forces that are parallel, opposite in direction, two metres apart and of 20 kN magnitude form a couple. Determine the magnitude of the couple.

2-102 Find the magnitude of the couple formed by two parallel forces that are opposite in direction and three metres apart. Each force is 700 N.

2-103 Determine the couple caused by the two forces shown in Fig. P2-103.

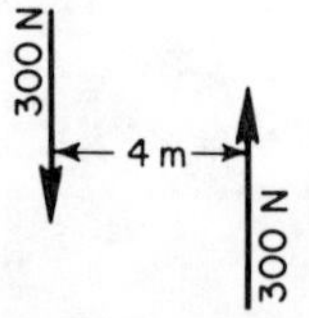

FIGURE P2-103

2-104 For the forces shown in Fig. P2-104, calculate the couple that is formed.

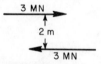

FIGURE P2-104

2-105 Evaluate the couple shown in Fig. P2-105.

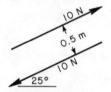

FIGURE P2-105

2-106 Determine the couple created by the force system shown in Fig. P2-106.

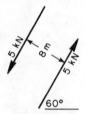

FIGURE P2-106

2-107 Calculate the couple formed by the forces shown in Fig. P2-107.

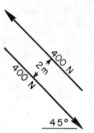

FIGURE P2-107

2-108 For the forces shown in Fig. P2-108, calculate the couple that is formed.

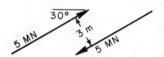

FIGURE P2-108

2-109 If the couple shown in Fig. P2-109 is 750 kN·m, determine the perpendicular distance between the two forces.

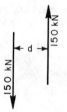

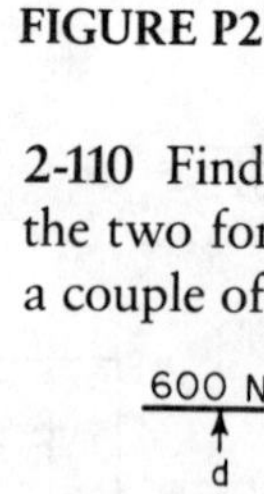

FIGURE P2-109

2-110 Find the perpendicular distance between the two forces shown in Fig. P2-110 if they cause a couple of –1800 N·m.

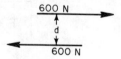

FIGURE P2-110

2-111 To loosen the nut on a wheel stud requires a torque of 300 N·m. What forces must be applied to the lug wrench shown in Fig. P2-111 in order to loosen the nut?

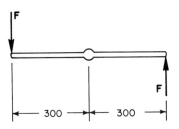

FIGURE P2-111

2-112 When tightening bolts, a specific torque is often called for. If the required torque for the bolt shown in Fig. P2-112 is 250 N·m, determine the magnitude of the force **P** that is exerted on the corners of the bolt head.

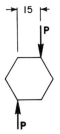

FIGURE P2-112

2-113 The flange shown in Fig. P2-113 is connected by six bolts. If the torque transmitted by the flange is 300 kN·m, determine the force carried by each bolt.

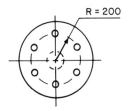

FIGURE P2-113

2-114 Determine the force that each bolt in the flange shown in Fig. P2-114 must carry if the torque transmitted by the flange is 12 kN·m.

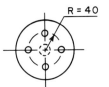

FIGURE P2-114

2-115 Determine the couple created by the system of forces shown in Fig. P2-115.

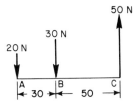

FIGURE P2-115

2-116 For the system of forces shown in Fig. P2-116, calculate the couple that is formed.

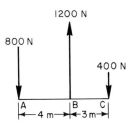

FIGURE P2-116

2-117 The forces shown in Fig. P2-117 form a couple of −60 kN·m. Determine the distance d.

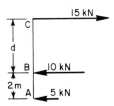

FIGURE P2-117

2-118 Find the distance *d* between the forces shown in Fig. P2-118 if the couple is 150 kN·m.

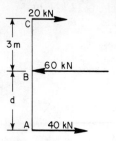

FIGURE P2-118

2-119 Calculate the couple formed by the system of forces shown in Fig. P2-119.

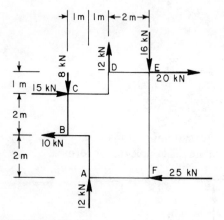

FIGURE P2-119

2-120 Determine the couple formed by the system of forces shown in Fig. P2-120.

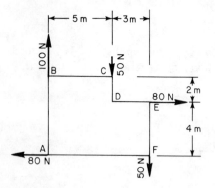

FIGURE P2-120

2-121 For the force system shown in Fig. P2-121, determine the couple that is formed.

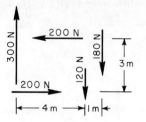

FIGURE P2-121

2-122 Find the couple created by the forces shown in Fig. P2-122.

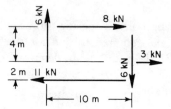

FIGURE P2-122

3 RESULTANTS

3-1 RESULTANT OF A SYSTEM OF FORCES

In many cases, the analysis of a problem in statics or dynamics can be simplified if the system of forces acting on a body is replaced by a simple equivalent system. The resultant of a system of forces is the simplest force system that can replace the original system of forces. This simplest system must have exactly the same effect on the body as the original system of forces. In other words, it must have the same tendency to cause translation (motion in a straight line) and the same tendency to cause rotation of the body. *Both* conditions must be satisfied.

The simplest system may consist of a single force or a couple. Although not truly a resultant, it is sometimes also convenient to replace a force system by a single force and a couple.

The design of the connection to the boat for the water skiers' tow ropes shown in Fig. 3-1 depends on the total or resultant force acting on the connection, rather than on the force from any one rope.

FIGURE 3-1 When designing the connection for the towropes, it is easier to work with one resultant force than with 20 separate forces. *Photo courtesy of Mercury Marine.*

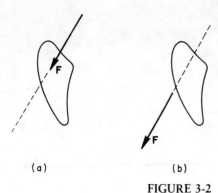

(a)   (b)

FIGURE 3-2

In determining a resultant, it is necessary to determine the magnitude and direction of the resultant force in order to have the resultant provide the same tendency to cause translation as the original force system. It is also necessary to locate the point of application of the resultant force so that the force will also have the same tendency to cause rotation as the original force system.

As stated previously, the discussion applies only to rigid bodies, or bodies that may be treated as rigid bodies without introducing any significant error.

To solve resultant problems, the *principle of transmissibility* is often used. This principle states that a force applied to a rigid body may be moved anywhere along its line of action without changing the effect of that force on the body. Figure 3-2(a) shows a force applied to a body, and Fig. 3-2(b) shows the same force at another point along the line of action of the first force. In both cases, the force would have the same effect on the rigid body. It will be shown in the next article that moving a force along its line of action will assist in simplifying the solution of many resultant problems.

3-2   PLANE, CONCURRENT FORCE SYSTEMS

A force system is a plane or coplanar system when all the forces lie in the same plane. It might also be described as a two-dimensional system. A system is concurrent if all the forces are concurrent, or intersect, at a common point. The force system shown in Fig. 3-3(a) is a plane, concurrent system, and point *A* is the point of concurrency. Similarly, Fig. 3-3(b) also shows a plane, concurrent force system, and point *B* is the point of concurrency. Although the forces shown in Fig. 3-3(b) do not appear to be concurrent at *B*, their lines of action are concurrent at *B*, and

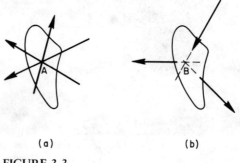

(a)   (b)

FIGURE 3-3

according to the principle of transmissibility the forces can be moved along their lines of action without changing their effect. Hence, *B* is the point of concurrency for the forces shown in Fig. 3-3(b).

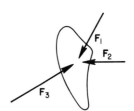

FIGURE 3-4

To determine the resultant of a concurrent force system, such as shown in Fig. 3-4, all that is necessary is to add the forces together using one of the methods of vector addition, such as the triangle rule, parallelogram rule, or the summation of components. The sum obtained will provide the same tendency to cause translation as the original system of forces. To ensure that the resultant will have the same tendency to cause rotation as the original system of forces, the resultant must be placed so that its line of action passes through the point of concurrency of the original system of forces.

To fully define the resultant force, its magnitude, direction and point of application must all be determined.

In general, the methods of Article 2-6 provide the best approach to determining the magnitude and direction of the resultant. The equations are modified somewhat, since all of the vectors are now force vectors.

Referring to the force system of Fig. 3-4, the *x* component of the resultant is

$$R_x = F_{x_1} + F_{x_2} + F_{x_3} + \ldots$$

or $\quad R_x = \Sigma F_{x_i}$ $\qquad$ (3-1)

Similarly

$$R_y = \Sigma F_{y_i} \qquad (3-2)$$

where R_x is the magnitude of the *x* component of the resultant of the force system,

R_y is the magnitude of the *y* component of the resultant of the force system,

ΣF_{x_i} is the algebraic summation of the *x* components of each force in the system, and

ΣF_{y_i} is the algebraic summation of the *y* components of each force in the system.

The *x* and *y* components of the resultant may be used to form a vector parallelogram to obtain **R**, as shown in Fig. 3-5. The magnitude of θ may be obtained from

$$\theta = \tan^{-1} \frac{R_y}{R_x} \qquad (3-3)$$

As mentioned previously, in this book θ is the angle between the *x* component of the resultant and the resultant, and thus is always less than 90°. R_x and R_y will be used without signs when

FIGURE 3-5

calculating θ. Similarly, when determining R, as shown below, R_y will be used without a sign so that R will always have a positive value.

$$R = \frac{R_y}{\sin \theta} \qquad (3\text{-}4)$$

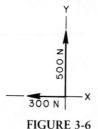

FIGURE 3-6

EXAMPLE 3-1

Determine the resultant of the system of two forces shown in Fig. 3-6.

SOLUTION

Since the two forces are at right angles to each other, the use of the triangle or parallelogram rules will provide the simplest, most direct solution. Figure 3-7 will assist in solving the problem, and if drawn to scale, it will provide a check on the calculations. Since θ is less than 90°, the magnitudes only of F_x and F_y are used to give a correct value to θ.

FIGURE 3-7

$$\theta = \tan^{-1} \frac{F_y}{F_x}$$

$$= \tan^{-1} \frac{500}{300}$$

$$= 59.04°$$

$$R = \frac{F_y}{\sin \theta}$$

$$= \frac{500}{\sin 59.04°}$$

$$= 583.1 \text{ kN}$$

Direction of $\vec{R}$ = 180.00° − 59.04°

$$= 120.96°$$

$$\boxed{\begin{array}{l} \vec{R} = 583 \text{ kN at } 120.96° \\ \text{through the origin} \end{array}}$$

*From the scale drawing of Fig. 3-7 the value for **R** can be found.*

$$\vec{R} = 583 \text{ kN at } 121°$$
$$\text{through the origin}$$

EXAMPLE 3-2

Find the resultant of the two coplanar forces F_1 = 125 kN at
110° and F_2 = 200 kN at 205°.

SOLUTION

*Since there are only two forces, they must intersect at some point
unless they are parallel. The magnitude and direction of the resultant may be obtained by use of the triangle rule. A drawing,
preferably to scale, as shown in* Fig. 3-8, *will help in applying
the triangle rule, and will provide a graphical check on the
solution.*

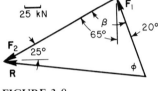

FIGURE 3-8

$$\beta = 20° + 65°$$

$$= 85°$$

$$R^2 = F_1^2 + F_2^2 - 2F_1F_2 \cos \beta$$

$$= 125^2 + 200^2 - 2 \times 125 \times 200 \cos 85°$$

$$= 15\ 625.0 + 40\ 000.0 - 4\ 357.8$$

$$= 51\ 267.2$$

$$R = 226.42 \text{ kN}$$

$$\frac{\sin \phi}{F_2} = \frac{\sin \beta}{R}$$

$$\sin \phi = \frac{200 \sin 85°}{226.42}$$

$$= 0.879\ 95$$

$$\phi = 61.64°$$

$$\text{Direction of } \vec{R} = 110.00° + 61.64°$$

$$= 171.64°$$

> $\vec{R}$ = 226 kN at 171.64°
> at point of concurrency

By scaling from Fig. 3-8, *the value for* **R** *is found to be*

$$\vec{R} = 226 \text{ kN at } 172°$$

This problem may also be solved by obtaining the sum of the components of the forces.

$$R_x = \Sigma F_{x_i}$$
$$= -125 \cos 70° - 200 \cos 25°$$
$$= -42.75 - 181.26$$
$$= -224.01 \text{ kN}$$
$$R_y = \Sigma F_{y_i}$$
$$= 125 \sin 70° - 200 \sin 25°$$
$$= 117.46 - 84.52$$
$$= 32.94 \text{ kN}$$

A sketch with the components of the resultant drawn to scale, as shown in Fig. 3-9, *is recommended. Since the angle that will be determined is* θ, *only the magnitudes (and not the signs) of* R_x *and* R_y *are used.*

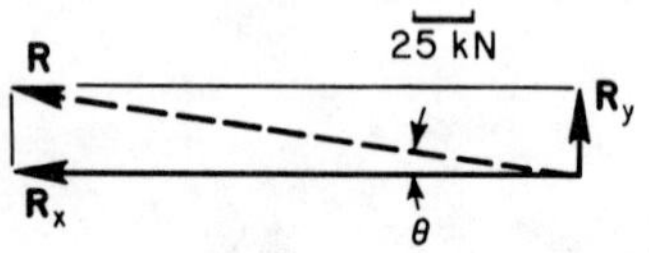

FIGURE 3-9

$$\theta = \tan^{-1}\frac{R_y}{R_x}$$
$$= \tan^{-1}\frac{32.94}{224.01}$$
$$= 8.37°$$

Direction of $\vec{R} = 180.00° - 8.37°$
$$= 171.63°$$

$$R = \frac{R_y}{\sin \theta}$$
$$= \frac{32.94}{\sin 8.37°}$$
$$= 226.29 \text{ kN}$$

$$\boxed{\begin{array}{l} \vec{R} = 226 \text{ kN at } 171.63° \\ \text{at point of concurrency} \end{array}}$$

EXAMPLE 3-3

Three forces acting on a body are shown in Fig. 3-10. Determine their resultant.

SOLUTION

The best analytical approach is to determine the components of the resultant by summing the components of the individual forces.

$$R_x = \Sigma F_{x_i}$$
$$= -4 + 3 \cos 50° + 5 \cos 60°$$
$$= -4.0000 + 1.9284 + 2.5000$$
$$= 0.4284 \text{ MN}$$

$$R_y = \Sigma F_{y_i}$$
$$= 3 \sin 50° - 5 \sin 60°$$
$$= 2.298 - 4.330$$
$$= -2.032 \text{ MN}$$

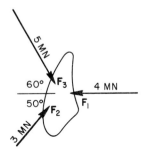

FIGURE 3-10

A drawing showing R_x and R_y, as shown in Fig. 3-11, should be made as an aid to determining the magnitude and direction of the resultant. Note that since the angle θ has been chosen, as shown, only the magnitudes of R_x and R_y, and not the signs, are used in calculating θ.

$$\theta = \tan^{-1} \frac{R_y}{R_x}$$

$$= \tan^{-1} \frac{2.032}{0.4284}$$

$$= 78.09°$$

Direction of $\vec{R}$ = 360.00° − 78.09°

$$= 281.91°$$

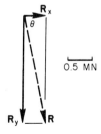

FIGURE 3-11

$$R = \frac{R_y}{\sin \theta}$$

$$= \frac{2.032}{\sin 78.09°}$$

$$= 2.077 \text{ MN}$$

$$\boxed{\begin{array}{l} \vec{R} = 2.08 \text{ MN at } 281.91° \\ \text{at point of concurrency} \end{array}}$$

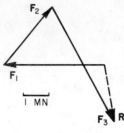

*The problem can be solved graphically by drawing a vector polygon, to scale, as shown in Fig. 3-12. The polygon method is strongly recommended as a check on the analytical solution. The magnitude and direction of **R** can be obtained using scale and protractor.*

FIGURE 3-12

$$\vec{R} = 2.08 \text{ MN at } 282°$$

at point of concurrency

PROBLEMS

3-1 For the forces shown in Fig. P3-1, determine the resultant.

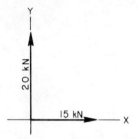

FIGURE P3-1

3-2 Find the resultant of the two forces shown in Fig. P3-2.

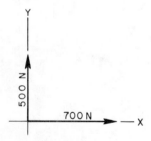

FIGURE P3-2

3-3 Find the resultant of forces $F_1 = 3$ MN at 90° and $F_2 = 2$ MN at 180°.

3-4 For the forces $F_1 = 80$ kN at 180° and $F_2 = 110$ kN at 270°, determine the resultant.

3-5 Calculate the resultant of F_1 and F_2 if $F_1 = 250$ kN at 270° and $F_2 = 225$ kN at 0°.

3-6 For $F_1 = 120$ N at 0° and $F_2 = 90$ N at 270°, determine the resultant force.

3-7 Find the resultant of the system of two forces shown in Fig. P3-7.

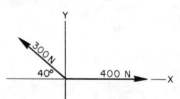

FIGURE P3-7

3-8 For the system of forces shown in Fig. P3-8, determine the resultant.

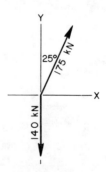

FIGURE P3-8

3-9 Determine the resultant of the system of forces shown in Fig. P3-9.

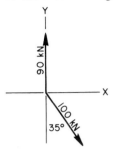

FIGURE P3-9

3-10 Calculate the resultant of the force system shown in Fig. P3-10.

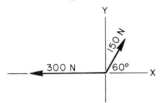

FIGURE P3-10

3-11 The load on the axle of a block or pulley is the resultant of the tensions in the ropes over the block. If the tension in both A and B is 750 N, determine the force on the axle at C of the block shown in Fig. P3-11.

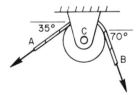

FIGURE P3-11

3-12 In Fig. P3-12, the forces shown in members AC and BC act on the pin at C. Determine the resultant of the two forces.

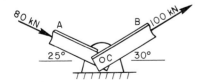

FIGURE P3-12

3-13 Two guy wires are attached to a utility pole as shown in Fig. P3-13. If the tension in guy wire AC is 5 kN and in BC is 4 kN, determine the resultant force acting on the anchor at C.

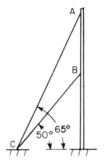

FIGURE P3-13

3-14 A powerboat tows two water skiers. If the tow rope for skier A exerts a force of 200 N at an angle of $+15°$ with the longitudinal axis of the boat and the tow rope for skier B exerts a force of 130 N at an angle of $-20°$ with the longitudinal axis, determine the resultant of the two forces exerted by the tow ropes on the boat.

3-15 Determine the resultant of the system of three forces shown in Fig. P3-15.

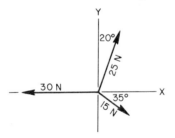

FIGURE P3-15

3-16 Calculate the resultant of the three forces shown in Fig. P3-16.

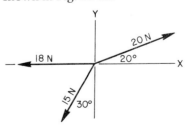

FIGURE P3-16

3-17 The three forces shown in Fig. P3-17 act on a pin in a structure. Determine the total force acting on the pin.

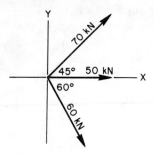

FIGURE P3-17

3-18 Determine the resultant of the concurrent force system shown in Fig. P3-18.

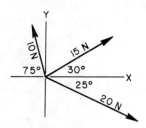

FIGURE P3-18

3-19 The forces acting on a ring used in rigging are shown in Fig. P3-19. Determine the resultant of the three forces.

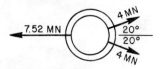

FIGURE P3-19

3-20 A drill bit is gripped in a chuck, and the forces shown in Fig. P3-20 are exerted on the bit. Determine the resultant of the three forces acting on the bit if each force is 1.2 kN.

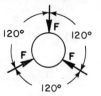

FIGURE P3-20

3-21 The forces in three members acting on a pin at the base of a structure are shown in Fig. P3-21. Determine the resultant of the three forces.

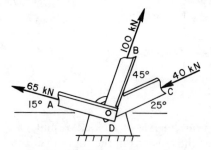

FIGURE P3-21

3-22 The forces shown in Fig. P3-22 are applied to an eye bolt. Determine the resultant of the forces acting on the bolt.

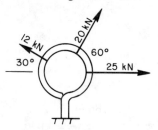

FIGURE P3-22

3-3 PLANE, PARALLEL FORCE SYSTEMS

A system of plane, parallel forces is shown in Fig. 3-13, along with the resultant **R**. The resultant of this system must produce the same tendency to cause linear translation as the original system, and it must also produce the same tendency to cause rotation as the original system.

For the resultant to provide the same tendency to cause linear translation, the magnitude of the resultant must be

$$R = F_1 + F_2 + F_3 + \ldots$$

or
$$R = \Sigma F_i \tag{3-5}$$

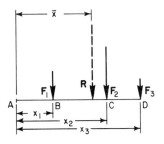

FIGURE 3-13

where R is the magnitude of the resultant force, and
ΣF_i is the algebraic sum of the original system of forces.

The above is a simple summation of the forces, since all the forces are parallel. Attention must be paid to the direction of the forces so that the correct sign is used with each force.

If the resultant force is to provide the same tendency to cause rotation about any axis as the original system of forces, then both the resultant and the original system must have the same moment about any axis. Taking moments about A:

M_A:

$$R\bar{x} = F_1 x_1 + F_2 x_2 + F_3 x_3 + \ldots$$

$$R\bar{x} = \Sigma (F_i x_i) \tag{3-6}$$

$$\bar{x} = \frac{\Sigma (F_i x_i)}{R}$$

but $R = \Sigma F_i$

thus
$$\bar{x} = \frac{\Sigma (F_i x_i)}{\Sigma F_i} \tag{3-7}$$

where $\bar{x}$ is the perpendicular distance from the reference axis to the resultant,
$\Sigma (F_i x_i)$ is the algebraic sum of the moments of each of the original forces about the reference axis, and
ΣF_i is the algebraic sum of the original system of forces.
When both R and $\bar{x}$ are determined, the resultant of the force system is then fully defined. It should be noted that if the calculations for $\bar{x}$ give a negative value for $\bar{x}$, this indicates that $\bar{x}$ is located to the opposite side of the axis of rotation from that assumed. However, the magnitude of $\bar{x}$ will be as calculated.

Because of the possibility of assuming an incorrect location for the resultant, it is important to be explicit in assuming the location of the resultant when working with Eq. (3-6) or Eq. (3-7). If the value obtained for the location is positive, the assumed location is correct.

If the resultant is always assumed to be to the positive side of the axis of rotation (that is, either to the right or above the axis of rotation), then the sign that is obtained for the distance to the resultant will always be consistent with the sign convention for an imaginary coordinate system with origin at the axis of rotation.

EXAMPLE 3-4

Determine the resultant of the two forces shown in Fig. 3-14.

SOLUTION

The calculation of the magnitude of the resultant is a straight-forward summation of forces.

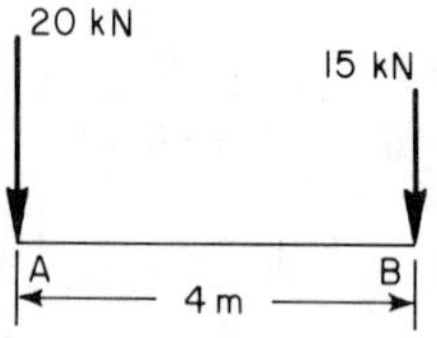

$$R = \Sigma\, F_i$$
$$= -20.00 - 15.00$$
$$= -35.00 \text{ kN}$$

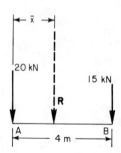

FIGURE 3-14

To calculate the location of the resultant, it is recommended that a diagram be drawn, such as **Fig. 3-15,** *showing the assumed location of* **R.** *Moments are taken about A, since this eliminates the moment of the 20 kN force from the moment equation. The usual rule for the sign of the moment must be applied to each term.*

$$M_A:$$
$$R\bar{x} = \Sigma\,(F_i\, x_i)$$
$$-(35.0 \times \bar{x}) = -(15.0 \times 4.0)$$
$$\bar{x} = \frac{15.0 \times 4.0}{35.0}$$
$$= 1.714 \text{ m}$$

FIGURE 3-15

Since the value obtained for $\bar{x}$ *is positive, the resultant is located to the right of A as assumed.*

$$\boxed{\begin{array}{l} \vec{R} = 35.0 \text{ kN at } 270.00°, \\ 1.71 \text{ m right of A} \end{array}}$$

EXAMPLE 3-5

Find the resultant of the system of three parallel forces shown in Fig. 3-16.

SOLUTION

The magnitude of the resultant is a simple algebraic summation of the forces.

$$R = \Sigma F_i$$
$$= 500 - 300 + 400$$
$$= 600 \text{ N}$$

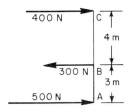

FIGURE 3-16

The location of R can be determined by taking moments about A, thus eliminating the 500 N force from the moment equation. The assumed location of the resultant may be shown on a sketch, such as Fig. 3-17, to aid in determining the signs of the moments.

M_A:

$$R\bar{y} = \Sigma (F_i y_i)$$
$$-(600 \times \bar{y}) = 300 \times 3.0 - 400 \times 7.0$$
$$\bar{y} = \frac{300 \times 3.0 - 400 \times 7.0}{-600}$$
$$= \frac{900 - 2800}{-600}$$
$$= 3.1667 \text{ m}$$

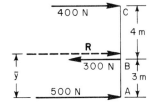

FIGURE 3-17

The fact that a positive value was obtained for $\bar{y}$ indicates that the resultant was above A, as assumed.

$$\vec{R} = 600 \text{ N at } 0.00°,$$
$$3.17 \text{ m above A}$$

EXAMPLE 3-6

For the system shown in Fig. 3-18, determine the resultant.

SOLUTION

To find the resultant, the forces are simply added, with due regard to their signs.

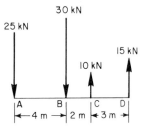

FIGURE 3-18

$$R = \Sigma\, F_i$$

$$= -25.0 - 30.0 + 10.0 + 15.0$$

$$= -30.0 \text{ kN}$$

To determine the location of the resultant, moments are taken about an axis through A to eliminate the force at A from the moment equation. The assumed location of the resultant may be shown in a diagram, such as Fig. 3-19, *as an aid to determining the signs of the moments.*

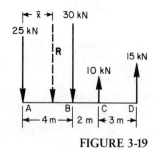

FIGURE 3-19

M_A:

$$R\bar{x} = \Sigma\, (F_i\, x_i)$$

$$- (30.0 \times \bar{x}) = -(30.0 \times 4.0) + 10.0 \times 6.0$$

$$+ 15.0 \times 9.0$$

$$\bar{x} = \frac{-(30.0 \times 4.0) + 10.0 \times 6.0 + 15.0 \times 9.0}{-30.0}$$

$$= \frac{-120.0 + 60.0 + 135.0}{-30.0}$$

$$= \frac{75.0}{-30.0}$$

$$= -2.50 \text{ m}$$

$$\bar{x} = 2.50 \text{ m left of A}$$

$$\boxed{\begin{array}{l} \vec{R} = 30.0 \text{ kN at } 270.00°, \\ 2.50 \text{ m left of A} \end{array}}$$

Since the calculated value of $\bar{x}$ was negative, then the actual location of the resultant is to the opposite side of A from that assumed. In other words, it must be to the left of A. Although it is not generally necessary to redraw the figure showing the correct location of the resultant, it is shown in Fig. 3-20.

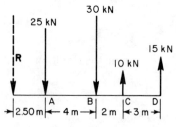

FIGURE 3-20

PROBLEMS

3-23 Replace the forces shown in Fig. P3-23 by a single force.

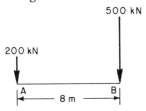

FIGURE P3-23

3-24 For the two loads shown in Fig. P3-24, find the single force that will replace them.

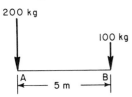

FIGURE P3-24

3-25 Find the single force that will replace the two loads shown in Fig. P3-25.

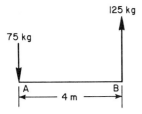

FIGURE P3-25

3-26 Replace the system of forces shown in Fig. P3-26 by a single force.

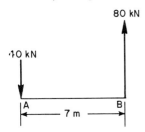

FIGURE P3-26

3-27 Find the single force that will replace the two forces shown in Fig. P3-27.

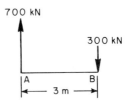

FIGURE P3-27

3-28 Calculate the single force that will replace the two loads shown in Fig. P3-28.

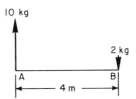

FIGURE P3-28

3-29 Replace the two forces shown in Fig. P3-29 by a single force.

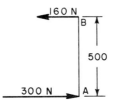

FIGURE P3-29

3-30 Find the replacement force for the loads shown in Fig. P3-30.

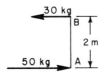

FIGURE P3-30

3-31 Replace the system of three forces shown in Fig. P3-31 by a single force.

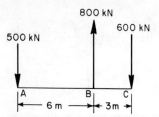

FIGURE P3-31

3-32 Find the single force that will replace the three forces shown in Fig. P3-32.

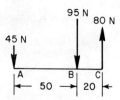

FIGURE P3-32

3-33 Find the resultant of the three forces shown in Fig. P3-33.

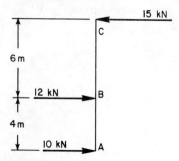

FIGURE P3-33

3-34 Replace the three forces shown in Fig. P3-34 by a single force.

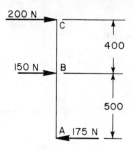

FIGURE P3-34

3-35 For the force system shown in Fig. P3-35, find the resultant.

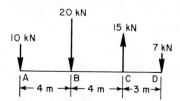

FIGURE P3-35

3-36 Determine the single replacement force for the four forces shown in Fig. P3-36.

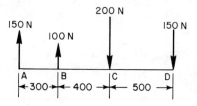

FIGURE P3-36

3-4 DISTRIBUTED LOADS

One system of parallel loads that is encountered with some frequency is the distributed load. Two common types of distributed loads are shown in Fig. 3-21. For the uniform distributed load shown in Fig. 3-21(a), the load has the same intensity per unit of length. Figure 3-21(b) shows a triangular load distribution, in which the load varies from zero to some specific value per unit of length.

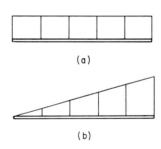

(a)

(b)

FIGURE 3-21

In reality, the distributed loads shown in Fig. 3-21 represent load graphs, as shown in Fig. 3-22, with the horizontal axis being the distance along the beam from the left end, and the vertical axis being the load intensity per unit of length. The distributed load shown by such a graph may be replaced by a single concentrated load for many calculation purposes. The magnitude of this replacement load is equal to the area under the load diagram or graph. Note that the units of area for the graph of Fig. 3-22 are

$$\text{Area} = \text{length} \times \text{height}$$

$$= \text{m} \times \frac{\text{N}}{\text{m}}$$

$$= \text{N}$$

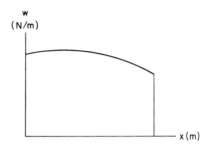

FIGURE 3-22

The replacement load for the distributed load is placed at the center of gravity of the distributed load, which is at the center of the uniform distributed load, as shown in Fig. 3-23(a), and one third of the base length from the maximum in the case of the triangular loading, as shown in Fig. 3-23(b).

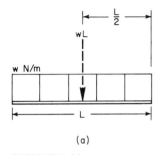

(a)

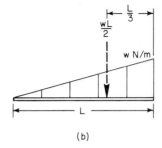

(b)

FIGURE 3-23

Distributed loads may have forms other than uniform or triangular, although these two forms are the most common. One other common form is trapezoidal. However, such a form is simply a triangular load superimposed on a uniform load.

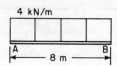

FIGURE 3-24

EXAMPLE 3-7

Replace the distributed load shown in Fig. 3-24 by a single concentrated load.

SOLUTION

The total load is equal to the area under the load diagram.

$$R = wL$$

$$= -(4.0 \times 8.0)$$

$$= -32.0 \text{ kN}$$

The location of the resultant is at half the length of the load from either end.

$$\bar{x} = \frac{L}{2}$$

$$= \frac{8.00}{2}$$

$$= 4.00 \text{ m}$$

$$\boxed{\bar{R} = 32.0 \text{ kN at } 270.00°, \\ 4.00 \text{ m right of A}}$$

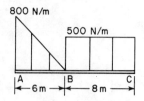

FIGURE 3-25

EXAMPLE 3-8

Find the single concentrated force required to replace the system of two distributed loads shown in Fig. 3-25.

SOLUTION

The two distributed loads can be replaced by two concentrated loads, and then the two loads can be replaced by their resultant, as indicated in Fig. 3-26.

$$R = P_1 + P_2$$

$$= -\frac{1}{2} \times 6.0 \times 800 - 8.0 \times 500$$

$$= -2400 - 4000$$

$$= -6400 \text{ N}$$

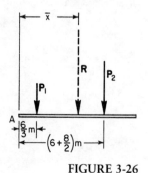

FIGURE 3-26

*The location of the resultant can be obtained by using the con-
centrated loads, and by using* Fig. 3-26. *Note that since moments are being calculated, each perpendicular distance must
be measured from the same axis of rotation.*

M_A:

$$R\bar{x} = \Sigma \, (F_i \, x_i)$$

$$- (6400 \times \bar{x}) = -\left(\frac{1}{2} \times 6.0 \times 800\right)\frac{6.0}{3}$$

$$- 500 \times 8.0 \left(6.0 + \frac{8.0}{2}\right)$$

$$\bar{x} = \frac{-4\,800 - 40\,000}{-6\,400}$$

$$= 7.000 \text{ m}$$

$$\boxed{\begin{array}{l} \vec{R} = 6400 \text{ N at } 270.00°, \\ 7.000 \text{ m right of A} \end{array}}$$

EXAMPLE 3-9

Determine the resultant of the distributed load system shown in
Fig. 3-27.

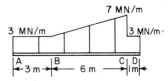

FIGURE 3-27

SOLUTION

*The distributed load is made up of a triangular load on top of a
uniform distributed load. Each of the distributed loads may be
replaced by a concentrated load, and the two concentrated loads
then may be replaced by a single resultant, as shown in* Fig. 3-28.

$$R = P_1 + P_2$$

$$= -3.0 \times 10.0 - \frac{1}{2} \times 6.0 \times 4.0$$

$$= -30.0 - 12.0$$

$$= -42.0 \text{ MN}$$

*The location of the resultant can be obtained by locating the
resultant of the two concentrated loads that replaced the two
distributed loads.*

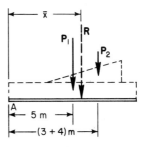

FIGURE 3-28

M_A:

$$R\bar{x} = \Sigma (F_i x_i)$$

$$- (42.0 \times \bar{x}) = -(3.0 \times 10.0)5.0 - \left(\frac{1}{2} \times 6.0 \times 4.0\right)(3.0 + 4.0)$$

$$\bar{x} = \frac{-150.0 - 84.0}{-42.0}$$

$$= \frac{-234.0}{-42.0}$$

$$= 5.571 \text{ m}$$

$$\boxed{\begin{array}{l} \vec{R} = 42.0 \text{ MN at } 270.00°, \\ 5.57 \text{ m right of A} \end{array}}$$

PROBLEMS

3-37 Replace the distributed load shown in Fig. P3-37 by a single force.

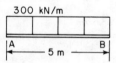

300 kN/m

FIGURE P3-37

3-38 Find the single force that will replace the distributed load shown in Fig. P3-38.

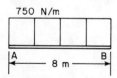

750 N/m

FIGURE P3-38

3-39 Calculate the single force that will replace the distributed load shown in Fig. P3-39.

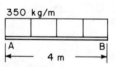

350 kg/m

FIGURE P3-39

3-40 Replace the distributed load shown in Fig. P3-40 by a single concentrated force.

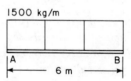

1500 kg/m

FIGURE P3-40

3-41 Replace the distributed load shown in Fig. P3-41 by a single force.

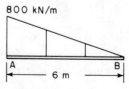

800 kN/m

FIGURE P3-41

3-42 For the distributed load shown in Fig. P3-42, determine the single force that will act as a replacement.

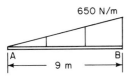

FIGURE P3-42

3-43 Find the single force that will replace the distributed load shown in Fig. P3-43.

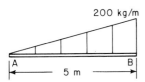

FIGURE P3-43

3-44 Calculate the single force that may be used to replace the distributed load shown in Fig. P3-44.

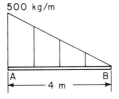

FIGURE P3-44

3-45 Replace the system of distributed loads shown in Fig. P3-45 by a single force.

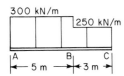

FIGURE P3-45

3-46 Find the single force that will replace the distributed loads shown in Fig. P3-46.

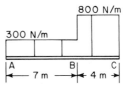

FIGURE P3-46

3-47 Replace the distributed loads shown in Fig. P3-47 by a single force.

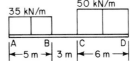

FIGURE P3-47

3-48 Determine the single force required to replace the distributed loads shown in Fig. P3-48.

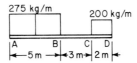

FIGURE P3-48

3-49 Replace the distributed loads shown in Fig. P3-49 by a single force.

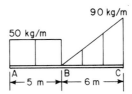

FIGURE P3-49

3-50 For the load system shown in Fig. P3-50, replace the system by a single force.

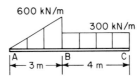

FIGURE P3-50

3-51 For the distributed load shown in Fig. P3-51, determine the resultant.

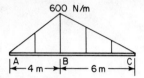

FIGURE P3-51

3-52 Determine the resultant of the distributed load shown in Fig. P3-52.

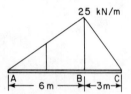

FIGURE P3-52

3-53 Replace the distributed load shown in Fig. P3-53 by a single force.

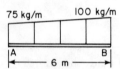

FIGURE P3-53

3-54 Find the single force that may be used to replace the distributed load shown in Fig. P3-54.

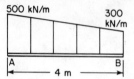

FIGURE P3-54

3-55 Determine the resultant for the system of distributed loads shown in Fig. P3-55.

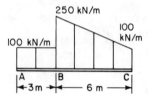

FIGURE P3-55

3-56 For the distributed load system shown in Fig. P3-56, find the resultant.

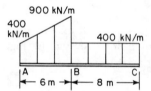

FIGURE P3-56

3-5 PLANE, NON-PARALLEL, NON-CONCURRENT FORCE SYSTEMS

A non-parallel, non-concurrent force system in a plane, such as shown in Fig. 3-29, is the most general plane force system. To determine the resultant of such a system, the single force must be determined that will create the same tendency to cause linear translation, and the same tendency to cause rotation, as the original system of forces.

The equivalent single force may be obtained by summing all the forces in the system.

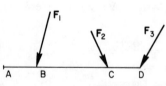

FIGURE 3-29

$$R = F_1 + F_2 + F_3 + \cdots$$

$$R = \Sigma\, F_i \qquad (3\text{-}8)$$

In actual application, the most simple approach for calculating the resultant usually is to use the method of summation of the components of the forces in the system.

The determination of the location of the resultant is based on the requirement that the resultant create the same tendency for rotation about any axis as the initial system of forces. When taking moments about the chosen axis, Varignon's theorem is almost always used to simplify the calculation. Referring to Fig. 3-30:

$$M_A:$$

$$R_y \bar{x} = F_{y_1} x_1 + F_{y_2} x_2 + F_{y_3} x_3 + \cdots$$

$$R_y \bar{x} = \Sigma\,(F_{y_i} x_i) \qquad (3\text{-}9)$$

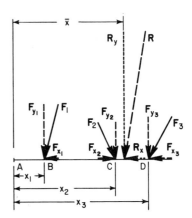

FIGURE 3-30

Equation (3-9) sets the moment of the resultant equal to the total moment of the original system of forces, providing that all the x components have been placed so that they are collinear with the axis of rotation. Equation (3-9) may thus be solved for $\bar{x}$.

In the case of a force system intersecting the y axis, a similar procedure may be used to find $\bar{y}$ by summing the moments of the x components about the axis of rotation.

If it is not convenient to set all of one parallel set of components collinear with the axis of rotation, then the moment of every component must be taken into account, since each component may have a moment about the axis of rotation.

EXAMPLE 3-10

Calculate the resultant for the system of forces shown in Fig. 3-31.

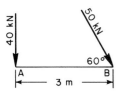

FIGURE 3-31

SOLUTION

The magnitude and direction of the resultant may be obtained by summing the components of the original system of forces.

$$R_x = \Sigma\ F_{x_i}$$

$$= 50 \cos 60°$$

$$= 25.00\ \text{kN}$$

$$R_y = \Sigma\ F_{y_i}$$

$$= -40 - 50 \sin 60°$$

$$= -40.00 - 43.30$$

$$= -83.30\ \text{kN}$$

A sketch, showing R_x, R_y, R and θ, as shown in Fig. 3-32, *is recommended as an aid in obtaining R and θ.*

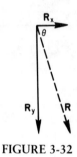

FIGURE 3-32

$$\theta = \tan^{-1} \frac{R_y}{R_x}$$

$$= \tan^{-1} \frac{83.30}{25.00}$$

$$= 73.29°$$

$$R = \frac{R_y}{\sin \theta}$$

$$= \frac{83.30}{\sin 73.29°}$$

$$= 86.97\ \text{kN}$$

Direction of $\bar{R} = 360.00° - 73.29°$

$$= 286.71°$$

To locate the resultant, moments are taken about an axis through A, since this will eliminate the 40 kN force from the moment equation. A drawing showing all forces, such as Fig. 3-33, may help in setting up the moment equation.

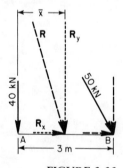

FIGURE 3-33

M_A:

$$R_y \bar{x} = \Sigma\ (F_{y_i} x_i)$$

$$-(83.30 \times \bar{x}) = -(50 \sin 60° \times 3)$$

$$\bar{x} = \frac{-50 \sin 60° \times 3}{-83.30}$$

$$= 1.559\ \text{m}$$

$$\vec{R} = 87.0 \text{ kN at } 286.71°,$$
$$1.56 \text{ m right of A}$$

EXAMPLE 3-11

Determine the resultant of the force system shown in Fig. 3-34.

SOLUTION

The first step is to determine the magnitude and direction of the resultant by summing the components of the forces in the x and y directions.

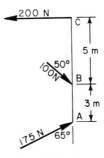

FIGURE 3-34

$$R_x = \Sigma F_{x_i}$$
$$= 175 \sin 65° + 100 \sin 50° - 200$$
$$= 158.60 + 76.60 - 200.00$$
$$= 35.20 \text{ N}$$

$$R_y = \Sigma F_{y_i}$$
$$= 175 \cos 65° - 100 \cos 50°$$
$$= 73.96 - 64.28$$
$$= 9.68 \text{ N}$$

To determine R, θ and the direction, a sketch such as Fig. 3-35 can be helpful.

$$\theta = \tan^{-1} \frac{R_y}{R_x}$$
$$= \tan^{-1} \frac{9.68}{35.20}$$
$$= 15.38°$$

Direction of $\vec{R} = 15.38°$

$$R = \frac{R_y}{\sin \theta}$$
$$= \frac{9.68}{\sin 15.38°}$$
$$= 36.50 \text{ N}$$

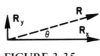

FIGURE 3-35

To determine the location of the resultant, the moments of all of the forces about an axis through A are set equal to the moment of the resultant about A. Figure 3-36 can be helpful in setting up the moment equation.

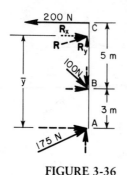

FIGURE 3-36

M_A:

$$R_x \bar{y} = \Sigma (F_{x_i} y_i)$$

$$-(35.20 \times \bar{y}) = -(100 \sin 50° \times 3) + 200 \times 8$$

$$\bar{y} = \frac{-229.81 + 1600.00}{-35.20}$$

$$= \frac{1370.19}{-35.20}$$

$$= -38.93 \text{ m}$$

*The negative value obtained for $\bar{y}$ indicates that the assumption that **R** is above A is incorrect. It is really 38.93 m below A.*

$$\boxed{\begin{array}{l} \vec{R} = 36.5 \text{ N at } 15.38°, \\ 38.9 \text{ m below A} \end{array}}$$

EXAMPLE 3-12

Find the single force passing through the *x* axis that is equivalent to the two forces shown in Fig. 3-37.

SOLUTION

The magnitude and direction of the resultant may be obtained by summing the x and y components of the two given forces.

$$R_x = \Sigma F_{x_i}$$

$$= 60 \cos 30° - 40 \cos 50°$$

$$= 51.96 - 25.71$$

$$= 26.25 \text{ kN}$$

$$R_y = \Sigma F_{y_i}$$

$$= -60 \sin 30° - 40 \sin 50°$$

$$= -30.00 - 30.64$$

$$= -60.64 \text{ kN}$$

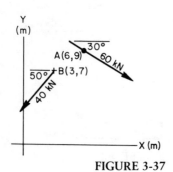

FIGURE 3-37

*Calculations for R, θ and the direction of **R** can be aided by a drawing such as Fig. 3-38.*

$$\theta = \tan^{-1} \frac{R_y}{R_x}$$

$$= \tan^{-1} \frac{60.64}{26.25}$$

$$= 66.59°$$

Direction of $\vec{R}$ = 360.00° − 66.59°

$$= 293.41°$$

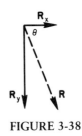

FIGURE 3-38

$$R = \frac{R_y}{\sin \theta}$$

$$= \frac{60.64}{\sin 66.59°}$$

$$= 66.08 \text{ kN}$$

To determine where the resultant crosses the x axis, the moment of the resultant is set equal to the sum of the moments of the original system of forces about an axis through the origin. Note that in this case, both the x and y components of the original forces will have moments about the origin. Figure 3-39, showing all the components, should help in setting up the moment equation.

M_0:

$$-(60.64 \times \bar{x}) = -(60 \cos 30° \times 9) - 60 \sin 30° \times 6$$
$$+ 40 \cos 50° \times 7 - 40 \sin 50° \times 3$$

$$-60.64 \bar{x} = -467.65 - 180.00 + 179.98 - 91.93$$

$$\bar{x} = \frac{-559.60}{-60.64}$$

$$= 9.228 \text{ m}$$

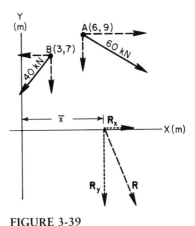

FIGURE 3-39

$$\boxed{\begin{array}{l} \vec{R} = 66.1 \text{ kN at } 293.41°, \\ \text{through (9.23, 0.00)} \end{array}}$$

PROBLEMS

3-57 Calculate the single force that will replace the two forces shown in Fig. P3-57.

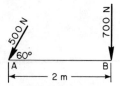

FIGURE P3-57

3-58 Replace the two forces shown in Fig. P3-58 by a single force.

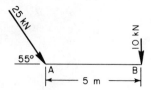

FIGURE P3-58

3-59 Determine the single force that may be used to replace the system of two forces shown in Fig. P3-59.

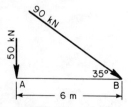

FIGURE P3-59

3-60 For the two forces shown in Fig. P3-60, find the single force that may be used as a replacement.

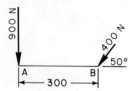

FIGURE P3-60

3-61 Determine the resultant of the system of loads shown in Fig. P3-61.

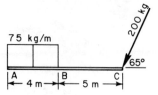

FIGURE P3-61

3-62 Replace the load system shown in Fig. P3-62 by a single concentrated force.

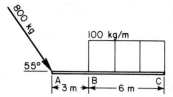

FIGURE P3-62

3-63 Determine the resultant of the load system shown in Fig. P3-63.

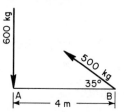

FIGURE P3-63

3-64 For the system of loads shown in Fig. P3-64, find the resultant.

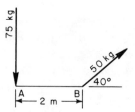

FIGURE P3-64

3-65 Determine the resultant of the two forces shown in Fig. P3-65.

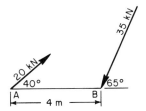

FIGURE P3-65

3-66 Find the resultant of the system of forces shown in Fig. P3-66.

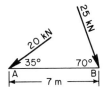

FIGURE P3-66

3-67 Find the force that will replace the two forces shown in Fig. P3-67.

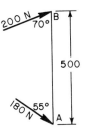

FIGURE P3-67

3-68 Replace the system of two forces shown in Fig. P3-68 by a single force.

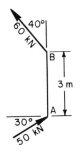

FIGURE P3-68

3-69 Determine the resultant of the system of forces shown in Fig. P3-69.

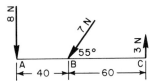

FIGURE P3-69

3-70 Find the resultant of the forces shown in Fig. P3-70.

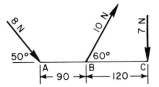

FIGURE P3-70

3-71 For the system of forces shown in Fig. P3-71, replace the forces by a single force.

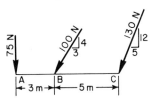

FIGURE P3-71

3-72 Calculate the resultant of the force system shown in Fig. P3-72.

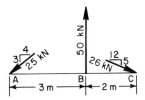

FIGURE P3-72

3-73 Find the resultant for the force system shown in Fig. P3-73.

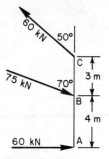

FIGURE P3-73

3-74 Determine the single force that will replace the three forces shown in Fig. P3-74.

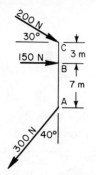

FIGURE P3-74

3-75 For the loading system shown in Fig. P3-75, determine the resultant and the point where it intersects the *y* axis.

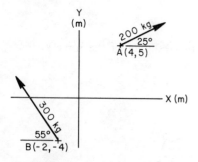

FIGURE P3-75

3-76 Find the resultant of the load system shown in Fig. P3-76. Give its location by determining where it crosses the *x* axis.

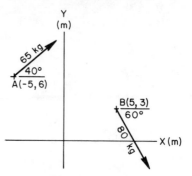

FIGURE P3-76

3-77 Determine the resultant for the system of forces shown in Fig. P3-77, and the point where it intersects the *x* axis.

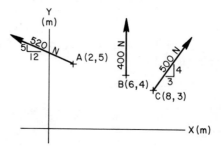

FIGURE P3-77

3-78 For the force system shown in Fig. P3-78, determine its resultant and its point of intersection with the *y* axis.

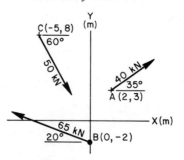

FIGURE P3-78

3-6 REPLACING A FORCE BY A FORCE AND A COUPLE

Up to this point, the emphasis has been on finding the resultant of a force system, the resultant being the simplest replacement of the original system. However, there are a number of situations where it is desirable or required that a force system be replaced by a single force at a specified location, and a couple. In some cases this may actually be a more complicated system than the original force system.

Figure 3-40(a) shows a column with the load **P** from a beam applied to a bracket. The design of the column is simplified if the load on the column consists of an axial load and a couple, as shown in Fig. 3-40(b). Note that the couple in this situation is popularly, but incorrectly, called a moment. The analysis of the motion of bodies can often be simplified by replacing the force acting on the body by a force through the center of gravity and a couple, as shown in Fig. 3-41. These are just two illustrations of situations where it may be necessary or desirable to replace a force by a force and a couple.

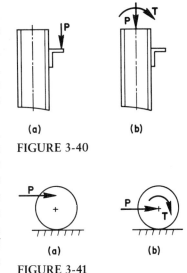

(a)   (b)

FIGURE 3-40

(a)   (b)

FIGURE 3-41

The process used to replace a force by a force and a couple is illustrated in Fig. 3-42. In Fig. 3-42(a) a force **P** is shown applied to point A. However, it is required that the force be applied to point B *without changing the effect of the force on the body*. In Fig. 3-42(b), the force is shown applied to point B, along with $-\mathbf{P}$, also applied to point B. The sum $\mathbf{P} - \mathbf{P} = 0$, so the net effect of the system in Fig. 3-42(b) is the same as the original system shown in Fig. 3-42(a). However, if the two forces enclosed by

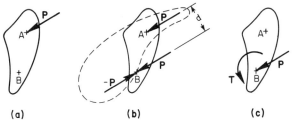

(a)   (b)   (c)

FIGURE 3-42

the dashed line are analyzed, it is noted that they form a couple, leaving a force of **P** at point B. The final system can thus be described as shown in Fig. 3-42(c), that is a force **P** at B and a couple equal to Pd.

Any system of forces can be replaced by a force at a point and a couple. If there are two or more forces involved, the resultant force is calculated, and Varignon's theorem is used in calculating the couple.

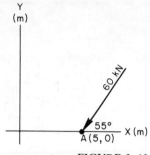

FIGURE 3-43

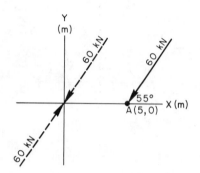

FIGURE 3-44

EXAMPLE 3-13

Replace the force shown in Fig. 3-43 by a force at the origin and a couple.

SOLUTION

Although it is not absolutely necessary, it may be helpful to draw in the 60 kN force placed at the origin, along with the opposite 60 kN force at the origin, as shown in Fig. 3-44, as an aid to visualizing the solution of the problem. The original force with the force shown below the x axis forms the required couple.

$$F = 60.0 \text{ kN}$$

$$\text{Direction of } \vec{F} = 180° + 55°$$

$$= 235.00°$$

Calculation of the couple is simplified by breaking the 60 kN force into its components and using Varignon's theorem. If the two components are concurrent at A, the x component will have no moment about an axis through the origin.

$$T = -(60 \sin 55° \times 5)$$

$$= -245.75 \text{ kN·m}$$

$$\boxed{\begin{aligned} \vec{F} &= 60.0 \text{ kN at } 235.00° \\ T &= -246 \text{ kN·m} \end{aligned}}$$

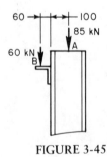

FIGURE 3-45

EXAMPLE 3-14

Find the single force at A and couple that will replace the system of two forces shown in Fig. 3-45.

SOLUTION

The force at B is moved to A and added to the force at A.

$$R = \Sigma F_i$$

$$= -85.0 - 60.0$$

$$= -145.0 \text{ kN}$$

The opposite 60 kN force placed at A along with the original 60 kN force form a couple. Since the 85 kN force was originally

at A, it will have no effect on the magnitude of the couple. The
final system is shown in Fig. 3-46.

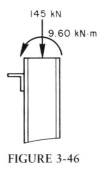

$$T = Fd$$
$$= 60 \times 0.16$$
$$= 9.60 \text{ kN} \cdot \text{m}$$

$$\vec{R} = 145 \text{ kN at } 270.00°$$
$$T = 9.60 \text{ kN} \cdot \text{m}$$

FIGURE 3-46

EXAMPLE 3-15

Replace the system of two forces shown in Fig 3-47 by a force at
C and a couple.

SOLUTION

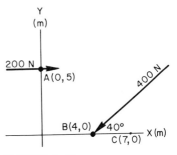

FIGURE 3-47

The two forces, when placed at C, would form a concurrent
force system, and their resultant may be determined in the usual
fashion for obtaining the resultant of a concurrent force system,
that is, by summing the components:

$$R_x = \Sigma F_{x_i}$$
$$= 200 - 400 \cos 40°$$
$$= 200.00 - 306.42$$
$$= -106.42 \text{ N}$$
$$R_y = \Sigma F_{y_i}$$
$$= -400 \sin 40°$$
$$= -257.12 \text{ N}$$

A sketch, such as Fig. 3-48, is an aid to obtaining the correct
value for **R** and its direction.

$$\theta = \tan^{-1} \frac{R_y}{R_x}$$
$$= \tan^{-1} \frac{257.12}{106.42}$$
$$= 67.52°$$
$$\text{Direction of } \vec{R} = 180.00° + 67.52°$$
$$= 247.52°$$

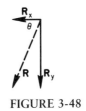

FIGURE 3-48

$$R = \frac{R_y}{\sin \theta}$$

$$= \frac{257.12}{\sin 67.52°}$$

$$= 278.27 \text{ N}$$

Each of the original forces and its opposite at point C form a couple. The sum of the couples produced, or the total couple, can be obtained by using Varignon's theorem. Note that the x component of the 400 N force will not tend to cause rotation about C.

$$T = -(200 \times 5) + 400 \sin 40° \times 3$$

$$= -1000.00 + 771.35$$

$$= -228.65 \text{ N·m}$$

$$\vec{R} = 278 \text{ N at } 247.52°$$
$$T = -229 \text{ N·m}$$

PROBLEMS

3-79 Replace the force shown in Fig. P3-79 by a force at the origin and a couple.

3-80 Find the force at the origin and the couple that will replace the force shown in Fig. P3-80.

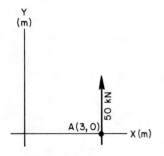

FIGURE P3-79

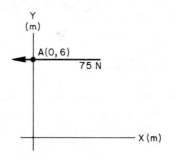

FIGURE P3-80

3-81 Determine the force through the origin and the couple that will replace the force shown in Fig. P3-81.

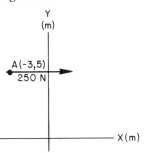

FIGURE P3-81

3-82 Replace the force shown in Fig. P3-82 by a force at the origin and a couple.

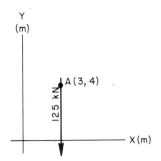

FIGURE P3-82

3-83 Determine the force at *A* and the couple that will replace the force shown in Fig. P3-83.

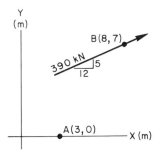

FIGURE P3-83

3-84 Replace the force shown in Fig. P3-84 by a force at *A* and a couple.

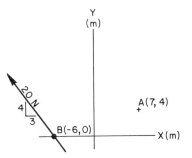

FIGURE P3-84

3-85 Replace the force shown in Fig. P3-85 by a force at *B* and a couple.

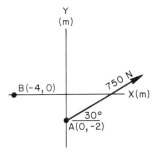

FIGURE P3-85

3-86 Determine the force at *B* and the couple that will replace the force shown in Fig. P3-86.

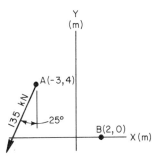

FIGURE P3-86

3-87 For the system of three forces shown in Fig. P3-87, find the couple and the force at A that will be equivalent.

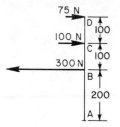

FIGURE P3-87

3-88 Replace the system of forces shown in Fig. P3-88 by a force at A and a couple.

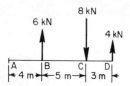

FIGURE P3-88

3-89 Find the single force at A and the couple that will replace the two forces shown in Fig. P3-89.

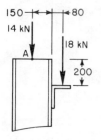

FIGURE P3-89

3-90 To design the base connection at A for the highway light standard shown in Fig. P3-90, the gravitational forces acting on the lamp are replaced by a force at A and a couple. If the luminaire C has a mass of 15 kg, the arm BC has a

mass of 10 kg acting at its center, and the standard AB has a mass of 35 kg, determine the force at A and the couple that will replace the given system.

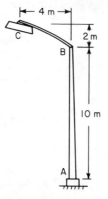

FIGURE P3-90

3-91 The beam shown in Fig. P3-91 has a mass of 65 kg/m. Replace the load of the beam and the applied load by a single force at A and a couple.

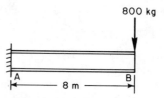

FIGURE P3-91

3-92 Replace the force due to the beam's mass and the 1000 kg load by a single force at C and a couple. The beam shown in Fig. P3-92 has a mass of 50 kg/m.

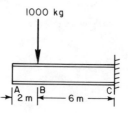

FIGURE P3-92

3-93 In Fig. P3-93, the connection at *A* that supports the cantilever beam *AC* is designed by replacing the two forces shown by a force at *A* and a couple. Calculate the required force at *A* and couple. The mass of the beam may be neglected.

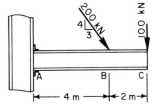

FIGURE P3-93

3-94 To determine the potential motion for the cabinet shown in Fig. P3-94, the 250 N force and the force due to the 50 kg mass of the cabinet should be replaced by a single force at *D* at the center of the cabinet, and a couple. The force due to the mass acts at *D*. Calculate the total force at *D* and the couple.

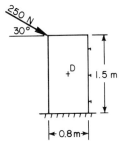

FIGURE P3-94

3-95 Replace the two forces shown in Fig. P3-95 by a single force at the origin and a couple.

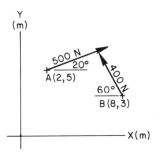

FIGURE P3-95

3-96 Find the force at the origin and the couple that will replace the system of two forces shown in Fig. P3-96.

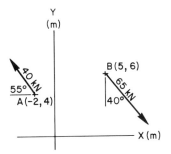

FIGURE P3-96

4 EQUILIBRIUM

4-1 PRINCIPLES OF EQUILIBRIUM

A body at rest or moving at constant speed in a straight line is said to be in equilibrium. Isaac Newton's first law is the basic equilibrium statement, and says that a body will remain at rest, and a body in motion will continue in motion with constant speed in a straight line, as long as no net force acts on it.

Mathematically, the equilibrium conditions may be stated as:

$$\Sigma \mathbf{F} = 0 \tag{4-1}$$

$$\Sigma \mathbf{M} = 0 \tag{4-2}$$

These equations state that the sum of all of the forces acting *on* a body in equilibrium must be zero, and that the sum of all the moments about any axis must also be zero. Equations (4-1) and (4-2) are vector equations, which can be expressed in terms of the components in the *x, y* and *z* directions.

$$\Sigma F_x = 0 \tag{4-3}$$

$$\Sigma F_y = 0 \tag{4-4}$$

$$\Sigma F_z = 0 \tag{4-5}$$

$$\Sigma M_x = 0 \tag{4-6}$$

$$\Sigma M_y = 0 \tag{4-7}$$

$$\Sigma M_z = 0 \tag{4-8}$$

For the plane or two-dimensional case, only Eqs. (4-3), (4-4) and (4-8) apply. Thus, for a body in equilibrium in a plane, the conditions for equilibrium are:

$$\Sigma F_x = 0 \tag{4-3}$$

$$\Sigma F_y = 0 \tag{4-4}$$

$$\Sigma M_z = 0 \tag{4-8}$$

Note that in using Eq. (4-8), moments may be taken about any axis parallel to the *z* axis, rather than just about the *z* axis.

FIGURE 4-1 An aircraft flying at a constant speed in a straight line is one example of a body in equilibrium. *Photo courtesy of Boeing Company.*

It cannot be overemphasized that all three equations must be satisfied for a body to be in equilibrium in a plane.

One of the more dramatic examples of a body in equilibrium is a large aircraft, such as shown in Fig. 4-1. Note that the aircraft will be in equilibrium *only* when flying at constant speed in a straight line, or when at rest on the ground. At other times, it will not be in equilibrium.

The solution of equilibrium problems is the basis for the analysis of all frames and machines, and hence is necessary for an understanding of both structural and machine design.

4-2 FREE-BODY DIAGRAMS

Perhaps the most important aid to solving equilibrium problems is the free-body diagram. A free-body diagram is a drawing showing the body being analyzed. The body is drawn with the supports removed and replaced by the forces the supports exert on the body. In addition, all other forces acting on the body are shown. It is important to note that *all* forces acting *on* the body must be shown. Forces acting in the body, or internal forces, must not be shown.

A mass suspended from a cable is shown in Fig. 4-2(a), and a free-body diagram of the mass is shown in Fig. 4-2(b). All the forces acting on the mass must be shown. In this case there are two forces shown, the tension **F** in the cable that supports the mass, and the gravitational attraction **W** acting on the mass. The force representing the gravitational attraction passes through the center of gravity of the mass, which will be at the

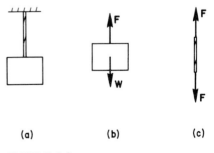

(a) (b) (c)

FIGURE 4-2

center of homogeneous bodies. Figure 4-2(c) is a free-body diagram of the cable. Note that the ceiling is a support and the upper force represents the force that the ceiling exerts on the cable. Similarly, the lower force represents the force that the gravitational attraction of the earth transmits to the cable.

4-3 CONVENTIONS FOR FREE-BODY DIAGRAMS

A number of standardized methods of representing forces in free-body diagrams are shown in Fig. 4-3. The force due to gravity is shown in Fig. 4-3(a). As mentioned earlier, it acts through the center of gravity, G, of the body. The force due to gravity is always directed towards the earth's center, and thus will point vertically down. The force in a cable due to an applied load is shown in Fig. 4-3(b). Such a force is always along the axis of the cable. The body on a smooth surface shown in Fig. 4-3(c) has a force perpendicular to the surface acting on it. In the case of any smooth or frictionless surface, the force exerted by the surface

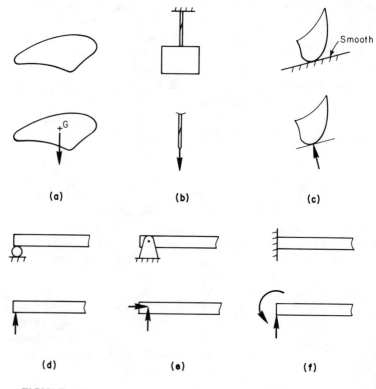

(a)   (b)   (c)

(d)   (e)   (f)

FIGURE 4-3

will be normal to or perpendicular to a line which is tangent to the surface at the point of contact.

Supports for beams are shown in Figs. 4-3(d), (e) and (f). In the case of the roller shown in Fig. 4-3(d), the force the roller exerts on the beam must be perpendicular to the surface of the beam. Any other direction of the force would tend to involve rotation of the roller, and if the roller is rotating, it is not in equilibrium. Note that it is a simple matter to design a roller that will resist upward forces, as well as downward forces. It is customary to show the forces acting on a beam due to a pin in terms of the x and y components, as shown in Fig. 4-3(e). This approach usually gives a simpler problem solution than would be obtained by showing the single force at some unknown angle θ. The fixed support shown in Fig. 4-3(f) usually requires both a force and a couple (usually called a moment) at the support to maintain equilibrium.

The force acting at the support for a body is often called the *reaction force* or *reaction*.

4-4 PLANE, CONCURRENT FORCE SYSTEMS

If the lines of action of all forces acting on a body pass through a common point, the force system is concurrent. In such a system, as shown in Fig. 4-4, if moments are taken about an axis through the point of concurrency, C, none of the forces would cause a moment about that axis. In most cases, moment equations are not useful when attempting to find the unknown forces. Thus, in dealing with a concurrent force system, only two of the equilibrium equations are usually useful:

$$\Sigma F_x = 0 \qquad (4\text{-}3)$$

$$\Sigma F_y = 0 \qquad (4\text{-}4)$$

As a result, in a plane, concurrent force system, no more than two unknown forces or combinations of unknown forces and directions can be obtained.

If F_1 and F_2, in Fig. 4-4, are both known forces, it would be possible to calculate the magnitude and direction of F_3. If F_1 is known, and if the directions of F_2 and F_3 are known, it would be possible to calculate the magnitudes of F_2 and F_3. Other combinations of known and unknown quantities may be made, but it is not possible to calculate more than two unknown quantities.

Any system that consists of only three non-parallel forces in equilibrium must be a concurrent system. A beam with three

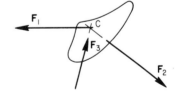

FIGURE 4-4

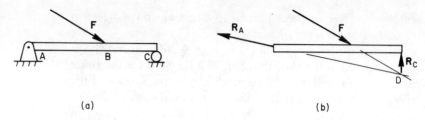

(a)   (b)

FIGURE 4-5

non-parallel forces acting on it is shown in Fig. 4-5(a), and its free-body diagram is shown in Fig. 4-5(b). **F** is a known force, and R_C must be vertical, since the support at C is a roller. The force R_A must be concurrent with **F** and R_C at D. If it is not also concurrent at D, it would cause a moment about D, and one of the conditions for equilibrium would not be satisfied. The ability to locate the point of concurrency of such a system because of the known direction of two forces sometimes assists in the solution of problems. Note that the carefully drawn free-body diagram provides the necessary clues to the direction of R_A.

EXAMPLE 4-1

A mass of 200 kg is suspended from two cables, as shown in Fig. 4-6. Determine the force in each cable.

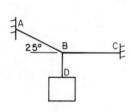

FIGURE 4-6

SOLUTION

The first step in the solution of the problem is to draw a suitable free-body diagram, as shown in Fig. 4-7. *In this case, the free body is the point B, where cables AB, BC and BD interconnect. Since the forces at B are all caused by cables, the line of action of each force must be along the axis of the cable. Since cables can only exert a pull (tension), the direction of the force is also fixed.*

From the free-body diagram it is observed that there are two unknown forces (components) in the x direction, and only one unknown force (component) in the y direction. By summing forces in the y direction, an equation with one unknown term would be obtained.

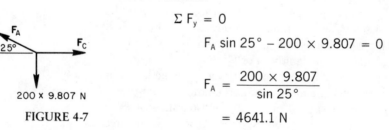

200 × 9.807 N

FIGURE 4-7

$$\Sigma F_y = 0$$

$$F_A \sin 25° - 200 \times 9.807 = 0$$

$$F_A = \frac{200 \times 9.807}{\sin 25°}$$

$$= 4641.1 \text{ N}$$

The direction is fixed by the cable.

$$\text{Direction of } F_A = 180° - 25°$$

$$= 155.00°$$

Now that F_A has been found, there would be only one unknown left in the x direction, and forces may then be summed in the x direction.

$$\Sigma F_x = 0$$

$$-4641.1 \cos 25° + F_C = 0$$

$$F_C = 4206.2 \text{ N}$$

$$\boxed{\begin{aligned} \vec{F}_A &= 4640 \text{ N at } 155.00° \\ \vec{F}_C &= 4210 \text{ N at } 0.00° \end{aligned}}$$

The problem can be solved or checked graphically by drawing a scale drawing of all the forces acting on B, as shown in Fig. 4-8. Since $\Sigma F = 0$, the sum of all the forces in the vector triangle must also be zero. Such a graphical check is strongly recommended.

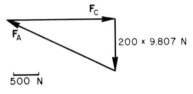

500 N

FIGURE 4-8

EXAMPLE 4-2

A barrel with a mass of 125 kg is supported by a rack, as shown in Fig. 4-9. Determine the force on the barrel at each of the contact points, A and B.

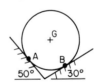

FIGURE 4-9

SOLUTION

The required free-body diagram is shown in Fig. 4-10. The force due to gravity acts vertically through the center of the body. The reactions at A and B are directed perpendicular to the support surfaces. Note that all three forces are concurrent at G. Since there are unknown forces (components) in both the x and y directions, it would appear necessary to write the equations summing forces in both the x and y directions and solve them simultaneously to calculate F_A and F_B.

$$\Sigma F_x = 0$$

$$F_A \cos 40° - F_B \cos 60° = 0$$

$$F_A = \frac{F_B \cos 60°}{\cos 40°}$$

$$F_A = 0.652\ 70\ F_B \qquad \text{Eq. (a)}$$

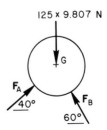

FIGURE 4-10

$$\Sigma F_y = 0$$

$$-125 \times 9.807 + F_A \sin 40° + F_B \sin 60° = 0 \quad \text{Eq. (b)}$$

Substitute Eq. (a) in Eq. (b)

$$-125 \times 9.807 + (0.652\ 70\ F_B) \sin 40° + F_B \sin 60° = 0$$

$$-1225.88 + 0.419\ 55\ F_B + 0.866\ 03\ F_B = 0$$

$$F_B = \frac{1225.88}{0.419\ 55 + 0.866\ 03}$$

$$= \frac{1225.88}{1.285\ 58}$$

$$= 953.56 \text{ N}$$

From Eq. (a)

$$F_A = 0.652\ 70 \times 953.56$$

$$= 622.39 \text{ N}$$

$$\text{Direction of } \vec{F}_A = 40.00°$$

$$\text{Direction of } \vec{F}_B = 180° - 60°$$

$$= 120.00°$$

$$\boxed{\begin{aligned} \vec{F}_A &= 622 \text{ N at } 40.00° \\ \vec{F}_B &= 954 \text{ N at } 120.00° \end{aligned}}$$

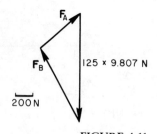

125 × 9.807 N

200 N

FIGURE 4-11

Since $\Sigma F = 0$, the forces can be drawn graphically to scale as a check, as shown in Fig. 4-11. If the vector triangle closes, the above solution may well be correct. The vector triangle may in itself also be used as a graphical solution to the problem.

EXAMPLE 4-3

Determine the force at A and the angle θ for the system shown in Fig. 4-12 if the tension in *BC* has been found to be 6000 N.

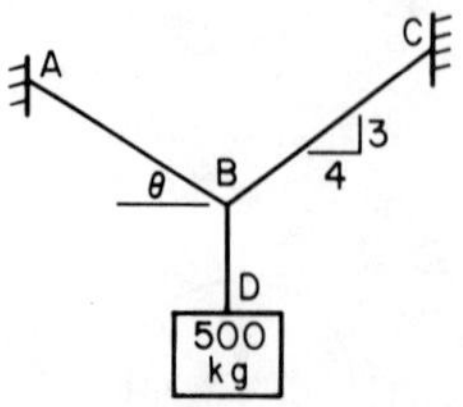

SOLUTION

The free-body diagram of the connection of the three cables at B is shown in Fig. 4-13. Each of the forces must have the same line of action as the cable. It will be simpler to work with the x and y components of F_A, rather than with F_A and θ. Once A_x and A_y have been found, F_A and θ can be calculated.

FIGURE 4-12

If the components of F_A are used, as shown, then there will be only one unknown in the equation if the forces are summed in the x direction.

$$\Sigma F_x = 0$$

$$-A_x + \frac{4}{5} \times 6000 = 0$$

$$A_x = 4800.0 \text{ N}$$

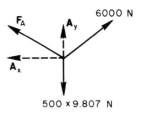

FIGURE 4-13

Similarly, in the y direction, there is only one unknown.

$$\Sigma F_y = 0$$

$$A_y + \frac{3}{5} \times 6000 - 500 \times 9.807 = 0$$

$$A_y = 4903.5 - 3600.0$$

$$= 1303.5 \text{ N}$$

A sketch such as Fig. 4-14, *showing* A_x *and* A_y, *will help in finding* F_A *and* θ.

$$\theta = \tan^{-1}\frac{A_y}{A_x}$$

$$= \tan^{-1}\frac{1303.5}{4800.0}$$

$$= 15.19°$$

FIGURE 4-14

$$F_A = \frac{A_y}{\sin \theta}$$

$$= \frac{1303.5}{\sin 15.19°}$$

$$= 4974.8 \text{ N}$$

$$F_A = 4970 \text{ N}$$
$$\theta = 15.19°$$

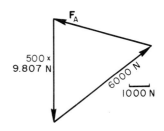

FIGURE 4-15

Since $\Sigma F = 0$, *a vector triangle showing all the forces acting on B can be drawn to scale, as shown in* Fig. 4-15. *This scale drawing can serve as a quick and accurate check of the analytical calculations, or as a separate solution.*

PROBLEMS

4-1 Find the tension in cables AB and BC for the system shown in Fig. P4-1.

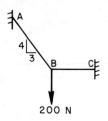

200 N

FIGURE P4-1

4-2 Calculate the tension in AB and BC for the system shown in Fig. P4-2.

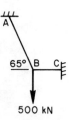

500 kN

FIGURE P4-2

4-3 Determine the force **P** if the tension in cable BC shown in Fig. P4-3 is found to be 500 kN.

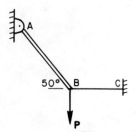

FIGURE P4-3

4-4 If the tension in AB, shown in Fig. P4-4, is 180 N, determine the size of the force **P**.

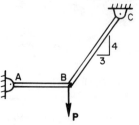

FIGURE P4-4

4-5 If the tension in cable BC, shown in Fig. P4-5, is found to be 80 kN, find the tension in AB and the angle θ

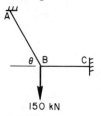

150 kN

FIGURE P4-5

4-6 For the system shown in Fig. P4-6, the tension in AB was found to be 800 N. Calculate the tension in BC and the angle θ.

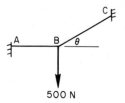

500 N

FIGURE P4-6

4-7 A solid cylinder has a radius of 0.75 m, a mass of 800 kg, and is supported as shown in Fig. P4-7. Calculate the reactions at A and B.

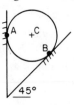

FIGURE P4-7

4-8 A rack is used to support a length of pipe with a mass of 200 kg. If the mass of the pipe acts at its center, find the reactions at contact points *A* and *B* as shown in Fig. P4-8.

FIGURE P4-8

4-9 Calculate the tension in *AB* and *BC* for the system shown in Fig. P4-9.

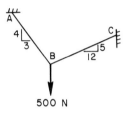

FIGURE P4-9

4-10 For the system shown in Fig. P4-10, find the tension in *AB* and *BC*.

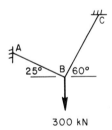

FIGURE P4-10

4-11 A fork lift is used to pick up a drum with a mass of 400 kg. Determine the force on the drum at contact points *A* and *B*, shown in Fig. P4-11. Each part of the fork will support half of the mass of the drum.

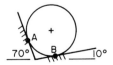

FIGURE P4-11

4-12 A billet with a mass of 2500 kg is supported, as shown in Fig. P4-12. Determine the force exerted on the billet at contact points *A* and *B*.

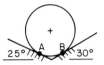

FIGURE P4-12

4-13 If the maximum compressive force in the boom *AB*, shown in Fig. P4-13, is 3 kN, determine the maximum possible value for the force *P*.

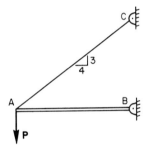

FIGURE P4-13

4-14 On some construction sites, a car suspended from a cable is used for transporting materials, as shown in Fig. P4-14. Determine the tension in the cable when the car, *B*, is at midspan if the car and contents have a mass of 8000 kg.

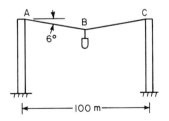

FIGURE P4-14

4-15 The force in the strut *BD*, shown in Fig. P4-15, is 500 kN compression. Calculate the tension in cables *AB* and *BC*.

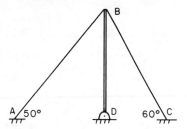

FIGURE P4-15

4-16 Springs are used to control the force **F** in member *BD*, as shown in Fig. P4-16. If the force in member *BD* is 500 N, determine the force in springs *AB* and *BC*.

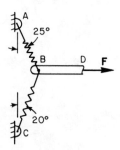

FIGURE P4-16

4-17 For the beam shown in Fig. P4-17, determine the reactions at *A* and *C*.

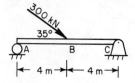

FIGURE P4-17

4-18 Find the reactions at *A* and *B* for the beam shown in Fig. P4-18.

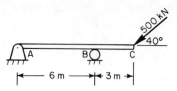

FIGURE P4-18

4-19 Determine the reactions at *A* and *B* for the member shown in Fig. P4-19.

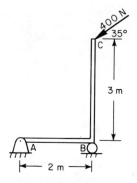

FIGURE P4-19

4-20 For the member shown in Fig. P4-20, determine the reactions at *A* and *C*.

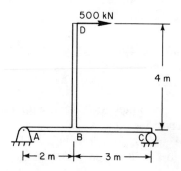

FIGURE P4-20

4-5 PLANE, PARALLEL FORCE SYSTEMS

A beam with a number of parallel forces applied to it is shown in Fig. 4-16(a). The free-body diagram for the beam is shown in Fig. 4-16(b). The support at A is a pin, and a pin can exert forces in both the x and y direction on the beam, so both components are shown. The support at D is a roller, which can exert a force perpendicular to the beam only. In general, unknown forces such as A_x, A_y and D_y will be shown pointing in the positive direction. Although their directions are fairly obvious in this case, in some cases the directions of unknown forces must be assumed, so the habit of assuming a positive direction may as well be cultivated now. When calculating the magnitude of an unknown force, if the answer has a positive value the direction assumed was correct.

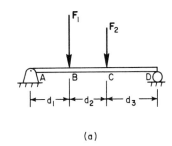

(a)

In the free-body diagram shown in Fig. 4-16(b), there are three unknown forces, A_x, A_y and D_y. It will be recalled that, for a plane system in equilibrium, there are three equilibrium equations available to aid in determining the unknown forces. They are

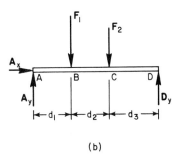

(b)

FIGURE 4-16

$$\Sigma F_x = 0 \tag{4-3}$$

$$\Sigma F_y = 0 \tag{4-4}$$

$$\Sigma M_z = 0 \tag{4-8}$$

If forces for the beam of Fig. 4-16(b) are summed in the x direction:

$$\Sigma F_x = 0$$

then

$$A_x = 0$$

Thus, for equilibrium in the x direction, A_x must be equal to zero, and *all* the actual forces acting on the body will be parallel.

In this instance, there are two unknown forces acting in the y direction, so the summation of forces in the y direction would give an equation with two unknown terms. However, if moments are taken about some convenient reference axis, a moment equation with one unknown can be written. Thus, if moments are taken about an axis passing through A, A_y will have no moment, and the only unknown term in the moment equation will be D_y. After D_y is obtained, then A_y can be determined by the summation of forces in the y direction.

When taking moments for an equilibrium equation, as a general rule, the chosen axis should be on the line of action of one of

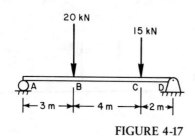

20 kN

15 kN

A   B   C D

|← 3 m →|← 4 m →|←2 m→|

FIGURE 4-17

the unknown forces. This will eliminate that unknown force from the moment equation.

EXAMPLE 4-4

Determine the reactions at the supports for the beam shown in Fig. 4-17.

SOLUTION

The first step is to draw the free-body diagram, as shown in Fig. 4-18. *Since the support at A is a roller, the force is shown as being vertically up. At pin D, only the y component is shown, since there are no other forces in the x direction, and thus there will be no x component at D.*

Since there are two unknown forces in the y direction, moments will be taken about an axis through D in order to calculate A_y. *Moments may also be taken about an axis through A to find* D_y.

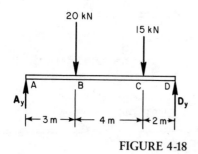

20 kN

15 kN

A   B   C   D

A_y D_y

|← 3 m →|← 4 m →|←2 m→|

FIGURE 4-18

$$\Sigma M_D = 0$$

$$-(A_y \times 9) + 20 \times 6 + 15 \times 2 = 0$$

$$A_y = \frac{120.00 + 30.00}{9.00}$$

$$= \frac{150.00}{9.00}$$

$$= 16.67 \text{ kN}$$

Now that A_y *has been found, the forces in the y direction may be summed to find* D_y.

$$\Sigma F_y = 0$$

$$16.67 - 20 - 15 + D_y = 0$$

$$D_y = 35.00 - 16.67$$

$$= 18.33 \text{ kN}$$

If moments are taken about A to find D_y, *this can serve as a check on the above calculation of* D_y.

In both cases, A_y *and* D_y *were positive, indicating that the assumed directions were correct. Since there were no x components,* $R_A = A_y$ *and* $R_D = D_y$.

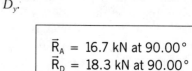

$$\vec{R}_A = 16.7 \text{ kN at } 90.00°$$
$$\vec{R}_D = 18.3 \text{ kN at } 90.00°$$

EXAMPLE 4-5

For the beam shown in Fig. 4-19, find the forces that the supports at A and C exert on the beam.

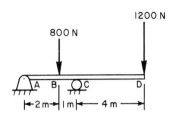

FIGURE 4-19

SOLUTION

The free-body diagram is drawn as shown in Fig. 4-20. Since the roller at C can only exert a vertical force, there will be no x component exerted by the pin at A, because all of the other forces acting on the beam are vertical.

There are two unknown forces in the y direction. If moments are taken about A, there will be only one unknown term in the moment equation.

$$\Sigma\, M_A = 0$$

$$-(800 \times 2) + C_y \times 3 - 1200 \times 7 = 0$$

$$C_y = \frac{1600 + 8400}{3.00}$$

$$= 3333 \text{ N}$$

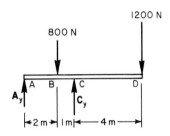

FIGURE 4-20

If forces in the y direction are now summed, there will be only one unknown term.

$$\Sigma\, F_y = 0$$

$$A_y - 800 + 3333 - 1200 = 0$$

$$A_y = 2000 - 3333$$

$$= -1333$$

The negative sign for A_y indicates that the assumed direction was incorrect. In reality, A_y is 1333 N down.

Since there were no x components at either support, $R_A = A_y$ and $R_C = C_y$.

$$\vec{R}_A = 1330 \text{ N at } 270.00°$$
$$\vec{R}_C = 3330 \text{ N at } 90.00°$$

EXAMPLE 4-6

Determine the reactions from the supports at A and E on the member shown in Fig. 4-21.

SOLUTION

Step number one is to draw the free-body diagram of the member as shown in Fig. 4-22. Since A is a roller, the force from A

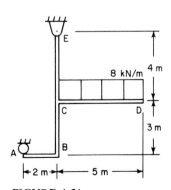

FIGURE 4-21

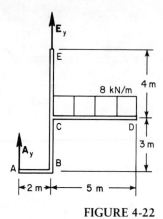

FIGURE 4-22

must be vertical. There are no forces applied in the x direction, so there will be no x component of the reaction at E.

There are two unknown forces in the y direction, so moments could be taken about an axis through E to obtain an equilibrium equation with only one unknown term.

$$\Sigma \, M_E = 0$$

$$-(A_y \times 2) - 8 \times 5 \times 2.5 = 0$$

$$A_y = \frac{100.0}{-2.00}$$

$$= -50.0 \text{ kN}$$

The negative sign indicates that A_y really points down, not up as assumed.

When summing forces in the y direction to find E_y, the actual direction, not the assumed direction, of A_y must be used in the equation.

$$\Sigma \, F_y = 0$$

$$-50.0 + E_y - 8 \times 5 = 0$$

$$E_y = 50.0 + 40.0$$

$$= 90.0 \text{ kN}$$

Since there are no x components for either reaction, the total reactions at A and E will be the same as the y components.

$$\vec{R}_A = 50.0 \text{ kN at } 270.00°$$
$$\vec{R}_E = 90.0 \text{ kN at } 90.00°$$

PROBLEMS

4-21 For the beam shown in Fig. P4-21, determine the reactions at *A* and *C*.

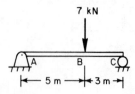

FIGURE P4-21

4-22 Calculate the reactions at *A* and *C* for the beam shown in Fig. P4-22.

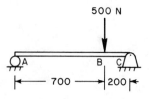

FIGURE P4-22

4-23 Determine the reactions at supports *A* and *C* for the beam shown in Fig. P4-23.

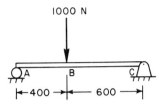

FIGURE P4-23

4-24 For the beam shown in Fig. P4-24, find the reactions at the supports at *A* and *C*.

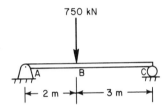

FIGURE P4-24

4-25 Determine the reactions at the supports for the beam shown in Fig. P4-25.

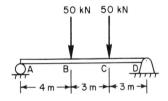

FIGURE P4-25

4-26 Find the reactions at supports *A* and *D* for the beam shown in Fig. P4-26.

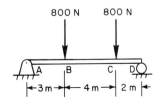

FIGURE P4-26

4-27 Calculate the reactions at the supports for the member shown in Fig. P4-27.

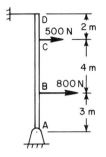

FIGURE P4-27

4-28 For the beam shown in Fig. P4-28, determine the reactions at the supports.

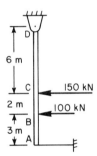

FIGURE P4-28

4-29 Evaluate the reactions at the supports *A* and *D* for the beam shown in Fig. P4-29.

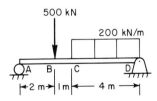

FIGURE P4-29

4-30 For the beam shown in Fig. P4-30, calculate the reactions at the supports.

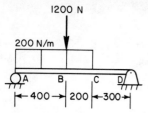

FIGURE P4-30

4-31 For the beam shown in Fig. P4-31, determine the reactions at supports B and D.

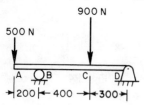

FIGURE P4-31

4-32 Evaluate the reactions at the supports for the beam shown in Fig. P4-32.

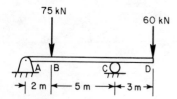

FIGURE P4-32

4-33 Find the reactions at the supports for the member shown in Fig. P4-33.

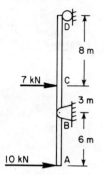

FIGURE P4-33

4-34 Calculate the reactions at A and C for the member shown in Fig. P4-34.

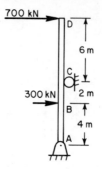

FIGURE P4-34

4-35 For the member shown in Fig. P4-35, find the reactions at C and D.

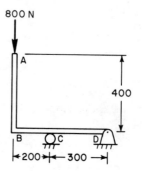

FIGURE P4-35

4-36 Determine the reactions at A and D for the member shown in Fig. P4-36.

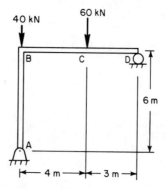

FIGURE P4-36

4-37 Calculate the reactions at *A* and *E* for the member shown in Fig. P4-37.

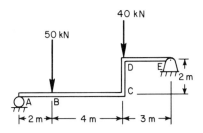

FIGURE P4-37

4-38 Find the reactions at *A* and *B* for the member shown in Fig. P4-38.

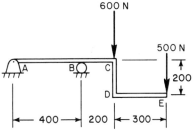

FIGURE P4-38

4-6   MOMENTS AND COUPLES

The only support for a cantilever beam, as shown in Fig. 4-23(a), is at the wall. If a single support force is shown at *A* in the free-body diagram in Fig. 4-23(b), the beam would not be in equilibrium, for the two forces shown would form a couple. To maintain equilibrium, it is necessary that the wall cause a couple equal in magnitude and opposite in direction to the couple caused by **P** and **A**$_y$. The required couple is shown as **M**$_S$ in Fig. 4-23(c). Although **M**$_S$ is actually a couple, it is commonly called a moment; that tradition will be maintained in this book, and the reaction at the support of a cantilever beam will be considered to consist of a force and a moment.

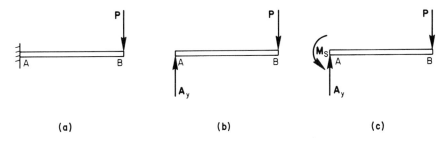

FIGURE 4-23

The magnitude of the moment at the support is usually found by utilizing the equilibrium equation for moments:

$$\Sigma M_z = 0 \qquad (4\text{-}8)$$

In general, the axis of rotation used for calculating the magnitude of the moment will be at the support of the cantilever beam.

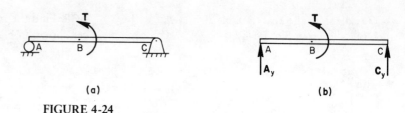

(a)   (b)

FIGURE 4-24

Once in a while the loading on a beam will actually be a couple, as shown in Fig. 4-24(a). The free-body diagram for the beam is shown in Fig. 4-24(b). For the beam to be in equilibrium, A_y and C_y must form a couple that opposes the applied couple T. The reactions at A and C may be obtained by taking moments about either A or C and then summing forces in the y direction to find the second force. When working with a couple, it should be kept in mind that, when calculating moments, the couple has the same value regardless of the axis used. Also, a couple does not form part of any equilibrium equation involving the summation of forces.

EXAMPLE 4-7

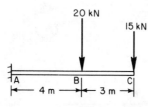

FIGURE 4-25

Determine the reaction at the support for the cantilever beam shown in Fig. 4-25.

SOLUTION

Drawing a free-body diagram of the beam, as shown in Fig. 4-26, is the suggested first step. Since the beam is a cantilever, there must be a vertical force at A as well as a moment. Both the force and the moment are assumed to be positive.

The value for A_y can be obtained by summing forces in the y direction.

$$\Sigma\,F_y = 0$$

$$A_y - 20 - 15 = 0$$

$$A_y = 35.0 \text{ kN}$$

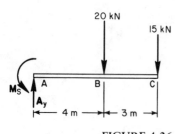

FIGURE 4-26

To determine M_S, moments are usually taken about an axis passing through the support, since taking moments about an axis at the support eliminates the vertical force at the support from the moment equation.

$$\Sigma\,M_A = 0$$

$$M_S - 20 \times 4 - 15 \times 7 = 0$$

$$M_S = 80.0 + 105.0$$

$$= 185.0 \text{ kN·m}$$

Since A_y is the magnitude of the total force at support A, A_y will also be equal to R_A. The sign of the moment will be based on the accepted sign convention (counterclockwise is positive and clockwise is negative). The signs obtained for both A_y and M_S were positive, indicating that the assumption of positive directions was correct.

$$\vec{R}_A = 35.0 \text{ kN at } 90.00°$$
$$M_S = 185 \text{ kN·m}$$

EXAMPLE 4-8

For the beam shown in Fig. 4-27, determine the reaction at the wall.

SOLUTION

The free-body diagram shown in Fig. 4-28 shows a vertical force at the support and a moment. It is assumed that both the force and the moment have a positive direction.

The value for D_y can be obtained by summing forces in the y direction, since D_y is the only unknown term in the y direction.

$$\Sigma F_y = 0$$
$$-300 \times 4 - 800 + D_y = 0$$
$$D_y = 1200 + 800$$
$$= 2000 \text{ N}$$

The value of M_S can be obtained by taking moments about D. M_S will be the only unknown term in the moment equation.

$$\Sigma M_D = 0$$
$$300 \times 4 \times 7 + 800 \times 3 + M_S = 0$$
$$M_S = -8400 - 2400$$
$$= -10\ 800 \text{ N·m}$$

The sign obtained for D_y was positive, so the assumed direction was correct. D_y is the magnitude of the total force at D, so $R_D = D_y$. The sign obtained for M_S was negative, indicating that the assumed positive direction was incorrect, and that M_S is actually a negative moment.

$$\vec{R}_D = 2000 \text{ N at } 90.00°$$
$$M_S = -10\ 800 \text{ N·m}$$

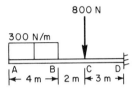

FIGURE 4-27

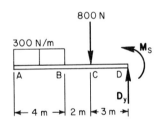

FIGURE 4-28

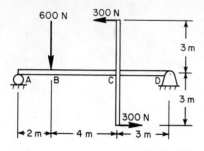

FIGURE 4-29

EXAMPLE 4-9

Find the forces that the supports at *A* and *D* exert on the beam shown in Fig. 4-29.

SOLUTION

The free-body diagram of the beam, as shown in Fig. 4-30, *should be drawn as the first step in the solution. The force at the roller at A is assumed to be vertically up. At the pin at D, only the vertical force is shown, as the two given forces in the x direction form a couple, and their sum is equal to zero. The direction of* D_y *is assumed to be positive.*

To determine one of the reactions, it will be necessary to take moments about an axis through either A or D. The couple can be calculated separately, and then used in the equilibrium moment equation.

$$T = Fd$$
$$= 300 \times 6$$
$$= 1800 \text{ N·m}$$
$$\Sigma M_D = 0$$
$$-(A_y \times 9) + 600 \times 7 + 1800 = 0$$
$$A_y = \frac{4200 + 1800}{9.00}$$
$$= 666.67 \text{ N}$$

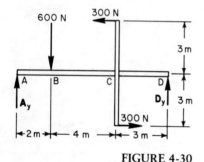

FIGURE 4-30

The value for D_y *may now be obtained by summing forces in the y direction.*

$$\Sigma F_y = 0$$
$$666.67 - 600 + D_y = 0$$
$$D_y = -666.67 + 600.00$$
$$= -66.67 \text{ N}$$

The negative sign for D_y *indicates that the assumed positive direction is incorrect, and that* D_y *actually points down. Since there is no x component at D,* $D_y = R_D$.

$$\vec{R}_A = 667 \text{ N at } 90.00°$$
$$\vec{R}_D = 66.7 \text{ N at } 270.00°$$

PROBLEMS

4-39 For the beam shown in Fig. P4-39, determine the reaction at the support.

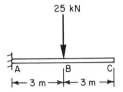

FIGURE P4-39

4-40 Determine the reaction at the support for the beam shown in Fig. P4-40.

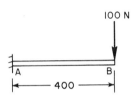

FIGURE P4-40

4-41 Find the reaction at *B* for the beam shown in Fig. P4-41.

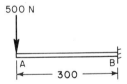

FIGURE P4-41

4-42 For the beam shown in Fig. P4-42, determine the reaction at the support.

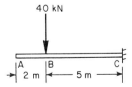

FIGURE P4-42

4-43 Calculate the reaction at the support for the beam shown in Fig. P4-43.

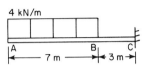

FIGURE P4-43

4-44 Find the reaction at *A* for the beam shown in Fig. P4-44.

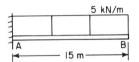

FIGURE P4-44

4-45 For the beam shown in Fig. P4-45, determine the reaction at the support.

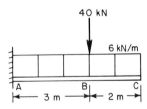

FIGURE P4-45

4-46 Calculate the reaction at the support for the beam shown in Fig. P4-46.

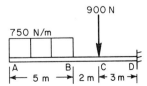

FIGURE P4-46

4-47 Determine the reactions at the supports for the beam shown in Fig. P4-47.

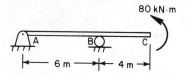

FIGURE P4-47

4-48 For the beam shown in Fig. P4-48, calculate the reactions at the two supports.

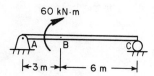

FIGURE P4-48

4-49 Calculate the reactions at the supports for the beam shown in Fig. P4-49.

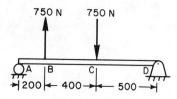

FIGURE P4-49

4-50 For the beam shown in Fig. P4-50, determine the reactions at the supports.

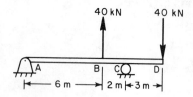

FIGURE P4-50

4-51 Determine the reactions at the supports B and D for the beam shown in Fig. P4-51.

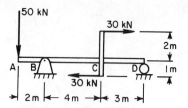

FIGURE P4-51

4-52 Find the reactions at A and D for the beam shown in Fig. P4-52.

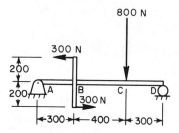

FIGURE P4-52

4-53 For the beam shown in Fig. P4-53, find the reactions at the supports.

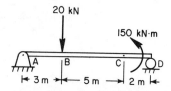

FIGURE P4-53

4-54 Determine the reactions at the supports for the beam shown in Fig. P4-54.

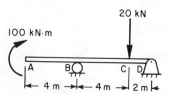

FIGURE P4-54

4-7 PLANE, NON-PARALLEL, NON-CONCURRENT FORCE SYSTEMS

The most general system of forces in a plane is the non-parallel, non-concurrent force system. Such a system is shown in Fig. 4-31(a). The free-body diagram for the beam in Fig. 4-31(a) is shown in Fig. 4-31(b). For the pin at A, there will be both x and y components of the reaction, since at least one of the applied loads has an x component. At D, the only component of the reaction will be in the vertical direction, since D is a roller. The unknown components of forces or reactions are shown pointing in the positive direction. If they are actually positive, the sign of the value obtained will be positive. If the force is actually pointing in the negative direction, the sign of the value obtained will be negative.

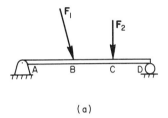

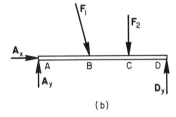

(a)   (b)

FIGURE 4-31

The free-body diagram in Fig. 4-31(b) has three unknown forces, A_x, A_y and D_y. To determine three unknown forces will require the use of the three available equilibrium equations:

$$\Sigma F_x = 0 \qquad (4\text{-}3)$$

$$\Sigma F_y = 0 \qquad (4\text{-}4)$$

$$\Sigma M_z = 0 \qquad (4\text{-}8)$$

The value for A_x may be obtained directly by summing forces in the x direction. In the y direction, there are two unknown terms, so moments must be taken about an axis through either A or D. Generally, the preferred axis of rotation for the moment equilibrium equation is at a point where two unknown forces intersect, in this case point A. It is usually most efficient to use Varignon's theorem when calculating moments in such a problem. Once one of the unknown forces in the y direction has been obtained, then forces may be summed in the y direction to find the remaining unknown force. The total reaction at A and its direction may be found by determining the resultant of A_x and A_y.

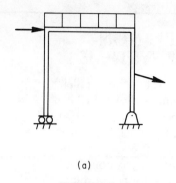

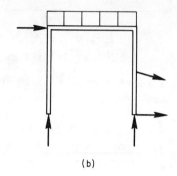

(a)   (b)

FIGURE 4-32

A beam is only one of many shapes that may support a non-parallel non-concurrent force system. A frame such as that shown in Fig. 4-32(a) also carries such a system. The free-body diagram for the frame is shown in Fig. 4-32(b). The analysis of this problem is little different from the analysis of a beam, except that, when writing moment equations, care must be taken to account for the moment caused by every component of every force.

EXAMPLE 4-10

Determine the reactions at A and D for the beam shown in Fig. 4-33.

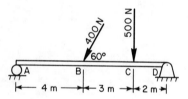

FIGURE 4-33

SOLUTION

Drawing the free-body diagram is the usual, and necessary, first step for solving equilibrium problems. Figure 4-34 *shows the free-body diagram. Since A is a roller, there is a single vertical force acting at A. At the pin, D, the x and y components are shown. Both components are assumed to be acting in the positive direction.*

Since there is only one unknown force in the x direction, the simplest step in the analysis would be to sum forces in the x direction to determine D_x.

$$\Sigma F_x = 0$$

$$-400 \cos 60° + D_x = 0$$

$$D_x = 200.00 \text{ N}$$

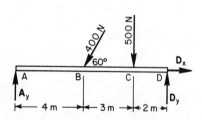

FIGURE 4-34

Moments may now be taken about D to find A_y. *The x component of the 400 N force will have no moment about D if components are concurrent on the beam axis, for the x component would then be collinear with D.*

$$\Sigma M_D = 0$$

$$-(A_y \times 9) + 400 \sin 60° \times 5 + 500 \times 2 = 0$$

$$A_y = \frac{1732.05 + 1000.00}{9.00}$$

$$= 303.56 \text{ N}$$

D_y *may now be obtained by summing forces in the y direction.*

$$\Sigma F_y = 0$$

$$303.56 - 400 \sin 60° - 500 + D_y = 0$$

$$D_y = -303.56 + 346.41 + 500.00$$

$$= 542.85 \text{ N}$$

All the unknown forces were found to have positive values, so their assumed positive directions were correct.

To determine R_D and its direction, a sketch, such as Fig. 4-35, should be drawn as an aid.

$$\theta = \tan^{-1} \frac{D_y}{D_x}$$

$$= \tan^{-1} \frac{542.85}{200.00}$$

$$= 69.78°$$

Direction of $\vec{R}_D = 69.78°$

$$R_D = \frac{D_y}{\sin \theta}$$

$$= \frac{542.85}{\sin 69.78°}$$

$$= 578.50 \text{ N}$$

FIGURE 4-35

$$\boxed{\begin{array}{l} \vec{R}_A = 304 \text{ N at } 90.00° \\ \vec{R}_D = 578 \text{ N at } 69.78° \end{array}}$$

It would also have been possible, and correct, to solve this problem by taking moments about A to solve for D_y first, and then to sum forces in the y direction to find A_y.

EXAMPLE 4-11

For the beam shown in Fig. 4-36, find the reactions at A and D. The surface at D is smooth.

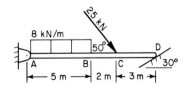

FIGURE 4-36

SOLUTION

The free-body diagram of the beam, as shown in Fig. 4-37, should be drawn first. The pin A will probably have reaction components in both the x and y directions, so both components have been shown. Their assumed direction is positive. The surface at D is smooth, so the reaction must be perpendicular to the surface. Thus the direction of the force at D is fixed.

At first glance, it appears that there are two unknown terms in both the x and y directions. However, if moments are taken about A, R_D may be obtained directly, since the angle of R_D is known.

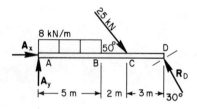

FIGURE 4-37

$$\Sigma\ M_A = 0$$

$$-(8 \times 5 \times 2.5) - 25 \sin 50° \times 7 + R_D \cos 30° \times 10 = 0$$

$$R_D = \frac{100.00 + 134.06}{10 \cos 30°}$$

$$= 27.03\ \text{kN}$$

Direction of $\vec{R}_D = 90° + 30°$

$$= 120.00°$$

It is now possible to sum forces in the y direction, to obtain A_y.

$$\Sigma\ F_y = 0$$

$$A_y - 8 \times 5 - 25 \sin 50° + 27.03 \cos 30° = 0$$

$$A_y = 40.00 + 19.15 - 23.41$$

$$= 34.74\ \text{kN}$$

By summing forces in the x direction, A_x may now be found.

$$\Sigma\ F_x = 0$$

$$A_x + 25 \cos 50° - 27.03 \sin 30° = 0$$

$$A_x = -16.07 + 13.52$$

$$= -2.55\ \text{kN}$$

The value obtained for A_y was positive; thus the assumed positive direction for the y component was correct. The value for A_x was negative so it must actually point to the left. It is worthwhile to draw a sketch as shown in Fig. 4-38, *as an aid to the determination of R_A and θ.*

$$\theta = \tan^{-1} \frac{A_y}{A_x}$$

$$= \tan^{-1} \frac{35.74}{2.55}$$

$$= 85.92°$$

Direction of $\vec{R}_A = 180.00° - 85.92°$

$$= 94.08°$$

$$R_A = \frac{A_y}{\sin \theta}$$

$$= \frac{35.74}{\sin 85.92°}$$

$$= 35.83 \text{ kN}$$

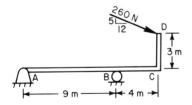

FIGURE 4-38

> $\vec{R}_A = 35.8 \text{ kN at } 94.08°$
> $\vec{R}_D = 27.0 \text{ kN at } 120.00°$

Other approaches could have been correctly and successfully used to solve this problem. Moments could have been taken about D to solve for A_y. Forces could then have been summed in the y direction to obtain R_D. It would then be possible to sum forces in the x direction to find A_x. It will be found that many problems have two or more correct methods available for their solution.

EXAMPLE 4-12

Determine the reactions at supports *A* and *B* for the member shown in Fig. 4-39.

FIGURE 4-39

SOLUTION

The free-body diagram, as shown in **Fig. 4-40,** *should be drawn as the first step. The force exerted by the roller at B must be* vertical. *The x and y components of the force from the pin at A are both assumed to be positive.*

If moments are taken about A, then B_y will be the only unknown term in the moment equation. Note that both the x and y components of the 260 N force will have a moment about A.

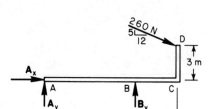

FIGURE 4-40

$$\Sigma M_A = 0$$

$$B_y \times 9 - \frac{12}{13} \times 260 \times 3 - \frac{5}{13} \times 260 \times 13 = 0$$

$$B_y = \frac{720.0 + 1300.0}{9.00}$$

$$= 224.44 \text{ N}$$

Since the value for B_y is positive, its actual direction is positive, as assumed.

It is now possible to determine A_y by summing forces in the y direction.

$$\Sigma F_y = 0$$

$$A_y + 224.44 - \frac{5}{13} \times 260 = 0$$

$$A_y = -224.44 + 100.00$$

$$= -124.44 \text{ N}$$

The value for A_x may be obtained by summing forces in the x direction.

$$\Sigma F_x = 0$$

$$A_x + \frac{12}{13} \times 260 = 0$$

$$A_x = -240.00 \text{ N}$$

The values for both A_x and A_y are negative, indicating that both of these components are actually pointing in the negative direction. A sketch, such as Fig. 4-41, *should be made as an aid to the determination of R_A and θ.*

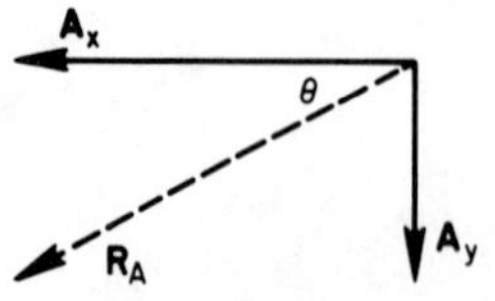

FIGURE 4-41

$$\theta = \tan^{-1} \frac{A_y}{A_x}$$

$$= \tan^{-1} \frac{124.44}{240.00}$$

$$= 27.41°$$

Direction of $\bar{R}_A$ = 180.00° + 27.41°

$$= 207.41°$$

$$R_A = \frac{A_y}{\sin \theta}$$

$$= \frac{124.44}{\sin 27.41°}$$

$$= 270.34 \text{ N}$$

$\bar{R}_A$ = 270 N at 207.41°
$\bar{R}_B$ = 224 N at 90.00°

This problem could also have been solved by first taking moments about B to obtain A_y. A_x and B_y could then be found by summing forces in the x and y directions respectively.

PROBLEMS

4-55 Calculate the reactions at *A* and *C* for the beam shown in Fig. P4-55.

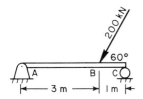

FIGURE P4-55

4-56 Determine the forces at supports *A* and *C* for the beam shown in Fig. P4-56.

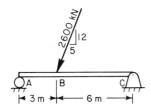

FIGURE P4-56

4-57 For the beam shown in Fig. P4-57, find the reactions at *A* and *C*.

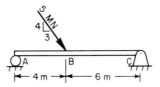

FIGURE P4-57

4-58 Calculate the reactions at supports *A* and *C* for the beam shown in Fig. P4-58.

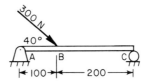

FIGURE P4-58

4-59 For the beam shown in Fig. P4-59, find the reactions at supports *A* and *B*.

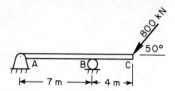

FIGURE P4-59

4-60 Find the reactions at *B* and *C* for the beam shown in Fig. P4-60.

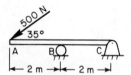

FIGURE P4-60

4-61 Find the reactions at the supports for the beam shown in Fig. P4-61.

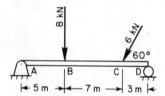

FIGURE P4-61

4-62 Determine the reactions at the supports for the beam shown in Fig. P4-62.

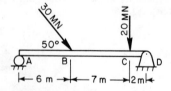

FIGURE P4-62

4-63 Calculate the reactions at the supports for the beam shown in Fig. P4-63.

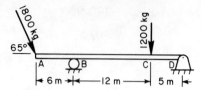

FIGURE P4-63

4-64 Determine the reactions at *B* and *D* for the beam shown in Fig. P4-64.

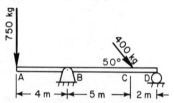

FIGURE P4-64

4-65 Determine the reaction at *A* for the beam shown in Fig. P4-65.

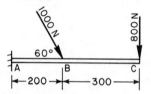

FIGURE P4-65

4-66 For the beam shown in Fig. P4-66, find the reaction at *C*.

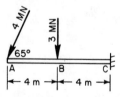

FIGURE P4-66

4-67 For the beam shown in Fig. P4-67, calculate the reaction at the wall.

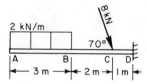

FIGURE P4-67

4-68 Find the reaction at *A* for the beam shown in Fig. P4-68.

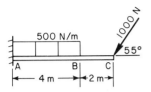

FIGURE P4-68

4-69 Calculate the reactions at the supports for the beam shown in Fig. P4-69.

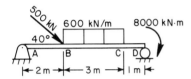

FIGURE P4-69

4-70 Find the reactions at *A* and *E* for the beam shown in Fig. P4-70.

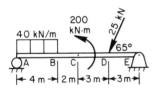

FIGURE P4-70

4-71 If the surface at *C* is smooth, determine the reactions at *A* and *C* for the beam shown in Fig. P4-71.

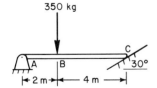

FIGURE P4-71

4-72 Determine the reaction at *A* and the tension in cable *CD* for the beam shown in Fig. P4-72.

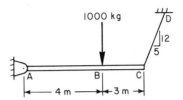

FIGURE P4-72

4-73 Find the reactions at *A* and *C* for the member shown in Fig. P4-73 if the surface at *C* is smooth.

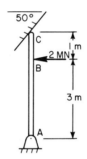

FIGURE P4-73

4-74 The 500 N load shown in Fig. P4-74 is applied at the midpoint of member *AC*. If the surface at *C* is smooth, determine the reactions at *A* and *C*.

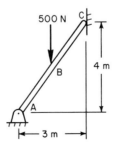

FIGURE P4-74

4-75 Find the reactions at *A* and *D* for the member shown in Fig. P4-75.

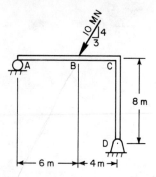

FIGURE P4-75

4-76 Find the reactions at supports *A* and *B* for the member shown in Fig. P4-76.

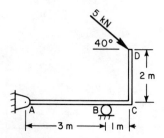

FIGURE P4-76

4-77 Find the reactions at *A* and *B* for the member shown in Fig. P4-77.

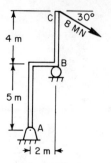

FIGURE P4-77

4-78 For the member shown in Fig. P4-78, determine the reactions at the supports.

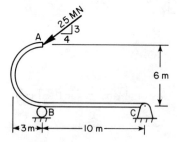

FIGURE P4-78

5 FRAMES AND MACHINES

5-1 FRAMES AND MACHINES

The determination or analysis of the forces in frames and machines by means of the equilibrium equations is one of the primary objectives of statics, for the ability to design frames and machines is dependent on a knowledge of the forces acting on each part of the frame or machine.

A frame may be defined as a system of two or more members designed to carry a load. A machine may be defined as a system of two or more members designed to transmit a force. There is not necessarily a clear difference between a frame and a machine, for in some instances a system combines the functions of both frame and machine.

The steel skeleton of a building is a rather obvious example of a frame. The skeleton carries the loads from the floors, the building contents, the wind and the frame itself, as well as other loads that may be applied. A pair of pliers, designed to transmit a force from the hand to the piece being held by the pliers, is a relatively simple machine. The human body, with its combination of skeleton and muscles, is a rather interesting system that operates as both frame and machine. The forces exerted in the

FIGURE 5-1 This small bascule bridge functions as a frame when it is in the closed position, and as a combination of frame and machine when in the open position. The drive mechanism is hidden in the abutments. *Photo courtesy of The Ontario Ministry of Transportation and Communications.*

body can be analyzed in the same manner as forces in any other frame or machine.

The small bascule bridge shown in Fig. 5-1 is an example of a structure that is both frame and machine. In the closed position, the bridge carries the load from vehicles as well as the load caused by its own mass. The machine portion of the system, which lifts the bridge, is hidden from view within the abutment.

Although frames and machines are discussed in separate sections in this book, some of the classification is arbitrary and has been done simply to break the material up into smaller sections. A clear-cut difference between frames and machines does not always exist in reality.

In analyzing frame and machine problems, it will be the practice to ignore the mass of the members, unless there are clear indications that the mass of a particular member must be taken into account. This approach will simplify problem calculations. In actual practice, the mass of the member will be omitted from the analysis only if that mass is small relative to the other loads that are applied.

5-2   TWO-FORCE MEMBERS

FIGURE 5-2

The analysis of many frame and machine problems is simplified by the recognition of two-force members as components of the frame or machine. A truss, which is one type of frame, is made up entirely of two-force members.

A two-force member is defined as a member with two forces acting on it. Such a member is shown in Fig. 5-2. For the member to be in equilibrium, the two forces acting on it must be equal in magnitude, opposite in direction, and collinear. If the two forces are not collinear, as shown in Fig. 5-3(a), there would be a tendency to rotate about an axis, and the member would not be in equilibrium. If the forces are in the same direction, as shown in Fig. 5-3(b), the sum of the forces would not be zero,

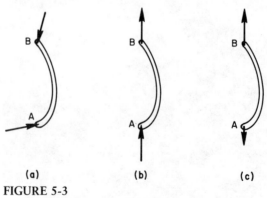

(a)   (b)   (c)

FIGURE 5-3

and again the member would not be in equilibrium. Similarly, if the magnitude of the forces is not the same, as shown in Fig. 5-3(c), the sum of the forces would not be zero, and equilibrium would not exist.

Whenever a two-force member is recognized, it should be observed that the line of action of the two forces involved will be collinear with the line connecting the points of application of the two forces. Thus, the line of action of the forces applied to a two-force member can be obtained by finding the orientation of the member. As a practical matter, most two-force members are straight, but there is no requirement that they be straight.

Any straight two-force member will be in simple *tension*, which is a pull, or *compression*, which is a push. In problem analysis, it is customary to assume that the unknown force in a two-force member is in tension. Rather than write out *tension* or *compression* with the magnitude of a force for a two-force member, it is common practice to use a plus sign (+) to indicate tension and a minus sign (−) to indicate compression. Thus, if the force in a two-force member is said to be −25 kN, it is understood that this is a compression force of 25 kN in that member. Similarly, a force of + 500 N indicates a tensile force of 500 N. Although mathematically it is understood that no sign implies a positive number, it is suggested that when dealing with forces in two-force members, the appropriate sign should always be included.

Note that if the unknown force in a two-force member is assumed to be in tension, the sign associated with the answer when the force is calculated will correctly indicate whether the force is actually tension (+) or compression (−).

5-3 MACHINES

There is no simple pattern to follow in the analysis of forces acting on the various parts of a machine. This may be one reason that the study of frames and machines is considered useful for developing analytical skills, as well as for the direct application related to structural and machine design.

The following series of steps is offered for consideration for analyzing machine problems. It can be modified to suit the particular problem being analyzed.

1. Draw a free-body diagram. Isolate the body or that part of the system that is to be analyzed. Any supports are replaced by the forces they exert on the body. It is recommended that, in the case of two-force members, the unknown force should be assumed to be tension. In the case of the x and y components of a force at a support, it is usually a good idea to assume that their

directions are positive. If these assumptions are made, the sign of the answer will give the correct sign for the direction of the force.

2. Think. Determine precisely what information is required. *Mentally* go through the equilibrium equations that might help you obtain the required information. Be constructively lazy. It is usually easier to solve one equation with one unknown term than two equations with two unknowns. If a moment equation is to be used, the best axis of rotation is often at the point of concurrency of two unknown forces. It will sometimes be necessary to draw supplementary free-body diagrams to determine the forces on a particular part of the machine. If supplementary free-body diagrams are necessary, the forces shown on them must be consistent with those shown on existing free-body diagrams. Thus, if a pin is pushing on a member, that same member is pushing (not pulling) on the pin.

3. Write the required equilibrium equations.

4. Solve the equilibrium equations.

5. Check the solution.

These are suggestions, not rules. Every problem is different, and each will require a somewhat different approach. A few example problems will give some guidance on the approach used in the solution of machine problems.

EXAMPLE 5-1

Determine the force the axle at *A* exerts on the pulley shown in Fig. 5-4. The pulley is smooth.

SOLUTION

Start with an appropriate free-body diagram. In this instance, a free-body diagram of the pulley would show the loads in the cable as well as the unknown force the axle applies to the pulley. The free-body diagram is shown in Fig. 5-5. *Since the cable is continuous, it will have the same tension at each end. The pulley serves only to change the direction of the force in the cable. (If moments are taken about A, it can be shown that the force in both parts of the cable has the same magnitude, as long as the radius of the pulley is constant.) The x and y components of the force from the axle are shown, since the direction of the force is unknown. The direction of both components has been assumed to be positive.*

The system shown in Fig. 5-5 *contains two unknown forces,* A_x *and* A_y, *which may be found by using the equilibrium equations to sum forces in the x and y directions.*

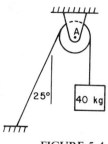

FIGURE 5-4

$$\Sigma \, F_x = 0$$

$$A_x - 40 \times 9.807 \sin 25° = 0$$

$$A_x = 165.78 \text{ N}$$

$$\Sigma \, F_y = 0$$

$$A_y - 40 \times 9.807 \cos 25° - 40 \times 9.807 = 0$$

$$A_y = 355.53 + 392.28$$

$$= 747.81 \text{ N}$$

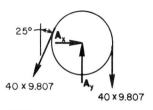

FIGURE 5-5

The total force from the axle is required, so the resultant of the two components should be calculated. Figure 5-6, which shows the two components and their resultant, will aid in the calculation.

$$\theta = \tan^{-1} \frac{A_y}{A_x}$$

$$= \tan^{-1} \frac{747.81}{165.78}$$

$$= 77.50°$$

Direction of $\vec{R}_A = 77.50°$

$$R_A = \frac{A_y}{\sin \theta}$$

$$= \frac{747.81}{\sin 77.50°}$$

$$= 765.97 \text{ N}$$

$$\boxed{\vec{R}_A = 766 \text{ N at } 77.50°}$$

FIGURE 5-6

EXAMPLE 5-2

An end view for a three-hole paper punch is shown in Fig. 5-7. If a 20 N force is required to operate the mechanism, determine the magnitude of the force acting on each of the three punches aligned at C and the magnitude of the force acting on each of the two pins aligned at B.

SOLUTION

A free-body-diagram of part AB would show all of the known and required forces. Since there are three punches, the force at C is shown as $3F_C$, so that F_C will be the force in each punch.

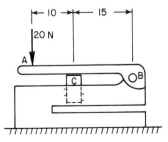

FIGURE 5-7

Similarly, the force at B is shown as 2F$_B$*, since there are two pins at B. The required free-body diagram is shown in* Fig. 5-8.

It makes no difference whether B or C is chosen as an axis of rotation to determine one of the unknown forces.

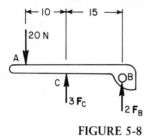

FIGURE 5-8

$$\Sigma\, M_B = 0$$

$$20 \times 25 - 3F_C \times 15 = 0$$

$$F_C = \frac{20 \times 25}{3 \times 15}$$

$$= 11.111 \text{ N}$$

$$\Sigma\, F_y = 0$$

$$-20.00 + 3 \times 11.111 + 2F_B = 0$$

$$F_B = \frac{20.00 - 33.33}{2}$$

$$= -6.667 \text{ N}$$

The negative sign indicates that **F**$_B$ *is actually acting down on member AB.*

$$\boxed{\begin{array}{l} F_C = 11.1 \text{ N} \\ F_B = 6.67 \text{ N} \end{array}}$$

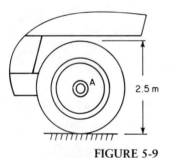

FIGURE 5-9

EXAMPLE 5-3

The wheel of the off-highway construction vehicle shown in Fig. 5-9 is powered by a direct-drive electric motor. If the tractive force between the tire and the ground required to move the vehicle at a steady speed is 15 000 N, determine the torque the motor must supply to the axle.

SOLUTION

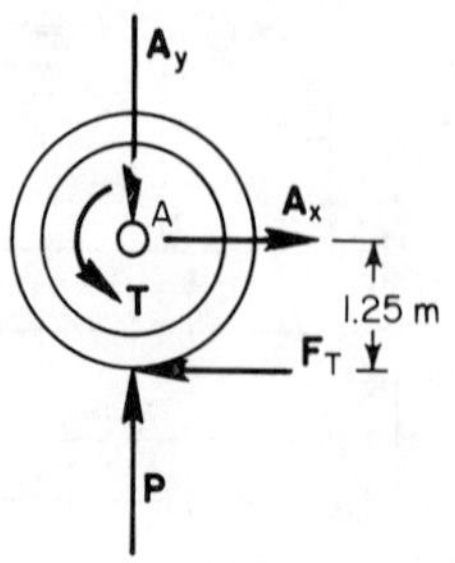

The starting point for the solution to this problem is the free-body diagram, as shown in Fig. 5-10. *As a matter of fact, once an accurate and complete free-body diagram is drawn, the actual calculations are quite simple. At the axle, there is a vertical force applied, due to the mass of the vehicle, a horizontal force from the frame, and the torque from the motor. At the ground there is the vertical force supporting the wheel as well as the tractive force represented by* **F**$_T$*. Although all forces but* **F**$_T$ *are unknown, if moments are taken about an axis through A, three of the unknown forces will not enter into the moment equation.*

FIGURE 5-10

$$\Sigma \ M_A = 0$$
$$T - 15\ 000 \times 1.25 = 0$$
$$T = 18\ 750\ \text{N·m}$$

$$\boxed{T = 18\ 800\ \text{N·m}}$$

EXAMPLE 5-4

The pin at D in the crank mechanism shown in Fig. 5-11 is to apply a horizontal force of 700 N to the right. Determine the magnitude of the torque or couple required to cause this force. The slot at D is smooth.

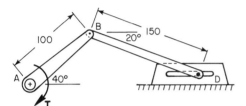

FIGURE 5-11

SOLUTION

If one starts with a free-body diagram of the mechanism, as shown in Fig. 5-12, *it is possible to determine the magnitude of the couple. In drawing the free-body diagram, note that if the pin is to apply a force of 700 N to the right, then the force acting on the pin must be 700 N to the left. There must also be a vertical force at D acting on the pin, since BD is a two-force member. If there are two components of the force at D, then there must also be x and y components of the force at A to maintain equilibrium in the x and y direction.*

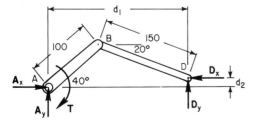

FIGURE 5-12

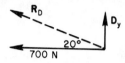

FIGURE 5-13

No forces are shown at B, since all forces acting at B are internal. (It must be remembered that only forces acting on the body, and not those acting in the body, are shown on a free-body diagram.)

Since BD is a two-force member, then R_D must be oriented as shown in Fig. 5-13, and the magnitude of D_y can be calculated as follows:

Since BD is a two-force member:

$$\frac{D_y}{700} = \tan 20°$$

$$D_y = 700 \tan 20°$$

$$= 254.78 \text{ N}$$

To calculate moments about an axis through A, it will be necessary to have both distances d_1 and d_2. It is often a good idea to calculate such distances separately.

$$d_1 = 100 \cos 40° + 150 \cos 20°$$

$$= 76.60 + 140.95$$

$$= 217.55 \text{ mm}$$

$$d_2 = 100 \sin 40° - 150 \sin 20°$$

$$= 64.28 - 51.30$$

$$= 12.98 \text{ mm}$$

Now moments may be taken about an axis through A to determine the magnitude of the couple. Note that distances are converted to metres to obtain the couple in newton metres.

$$\Sigma M_A = 0$$

$$700 \times 0.012\,98 + 254.78 \times 0.217\,55 - T = 0$$

$$T = 9.09 + 55.43$$

$$= 64.52 \text{ N·m}$$

$$T = 64.5 \text{ N·m}$$

EXAMPLE 5-5

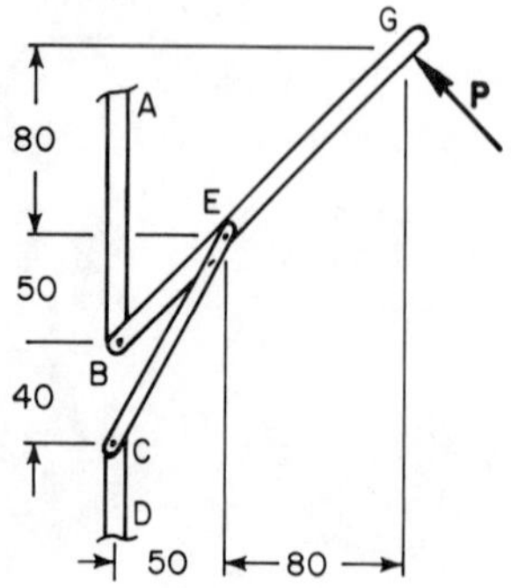

Many clamping devices employ a toggle system, similar to that shown in Fig. 5-14, to tighten strapping, chains or cable. If the force **P** applied perpendicular to BG at G is 100 N, determine

FIGURE 5-14

the tension in part *CE* and the force the pin at *B* applies in the direction of *AB*.

SOLUTION

The mechanism consists of two parts, BG and CE. A free-body diagram could be drawn of the two parts. However, CE is a two-force member, so it would appear practical to draw a free-body diagram of member BG only, since the line of action of the force at E is known. (It must be along the line CE.) The free-body diagram is shown in Fig. 5-15. There are three unknown forces acting on BG. The force in CE may be obtained directly by taking moments about an axis through B.

The angles ϕ and θ should be found, since knowing these angles will simplify writing the necessary moment equation.

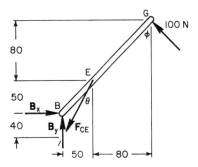

FIGURE 5-15

$$\phi = \tan^{-1}\frac{130}{130}$$

$$= 45.00°$$

$$\theta = \tan^{-1}\frac{50}{90}$$

$$= 29.05°$$

Moments may now be taken about an axis through B to find the force in CE. The perpendicular distance from B to G can be readily found. However, to find the moment of F_{CE} with respect to an axis through B, it is probably easier to use Varignon's theorem, and the components of F_{CE}.

$$\Sigma M_B = 0$$

$$100 \times \frac{130}{\sin 45.00°} - F_{CE} \cos 29.05° \times 50$$

$$+ F_{CE} \sin 29.05° \times 50 = 0$$

$$18\ 385 - 43.710\ F_{CE} + 24.279\ F_{CE} = 0$$

$$F_{CE} = \frac{18\ 385}{43.710 - 24.279}$$

$$= \frac{18\ 385}{19.431}$$

$$= 946.17\ \text{N}$$

The value for B_y, which will be the same as the magnitude of the force exerted by the pin at B along the line of AB, may be obtained by summing forces in the y direction.

$$\Sigma F_y = 0$$

$$B_y - 946.17 \cos 29.05° + 100 \sin 45.00° = 0$$

$$B_y = 827.14 - 70.71$$

$$= 756.43 \text{ N}$$

$$\boxed{\begin{aligned} F_{CE} &= 946 \text{ N} \\ B_y &= 756 \text{ N} \end{aligned}}$$

PROBLEMS

5-1 For the pulley shown in Fig. P5-1, determine the force that will be applied by the pin at *A* to the pulley.

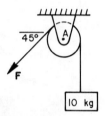

FIGURE P5-1

5-3 Determine the force exerted by the axle at *A* on the pulley shown in Fig. P5-2.

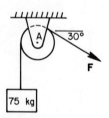

FIGURE P5-2

5-3 If the force **F** applied to the rope shown in Fig. P5-3 is 250 N, determine the force the axle *A* of the pulley must exert on the pulley.

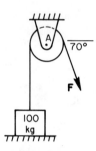

FIGURE P5-3

5-4 Determine the force applied by the axle at *A* on the pulley shown in Fig. P5-4 if the force in the cable is 800 N.

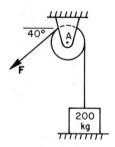

FIGURE P5-4

5-5 Determine the mass *m* that can be supported by the block system shown in Fig. P5-5 if the force applied to the cable is 500 N.

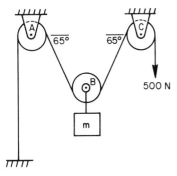

FIGURE P5-5

5-6 If the magnitude of $\mathbf{F}_A$, as shown in Fig. P5-6, is 5000 N, determine the magnitude of **F**.

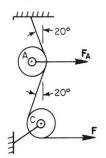

FIGURE P5-6

5-7 Determine the magnitude and direction of the force that cable *AB* exerts on the pin at *A* of the pulley shown in Fig. P5-7. The magnitude of the force **F** is 600 N. The 200 kg block does not slide.

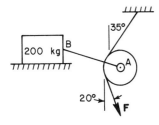

FIGURE P5-7

5-8 If the force **F** shown in Fig. P5-8 is 700 N, determine the magnitude and direction of the force that cable *AB* exerts on the pulley. The 500 kg mass does not slide.

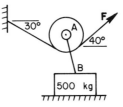

FIGURE P5-8

5-9 What force **F** is required to lift the 80 kg mass shown in Fig. P5-9?

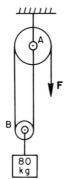

FIGURE P5-9

5-10 If the force **F**, shown in Fig. P5-10, is 1200 N, determine the tension in cable *AB*. The 500 kg block does not slide.

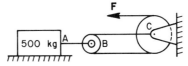

FIGURE P5-10

5-11 For the pulley system shown in Fig. P5-11, determine the tension **P**.

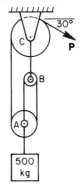

FIGURE P5-11

5-12 For the pulley system shown in Fig. P5-12, determine the force F required to lift the mass of 300 kg.

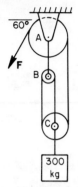

FIGURE P5-12

5-13 A bulldozer blade, as shown in Fig. P5-13, must overcome a resistance of 25 kN/m of blade length at the lower edge of the blade when cutting a certain type of soil. If the blade is 2 m long, determine the force in the tilt control link *AB*.

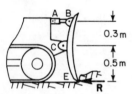

FIGURE P5-13

5-14 If there is an effective downward force of 200 N on the piston *D*, shown in Fig. P5-14, determine the force P required to maintain equilibrium.

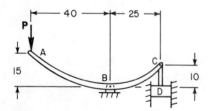

FIGURE P5-14

5-15 The force acting on the bolt at *A*, shown in Fig. P5-15, must be 80 N to keep the bolt from slipping. Determine the magnitude of the force that must be applied to the grips of the pliers at *C* and *D*.

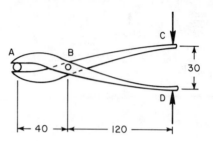

FIGURE P5-15

5-16 The woodworker's clamp shown in Fig. P5-16 exerts a force of 600 N on the piece, *CD*, being held. Determine the forces in screws *AF* and *BE*.

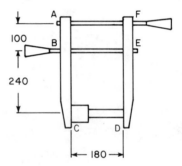

FIGURE P5-16

5-17 The frame and box for a dumptruck are shown in Fig. P5-17. If the combined mass of the box and contents is 15 000 kg, and if its center of gravity is located at *C*, determine the force the hydraulic hoist *AB* must apply at *B* to start to tilt the box.

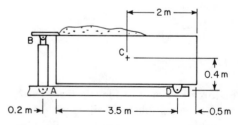

FIGURE P5-17

5-18 The suspension for a filing-cabinet drawer consists of a track and a pair of rollers on each side of the drawer, as shown in Fig. P5-18. If the mass of the drawer and contents is 20 kg and is assumed to be located at C, determine the reactions for each of the two rollers located at A and each of the two rollers located at B.

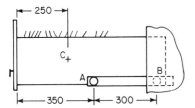

FIGURE P5-18

5-19 The tractive force at D for the drive wheel shown in Fig. P5-19 must be 75 kN. Determine the force F that must be applied by rod AB. B is a pin, and part BC is fixed to the wheel.

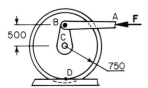

FIGURE P5-19

5-20 An end view of a rotary pump is shown in Fig. P5-20. If the output torque is 1500 N·m, determine the tension in each of the two hold-down clamps at B.

FIGURE P5-20

5-21 The winch drum shown in Fig. P5-21 has a radius of 150 mm. Determine the magnitude of the torque that must be applied by the axle A to hold the 500 kg mass.

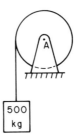

FIGURE P5-21

5-22 The winch shown in Fig. P5-22 is in a crane being used to lift a 500 kg mass. If there is no mechanical advantage in the crane system, and if the radius of the winch drum is 0.65 m, determine the torque that must be applied to the axle A of the winch.

FIGURE P5-22

5-23 The tension in side CD of the belt shown in Fig. P5-23 was found to be 8000 N, and the tension in EF was found to be 17 000 N. Determine the torque developed by the axle at A if the diameter of the pulley at A is 800 mm and the diameter of the pulley at B is 500 mm.

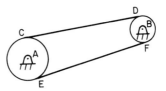

FIGURE P5-23

5-24 If the torque applied to the shaft at *A* for the pulley system shown in Fig. P5-24 is 200 N·m, determine the torque delivered to the shaft at *B* if there is no slipping of the belt, and if pulley *A* has a radius of 60 mm and pulley *B* has a radius of 90 mm. Assume no tension in the slack side of the belt.

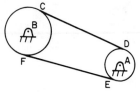

FIGURE P5-24

5-25 The torque applied to the shaft of gear *B* shown in Fig. P5-25 is 750 N·m. If the radius of *B* is 60 mm and the radius of *A* is 150 mm, determine the magnitude of the torque delivered to the shaft of gear *A*.

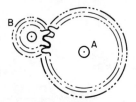

FIGURE P5-25

5-26 For the gears shown in Fig. P5-26, determine the magnitude of the force that a tooth from gear *A* would exert on a tooth of gear *B* if the diameter of *A* is 250 mm and the diameter of *B* is 350 mm. The torque applied to the hub of gear *A* is 2000 N·m.

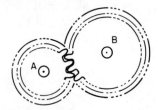

FIGURE P5-26

5-27 If the force **P** applied to the piston *A* as shown in Fig. P5-27 is 2.5 kN, determine the magnitude of the torque, **T**, applied by the

crankshaft. Assume that the cylinder wall is smooth.

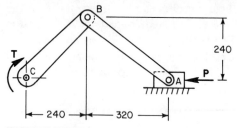

FIGURE P5-27

5-28 Determine the compressive force in connecting rod *BC* for the assembly shown in Fig. P5-28, if the torque acting on the shaft at *A* is 3 kN·m. The cylinder wall is smooth.

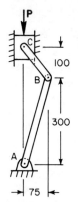

FIGURE P5-28

5-29 Determine the torque supplied by the shaft at *C* for the crank mechanism shown in Fig. P5-29. The force **P** is 1200 N and the slot in which pin *A* moves is smooth.

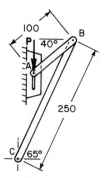

FIGURE P5-29

5-30 For the slider-crank mechanism shown in Fig. P5-30, calculate the force **F** if the magnitude of the torque **T** is 1500 N·m. The length of the crank *BC* is 400 mm. The cylinder wall is frictionless.

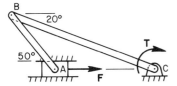

FIGURE P5-30

5-31 Determine the force **P**, parallel to the smooth slot at *C*, applied to the pin at *C* as shown in Fig. P5-31. The torque applied at *A* is 225 N·m.

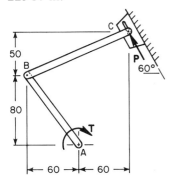

FIGURE P5-31

5-32 Calculate the force **P** that is resisted by the piston at *A*, which slides on the smooth plane as shown in Fig. P5-32.

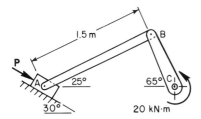

FIGURE P5-32

5-33 The crane shown in Fig. P5-33 has a 30 m boom and is lifting a mass of 10 000 kg. The cable *DAE* passes over a small pulley at *A*, and part *AE* may be assumed to be parallel to the boom *AB*. Cable *AC* is clamped to the end of the boom at *A*. Determine the force in the boom *AB*.

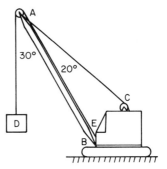

FIGURE P5-33

5-34 On some small sailboats, the mast *AB* is raised by means of a gin pole, *BC*, and a cable attached at *C*, as shown in Fig. P5-34. If the mast has a mass of 4 kg/m, determine the tension, *P*, when the mast is horizontal.

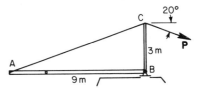

FIGURE P5-34

5-35 The maximum force that can be developed in the hydraulic ram *CD* of the crane shown in Fig. P5-35 is 750 kN. Determine the maximum mass that may be lifted when the boom *AB* is in the position shown. The diameter of the block at *A* may be neglected. The cable from the block to the winch drum is parallel to the boom.

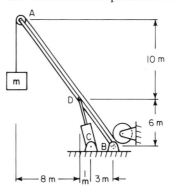

FIGURE P5-35

5-36 Determine the force in the jack *AD* for the shop crane, shown in Fig. P5-36, when it is supporting a mass of 200 kg.

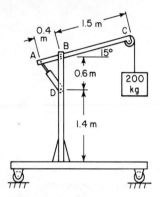

FIGURE P5-36

5-37 The tilt of the bucket of a front-end loader is controlled by two links, such as *AB*, as shown in Fig. P5-37. Determine the tension in each link, when the bucket is in the position shown, if the center of gravity of the combined mass of bucket and contents, which is 1900 kg, is located at *E*.

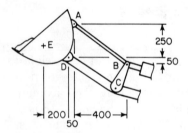

FIGURE P5-37

5-38 Calculate the force pin *A* exerts on part *BD* of the pliers shown in Fig. P5-38.

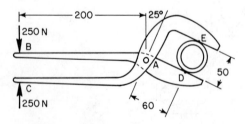

FIGURE P5-38

5-39 Determine the tension in the screw between *D* and *E* if the scissors jack shown in Fig. P5-39 is supporting a mass of 500 kg. The slots at *B* and *K* and all the pin connections are smooth.

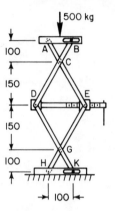

FIGURE P5-39

5-40 Figure P5-40 shows a type of scale in which a 2 kg mass is moved along the beam *AC* to balance the mass *m* in the pan at *G*. Determine the mass *m* if the scale is in balance in the position shown.

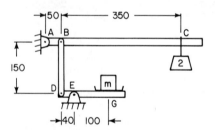

FIGURE P5-40

5-41 A motor drives a belt, with the tensions as shown in Fig. P5-41. If there are two hold-down bolts at *B*, determine the tension in each of the bolts. The holes at *B* are slotted so that the horizontal forces at *B* may be neglected, and positioned so that both bolts have the same tension. The radius of the pulley at *C* is 40 mm.

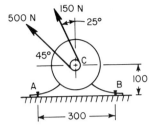

FIGURE P5-42

5-42 A plan view of a winch used on some machinery and on sailboats is shown in Fig. P5-42. If *A* and *B* are the bolts that fasten the winch to the base, determine the force each bolt applies to the winch base if the *x* component of each force is the same. Note that for this type of winch, the line or cable is wrapped around the winch drum and is not fastened to the winch.

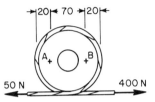

FIGURE P5-41

5-4 FRAMES

A frame has been defined as a structure consisting of two or more members that carry a load. Unlike a machine, parts in a frame do not tend to move relative to one another. In many respects, however, the frame and the machine are very similar, and the analysis of forces on both follows a similar pattern.

The following steps are suggested for the analysis of forces acting on the various parts of a frame.

1. Draw a free-body diagram of the frame, or that portion of the frame that is to be analyzed. The free-body diagram will usually help to provide a clear perspective of what information is available and what information is required. Make certain that only forces acting *on* the free body are shown. This includes forces due to gravity, applied loads and the action of supports.

2. Think. The problem should be solved mentally before the pencil and calculator are used. Always look for the simplest method of solution; the simplest method will save time and will also reduce the risk of error. If it is necessary to write a moment equation, an axis through the point of concurrency of two unknown forces is frequently the best axis of rotation to use. It may be necessary to separate the structure into separate parts and to draw additional free-body diagrams to solve the problem. Note that in drawing supplementary free-body diagrams, assumptions made on the direction of forces must be consistent. In other words, a member that pulls on another member will, in turn, be pulled on by that second member.

3. Write the equilibrium equations required to solve for the unknown forces.

4. Solve the equations.
5. Check the calculations.

These are general guidelines for the solution of frame problems. Since each problem is different, the method of approach may have to be modified for each problem. A few example problems will provide some additional guidance on the solution of frame problems.

EXAMPLE 5-6

Determine the force in member *BD* and the force the pin at *C* applies to member *AC* in the frame shown in Fig. 5-16.

SOLUTION

The free-body diagram, as shown in Fig. 5-17, *should be drawn. The direction of the force due to the pin at C is unknown, so the two components have been shown, and both have been assumed to be positive.*

Member BD is recognized as a two-force member, so the force due to member BD is shown in its known line of action acting at B. It is assumed to be in tension.

The free-body diagram now shows a system of three unknown forces. Of the three equilibrium equations available for solving for the unknown forces, both $\Sigma F_x = 0$ and $\Sigma F_y = 0$ would give equations with two unknown terms in each. Moments could be taken about an axis through either B or C, and either moment equation would provide an equation with only one unknown term.

Since C is a point of concurrency for two unknown forces, it is suggested that it should be used as the axis of rotation.

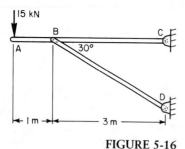

FIGURE 5-16

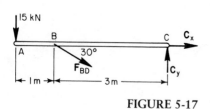

FIGURE 5-17

$$\Sigma\ M_C = 0$$

$$F_{BD} \sin 30° \times 3 + 15 \times 4 = 0$$

$$F_{BD} = \frac{-(15 \times 4)}{\sin 30° \times 3}$$

$$= -40.00 \text{ kN}$$

The negative sign indicates that the force in BD is opposite to that assumed. The force in BD is really 40.0 kN compression.

Now forces may be summed in the x and y directions to determine the values of C_x and C_y. Note that when using the calculated value for F_{BD}, its true direction must be used in all subsequent equations where F_{BD} is treated as a known quantity.

$$\Sigma\, F_x = 0$$

$$-40.00 \cos 30° + C_x = 0$$

$$C_x = 34.641 \text{ kN}$$

$$\Sigma\, F_y = 0$$

$$-15.00 + 40.00 \sin 30° + C_y = 0$$

$$C_y = 15.00 - 20.00$$

$$= -5.00 \text{ kN}$$

The total force applied by the pin at C may now be found. The sketch of the components, as shown in Fig. 5-18, should first be drawn.

$$\theta = \tan^{-1} \frac{C_y}{C_x}$$

$$= \tan^{-1} \frac{5.00}{34.641}$$

$$= 8.21°$$

Direction of $\vec{R}_C = 360.00° - 8.21°$

$$= 351.79°$$

$$R_C = \frac{C_y}{\sin \theta}$$

$$= \frac{5.00}{\sin 8.21°}$$

$$= 35.00 \text{ kN}$$

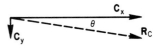

FIGURE 5-18

$$\boxed{\begin{array}{l} F_{BD} = -40.0 \text{ kN} \\ \vec{R}_C = 35.0 \text{ kN at } 351.79° \end{array}}$$

EXAMPLE 5-7

Determine the force in each member of the frame shown in Fig. 5-19.

SOLUTION

A free-body diagram should be drawn as an aid to the solution of the problem. First, it is necessary to recognize that both BC and AB are two-force members, so the line of action of the force

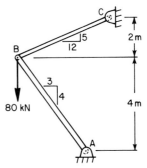

FIGURE 5-19

in each is known. It is correct to draw either a free-body diagram of the entire frame, removing the support of A and C, as shown in Fig. 5-20 or a free-body diagram of the pin at B, as shown in Fig. 5-21. In either case, the unknown forces have been assumed to be in tension. Both free-body diagrams are valid for the following solution. However, the free-body diagram of the pin at B is recommended because it is simpler.

The force system should be recognized as a concurrent force system. As a consequence, there are only two useful equilibrium equations available. It will be noted that there are two unknown terms in both the x and y directions. It will thus be necessary to write and solve a system of two equations with two unknown terms.

If forces are first summed in the x direction, it is possible to obtain a fairly simple expression for F_{AB} in terms of F_{BC}.

$$\Sigma \, F_x = 0$$

$$\frac{3}{5} \, F_{AB} + \frac{12}{13} \, F_{BC} = 0$$

$$F_{AB} = -\left(\frac{5}{3}\right) \frac{12}{13} \, F_{BC}$$

$$F_{AB} = -1.5385 \, F_{BC} \qquad \text{Eq. (a)}$$

Forces may now be summed in the y direction to obtain a second equation.

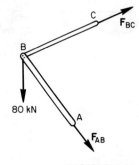

FIGURE 5-20

$$\Sigma \, F_y = 0$$

$$-80.0 - \frac{4}{5} \, F_{AB} + \frac{5}{13} \, F_{BC} = 0 \qquad \text{Eq. (b)}$$

FIGURE 5-21

Substituting Eq. (a) in Eq. (b):

$$-80.0 - \frac{4}{5}\left(-1.5385 \, F_{BC}\right) + \frac{5}{13} \, F_{BC} = 0$$

$$-80.0 + 1.2307 \, F_{BC} + 0.3846 \, F_{BC} = 0$$

$$1.6153 \, F_{BC} = 80.0$$

$$F_{BC} = \frac{80.0}{1.6153}$$

$$= 49.526 \text{ kN}$$

Substituting for F_{BC} in Eq. (a):

$$F_{AB} = -1.5385 \times 49.526$$

$$= -76.196 \text{ kN}$$

i.e. F_{AB} is in compression

$$\boxed{\begin{aligned} F_{AB} &= -76.2 \text{ kN} \\ F_{BC} &= +49.5 \text{ kN} \end{aligned}}$$

EXAMPLE 5-8

Determine the reactions from the supports at A and G for the frame shown in Fig. 5-22 if the surface at G is smooth. Also find the force the pin at B applies to member AC.

SOLUTION

Drawing a free-body diagram of the entire frame, as shown in Fig. 5-23, is a first step to the solution of the problem. Since the surface at G is smooth, the force acting at G must be perpendicular to the tangent at the point of contact. At A there is a pin, so both the x and y components of the force at A have been shown. No force is shown at B, because any force at B is internal to the free body. In other words, no external force is applied to the body at B.

From Fig. 5-23, it can be seen that there are three unknown forces. It is possible to proceed with the calculation of R_A and R_G and to save the calculation of the force due to the pin at B for later.

Since it is expected that there will be additional free-body diagrams, each diagram should be numbered.

If moments are taken about an axis through A, the reaction at G may be found directly. Before writing the moment equation, it might be a good idea to calculate the distance AG.

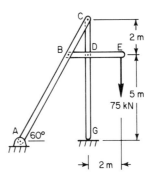

FIGURE 5-22

$$AG = \frac{7}{\tan 60°}$$

$$= 4.0414 \text{ m}$$

$$\Sigma M_A = 0$$

$$G_y \times 4.0414 - 75 \times 6.0414 = 0$$

$$G_y = \frac{75 \times 6.0414}{4.0414}$$

$$= 112.115 \text{ kN}$$

Now the equilibrium equations for the x and y directions may be used to determine A_x and A_y.

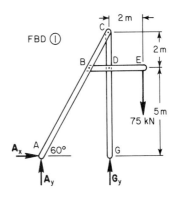

FIGURE 5-23

$$\Sigma \, F_x = 0$$

$$A_x = 0$$

$$\Sigma \, F_y = 0$$

$$A_y + 112.115 - 75.00 = 0$$

$$A_y = -37.115 \text{ kN}$$

i.e. A_y is 37.115 kN downwards

To determine the force the pin at B applies to member AC, a free-body diagram of AC showing the required force is necessary. Figure 5-24 shows the required free-body diagram. Note that there are four unknown forces on this free-body diagram, and thus the member appears to be statically indeterminate. In addition, a free-body diagram of member BE can be drawn, as shown in Fig. 5-25. Note that the forces at B in Fig. 5-25 (FBD 3) must be consistent with the assumptions made in Fig. 5-24 (FBD 2). Thus, if the pin at B pulls to the right on member AC, it must pull to the left on member BE.

If moments are taken about an axis through D using Fig. 5-25 (FBD 3), then the value for B_y can be obtained directly.

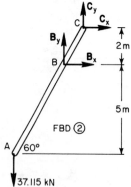

FIGURE 5-24

FBD ③

FIGURE 5-25

$$BD = \frac{2}{\tan 60°}$$

$$= 1.1547 \text{ m}$$

From FBD 3

$$\Sigma \, M_D = 0$$

$$B_y \times 1.1547 - 75 \times 2 = 0$$

$$B_y = \frac{75 \times 2}{1.1547}$$

$$= 129.90 \text{ kN}$$

The positive sign obtained for the value of B_y indicates that the assumed direction of B_y is correct, that is, down in FBD 3 and up in FBD 2.

Since B_y is now known, Fig. 5-24 (FBD 2) can now be used to determine B_x by taking moments about an axis through C.

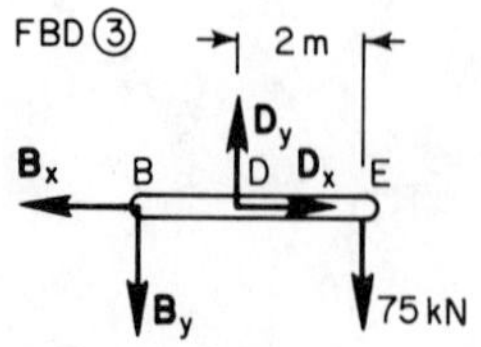

From FBD 2

$$\Sigma \, M_C = 0$$

$$-(129.90 \times 1.1547) + B_x \times 2 + 37.115 \times 4.0414 = 0$$

$$-149.996 + 2 \, B_x + 149.996 = 0$$

$B_x = 0$

$$\vec{R}_A = 37.1 \text{ kN at } 270.00°$$
$$\vec{R}_G = 112 \text{ kN at } 90.00°$$
$$\vec{R}_B = 130 \text{ kN at } 90.00°$$

EXAMPLE 5-9

For the three-hinged arch shown in Fig. 5-26, determine the re-actions at A and E. The forces at B and D are applied at midspan of the members.

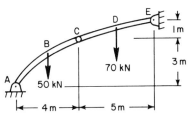

FIGURE 5-26

SOLUTION

Since the structure is supported by two pin connections, it is anticipated that it will be statically indeterminate, because the free-body diagram, as shown in Fig. 5-27, *shows four unknown forces. However, with a bit of ingenuity, it is possible to set up a second free-body diagram that will aid in the solution. If a free-body diagram of member CE is drawn, as shown in* Fig. 5-28, *the system set up will provide a mechanism for solving the prob-lem. Using* Fig. 5-27 (FBD 1), *moments can be taken about an axis through A, which will give an equation with E_x and E_y as unknown terms. Similarly, using* Fig. 5-28 (FBD 2), *moments can be taken about an axis through C, which will give an equa-tion with the same two unknown terms, E_x and E_y. Since E_x and E_y are the same in both equations, the two equations may be solved simultaneously to obtain values for E_x and E_y.*

From FBD 1:

$\Sigma M_A = 0$

$-(50 \times 2) - 70 \times 6.5 - E_x \times 4 + E_y \times 9 = 0$

$-4 E_x + 9 E_y - 100 - 455 = 0$

$-4 E_x + 9 E_y - 555 = 0$ Eq. (a)

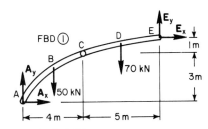

FIGURE 5-27

From FBD 2:

$\Sigma M_C = 0$

$-(70 \times 2.5) - E_x \times 1 + E_y \times 5 = 0$

$E_x = 5 E_y - 175$ Eq. (b)

Substituting Eq. (b) in Eq. (a):

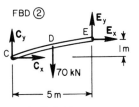

FIGURE 5-28

$$-4(5\,E_y - 175) + 9\,E_y - 555 = 0$$

$$-20\,E_y + 700 + 9\,E_y - 555 = 0$$

$$-11\,E_y + 145 = 0$$

$$E_y = \frac{145}{11}$$

$$= 13.182 \text{ kN}$$

Substituting for E_y in Eq. (b):

$$E_x = 5 \times 13.182 - 175$$

$$= 65.909 - 175$$

$$= -109.09 \text{ kN}$$

To obtain the magnitude and direction of $\boldsymbol{R}_E$, draw the sketch of the components as shown in Fig. 5-29.

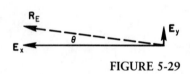

FIGURE 5-29

$$\theta = \tan^{-1} \frac{E_y}{E_x}$$

$$= \tan^{-1} \frac{13.182}{109.09}$$

$$= 6.89°$$

Direction of $\vec{R}_E = 180.00° - 6.89°$

$$= 173.11°$$

$$R_E = \frac{E_y}{\sin \theta}$$

$$= \frac{13.182}{\sin 6.89°}$$

$$= 109.88 \text{ kN}$$

Now the components of the reaction at A can be determined using Fig. 5-27 (FBD 1). Note that the actual calculated directions of E_x and E_y must be used in the following calculations.

$$\Sigma\,F_x = 0$$

$$A_x - 109.09 = 0$$

$$A_x = 109.09 \text{ kN}$$

$$\Sigma\,F_y = 0$$

$$A_y - 50 - 70 + 13.182 = 0$$

$$A_y = 120.00 - 13.182$$

$$= 106.818 \text{ kN}$$

A drawing of the components for the force at A, as shown in Fig. 5-30, *will assist in determining the magnitude and direction of* R_A.

$$\theta = \tan^{-1} \frac{A_y}{A_x}.$$

$$= \tan^{-1} \frac{106.818}{109.09}$$

$$= 44.40°$$

Direction of $\vec{R}_A = 44.40°$

$$R_A = \frac{A_y}{\sin \theta}$$

$$= \frac{106.818}{\sin 44.40°}$$

$$= 152.67 \text{ kN}$$

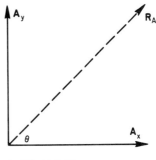

FIGURE 5-30

$$\boxed{\begin{array}{l} \vec{R}_A = 153 \text{ kN at } 44.40° \\ \vec{R}_E = 110 \text{ kN at } 173.11° \end{array}}$$

PROBLEMS

5-43 For the frame shown in Fig. P5-43, find the reactions at *A* and *D*.

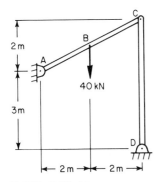

FIGURE P5-43

5-44 Find the reactions at *A* and *D* for the frame shown in Fig. P5-44.

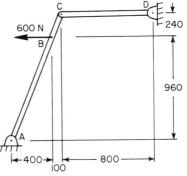

FIGURE P5-44

5-45 Find the reactions at *A* and *D* for the frame shown in Fig. P5-45.

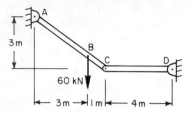

FIGURE P5-45

5-46 For the frame shown in Fig. P5-46, calculate the reactions at *A* and *D*.

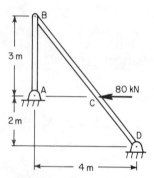

FIGURE P5-46

5-47 Determine the force in member *BC* and the reaction at *A* for the frame shown in Fig. P5-47.

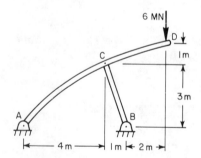

FIGURE P5-47

5-48 Determine the reaction at *D* for the frame shown in Fig. P5-48.

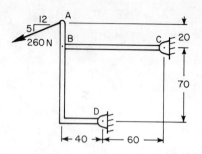

FIGURE P5-48

5-49 Determine the forces the pins at *A* and *G* apply to the frame shown in Fig. P5-49.

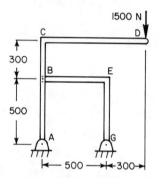

FIGURE P5-49

5-50 Determine the reactions acting on the frame shown in Fig. P5-50 at *A* and *D*.

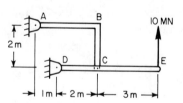

FIGURE P5-50

5-51 Find the force the pin at *A* exerts on the beam shown in Fig. P5-51, and find the force in member *BD*.

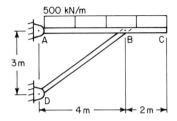

FIGURE P5-51

5-52 Find the tension in cable *AB* and the reaction at *C* for the member shown in Fig. P5-52.

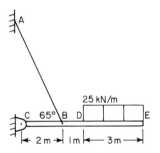

FIGURE P5-52

5-53 Each member in the frame shown in Fig. P5-53 has a mass of 50 kg/m. Determine the reactions at *A* and *B*.

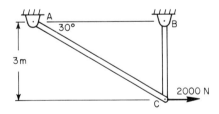

FIGURE P5-53

5-54 If each member of the frame shown in Fig. P5-54 has a mass of 150 kg/m, determine the reactions at *A* and *C*.

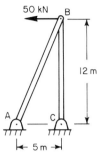

FIGURE P5-54

5-55 The cable *CD*, for the loading boom shown in Fig. P5-55, will fail if the tension exceeds 110 kN. Determine the minimum value for *x* at which failure will occur if the mass *m* is 5000 kg.

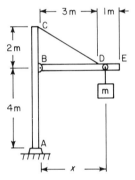

FIGURE P5-55

5-56 The pin at *C* in the boom shown in Fig. P5-56 will fail if the *y* component of the force on it exceeds 30 kN. If the mass suspended at *E* is 4000 kg, determine the minimum distance that *E* may be from *C* without causing failure.

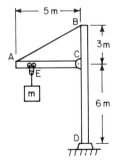

FIGURE P5-56

5-57 For the frame shown in Fig. P5-57, find the forces in members *AB* and *BC*.

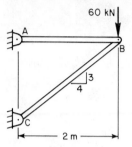

FIGURE P5-57

5-58 Determine the forces in members *AB* and *BC* of the frame shown in Fig. P5-58.

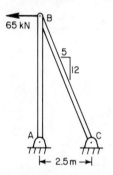

FIGURE P5-58

5-59 Calculate the force in each of the three members of the frame shown in Fig. P5-59.

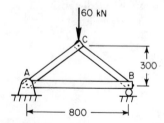

FIGURE P5-59

5-60 Boats and other irregularly shaped objects are lifted using a spreader, such as *BC*, as shown in Fig. P5-60, so that the load in the slings will be vertical. Determine the force in spreader *BC* if

the boat being lifted has a mass of 5000 kg. There are two slings, and each may be assumed to carry half the load.

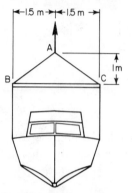

FIGURE P5-60

5-61 Determine the forces in members *AC* and *BC* for the frame shown in Fig. P5-61. The mass *m* is 1000 kg.

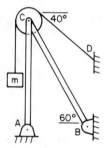

FIGURE P5-61

5-62 For the frame shown in Fig. P5-62, calculate the reactions at *C* and *D* if the mass *m* is 3000 kg.

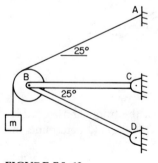

FIGURE P5-62

5-63 If cylinder *A* has a mass of 200 kg and cylinder *B* has a mass of 100 kg, determine the magnitude of the force at each of the points of contact where the cylinders are supported by the bracket shown in Fig. P5-63.

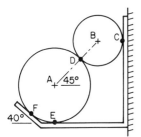

FIGURE P5-63

5-64 In Fig. P5-64, cylinder *A* has a mass of 75 kg and cylinder *B* has a mass of 150 kg. Determine the magnitude of the force at contact point *E*.

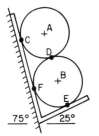

FIGURE P5-64

5-65 For the frame shown in Fig. P5-65, calculate the force pin *A* exerts on member *AC* and the force pin *C* exerts on member *CE*.

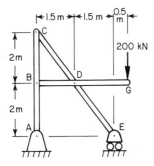

FIGURE P5-65

5-66 Find the reaction at *G* and the force the pin at *C* applies to member *CG* for the frame shown in Fig. P5-66. The surface at *A* is smooth.

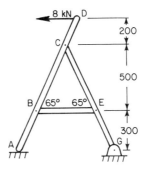

FIGURE P5-66

5-67 Find the total force pin *A* exerts on member *AC* in the frame shown in Fig. P5-67. *BGD* is a cable.

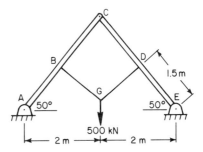

FIGURE P5-67

5-68 For the frame shown in Fig. P5-68, determine the reaction at support *E* if the magnitude of **F** acting on cable *BGD* is 4 MN.

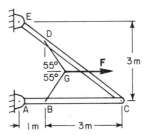

FIGURE P5-68

5-69 For the beam shown in Fig. P5-69, determine the tension in cable *BC* if the block resting on the beam at *B* has a mass of 800 kg and the beam has a mass of 40 kg/m.

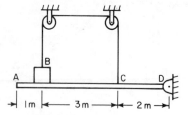

FIGURE P5-69

5-70 A rigid uniform beam with a mass of 200 kg, as shown in Fig. P5-70, is supported by a hinge at *A* and a cable at *C*. The cable runs over a pulley at *D* and is attached to a 500 kg mass, *B*, which rests on top of the beam when it is horizontal. Determine the tension in the cable.

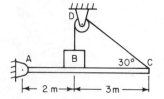

FIGURE P5-70

5-71 For the three-hinged arch shown in Fig. P5-71, find the reaction at *A* and the force that member *CE* exerts on the pin at *C*.

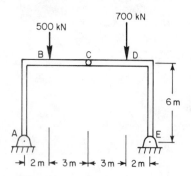

FIGURE P5-71

5-72 Calculate the reactions at *A* and *E* for the three-hinged arch shown in Fig. P5-72.

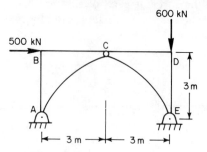

FIGURE P5-72

5-73 Find the reaction at pin *E* and the force pin *C* exerts on member *CE* of the arch shown in Fig. P5-73.

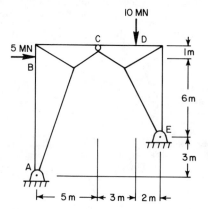

FIGURE P5-73

5-74 For the arch shown in Fig. P5-74, determine the reactions at pins *A* and *F*.

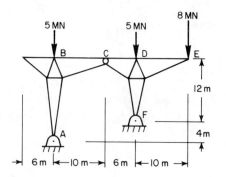

FIGURE P5-74

5-75 A man with a mass of 70 kg stands on an extension ladder at *B*, as shown in Fig. P5-75. If the two supports for the upper section at *D* act as pins and the two guides at *C* apply forces perpendicular to the longitudinal axis of the ladder, determine the magnitude of the force in each of the two supports at *D* and the two guides at *C*. The wall at *A* is smooth and the surface at *E* is rough enough to prevent sliding. The mass of the ladder may be neglected.

5-76 The cylinder shown in Fig. P5-76 has a mass of 500 kg. If it is supported by two frames, such as *BC*, determine the tension in each of the cables *AB*.

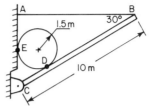

FIGURE P5-76

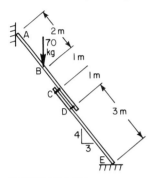

FIGURE P5-75

5-5 TRUSSES

A truss is a structure made up entirely of two-force members. Trusses were developed to carry loads over long spans, as is required in many bridges and roofs. In many long-span structures, the mass of the structure became the most significant load carried, and the truss was developed to provide a relatively lightweight structure to carry the loads. Trusses are also used in mechanical and other applications because of their weight-saving characteristics. Some typical trusses are shown in Fig. 5-31. Many special types of trusses have been developed over the years, and they often carry the name of the original designer. However, truss classifications can be left for studies in structural analysis.

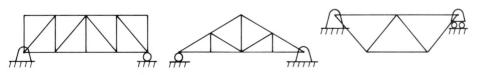

FIGURE 5-31

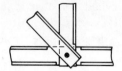

FIGURE 5-32

The ideal truss is made up entirely of two-force members and is assumed to have frictionless pin connections at the joints where members are connected. Figure 5-32 shows a joint where several members meet. Many early trusses actually were pin-connected, but modern trusses are usually bolted or welded. Some old trusses have riveted connections. Regardless of the actual method of connection, the joint is assumed to be pin-connected for purposes of the analysis of the forces in the structure. One consequence of the pin connections is that, for the structure to be stable, the members must usually form triangle-shaped sections. Otherwise, the structure is likely to be unstable, as illustrated in Fig. 5-33. An unstable structure does not maintain its shape when a load is applied.

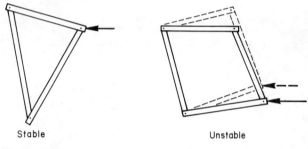

Stable   Unstable

FIGURE 5-33

Since all the members of a truss are two-force members, the line of action of the force in each member must be along a line joining the pins at each end of the member. From this fact a method of analyzing forces in members is developed, for each pin is the point of concurrency for a system of concurrent forces. This method of analysis is called the *method of joints*. A second method is also based on the fact that all members are two-force members, but in the second method, called *method of sections*, whole sections of the truss are analyzed.

If all members of a truss are two-force members, then each member of the truss is either in tension (a pull) or in compression (a push). It has become common practice, when giving the forces in members of a truss, to indicate the member in tension with a plus (+) sign and the member in compression with a minus (−) sign. Thus, if the force in a member is + 75.6 kN, it should be understood that the member is in tension; if the force in a member is −16.3 kN, it should be understood that the member is in compression.

It tends to simplify free-body diagrams and calculations if all unknown forces are shown as being in tension. If this practice is followed, the correct sign to represent tension or compression will automatically be obtained when solving for the force in each member.

It may be helpful to know the names for the various parts of the truss. The lower outside members, such as *AJ* and *GH* in Fig. 5-34, form the *lower chord*, while the upper outside members, such as *BC* and *CD*, form the *upper chord*. The interior members are called *web members*. The web members are called *verticals* or *diagonals*, depending on their orientation. A *panel* is one section of the truss, such as *BCHJ*.

Note that the loads must be applied at the joints of the truss. If they are not, the members will not be two-force members, and the structure will be a frame and not a truss.

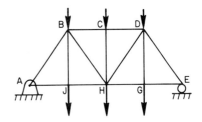

FIGURE 5-34

5-6   METHOD OF JOINTS

Trusses are structures made up entirely of two-force members, so if a free-body diagram is drawn of the pin at any joint, the forces acting on that pin must form a concurrent force system. This fact is the basis of the method of joints for the analysis of the forces in members of a truss.

Before analyzing the forces in the individual members of a truss, it is usually necessary to determine the reactions at the supports of the truss, utilizing a free-body diagram and the equilibrium equations.

A truss with its applied loads is shown in Fig. 5-35(a) and its corresponding free-body diagram is shown in Fig. 5-35(b). The analysis of the reactions on a truss follows the same general procedure that is followed for determining the reactions on a beam, with one significant difference. For most beams, the depth of the beam may be neglected because it is small relative to the length of the beam. However, for trusses, the height of the truss must be taken into account when writing moment equations as part of the determination of the reactions.

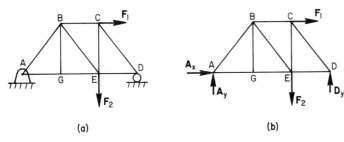

(a)   (b)

FIGURE 5-35

Once the reactions on the truss have been determined, the forces in members of the truss may be analyzed by proceeding

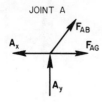

JOINT A

FIGURE 5-36

JOINT G

FIGURE 5-37

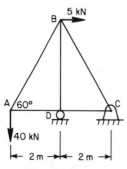

5 kN

40 kN

FIGURE 5-38

joint by joint through the truss. The usual starting point is the joint at one of the supports, since once the reactions are known, then at least there is one known force at that joint. Providing there are no more than two unknown forces at the joint, the unknown forces may be calculated using the equilibrium equations. Figure 5-36 shows joint A from the truss of Fig. 5-35. Note that once the reactions have been determined, their actual values and directions are shown on the free-body diagram of the joint. By assuming each unknown force to be in tension, the correct sign of the force in the member will automatically be obtained.

When analyzing the forces shown in Fig. 5-36, if forces are summed in the y direction, there will be only one unknown term (assuming that A_x and A_y have previously been obtained), so F_{AB} can then be obtained. After calculating F_{AB}, it would then be possible to sum forces in the x direction to obtain F_{AG}. Note that the actual direction of F_{AB} must be used in the calculation for F_{AG}.

After completing the analysis of joint A, the next step is to proceed to another joint. The next joint chosen is usually adjacent to the first one, but it must also be one at which there are no more than two unknown forces. This means that the next joint to be analyzed should be joint G, as shown in Fig. 5-37. Joint B would not be a satisfactory second joint because the forces in BG, BE and BC are unknown. However, after joint G is analyzed, the force in BG would be known, and the forces at joint B could be analyzed as the following step. The analysis then proceeds, joint by joint, until the force in each member of the truss has been determined.

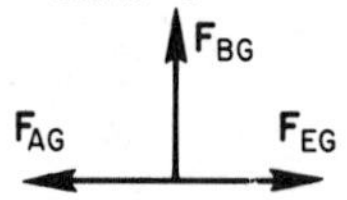

It will be noticed from the free-body diagram of the pin at G, shown in Fig. 5-37, that when forces are summed in the y direction the force in member BG will be found to be zero. Members such as BG, which have no force in them, are called *redundant members*.

Two final steps are recommended. There is usually one joint that need not be analyzed. Analyze this joint to see if it is in equilibrium. If it is, then the previous calculations are probably correct. If not, there is an error to be corrected. Finally, results should be tabulated in a neat form, both as a means of summarizing results and as a means of checking to make certain that no member has been omitted from the calculations.

EXAMPLE 5-10

For the truss shown in Fig. 5-38, find the force in each member.

SOLUTION

Although it is possible to start an analysis of the forces in the truss by analyzing the forces at joint A, it is recommended that the reactions be obtained first. A free-body diagram of the truss, as shown in Fig. 5-39, is drawn as an aid in finding the reactions.

The reaction at D may be obtained by taking the moments of all forces about an axis through C. C_x and C_y may then be obtained by summing forces in the x and y directions.

$$\Sigma\, M_C = 0$$

$$40 \times 4 - 5 \times 2 \tan 60° - D_y \times 2 = 0$$

$$D_y = \frac{40 \times 4 - 5 \times 2 \tan 60°}{2}$$

$$= \frac{160.00 - 17.32}{2}$$

$$= \frac{142.68}{2}$$

$$= 71.34 \text{ kN}$$

$$\Sigma\, F_y = 0$$

$$-40.00 + 71.34 + C_y = 0$$

$$C_y = 40.00 - 71.34$$

$$= -31.34 \text{ kN}$$

$$C_y = 31.34 \text{ kN down}$$

$$\Sigma\, F_x = 0$$

$$C_x + 5.00 = 0$$

$$C_x = -5.00 \text{ kN}$$

$$C_x = 5.00 \text{ kN left}$$

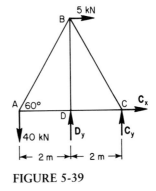

FIGURE 5-39

It is now possible to proceed with the analysis of the forces in the members by analyzing the forces acting on each joint of the truss. The analysis could start with either joint A or joint C, where there are two unknown forces acting on the joint, along with the known forces. Since joint A involves the use of fewer forces in the analysis, it will be used as a starting point.

The free-body diagram of joint A, as shown in Fig. 5-40, is drawn, showing the unknown forces in tension. Since there is only one unknown term in the y direction, forces will be summed in the y direction first to obtain the force in member

AB. Following this, forces are summed in the x direction to find the force in member AD.

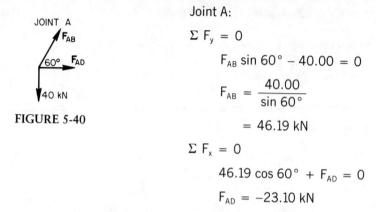

JOINT A

FIGURE 5-40

Joint A:

$$\Sigma F_y = 0$$

$$F_{AB} \sin 60° - 40.00 = 0$$

$$F_{AB} = \frac{40.00}{\sin 60°}$$

$$= 46.19 \text{ kN}$$

$$\Sigma F_x = 0$$

$$46.19 \cos 60° + F_{AD} = 0$$

$$F_{AD} = -23.10 \text{ kN}$$

The negative sign for F_{AD} indicates that the member is really in compression. Values for the forces in both of these members should be entered in the table at the end of the problem solution.

At joints B and D there are now only two unknown forces. However, since all the forces at D are parallel to the x or y axes, the analysis of the forces at D is more simple. A free-body diagram of the pin at D is drawn, as shown in Fig. 5-41. *The force in member AD was found to be in compression, so it must be shown as a compressive force, or push, on joint D. Forces may be summed in the x and y directions to find the forces in members CD and BD.*

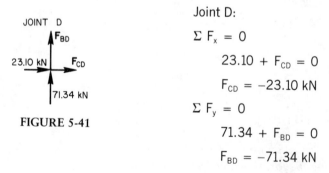

JOINT D

FIGURE 5-41

Joint D:

$$\Sigma F_x = 0$$

$$23.10 + F_{CD} = 0$$

$$F_{CD} = -23.10 \text{ kN}$$

$$\Sigma F_y = 0$$

$$71.34 + F_{BD} = 0$$

$$F_{BD} = -71.34 \text{ kN}$$

The negative sign for both forces indicates that both members are in compression. The values of the forces should be entered in the table at the end of the problem solution.

The force in member BC has not yet been found. It could be found by analyzing the forces on pin B or pin C. Pin C has been chosen, and the free-body diagram of the pin is shown in Fig. 5-42. *The forces that have already been determined must be shown in their true direction. Thus, the 23.10 kN force in CD is* a compression force, the 31.34 kN vertical component of the reaction at C is pulling down, and the horizontal reaction is pushing to the left, as previously determined. If forces are summed in the y direction to find the force in member BC, there will be only two terms in the equation, rather than the three terms that would occur in the equation for summing forces in the x direction.

Joint C:

$$\Sigma F_y = 0$$

$$F_{BC} \sin 60° - 31.34 = 0$$

$$F_{BC} = \frac{31.34}{\sin 60°}$$

$$= 36.19 \text{ kN}$$

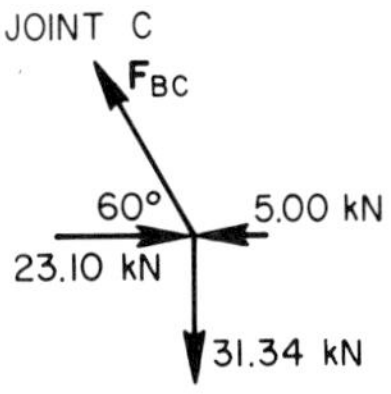

JOINT C

FIGURE 5-42

This value should be entered in the table at the end of the solution, which will complete the table.

Joint B has not been analyzed in the solution of the problem. It may now be used as a check. If it is in equilibrium, as it should be, then the previous calculations may be correct. A free-body diagram of joint B, as shown in Fig. 5-43, is drawn, and all the forces, with their known values and directions, are shown.

Joint B:

$$\Sigma F_x = -46.19 \cos 60° + 36.19 \cos 60° + 5.00$$

$$= -23.09 + 18.09 + 5.00$$

$$= 0.00 \qquad \text{Check}$$

$$\Sigma F_y = -46.19 \sin 60° + 71.34 - 36.19 \sin 60°$$

$$= -40.00 + 71.34 - 31.34$$

$$= 0.00 \qquad \text{Check}$$

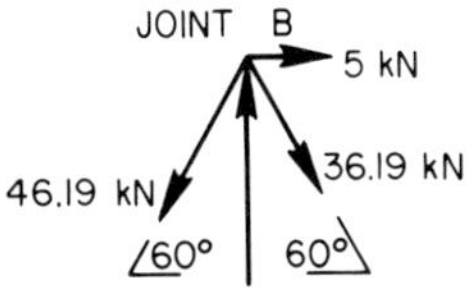

JOINT B

FIGURE 5-43

Unless there are some compensating errors in the calculation, the check indicates that the calculations are correct.

The table summarizing results is shown at the end of the problem solution.

Member	Force (kN)
AB	+46.2
BC	+36.2
CD	-23.1
AD	-23.1
BD	-71.3

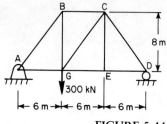

FIGURE 5-44

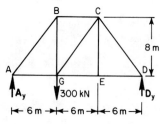

FIGURE 5-45

EXAMPLE 5-11

Determine the force in each member of the truss shown in Fig. 5-44.

SOLUTION

The free-body diagram for the structure, as shown in Fig. 5-45, should be drawn, and the reactions at the supports should be calculated. Since there is no external load applied with a component in the x direction, there will be no x component of the reaction at the pin at A. The reaction at D may be obtained by taking moments about an axis through A, and then the reaction at A may be found by summing forces in the y direction.

$$\Sigma\ M_A = 0$$

$$-(300 \times 6) + D_y \times 18 = 0$$

$$D_y = \frac{300 \times 6}{18}$$

$$= 100.00\ kN$$

$$\Sigma\ F_y = 0$$

$$A_y - 300.00 + 100.00 = 0$$

$$A_y = 200.00\ kN$$

Now it is possible to examine one joint and analyze the forces acting on it. Either joint A or joint D could be used first, since there is now a known force at each joint, and there would be only two unknown forces acting at each joint. For the purposes of illustration, joint A will be chosen to start the analysis.

A free-body diagram, as shown in Fig. 5-46, is drawn showing the forces acting on the pin at joint A. The two unknown forces F_{AB} and F_{AG} are both assumed to be in tension. In the concurrent force system shown, there is only one unknown term in the y direction, so forces may be summed in the y direction to obtain F_{AB}.

Joint A:

$$\Sigma\ F_y = 0$$

$$\frac{4}{5}\ F_{AB} + 200.00 = 0$$

$$F_{AB} = -\frac{5}{4} \times 200.00$$

$$= -250.00\ kN$$

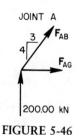

JOINT A

FIGURE 5-46

The negative sign in the answer indicates that the force in AB is opposite to that assumed, and is really compression. It is recommended that a table summarizing results be set up, as shown at the end of the problem solution, and that values for the forces be written in as obtained.

The force in member AG may now be obtained by summing forces in the x direction. The fact that the force in AB is compression must be taken into account when doing the calculations. The x component of F_{AB} really points to the left, and is thus a negative term in the equation.

$$\Sigma\ F_x = 0$$

$$F_{AG} - \frac{3}{5} \times 250.00 = 0$$

$$F_{AG} = 150.00\ kN$$

The positive sign for F_{AG} indicates that the force is actually tension, as assumed. The value should be added to the table at the end of the solution.

The next joint to be analyzed is usually one of those at the end of one of the members analyzed. Either joint B or joint G might be possible. However, there are three members at G in which the forces are unknown. At joint B there are only two members with unknown forces in them, so this joint can be analyzed.

The free-body diagram for joint B as shown in **Fig. 5-47** *is drawn. The unknown forces acting on the pin are assumed to be in tension. The 250.00 kN force from member AB must be shown in its true direction of compression, as was determined in the previous calculations. If its true direction is not used, subsequent calculations will be incorrect. The unknown forces in this concurrent system may be obtained by summing forces in the x and y directions.*

Joint B:

$$\Sigma\ F_x = 0$$

$$\frac{3}{5} \times 250.00 + F_{BC} = 0$$

$$F_{BC} = -150.00\ kN$$

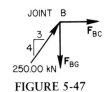

JOINT B

FIGURE 5-47

The negative sign for the answer indicates that member BC is actually in compression. Enter this value, along with its sign, in the table of results at the end of the problem solution.

$$\Sigma \ F_y = 0$$

$$\frac{4}{5} \times 250.00 - F_{BG} = 0$$

$$F_{BG} = 200.00 \text{ kN}$$

The force in BG is tensile, as indicated by the positive sign in the answer. Enter the value in the table of results.

Since the force in BG has been determined, there will now be only two unknown forces acting on the pin at G, so a free-body diagram of the joint at G can be drawn, as shown in Fig. 5-48, *and the forces acting on the joint can be analyzed. It is important to show the forces in AG and BG in their correct directions, as determined in previous calculations.*

The unknown forces may be obtained by summing forces in the x and y directions. Forces in the y direction should be summed first, since there is only one unknown term in the y direction.

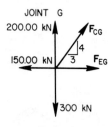

JOINT G

FIGURE 5-48

Joint G:

$$\Sigma \ F_y = 0$$

$$200.00 + \frac{4}{5} \times F_{CG} - 300.00 = 0$$

$$F_{CG} = \frac{5}{4}(300.00 - 200.00)$$

$$= \frac{5}{4} \times 100.00$$

$$= 125.00 \text{ kN}$$

$$\Sigma \ F_x = 0$$

$$-150.00 + \frac{3}{5} \times 125.00 + F_{EG} = 0$$

$$F_{EG} = 150.00 - 75.00$$

$$= 75.00 \text{ kN}$$

These values should be added to the table of results at the end of the problem solution.

There are two unknown forces acting at joint C and joint E. The easier joint to analyze is joint E, since all the members are mutually perpendicular. It will also be observed that the actual solution is quite simple for joint E. The analysis starts with the free-body diagram, as shown in Fig. 5-49. *By summing forces in the x direction,* F_{DE} *may be obtained.*

Joint E:

$$\Sigma F_x = 0$$

$$-75.00 + F_{DE} = 0$$

$$F_{DE} = 75.00 \text{ kN}$$

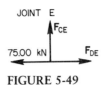

JOINT E

FIGURE 5-49

If forces are summed in the y direction, the force in CE may also be obtained.

$$\Sigma F_y = 0$$

$$F_{CE} = 0$$

The equilibrium equation solution gives the value for F_{CE} directly. Logic should also make it clear that if there is no external force in the y direction at E, then there is no force for the member CE to resist, and the force in CE must be zero.

Add the results to the table of results.

It makes no real difference whether joint D or joint C is the next one analyzed. Joint D has been chosen, and a free-body diagram of joint D is drawn, as shown in Fig. 5-50. *The single unknown force may be obtained by summing forces in the y direction.*

Joint D:

$$\Sigma F_y = 0$$

$$\frac{4}{5} F_{CD} + 100.00 = 0$$

$$F_{CD} = -\frac{5}{4} \times 100.00$$

$$= -125.00 \text{ kN}$$

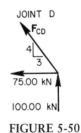

JOINT D

FIGURE 5-50

The force in CD is actually opposite to that assumed, and is a compressive force. When the value for F_{CD} is added to the table at the end of the solution, the table will be complete, for the force in each member has now been found.

A check of the solution may be made by determining if joint C is in equilibrium. A free-body diagram of joint C, as shown in Fig. 5-51, *is drawn. Each force must be shown in its actual direction. If forces are summed in the x and y directions, and it is found that the joint is in equilibrium, then the previous calculations are probably correct.*

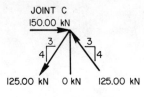

JOINT C
150.00 kN

125.00 kN   0 kN   125.00 kN

FIGURE 5-51

Joint C:

$$\Sigma F_x = 150.00 - \frac{3}{5} \times 125.00 - \frac{3}{5} \times 125.00$$

$$= 150.00 - 75.00 - 75.00$$

$$= 0.00 \qquad\qquad \text{Check}$$

$$\Sigma F_y = -\frac{4}{5} \times 125.00 + \frac{4}{5} \times 125.00$$

$$= 0.00 \qquad\qquad \text{Check}$$

The summary of results is an important part of the problem solution.

Member	Force (kN)
AB	−250
BC	−150
CD	−125
DE	+75.0
EG	+75.0
AG	+150
BG	+200
CG	+125
CE	0

EXAMPLE 5-12

Find the force in each member of the truss shown in Fig. 5-52.

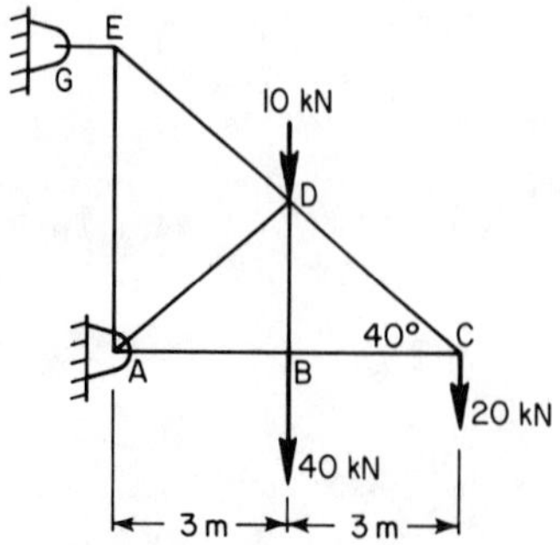

SOLUTION

It is possible to start the analysis of the forces in the members of the truss at joint C. In fact, joint C is probably the preferred starting point. However, before analyzing the joints, the reactions at the supports will be obtained, since they will be needed in the analysis. The required free-body diagram for finding the reactions is shown in Fig. 5-53. Moments are first taken about an axis through A to find the force in EG. The forces may then be summed in the x and y directions to find the components of the reactions at A.

$$\Sigma M_A = 0$$

FIGURE 5-52

$$-(40 \times 3) - 20 \times 6 - 10 \times 3 + F_{EG} \times 6 \tan 40° = 0$$

$$F_{EG} = \frac{120.00 + 120.00 + 30.00}{6 \tan 40°}$$

$$= \frac{270.00}{6 \tan 40°}$$

$$= 53.63 \text{ kN}$$

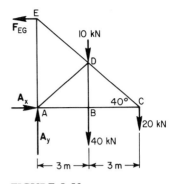

FIGURE 5-53

$\Sigma F_x = 0$

$\quad A_x - 53.63 = 0$

$\quad A_x = 53.63 \text{ kN}$

$\Sigma F_y = 0$

$\quad A_y - 40 - 20 - 10 = 0$

$\quad A_y = 70.00 \text{ kN}$

The analysis of the force in each member may start with either joint C or joint E, since both joints now have one known force and two unknown forces acting on them. Since the known force at C is given, rather than calculated, joint C is the preferred starting point.

Draw a free-body diagram of joint C, as shown in Fig. 5-54. *The unknown forces in members BC and CD are assumed to be in tension. Since there is only one unknown term in the y direction, the forces are first summed in the y direction to obtain the force in member CD.*

Joint C:

$\quad \Sigma F_y = 0$

$\quad\quad F_{CD} \sin 40° - 20 = 0$

$\quad\quad F_{CD} = \dfrac{20}{\sin 40°}$

$\quad\quad = 31.11 \text{ kN}$

JOINT C

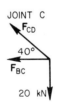

FIGURE 5-54

Forces may now be summed in the x direction to find the force in member BC.

$\quad \Sigma F_x = 0$

$\quad\quad -F_{BC} - 31.11 \cos 40° = 0$

$\quad\quad F_{BC} = -23.83 \text{ kN}$

The negative value for F_{BC} indicates that the member is in compression. Enter these values in the table at the end of the problem solution.

At joint B there are now only two unknown forces. The free-body diagram, as shown in **Fig. 5-55,** is used for analyzing the forces acting on the pin at B. Note that the force in member BC was found to be in compression, so it must show as a compressive force on the pin at B. The forces in AB and BD may be found by summing forces in the x and y directions.

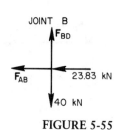

JOINT B

FIGURE 5-55

Joint B:

$$\Sigma F_x = 0$$

$$-F_{AB} - 23.83 = 0$$

$$F_{AB} = -23.83 \text{ kN}$$

$$\Sigma F_y = 0$$

$$F_{BD} - 40 = 0$$

$$F_{BD} = 40.00 \text{ kN}$$

The negative value for F_{AB} indicates that the member is in compression. Enter the values for F_{AB} and F_{BD} in the table at the end of the problem solution.

The careful observer will notice that the analysis of forces in the truss can be completed by analyzing joint A and then joint E; joint D need not be analyzed. However, since the analysis of joints such as D cannot always be avoided, it will be analyzed next to demonstrate a technique for analyzing such joints.

To analyze joint D, a free-body diagram of the joint, as shown in **Fig. 5-56,** is first drawn. Both unknown forces have components in both the x and y directions. Solving for F_{DE} and F_{AD} may involve the solution of two equations with two unknown terms, but this is only one way of solving the problem.

It is also possible to solve the problem using one equation with one unknown by the technique of rotating the axes. The axis system is rotated so that there is an m and an n axis, as shown in **Fig. 5-56,** where the m axis is drawn parallel to the force in member DE (an unknown term) and the n axis is drawn perpendicular to the m axis. If forces are summed in the n direction, there will be only one unknown term in the equation. Angles have been carefully added to the free-body diagram as an aid in writing the necessary equations. It is strongly recommended that the free-body diagram be accurately drawn as an aid to correctly obtaining all the necessary angles. Once the angles are obtained, the forces may be summed in the n direction.

Joint D:

$$\Sigma F_n = 0$$

$$-10 \sin 50° - F_{AD} \cos 10° - 40.00 \cos 40° = 0$$

$$F_{AD} = \frac{-7.66 - 30.64}{\cos 10°}$$

$$= \frac{-38.30}{\cos 10°}$$

$$= -38.89 \text{ kN}$$

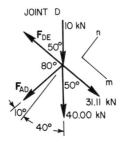

JOINT D

FIGURE 5-56

The negative sign indicates that member AD is actually in compression. The true direction of the force in AD must be used when forces are summed in the m direction to find F_{DE}.

$$\Sigma F_m = 0$$

$$-F_{DE} + 10 \cos 50° + 38.89 \cos 80°$$

$$+ 40.00 \sin 40° + 31.11 = 0$$

$$F_{DE} = 6.43 + 6.75 + 25.71 + 31.11$$

$$= 70.00 \text{ kN}$$

Enter the values for F_{AD} and F_{DE} in the table at the end of the problem solution.

The only force still required is the force in member AE. This may be obtained by drawing a free-body diagram of joint E, as shown in **Fig. 5-57.** *Forces may be summed in the y direction to find the force in member AE.*

Joint E:

$$\Sigma F_y = 0$$

$$-F_{AE} - 70.00 \cos 50° = 0$$

$$F_{AE} = -45.00 \text{ kN}$$

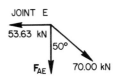

JOINT E

FIGURE 5-57

The negative sign indicates that the force in AE is actually compression. The value should be entered in the table at the end of the problem solution.

The accuracy of the solution may be checked by analyzing joint A, which was not previously analyzed, to determine if it is in equilibrium. The necessary free-body diagram for the check is shown in **Fig. 5-58.**

Joint A:

$$\Sigma F_x = 53.63 - 38.89 \cos 40° - 23.83$$

$$= 53.63 - 26.79 - 23.83$$

$$= 0.01 \text{ kN} \qquad \text{Check}$$

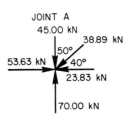

JOINT A

FIGURE 5-58

The size of 0.01 kN is small relative to the forces involved, and represents only rounding-off errors. It does not indicate an error in the calculations.

$$\Sigma F_y = 70.00 - 45.00 - 38.89 \sin 40°$$

$$= 70.00 - 45.00 - 25.00$$

$$= 0.00 \qquad \text{Check}$$

The table summarizing results is considered to be an important part of the problem solution.

Member	Force (kN)
AB	−23.8
BC	−23.8
CD	+31.1
DE	+70.0
AE	−45.0
AD	−38.9
BD	+40.0

PROBLEMS

5-77 Calculate the reactions at the supports and the force in each member of the truss shown in Fig. P5-77.

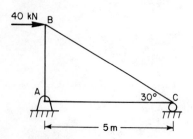

FIGURE P5-77

5-78 For the truss shown in Fig. P5-78, determine the reaction at each support and the force in each member.

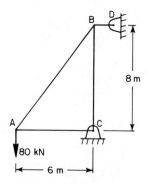

FIGURE P5-78

5-79 For the truss shown in Fig. P5-79, find the force in each member.

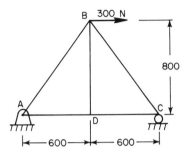

FIGURE P5-79

5-80 Determine the force in each member of the truss shown in Fig. P5-80.

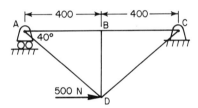

FIGURE P5-80

5-81 Calculate the force in each member of the truss shown in Fig. P5-81.

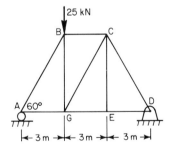

FIGURE P5-81

5-82 Find the force in each member of the truss shown in Fig. P5-82.

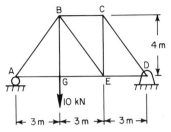

FIGURE P5-82

5-83 For the truss shown in Fig. P5-83, calculate the force in each member.

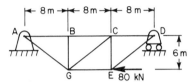

FIGURE P5-83

5-84 Determine the force in each member of the truss shown in Fig. P5-84

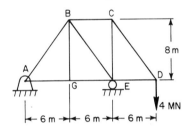

FIGURE P5-84

5-85 Calculate the force in each member of the truss shown in Fig. P5-85.

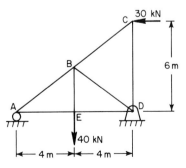

FIGURE P5-85

5-86 For the truss shown in Fig. P5-86, determine the force in each member.

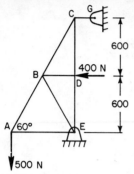

500 N

FIGURE P5-86

5-87 Find the force in each member of the truss shown in Fig. P5-87.

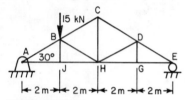

FIGURE P5-87

5-88 Calculate the force in each member of the truss shown in Fig. P5-88.

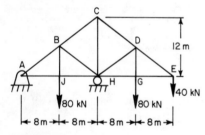

FIGURE P5-88

5-89 For the truss shown in Fig. P5-89, calculate the force in each member.

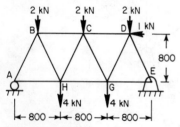

FIGURE P5-89

5-90 Determine the force in each member of the truss shown in Fig. P5-90.

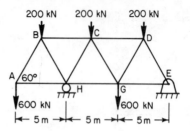

FIGURE P5-90

5-91 Calculate the force in each member of the truss shown in Fig. P5-91.

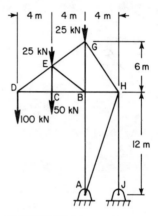

FIGURE P5-91

5-92 For the truss structure shown in Fig. 5-92, calculate the force in each member.

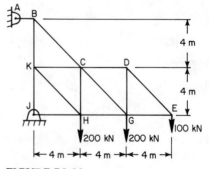

FIGURE P5-92

5-93 For the truss shown in Fig. P5-93, determine the force in each member.

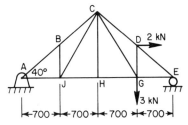

FIGURE P5-93

5-94 Calculate the force in each member of the truss shown in Fig. P5-94.

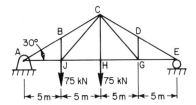

FIGURE P5-94

5-95 Find the force in each member of the truss shown in Fig. P5-95.

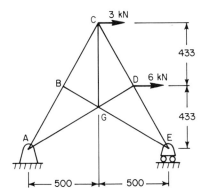

FIGURE P5-95

5-96 Calculate the force in each member of the truss shown in Fig. P5-96.

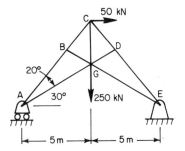

FIGURE P5-96

5-97 Calculate the force in each member to the right of *CK* for the truss shown in Fig. P5-97.

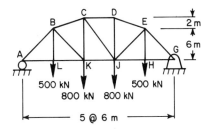

FIGURE P5-97

5-98 Determine the force in each member to the left of *DJ* for the truss shown in Fig. P5-98.

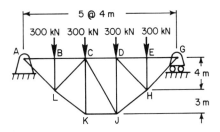

FIGURE P5-98

5-7 METHOD OF SECTIONS

To analyze the forces in members of a truss using the method of sections, pass a section through the truss in such a manner that the section cuts the member to be analyzed and usually no more than two additional members. A free-body diagram is then made of the portion to one side of the section, and the forces acting on the free body are analyzed. The cut members now act as supports for the rest of the truss, and the forces in the supports can be determined using the principles of equilibrium.

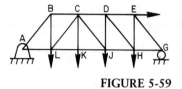

FIGURE 5-59

To find the force in member CL of the truss shown in Fig. 5-59, draw a free-body diagram of the truss, as shown in Fig. 5-60(a). A section, QR, is drawn, which cuts through member CL as well as members BC and KL. The free-body diagram

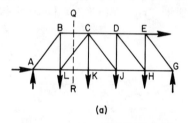

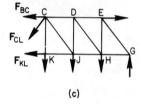

(a)   (b)   (c)

FIGURE 5-60

shown in Fig. 5-60(a) is used to determine the reactions at the supports. Another free-body diagram, of the part to either the left or right of the section is drawn, as shown in Figs. 5-60(b) and 5-60(c). Normally, only one of these, the simpler free-body diagram, would be drawn, which in this case is Fig. 5-60(b). The free-body diagram of the right-hand portion has been drawn to make it possible to compare the two free-body diagrams.

If the applied loads are known, and the reaction at A has been found, then the force in member CL can be found simply by summing forces in the y direction. Similarly, if it is required to find the force in BC, the same section can be used, moments can be taken about an axis through L, and F_{BC} can be obtained directly. If the force in KL is to be determined, then moments are taken about an axis through C, and the force in KL will be the only unknown term in the moment equation.

Thus, the forces in most members of a truss can be found by first making a section that cuts through the desired member; then either sum forces in the x or y directions, or take moments, usually about an axis through the point of concurrency of the two other unknown forces. Since it is possible to determine a maximum of three unknown terms for a plane force system, the section must usually cut through not more than three members whose forces are unknown.

Because a truss is made up of two-force members, the line of action of each force is known. Usually, the members are all assumed to act in tension; whether the actual force is tension or compression can then be determined from the sign at the answer.

The method of sections is particularly useful as a check on calculations made using the method of joints, for it permits checking before the entire truss has been analyzed. It is also useful for the situation where for some reason, such as failure of a member, it is only necessary to find the force in one or two interior members of the truss. For these reasons, it is necessary to become familiar with both the method of joints and the method of sections for determining the forces in members of a truss.

EXAMPLE 5-13

Calculate the forces in members *DE, EK* and *JK* of the truss shown in Fig. 5-61.

SOLUTION

To determine the necessary reactions at the supports, a free-body diagram of the truss, as shown in Fig. 5-62, is drawn. A section MN, which cuts the members in which the forces are to be found, is also shown on the free-body diagram. Since the part of the truss to the right of the section will probably be simpler than the one to the left, only the reaction at H will be calculated; it is the only reaction that will be on the required free-body diagram of the section.

The reaction at H may be obtained by taking moments about an axis through A.

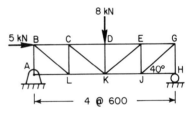

FIGURE 5-61

$$\Sigma M_A = 0$$

$$-(5 \times 600 \tan 40°) - 8 \times 1200 + H_y \times 2400 = 0$$

$$H_y = \frac{2517.3 + 9600.0}{2400.0}$$

$$= \frac{12\ 117.3}{2400.0}$$

$$= 5.0489 \text{ kN}$$

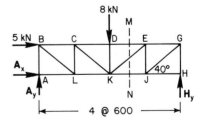

FIGURE 5-62

The free-body diagram of the part of the truss to the right of the section is now drawn, as shown in Fig. 5-63. *Members, DE, EK and JK and the roller at H are acting as supports for the panel*

EGHJ. The forces in the cut members are all assumed to be tension. If they are actually compression, the sign of the magnitude of the force calculated in the member will be negative.

The body shown in Fig 5-63 has three unknown forces acting on it. The line of action of each force is known, since each force is acting in a two-force member. The force in member EK can be obtained by summing forces in the y direction.

$$\Sigma\ F_y = 0$$

$$5.0489 - F_{EK}\ \sin 40° = 0$$

$$F_{EK} = \frac{5.0489}{\sin 40°}$$

$$= 7.8547 \text{ kN}$$

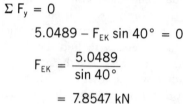

FIGURE 5-63

The positive value for F_{EK} indicates that the member is in tension as assumed.

Since both $\mathbf{F}_{DE}$ and $\mathbf{F}_{JK}$ are in the x direction, it will be necessary to take moments about some axis to find one or the other. There are a couple of suitable axes. If moments are taken about an axis through E, the only unknown term in the moment equation will be F_{JK}.

$$\Sigma\ M_E = 0$$

$$5.0489 \times 600 - F_{JK} \times 600 \tan 40° = 0$$

$$F_{JK} = \frac{5.0489 \times 600}{600 \tan 40°}$$

$$= 6.0170 \text{ kN}$$

Since a positive sign was obtained for F_{JK}, the member is in tension, as assumed.

Now the forces may be summed in the x direction to find the force in member DE.

$$\Sigma\ F_x = 0$$

$$-F_{DE} - 7.8547 \cos 40° - 6.0170 = 0$$

$$F_{DE} = -6.0170 - 6.0170$$

$$= -12.0340 \text{ kN}$$

The negative value for the answer indicates that member DE actually is in compression.

As usual, results should be summarized at the end of the problem solution.

$$F_{DE} = -12.0 \text{ kN}$$
$$F_{EK} = +7.85 \text{ kN}$$
$$F_{JK} = +6.02 \text{ kN}$$

EXAMPLE 5-14

For the truss shown in Fig. 5-64, determine the forces in members CD, CG and GH.

SOLUTION

In this case it will not be necessary to determine the reactions at the supports. A section can be cut through members CD, CG and GH and the portion of the truss to the right of the section can be analyzed, eliminating the need to calculate the reactions at the supports. The free-body diagram for the right portion of the truss is shown in Fig. 5-65. *Members CD, CG and GH act as supports for panel DEG, and the forces these supports apply to the panel are shown in the free-body diagram. They have all been assumed to be tensile forces.*

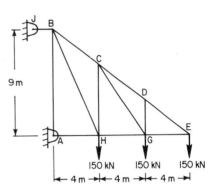

FIGURE 5-64

The free-body diagram shows three unknown forces. If forces are summed in the x direction there are three unknown terms in the equation; if forces are summed in the y direction there are two unknown terms in the equation. A moment equation would appear to be a necessity. If moments are taken about an axis through E, two of the unknown forces are concurrent at E, so an equation with only one unknown term can be obtained.

Before writing the moment equation, it is helpful to obtain the angle θ that member CG makes with member GH, as shown in Fig. 5-66. *By similar triangles, it can be shown that CH is 6 m.*

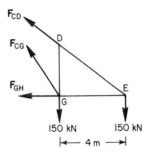

FIGURE 5-65

$$\theta = \tan^{-1} \frac{6}{4}$$

$$= 56.31°$$

$$\Sigma M_E = 0$$

$$150 \times 4 - F_{CG} \sin 56.31° \times 4 = 0$$

$$F_{CG} = \frac{150 \times 4}{\sin 56.31° \times 4}$$

$$= 180.28 \text{ kN}$$

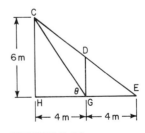

FIGURE 5-66

The positive value indicates that CG is in tension, as assumed.

Now forces may be summed in the y direction to find the force in member CD. Note that the slope of member CD is 3:4.

$$\Sigma F_y = 0$$

$$\frac{3}{5} F_{CD} + 180.28 \sin 56.31° - 150 - 150 = 0$$

$$F_{CD} = \frac{5}{3} \left(-150.00 + 150.00 + 150.00 \right)$$

$$= \frac{5}{3} \times 150.00$$

$$= 250.00 \text{ kN}$$

F_{CD} *is a tensile force, as assumed, since the value obtained is positive.*

To find the force in member GH, forces may now be summed in the x direction.

$$\Sigma F_x = 0$$

$$-F_{GH} - 180.28 \cos 56.31° - \frac{4}{5} \times 250.00 = 0$$

$$F_{GH} = 100.00 - 200.00$$

$$= -300.00 \text{ kN}$$

The negative sign indicates that member GH is in compression.

$$\boxed{\begin{array}{l} F_{CD} = +250 \text{ kN} \\ F_{CG} = +180 \text{ kN} \\ F_{GH} = -300 \text{ kN} \end{array}}$$

EXAMPLE 5-15

Find the force in member *CH* for the truss shown in Fig. 5-67.

SOLUTION

A section can be cut through members BC, CH and GH, and a free-body diagram of the part of the truss to the left of the section can be drawn, as shown in Fig. 5-68. Since only the force in member CH is required, moments could be taken about an axis through the point of concurrency of the forces in BC and GH. This point is P, as shown in Fig. 5-68.

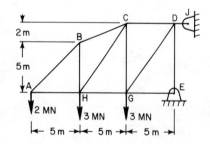

FIGURE 5-67

To determine the moment of F_{CH} about an axis through P, it is necessary to find the angle θ and the distance PH. Figure 5-69 will aid in these calculations.

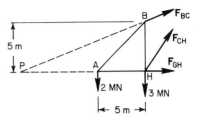

FIGURE 5-68

$$\theta = \tan^{-1}\frac{7}{5}$$

$$= 54.46°$$

From similar triangles:

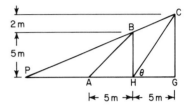

FIGURE 5-69

$$\frac{PH}{5} = \frac{PG}{7}$$

But PG = PH + 5

$$\frac{PH}{5} = \frac{PH + 5}{7}$$

$$7\,PH = 5\,PH + 25$$

$$2\,PH = 25$$

$$PH = \frac{25}{2}$$

$$= 12.50 \text{ m}$$

There is now enough information to take moments about an axis through P to find F_{CH}.

$\Sigma\,M_P = 0$

$$-2(12.50-5)-3 \times 12.50 + F_{CH}\sin 54.46° \times 12.50 = 0$$

$$F_{CH} = \frac{2 \times 7.50 + 3 \times 12.50}{\sin 54.46° \times 12.50}$$

$$= \frac{15.00 + 37.50}{\sin 54.46° \times 12.50}$$

$$= \frac{52.50}{\sin 54.46° \times 12.50}$$

$$= 5.1615 \text{ MN}$$

$$\boxed{F_{CH} = +5.16 \text{ MN}}$$

PROBLEMS

5-99 For the truss shown in Fig. P5-99, determine the forces in members *BC, BE* and *EG*.

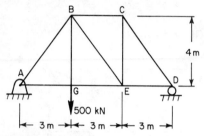

FIGURE P5-99

5-100 Calculate the forces in members *BC, CG* and *EG* of the truss shown in Fig. P5-100.

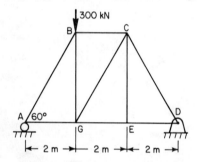

FIGURE P5-100

5-101 For the truss shown in Fig. P5-101, find the forces in members *CD, CE* and *EG* using the method of sections.

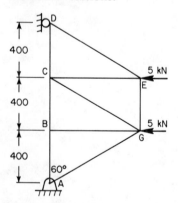

FIGURE P5-101

5-102 Use the method of sections to find the forces in *BC, BG* and *AG* for the truss shown in Fig. P5-102.

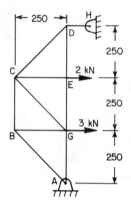

FIGURE P5-102

5-103 Calculate the forces in members *BC, CH* and *GH* of the truss shown in Fig. P5-103.

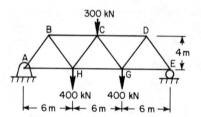

FIGURE P5-103

5-104 For the truss shown in Fig. P5-104, find the forces in members *CD, CG* and *GH*.

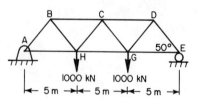

FIGURE P5-104

5-105 Calculate the forces in members *BC*, *CG* and *EG* for the truss shown in Fig. P5-105. Each panel has the same length.

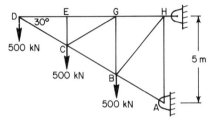

FIGURE P5-105

5-106 For the truss shown in Fig. P5-106, find the forces in members *BC*, *BE* and *EG*. The length of each panel is the same.

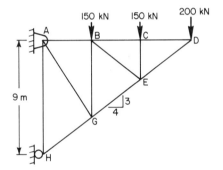

FIGURE P5-106

5-107 Determine the forces in members *CD*, *DH* and *GH* of the truss shown in Fig. P5-107.

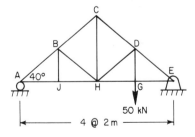

FIGURE P5-107

5-108 For the truss shown in Fig. P5-108, calculate the forces in members *BC*, *CJ* and *HJ*.

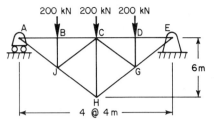

FIGURE P5-108

5-109 Determine the forces in members *AB*, *BE* and *DE* using the method of sections for the truss shown in Fig. P5-109.

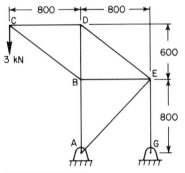

FIGURE P5-109

5-110 Use the method of sections to determine the forces in members *BC*, *CG* and *EG* for the truss shown in Fig. P5-110.

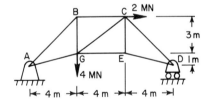

FIGURE P5-110

5-111 Find the forces in members *BC*, *CE* and *DE* for the truss shown in Fig. P5-111.

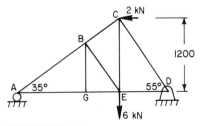

FIGURE P5-111

5-112 Determine the forces in members *CD, DH* and *GH* for the truss shown in Fig. P5-112.

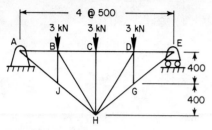

FIGURE P5-112

5-113 If the force in member *EG* of the truss shown in Fig. P5-113 is −12.0 kN, calculate the magnitude of the force **P**.

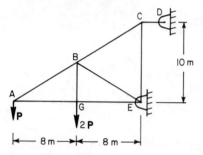

FIGURE P5-113

5-114 For the truss shown in Fig. P5-114, the force in member *EG* was found to be −15.0 kN. Use the method of sections to find the magnitude of **P**.

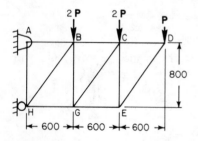

FIGURE P5-114

5-115 For the truss shown in Fig. P5-115, member *CE* was found to have a force of +250 kN. Determine the magnitude of **P**.

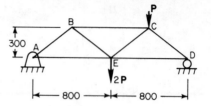

FIGURE P5-115

5-116 The force in member *KL* for the truss shown in Fig. P5-116 was found to be +175 kN. Determine the magnitude of **P**.

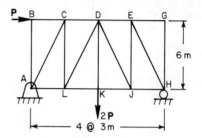

FIGURE P5-116

5-117 Calculate the force in member *BE* for the truss shown in Fig. P5-117.

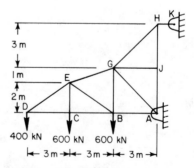

FIGURE P5-117

5-118 Find the force in member *CH* for the truss shown in Fig. P5-118.

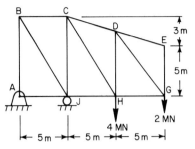

FIGURE P5-118

5-119 For the truss shown in Fig. P5-119, calculate the force in member *GM*.

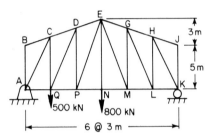

FIGURE P5-119

5-120 Use the method of sections to determine the force in member *CK* of the truss shown in Fig. P5-120.

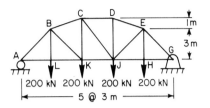

FIGURE P5-120

6 THREE-DIMENSIONAL STATICS

6-1 THREE-DIMENSIONAL SYSTEMS

We live in a three-dimensional world. Although it is possible to solve many statics problems using a plane or two-dimensional system, in some situations it is necessary to work with all three dimensions. The dockside derrick shown in Fig. 6-1 is an illustration of a system that cannot be analyzed by considering any one plane. To determine the forces acting on this structure, it is necessary to work with a three-dimensional system.

FIGURE 6-1 Forces in this dockside crane, which can lift a mass of over 200 000 kg, may be analyzed using the methods of three-dimensional statics. *Photo courtesy of the Port of Vancouver.*

To locate points in a three-dimensional system, it is customary to use an axis system as shown in Fig. 6-2. The positive ends of the axes are labelled. The axis system may be reoriented in space, but the positive ends of the x, y and z axes should always have the same positions relative to each other.

Drawing a meaningful vector in three dimensions is somewhat difficult, but the task may be greatly simplified by showing the vector as the diagonal of a rectangular parallelepiped, as shown in Fig. 6-3. The lengths of the sides of the parallelepiped are in proportion to the x, y and z components of the vector. This procedure helps to visualize the proportions of the vector in the x, y and z directions.

The procedures for calculations in three-dimensional systems are similar to those used for plane or two-dimensional systems; there will be some modifications to allow for the fact that the system is three-dimensional.

6-2 COMPONENTS IN THREE DIMENSIONS

The solving of many three-dimensional problems will involve the calculation of the orthogonal or mutually perpendicular components of the vector. The orthogonal components that will most frequently be used will be the x, y and z components. Although the discussion here will be in terms of force vectors, the procedure for calculating components of any vector will be the same.

A vector **F** is shown in Fig. 6-4. It forms the diagonal of the rectangular parallelepiped shown. The lengths of the sides of the parallelepiped are d_x, d_y and d_z, and the length of the diagonal is d. The direction angles, θ_x, θ_y and θ_z, are also shown. They are measured from the positive x, y and z axes to the vector. The components of the vector may be obtained using the direction angles. In Fig. 6-4, it is most apparent for the y component that $F_y = F \cos \theta_y$. Angle ABO is a right angle; and the force **F**, the y axis and the triangle ABO are all contained in the same plane. Thus, in that plane system, the y component of **F** must be $F \cos \theta_y$. (This plane system is the type of system discussed in Chap. 2.) The same approach may be used to show that the three components of the vector are:

$$F_x = F \cos \theta_x \qquad (6\text{-}1)$$

$$F_y = F \cos \theta_y \qquad (6\text{-}1)$$

$$F_z = F \cos \theta_z \qquad (6\text{-}3)$$

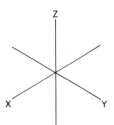

FIGURE 6-2

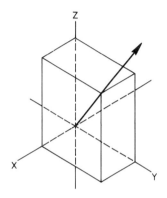

FIGURE 6-3

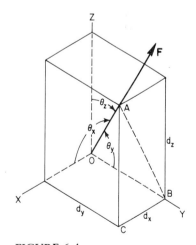

FIGURE 6-4

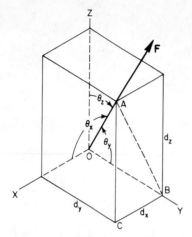

FIGURE 6-4 *Repeated*

where F is the magnitude of the force vector **F**,

F_x, F_y and F_z are the magnitudes of the x, y and z components of the force vector **F**, and

$\cos \theta_x$, $\cos \theta_y$ and $\cos \theta_z$ are the x, y and z direction cosines of the force vector **F**.

The direction cosines are the cosines of the direction angles. Usually, it is the direction cosines that are calculated, rather than the direction angles, since the direction cosines are used directly in the calculation of the components.

Figure 6-4 may be used as an aid in determining the direction cosines. From the right-angled triangle ABC, it can be seen that

$$(AB)^2 = d_x^2 + d_z^2$$

Then, from the right-angled triangle ABO, it is seen that

$$(OA)^2 = (AB)^2 + d_y^2$$

but

$$(AB)^2 = d_x^2 + d_z^2$$

thus

$$(OA)^2 = d_x^2 + d_z^2 + d_y^2$$

If we let the diagonal distance $d = OA$, we have

$$d^2 = d_x^2 + d_y^2 + d_z^2$$

or

$$d = (d_x^2 + d_y^2 + d_z^2)^{1/2} \tag{6-4}$$

and the direction cosines will be

$$\cos \theta_x = \frac{d_x}{d} \tag{6-5}$$

$$\cos \theta_y = \frac{d_y}{d} \tag{6-6}$$

$$\cos \theta_z = \frac{d_z}{d} \tag{6-7}$$

where d is the length of the diagonal of the rectangular parallelepiped,

d_x, d_y and d_z are the lengths of the sides of the rectangular parallelepiped, and

$\cos \theta_x$, $\cos \theta_y$ and $\cos \theta_z$ are the direction cosines for the diagonal of the rectangular parallelepiped.

In the case of a triangle, it is known that the sum of the three interior angles is 180°. In the case of a vector in space, the following relationship applies to the direction angles:

$$\cos^2 \theta_x + \cos^2 \theta_y + \cos^2 \theta_z = 1 \qquad (6\text{-}8)$$

Substituting Eqs. (6-5) through (6-7) in Eq. (6-8), the following is obtained:

$$\left(\frac{d_x}{d}\right)^2 + \left(\frac{d_y}{d}\right)^2 + \left(\frac{d_z}{d}\right)^2 = \frac{d_x^2 + d_y^2 + d_z^2}{d^2}$$

but

$$d_x^2 + d_y^2 + d_z^2 = d^2$$

thus

$$\cos^2 \theta_x + \cos^2 \theta_y + \cos^2 \theta_z = \frac{d^2}{d^2} = 1$$

Equation (6-8) provides a form of check on the calculations for the values of the direction cosines.

When working with direction cosines, use the same sign rules that were used with plane angles. The cosine is negative if the angle is between 90° and 180°. It should also be noted that direction angles are never greater than 180°.

EXAMPLE 6-1

Find the length of the diagonal of the rectangular parallelepiped shown in Fig. 6-5.

SOLUTION

The length of the diagonal may be obtained by direct substitution of the lengths of the sides of the parallelepiped into Eq. (6-4).

$$\begin{aligned}
d &= (d_x^2 + d_y^2 + d_z^2)^{1/2} \\
&= (3^2 + 6^2 + 4^2)^{1/2} \\
&= (9 + 36 + 16)^{1/2} \\
&= 61^{1/2} \\
&= 7.8102 \text{ m}
\end{aligned}$$

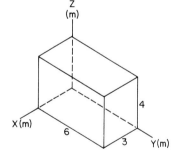

FIGURE 6-5

$$\boxed{d = 7.81 \text{ m}}$$

EXAMPLE 6-2

For the force shown in Fig. 6-6, determine the direction cosines and *x, y* and *z* components.

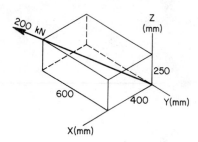

FIGURE 6-6

SOLUTION

The direction cosines may be obtained first, using Eqs. (6-5) *through* (6-7). *However, before finding the direction cosines, it is necessary to find the length of the diagonal using* Eq. (6-4).

$$d = (d_x^2 + d_y^2 + d_z^2)^{1/2}$$

$$= \left[400^2 + (-600)^2 + 250^2\right]^{1/2}$$

$$= (160\ 000 + 360\ 000 + 62\ 500)^{1/2}$$

$$= 582\ 500^{1/2}$$

$$= 763.217 \text{ mm}$$

Now the direction cosines may be obtained.

$$\cos \theta_y = \frac{d_y}{d}$$

$$= \frac{400}{763.217}$$

$$= 0.524\ 097$$

The value for d_y is negative since the y component of the force is directed towards the negative end of the y axis. As a result, $\cos \theta_y$ *will have a negative value.*

$$\cos \theta_y = \frac{d_y}{d}$$

$$= \frac{-600}{763.217}$$

$$= -0.786\ 146$$

$$\cos \theta_z = \frac{d_z}{d}$$

$$= \frac{250}{763.217}$$

$$= 0.327\ 561$$

These calculations may be checked by using Eq. (6-8)

$$\cos^2 \theta_x + \cos^2 \theta_y + \cos^2 \theta_z$$

$$= 0.524\ 097^2 + (-0.786\ 146)^2 + 0.327\ 561^2$$

$$= 0.274\ 678 + 0.618\ 026 + 0.107\ 296$$

$$= 1.000\ 000 \qquad\qquad \text{Check}$$

The components may now be obtained using Eqs. (6-1) *through* (6-3).

$$F_x = F \cos \theta_x$$
$$= 200 \times 0.524\ 097$$
$$= 104.819 \text{ kN}$$

$$F_y = F \cos \theta_y$$
$$= 200 \times (-0.786\ 146)$$
$$= -157.229 \text{ kN}$$

$$F_z = F \cos \theta_z$$
$$= 200 \times 0.327\ 561$$
$$= 65.512 \text{ kN}$$

$$
\boxed{
\begin{aligned}
\cos \theta_x &= 0.524 \\
\cos \theta_y &= -0.786 \\
\cos \theta_z &= 0.328 \\
F_x &= 105 \text{ kN} \\
F_y &= -157 \text{ kN} \\
F_z &= 65.5 \text{ kN}
\end{aligned}
}
$$

EXAMPLE 6-3

A velocity vector of 140 m/s starts from point A (3, –2, 4) and passes through point B (6, –7, 2). Determine the x, y and z components of the vector. Coordinate distances are in metres.

SOLUTION

To visualize the problem, a drawing, as shown in Fig. 6-7, *may be helpful. The diagonal distance should be calculated first using* Eq. (6-4). *From* Fig. 6-7, *it may be observed that* $d_x = x_B - x_A$, $d_y = y_B - y_A$ *and* $d_z = z_B - z_A$.

$$d = \left[(x_B - x_A)^2 + (y_B - y_A)^2 + (z_B - z_A)^2 \right]^{1/2}$$
$$= \left\{ (6 - 3)^2 + \left[-7 - (-2) \right]^2 + (2 - 4)^2 \right\}^{1/2}$$
$$= \left[3^2 + (-5)^2 + (-2)^2 \right]^{1/2}$$
$$= (9.00 + 25.00 + 4.00)^{1/2}$$
$$= 38.00^{1/2}$$
$$= 6.1644 \text{ m}$$

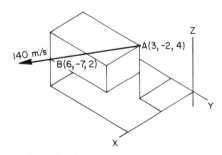

FIGURE 6-7

Now the components may be calculated using Eqs. (6-1) *through* (6-3) *and* Eqs. (6-4) *through* (6-6) *in a combined form.*

$$v_x = v \cos \theta_x = v \frac{d_x}{d}$$

$$= 140 \times \frac{(6 - 3)}{6.1644}$$

$$= 140 \times \frac{3}{6.1644}$$

$$= 68.133 \text{ m/s}$$

$$v_y = v \cos \theta_y = v \frac{d_y}{d}$$

$$= 140 \times \frac{[-7 - (-2)]}{6.1644}$$

$$= 140 \times \frac{(-5)}{6.1644}$$

$$= -113.555 \text{ m/s}$$

$$v_z = v \cos \theta_z = v \frac{d_z}{d}$$

$$= 140 \times \frac{(2 - 4)}{6.1644}$$

$$= 140 \times \frac{(-2)}{6.1644}$$

$$= -45.422 \text{ m/s}$$

$$\boxed{\begin{aligned} v_x &= -114 \text{ m/s} \\ v_y &= 68.1 \text{ m/s} \\ v_z &= -45.4 \text{ m/s} \end{aligned}}$$

PROBLEMS

6-1 Find the length of the diagonal for the rectangular parallelepiped shown in Fig. P6-1.

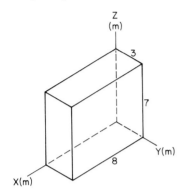

FIGURE P6-1

6-2 For the rectangular parallelpiped shown in Fig. P6-2, determine the length of the diagonal.

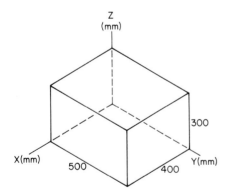

FIGURE P6-2

6-3 For the rectangular parallelepiped shown in Fig. P6-3, calculate the diagonal.

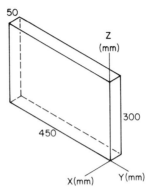

FIGURE P6-3

6-4 Find the length of the diagonal for the rectangular parallelepiped shown in Fig. P6-4.

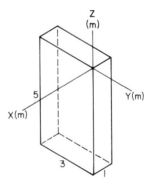

FIGURE P6-4

6-5 Determine the length of a line that runs from the origin at $(0, 0, 0)$ to the point $(4, 8, -6)$. Coordinate dimensions are in metres.

6-6 A line runs from point A at $(-2, 6, -3)$ to point B at $(4, 7, -7)$. Determine the length of the line if the coordinates are in metres.

6-7 Determine the x, y and z components of the force shown in Fig. P6-7.

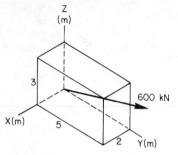

FIGURE P6-7

6-8 Find the x, y and z components of the force shown in Fig. P6-8.

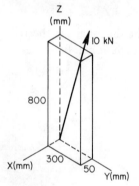

FIGURE P6-8

6-9 Calculate the x, y and z components and the direction cosines for the force shown in Fig. P6-9.

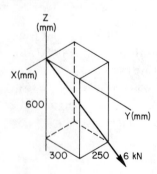

FIGURE P6-9

6-10 For the force shown in Fig. P6-10, determine the rectangular components and the direction cosines.

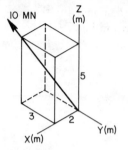

FIGURE P6-10

6-11 Calculate the x, y and z components of the vector shown in Fig. P6-11.

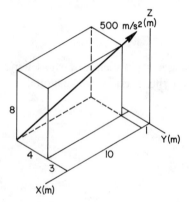

FIGURE P6-11

6-12 For the vector shown in Fig. P6-12, determine the x, y and z components.

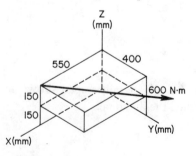

FIGURE P6-12

6-13 A force of 30 MN has its tail at $(3, 4, -2)$ and passes through the point $(-4, -1, 5)$. Determine the x, y and z components of the force. The coordinates are in metres.

6-14 Calculate the x, y and z components for a 200 N force that starts at $(20, 35, 15)$ and passes through $(-10, -30, 25)$. Coordinate distances are in millimetres.

6-3 MOMENT OF A FORCE IN THREE DIMENSIONS

The moment of a force was defined in Chap. 2 as a tendency of that force to cause rotation about an axis. The magnitude of the moment was obtained from

$$M_A = Fd \qquad (2\text{-}9)$$

As can be seen from Fig. 6-8, the calculation of the perpendicular distance from an axis, such as the x axis, to the line of action of the force, could be somewhat complex. However, the perpendicular distance from an axis such as x to the components of the force can usually be readily obtained, and the moment of each of the components about the axis can be calculated. From Fig. 6-8 it will be noted that $\mathbf{F}_x$ has no moment about the x axis, since it is parallel to the x axis. The right-hand rule, which was introduced in Chap. 2, states that when the fingers of the right hand curl in the direction of rotation, if the thumb points to the positive end of the axis of rotation, then the moment is positive. On this basis, $\mathbf{F}_y$ would cause a negative moment about the x axis, and $\mathbf{F}_z$ would cause a positive moment about the x axis. The moments due to both $\mathbf{F}_y$ and $\mathbf{F}_z$ may be added algebraically, since both moment vectors are parallel.

It will be recalled that Varignon's theorem stated that the moment of a force about an axis is equal to the sum of the moments of the components of the force about the same axis. Varignon's theorem is valid for forces in three dimensions, as well as for forces in two dimensions.

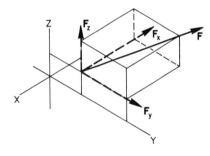

FIGURE 6-8

EXAMPLE 6-4

Determine the moment about the z axis for the force shown in Fig. 6-9.

SOLUTION

A sketch showing the components of the force, as shown in Fig. 6-10, *will help in visualizing the solution. It can be seen from* Fig. 6-10 *that F_x will have a positive moment about the z axis, but*

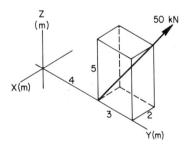

FIGURE 6-9

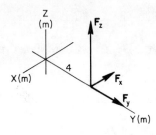

FIGURE 6-10

that F_y will have no moment about the z axis, since its line of action passes through the z axis. Nor will F_z have a moment about the z axis, since it is parallel to the axis. Thus, the only component that needs to be calculated is F_x. First the diagonal distance must be calculated, using Fig. (6-4), and then the component may be calculated using Eqs. (6-1) and (6-5).

$$d = (d_x^2 + d_y^2 + d_z^2)^{1/2}$$
$$= \left[(-2)^2 + 3^2 + 5^2 \right]^{1/2}$$
$$= (4 + 9 + 25)^{1/2}$$
$$= 38^{1/2}$$
$$= 6.1644 \text{ m}$$
$$F_x = F \cos \theta_x$$
$$= 50 \times \frac{-2}{6.1644}$$
$$= -16.222 \text{ kN}$$

The moment of the force may be obtained from Eq. (2-9).

$$M_z = Fd$$
$$= 16.222 \times 4$$
$$= 64.888 \text{ kN} \cdot \text{m}$$

$$\boxed{M_z = 64.9 \text{ kN} \cdot \text{m}}$$

Remember that the sign of the moment is based on the right-hand rule, and not on the sign of the component.

EXAMPLE 6-5

For the force shown in Fig. 6-11, determine the moment about an axis AA, which is parallel to the y axis and lies in the y-z plane.

SOLUTION

To aid in visualizing the solution, a sketch of the components of the force, as shown in Fig. 6-12, may be helpful. Since F_y is parallel to axis AA it will have no moment about the axis, but both F_x and F_z will have moments about AA. It will be necessary to calculate the length of the diagonal of the parallelepiped, using Eq. (6-4), before using Eqs. (6-1), (6-3), (6-5) and (6-7) to determine F_x and F_z.

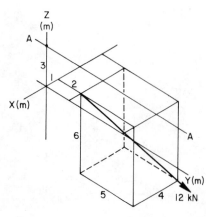

FIGURE 6-11

$$d = (d_x^2 + d_y^2 + d_z^2)^{1/2}$$

$$= \left[(-4)^2 + 5^2 + (-6)^2\right]^{1/2}$$

$$= (16 + 25 + 36)^{1/2}$$

$$= 77^{1/2}$$

$$= 8.7750 \text{ m}$$

$$F_x = F \cos \theta_x$$

$$= 12 \times \frac{-4}{8.7750}$$

$$= -5.4701 \text{ kN}$$

$$F_z = F \cos \theta_z$$

$$= 12 \times \frac{-6}{8.7750}$$

$$= -8.2051 \text{ kN}$$

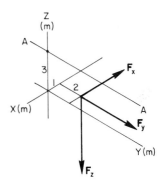

FIGURE 6-12

The total moment is the sum of the moments of the components. Using the right-hand rule, F_x will cause a positive moment about AA and F_z will cause a negative moment about AA. (Note that the positive end of an axis is assumed to be at the same end as the positive end of the coordinate axis.) Remember that the sign of a moment depends on the right-hand rule, and not on the sign of the component.

$$M_{AA} = \Sigma Fd$$

$$= 5.4701 \times 3 - (8.2051 \times 1)$$

$$= 16.4103 - 8.2051$$

$$= 8.2052 \text{ kN} \cdot \text{m}$$

$$\boxed{M_{AA} = 8.21 \text{ kN} \cdot \text{m}}$$

EXAMPLE 6-6

Find the moment about the x axis that is caused by the force shown in Fig. 6-13.

SOLUTION

A sketch showing the components will help in determining the magnitude and signs of the moments. Such a sketch is shown in Fig. 6-14. There will be no moment caused by F_x, since it is

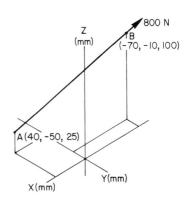

FIGURE 6-13

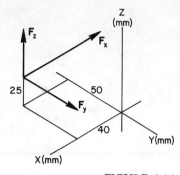

FIGURE 6-14

parallel to the x axis. Both F_y and F_z will cause negative moments about the x axis.

Before calculating the moment, the diagonal distance from A to B must be found using Eq. (6-4), and then the values for F_y and F_z are found using Eqs. (6-2), (6-3), (6-6) and (6-7).

$$d = \left[(x_B - x_A)^2 + (y_B - y_A)^2 + (z_B - z_A)^2\right]^{1/2}$$

$$= \left\{(-70 - 40)^2 + \left[-10 - (-50)\right]^2 + (100 - 25)^2\right\}^{1/2}$$

$$= \left[(-110)^2 + 40^2 + 75^2\right]^{1/2}$$

$$= (12\ 100 + 1\ 600 + 5\ 625)^{1/2}$$

$$= 19\ 325^{1/2}$$

$$= 139.01 \text{ mm}$$

$$F_y = F \cos \theta_y$$

$$= 800 \times \frac{-10 - (-50)}{139.01}$$

$$= 800 \times \frac{40}{139.01}$$

$$= 230.20 \text{ N}$$

$$F_z = F \cos \theta_z$$

$$= 800 \times \frac{100 - 25}{139.01}$$

$$= 800 \times \frac{75}{139.01}$$

$$= 431.62 \text{ N}$$

The moment is calculated making use of Varignon's theorem.

$$M_x = Fd$$

$$= -(230.20 \times 25) - (431.62 \times 50)$$

$$= -5\ 755 - 21\ 581$$

$$= -27\ 336 \text{ N·mm}$$

$$= -27.336 \text{ N·m}$$

$$\boxed{M_x = -27.3 \text{ N·m}}$$

PROBLEMS

6-15 For the force shown in Fig. P6-15, determine the moment about the x axis.

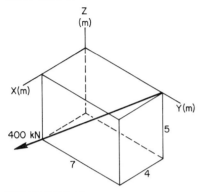

FIGURE P6-15

6-16 Calculate the moment of the force shown in Fig. P6-16 with respect to the z axis.

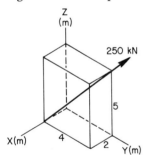

FIGURE P6-16

6-17 For the force shown in Fig. P6-17, find the moment about the x axis.

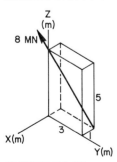

FIGURE P6-17

6-18 Find the moment of the force shown in Fig. P6-18 with respect to the y axis.

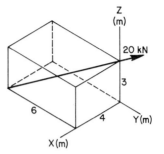

FIGURE P6-18

6-19 Determine the moment about the z axis caused by the force shown in Fig. P6-19.

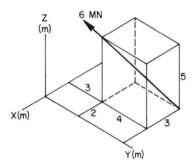

FIGURE P6-19

6-20 For the force shown in Fig. P6-20, find the moment about the x axis.

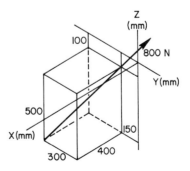

FIGURE P6-20

6-21 Find the moment about axis *AA* for the force shown in Fig. P6-21. Axis *AA* is parallel to the *y* axis, and is in the *y-z* plane.

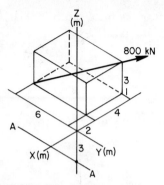

FIGURE P6-21

6-22 For the force shown in Fig. P6-22, determine the moment about the axis *AA*, which is parallel to the *z* axis and lies in the *y-z* plane.

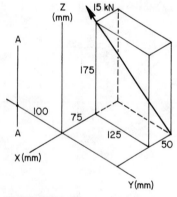

FIGURE P6-22

6-23 For the force shown in Fig. P6-23, calculate the moment about the *y* axis.

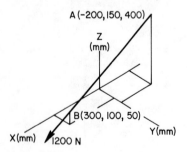

FIGURE P6-23

6-24 Calculate the moment of the force shown in Fig. P6-24 with respect to the *z* axis.

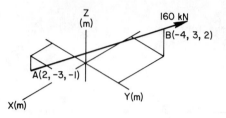

FIGURE P6-24

6-25 Determine the moment about the *x* axis due to the force shown in Fig. P6-25.

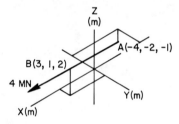

FIGURE P6-25

6-26 For the force shown in Fig. P6-26, find the moment about the *y* axis.

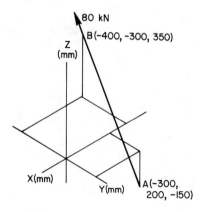

FIGURE P6-26

6-27 For the force shown in Fig. P6-27, determine the moment about the axis AA, which is parallel to the z axis and is in the y-z plane.

6-28 Determine the moment of the force shown in Fig. P6-28 with respect to the axis AA, which is parallel to the x axis and is in the x-y plane.

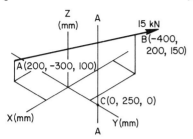

FIGURE P6-27

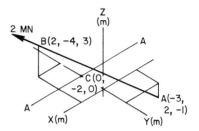

FIGURE P6-28

6-4 RESULTANT OF A CONCURRENT FORCE SYSTEM

Two or more forces whose lines of action intersect at a common point form a concurrent force system. An example of such a system is shown in Fig. 6-15, where point A in the x-y plane is the point of concurrency of the three forces shown.

In some instances, the resultant of such a concurrent force system must be calculated. The resultant may be obtained by summing the rectangular components and then finding the resultant of the components using a procedure similar to that used for calculating the resultant of a plane system of concurrent forces. Note that some of the equations used in the two procedures are identical.

Parallel components of forces may be added algebraically, so the components of the resultant are

$$R_x = F_{x_1} + F_{x_2} + F_{x_3} + \ldots$$
$$R_x = \Sigma F_{x_i} \qquad (3\text{-}1)$$

Similarly

$$R_y = \Sigma F_{y_i} \qquad (3\text{-}2)$$
$$R_z = \Sigma F_{z_i} \qquad (6\text{-}9)$$

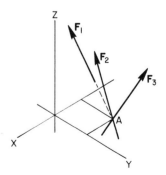

FIGURE 6-15

where R_x is the magnitude of the x component of the resultant of the force system

R_y is the magnitude of the y component of the resultant of the force system,

R_z is the magnitude of the z component of the resultant of the force system,

ΣF_{x_i} is the algebraic summation of the x components of each force in the system,

ΣF_{y_i} is the algebraic summation of the y components of each force in the system, and

ΣF_{z_i} is the algebraic summation of the z components of each force in the system.

The magnitude of the resultant may be obtained by using the Pythagorean theorem for a three-dimensional system.

$$R = (R_x^2 + R_y^2 + R_z^2)^{1/2} \qquad (6\text{-}10)$$

where R is the magnitude of the resultant of the system of concurrent forces, and

R_x, R_y and R_z are the magnitudes of the components of the resultant.

The direction of the resultant is usually expressed in terms of the direction cosines, which may be expressed as follows:

$$\cos \theta_x = \frac{R_x}{R} \qquad (6\text{-}11)$$

$$\cos \theta_y = \frac{R_y}{R} \qquad (6\text{-}12)$$

$$\cos \theta_z = \frac{R_z}{R} \qquad (6\text{-}13)$$

where θ_x, θ_y and θ_z are the direction angles measured from the positive ends of the axes to the resultant,

R is the magnitude of the resultant, and

R_x, R_y and R_z are the magnitudes of the components of the resultant.

The resultant of a concurrent force system in space may be fully defined by giving its magnitude and its direction in terms of the direction cosines. It must be located so that its line of action passes through the point of concurrency of the original system of forces.

EXAMPLE 6-7

Find the resultant of the system of two concurrent forces shown in Fig. 6-16.

SOLUTION

To find the resultant of the force system, it is first necessary to determine the x, y and z components for each of the forces. Prior to calculating the components, it is necessary to determine the diagonal distance for each parallelepiped, using Eq. (6-4).

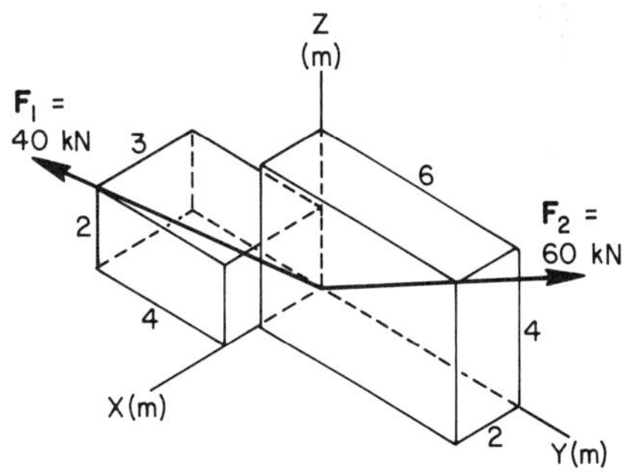

$$d_1 = (d_{x_1}^2 + d_{y_1}^2 + d_{z_1}^2)^{1/2}$$

$$= \left[3^2 + (-4)^2 + 2^2\right]^{1/2}$$

$$= (9 + 16 + 4)^{1/2}$$

$$= 29^{1/2}$$

$$= 5.3852 \text{ m}$$

$$d_2 = (d_{x_2}^2 + d_{y_2}^2 + d_{z_2}^2)^{1/2}$$

$$= (2^2 + 6^2 + 4^2)^{1/2}$$

$$= (4 + 36 + 16)^{1/2}$$

$$= 56^{1/2}$$

$$= 7.4833 \text{ m}$$

FIGURE 6-16

The components of the resultant are obtained by calculating the algebraic sum of the components of each force. To save calculation space, it is convenient to calculate the components in the equations summing the components. Equations (6-1), (6-2), (6-3) and (6-5), (6-6) and (6-7) are combined to provide the necessary information.

$$R_x = \Sigma F_{x_i}$$

$$= F_1 \cos \theta_{x_1} + F_2 \cos \theta_{x_2}$$

$$= 40 \times \frac{3}{5.3852} + 60 \times \frac{2}{7.4833}$$

$$= 22.2833 + 16.0357$$

$$= 38.3190 \text{ kN}$$

$$R_y = \Sigma F_{y_i}$$

$$= F_1 \cos \theta_{y_1} + F_2 \cos \theta_{y_2}$$

$$= 40 \times \frac{-4}{5.3852} + 60 \times \frac{6}{7.4833}$$

$$= -29.7110 + 48.1071$$

$$= 18.3961 \text{ kN}$$

$$R_z = \Sigma F_{z_i}$$

$$= F_1 \cos \theta_{z_1} + F_2 \cos \theta_{z_2}$$

$$= 40 \times \frac{2}{5.3852} + 60 \times \frac{4}{7.4833}$$

$$= 14.8555 + 32.0714$$

$$= 46.9269 \text{ kN}$$

The magnitude of the resultant may now be calculated using the Pythagorean theorem for three dimensions, Eq. (6-10).

$$R = (R_x^2 + R_y^2 + R_z^2)^{1/2}$$

$$= (38.3190^2 + 18.3961^2 + 46.9269^2)^{1/2}$$

$$= (1468.346 + 338.416 + 2202.143)^{1/2}$$

$$= 4008.896^{1/2}$$

$$= 63.3159 \text{ kN}$$

The direction of the resultant is described by means of the direction cosines, as obtained from Eqs. (6-11), (6-12) *and* (6-13).

$$\cos \theta_x = \frac{R_x}{R}$$

$$= \frac{38.3190}{63.3159}$$

$$= 0.605\ 20$$

$$\cos \theta_y = \frac{R_y}{R}$$

$$= \frac{18.3961}{63.3159}$$

$$= 0.290\ 55$$

$$\cos \theta_z = \frac{R_z}{R}$$

$$= \frac{46.9269}{63.3159}$$

$$= 0.741\ 16$$

$$\boxed{\begin{aligned} R &= 63.3 \text{ kN} \\ \cos \theta_x &= 0.605 \\ \cos \theta_y &= 0.291 \\ \cos \theta_z &= 0.741 \end{aligned}}$$

EXAMPLE 6-8

For the two forces shown in Fig. 6-17, calculate the resultant.

SOLUTION

The first step will be to calculate the distances along two points on the vectors, which will be used in calculating the components of the vectors. Equation (6-4) is used for making this calculation. Note that for d_1, $d_{x_1} = x_A - x_C$; $d_{y_1} = y_A - y_C$; and $d_{z_1} = z_A - z_C$; and that for d_2, $d_{x_2} = x_B - x_C$; $d_{y_2} = y_B - y_C$; and $d_{z_2} = z_B - z_C$.

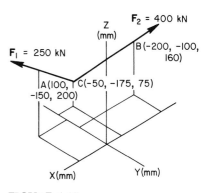

FIGURE 6-17

$$d_1 = \left[(x_A - x_C)^2 + (y_A - y_C)^2 + (z_A - z_C)^2\right]^{1/2}$$

$$= \left\{\left[100 - (-50)\right]^2 + \left[-150 - (-175)\right]^2 + (200 - 75)^2\right\}^{1/2}$$

$$= (150^2 + 25^2 + 125^2)^{1/2}$$

$$= (22\ 500 + 625 + 15\ 625)^{1/2}$$

$$= 38\ 750^{1/2}$$

$$= 196.850 \text{ mm}$$

$$d_2 = \left[(x_B - x_C)^2 + (y_B - y_C)^2 + (z_B - z_C)^2\right]^{1/2}$$

$$= \left\{\left[-200 - (-50)\right]^2 + \left[-100 - (-175)\right]^2 + (160 - 75)^2\right\}^{1/2}$$

$$= \left[(-150)^2 + 75^2 + 85^2\right]^{1/2}$$

$$= (22\ 500 + 5\ 625 + 7\ 225)^{1/2}$$

$$= 35\ 350^{1/2}$$

$$= 188.016 \text{ mm}$$

The components of the resultant may now be obtained by summing the components of each of the forces. The individual components are calculated using Eqs. (6-1), (6-2) and (6-3), and Eqs. (6-5), (6-6) and (6-7).

$$R_x = \Sigma F_{x_i}$$

$$= F_1 \cos \theta_{x_1} + F_2 \cos \theta_{x_2}$$

$$= 250 \times \frac{150}{196.850} + 400 \times \frac{-150}{188.016}$$

$$= 190.500 - 319.122$$

$$= -128.622 \text{ kN}$$

$$R_y = \Sigma F_{y_i}$$

$$= F_1 \cos \theta_{y_1} + F_2 \cos \theta_{y_2}$$

$$= 250 \times \frac{25}{196.850} + 400 \times \frac{75}{188.016}$$

$$= 31.750 + 159.561$$

$$= 191.311 \text{ kN}$$

$$R_z = \Sigma F_{z_i}$$

$$= F_1 \cos \theta_{z_1} + F_2 \cos \theta_{z_2}$$

$$= 250 \times \frac{125}{196.850} + 400 \times \frac{85}{188.016}$$

$$= 158.750 + 180.836$$

$$= 339.586 \text{ kN}$$

Now the magnitude of the resultant may be calculated by using Eq. (6-10).

$$R = (R_x^2 + R_y^2 + R_z^2)^{1/2}$$

$$= \left[(-128.622)^2 + 191.311^2 + 339.586^2\right]^{1/2}$$

$$= (16\ 543.4 + 36\ 599.9 + 115\ 318.7)^{1/2}$$

$$= 168\ 462.0^{1/2}$$

$$= 410.441 \text{ kN}$$

To describe the direction of the resultant, the direction cosines are obtained, using Eqs. (6-11), (6-12) and (6-13).

$$\cos \theta_x = \frac{R_x}{R}$$

$$= \frac{-128.622}{410.441}$$

$$= -0.313\ 375$$

$$\cos \theta_y = \frac{R_y}{R}$$

$$= \frac{191.311}{410.441}$$

$$= 0.466\ 111$$

$$\cos \theta_z = \frac{R_z}{R}$$

$$= \frac{339.586}{410.441}$$

$$= 0.827\ 369$$

> R = 410 kN
> $\cos \theta_x = -0.313$
> $\cos \theta_y = 0.466$
> $\cos \theta_z = 0.827$

EXAMPLE 6-9

Guys from two towers have been led to a common anchor, as shown in Fig. 6-18. Determine the total vertical force on the anchor, as well as the total horizontal force acting on the anchor.

SOLUTION

The diagonal distance, determined from the slope of each of the forces, must first be calculated, using Eq. (6-4), *since the diagonal distance is necessary in order to calculate the direction cosines.*

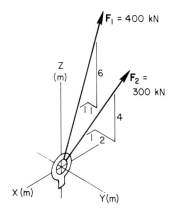

FIGURE 6-18

$$d_1 = (d_{x_1}^2 + d_{y_1}^2 + d_{z_1}^2)^{1/2}$$

$$= \left[(-1)^2 + 1^2 + 6^2\right]^{1/2}$$

$$= (1 + 1 + 36)^{1/2}$$

$$= 38^{1/2}$$

$$= 6.1644 \text{ m}$$

$$d_2 = (d_{x_2}^2 + d_{y_2}^2 + d_{z_2}^2)^{1/2}$$

$$= \left[(-1)^2 + 2^2 + 4^2\right]^{1/2}$$

$$= (1 + 4 + 16)^{1/2}$$

$$= 21^{1/2}$$

$$= 4.5826 \text{ m}$$

The total vertical force will be the sum of the z components of the two forces. This may be obtained by using Eqs. (6-3) and (6-7).

$$R_V = \Sigma F_{z_i}$$

$$= F_1 \cos \theta_{z_1} + F_2 \cos \theta_{z_2}$$

$$= 400 \times \frac{6}{6.1644} + 300 \times \frac{4}{4.5826}$$

$$= 389.332 + 261.860$$

$$= 651.192 \text{ kN}$$

The total horizontal force acting on the anchor will be the resultant of R_x and R_y. R_x and R_y may be obtained from Eqs. (6-1), (6-2), (6-5) and (6-6).

$$R_x = \Sigma F_{x_i}$$

$$= F_1 \cos \theta_{x_1} + F_2 \cos \theta_{x_2}$$

$$= 400 \times \frac{-1}{6.1644} + 300 \times \frac{-1}{4.5826}$$

$$= -64.8887 - 65.4650$$

$$= -130.3537 \text{ kN}$$

$$R_y = \Sigma F_{y_i}$$

$$= F_1 \cos \theta_{y_1} + F_2 \cos \theta_{y_2}$$

$$= 400 \times \frac{1}{6.1644} + 300 \times \frac{2}{4.5826}$$

$$= 64.8887 + 130.9300$$

$$= 195.8187 \text{ kN}$$

The direction in the x-y plane may be obtained from Fig. 6-19 *and* Eq. (3-3).

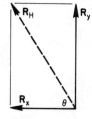

FIGURE 6-19

$$\theta = \tan^{-1} \frac{R_y}{R_x}$$

$$= \tan^{-1} \frac{195.8187}{130.3537}$$

$$= 56.35°$$

Direction of $R_H = 180.00° - 56.35°$

$$= 123.65°$$

The magnitude of the total horizontal force may be calculated from Eq. (3-4).

$$R_H = \frac{R_y}{\sin \theta}$$

$$= \frac{195.8187}{\sin 56.35°}$$

$$= 235.235 \text{ kN}$$

$$R_V = 651 \text{ kN}$$
$$\vec{R}_H = 235 \text{ kN at } 123.65°$$

PROBLEMS

6-29 For the force system shown in Fig. P6-29, determine the resultant.

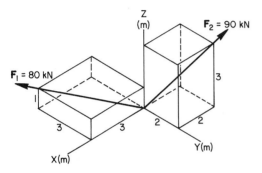

FIGURE P6-29

6-30 For the system of forces shown in Fig. P6-30, calculate the resultant.

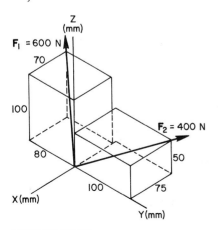

FIGURE P6-30

6-31 Determine the resultant of the forces shown in Fig. P6-31.

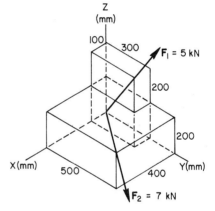

FIGURE P6-31

6-32 Find the resultant of the forces shown in Fig. P6-32

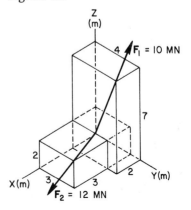

FIGURE P6-32

6-33 For the force system shown in Fig. P6-33, determine the resultant.

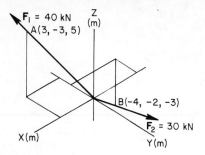

FIGURE P6-33

6-34 Calculate the resultant of the two forces shown in Fig. P6-34

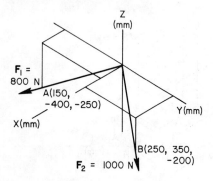

FIGURE P6-34

6-35 Calculate the resultant of the system of forces shown in Fig. P6-35.

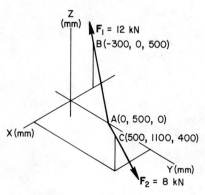

FIGURE P6-35

6-36 For the forces shown in Fig. P6-36, determine the resultant.

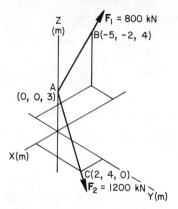

FIGURE P6-36

6-37 Determine the resultant of the three forces shown in Fig. P6-37.

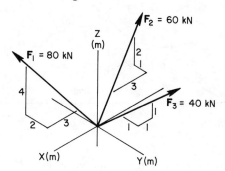

FIGURE P6-37

6-38 For the system of forces shown in Fig. P6-38, determine the resultant.

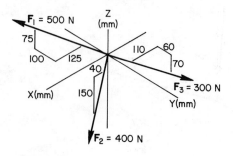

FIGURE P6-38

6-39 For the gin pole shown in Fig. P6-39, determine the resultant of the 50 kN load, **P**, and the tension in the two guys, *AB* and *AC*, if the tension in each guy is 35 kN.

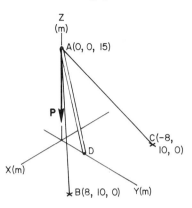

FIGURE P6-39

6-40 Three cables, as shown in Fig. P6-40, support a load, **P**. If the tension in cable *AD* is 700 kN, in *BD* is 700 kN, and in *CD* is 900 kN, determine the resultant of the tensions in the three cables.

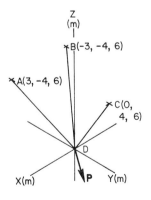

FIGURE P6-40

6-41 An anchor bolt for two tie-bars is located in a wall in the *x-z* plane at *A*, as shown in Fig. P6-41. If the tension in tie *AB* is 75 kN and the tension in tie *AC* is 40 kN, determine the tension on the bolt (the total force in the *y* direction) and the magnitude of the shear on the bolt (the total force in the *x-z* plane).

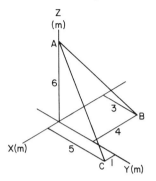

FIGURE P6-41

6-42 Two support brackets are welded to a common point, *A*, as shown in Fig. P6-42. If the force in *AB* is 800 N compression, and if the force in *AC* is 1500 N tension, determine the magnitude of the total shear force on the weld at *A* (that is, the total force in the *x-y* plane).

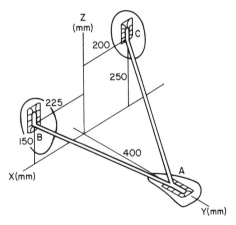

FIGURE P6-42

6-5 RESULTANT OF A PARALLEL FORCE SYSTEM

One of the most common force systems is the parallel force system. It is most often encountered when dealing with forces caused by gravity, such as vehicle loads on a bridge or building footings on soil. One parallel force system is shown in Fig. 6-20(a), and the same system, along with its resultant, is shown in Fig. 6-20(b).

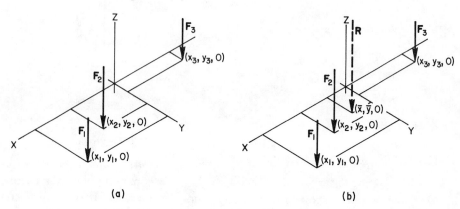

(a)   (b)

FIGURE 6-20

A resultant was defined as the simplest force system that will replace the original force system. The information on the resultant must include its magnitude, direction and point of application, for the resultant must cause the same tendency for both translation and rotation as does the original force system.

The magnitude and direction of the resultant may be obtained from

$$R = \Sigma F_i \qquad (3\text{-}5)$$

where R is the magitude of the resultant, and
ΣF_i is the algebraic sum of the magnitudes of each individual force.

Since all the forces are parallel, the correct sign for the resultant will be obtained by the use of the usual sign convention for each of the forces.

Perhaps the easiest method for determining the x coordinate of the location of the resultant is to view the system along the y axis, as shown in Fig. 6-21. The resultant, **R**, must cause the same moment about any axis as the original force system. Generally, the reference axis chosen is the y axis, since it is usually the most convenient.

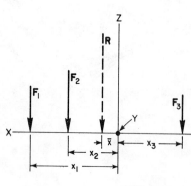

FIGURE 6-21

M_y:

$$R\bar{x} = F_1x_1 + F_2x_2 + F_3x_3 + \ldots$$

$$R\bar{x} = \Sigma \ (F_ix_i) \qquad\qquad (3\text{-}6)$$

$$\bar{x} = \frac{\Sigma \ (F_ix_i)}{R}$$

but $R = \Sigma \ F_i$

thus $\bar{x} = \dfrac{\Sigma \ (F_ix_i)}{\Sigma \ F_i} \qquad\qquad (3\text{-}7)$

where $\bar{x}$ is the perpendicular distance from the reference axis to the resultant,

$\Sigma \ (F_ix_i)$ is the algebraic sum of the moments of each of the original forces about the reference axis, and

$\Sigma \ F_i$ is the algebraic sum of the original system of forces.

For Eq. (3-7) to be used, the usual rules regarding signs for moments must be observed.

In a similar fashion, it may be shown that the value for the y coordinate of the location of the resultant may be obtained from

$$R\bar{y} = \Sigma \ (F_iy_i) \qquad\qquad (6\text{-}14)$$

and that

$$\bar{y} = \frac{\Sigma \ (F_iy_i)}{\Sigma \ F_i} \qquad\qquad (6\text{-}15)$$

where $\bar{y}$ is the perpendicular distance from the reference axis to the resultant,

$\Sigma \ (F_iy_i)$ is the algebraic sum of the moments of each of the original forces about the reference axis, and

$\Sigma \ F_i$ is the algebraic sum of the original system of forces.

When using Eqs. (3-6), (3-7), (6-14) and (6-15), the sign of the moment in each term must be carefully observed. To solve the equations, assume that the resultant is located so that both the x and y coordinates have positive values. The sign obtained in the solution will then be the correct sign for the coordinate.

EXAMPLE 6-10

Find the resultant of the system of three forces shown in Fig. 6-22.

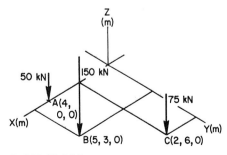

FIGURE 6-22

SOLUTION

The magnitude of the resultant can be quickly obtained by using Eq. (3-5) *to sum the forces.*

$$R = \Sigma F_i$$
$$= -50 - 150 - 75$$
$$= -275 \text{ kN}$$

The negative sign indicates that the resultant points down.

   To obtain the location of the resultant, moments are first taken about the y axis to find $\bar{x}$, as indicated in Eq. (3-6). *Figure 6-23 will be of help in determining the signs of the moments, particularly that of the resultant.*

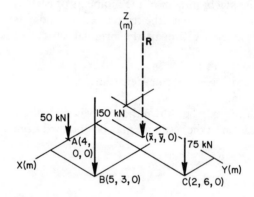

FIGURE 6-23

$$M_y:$$
$$R\bar{x} = \Sigma (F_i x_i)$$
$$275 \times \bar{x} = 50 \times 4 + 150 \times 5 + 75 \times 2$$
$$= 200 + 750 + 150$$
$$= 1100$$
$$\bar{x} = \frac{1100}{275}$$
$$= 4.0000 \text{ m}$$

The value for $\bar{y}$ may be obtained by using Eq. (6-14). *Note that, according to the right-hand rule, the moments about the x axis of each force in the system will be negative.*

$$M_x:$$
$$R\bar{y} = \Sigma (F_i y_i)$$

$$-(275 \times \bar{y}) = 50 \times 0 - 150 \times 3 - 75 \times 6$$
$$= 0 - 450 - 450$$
$$= -900$$

$$\bar{y} = \frac{900}{275}$$
$$= 3.2727 \text{ m}$$

The positive values for both $\bar{x}$ and $\bar{y}$ confirm that their coordinate values are positive, as assumed in Fig. 6-23.

$$\bar{R} = 275 \text{ kN down,}$$
$$\text{at } (4.00, 3.27, 0.00)$$

EXAMPLE 6-11

For the system of forces shown in Fig. 6-24, determine the resultant.

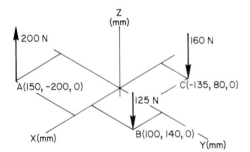

FIGURE 6-24

SOLUTION

The first step is to determine the magnitude and direction of the resultant by summing forces, using Eq. (3-5).

$$R = \Sigma F_i$$
$$= 200 - 125 - 160$$
$$= -85.00 \text{ N}$$

The negative sign indicates that the resultant points down.

To determine the location of the resultant, moments are first taken about the y axis to find $\bar{x}$. Equation (3-6) is used. The assumed location of the resultant is shown in Fig. 6-25, *as an aid to obtaining the correct signs in the equations.*

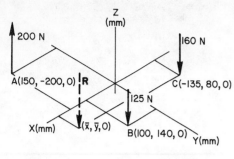

FIGURE 6-25

M_y:

$$R\bar{x} = \Sigma\,(F_i x_i)$$

$$85.00 \times \bar{x} = -(200 \times 150) + 125 \times 100 - 160 \times 135$$

$$= -30\,000 + 12\,500 - 21\,600$$

$$= -39\,100$$

$$\bar{x} = \frac{-39\,100}{85.00}$$

$$= -460.00 \text{ mm}$$

The negative sign indicates that the x coordinate of the resultant is negative and not positive as assumed.

Moments may now be taken about the x axis, using Eq. (6-14), to find $\bar{y}$.

M_x:

$$R\bar{y} = \Sigma\,(F_i y_i)$$

$$-(85.00 \times \bar{y}) = -(200 \times 200) - 125 \times 140 - 160 \times 80$$

$$= -40\,000 - 17\,500 - 12\,800$$

$$= -70\,300$$

$$\bar{y} = \frac{-70\,300}{-85.00}$$

$$= 827.06 \text{ mm}$$

The positive sign for $\bar{y}$ indicates that the resultant is on the positive end of the y axis, as assumed.

$$\boxed{\begin{array}{c} \vec{R} = 85.0 \text{ N down,} \\ \text{at } (-460, 827, 0.00) \end{array}}$$

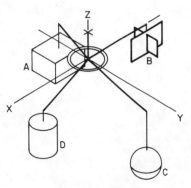

FIGURE 6-26

EXAMPLE 6-12

A large, decorative mobile designed to hang in the lobby of a hotel is shown in Fig. 6-26. Determine the x and y coordinates for the location of the 80 kg part D if the masses and locations of the other parts are A: 60 kg at $(-1, -3, -2)$; B: 45 kg at $(-4, 0, -1)$ and C: 75 kg at $(1, 5, -3)$. For the mobile to hang properly, the resultant of the four gravitational forces must pass through the origin.

SOLUTION

The lines of action of all gravitational forces will be parallel and will pass through the x-y plane, so the z coordinates of the center of gravity will not affect the calculations. The problem solution may be somewhat easier to set up if the gravitional forces and their locations are shown in a sketch, as shown in Fig. 6-27.

It is known that both the x and y coordinates of the location of the resultant must be zero; that is, $\bar{x} = 0$ and $\bar{y} = 0$. If moments are taken about the y axis, the moment of the resultant about the y axis must equal the moment of the original force system about the y axis. This will give an equation with one unknown term in it, the unknown term being x, which is the x coordinate of the gravitational attraction on D. The sign for each term in the equation is obtained by use of the right-hand rule.

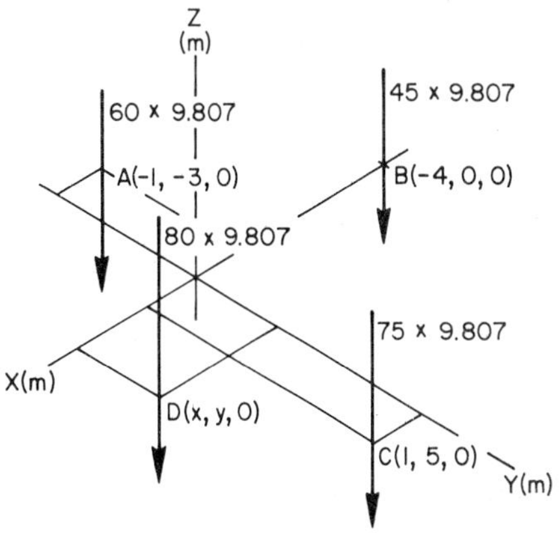

FIGURE 6-27

M_y:

$$R\bar{x} = \Sigma (F_i x_i)$$

$$0 = -(60 \times 9.807 \times 1) - 45 \times 9.807 \times 4$$
$$+ 75 \times 9.807 \times 1 + 80 \times 9.807 \times x$$

$$0 = -60.00 - 180.00 + 75.00 + 80.00 x$$

$$x = \frac{60.00 + 180.00 - 75.00}{80.00}$$

$$= \frac{165.00}{80.00}$$

$$= 2.0625 \text{ m}$$

In a similar fashion, moments may be taken about the x axis to obtain the y coordinate for the location of D.

M_x:

$$R\bar{y} = \Sigma (F_i y_i)$$

$$0 = 60 \times 9.807 \times 3 + 45 \times 9.807 \times 0$$
$$- 75 \times 9.807 \times 5 - 80 \times 9.807 \times y$$

$$0 = 180.00 + 0 - 375.00 - 80.00 y$$

$$y = \frac{180.00 - 375.00}{80.00}$$

$$= \frac{-195.00}{80.00}$$

$$= -2.4375 \text{ m}$$

The negative sign indicates that the y coordinate should actually have a negative value, rather than the positive value assumed when drawing Fig. 6-27.

Since the z coordinate is not of importance, the final answer shows it simply as z.

D: (2.06, −2.44, z)

PROBLEMS

6-43 For the system of two forces shown in Fig. P6-43, find the resultant.

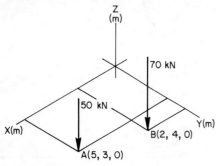

FIGURE P6-43

6-44 Determine the resultant of the two forces shown in Fig. P6-44.

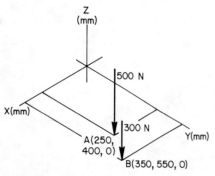

FIGURE P6-44

6-45 Find the resultant of the system of three forces shown in Fig. P6-45.

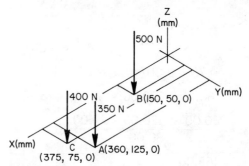

FIGURE P6-45

6-46 For the system of forces shown in Fig. P6-46, determine the resultant.

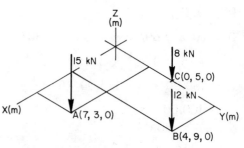

FIGURE P6-46

6-47 For the system of forces shown in Fig. P6-47, find the resultant.

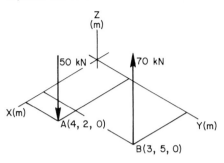

FIGURE P6-47

6-48 Calculate the resultant for the system of forces shown in Fig. P6-48.

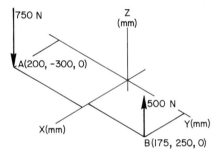

FIGURE P6-48

6-49 Find the resultant for the system of forces shown in Fig. P6-49.

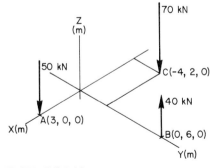

FIGURE P6-49

6-50 Determine the resultant of the system of forces shown in Fig. P6-50.

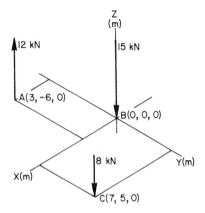

FIGURE P6-50

6-51 Figure P6-51 shows the arrangement of some heavy equipment in the hold of an aircraft. Determine where load D should be placed so that the resultant load passes through the origin.

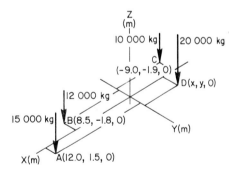

FIGURE P6-51

6-52 Figure P6-52 represents pieces of heavy construction equipment loaded on a barge. If the barge is to float level, the resultant of the four loads must pass through the origin. Determine where load D should be located.

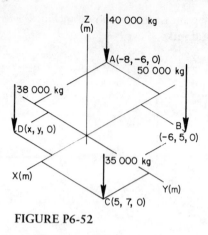

FIGURE P6-52

6-6 EQUILIBRIUM IN THREE DIMENSIONS

The concept of Newton's first law and equilibrium was first introduced in Chap. 4. According to Newton's first law, a body will remain at rest, or will continue in motion in a straight line at constant speed, so long as no net force acts on the body. Thus, for a body to be in equilibrium, the following two conditions must be satisfied:

$$\Sigma \mathbf{F} = 0 \qquad (4\text{-}1)$$

$$\Sigma \mathbf{M} = 0 \qquad (4\text{-}2)$$

These two vector equations state that the sum of all the forces acting *on* a body in equilibrium must be zero, and that the sum of all the moments about any axis acting *on* the body must also be zero. It was found more convenient to express Eqs. (4-1) and (4-2) in terms of the components in the x, y and z directions.

$$\Sigma F_x = 0 \qquad (4\text{-}3)$$

$$\Sigma F_y = 0 \qquad (4\text{-}4)$$

$$\Sigma F_z = 0 \qquad (4\text{-}5)$$

$$\Sigma M_x = 0 \qquad (4\text{-}6)$$

$$\Sigma M_y = 0 \qquad (4\text{-}7)$$

$$\Sigma M_z = 0 \qquad (4\text{-}8)$$

In the case of the plane or two-dimensional force system, as discussed in Chaps. 4 and 5, only Eqs. (4-3), (4-4) and (4-8) were used. However, for a force system in space or a three-dimensional force system, it may be necessary to use all six equations to solve for up to six unknown terms in a three-dimensional system. In most cases, the unknown terms will be components of forces, although they could be moments or couples.

The procedure for solving three-dimensional equilibrium problems is very much like the procedure outlined for frame and machine problems in Chap. 5.

1. Draw a free-body diagram of the object to be analyzed. In some problems it is a temptation to overlook this step. However, the free-body diagram helps to clarify the information that is known and to point out what is required. As a minimum, it will help to assure consistency on the assumption of directions of any unknown forces.

2. Think. Many problems can be solved correctly in more than one way. However, some correct solutions take much longer than others. Before writing any equations, decide which equations will provide the easiest solution. Most people would prefer to set up and solve six equations, with one unknown term each, than to solve a system of six equations with six unknown terms.

3. Write the required equilibrium equations.

4. Solve the equations.

5. Check the solution.

A few examples illustrate three different types of three-dimensional force systems: concurrent, parallel and the general non-concurrent, non-parallel system.

6-7 EQUILIBRIUM FOR THREE-DIMENSIONAL CONCURRENT FORCE SYSTEMS

In a concurrent force system the lines of action of all forces pass through one common point. If moments are taken about an axis passing through the point of concurrency, the moment equation would give $0 = 0$, which is not very useful. Generally, there are only three useful equilibrium equations, Eqs. (4-3), (4-4) and (4-5), which would indicate that the maximum number of unknown terms that can be determined is three. It is often necessary to set up a system of three equations, each with three unknown terms, and these equations must then be solved simultaneously.

In spite of the earlier statement about using moment equations to solve equilibrium problems for a concurrent force system, there are some cases where you can draw a convenient axis that passes through the line of action of only two of the unknown forces; moments can be taken about this axis. This would give an equation with only one unknown term. Example 6-13 illustrates the process. Note that even though a moment equation may be used for solving an equilibrium problem for a three-dimensional concurrent force system, the maximum number of unknown terms that may be obtained is still limited to three, since only three *independent* equations can be written.

EXAMPLE 6-13

The gin pole *AB*, in Fig. 6-28, will fail if the compressive force in it exceeds 70 kN. Determine the magnitude of the maximum vertical load, **P**, which may be supported.

SOLUTION

For the structure shown in Fig. 6-28, *the y-z plane is a plane of symmetry. Both* **P** *and* F_{AB} *are contained in the y-z plane. A free-body diagram is shown of the side view of the structure in* Fig. 6-29. *(This is a view obtained by looking along the x axis.) The perpendicular distance from the line CD to* **P** *and the y and z components of* F_{AB} *can be readily obtained from* Fig. 6-29. *If moments are taken about an axis through CD, neither* F_{BC} *or* F_{BD} *will have a moment about the axis CD.*

To determine the components of F_{AB}, *the length of AB should be determined.*

$$
\begin{aligned}
d_{AB} &= \left[(-5)^2 + 12^2 \right]^{1/2} \\
&= (25 + 144)^{1/2} \\
&= 169^{1/2} \\
&= 13.00 \text{ m}
\end{aligned}
$$

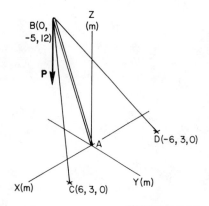

FIGURE 6-28

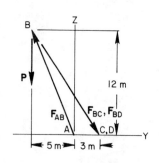

FIGURE 6-29

Since the maximum value of P is to be obtained, the maximum force in AB of 70 kN will be assumed to exist in AB. Moments may be taken about an axis through CD to find P.

Note that if the components of F_{AB} *are placed at A, only the z component will have a moment about CD. However, if the components are placed at B, both the y and z components will have moments about CD.*

$$
\Sigma M_{CD} = 0
$$

$$P \times 8 - \frac{12}{13} \times 70 \times 3 = 0$$

$$P = \frac{12 \times 70 \times 3}{13 \times 8}$$

$$= 24.231 \text{ kN}$$

$$\boxed{P = 24.2 \text{ kN}}$$

EXAMPLE 6-14

A 5000 kg mass is suspended by three cables, as shown in Fig. 6-30. Determine the tension in each cable.

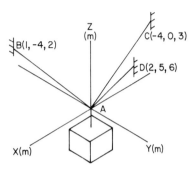

FIGURE 6-30

SOLUTION

The point where all the cables meet, point A, is the logical body to use for a free-body diagram, since it is the point of concurrency of all forces. The free-body diagram is shown in Fig. 6-31. *In this problem there does not appear to be any convenient axis that could be chosen for taking moments, so it will be necessary to use the equilibrium equations for forces. To write the equations, the lengths of the cables must be determined so that the x, y and z components of the forces in each cable may be found.*

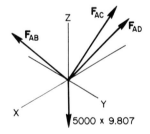

FIGURE 6-31

$$d_{AB} = \left[1^2 + (-4)^2 + 2^2\right]^{\frac{1}{2}}$$

$$= (1 + 16 + 4)^{\frac{1}{2}}$$

$$= 21^{\frac{1}{2}}$$

$$= 4.5826 \text{ m}$$

$$d_{AC} = \left[(-4)^2 + 3^2\right]^{\frac{1}{2}}$$

$$= (16 + 9)^{\frac{1}{2}}$$

$$= 25^{\frac{1}{2}}$$

$$= 5.0000 \text{ m}$$

$$d_{AD} = (2^2 + 5^2 + 6^2)^{\frac{1}{2}}$$

$$= (4 + 25 + 36)^{\frac{1}{2}}$$

$$= 65^{\frac{1}{2}}$$

$$= 8.0623 \text{ m}$$

Because F_{AC} lies in the x-z plane, it will have no y component. Thus, if forces are summed in the y direction, one equation relating F_{AB} and F_{AD} can be obtained.

$$\Sigma \, F_y = 0$$

$$\frac{-4}{4.5826} \, F_{AB} + \frac{5}{8.0623} \, F_{AD} = 0$$

$$F_{AB} = \frac{4.5826}{4} \times \frac{5}{8.0623} \, F_{AD}$$

$$F_{AB} = 0.710 \, 50 \, F_{AD} \qquad\qquad \text{Eq. (a)}$$

If forces are summed in the x direction, the values for F_{AB}, F_{AC} and F_{AD} can be related.

$$\Sigma \, F_x = 0$$

$$\frac{1}{4.5826} \, F_{AB} - \frac{4}{5} \, F_{AC} + \frac{2}{8.0623} \, F_{AD} = 0 \qquad \text{Eq. (b)}$$

Substitute Eq. (a) in Eq. (b):

$$\frac{1}{4.5826} \Big(0.710 \, 50 \, F_{AD} \Big) - \frac{4}{5} F_{AC} + \frac{2}{8.0623} F_{AD} = 0$$

$$0.155 \, 04 \, F_{AD} - 0.800 \, 00 \, F_{AC} + 0.248 \, 07 \, F_{AD} = 0$$

$$0.403 \, 11 \, F_{AD} - 0.800 \, 00 \, F_{AC} = 0$$

$$F_{AC} = \frac{0.403 \, 11}{0.800 \, 00} \, F_{AD}$$

$$F_{AC} = 0.503 \, 89 \, F_{AD} \qquad\qquad \text{Eq. (c)}$$

If forces are now summed in the z direction, Eqs. (a) and (c) may be substituted into the resulting equation to solve the problem.

$$\Sigma \, F_z = 0$$

$$\frac{2}{4.5826} \, F_{AB} + \frac{3}{5} \, F_{AC} + \frac{6}{8.0623} F_{AD} - 5000 \times 9.807 = 0$$
$$\text{Eq. (d)}$$

Substitute Eq. (a) and Eq. (c) in Eq. (d):

$$\frac{2}{4.5826} \Big(0.710 \, 50 \, F_{AD} \Big) + \frac{3}{5} \Big(0.503 \, 89 \, F_{AD} \Big) + \frac{6}{8.0623} \, F_{AD}$$

$$- 5000 \times 9.807 = 0$$

$$0.310 \, 09 \, F_{AD} + 0.302 \, 33 \, F_{AD} + 0.744 \, 21 \, F_{AD} = 49 \, 035$$

$$1.356 \, 63 \, F_{AD} = 49 \, 035$$

$$F_{AD} = \frac{49 \, 035}{1.356 \, 63}$$

$$= 36 \, 145 \text{ N}$$

From Eq. (a)

F_{AB} = 0.710 50 F_{AD}

    = 0.710 50 × 36 145

    = 25 681 N

From Eq. (c)

F_{AC} = 0.503 89 F_{AD}

    = 0.503 89 × 36 145

    = 18 213 N

$$
\boxed{
\begin{array}{l}
F_{AB} = 25.7 \text{ kN} \\
F_{AC} = 18.2 \text{ kN} \\
F_{AD} = 36.1 \text{ kN}
\end{array}
}
$$

PROBLEMS

6-53 Determine the force in the mast *AB* shown in Fig. P6-53.

6-54 Calculate the compressive force in member *CD* of the system shown in Fig. P6-54.

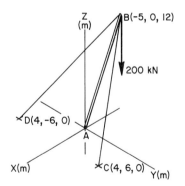

FIGURE P6-53

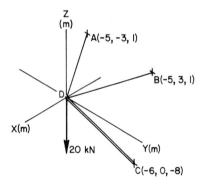

FIGURE P6-54

6-55 For the boom shown in Fig. P6-55, determine the tension in cables *AC* and *AD* and the force in boom *AB*.

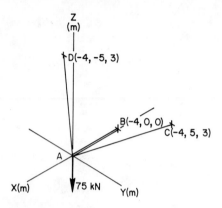

FIGURE P6-55

6-56 Determine the force in the gin pole *AB* and in the cables *BC* and *BD* shown in Fig. P6-56.

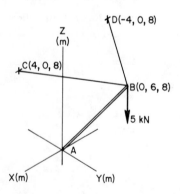

FIGURE P6-56

6-57 The cable *AD* shown in Fig. P6-57 will fail if the tension in it exceeds 1500 N. Determine the maximum possible magnitude of the vertical load **P** that may be supported by the system shown.

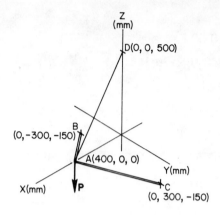

FIGURE P6-57

6-58 The strut *CD*, shown in Fig. P6-58, will fail if the force in it exceeds 20 kN. Find the maximum magnitude of the vertical force **P** that may be carried without causing failure of *CD*.

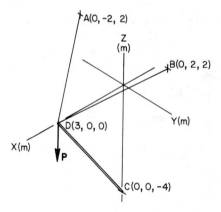

FIGURE P6-58

6-59 Determine the force in each member of the structure shown in Fig. P6-59. The 1500 N force is parallel to the *x* axis.

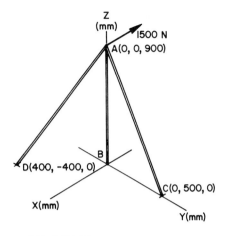

FIGURE P6-59

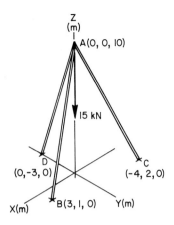

FIGURE P6-61

6-60 Find the tension in each of the three cables that support the 25 kN force shown in Fig. P6-60.

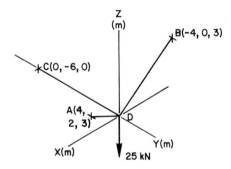

FIGURE P6-60

6-61 For the diamond-drill tripod shown in Fig. P6-61, which supports a vertical load caused by the drill rod, determine the force in each leg.

6-62 If the 3 MN force applied to the strut shown in Fig. P6-62 is parallel to the y axis, determine the force in the strut AD and in the cables AB and AC.

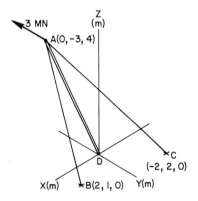

FIGURE P6-62

6-63 If the maximum load (tension or compression) that may be carried by any member in the system shown in Fig. P6-63 is 12 kN, determine the maximum allowable value for **P**.

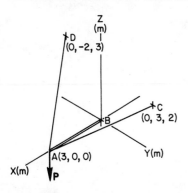

FIGURE P6-63

6-64 Find the maximum value for **P** if the maximum force that can be supported by any leg of the tripod shown in Fig. P6-64 is 4000 N.

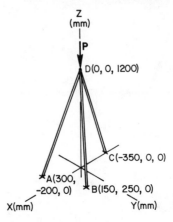

FIGURE P6-64

6-8 EQUILIBRIUM FOR THREE-DIMENSIONAL PARALLEL FORCE SYSTEMS

If all forces in a system are parallel, it will be possible to find a maximum of three unknown terms, since there will be only three independent equilibrium equations available. It is possible to sum forces in the direction of the parallel forces in the system and to take moments about two axes perpendicular to the parallel force system.

Generally, when determining unknown forces in a parallel force system, one looks for a convenient axis of rotation through which two unknown forces pass. If such an axis is located, then an equation can be written containing only one unknown term. By careful selection of axes, a second equation can be found so that a second force can be calculated and, finally, forces may be summed in the direction parallel to the force system to find the third force.

If no convenient axis can be found, and an equation with only one unknown term can not be written, then it will be necessary to write the three equilibrium equations and solve them simultaneously for the unknown terms.

Examples 6-15 and 6-16 illustrate the procedure for solving equilibrium problems involving parallel force systems.

EXAMPLE 6-15

The plate shown in Fig. 6-32 has a mass of 72 000 kg and is suspended by vertical cables at A, B and E. Determine the tension in each of the three cables. The force due to the mass of the plate acts at the center of the plate.

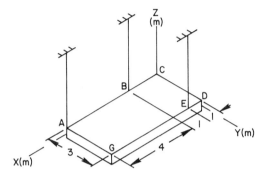

FIGURE 6-32

SOLUTION

If the plate is viewed from along the x axis, F_A and F_B would both appear to be along the same line. A free-body diagram is drawn showing an edge view of the plate as viewed from along the x axis, as in Fig. 6-33. If moments are taken about the x axis, an equation would be obtained with only one unknown term.

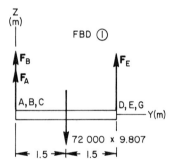

FIGURE 6-33

From FBD 1:

$$\Sigma M_x = 0$$

$$-(72\ 000 \times 9.807 \times 1.5) + F_E \times 3 = 0$$

$$F_E = \frac{72\ 000 \times 9.807 \times 1.5}{3}$$

$$= 353\ 052\ N$$

Now if the plate is viewed from along the y axis, a different free-body diagram can be drawn, as shown in Fig. 6-34. If moments are taken about axis AG, there would be only one unknown term in the equation, since the value for F_E has already been found.

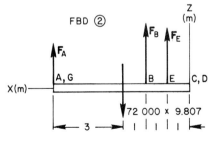

FIGURE 6-34

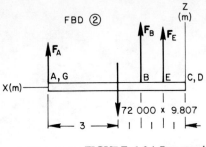

FBD ②

FIGURE 6-34 *Repeated*

From FBD 2:

$$\Sigma M_{AG} = 0$$

$$-(72\ 000 \times 9.807 \times 3) + F_B \times 4 + 353\ 052 \times 5 = 0$$

$$F_B = \frac{2\ 118\ 312 - 1\ 765\ 260}{4}$$

$$= \frac{353\ 052}{4}$$

$$= 88\ 263\ \text{N}$$

The remaining unknown force, in the cable at A, may now be determined by summing forces in the z direction.

From FBD 2:

$$\Sigma F_z = 0$$

$$F_A + 88\ 263 + 353\ 052 - 72\ 000 \times 9.807 = 0$$

$$F_A = 706\ 104 - 88\ 263 - 353\ 052$$

$$= 264\ 789\ \text{N}$$

$$\boxed{\begin{aligned} F_A &= 265\ \text{kN} \\ F_B &= 88.3\ \text{kN} \\ F_E &= 353\ \text{kN} \end{aligned}}$$

EXAMPLE 6-16

The two forces shown in Fig. 6-35 act on a plate supported at points *C*, *E* and *H*. If the mass of the plate is 30 kg, determine the reactions at each of the three supports. The force due to the mass of the plate acts at the center of the plate.

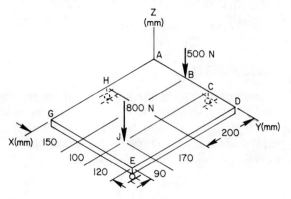

FIGURE 6-35

SOLUTION

There does not appear to be any convenient axis that passes through two of the supports about which moments could be taken. If moments are taken about an axis DE, an equation would be obtained with the unknown terms R_C and R_H. Similarly, if moments are taken about an axis EG, an equation with unknown terms R_C and R_H would be obtained. These two equations with the same two unknown terms can be solved for R_C and R_H.

A free-body diagram, as shown in Fig. 6-36, obtained by looking along the x axis, would help in writing the moment equation for moments about axis DE.

From FBD 1:

$$\Sigma\, M_{DE} = 0$$

$$500 \times 220 + 30 \times 9.807 \times 185 + 800 \times 120$$
$$- R_H \times 370 - R_C \times 120 = 0$$
$$110\,000 + 54\,429 + 96\,000 - 370\,R_H - 120\,R_C = 0$$
$$260\,429 - 370\,R_H - 120\,R_C = 0 \qquad \text{Eq. (a)}$$

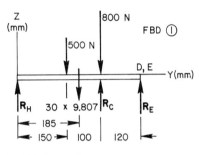

FIGURE 6-36

To write the moment equation about an axis through EG, a free-body diagram drawn by looking along the y axis, as shown in Fig. 6-37, will be helpful.

From FBD 2:

$$\Sigma\, M_{EG} = 0$$

$$-(800 \times 90) - 30 \times 9.807 \times 230 - 500 \times 460$$
$$+ R_H \times 260 + R_C \times 460 = 0$$
$$-72\,000 - 67\,668 - 230\,000 + 260\,R_H$$
$$+ 460\,R_C = 0$$
$$-369\,668 + 260\,R_H + 460\,R_C = 0 \qquad \text{Eq. (b)}$$

It is now necessary to solve Eqs. (a) and (b) simultaneously.

Dividing Eq. (a) by 370:

$$\frac{260\,429}{370} - \frac{370}{370}\,R_H - \frac{120}{370}\,R_C = 0$$

$$703.86 - R_H - 0.324\,32\,R_C = 0 \qquad \text{Eq. (c)}$$

Dividing Eq. (b) by 260:

$$\frac{-369\,668}{260} + \frac{260}{260}\,R_H + \frac{460}{260}\,R_C = 0$$

$$-1421.80 + R_H + 1.769\,23\,R_C = 0 \qquad \text{Eq. (d)}$$

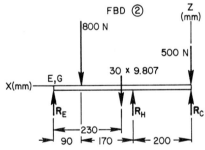

FIGURE 6-37

Adding Eq. (c) and Eq. (d):

$$703.86 - R_H - 0.324\ 32\ R_C = 0$$

$$\underline{-1421.80 + R_H + 1.769\ 23\ R_C = 0}$$

$$-717.94 \qquad + 1.444\ 91\ R_C = 0$$

$$R_C = \frac{717.94}{1.444\ 91}$$

$$= 496.88\ N$$

Substituting in Eq. (c):

$$703.86 - R_H - 0.324\ 32 \times 496.88 = 0$$

$$R_H = 703.86 - 161.15$$

$$= 542.71\ N$$

It is now possible to find R_E by summing forces in the z direction. Free-body diagram (1) or (2) may be used.

From FBD 1:

$$\Sigma\ F_z = 0$$

$$-500 - 30 \times 9.807 - 800 + 542.71 + 496.88$$
$$+ R_E = 0$$

$$R_E = 500 + 294.21 + 800 - 542.71 - 496.88$$

$$= 554.62\ N$$

$$\boxed{\begin{aligned} R_C &= 497\ N \\ R_E &= 555\ N \\ R_H &= 543\ N \end{aligned}}$$

PROBLEMS

6-65 Determine the tension in each of the three cables supporting the plate shown in Fig. P6-65. The mass of the plate may be neglected.

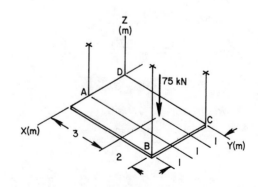

FIGURE P6-65

6-66 Find the vertical reactions at supports *B, D* and *E* for the plate shown in Fig. P6-66. The mass of the plate may be neglected.

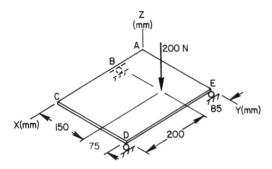

FIGURE P6-66

6-67 The 200 kg uniform plate is suspended by three cables, as shown in Fig. P6-67. Determine the tension in each cable if the mass of the plate may be assumed to act at the center of the plate.

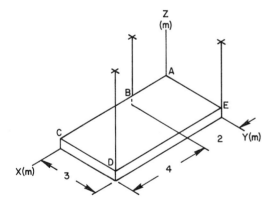

FIGURE P6-67

6-68 A triangle-shaped platform with a mass of 1200 kg is suspended by three cables as shown in Fig. P6-68. Determine the tension in each cable if the mass of the platform acts at (1.33, 1.00, 0.00).

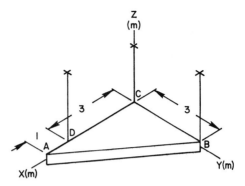

FIGURE P6-68

6-69 For the plate shown in Fig. P6-69, with supports at *A, B* and *D*, calculate the vertical reactions at the supports caused by the two loads.

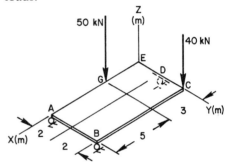

FIGURE P6-69

6-70 The plate shown in Fig. P6-70 is supported by three supports at *A, C* and *E*. Determine the reaction at each of the three supports, if the mass of the plate may be neglected.

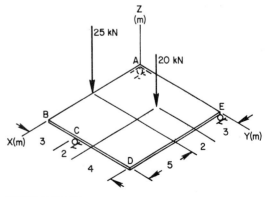

FIGURE P6-70

6-71 Find the reactions at supports *B, D* and *G* for the plate shown in Fig. P6-71. The mass of the plate is negligible.

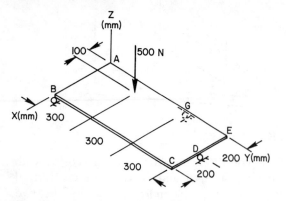

FIGURE P6-71

6-72 Calculate the tension in each cable supporting the plate shown in Fig. P6-72, if the mass of the plate may be neglected.

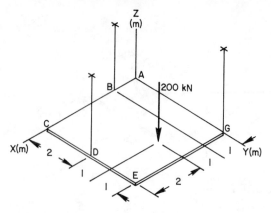

FIGURE P6-72

6-9 EQUILIBRIUM FOR THREE-DIMENSIONAL, NON-PARALLEL, NON-CONCURRENT FORCE SYSTEMS

The most general type of equilibrium problem is the three-dimensional, non-parallel, non-concurrent force system. In this system, up to six unknown terms may occur. Thus it may be necessary to solve up to six equations simultaneously. Fortunately with a combination of care, planning and thinking it is seldom necessary to solve six equations simultaneously, although it may often be necessary to solve six equations.

Since each problem does tend to be different, there are few general guidelines available for the solution of these problems. As usual, a free-body diagram is a necessity. To keep directions sorted out, it is recommended that all unknown forces in two-force members be shown as tension, and that all unknown components of forces be shown as acting in the positive direction. A positive sign in the solution will indicate that the force is tension or that the component is positive, and a negative sign will indicate that the force is compression, or that the component is negative.

The thinking step is a critical step for the solution of these problems. For example, by the careful choice of axis for a moment equation, it may be possible to write one equation with one unknown term. If you do not think, you might make the problem solution much more difficult and time-consuming, for you may end up unnecessarily solving equations simultaneously.

Some example problems will illustrate an approach to solving general three-dimensional equilibrium problems.

EXAMPLE 6-17

For the boom AB shown in Fig. 6-38, determine the components of the reaction at the ball-and-socket support at A and the tension in cables BC and BD. The 5 kN load is supported at the midpoint of the boom.

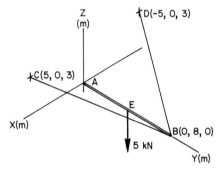

FIGURE 6-38

SOLUTION

The best starting point for the solution of this problem is the construction of a free-body diagram, as shown in Fig. 6-39. The free-body diagram shows the boom AB and the forces acting on the boom. No x component of the reaction is shown at A, since $A_x = 0$. *This can be proven by taking moments about a z axis passing through B.*

It is generally a good idea to assume that unknown forces in two-force members are tension, and that unknown components of reactions are positive. As usual, a negative value in a calculated solution will indicate that the correct direction is opposite to that assumed. Thus, by initially assuming positive values, it should help in obtaining the correct sign for the final answer for the problem.

Due to symmetry with respect to the y-z plane, $F_{BC} = F_{BD}$. *This can also be proven using the equilibrium equation summing forces in the x direction.*

If moments are taken about the x axis, the values for F_{BC} *and* F_{BD} *may be obtained. Before doing this calculation, the lengths of BC and BD will be required for computing the components.*

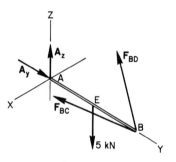

FIGURE 6-39

$$d_{BC} = d_{BD} = (5^2 + 8^2 + 3^2)^{1/2}$$

$$= (25 + 64 + 9)^{1/2}$$

$$= 98^{1/2}$$

$$= 9.8995 \text{ m}$$

$$\Sigma M_x = 0$$

$$-(5 \times 4) + \frac{3}{9.8995} F_{BC} \times 8 + \frac{3}{9.8995} F_{BD} \times 8 = 0$$

But $F_{BC} = F_{BD}$

$$-20.000 + 2.4244\ F_{BC} + 2.4244\ F_{BC} = 0$$

$$4.8488\ F_{BC} = 20.000$$

$$F_{BC} = \frac{20.000}{4.8488}$$

$$= 4.1247\ \text{kN} = F_{BD}$$

Forces may now be summed in the z direction to find A_z.

$$\Sigma\ F_z = 0$$

$$\frac{3}{9.8995} \times 4.1247 + \frac{3}{9.8995} \times 4.1247 - 5.0000 + A_z = 0$$

$$1.2500 + 1.2500 - 5.0000 + A_z = 0$$

$$A_z = -2.5000 + 5.0000$$

$$= 2.5000\ \text{kN}$$

To find A_y, forces may be summed in the y direction.

$$\Sigma\ F_y = 0$$

$$A_y - \frac{8}{9.8995} \times 4.1247 - \frac{8}{9.8995} \times 4.1247 = 0$$

$$A_y = 3.3333 + 3.3333$$

$$= 6.6666\ \text{kN}$$

FIGURE 6-40

$$
\boxed{
\begin{aligned}
A_x &= 0 \\
A_y &= 6.67\ \text{kN} \\
A_z &= 2.50\ \text{kN} \\
F_{BC} &= 4.12\ \text{kN} \\
F_{BD} &= 4.12\ \text{kN}
\end{aligned}
}
$$

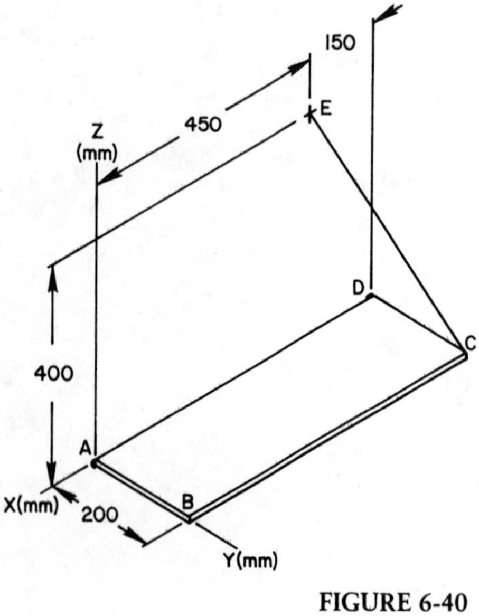

EXAMPLE 6-18

A 175 kg plate, shown in Fig. 6-40, is supported by a cable CE, by a ball-and-socket connection at A, which can resist forces in the x, y and z directions, and a hinge at D, which can resist forces in the y and z directions only. If the mass of the plate is assumed to act at its center, determine the tension in the cable and find the components of the reactions at A and D.

SOLUTION

The best approach to solving this problem is to start with the free-body diagram of the plate, as shown in Fig. 6-41. *There are six unknown forces or components acting on the plate, and each is assumed to be acting in the positive direction.*

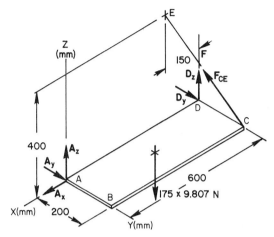

FIGURE 6-41

If moments are taken about the x axis, only one unknown term, F_{CE}, will appear in the moment equation. This is not the only possible first step, for if moments are taken about an axis CD, the only unknown term that would appear in that moment equation is A_z.

To take moments about the x axis, the length of CE must be calculated to obtain the components of F_{CE}. If the components of F_{CE} are located at C, only the z component will have a moment about the x axis.

$$d_{CE} = (150^2 + 200^2 + 400^2)^{1/2}$$

$$= (22\ 500 + 40\ 000 + 160\ 000)^{1/2}$$

$$= 222\ 500^{1/2}$$

$$= 471.70 \text{ mm}$$

$\Sigma\ M_x = 0$

$$-\left(175 \times 9.807 \times 100\right) + \frac{400}{471.70}\ F_{CE} \times 200 = 0$$

$$F_{CE} = \frac{175 \times 9.807 \times 100 \times 471.70}{400 \times 200}$$

$$= 1011.93 \text{ N}$$

Since there is only one other component in the x direction besides the x component of the force in CE, forces may be summed in the x direction as a convenient second step.

$$\Sigma F_x = 0$$

$$A_x + \frac{150}{471.70} \times 1011.93 = 0$$

$$A_x = -321.79 \text{ N}$$

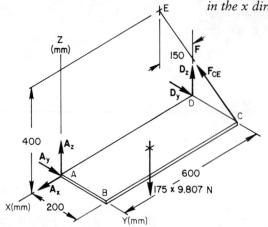

FIGURE 6-41 *Repeated*

The negative sign in the answer shows that the actual direction of A_x is opposite to that assumed.

For a third step, several different axes of rotation could be chosen that would lead to an equation with only one unknown term. Moments could be taken about CD, about z, about y, or about an axis passing through D and parallel to the z axis, to name some possibilities. Perhaps the simplest equation to set up is the moment equation about the axis CD.

$$\Sigma M_{CD} = 0$$

$$-(A_z \times 600) + 175 \times 9.807 \times 300 = 0$$

$$A_z = \frac{175 \times 9.807 \times 300}{600}$$

$$= 858.11 \text{ N}$$

The positive value for A_z indicates that A_z is actually pointing in the positive direction, as assumed.

Forces may now be summed in the z direction to calculate D_z.

$$\Sigma F_z = 0$$

$$858.11 - 175 \times 9.807 + \frac{400}{471.70} \times 1011.93 + D_z = 0$$

$$D_z = -858.11 + 1716.22 - 858.11$$

$$= 0.00$$

If moments are taken about an axis through C, parallel to the z axis, the only unknown in the equation will be A_y.

$$\Sigma M_{z_C} = 0$$

$$A_y \times 600 - 321.79 \times 200 = 0$$

$$A_y = \frac{321.79 \times 200}{600}$$

$$= 107.26 \text{ N}$$

Only D_y remains to be found. This can be calculated by summing forces in the y direction.

$$\Sigma F_y = 0$$

$$107.26 + D_y - \frac{200}{471.70} \times 1011.93 = 0$$

$$D_y = -107.26 + 429.06$$

$$= 321.80 \text{ N}$$

$$
\begin{array}{l}
A_x = -322 \text{ N} \\
A_y = 107 \text{ N} \\
A_z = 858 \text{ N} \\
D_y = 322 \text{ N} \\
D_z = 0 \text{ N} \\
F_{CE} = 1010 \text{ N}
\end{array}
$$

PROBLEMS

6-73 For the mast shown in Fig. P6-73, determine the tension in each of the cables and find the x and z components of the reaction at A. The 12 kN force is parallel to the x axis.

6-74 For the boom shown in Fig. P6-74, calculate the x and z components of the reaction at the ball-and-socket at A and the tensions in cables BD and BE.

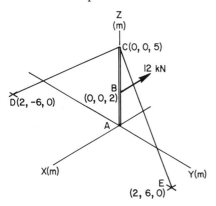

FIGURE P6-73

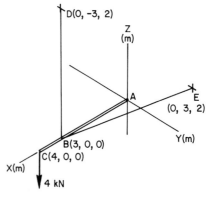

FIGURE P6-74

6-75 The mast shown in Fig. P6-75 is supported by a ball-and-socket joint at A and two cables at B. If the applied load lines up with point D, determine the components of the reaction at A and the tension in each cable.

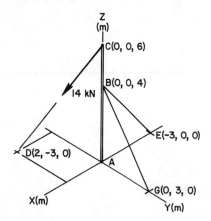

FIGURE P6-75

6-76 For the boom shown in Fig. P6-76, determine the tension in cables CE and AG and find the x, y and z components of the reaction at the ball-and-socket connection at D.

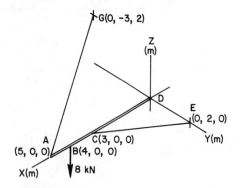

FIGURE P6-76

6-77 The plate shown in Fig. P6-77 has a mass of 15 kg acting at its center, and it is supported by the cable CH and hinges at E and G. Determine the tension in the cable and the y and z components of the force in each hinge.

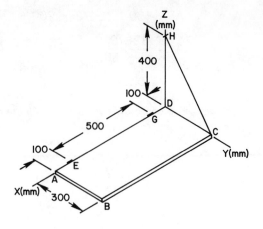

FIGURE P6-77

6-78 A ramp is supported by only one cable, as shown in Fig. P6-78. Determine the tension in the cable BJ and the x and z components of the reactions at the hinges G and H due to the 25 kN load at D.

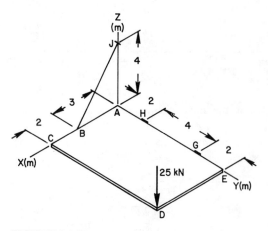

FIGURE P6-78

6-79 Determine the tension in cable DE, the y and z components of the reaction of the pin at A and the x, y and z components of the ball-and-socket at B for the canopy shown in Fig. P6-79. The mass of the canopy is 1800 kg, and may be assumed to act at the center of the canopy.

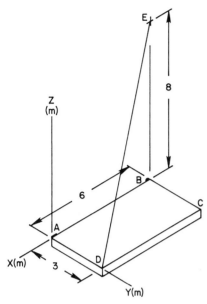

FIGURE P6-79

6-80 The bin shown in Fig. P6-80, combined with its contents, has a mass of 250 kg, which may be located at the geometric center of the bin. If the support at A is a ball and socket, which may resist force in any direction, and if the support at D is a hinge with the pin along the x axis, determine the tension in cable CG and the components of the reactions at A and D.

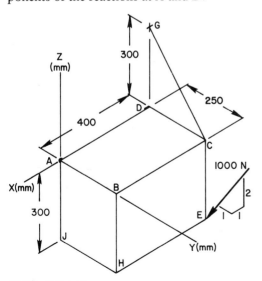

FIGURE P6-80

6-81 If a torque of 300 N·m is applied at C to the shaft shown in Fig. P6-81, determine the y and z components of the reactions at A and C and the magnitude of F_2 if the magnitude of F_1 is 4500 N.

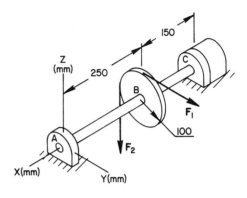

FIGURE P6-81

6-82 If the tension in each belt in Fig. P6-82 is 2000 N, determine the y and z components of the reactions at bearings B and C for the shaft.

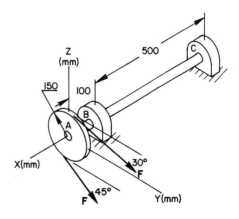

FIGURE P6-82

7 FRICTION

7-1 BASIC CONCEPTS OF FRICTION

Friction is a force that exists between any two bodies in contact that attempt to move relative to one another parallel to their contact surfaces. This force is tangent to or parallel to the contact surfaces of the two bodies. As long as there is a force attempting to cause two bodies to move relative to one another along the contact surface, there will be a friction force. If there is no force tending to cause motion, there will be no friction force.

Friction can be both beneficial and detrimental. If there were no friction between the soles of your shoes and the floor, you would not be able to walk; you would find standing difficult — if you could get to a standing position in the first place. Without friction, the inclined moving sidewalk shown in Fig. 7-1 would not operate. On the other hand, much effort and money is spent in attempting to overcome friction in some situations. Friction between a piston and the walls of a cylinder leads to wear and energy losses. Friction in a wheel bearing is undesirable, yet friction between a brake drum and brake pads is a necessity.

FIGURE 7-1 The successful operation of this inclined moving sidewalk depends on friction between the belt and shoes for moving people, and between the drive pulley and the belt for moving the belt. *Photo courtesy of Sandvik Process Systems Canada Ltd.*

In this chapter, the study of friction will be limited to one special case, dry friction, which is sometimes called Coulomb friction. Friction between lubricated surfaces is a complex study and will not be undertaken here.

The cause of friction is irregularities that appear on any surface, no matter how highly polished. Figure 7-2(a) shows a block, *B*, resting on the surface of a table, *T*. The force **P** is attempting to slide the block to the right. If the surfaces of the block and table were highly magnified, they would appear as shown in Fig. 7-2(b). The peaks and valleys of the surfaces would tend to prevent motion. However, if the force **P** is large enough, it can cause the block to ride up and over some of the peaks, and to shave others off, and hence cause motion. Of course, this is also the process that leads to wear between two moving surfaces in contact.

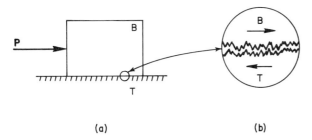

(a)   (b)

FIGURE 7-2

A free-body diagram of block *B* is shown in Fig. 7-3. The forces shown are the applied force **P**, the force due to gravity, the friction force F_r, which is parallel to the contact surface and opposite in direction to the motion **P** attempts to cause, and the normal force **N**. The normal force is normal to or perpendicular to the surface on which the friction force acts.

(It should be noted that, with basic friction problems, the forces acting on the body are treated as though the body is a point and the forces are treated as if they were concurrent.)

From the definition of equilibrium, we know that as long as there is no motion, the magnitude of **P** must equal that of F_r. Thus, as **P** increases F_r will increase, until at some point the block will start to slide and equilibrium may no longer exist. Figure 7-4 shows a graph of how F_r will vary with *P*. Note that as soon as motion starts, the friction force drops significantly. Just immediately before motion commences the block is in a condition called *impending motion*, a rather critical condition for many calculations involving friction. The section of the

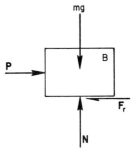

FIGURE 7-3

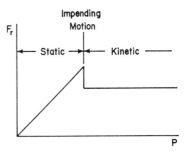

FIGURE 7-4

graph to the left of impending motion shows the static friction condition, and the section to the right shows the kinetic friction condition.

7-2   THE COEFFICIENT OF FRICTION

The static coefficient of friction is defined as follows:

$$\mu_s = \frac{F_r}{N} \tag{7-1}$$

This may be rewritten to give the magnitude of the friction force as

$$F_r = \mu_s N \tag{7-2}$$

where μ_s is the static coefficient of friction
F_r is the magnitude of the friction force *when motion impends*, and
N is the magnitude of the normal force acting on the body.

It cannot be overemphasized that the value for F_r associated with μ_s must be the friction force when motion impends.

For the case of the kinetic coefficient of friction, it is defined as:

$$\mu_k = \frac{F_r}{N} \tag{7-3}$$

This may be rewritten to give the magnitude of the friction force as

$$F_r = \mu_k N \tag{7-4}$$

where μ_k is the kinetic coefficient of friction
F_r is the magnitude of the friction force when the body is in motion, and
N is the magnitude of the normal force acting on the body.

Table 7-1 lists some typical values for the coefficient of friction. The coefficient of friction will differ for any combination of two materials that make up the contact surfaces and for any differences in quality of surface finish. The values shown are for dry or unlubricated surfaces. Although most values of μ are less than 1.0, there is nothing to prevent μ from having a value greater than 1.0, given a suitable combination of materials.

The classic experiment for determining the coefficient of static friction between two materials is to set a block of one material on an inclinable plane made of the second material, as shown in

TABLE 7-1
TYPICAL COEFFICIENTS OF FRICTION

MATERIALS	μ_s	μ_k
Aluminum on aluminum	1.4	
Asbestos fabric on cast iron	0.40	0.35
Cast iron on steel	0.40	0.25
Leather on oak	0.61	0.52
Oak on cast iron		0.30
Rubber on concrete	0.90	0.85
Steel on babbitt	0.42	0.35
Steel on ice		0.02
Teflon on Teflon	0.07	

Fig. 7-5. The plane is inclined until the block starts to slide, at which point the angle θ, between the plane and the horizontal, is measured. The analysis of the block at the point of impending motion provides some useful information. A free-body diagram of the block is shown in Fig. 7-6. A normal axis, n, and a tangential axis, t, are shown on the diagram.

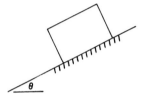

FIGURE 7-5

Using the equilibrium equations in the n and t directions, the following relationships are obtained:

$$\Sigma F_n = 0$$

$$N - mg \cos \theta = 0$$

$$N = mg \cos \theta \qquad (7\text{-}5)$$

$$\Sigma F_t = 0$$

$$F_r - mg \sin \theta = 0$$

$$F_r = mg \sin \theta \qquad (7\text{-}6)$$

FIGURE 7-6

If the left side of Eq. (7-6) is divided by the left side of Eq. (7-5), and if the right side of Eq. (7-6) is divided by the right side of Eq. (7-5), the two quotients equal each other.

$$\frac{F_r}{N} = \frac{mg \sin \theta}{mg \cos \theta} = \frac{\sin \theta}{\cos \theta}$$

but $\dfrac{F_r}{N} = \mu_s$ for impending motion, which exists in this case,

and

$$\frac{\sin \theta}{\cos \theta} = \tan \theta$$

thus

$$\frac{F_r}{N} = \mu_s = \frac{\sin \theta}{\cos \theta} = \tan \theta$$

or

$$\mu_s = \tan \theta \qquad (7\text{-}7)$$

From this equation, it is seen that the tangent of the angle when motion impends on an inclined plane is equal to the static coefficient of friction for the two materials. The angle of inclination for impending motion is called the *angle of repose* or *angle of static friction*.

7-3   LAWS OF FRICTION

Experiments with friction have led to the development of several laws of friction:

1. For impending motion, the friction force is proportional to the normal force. The constant of proportionality is called the static coefficient of friction.

2. The friction force is independent of the contact area.

3. The friction force when motion impends is larger than the friction force when the body is in motion.

4. For a body in motion, the friction force is independent of speed for moderate speeds.

Laws 1 and 3 have already been discussed. Laws 2 and 4 are presented for information. The two laws explain why neither the contact area nor the speed of a sliding body enters into any of the sample friction problems.

EXAMPLE   7-1

An iron casting with a mass of 160 kg is sitting on the steel bed of a shaper, which is horizontal. Determine the magnitude of the horizontal force required to just start to move the iron casting.

SOLUTION

This is an equilibrium problem, so a free-body diagram of the casting, as shown in Fig. 7-7, *should be used to start the solution. If motion is impending, it is known that* $F_r = \mu_s N$, *from* Eq. (7-2). *The value for* μ_s *is* 0.40, *from* Table 7-1. *To obtain* N, *forces are summed in the normal* (n) *direction.*

$$\Sigma F_n = 0$$

$$N - 160 \times 9.807 = 0$$

$$N = 1569.1 \text{ N}$$

For impending motion

$$F_r = \mu_s N$$

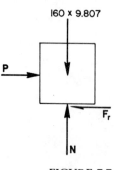

160 x 9.807

P

F_r

N

FIGURE 7-7

$$= 0.40 \times 1569.1$$

$$= 627.64 \text{ N}$$

Since the body is still in equilibrium when motion impends, forces may be summed in the tangential (t) direction to find the magnitude of the force required to initiate motion.

$$\Sigma F_t = 0$$

$$P - F_r = 0$$

$$P - 627.64 = 0$$

$$P = 627.64 \text{ N}$$

$$\boxed{P = 628 \text{ N}}$$

EXAMPLE 7-2

A farmer finds that corn will not flow or slide in a steel chute if the angle of the chute is less than 21°. What is the coefficient of static friction between steel and corn?

SOLUTION

Find the coefficient of friction by using the inclined plane (the chute). The coefficient of friction may be calculated by substitution in Eq. (7-7).

$$\mu_s = \tan \theta$$

$$= \tan 21°$$

$$= 0.383\ 86$$

$$\boxed{\mu_s = 0.384}$$

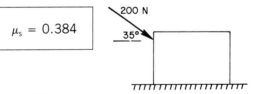

FIGURE 7-8

EXAMPLE 7-3

The block shown in Fig. 7-8 has a mass of 40 kg, and the static coefficient of friction between the block and the floor is 0.40. Calculate the friction force acting on the block.

SOLUTION

A free-body diagram of the block, as shown in Fig. 7-9, *should be drawn. The equilibrium equations can be used to calculate* F_r *and N. Note that the friction force has been drawn so that it*

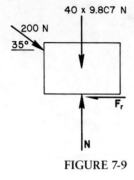

40 x 9.8C7 N

200 N

35°

F_r

N

FIGURE 7-9

opposes potential motion. (Again, in this problem solution, an n and t axis system will be used, since it is more convenient than any other axis system.)

If the block is not in motion, it must be in equilibrium; F_r may be obtained by summing forces in the t direction.

Assuming no motion:

$$\Sigma F_t = 0$$

$$200 \cos 35° - F_r = 0$$

$$F_r = 163.83 \text{ N}$$

At this point we do not know whether the block is sliding. The friction force for impending motion must be determined to see if the actual friction is more or less than that for impending motion. If the friction force, as determined above, is less than the friction force for impending motion, then the block is in equilibrium, as assumed, and the friction force calculated above is the actual friction force acting on the block. If the friction force determined above is larger than that for impending motion, the block will be sliding, and it would be necessary to know the coefficient of kinetic friction to determine the actual friction force acting on the block.

To calculate the friction force for impending motion, it is necessary to calculate N first. Note that the applied force of 200 N will have an effect on the magnitude of N.

$$\Sigma F_n = 0$$

$$N - 200 \sin 35° - 40 \times 9.807 = 0$$

$$N = 114.72 + 392.28$$

$$= 507.00 \text{ N}$$

For impending motion:

$$F_r = \mu_s N$$

$$= 0.40 \times 507.00$$

$$= 202.80 \text{ N}$$

Block will not slide unless F_r exceeds 202.80 N.

$$\boxed{F_r = 164 \text{ N}}$$

EXAMPLE 7-4

Determine the magnitude of a force **P** that will just cause motion to impend if the static coefficient of friction between the floor and the block shown in Fig. 7-10 is 0.25.

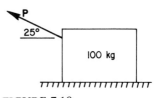

FIGURE 7-10

SOLUTION

The free-body diagram of the block, as shown in Fig. 7-11, *is the best starting point for the solution. Since the friction force for impending motion depends on the normal force, finding the normal force would apparently be the first step. Note that* **P** *will influence the magnitude of the normal force.*

$$\Sigma F_n = 0$$

$$N - 100 \times 9.807 + P \sin 25° = 0$$

$$N = 980.7 - 0.422\ 62\ P$$

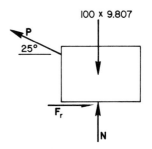

FIGURE 7-11

At first glance, it appears that there may be too many unknown terms. However, if forces are summed in the tangential direction, F_r *may be written in terms of P. But* F_r *and N are related by* μ_s. *This relationship leads to a method of solution.*

$$\Sigma F_t = 0$$

$$F_r - P \cos 25° = 0$$

$$F_r = 0.906\ 31\ P$$

But $\mu_s = \dfrac{F_r}{N}$

$$0.25 = \frac{F_r}{N} = \frac{0.906\ 31\ P}{980.7 - 0.422\ 62\ P}$$

$$0.25(980.7 - 0.422\ 62\ P) = 0.906\ 31\ P$$

$$245.18 - 0.105\ 66\ P = 0.906\ 31\ P$$

$$245.18 = 1.011\ 97\ P$$

$$P = \frac{245.18}{1.011\ 97}$$

$$= 242.28\ N$$

$$P = 242\ N$$

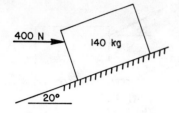

FIGURE 7-12

EXAMPLE 7-5

For the block shown in Fig. 7-12, calculate the magnitude and direction of the friction force and indicate whether the block is at rest or moving up or down the plane. The coefficient of static friction between the block and plane is 0.15 and the coefficient of kinetic friction is 0.12.

SOLUTION

The free-body diagram of the block is the logical starting point. In this case, it is not readily apparent whether the block will tend to slide up the plane or down the plane, so it has been assumed that the block is tending to slide up the plane, as shown in the free-body diagram, Fig. 7-13, where the friction force points down the plane.

If the block is not moving, it is in equilibrium. The friction force can be calculated by summing forces in the t direction.

$$\Sigma F_t = 0$$

$$-F_r + 400 \cos 20° - 140 \times 9.807 \sin 20° = 0$$

$$F_r = 375.877 - 469.587$$

$$= -93.710 \text{ N}$$

The negative sign for the value of F_r indicates that the wrong direction was assumed. Actually, for equilibrium, the friction force must point down the plane. However, its magnitude is still 93.710 N.

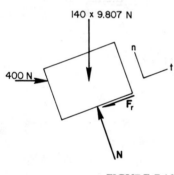

FIGURE 7-13

*The next step is to determine the magnitude of the friction force for impending motion to determine whether the block is sliding. It is first necessary to find the magnitude of **N**.*

$$\Sigma F_n = 0$$

$$N - 400 \sin 20° - 140 \times 9.807 \cos 20° = 0$$

$$N = 136.81 + 1290.18$$

$$= 1426.99 \text{ N}$$

For impending motion

$$F_r = \mu_s N$$

$$= 0.15 \times 1426.99$$

$$= 214.05 \text{ N}$$

Since the actual friction force is less than the friction force for impending motion, the block remains at rest.

$F_r = 93.7$ N up the plane
Block is at rest

PROBLEMS

7-1 A Teflon-coverd steel plate with a mass of 12 kg is at rest on a horizontal Teflon-coated surface. What friction force will exist between the two surfaces if a horizontal force is applied to the plate so that motion is impending?

7-2 An aluminum plate with a mass of 35 kg is on top of a stack of similar plates. If a horizontal force that just initiates motion is applied to the top plate, what will be the friction force between the two top plates?

7-3 A 50 kg crate rests on a horizontal floor. If the coefficient of static friction between the crate and the floor is 0.35, determine the magnitude of the horizontal force required to just start to move the crate.

7-4 A 1200 kg automobile with rubber tires is parked on level concrete pavement. Calculate the magnitude of the horizontal force required to cause the automobile to start to move if the brakes are locked on all four wheels.

7-5 If the coefficient of static friction between the floor and the 75 kg block shown in Fig. P7-5 is 0.25, determine the magnitude of the friction force.

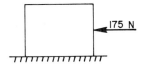

FIGURE P7-5

7-6 For the block shown in Fig. P7-6, determine the friction force if $\mu_s = 0.35$.

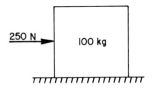

FIGURE P7-6

7-7 A rubber tire from an earth mover is lying on a concrete shop floor. The tire has a mass of 620 kg. Determine the friction force between the tire and the floor if a horizontal force of 6000 N is applied to the tire.

7-8 A horizontal force of 180 N is applied to a 30 kg block with a leather-covered bottom. The block is supported on a horizontal oak board. Determine the friction force between the block and the board.

7-9 If the coefficient of static friction between belting on a conveyor and a cardboard box is 0.65, determine the maximum angle of elevation the conveyor may have if the box is not to slip.

7-10 If the coefficient of static friction between a block and a plane is 0.364, what will be the maximum angle to which the plane can be raised before the block starts to slide?

7-11 A block with a mass of 50 kg is about to slide down a plane that is inclined at an angle of 25° with the horizontal. Determine the static coefficient of friction.

7-12 When attempting to stand on a slope of 5°, a skier starts to slide. What is the value for the static coefficient of friction between the wooden skis and the snow?

7-13 Find the magnitude of the force required to initiate motion for the system of two blocks shown in Fig. P7-13 if the coefficient of static friction between block *A* and the floor is 0.25 and between block *B* and the floor is 0.40.

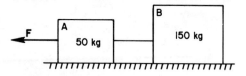

FIGURE P7-13

7-14 Determine the magnitude of the force **P** required to initiate motion for block *B* shown in Fig. P7-14 if μ_s for blocks *A* and *B* is 0.30 and μ_s for block *B* and the floor is 0.20.

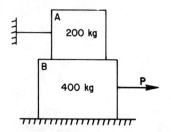

FIGURE P7-14

7-15 For the 25 kg block shown in Fig. P7-15, the coefficient of static friction between the block and the floor is 0.55. Determine the friction force between the block and the floor.

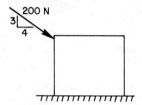

FIGURE P7-15

7-16 If the coefficient of static friction between the block shown in Fig. P7-16 and the floor is 0.15, determine the magnitude of the friction force acting on the block.

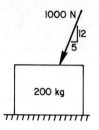

FIGURE P7-16

7-17 Calculate the magnitude of the friction force between the block shown in Fig. P7-17 and the floor if the coefficient of static friction is 0.35.

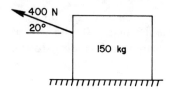

FIGURE P7-17

7-18 Find the magnitude of the friction force between the 60 kg block shown in Fig. P7-18 and the floor if the coefficient of static friction is 0.65.

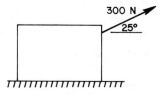

FIGURE P7-18

7-19 Determine the force **P** that will just cause motion for the block shown in Fig. P7-19 if $\mu_s = 0.30$.

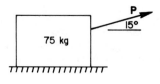

FIGURE P7-19

7-20 If the static coefficient of friction between the 50 kg block shown in Fig. P7-20 and the floor is 0.35, determine the magnitude of the force **P** that will initiate motion.

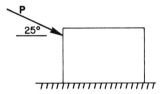

FIGURE P7-20

7-21 If the 120 kg block shown in Fig. P7-21 is made of cast iron, and if it is sliding at a constant speed on a steel surface, determine the magnitude of the force **P** required to maintain that constant speed.

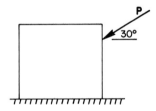

FIGURE P7-21

7-22 The block of ice shown in Fig. P7-22 is on the steel deck of a truck. If the block has been set in motion, determine the magnitude of the force **P** required to keep the block moving at a constant speed.

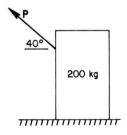

FIGURE P7-22

7-23 Determine the minimum horizontal force **F** required to prevent the 50 kg block shown in Fig. P7-23 from sliding down the plane if $\mu_s = 0.35$.

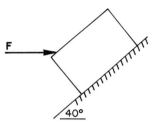

FIGURE P7-23

7-24 For the 125 kg block shown in Fig. P7-24, determine the magnitude of the horizontal force **F** that will just initiate motion up the plane. The static coefficient of friction between the block and the plane is 0.35.

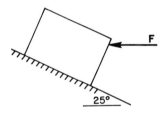

FIGURE P7-24

7-25 For the block shown in Fig. P7-25, determine the friction force acting on the block. Determine whether the block is at rest or is sliding up or down the plane. The coefficient of static friction between the block and the plane is 0.35 and the coefficient of kinetic friction is 0.30.

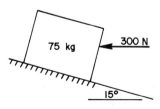

FIGURE P7-25

7-26 If μ_s for the block and plane shown in Fig. P7-26 is 0.40, and if $\mu_k = 0.30$, determine the friction force acting on the block and determine whether the block is at rest or is sliding up or down the plane.

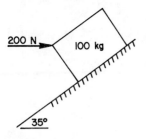

FIGURE P7-26

7-27 If motion is impending for the system shown in Fig. P7-27, determine μ_s for the 400 kg mass and the surface on which it rests.

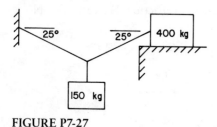

FIGURE P7-27

7-28 The beam shown in Fig. P7-28 has a mass of 60 kg acting at its center, and the block at *B* has a mass of 100 kg. Determine the minimum static coefficient of friction required to maintain equilibrium

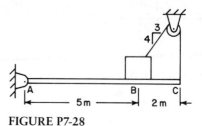

FIGURE P7-28

7-4   WEDGES

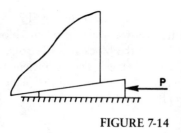

FIGURE 7-14

A wedge is an ancient device used for creating mechanical advantage. As shown in Fig. 7-14, a wedge can be placed under a corner of a heavy piece of machinery and a relatively small force, **P**, can be applied to the wedge to lift a relatively heavy load. A wedge can also be used to provide precision in positioning machinery or other bodies that must be exactly located. It can be deduced from Fig. 7-14 that a large horizontal movement of the wedge would lead to a relatively small vertical movement of the load being supported.

The performance of a wedge depends on the angle of the wedge and on the friction forces involved at the surfaces of contact. Since the initiation of motion of the wedge is usually critical, in most wedge problems it is the condition of impending motion that is analyzed. When analyzing wedges and the bodies with which they are in contact, the force systems involved are usually treated as concurrent force systems.

To analyze the forces on a wedge, the relationship between the normal force, the friction force and the resultant of these two forces must be understood. When motion impends for a body, $\mu_s = F_r/N$. In Fig. 7-15, θ is the angle between the resultant, $\mathbf{R}$, and the normal force, $\mathbf{N}$. It is observed from the figure that $F_r/N = \tan \theta$. Thus, when motion impends, the angle between the normal force and the resultant is θ, since $\mu_s = F_r/N = \tan \theta$.

The actual analysis of forces acting on a wedge is best illustrated by means of some example problems.

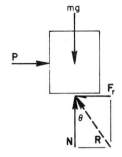

FIGURE 7-15

EXAMPLE 7-6

Calculate the magnitude of the force $\mathbf{P}$ required to start to raise the box shown in Fig. 7-16. The wall is smooth, and the static coefficient of friction between the surfaces of the wedge and the box and floor is 0.30.

SOLUTION

An impending motion friction problem is an equilibrium problem, and usually one begins the analysis of an equilibrium problem with a free-body diagram. It is not readily apparent whether one should draw a free-body diagram of the wedge or of the box being lifted. There is merit in drawing both free-body diagrams, as shown in Fig. 7-17; both will be used in due course. Figure 7-17 (a) is the free-body diagram of the box. The forces acting are the gravitational attraction, the normal force at the wall and the force on the base. There is no friction force at the wall, since it is smooth. At the base of the box is shown a normal force and the friction force. The direction of the friction force may not be

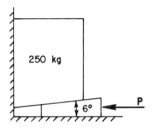

FIGURE 7-16

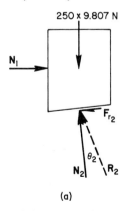

(a)

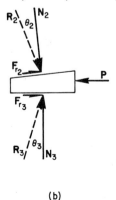

(b)

FIGURE 7-17

readily apparent. The friction force tends to oppose motion be-tween the two contacting surfaces. Since the box would tend to move to the right relative to the wedge, the friction force on the box must point to the left. R_2 is simply the resultant of F_{r_2} and N_2.

The free-body diagram of the wedge, as shown in Fig. 7-17(b), shows the applied force P, the two normal forces and the two friction forces. The directions of the friction forces oppose the motion of the wedge. Note that if F_{r_2} on the wedge is to the right, then F_{r_2} on the box must be equal and opposite. Again, R_2 and R_3 are simply the resultants of N_2 and F_{r_2} and N_3 and F_{r_3}. Because of the number of normal forces, friction forces and re-sultants involved, it is imperative that the force symbols be given subscripts, to keep track of which is which. There are no known forces in the free-body diagram of the wedge, but in the free-body diagram of the box there is one known force, so the box is the starting point for analysis. The forces acting on the box form a concurrent force system, and the vector triangle for the forces is shown in Fig. 7-18. As a convenient check on calculations, the vector triangle should be drawn to scale. Since motion is im-pending, $\mu_{s_2} = \tan \theta_2$.

$$\theta_2 = \tan^{-1} \mu_{s_2}$$
$$= \tan^{-1} 0.30$$
$$= 16.70°$$

The vector triangle shown in Fig. 7-18 is a right-angled triangle, which can be solved for R_2.

From the vector triangle for the box:

$$\alpha = 6° + 16.70°$$
$$= 22.70°$$
$$\frac{250 \times 9.807}{R_2} = \cos 22.70°$$
$$R_2 = \frac{250 \times 9.807}{\cos 22.70°}$$
$$= 2657.6 \text{ N}$$

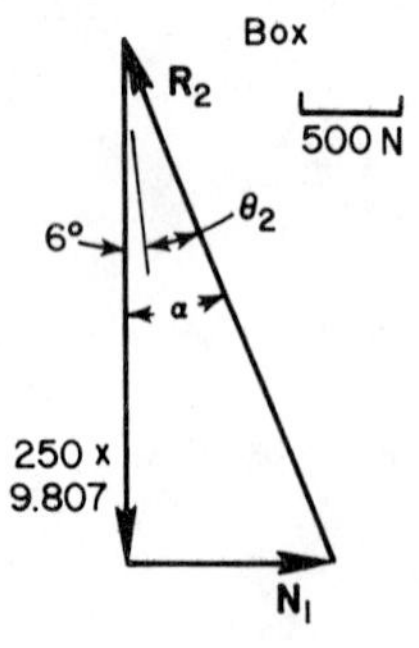

FIGURE 7-18

The value for N_1 is not calculated, since it will not be used in any following calculations.

If the vector triangle for the wedge is drawn, it will appear as shown in Fig. 7-19. Since R_2 has been calculated, it is a known quantity in the vector triangle. The vector triangle can be solved using the sine law to find P once β and ϕ have been found.

$$\theta_3 = \tan^{-1}\mu_{s3}$$

$$= \tan^{-1} 0.30$$

$$= 16.70°$$

$$\beta = \theta_2 + \theta_3 + 6°$$

$$= 16.70° + 16.70° + 6°$$

$$= 39.40°$$

$$\phi = 90° - 16.70°$$

$$= 73.30°$$

$$\frac{P}{\sin \beta} = \frac{R_2}{\sin \phi}$$

$$P = \frac{R_2 \sin \beta}{\sin \phi}$$

$$= \frac{2657.6 \sin 39.40°}{\sin 73.30°}$$

$$= 1761.1 \text{ N}$$

$$\boxed{P = 1760 \text{ N}}$$

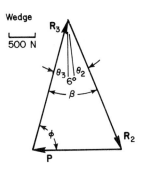

FIGURE 7-19

EXAMPLE 7-7

Figure 7-20 shows a pair of wedges used to separate a timber from some cribbing. If a force **P** of 500 N is needed to withdraw the wedge *A*, determine the magnitude of the normal force the spikes apply between the timber, *C*, and the wedge, *A*. The static coefficient of friction between all contact surfaces is 0.40. The spikes do not pass through the wedge but are beside the wedge.

SOLUTION

*Both the force to be determined, N_1, and the known applied force, **P**, appear on the free-body diagram of wedge A, shown in Fig. 7-21. Since the wedge tends to move up, the two friction forces must point down to oppose the motion. The vector triangle for the wedge is shown in Fig. 7-22. The angle between the normal force and the resultant must be calculated before attempting to draw the vector triangle to scale.*

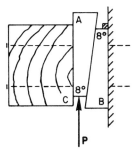

FIGURE 7-20

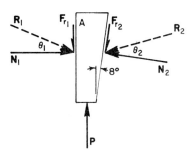

FIGURE 7-21

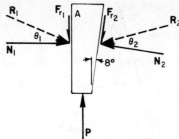

FIGURE 7-21   *Repeated*

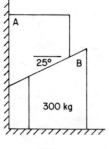

FIGURE 7-22

$$\theta_1 = \theta_2 = \tan^{-1} \mu_s$$
$$= \tan^{-1} 0.40$$
$$= 21.80°$$

From the free-body diagram of the wedge, it can be seen that the angle between the horizontal and R_2 may be obtained:

$$\phi = \theta_2 - 8°$$
$$= 21.80° - 8°$$
$$= 13.80°$$

After obtaining α and β, the sine law may be used to find R_1.

$$\alpha = \phi + \theta_1$$
$$= 13.80° + 21.80°$$
$$= 35.60°$$
$$\beta = 90° - \phi$$
$$= 90° - 13.80°$$
$$= 76.20°$$
$$\frac{R_1}{\sin \beta} = \frac{500}{\sin \alpha}$$
$$R_1 = \frac{500 \sin 76.20°}{\sin 35.60°}$$
$$= 834.13 \text{ N}$$

From Fig. 7-21, and from the knowledge that motion is impending, N_1 may be obtained.

$$N_1 = R_1 \cos \theta_1$$
$$= 834.13 \cos 21.80°$$
$$= 774.48 \text{ N}$$

$$\boxed{N = 774 \text{ N}}$$

EXAMPLE   7-8

Find the minimum mass for block A, shown in Fig. 7-23, that will just cause block B to slide if the static coefficient of friction for all surfaces in contact is 0.15.

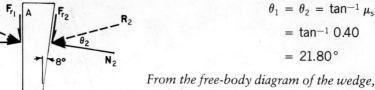

FIGURE 7-23

SOLUTION

Drawing the free-body diagram of the two blocks, as shown in Fig. 7-24, is the best place to start. Block B, as shown in Fig. 7-24(b), would tend to slide to the right, so both friction forces acting on it point to the left. On block A, F_{r_2} must thus point to the right to be opposite to F_{r_2} on block B. Since block A tends to slide down, F_{r_1} must point up.

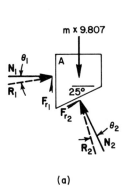

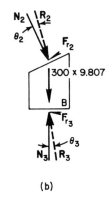

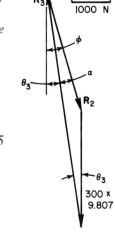

(a)   (b)

FIGURE 7-24

Block B has the one known force acting on it, so its vector triangle will be drawn to scale first, as shown in Fig. 7-25.

The angle between the normal force and the resultant will be the same for all three contact surfaces.

$$\theta_1 = \theta_2 = \theta_3 = \tan^{-1} \mu_s$$

$$= \tan^{-1} 0.15$$

$$= 8.53°$$

From Fig. 7-24(b) it may be seen that the value for ϕ in Fig. 7-25 is

$$\phi = 25° - \theta_2$$

$$= 25° - 8.53°$$

$$= 16.47°$$

$$\alpha = \phi - \theta_3$$

$$= 16.47° - 8.53°$$

$$= 7.94°$$

FIGURE 7-25

The sine law may be used to obtain R_2.

$$\frac{R_2}{\sin \theta_3} = \frac{300 \times 9.807}{\sin \alpha}$$

$$\frac{R_2}{\sin 8.53°} = \frac{300 \times 9.807}{\sin 7.94°}$$

$$R_2 = \frac{300 \times 9.807 \sin 8.53°}{\sin 7.94°}$$

$$= 3159.2 \text{ N}$$

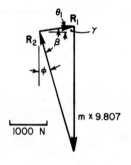

FIGURE 7-26

The vector triangle for block A may now be drawn to scale, as shown in Fig. 7-26. *From Fig. 7-26, the values of the angles β and γ may be obtained.*

$$\beta = (90° - \phi) + \theta_1$$

$$= 90° - 16.47° + 8.53°$$

$$= 82.06°$$

$$\gamma = 90° - \theta_1$$

$$= 90° - 8.53°$$

$$= 81.47°$$

The sine law may now be used to find the value of m.

$$\frac{m \times 9.807}{\sin \beta} = \frac{R_2}{\sin \gamma}$$

$$\frac{m \times 9.807}{\sin 82.06°} = \frac{3159.2}{\sin 81.47°}$$

$$m = \frac{3159.2 \sin 82.06°}{9.807 \sin 81.47°}$$

$$= 322.62 \text{ kg}$$

$$\boxed{m = 323 \text{ kg}}$$

PROBLEMS

7-29 For the wedge-and-block system shown in Fig. P7-29, calculate the magnitude of **P** required to just start to raise the block. The surface of the wall is smooth, and the static coefficient of friction between the contact surfaces and the wedge is 0.15.

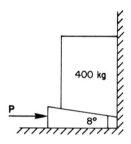

FIGURE P7-29

7-30 A 3° wedge, as shown in Fig. P7-30, is placed under one corner of a piece of machinery that has a mass of 4500 kg. If the wedge supports one quarter of the mass of the machinery, and if the machinery is prevented from sliding by a horizontal force, determine the magnitude of the force **P** required to start to raise the machinery. The coefficient of static friction between the wedge and the contact surfaces is 0.18.

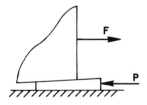

FIGURE P7-30

7-31 Determine the magnitude of the force **P** required to remove the 5° wedge, shown in Fig. P7-31, from under one end of a 900 kg beam. The beam is prevented from sliding by a horizontal force. The coefficient of static friction between the wedge and the contact surfaces is 0.25.

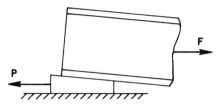

FIGURE P7-31

7-32 Determine the magnitude of the force **F** required to remove the wedge from beneath the 200 kg block shown in Fig. P7-32. The coefficient of static friction between block *A* and the wall is zero, and between all other surfaces is 0.25.

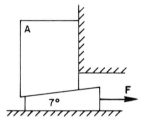

FIGURE P7-32

7-33 A 14° wedge is used for splitting logs, as shown in Fig. P7-33. If the coefficient of static friction between the wedge and the wood is 0.35, determine the magnitude of the normal force acting on the wood.

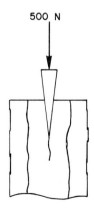

FIGURE P7-33

7-34 Alignment for a door frame can be obtained by the use of wedges, as shown in section in Fig. P7-34. If the pair of 7° wedges is beside a nail with a tension of 300 N, determine the magnitude of the force **P** required to drive the wedge. The coefficient of static friction is 0.25 for all surfaces.

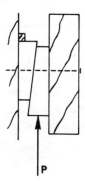

FIGURE P7-34

7-35 What force **P** is required to start to move the wedge in the system shown in Fig. P7-35? The coefficient of static friction between all surfaces is 0.15.

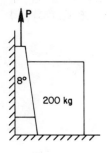

FIGURE P7-35

7-36 Calculate the magnitude of the force **P** required to start to move the 400 kg block shown in Fig. P7-36. The coefficient of friction between all surfaces is 0.25.

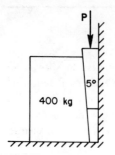

FIGURE P7-36

7-37 For the 800 kg block shown in Fig. P7-37, determine the magnitude of the force **P** required to remove the 12° wedge. The static coefficient of friction between the wedge and the floor is 0.40; between the wedge and the block it is 0.35, and between the block and the wall it is 0.20.

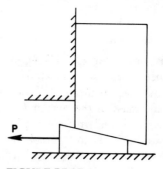

FIGURE P7-37

7-38 Determine the magnitude of the force **P** required to start to move the block shown in Fig. P7-38. The coefficients of friction are as follows: between the block and the wall $\mu_s = 0.20$; between the block and the wedge $\mu_s = 0.30$; and between the wedge and the floor $\mu_s = 0.40$.

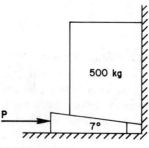

FIGURE P7-38

7-39 Find the minimum mass for block *B*, as shown in Fig. P7-39, that will cause motion to impend if μ_s for all surfaces in contact is 0.40.

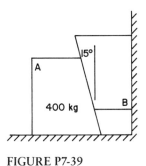

FIGURE P7-39

7-40 If wedge *A*, shown in Fig. P7-40, has a mass of 75 kg, determine the minimum mass required for block *B* to prevent motion. The static coefficient of friction between all surfaces is 0.35.

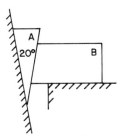

FIGURE P7-40

7-5 BELT FRICTION

A belt may be used to drive a shaft through a pulley, as shown in Fig. 7-27(a). There are friction forces acting on the contact surfaces between belt and pulley; those forces actually cause the rotation of the pulley. The friction forces and normal forces the pulley applies to the belt are shown in Fig. 7-27(b). The forces the belt applies to the pulley would be of equal magnitude and opposite direction.

It can be determined from Fig. 7-27(b) that F_1 must be the larger belt tension and F_2 the smaller. Neither the friction forces nor normal forces is uniform, and as a consequence, the analysis of the forces is complex. If a flat belt is about to slip, the relationship between the belt tension, coefficient of friction and angle of contact is

$$\ln \frac{F_1}{F_2} = \mu_s \theta \qquad (7\text{-}8)$$

which may also be expressed as

$$\frac{F_1}{F_2} = e^{\mu_s \theta} \qquad (7\text{-}9)$$

where F_1 is the magnitude of the larger belt tension when slipping impends,

F_2 is the magnitude of the smaller belt tension when slipping impends,

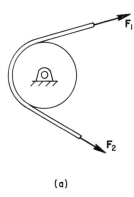

(a)

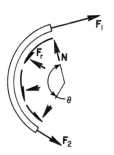

(b)

FIGURE 7-27

e is the Napierian constant 2.718 28,

μ_s is the static coefficient of friction,

θ is the angle of contact, *in radians*, between the belt and pulley, and

ln is the symbol for logarithms to the base *e*.

Equations (7-8) and (7-9) apply to a rope wrapped around a circular shaft that is about to slip, and would also apply to a band brake used for stopping a rotating shaft. However, in the case of the band brake, slipping is occuring, and μ_k would have to be used instead of μ_s. The equations do not apply in the case of vee belts.

EXAMPLE 7-9

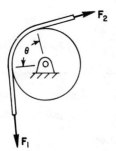

FIGURE 7-28

If the belt tension $\mathbf{F_1}$ for the system shown in Fig. 7-28 has a magnitude of 750 N, determine the magnitude of $\mathbf{F_2}$ if the belt is about to slip, and if $\mu_s = 0.40$ and $\theta = 80°$.

SOLUTION

The value for F_2 *may be obtained by direct substitution in* Eq. *(7-9). Note that the value for* θ *must be converted so that it is expressed in radians.*

$$\frac{F_1}{F_2} = e^{\mu_s \theta}$$

$$\frac{750}{F_2} = e^{0.40 \times 80\pi/180}$$

$$= 1.7481$$

$$F_2 = \frac{750}{1.7481}$$

$$= 429.04 \text{ N}$$

$$\boxed{F_2 = 429 \text{ N}}$$

EXAMPLE 7-10

A band brake and drum are shown in Fig. 7-29. If the magnitudes of $\mathbf{F_1}$ and $\mathbf{F_2}$ are 600 N and 200 N respectively, determine the value for the static coefficient of friction that will prevent motion if rotation of the drum is impending.

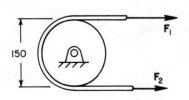

FIGURE 7-29

SOLUTION

The information required is μ_s, *and this may be obtained most directly by using* Eq. (7-8). *Note that the angle of contact between the band brake and the drum must be expressed in radians.*

$$\ln \frac{F_1}{F_2} = \mu_s \theta$$

$$\ln \frac{600}{200} = \mu_s \pi$$

$$1.0986 = \mu_s \pi$$

$$\mu_s = \frac{1.0986}{\pi}$$

$$= 0.349\ 70$$

$$\boxed{\mu_s = 0.350}$$

EXAMPLE 7-11

A rotating capstan is shown in Fig. 7-30. The capstan can be used to move loads when a cable or rope is wrapped around it. One end of the rope is attached to the load, represented by F_1; the free end of the rope is held, to apply a tension, as represented by F_2. If the magnitude of F_1 must be 4 kN to move a railway car on a siding, and if the person applying the tension can apply a maximum force of 250 N, determine the number of full turns of cable required around the capstan to move the car. The coefficient of friction between the cable and the capstan is 0.20.

SOLUTION

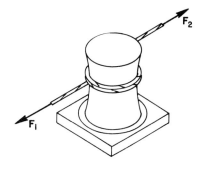

FIGURE 7-30

The angle subtended by the cable is required. Substitution in Eq. (7-8) *would probably provide the easier solution.*

$$\ln \frac{F_1}{F_2} = \mu_s \theta$$

$$\ln \frac{4000}{250} = 0.20\ \theta$$

$$2.772\ 59 = 0.20\ \theta$$

$$\theta = \frac{2.772\ 59}{0.20}$$

$$= 13.8629 \text{ radians}$$

To convert the angle to the number of turns of rope, use the fact that there are 2π radians in a full circle.

$$\text{Number of turns} = \frac{13.8629}{2\pi}$$

$$= 2.2064$$

Since the question requests the number of full turns required to prevent slipping, then the next whole number larger than 2.2064 is the answer.

Number of turns = 3

PROBLEMS

7-41 For the rope passing over the fixed shaft, as shown in Fig. P7-41, determine the magnitude of the force **P** required to start to raise the mass if the static coefficient of friction is 0.40.

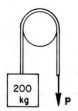

FIGURE P7-41

7-42 Find the magnitude of the force **F** required to just prevent the mass shown in Fig. P7-42 from dropping. The coefficient of static friction between the rope and the fixed shaft is 0.45.

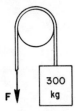

FIGURE P7-42

7-43 A mass of 60 kg is lowered by means of a rope passing over a fixed pipe, as shown in Fig.

P7-43. If the coefficient of static friction between the rope and the pipe is 0.25, determine the magnitude of the tension **F** when motion starts.

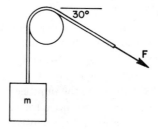

FIGURE P7-43

7-44 A mass of 40 kg is raised by means of a cable passing over a fixed pipe, as shown in Fig. P7-44. Find the magnitude of the tension **P** required to start to lift the mass if the coefficient of static friction between the cable and the pipe is 0.20.

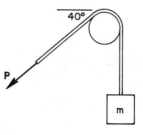

FIGURE P7-44

7-45 The brake drum shown in Fig. P7-45 is attached to a shaft transmitting a torque of −500 N·m. Determine the coefficient of friction if slippage is impending. The force F_B has a magnitude of 200 N and the angle of contact is 150°.

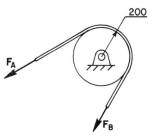

FIGURE P7-45

7-46 Find the minimum coefficient of friction required between the band brake, shown in Fig. P7-46, and the drum to prevent slipping if $F_2 = 0.4\ F_1$. The angle of contact between drum and brake is 260°.

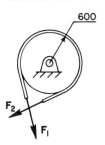

FIGURE P7-46

7-47 To find the coefficient of static friction between steel and nylon rope, a mass of 15 kg was tied to one end of the rope. Then the rope was wrapped one and one-half times around a horizontal steel pipe. A force of 200 N, applied to the free end of the rope, was required to start to raise the mass. What was the coefficient of friction?

7-48 A band of leather is draped over a 150 mm diameter oak pin, which is horizontal. If a mass of 25 kg is attached to one end of the band, and a force scale is attached to the other, determine the coefficient of friction between the oak and the leather if the mass starts to drop when the tension in the force scale is 50 N.

7-49 If an asbestos-fabric band is used to prevent a cast-iron drum from rotation, determine the minimum angle of contact required, in degrees, to prevent rotation. The tension on one end of the band is 150 N and the tension on the other end is 80 N.

7-50 If the coefficient of friction between a rope and a post is 0.20, determine the number of turns the rope must have around the post if a man who can apply a force of 400 N is to hold back an automobile that can apply a force of 2000 N.

7-51 A rubber belt passes over a fixed drum, as shown in Fig. P7-51. If the coefficient of friction between the belt and the drum is 0.65, and if the magnitudes of F_1 and F_2 are 750 N and 165 N respectively, determine the value of the angle ϕ at which slipping would impend.

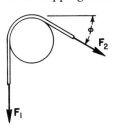

FIGURE P7-51

7-52 A rope is wrapped several times around a horizontal pipe, so that one end of the rope hangs down freely and the other end supports a mass, as shown in Fig. P7-52. If the free end of the rope has a mass of 0.20 kg, and if the mass of the other end of the rope plus the supported mass is 25 kg, determine the minimum total angle, in degrees, of contact between the rope and pipe. The coefficient of static friction is 0.15.

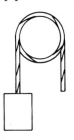

FIGURE P7-52

7-6 ROLLING RESISTANCE

A roller or wheel is rolling on a level surface, as shown in Fig. 7-31(a). To maintain rolling at a constant speed, some horizontal force **P** is necessary. The reason for the need for this force is that real materials deform, as shown in an exaggerated manner in Fig. 7-31(b), and the force is necessary to push aside the deformation. (Generally, up to this point, we have been assuming that the materials we deal with are rigid.)

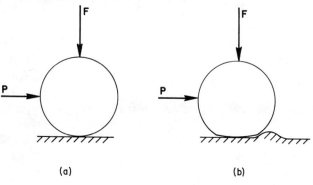

(a)   (b)

FIGURE 7-31

A free-body diagram of the roller or wheel is shown in Fig. 7-32. The point where the contact force **R** acts is offset a distance, a, from a point beneath the center of the roller. The distance a is called the coefficient of rolling resistance, and it is usually measured in mm. Typical values of the coefficient of rolling resistance are given in Table 7-2.

If moments are taken about point B in Fig. 7-32, the following equation is obtained;

$$\Sigma M_B = 0$$

$$Fa - Pr = 0$$

$$P = \frac{a}{r} F \qquad (7\text{-}10)$$

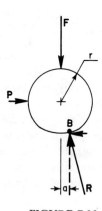

FIGURE 7-32

where P is the magnitude of the force required to overcome rolling resistance,
F is the magnitude of the load on the roller or wheel,
a is the coefficient of rolling resistance, and
r is the radius of the roller or wheel.

In deriving Eq. (7-10), it is assumed that a is sufficiently small that the perpendicular distance from B to the line of action of **P** closely approximates r.

It will be observed from Eq. (7-10) that if the radius of the wheel or roller is increased, the rolling resistance will decrease.

TABLE 7-2
TYPICAL COEFFICIENTS OF ROLLING RESISTANCE

Material	a (mm)
Steel on steel	0.18
Steel on wood	1.5
Pneumatic tire on smooth road	0.5
Hardwood on wood	1.8

Note that the force **P** is the force required to overcome rolling resistance. In the case of a wheel with an axle that uses some type of bearing, there would be friction forces in the bearing that would have to be overcome, in addition to the rolling resistance.

The topic of rolling resistance appears to be less well understood than many other topics in mechanics. Tabulated values for a, when they can be found, have a wide numeric range. In fact, the definition of the coefficient of rolling resistance is not standardized. Some authors define it as $\mu_r = a/r$, which is different from the definition used here. If you use values for the coefficient of rolling resistance from other sources, be certain to check the definition used in your sources.

EXAMPLE 7-12

An automobile with a mass of 900 kg is to be towed through loose snow on a horizontal road. If the rolling resistance for pneumatic tires in loose snow is 80 mm, and if the tire diameter is 400 mm, calculate the magnitude of the horizontal towing force required to overcome the rolling resistance.

SOLUTION

The value for the towing force required to overcome rolling resistance may be obtained by direct substitution in Eq. (7-10) *and by solving for P. Note that the number of wheels involved does not appear to affect the equation.*

$$P = \frac{a}{r} F$$

$$= \frac{80}{200} \times 900 \times 9.807$$

$$= 3530.5 \text{ N}$$

$$\boxed{P = 3530 \text{ N}}$$

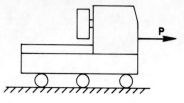

FIGURE 7-33

EXAMPLE 7-13

A machine with a mass of 250 kg has a steel base. It is being moved across a hardwood floor using 50 mm diameter steel rollers, as shown in Fig. 7-33. Determine the magnitude of the horizontal force **P** required to move the machine.

SOLUTION

Rolling resistance will occur at both contact surfaces of the rollers. The rolling resistance due to each contact can be calculated, and the total rolling resistance will be the sum of the two rolling resistances. Thus, Eq. (7-10) is used once for each combination of materials. The values for the coefficients of rolling resistance can be obtained from Table 7-2.

For steel rollers on steel:

$$P_1 = \frac{a}{r} F$$

$$= \frac{0.18}{25} \times 250 \times 9.807$$

$$= 17.653 \text{ N}$$

For steel rollers on wood:

$$P_2 = \frac{a}{r} F$$

$$= \frac{1.5}{25} \times 250 \times 9.807$$

$$= 147.105 \text{ N}$$

$$\text{Total resistance} = P_1 + P_2$$

$$= 17.653 + 147.105$$

$$= 164.758 \text{ N}$$

$$\boxed{P = 165 \text{ N}}$$

PROBLEMS

7-53 A railway car and its contents have a mass of 15 000 kg. If the car has eight steel wheels, each with a diameter of 650 mm, determine the magnitude of the force **P** required to overcome rolling resistance on horizontal steel rails.

7-54 What horizontal force must be applied to a 1000 kg automobile with 450 mm diameter pneumatic tires to overcome rolling resistance on a smooth road?

7-55 To keep an automobile wheel and tire rolling on a sand beach, a horizontal force of 15 N must be applied to the center of the wheel. Determine the coefficient of rolling resistance for the tire on the sand if the tire has a diameter of 600 mm and the wheel and tire have a mass of 18 kg.

7-56 An 80 kg roller with a steel drum that has a diameter of 500 mm is used for compacting soft asphalt for a sidewalk. If a horizontal push of 40 N must be applied to the roller to keep it moving on the level, what is the value of the coefficient of rolling resistance? Assume bearing friction is negligible.

7-57 An automobile towing a trailer with 400 mm diameter tires must apply a horizontal force of 25 N to overcome rolling resistance. What force would be required with the same trailer if the tires were changed to 600 mm diameter?

7-58 A concrete buggy and its contents have a mass of 175 kg. To push the buggy through a muddy construction site, a horizontal force of 100 N is required. Of this, 15 N is used to overcome bearing friction. If the 900 mm diameter pneumatic tires on the buggy were replaced by similar 600 mm diameter pneumatic tires, what horizontal force would be required to move the buggy on the same site?

7-59 A flat-bottomed wooden boat with a mass of 180 kg is moved across a sand beach on 150 mm diameter wooden rollers. If the coefficient of rolling resistance between the wood rollers and the sand is 3 mm, find the horizontal force necessary to keep the boat in motion.

7-60 Find the horizontal force required to move a 300 kg wooden crate across a level wooden floor if the crate is moved on four 50 mm diameter steel rollers.

8 CENTER OF GRAVITY AND CENTROID

8-1 CENTER OF GRAVITY

Every body is made up of many particles, all of which are attracted to the center of the earth by gravity. The resultant of all of these gravity forces acting on each particle is the single force that may be assumed to act on the body. The point of application of this resultant force is called the center of gravity of the body.

The location of the center of gravity is important in many situations. If the center of gravity of a crane and its load, such as that shown in Fig. 1-2, is not located between the wheels or outriggers, the crane will overturn. An important calculation for the design of an aircraft, such as the one in Fig. 4-1, is the determination of the location of the center of gravity. The center of gravity for an aircraft and its cargo depends on the distribution of cargo, and can affect the flying ability of the aircraft. The pilot will be concerned about the placement of cargo in the aircraft.

Calculations of the center of gravity also provide background for developing procedures for calculating centroids and area moments of inertia, which will be discussed in later sections.

8-2 CENTER OF GRAVITY FOR PARTICLES IN A PLANE

A system of particles in the x-y plane is shown in Fig. 8-1(a). The gravitational attraction acting on each particle and the resultant, W, of the gravitational forces are shown in Fig. 8-1(b). To locate the center of gravity of the system of particles, it is necessary to locate the point of application of the resultant of the system of forces.

Figure 8-1(b) shows a force system in space with each force passing through the x-y plane. It can also be seen as a parallel

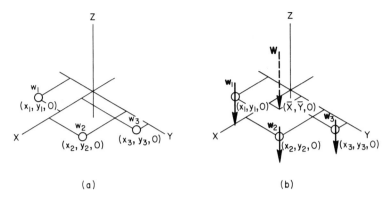

(a)   (b)

FIGURE 8-1

force system in a plane, and the resultant and its location can be obtained by following a procedure similar to that outlined in Article 3-3. Look along the y axis, so that the y axis appears as a point; the system will appear as shown in Fig. 8-2, which appears as a plane, parallel force system. When taking moments about the y axis, the distance between the forces and the x axis does not enter into the moment equation.

When taking moments about the y axis to locate the resultant force W, the moment of W about the y axis must be the same as the sum of the moments of the original system.

$$M_y:$$

$$W\overline{X} = w_1x_1 + w_2x_2 + w_3x_3 + \ldots$$

$$= \Sigma \, w_ix_i$$

but $W = \Sigma \, w_i$

thus $\overline{X} = \dfrac{\Sigma \, w_ix_i}{\Sigma \, w_i}$ \hfill (8-1)

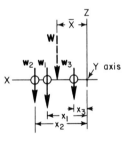

FIGURE 8-2

where $\overline{X}$ is the x coordinate of the center of gravity of the system of particles,

$\Sigma \, w_ix_i$ is the sum of the products of the gravitational force and the x coordinate of each particle, and

$\Sigma \, w_i$ is the sum of the gravitational forces acting on each particle.

In a similar manner, it may be shown that

$$\overline{Y} = \frac{\Sigma \, w_iy_i}{\Sigma \, w_i} \hfill (8-2)$$

Although Eqs. (8-1) and (8-2) are developed using moments, in this instance the right-hand rule is not used for determining signs, since all the forces have the same direction. It is more convenient to simply use the sign of the coordinates in Eqs. (8-1) and (8-2). By using this approach, the signs obtained for $\bar{X}$ and $\bar{Y}$ will automatically be the correct signs for the coordinates of the center of gravity.

EXAMPLE 8-1

Determine the location of the center of gravity of the system of two particles shown in Fig. 8-3.

SOLUTION

Both $\bar{X}$ and $\bar{Y}$ may be obtained by the use of Eqs. (8-1) and (8-2). Since the forces are gravitational forces, the mass has been multiplied by 9.807 to determine the gravitational force. Since 9.807 is a common factor, it is removed from the equation.

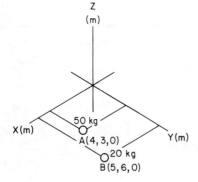

FIGURE 8-3

$$\bar{X} = \frac{\Sigma\, w_i x_i}{\Sigma\, w_i}$$

$$= \frac{50 \times 9.807 \times 4 + 20 \times 9.807 \times 5}{50 \times 9.807 + 20 \times 9.807}$$

$$= \frac{200.0 + 100.0}{50.0 + 20.0}$$

$$= \frac{300.0}{70.0}$$

$$= 4.286 \text{ m}$$

$$\bar{Y} = \frac{\Sigma\, w_i y_i}{\Sigma\, w_i}$$

$$= \frac{50 \times 9.807 \times 3 + 20 \times 9.807 \times 6}{50 \times 9.807 + 20 \times 9.807}$$

$$= \frac{150.0 + 120.0}{50.0 + 20.0}$$

$$= \frac{270.0}{70.0}$$

$$= 3.857 \text{ m}$$

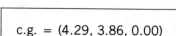

c.g. = (4.29, 3.86, 0.00)

Since each coordinate was positive, each term in the equation was positive, and the values obtained for $\overline{X}$ and $\overline{Y}$ are both positive. Although not absolutely necessary, the Z coordinate has been shown in the final answer. As long as the particles are in the x-y plane, the value for the Z coordinate of the center of gravity must be zero.

EXAMPLE 8-2

For the system of particles shown in Fig. 8-4, find the location of the center of gravity.

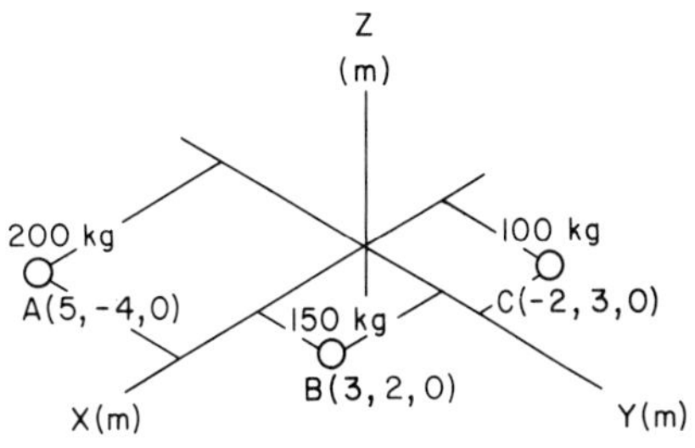

SOLUTION

The values for $\overline{X}$ and $\overline{Y}$ may be obtained by using Eqs. (8-1) and (8-2). The signs of the coordinates must be used when substituting in the equations, since this is what provides the sign for each term in the numerator.

FIGURE 8-4

$$\overline{X} = \frac{\Sigma w_i x_i}{\Sigma w_i}$$

$$= \frac{200 \times 9.807 \times 5 + 150 \times 9.807 \times 3 - 100 \times 9.807 \times 2}{200 \times 9.807 + 150 \times 9.807 + 100 \times 9.807}$$

$$= \frac{1000.0 + 450.0 - 200.0}{200.0 + 150.0 + 100.0}$$

$$= \frac{1250.0}{450.0}$$

$$= 2.778 \text{ m}$$

$$\overline{Y} = \frac{\Sigma w_i y_i}{\Sigma w_i}$$

$$= \frac{-(200 \times 9.807 \times 4) + 150 \times 9.807 \times 2 + 100 \times 9.807 \times 3}{200 \times 9.807 + 150 \times 9.807 + 100 \times 9.807}$$

$$= \frac{-800.0 + 300.0 + 300.0}{200.0 + 150.0 + 100.0}$$

$$= \frac{-200.0}{450.0}$$

$$= -0.4444 \text{ m}$$

c.g. = (2.78, −0.444, 0.00)

Since the value obtained for $\bar{Y}$ was negative, the actual coordinate value for $\bar{Y}$ will be negative, as shown.

EXAMPLE 8-3

Find the center of gravity for the following system of particles: $A = 1000$ kg at $(4,0,0)$; $B = 800$ kg at $(0,5,0)$; and $C = 1200$ kg at $(-3,-4,0)$. Coordinate distances are in metres.

SOLUTION

The values for $\bar{X}$ and $\bar{Y}$ may be obtained by application of Eqs. (8-1) and (8-2). Note that when calculating $\bar{X}$, the 800 kg particle will not add to the value of the numerator, since its x coordinate is zero, but it must still be included in the denominator, because it still contributes to the total gravitational attraction. Similarly, the 1000 kg particle will not influence the numerator when determining $\bar{Y}$.

$$\bar{X} = \frac{\Sigma \, w_i x_i}{\Sigma \, w_i}$$

$$= \frac{1000 \times 9.807 \times 4 + 800 \times 9.807 \times 0 - 1200 \times 9.807 \times 3}{1000 \times 9.807 + 800 \times 9.807 + 1200 \times 9.807}$$

$$= \frac{4000.0 + 0.0 - 3600.0}{1000.0 + 800.0 + 1200.0}$$

$$= \frac{400.0}{3000.0}$$

$$= 0.1333 \text{ m}$$

$$\bar{Y} = \frac{\Sigma \, w_i y_i}{\Sigma \, w_i}$$

$$= \frac{1000.0 \times 9.807 \times 0 + 800 \times 9.807 \times 5 - 1200 \times 9.807 \times 4}{1000 \times 9.807 + 800 \times 9.807 + 1200 \times 9.807}$$

$$= \frac{0.0 + 4000.0 - 4800.0}{1000.0 + 800.0 + 1200.0}$$

$$= \frac{-800.0}{3000.0}$$

$$= -0.2667 \text{ m}$$

$$\boxed{\text{c.g.} = (0.133, -0.267, 0.00)}$$

PROBLEMS

8-1 For the system of two particles shown in Fig. P8-1, determine the center of gravity.

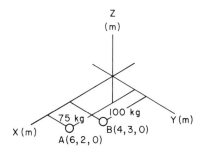

FIGURE P8-1

8-2 Locate the center of gravity of the system of two particles shown in Fig. P8-2.

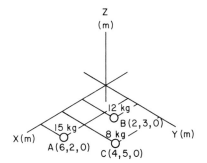

FIGURE P8-2

8-3 Find the center of gravity of the system of particles shown in Fig. P8-3.

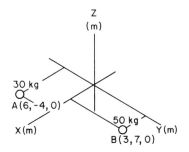

FIGURE P8-3

8-4 Determine the center of gravity of the system of particles shown in Fig. P8-4.

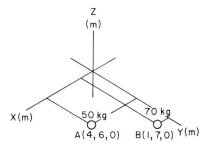

FIGURE P8-4

8-5 For the system shown in Fig. P8-5, locate the center of gravity.

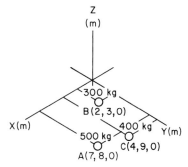

FIGURE P8-5

8-6 Calculate the center of gravity of the system shown in Fig. P8-6.

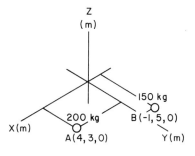

FIGURE P8-6

8-7 Find the center of gravity of $A = 7$ kg at $(3,-6,0)$; $B = 5$ kg at $(5,6,0)$; and $C = 8$ kg at $(-2,-3,0)$. Coordinate distances are in metres.

8-8 For particles $A = 500$ kg at $(4,-3,0)$; $B = 600$ kg at $(2,5,0)$; and $C = 700$ kg at $(-3,0,0)$, determine the center of gravity if distances are in metres.

8-9 Locate the center of gravity for the following system of particles: $A = 100$ kg at $(2,-3,0)$; $B = 95$ kg at $(0,0,0)$; and $C = 120$ kg at $(-3,-2,0)$. Distances are in metres.

8-10 Determine the center of gravity of $A = 40$ kg at $(5,7,0)$; $B = 50$ kg at $(-6,3,0)$; and $C = 60$ kg at $(-5,-6,0)$. Coordinates are in metres.

8-3 CENTER OF GRAVITY OF PARTICLES IN SPACE

Figure 8-5(a) shows a system of particles in space. The lines of action of the gravitational forces acting on the particles would continue to pass through the x-y plane, as shown in Fig. 8-5(b), so that the location of the x and y coordinates of the resultant force **W** may be obtained by using the equations developed in Article 8-2.

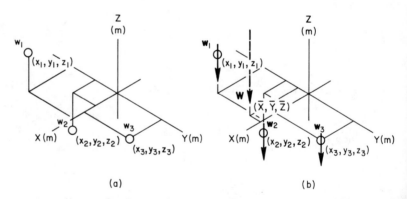

FIGURE 8-5

$$\bar{X} = \frac{\Sigma w_i x_i}{\Sigma w_i} \tag{8-1}$$

$$\bar{Y} = \frac{\Sigma w_i y_i}{\Sigma w_i} \tag{8-2}$$

The forces shown in Fig. 8-5(b) are all parallel to the z axis and thus have no moment about the z axis. Now imagine that the system shown in Fig. 8-5(a) is being rotated about the y axis, and that you are viewing it from the end of the y axis. The gravitational forces, which appear as shown in Fig. 8-6, now have a moment about the y axis, and moments can now be taken about the y axis to find $\bar{Z}$. Again following the procedure that was used in Article 8-2, it is found that

$$\bar{Z} = \frac{\Sigma \, w_i z_i}{\Sigma \, w_i} \qquad (8\text{-}3)$$

As with systems of particles in a plane, the signs of the coordinates are used in solving Eqs. (8-1), (8-2) and (8-3). Since all forces are parallel, this process will automatically give the correct sign for the coordinates of the center of gravity.

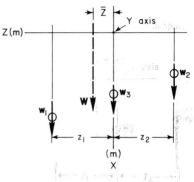

FIGURE 8-6

EXAMPLE 8-4

Find the center of gravity of the system of particles shown in Fig. 8-7.

SOLUTION

The calculation of the center of gravity is an application of Eqs. (8-1), (8-2) and (8-3). The signs of the coordinates of the particles must be used in the calculations to determine the sign for each term in the numerator. Note that 9.807 is a common factor in each term, and hence is eliminated from the calculation.

$$\bar{X} = \frac{\Sigma \, w_i x_i}{\Sigma \, w_i}$$

$$= \frac{30 \times 9.807 \times 4 + 25 \times 9.807 \times 6 - 40 \times 9.807 \times 3}{30 \times 9.807 + 25 \times 9.807 + 40 \times 9.807}$$

$$= \frac{120.0 + 150.0 - 120.0}{30.0 + 25.0 + 40.0}$$

$$= \frac{150.0}{95.0}$$

$$= 1.579 \text{ m}$$

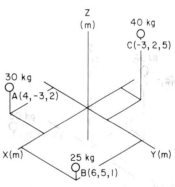

FIGURE 8-7

$$\bar{Y} = \frac{\Sigma \, w_i y_i}{\Sigma \, w_i}$$

$$= \frac{-(30 \times 9.807 \times 3) + 25 \times 9.807 \times 5 + 40 \times 9.807 \times 2}{30 \times 9.807 + 25 \times 9.807 + 40 \times 9.807}$$

$$= \frac{-90.0 + 125.0 + 80.0}{30.0 + 25.0 + 40.0}$$

$$= \frac{115.0}{95.0}$$

$$= 1.211 \text{ m}$$

$$\bar{Z} = \frac{\Sigma \, w_i z_i}{\Sigma \, w_i}$$

$$= \frac{30 \times 9.807 \times 2 + 25 \times 9.807 \times 1 + 40 \times 9.807 \times 5}{30 \times 9.807 + 25 \times 9.807 + 40 \times 9.807}$$

$$= \frac{60.0 + 25.0 + 200.0}{30.0 + 25.0 + 40.0}$$

$$= \frac{285.0}{95.0}$$

$$= 3.000 \text{ m}$$

$$\boxed{\text{c.g.} = (1.58, \, 1.21, \, 3.00)}$$

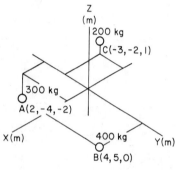

FIGURE 8-8

EXAMPLE 8-5

Determine the location of the center of gravity for the particles shown in Fig. 8-8.

SOLUTION

The coordinates of the center of gravity may be obtained by substitution into Eqs. (8-1), (8-2) and (8-3). Note that the sign of the coordinate of each particle must also be used in the equation to obtain the correct value for the center of gravity. When calculating $\bar{Z}$, the z coordinate for the 400 kg particle is zero. However, the force due to the 400 kg particle must still form part of the denominator of the equation.

$$\bar{X} = \frac{\Sigma \, w_i x_i}{\Sigma \, w_i}$$

$$= \frac{300 \times 9.807 \times 2 + 400 \times 9.807 \times 4 - 200 \times 9.807 \times 3}{300 \times 9.807 + 400 \times 9.807 + 200 \times 9.807}$$

$$= \frac{600.0 + 1600.0 - 600.0}{300.0 + 400.0 + 200.0}$$

$$= \frac{1600.0}{900.0}$$

$$= 1.778 \text{ m}$$

$$\bar{Y} = \frac{\Sigma \, w_i y_i}{\Sigma \, w_i}$$

$$= \frac{-(300 \times 9.807 \times 4) + 400 \times 9.807 \times 5 - 200 \times 9.807 \times 2}{300 \times 9.807 + 400 \times 9.807 + 200 \times 9.807}$$

$$= \frac{-1200.0 + 2000.0 - 400.0}{300.0 + 400.0 + 200.0}$$

$$= \frac{400.0}{900.0}$$

$$= 0.4444 \text{ m}$$

$$\bar{Z} = \frac{\Sigma w_i z_i}{\Sigma w_i}$$

$$= \frac{-(300 \times 9.807 \times 2) + 400 \times 9.807 \times 0 + 200 \times 9.807 \times 1}{300 \times 9.807 + 400 \times 9.807 + 200 \times 9.807}$$

$$= \frac{-600.0 + 0.0 + 200.0}{300.0 + 400.0 + 200.0}$$

$$= \frac{-400.0}{900.0}$$

$$= -0.4444 \text{ m}$$

$$\boxed{\text{c.g.} = (1.78, 0.444, -0.444)}$$

EXAMPLE 8-6

Locate the center of gravity for the following system of particles:
$A = 35$ kg at $(3,-5,2)$; $B = 60$ kg at $(-2,3,-4)$; $C = 50$ kg at
$(-4,-2,0)$; and $D = 20$ kg at $(0,0,0)$. Coordinates are in metres.

SOLUTION

By substituting into Eqs. (8-1), (8-2) *and* (8-3), *with due regard
for both values and signs, the location of the center of gravity
may be obtained.*

$$\bar{X} = \frac{\Sigma w_i x_i}{\Sigma w_i}$$

$$= \frac{35 \times 9.807 \times 3 - 60 \times 9.807 \times 2 - 50 \times 9.807 \times 4 + 20 \times 9.807 \times 0}{35 \times 9.807 + 60 \times 9.807 + 50 \times 9.807 + 20 \times 9.807}$$

$$= \frac{105.0 - 120.0 - 200.0 + 0.0}{35.0 + 60.0 + 50.0 + 20.0}$$

$$= \frac{-215.0}{165.0}$$

$$= -1.3030 \text{ m}$$

$$\bar{Y} = \frac{\Sigma w_i y_i}{\Sigma w_i}$$

$$= \frac{-(35 \times 9.807 \times 5) + 60 \times 9.807 \times 3 - 50 \times 9.807 \times 2 + 20 \times 9.807 \times 0}{35 \times 9.807 + 60 \times 9.807 + 50 \times 9.807 + 20 \times 9.807}$$

$$= \frac{-175.0 + 180.0 - 100.0 + 0.0}{35.0 + 60.0 + 50.0 + 20.0}$$

$$= \frac{-95.0}{165.0}$$

$$= -0.5758 \text{ m}$$

$$\bar{Z} = \frac{\Sigma w_i z_i}{\Sigma w_i}$$

$$= \frac{35 \times 9.807 \times 2 - 60 \times 9.807 \times 4 + 50 \times 9.807 \times 0 + 20 \times 9.807 \times 0}{35 \times 9.807 + 60 \times 9.807 + 50 \times 9.807 + 20 \times 9.807}$$

$$= \frac{70.0 - 240.0 + 0.0 + 0.0}{35.0 + 60.0 + 50.0 + 20.0}$$

$$= \frac{-170.0}{165.0}$$

$$= -1.0303 \text{ m}$$

c.g. = (−1.30, −0.576, −1.03)

PROBLEMS

8-11 Find the center of gravity of the two particles shown in Fig. P8-11

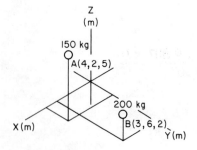

FIGURE P8-11

8-12 Locate the center of gravity for the two particles shown in Fig. P8-12.

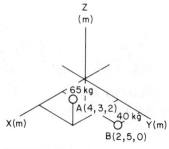

FIGURE P8-12

8-13 Find the center of gravity for the two particles shown in Fig. P8-13.

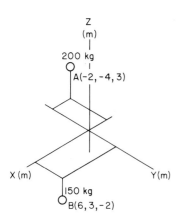

FIGURE P8-13

8-14 For the system of particles shown in Fig. P8-14, determine the location of the center of gravity.

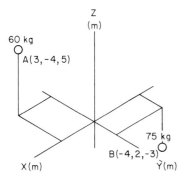

FIGURE P8-14

8-15 Locate the center of gravity of the system of particles shown in Fig. P8-15.

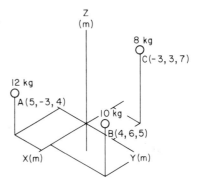

FIGURE P8-15

8-16 for the system of particles shown in Fig. P8-16, locate the center of gravity.

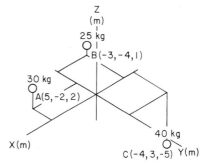

FIGURE P8-16

8-17 Determine the center of gravity for the following system of particles: $A = 150$ kg at $(5,0,0)$; $B = 200$ kg at $(3,2,-4)$; and $C = 250$ kg at $(-4,-1,2)$. Coordinates are in metres.

8-18 For the system of particles consisting of $A = 10$ kg at $(3,-2,4)$; $B = 15$ kg at $(0,0,5)$; and $C = 20$ kg at $(-2,4,0)$, calculate the center of gravity. Coordinates are in metres.

8-19 Find the center of gravity for four particles: $A = 60$ kg at $(7,8,10)$; $B = 25$ kg at $(-4,0,7)$; $C = 40$ kg at $(9,11,-3)$; and $D = 50$ kg at $(2,0,0)$. Distances are in metres.

8-20 For the particles $A = 200$ kg at $(-3,0,0)$; $B = 300$ kg at $(-4,5,1)$; $C = 400$ kg at $(2,0,-3)$; and $D = 100$ kg at $(0,-2,-2)$, locate the center of gravity. Distances are in metres.

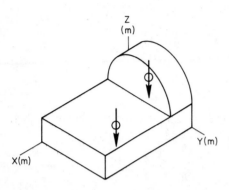

FIGURE 8-9

8-4 CENTER OF GRAVITY OF COMPOSITE BODIES

A composite body is a body made up of two or more simple shapes, such as spheres, cones or rectangular solids. The mass of each component or part may be assumed to be concentrated at the center of gravity of the component. The body could be treated as a system of particles in space, with the coordinates of each particle being the location of the center of gravity of each component, and the mass of each particle being the mass of each component.

If the material of each component is homogeneous, the center of gravity for each may be located by reference to Appendix B, which shows the center of gravity for a number of solid shapes and the volume of those shapes.

Figure 8-9 shows a simple composite body. It also shows the particles, and the gravitational attraction on them that may be assumed to replace the two components of the composite body. Once the location of the center of gravity of each particle is determined, then the location of the center of gravity of the composite body may be obtained using the procedures of Article 8-3.

The composite body shown in Fig. 8-10(a) consists of a rectangular solid with a cylinder removed, as shown in Fig. 8-10(b). The mass of the cylinder is treated as a negative mass, and is thus given a negative sign. The balance of the calculations proceed as outlined in Article 8-3.

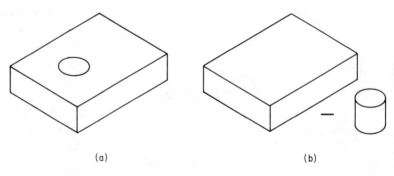

(a)   (b)

FIGURE 8-10

A plane of symmetry exists for some bodies. Such a plane of symmetry will contain the center of gravity, provided each of the components is homogeneous. If the coordinates of the center of gravity of each component are tabulated and it is found that all the coordinates for one axis have the same value, then it will not be necessary to calculate the coordinate for the center of gravity of that axis, for it will be the same as the common value for each of the component parts of the body.

EXAMPLE 8-7

Locate the center of gravity of the composite body shown in Fig. 8-11. The lower block has a density of 1200 kg/m³ and the upper block has a density of 2000 kg/m³.

SOLUTION

For purposes of labelling, the lower block will be Part 1 *and the upper block will be* Part 2. *The mass and center of gravity of each block should be obtained. Appendix B is used as an aid in obtaining this information.*

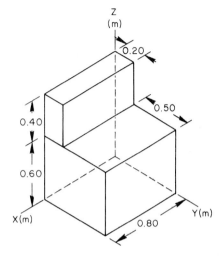

FIGURE 8-11

Lower Block — Part 1

$$m_1 = 0.80 \times 0.70 \times 0.60 \times 1200$$
$$= 403.2 \text{ kg}$$
$$x_1 = 0.40 \text{ m}$$
$$y_1 = 0.35 \text{ m}$$
$$z_1 = 0.30 \text{ m}$$

Upper block — Part 2

$$m_2 = 0.80 \times 0.20 \times 0.40 \times 2000$$
$$= 128.0 \text{ kg}$$
$$x_2 = 0.40 \text{ m}$$
$$y_2 = 0.10$$
$$z_2 = 0.60 + 0.20$$
$$= 0.80 \text{ m}$$

Note that z_2 is equal to the height of the lower block plus half the height of the upper block.

Both x_1 and x_2 are 0.40. A plane parallel to the y-z plane passing through x = 0.40 is a plane of symmetry. Thus $\bar{X}$ may be obtained by observation.

By symmetry:

$$\bar{X} = 0.400 \text{ m}$$

The value for $\bar{Y}$ may be obtained by substituting the values noted in Eq. (8-2). Although 9.807 turns out to be a common factor in each term, it is included as a reminder that the calculation is actually based on the forces due to gravity.

$$\overline{Y} = \frac{\Sigma\, w_i y_i}{\Sigma\, w_i}$$

$$= \frac{403.2 \times 9.807 \times 0.35 + 128.0 \times 9.807 \times 0.10}{403.2 \times 9.807 + 128.0 \times 9.807}$$

$$= \frac{141.1 + 12.8}{403.2 + 128.0}$$

$$= \frac{153.9}{531.2}$$

$$= 0.2897 \text{ m}$$

Similarly, the value for $\overline{Z}$ may be obtained using the values noted above and using Eq. (8-3).

$$\overline{Z} = \frac{\Sigma\, w_i z_i}{\Sigma\, w_i}$$

$$= \frac{403.2 \times 9.807 \times 0.30 + 128.0 \times 9.807 \times 0.80}{403.2 \times 9.807 + 128.0 \times 9.807}$$

$$= \frac{121.0 + 102.4}{403.2 + 128.0}$$

$$= \frac{223.4}{531.2}$$

$$= 0.4205 \text{ m}$$

> c.g. = (0.400, 0.290, 0.420)

EXAMPLE 8-8

Determine the location of the center of gravity of the body shown in Fig. 8-12. It is made of material with a density of 2700 kg/m³.

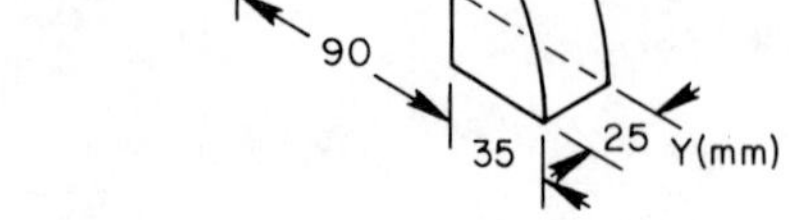

SOLUTION

The body is made up of a semicircular cylinder with a rectangular solid removed. The mass and center of gravity of each component should be determined, using the information from Appendix B.

Semicircular solid — Part 1

$$m_1 = \frac{\pi \times 80^2}{2} \times 25 \times \frac{2700}{10^9}$$

FIGURE 8-12

$$= 0.6786 \text{ kg}$$

$$x_1 = 12.5 \text{ mm}$$

$$y_1 = 80.0 \text{ mm}$$

$$z_1 = \frac{4 \times 80}{3\pi}$$

$$= 33.95 \text{ mm}$$

The center of gravity for the semicircular cylinder will be on the cylinder's plane of symmetry, and thus the y coordinate for the center of gravity will be at y = 80. Both quarter-circular cylinders have their z coordinates of the center of gravity at the same value (z = 33.95). Thus the z coordinate for the semicircular cylinder must also be at the same location. In the calculations of mass, the density is divided by 10^9 to convert from kg/m^3 to kg/mm^3.

Rectangular solid — Part 2

$$m_2 = -25 \times 90 \times 30 \times \frac{2700}{10^9}$$

$$= -0.1822 \text{ kg}$$

$$x_2 = 12.5 \text{ mm}$$

$$y_2 = 35 + 45$$

$$= 80.0 \text{ mm}$$

$$z_2 = 15.0 \text{ mm}$$

In calculating y_2, it should be noted that y_2 is equal to the distance from the x axis to the edge of the rectangular solid plus half the width of the rectangular solid.

In determining $\overline{X}$, note that both parts have the same x coordinate for the center of gravity. Hence, the center of gravity will be located at the common value. Also note that a plane passing through x = 12.5 and parallel to the y-z plane is a plane of symmetry, which must contain the center of gravity.

By symmetry:

$$\overline{X} = 12.5 \text{ mm}$$

The y coordinate for the center of gravity for each part has the same value, so the center of gravity for the entire body must also have that same value. It may also be observed that a plane of symmetry parallel to the x-z plane passes through y = 80.0.

By symmetry:

$$\bar{Y} = 80.0 \text{ mm}$$

To determine $\bar{Z}$, it is necessary to use the information developed above and to use Eq. (8-3). Note the use of the negative sign with Part 2, which is removed from the body. Since it is the center of gravity that is being obtained, the factor of 9.807 is used to convert mass to the force due to gravity.

$$
\begin{aligned}
\bar{Z} &= \frac{\Sigma \, w_i z_i}{\Sigma \, w_i} \\[2mm]
&= \frac{0.6786 \times 9.807 \times 33.95 - 0.1822 \times 9.807 \times 15.0}{0.6786 \times 9.807 - 0.1822 \times 9.807} \\[2mm]
&= \frac{23.041 - 2.734}{0.6786 - 0.1822} \\[2mm]
&= \frac{20.307}{0.4964} \\[2mm]
&= 40.91 \text{ mm}
\end{aligned}
$$

> c.g. = (12.5, 80.0, 40.9)

EXAMPLE   8-9

The base of the composite body shown in Fig. 8-13 is made of material with a density of 900 kg/m³; the hemisphere is made of material with a density of 1100 kg/m³. Determine the location of the center of gravity.

SOLUTION

The body can be made up by a rectangular solid base from which a triangular solid is removed. To the base is added a hemi-

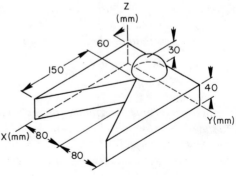

FIGURE 8-13

sphere. (It is also possible to treat the base as a rectangular solid to which two triangular solids are added.)

The first step is to determine the mass of each part and to locate the center of gravity of each part, using Appendix B.

Rectangular solid — Part 1

$$m_1 = 210 \times 160 \times 40 \times \frac{900}{10^9}$$

$$= 1.2096 \text{ kg}$$

$$x_1 = 105.0 \text{ mm}$$

$$y_1 = 80.0 \text{ mm}$$

$$z_1 = 20.0 \text{ mm}$$

Triangular solid — Part 2

$$m_2 = -\frac{1}{2} \times 160 \times 150 \times 40 \times \frac{900}{10^9}$$

$$= -0.4320 \text{ kg}$$

$$x_2 = 210 - \frac{150}{3}$$

$$= 210.0 - 50.0$$

$$= 160.0 \text{ mm}$$

$$y_2 = 80.0 \text{ mm}$$

$$z_2 = 20.0 \text{ mm}$$

When locating x_2, *the distance to the center of gravity of the triangular solid is measured from the base of the triangle, which is located at* $x = 210$.

Hemisphere — Part 3

$$m_3 = \frac{2}{3}\pi \times 30^3 \times \frac{1100}{10^9}$$

$$= 0.06220 \text{ kg}$$

$$x_3 = 30.0 \text{ mm}$$

$$y_3 = 80.0 \text{ mm}$$

$$z_3 = 40 + \frac{3}{8} \times 30$$

$$= 40.00 + 11.25$$

$$= 51.25 \text{ mm}$$

The value for z_3 is equal to the thickness of the rectangular solid plus the distance from the bottom of the hemisphere to its center of gravity.

The center of gravity of the composite body may now be calculated. Equation (8-1) is used to obtain $\overline{X}$. Since this is a calculation involving the gravitational forces, the mass is converted to force, even though the 9.807 is a common factor that disappears from the equation.

$$\overline{X} = \frac{\Sigma \, w_i x_i}{\Sigma \, w_i}$$

$$= \frac{1.2096 \times 9.807 \times 105.0 - 0.4320 \times 9.807 \times 160.0 + 0.06220 \times 9.807 \times 30.0}{1.2096 \times 9.807 - 0.4320 \times 9.807 + 0.06220 \times 9.807}$$

$$= \frac{127.008 - 69.120 + 1.866}{1.2096 - 0.4320 + 0.0622}$$

$$= \frac{59.754}{0.8398}$$

$$= 71.153 \text{ mm}$$

All three parts have the same value for the y coordinate for the center of gravity. It is fairly obvious that a plane of symmetry parallel to the x-z plane passes through $y = 80$.

By symmetry:

$$\overline{Y} = 80.0 \text{ mm}$$

The value for $\overline{Z}$ may be obtained by using the above information in Eq. (8-3).

$$\overline{Z} = \frac{\Sigma \, w_i z_i}{\Sigma \, w_i}$$

$$= \frac{1.2096 \times 9.807 \times 20.0 - 0.4320 \times 9.807 \times 20.0 + 0.06220 \times 9.807 \times 51.25}{1.2096 \times 9.807 - 0.4320 \times 9.807 + 0.06220 \times 9.807}$$

$$= \frac{24.192 - 8.640 + 3.188}{1.2096 - 0.4320 + 0.0622}$$

$$= \frac{18.74}{0.8398}$$

$$= 22.315 \text{ mm}$$

c.g. = (71.2, 80.0, 22.3)

PROBLEMS

8-21 The block shown in Fig. P8-21 is made of two materials. The part on the left has a density of 1000 kg/m³ and the part on the right has a density of 1500 kg/m³. Locate the block's center of gravity.

rial with a density of 2700 kg/m³. The *x-z* plane is a plane of symmetry and the *z* axis is on the surface of the upper cylinder. Determine the center of gravity.

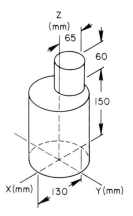

FIGURE P8-23

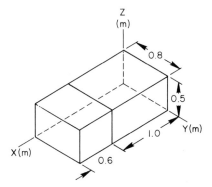

FIGURE P8-21

8-22 The cylinder in Fig. P8-22 has an upper part with a density of 8000 kg/m³ and a lower part with a density of 2700 kg/m³. Locate the cylinder's center of gravity.

8-24 Locate the center of gravity of the body shown in Fig. P8-24. The upper block is made of material with a density of 2700 kg/m³ and the lower portion is made of material with a density of 7200 kg/m³.

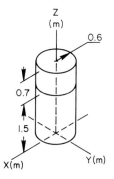

FIGURE P8-22

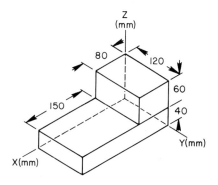

FIGURE P8-24

8-23 The lower part of the body shown in Fig. P8-23 is made of material with a density of 1200 kg/m³ and the upper part is made of mate-

8-25 For the body shown in Fig. P8-25, determine the location of the center of gravity. The base has a density of 8000 kg/m³ and the upper part has a density of 12 500 kg/m³.

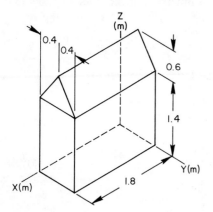

FIGURE P8-25

8-26 Find the location of the center of gravity for the body shown in Fig. P8-26. The rectangular solid has a density of 900 kg/m³ and the semicircular cylinder has a density of 1200 kg/m³.

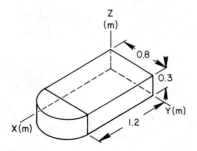

FIGURE P8-26

8-27 Determine the location of the center of gravity of the homogeneous block with a hole, as shown in Fig. P8-27.

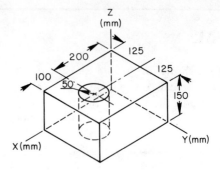

FIGURE P8-27

8-28 Determine the location of the center of gravity for the homogeneous body shown in Fig. P8-28.

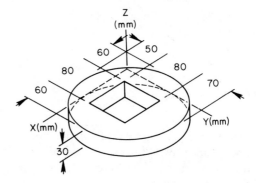

FIGURE P8-28

8-29 Find the center of gravity for the homogeneous solid shown in Fig. P8-29.

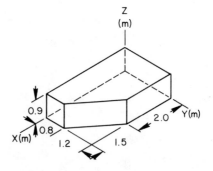

FIGURE P8-29

8-30 For the homogeneous body shown in Fig. P8-30, determine the center of gravity.

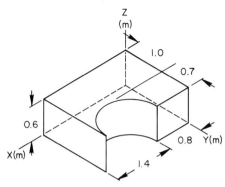

FIGURE P8-30

8-31 Locate the center of gravity for the truncated triangular solid shown in Fig. P8-31. The material has a density of 2400 kg/m³.

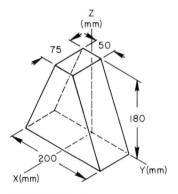

FIGURE P8-31

8-32 Locate the center of gravity of the truncated cone shown in Fig. P8-32. The material has a density of 8000 kg/m³.

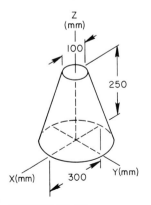

FIGURE P8-32

8-33 Locate the center of gravity for the body shown in Fig. P8-33. The cylinder has a density of 2700 kg/m³ and the cone has a density of 8000 kg/m³.

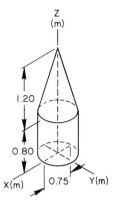

FIGURE P8-33

8-34 Find the center of gravity for the body shown in Fig. P8-34. The cylinder is made of material with a density of 2700 kg/m³ and the hemisphere is made of material with a density of 8000 kg/m³.

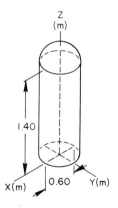

FIGURE P8-34

8-35 Locate the center of gravity for the bracket shown in Fig. P8-35. The vertical part has a density of 3500 kg/m³ and the base has a density of 3000 kg/m³.

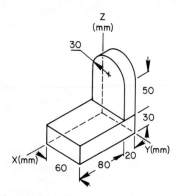

FIGURE P8-35

8-36 The cylinder shown in Fig. P8-36 has a density of 7000 kg/m³ and the arm to which it is fastened has a density of 8000 kg/m³. Locate the center of gravity for the body.

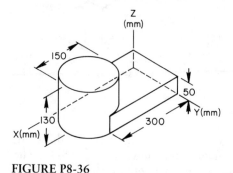

FIGURE P8-36

8-5   CENTROID OF AN AREA

The centroid of an area is a geometric property of the shape of the area, and is the geometric center of the area. You will need to locate centroids when calculating the area moment of inertia, which will be discussed in the next chapter. The area moment of inertia of the cross section is required for all calculations of stress and deflection in beams, as well as for calculations of the strength of columns.

The center of gravity of a body is a physical property of that body, and is the basis for calculating the centroid, as is shown in the following calculation. A plate in the x-y plane with uniform thickness, t, and constant density ρ, is shown in Fig. 8-14. The plate is made up of many small elements, each with a surface area of A_i and a thickness of t. The mass of each element of the plate is $A_i t \rho$. Consider the plate as a composite body. Following the procedures of Article 8-4, it is found that the x coordinate of the center of gravity of the uniform plate is

$$\bar{X} = \frac{\Sigma w_i x_i}{\Sigma w_i}$$

but $w_i = A_i t \rho$

thus $\bar{X} = \frac{\Sigma A_i t \rho x_i}{\Sigma A_i t \rho}$

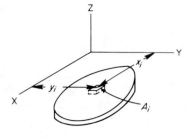

FIGURE 8-14

Since t and ρ are constants, they may be taken outside of the summation sign, so that the expression becomes

$$\bar{X} = \frac{t\rho \, \Sigma \, A_i x_i}{t\rho \, \Sigma \, A_i}$$

The terms t and ρ may now be treated as common factors in the numerator and denominator, giving

$$\bar{X} = \frac{\Sigma \, A_i x_i}{\Sigma \, A_i} \tag{8-4}$$

where $\bar{X}$ is the x coordinate of the centroid of the area,

$\Sigma \, A_i x_i$ is the sum of the products of each area and the x coordinate of the centroid of each individual area, and

$\Sigma \, A_i$ is the sum of all the individual areas making up the total area.

It will be noted that $\bar{X}$ is now expressed in terms of the area of the parts making up the total area, and thus $\bar{X}$ is the x coordinate of the centroid of the area rather than the x coordinate of the center of gravity of the mass.

In a similar fashion, it may be shown that

$$\bar{Y} = \frac{\Sigma \, A_i y_i}{\Sigma \, A_i} \tag{8-5}$$

The expressions $A_i x_i$ and $A_i y_i$ are sometimes called the first moment of area because the expression is an area times a distance.

When working with Eqs. (8-4) and (8-5), attention must be paid to the signs. Areas are positive unless they are being removed or subtracted from the shape, in which case the sign of the area will be negative. The actual sign of the coordinate of each simple area is used in the calculation. The sign of values obtained for $\bar{X}$ and $\bar{Y}$ will be the correct sign for each coordinate of the centroid. The areas and locations of the centroids for many simple areas are given in Appendix C, and these simple areas can be combined to make up a very large proportion of the common areas or shapes you will encounter.

If an area has an axis of symmetry, the centroid will lie on that axis. If the coordinate for the centroid of each area in the x and y direction has the same value, the common value for the centroid may be an axis of symmetry.

EXAMPLE 8-10

Find the centroid of the T section shown in Fig. 8-15.

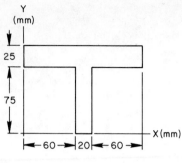

FIGURE 8-15

SOLUTION

The shape can be made up of a vertical rectangle and a horizontal rectangle. It will be easier to set up the solution if each area and its centroid are calculated before Eqs. (8-4) and (8-5) are used. Note that all values for the x and y coordinates of the centroids must be measured from the y and x axes, and not just from the edge of the rectangle.

Vertical rectangle — Part 1

$$A_1 = 20 \times 75$$

$$= 1500 \text{ mm}^2$$

$$x_1 = 60 + \frac{20}{2}$$

$$= 60.0 + 10.0$$

$$= 70.0 \text{ mm}$$

$$y_1 = \frac{75}{2}$$

$$= 37.5 \text{ mm}$$

Horizontal rectangle — Part 2

$$A_2 = 140 \times 25$$

$$= 3500 \text{ mm}^2$$

$$x_2 = \frac{140}{2}$$

$$= 70.0 \text{ mm}$$

$$y_2 = 75 + \frac{25}{2}$$

$$= 75.0 + 12.5$$

$$= 87.5 \text{ mm}$$

It is now possible to use Eq. (8-4) to find $\bar{X}$. However, note that x = 70.0 is an axis of symmetry, and also that both areas have their centroids at x = 70.0. Thus, the actual calculation for $\bar{X}$ is not necessary.

By symmetry:

$$\bar{X} = 70.00 \text{ mm}$$

To determine $\bar{Y}$, the information on areas and moments above is used in Eq. (8-5).

$$\overline{Y} = \frac{\Sigma\ A_iy_i}{\Sigma\ A_i}$$

$$= \frac{1500 \times 37.5 + 3500 \times 87.5}{1500 + 3500}$$

$$= \frac{56\ 250 + 306\ 250}{5\ 000}$$

$$= \frac{362\ 500}{5\ 000}$$

$$= 72.50\ \text{mm}$$

Centroid = (70.0, 72.5)

EXAMPLE 8-11

For the area shown in Fig. 8-16, locate the centroid.

SOLUTION

The area is a rectangle from which a quarter-circular area has been removed. The information from Appendix C is used to determine the areas and the centroids for the two parts.

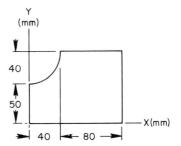

FIGURE 8-16

Rectangle — Part 1

$$A_1 = 120 \times 90$$

$$= 10\ 800\ \text{mm}^2$$

$$x_1 = \frac{120}{2}$$

$$= 60.00\ \text{mm}$$

$$y_1 = \frac{90}{2}$$

$$= 45.00\ \text{mm}$$

Quarter-circular area — Part 2

$$A_2 = \frac{\pi \times 40^2}{4}$$

$$= -1256.6\ \text{mm}^2$$

$$x_2 = \frac{4 \times 40}{3\pi}$$

$$= 16.98\ \text{mm}$$

$$y_2 = 90 - \frac{4 \times 40}{3\pi}$$

$$= 90.00 - 16.98$$

$$= 73.02 \text{ mm}$$

In calculating y_2, note that the table gives the distance from the base of the quarter-circular area to the centroid. The distance from the x axis to the base must be taken into account when determining the value for y_2, since it is the location of the centroid relative to the axis system for the composite area that is required.

The values for $\bar{X}$ and $\bar{Y}$ may be obtained by applying the area and centroid information in Eqs. (8-4) *and* (8-5). *Note that the negative sign is used with A_2, since the area is being removed.*

$$\bar{X} = \frac{\Sigma A_i x_i}{\Sigma A_i}$$

$$= \frac{10\ 800 \times 60.00 - 1\ 256.6 \times 16.98}{10\ 800 - 1\ 256.6}$$

$$= \frac{648\ 000.0 - 21\ 337.0}{9\ 543.4}$$

$$= \frac{626\ 663.0}{9\ 543.4}$$

$$= 65.66 \text{ mm}$$

$$\bar{Y} = \frac{\Sigma A_i y_i}{\Sigma A_i}$$

$$= \frac{10\ 800 \times 45.00 - 1\ 256.6 \times 73.02}{10\ 800 - 1\ 256.6}$$

$$= \frac{486\ 000.0 - 91\ 756.9}{9\ 543.4}$$

$$= \frac{394\ 243.1}{9\ 543.4}$$

$$= 41.31 \text{ mm}$$

Centroid = (65.7, 41.3)

EXAMPLE 8-12

Calculate the location of the centroid for the area shown in Fig. 8-17.

SOLUTION

This particular area may be broken up several different ways. For example, it may be a rectangle with a triangle added or a rectangle with a triangle removed. Probably the best way to treat this particular area is as two rectangles, one on each side of the y axis, and a triangle.

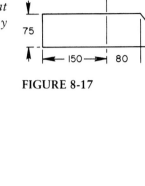

FIGURE 8-17

Left rectangle — Part 1

$$A_1 = 150 \times 75$$

$$= 11\ 250 \text{ mm}^2$$

$$x_1 = -\frac{150}{2}$$

$$= -75.0 \text{ mm}$$

$$y_1 = \frac{75}{2}$$

$$= 37.5 \text{ mm}$$

Right rectangle — Part 2

$$A_2 = 80 \times 75$$

$$= 6\ 000 \text{ mm}^2$$

$$x_2 = \frac{80}{2}$$

$$= 40.0 \text{ mm}$$

$$y_2 = \frac{75}{2}$$

$$= 37.5 \text{ mm}$$

(If the two rectangles had been treated as one, the centroid of the single rectangle would be at x = −35.0, and the area of the single rectangle is 17 250 mm².)

Triangle — Part 3

$$A_3 = \frac{1}{2} \times 60 \times 75$$

$$= 2\ 250 \text{ mm}^2$$

$$x_3 = 80 + \frac{60}{3}$$

$$= 80.0 + 20.0$$

$$= 100.0 \text{ mm}$$

$$y_3 = \frac{75}{3}$$

$$= 25.0 \text{ mm}$$

When calculating the location of a centroid, all measurements in one direction must be made from the same axis. Thus, when determining x_3, it is the distance from the y axis to the centroid of the triangle that is required, not just the distance from the base of the triangle to the centroid of the triangle.

$$\bar{X} = \frac{\Sigma A_i x_i}{\Sigma A_i}$$

$$= \frac{-(11\ 250 \times 75.0) + 6\ 000 \times 40.0 + 2\ 250 \times 100.0}{11\ 250 + 6\ 000 + 2\ 250}$$

$$= \frac{-843\ 750 + 240\ 000 + 225\ 000}{19\ 500}$$

$$= \frac{-378\ 750}{19\ 500}$$

$$= -19.42 \text{ mm}$$

$$\bar{Y} = \frac{\Sigma A_i y_i}{\Sigma A_i}$$

$$= \frac{11\ 250 \times 37.5 + 6\ 000 \times 37.5 + 2\ 250 \times 25.0}{11\ 250 + 6\ 000 + 2\ 250}$$

$$= \frac{421\ 875 + 225\ 000 + 56\ 250}{19\ 500}$$

$$= \frac{703\ 125}{19\ 500}$$

$$= 36.06 \text{ mm}$$

Centroid = (−19.4, 36.1)

PROBLEMS

8-37 Locate the centroid for the T section shown in Fig. P8-37.

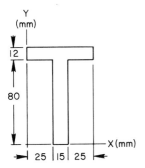

FIGURE P8-37

8-38 Find the centroid of the section shown in Fig. P8-38.

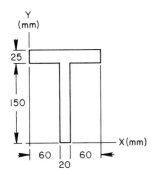

FIGURE P8-38

8-39 Find the centroid for the channel shown in Fig. P8-39.

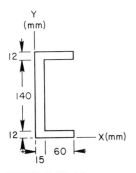

FIGURE P8-39

8-40 For the section shown in Fig. P8-40, determine the location of the centroid.

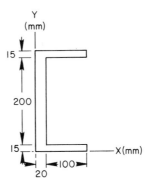

FIGURE P8-40

8-41 For the angle shown in Fig. P8-41, determine $\overline{X}$ and $\overline{Y}$.

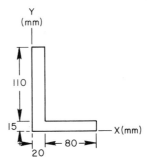

FIGURE P8-41

8-42 Find the centroid for the area shown in Fig. P8-42.

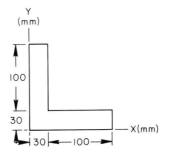

FIGURE P8-42

8-43 Calculate the location of the centroid for the Z section shown in Fig. P8-43.

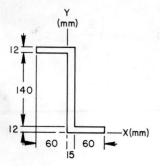

FIGURE P8-43

8-44 For the Z section shown in Fig. P8-44, determine the location of the centroid.

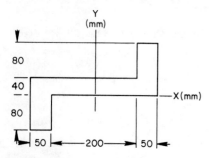

FIGURE P8-44

8-45 For the area shown in Fig. P8-45, determine the location of the centroid.

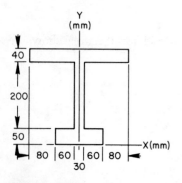

FIGURE P8-45

8-46 For the double-T beam section shown in Fig. P8-46, determine the centroid.

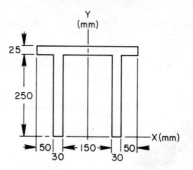

FIGURE P8-46

8-47 Find the centroid for the area shown in Fig. P8-47.

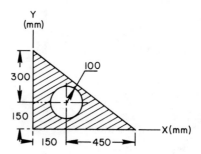

FIGURE P8-47

8-48 Calculate $\bar{X}$ and $\bar{Y}$ for the rectangular area with the hole shown in Fig. P8-48.

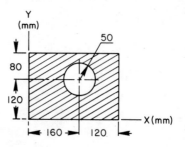

FIGURE P8-48

8-49 Determine the centroid for the area shown in Fig. P8-49.

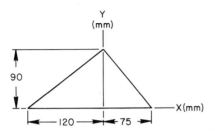

FIGURE P8-49

8-50 Find the centroid of the area shown in Fig. P8-50.

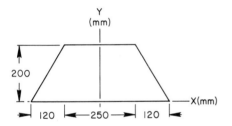

FIGURE P8-50

8-51 Locate the centroid for the area shown in Fig. P8-51.

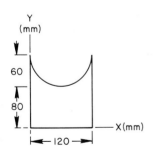

FIGURE P8-51

8-52 For the area shown in Fig. P8-52, locate the centroid.

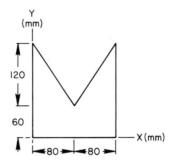

FIGURE P8-52

8-53 Calculate $\bar{X}$ and $\bar{Y}$ for the area shown in Fig. P8-53.

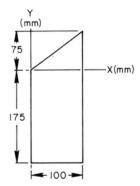

FIGURE P8-53

8-54 Determine the location of the centroid for the area shown in Fig. P8-54.

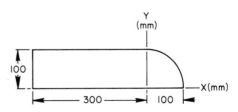

FIGURE P8-54

8-55 For the area shown in Fig. P8-55, determine the location of the centroid.

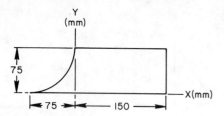

FIGURE P8-55

8-56 Find the location of the centroid for the area shown in Fig. P8-56.

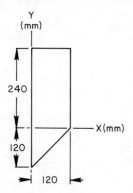

FIGURE P8-56

8-57 Determine the centroid for the area shown in Fig. P8-57.

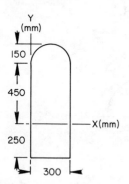

FIGURE P8-57

8-58 For the area shown in Fig. P8-58, determine the location of the centroid.

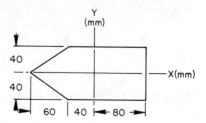

FIGURE P8-58

8-59 Calculate the location of the centroid for the area shown in Fig. P8-59.

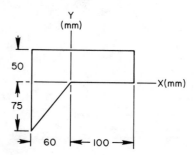

FIGURE P8-59

8-60 Find the centroid of the area shown in Fig. P8-60.

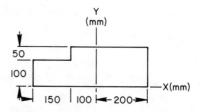

FIGURE P8-60

8-6 CENTROID OF A LINE

The centroid of a line is useful in at least two situations. The end view of a regular cylinder formed by a uniform sheet, as shown in Fig. 8-18(a), would appear as a line, as shown in Fig. 8-18(b). The center of gravity of the formed sheet could be determined by locating the centroid of the projected line or end view. Similarly, a system of uniform piping or conduit could be represented by a line and the centroid of the line would, for practical purposes, be at the center of gravity of the pipe system.

(a)   (b)

FIGURE 8-18

Note that centroid and center of gravity are not the same thing. However, if dealing with a thin, uniform sheet, or uniform small-diameter piping, the error introduced by assuming that the centroid of the line is the same as the center of gravity of the sheet or pipe is negligible.

Locating the centroid of a line is similar to locating the centroid of an area; a uniform thin cylindrical rod is used in place of a uniform thin plate. Using this procedure, the value for $\overline{X}$ obtained is

$$\overline{X} = \frac{\Sigma L_i x_i}{\Sigma L_i} \qquad (8\text{-}6)$$

where $\overline{X}$ is the x coordinate of the centroid of the line,
$\Sigma L_i x_i$ is the sum of the products of each line length and the x coordinate of the centroid of each line, and
ΣL_i is the sum of all the individual line lengths making up the total line.

In a similar fashion, it may also be shown that $\overline{Y}$ and $\overline{Z}$ are

$$\overline{Y} = \frac{\Sigma L_i y_i}{\Sigma L_i} \qquad (8\text{-}7)$$

$$\overline{Z} = \frac{\Sigma L_i z_i}{\Sigma L_i} \qquad (8\text{-}8)$$

In using Eqs. (8-6), (8-7) and (8-8), the sign of the coordinate for the centroid of each line must be used in order to successfully obtain the centroid for the total line. If there is an axis (or plane) of symmetry for the line, it may be expected that the centroid will be on the axis (or plane) of symmetry.

The centroids for several simple lines are given in Appendix D. Many complex lines can be made by adding two or more simple lines together.

EXAMPLE 8-13

Find the location of the centroid of the line shown in Fig. 8-19.

SOLUTION

The line shown consists of a horizontal straight line and an inclined straight line. The line lengths and the centroids should be summarized, with the aid of Appendix D, so that the information can be conveniently used in Eqs. (8-6) and (8-7).

Horizontal line — Part 1

$$L_1 = 150.0 \text{ mm}$$

$$x_1 = \frac{150}{2}$$

$$= 75.0 \text{ mm}$$

$$y_1 = 0.0 \text{ mm}$$

Inclined line — Part 2

$$L_2 = (80^2 + 60^2)^{1/2}$$

$$= 100.0 \text{ mm}$$

$$x_2 = 150 + \frac{80}{2}$$

$$= 150.0 + 40.0$$

$$= 190.0 \text{ mm}$$

$$y_2 = \frac{60}{2}$$

$$= 30.0 \text{ mm}$$

All centroids for the components or individual lines must be measured from the coordinate axis given. Thus x_2 is found to be the distance from the y axis to the midpoint of the inclined line; $x_2 = 150.0 + 40.0$ mm.

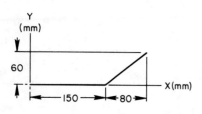

FIGURE 8-19

This information may now be used in Eqs. (8-6) *and* (8-7) *to determine* $\bar{X}$ *and* $\bar{Y}$.

$$\bar{X} = \frac{\Sigma \, L_i x_i}{\Sigma \, L_i}$$

$$= \frac{150.0 \times 75.0 + 100.0 \times 190.0}{150.0 + 100.0}$$

$$= \frac{11\ 250 + 19\ 000}{250.0}$$

$$= \frac{30\ 250}{250.0}$$

$$= 121.0 \text{ mm}$$

$$\bar{Y} = \frac{\Sigma \, L_i y_i}{\Sigma \, L_i}$$

$$= \frac{150.0 \times 0.0 + 100.0 \times 30.0}{150.0 + 100.0}$$

$$= \frac{0 + 3\ 000}{250.0}$$

$$= 12.00 \text{ mm}$$

$$\boxed{\text{Centroid} = (121,\ 12.0)}$$

Note that even though the horizontal line is on the x axis, and makes no contribution to the numerator of Eq. (8-7), *it still must be included in the denominator of* Eq. (8-7).

EXAMPLE   8-14

For the line shown in Fig. 8-20, calculate the centroid.

SOLUTION

The line is composed of a straight-line segment and a semicircular arc. The y coordinate of the centroid for the semicircular arc will be the same as for the quarter-circular arc shown in Appendix D. *Line lengths and centroid locations are tabulated so that* Eqs. (8-6) *and* (8-7) *may be used conveniently.*

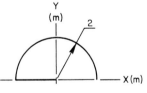

FIGURE 8-20

Horizontal Line — Part 1

$$L_1 = 2.00 \text{ m}$$

$$x_1 = -\frac{2}{2}$$

$$= -1.00 \text{ m}$$

$$y_1 = 0.00 \text{ m}$$

Semicircular arc — Part 2

$$L_2 = 2\pi$$

$$= 6.283 \text{ m}$$

$$x_2 = 0.00 \text{ m}$$

$$y_2 = \frac{2 \times 2}{\pi}$$

$$= 1.273 \text{ m}$$

Now Eqs. (8-6) and (8-7) may be used to determine $\bar{X}$ and $\bar{Y}$. Note that the signs of the centroids must be used in the equations.

$$\bar{X} = \frac{\Sigma L_i x_i}{\Sigma L_i}$$

$$= \frac{-(2.00 \times 1.00) + 6.283 \times 0.00}{2.00 + 6.283}$$

$$= \frac{-2.00 + 0.00}{8.283}$$

$$= -0.2414 \text{ m}$$

$$\bar{Y} = \frac{\Sigma L_i y_i}{\Sigma L_i}$$

$$= \frac{2.00 \times 0.00 + 6.283 \times 1.273}{2.00 + 6.283}$$

$$= \frac{0.00 + 7.998}{8.283}$$

$$= 0.9656 \text{ m}$$

Centroid = (−0.241, 0.966)

EXAMPLE 8-15

Find the centroid of the system of lines shown in Fig. 8-21.

SOLUTION

First, note the length of line and location of the centroid for each line segment. Since this is a three-dimensional system, it will be necessary to use Eqs. (8-6), (8-7) and (8-8). All measurements for the centroids must be made from the axis system given in the problem.

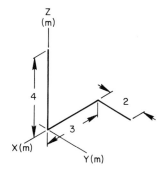

FIGURE 8-21

Line — x axis — Part 1

$L_1 = 3.00$ m

$x_1 = -\dfrac{3}{2}$

$\quad = -1.50$ m

$y_1 = 0.00$ m

$z_1 = 0.00$ m

Line — y axis — Part 2

$L_2 = 2.00$ m

$x_2 = -3.00$ m

$y_2 = \dfrac{2}{2}$

$\quad = 1.00$ m

$z_2 = 0.00$ m

Line — z axis — Part 3

$L_3 = 4.00$ m

$x_3 = 0.00$ m

$y_3 = 0.00$ m

$z_3 = \dfrac{4}{2}$

$\quad = 2.00$ m

$\bar{X} = \dfrac{\Sigma \, L_i x_i}{\Sigma \, L_i}$

$\quad = \dfrac{-(3.00 \times 1.50) - 2.00 \times 3.00 + 4.00 \times 0.00}{3.00 + 2.00 + 4.00}$

$\quad = \dfrac{-4.50 - 6.00 + 0.00}{9.00}$

$\quad = \dfrac{-10.50}{9.00}$

$$\bar{Y} = \frac{\Sigma\ L_i y_i}{\Sigma\ L_i}$$

$$= \frac{3.00 \times 0.00 + 2.00 \times 1.00 + 4.00 \times 0.00}{3.00 + 2.00 + 4.00}$$

$$= \frac{0.00 + 2.00 + 0.00}{9.00}$$

$$= \frac{2.00}{9.00}$$

$$= 0.2222 \text{ m}$$

$$\bar{Z} = \frac{\Sigma\ L_i z_i}{\Sigma\ L_i}$$

$$= \frac{3.00 \times 0.00 + 2.00 \times 0.00 + 4.00 \times 2.00}{3.00 + 2.00 + 4.00}$$

$$= \frac{0.00 + 0.00 + 8.00}{9.00}$$

$$= 0.8889 \text{ m}$$

Centroid = (−1.17, 0.222, 0.889)

EXAMPLE 8-16

Calculate the location of the centroid for the line shown in Fig. 8-22.

SOLUTION

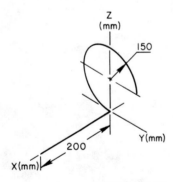

FIGURE 8-22

The line has two parts: a straight line along the x axis and a circle from which a quarter-circle arc has been removed. The line lengths, along with their centroids, should be tabulated so that the information may be used in Eqs. (8-6), (8-7) *and* (8-8).

Straight line — Part 1

$$L_1 = 200.0 \text{ mm}$$

$$x_1 = \frac{200}{2}$$

$$= 100.0 \text{ mm}$$

$$y_1 = 0.0 \text{ mm}$$

$$z_1 = 0.0 \text{ mm}$$

Circle — Part 2

$$L_2 = 2\pi \times 150$$

$$= 942.5 \text{ mm}$$

$$x_2 = 0.0 \text{ mm}$$

$$y_2 = 0.0 \text{ mm}$$

$$z_2 = 150.0 \text{ mm}$$

Quarter-circle arc — Part 3

$$L_3 = -\frac{\pi \times 150}{2}$$

$$= -235.6 \text{ mm}$$

$$x_3 = 0.0 \text{ mm}$$

$$y_3 = \frac{2 \times 150}{\pi}$$

$$= 95.49 \text{ mm}$$

$$z_3 = 150 - \frac{2 \times 150}{\pi}$$

$$= 150.00 - 95.49$$

$$= 54.51 \text{ mm}$$

Appendix D *gives the distance from an axis through the diameter to the centroid of the quarter-circle arc, rather than the distance from the x-y plane to the centroid, as required in determining* z_3.

The values for $\overline{X}$, $\overline{Y}$ and $\overline{Z}$ *may now be obtained using* Eqs. (8-6), (8-7) *and* (8-8).

$$\overline{X} = \frac{\Sigma L_i x_i}{\Sigma L_i}$$

$$= \frac{200.0 \times 100.0 + 942.5 \times 0.0 - 235.6 \times 0.0}{200.0 + 942.5 - 235.6}$$

$$= \frac{20\ 000 + 0 - 0}{906.9}$$

$$= 22.053 \text{ mm}$$

$$\overline{Y} = \frac{\Sigma L_i y_i}{\Sigma L_i}$$

$$= \frac{200.0 \times 0.0 + 942.5 \times 0.0 - 235.6 \times 95.49}{200.0 + 942.5 - 235.6}$$

$$= \frac{0 + 0 - 22\ 499}{906.9}$$

$$= -24.810 \text{ mm}$$

$$\overline{Z} = \frac{\Sigma\ L_i z_i}{\Sigma\ L_i}$$

$$= \frac{200.0 \times 0.0 + 942.5 \times 150.0 - 235.6 \times 54.51}{200.0 + 942.5 - 235.6}$$

$$= \frac{0 + 141\ 375 - 12\ 843}{906.9}$$

$$= \frac{128\ 532}{906.9}$$

$$= 141.73$$

$$\boxed{\text{Centroid} = (22.1,\ -24.8,\ 142)}$$

PROBLEMS

8-61 For the line shown in Fig. P8-61, determine the location of the centroid.

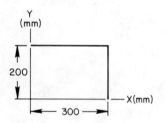

FIGURE P8-61

8-62 Calculate the centroid for the line shown in Fig. P8-62.

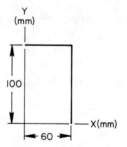

FIGURE P8-62

8-63 Find the centroid of the line shown in Fig. P8-63.

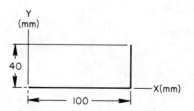

FIGURE P8-63

8-64 Determine the centroid for the line shown in Fig. P8-64.

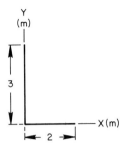

FIGURE P8-64

8-65 For the triangle-shaped line shown in Fig. P8-65, determine the location of the centroid.

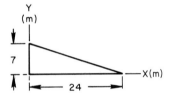

FIGURE P8-65

8-66 Locate the centroid of the line system shown in Fig. P8-66.

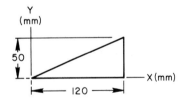

FIGURE P8-66

8-67 Determine the location of the centroid of the triangle-shaped line shown in Fig. P8-67.

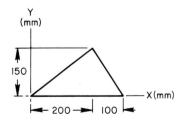

FIGURE P8-67

8-68 Locate the centroid of the line shown in Fig. P8-68.

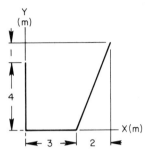

FIGURE P8-68

8-69 For the line system shown in Fig. P8-69, determine the location of the centroid.

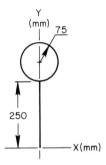

FIGURE P8-69

8-70 Calculate the centroid for the line shown in Fig. P8-70.

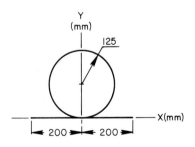

FIGURE P8-70

8-71 Find the location of the centroid for the shape shown in Fig. P8-71.

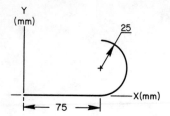

FIGURE P8-71

8-72 Locate the centroid of the shape shown in Fig. P8-72.

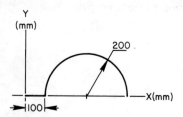

FIGURE P8-72

8-73 Find the centroid of the line shown in Fig. P8-73.

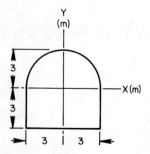

FIGURE P8-73

8-74 Determine the location of the centroid for the line shown in Fig. P8-74.

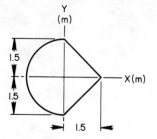

FIGURE P8-74

8-75 Find the location of the centroid for the line system shown in Fig. P8-75.

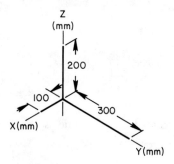

FIGURE P8-75

8-76 Determine the centroid of the line shown in Fig. P8-76.

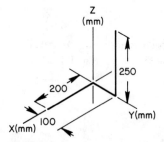

FIGURE P8-76

8-77 For the line shown in Fig. P8-77, calculate the centroid.

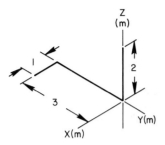

FIGURE P8-77

8-78 For the line system shown in Fig. P8-78, find the centroid.

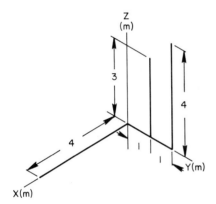

FIGURE P8-78

8-79 If the inclined portion of the line shown in Fig. P8-79 is in the *y-z* plane, calculate the centroid of the line.

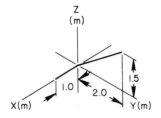

FIGURE P8-79

8-80 Locate the centroid of the line shown in Fig. P8-80.

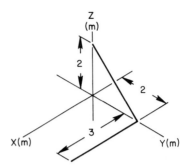

FIGURE P8-80

8-81 Determine the location of the centroid for the line shown in Fig. P8-81. The semicircular arc is in the *x-z* plane.

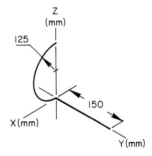

FIGURE P8-81

8-82 Find the centroid of the line system shown in Fig. P8-82.

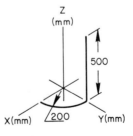

FIGURE P8-82

8-83 Find the centroid of the line system shown in Fig. P8-83. The two nonvertical bars are in the *x-y* plane.

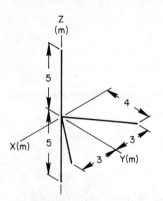

FIGURE P8-83

8-84 Find the centroid for the system shown in Fig. P8-84.

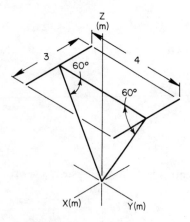

FIGURE P8-84

8-85 For the system shown in Fig. P8-85, determine the location of the centroid.

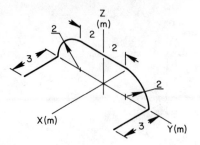

FIGURE P8-85

8-86 Determine the location of the centroid for the line system shown in Fig. P8-86.

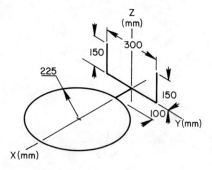

FIGURE P8-86

8-7 CENTROID OF A VOLUME

The concept of the centroid of a volume was dealt with indirectly in Article 8-4, which was about the center of gravity of bodies. In Appendix B, the center of gravity of a homogeneous body and the centroid of the same volume have the same value. For practical purposes, center of gravity and centroid are the same, although the center of gravity is really a physical property of the body, while the centroid is a geometric property of the shape of the volume.

To locate the centroid of a volume, it is possible to use a process similar to that used in Article 8-5, which dealt with the centroid of an area, in order to obtain the following equations:

$$\bar{X} = \frac{\Sigma\ V_i x_i}{\Sigma\ V_i} \qquad (8\text{-}9)$$

where $\bar{X}$ is the x coordinate of the centroid of the volume,

$\Sigma\ V_i x_i$ is the sum of the products of each volume and the x coordinate of the centroid of each volume, and

$\Sigma\ V_i$ is the sum of all the individual volumes making up the total volume.

Similarly,

$$\bar{Y} = \frac{\Sigma\ V_i y_i}{\Sigma\ V_i} \qquad (8\text{-}10)$$

$$\bar{Z} = \frac{\Sigma\ V_i z_i}{\Sigma\ V_i} \qquad (8\text{-}11)$$

If a volume is a composite volume, that is, one made up of two or more simple shapes such as shown in Appendix B, the above equations may be used to determine the location of the centroid. When using Eqs. (8-9), (8-10) and (8-11), the sign of each coordinate of each component volume must be used, along with its magnitude. If a component volume is removed in constructing the composite volume, the volume that is removed is treated as a negative volume. The sign obtained with $\bar{X}$, $\bar{Y}$ or $\bar{Z}$ is the actual sign of the coordinate for the centroid. If the volume has a plane of symmetry, the centroid will lie in that plane.

EXAMPLE 8-17

Determine the location of the centroid of the volume shown in Fig. 8-23.

SOLUTION

The volume given consists of a rectangular prism, with a quarter-circle cylinder on top of it. To efficiently use Eqs. (8-9), (8-10) and (8-11) it is suggested that each volume and its centroid be tabulated.

Rectangular prism — Part 1

$$V_1 = 2 \times 4 \times 3$$

$$= 24.00\ \text{m}^3$$

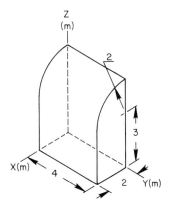

FIGURE 8-23

$$x_1 = \frac{2}{2}$$

$$= 1.000 \text{ m}$$

$$y_1 = \frac{4}{2}$$

$$= 2.000 \text{ m}$$

$$z_1 = \frac{3}{2}$$

$$= 1.500 \text{ m}$$

Quarter-circular cylinder — Part 2

$$V_2 = \frac{\pi \times 2^2}{4} \times 4$$

$$= 12.57 \text{ m}^3$$

$$x_2 = \frac{4 \times 2}{3\pi}$$

$$= 0.8488 \text{ m}$$

$$y_2 = \frac{4}{2}$$

$$= 2.000 \text{ m}$$

$$z_2 = 3 + \frac{4 \times 2}{3\pi}$$

$$= 3.000 + 0.849$$

$$= 3.849 \text{ m}$$

Note that z_2 *is the total distance from the x-y plane to the centroid, and not just the distance from the base of the quarter-circular cylinder.*

Now Eqs. (8-9), (8-10) *and* (8-11) *may be used to find* $\bar{X}$, $\bar{Y}$ *and* $\bar{Z}$.

$$\bar{X} = \frac{\Sigma V_i x_i}{\Sigma V_i}$$

$$= \frac{24.00 \times 1.000 + 12.57 \times 0.8488}{24.00 + 12.57}$$

$$= \frac{24.00 + 10.67}{36.57}$$

$$= \frac{34.67}{36.57}$$

$$= 0.9480 \text{ m}$$

By symmetry:

$$\overline{Y} = 2.000 \text{ m}$$

$$\overline{Z} = \frac{\Sigma V_i z_i}{\Sigma V_i}$$

$$= \frac{24.00 \times 1.500 + 12.57 \times 3.849}{24.00 + 12.57}$$

$$= \frac{36.00 + 48.38}{36.57}$$

$$= \frac{84.38}{36.57}$$

$$= 2.307 \text{ m}$$

Centroid = (0.948, 2.00, 2.31)

EXAMPLE 8-18

For the volume shown in Fig. 8-24, determine the location of the centroid.

SOLUTION

The volume can be constructed from a rectangular prism of 250 by 300 by 500 mm, from which a triangular prism with a base of 200 mm (at the top), a height of 500 mm and a depth of 250 mm is removed.

It is recommended that the volume and centroid of each part be determined with the aid of Appendix B; *that information can be used in* Eqs. (8-9), (8-10) *and* (8-11).

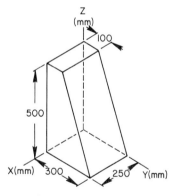

FIGURE 8-24

Rectangular prism — Part 1

$$V_1 = 250 \times 300 \times 500$$

$$= 37.50 \times 10^6 \text{ mm}^3$$

$$x_1 = \frac{250}{2}$$

$$= 125.0 \text{ mm}$$

$$y_1 = \frac{300}{2}$$

$$= 150.0 \text{ mm}$$

$$z_1 = \frac{500}{2}$$

$$= 250.0 \text{ mm}$$

Triangular prism — Part 2

$$V_2 = -\frac{1}{2} \times 200 \times 500 \times 250$$

$$= -12.50 \times 10^6 \text{ mm}^3$$

$$x_2 = \frac{250}{2}$$

$$= 125.0 \text{ mm}$$

$$y_2 = 300 - \frac{200}{3}$$

$$= 300.0 - 66.7$$

$$= 233.3 \text{ mm}$$

$$z_2 = 500 - \frac{500}{3}$$

$$= 500 - 166.7$$

$$= 333.3 \text{ mm}$$

When determining y_2, the base of the triangular prism is
300 mm *from the x-z plane. Thus the distance from the x-z
plane to the centroid will be* 300 mm *minus one third of the
height of the triangular prism. A similar approach is used in
calculating* z_2, *except in that case the base is* 200 mm *and the
height is* 500 mm.

By symmetry:

$$\bar{X} = 125.0 \text{ mm}$$

$$\bar{Y} = \frac{\Sigma V_i y_i}{\Sigma V_i}$$

$$= \frac{37.50 \times 10^6 \times 150.0 - 12.50 \times 10^6 \times 233.3}{37.50 \times 10^6 - 12.50 \times 10^6}$$

$$= \frac{5625 \times 10^6 - 2916 \times 10^6}{25.00 \times 10^6}$$

$$= \frac{2709 \times 10^6}{25.00 \times 10^6}$$

$$= 108.35 \text{ mm}$$

$$\bar{Z} = \frac{\Sigma \, V_i z_i}{\Sigma \, V_i}$$

$$= \frac{37.50 \times 10^6 \times 250.0 - 12.50 \times 10^6 \times 333.3}{37.50 \times 10^6 - 12.50 \times 10^6}$$

$$= \frac{9375 \times 10^6 - 4166 \times 10^6}{25.00 \times 10^6}$$

$$= \frac{5209 \times 10^6}{25.00 \times 10^6}$$

$$= 208.35 \text{ mm}$$

Centroid = (125, 108, 208)

EXAMPLE 8-19

Determine the location of the centroid for the volume shown in Fig. 8-25.

SOLUTION

The volume can be treated as a semicircular cylinder lying on a rectangular prism. A small rectangular prism has been removed from the large prism. The volume and centroid of each part should be tabulated with the aid of Appendix B *to expedite the use of* Eqs. (8-9), (8-10) *and* (8-11).

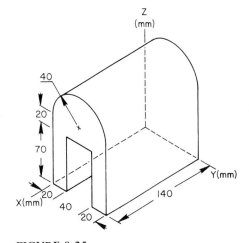

FIGURE 8-25

Large Rectangular prism — Part 1

$$V_1 = 140 \times 80 \times 90$$

$$= 1\ 008\ 000 \text{ mm}^3$$

$$x_1 = \frac{140}{2}$$

$$= 70.0 \text{ mm}$$

$$y_1 = \frac{80}{2}$$

$$= 40.0 \text{ mm}$$

$$z_1 = \frac{90}{2}$$

$$= 45.0 \text{ mm}$$

Small rectangular prism — Part 2

$$V_2 = -140 \times 40 \times 70$$

$$= -392\ 000\ mm^3$$

$$x_2 = \frac{140}{2}$$

$$= 70.0\ mm$$

$$y_2 = 20 + \frac{40}{2}$$

$$= 20.0 + 20.0$$

$$= 40.0$$

$$z_2 = \frac{70}{2}$$

$$= 35.0\ mm$$

Semicircular cylinder — Part 3

$$V_3 = \frac{\pi \times 40^2}{2} \times 140$$

$$= 351\ 900\ mm^3$$

$$x_3 = \frac{140}{2}$$

$$= 70.0\ mm$$

$$y_3 = \frac{80}{2}$$

$$= 40.0\ mm$$

$$z_3 = 90 + \frac{4 \times 40}{3\pi}$$

$$= 90.0 + 16.98$$

$$= 106.98\ mm$$

The distance z_3 to the centroid of the cylinder must be measured from the x-y plane and not from the side of the cylinder.

By symmetry:

$\bar{X} = 70.0\ mm$

$\bar{Y} = 40.0\ mm$

$$\bar{Z} = \frac{\Sigma\, V_i z_i}{\Sigma\, V_i}$$

$$= \frac{1\,008\,000 \times 45.0 - 392\,000 \times 35.0 + 351\,900 \times 106.98}{1\,008\,000 - 392\,000 + 351\,900}$$

$$= \frac{45.36 \times 10^6 - 13.72 \times 10^6 + 37.64 \times 10^6}{0.9679 \times 10^6}$$

$$= \frac{69.28 \times 10^6}{0.9679 \times 10^6}$$

$$= 71.58 \text{ mm}$$

Centroid = (70.0, 40.0, 71.6)

PROBLEMS

8-87 Find the centroid of the volume shown in Fig. P8-87.

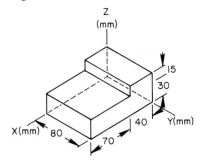

FIGURE P8-87

8-88 For the volume shown in Fig. P8-88, determine the location of the centroid.

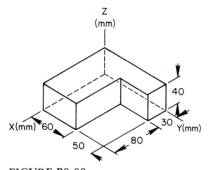

FIGURE P8-88

8-89 Determine the location of the centroid for the volume shown in Fig. P8-89.

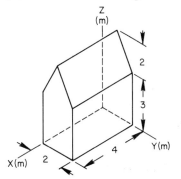

FIGURE P8-89

8-90 Locate the centroid for the shape shown in Fig. P8-90.

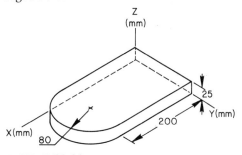

FIGURE P8-90

8-91 For the volume shown in Fig. P8-91, determine $\overline{X}$, $\overline{Y}$, and $\overline{Z}$.

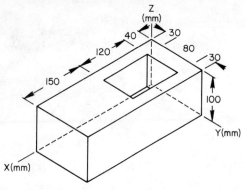

FIGURE P8-91

8-92 Locate the centroid for the volume shown in Fig. P8-92.

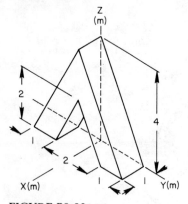

FIGURE P8-92

8-93 Determine the location of the centroid of the cylinder with the hemisphere removed shown in Fig. P8-93.

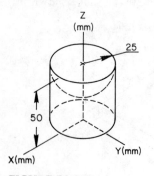

FIGURE P8-93

8-94 For the cylinder with the cone removed, shown in Fig. P8-94, determine the location of the centroid.

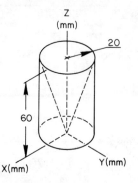

FIGURE P8-94

8-95 The shape shown in Fig. P8-95 is a truncated right circular cone. Calculate the location of its centroid.

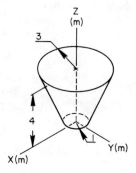

FIGURE P8-95

8-96 Locate the centroid of the truncated triangular prism shown in Fig. P8-96.

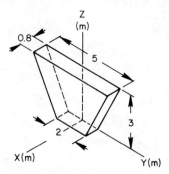

FIGURE P8-96

8-97 Find the centroid of the volume shown in Fig. P8-97.

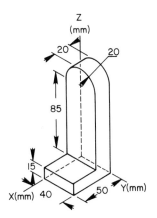

FIGURE P8-97

8-98 Determine the location of the centroid of the volume shown in Fig. P8-98.

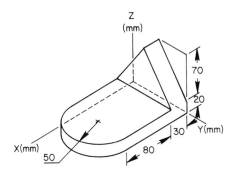

FIGURE P8-98

8-99 For the shape shown in Fig. P8-99, calculate the location of the centroid.

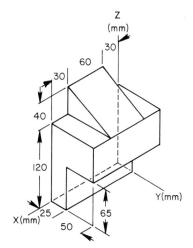

FIGURE P8-99

8-100 Determine $\bar{X}$, $\bar{Y}$ and $\bar{Z}$ for the shape shown in Fig. P8-100.

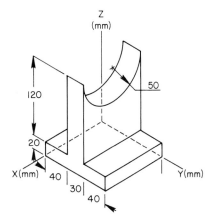

FIGURE P8-100

9 MOMENT OF INERTIA

9-1 TYPES OF MOMENT OF INERTIA

There are two different moments of inertia. They are quite unrelated except for the similarity in their mathematical expressions. The mass moment of inertia, which is a physical quantity, is a measure of a body's resistance to angular acceleration, and is used in dynamics. The area moment of inertia is a purely mathematical expression, and is used in stress analysis and fluid mechanics.

9-2 AREA MOMENT OF INERTIA

The area moment of inertia is not readily defined except in mathematical terms. Physically, the moment of inertia of the cross-sectional area of a beam is one of the factors that is a measure of a beam's resistance to bending. The larger the moment of inertia the greater the resistance to bending. For this reason, the calculation of the area moment of inertia is very important in the study of beams in stress analysis. The resistance of a column to buckling also depends, in part, on the moment of inertia of the cross-sectional area of the column; this will be studied in stress analysis. The area moment of inertia is also used in the analysis of forces on a submerged surface in fluid mechanics.

Actual values for the moment of inertia of simple areas are calculated precisely using the calculus, and the results of a number of these calculations are given in Appendix C. These precise values will be used in the problems that follow.

An approximate value for the moment of inertia with respect to the x axis may be obtained using Fig. 9-1. The moment of inertia of the small element of area A_i with respect to the x axis is $A_i y_i^2$. The moment of inertia of the total area with respect to the x axis is the sum of all of the products of A_i and y_i^2 for all the elements of area making up the total area. In other words, the approximate moment of inertia with respect to the x axis for the whole area is

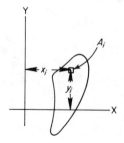

FIGURE 9-1

$$I_x = \Sigma A_i y_i^2 \tag{9-1}$$

Similarly, the approximate moment of inertia of the area with respect to the y axis is

$$I_y = \Sigma \, A_i x_i^2 \qquad (9\text{-}2)$$

Note that to obtain accurate values of the moment of inertia, it is necessary to break the area up into small elements of area. The calculus, which is beyond the scope of this book, provides a method of subdividing the area into a very large number of exceedingly small elements of area, and thus provides very precise values for I_x or I_y. Although the calculus is not used here, the results obtained using the calculus are shown, as mentioned, in Appendix C.

The expression $A_i y_i^2$ or $A_i x_i^2$ is an area times the square of a distance, and is sometimes referred to as the second moment of the area. (Compare with calculations of the centroid, where the expression $A_i y_i$ or $A_i x_i$ is sometimes referred to as the first moment of the area.)

In Eqs. (9-1) and (9-2), the units are length^2 × length^2. Since the dimensions will usually be mm, then the units of the moment of inertia of area will be mm^4. In view of the fact that the numeric values will tend to be large, calculations are usually expressed in terms of 10^6 mm^4, which will help to eliminate awkward numbers.

As might be expected from Eqs. (9-1) and (9-2), moments of inertia of different areas may be combined by adding or subtracting, provided they are all measured with respect to the same axis.

Figure 9-2 shows a number of structural shapes. To use these

FIGURE 9-2 This trailer load of steel shapes is for use in a structure. The moment of inertia of the cross section of each shape was required before the shape could be used in the design of the structure. *Photo courtesy of Canadian Steel Service Centre Institute.*

shapes to design, the designer must know the area moment of inertia of the cross section with respect to an axis passing through the centroid of the area. Thus, calculation of the area moment of inertia will usually also require calculation of the centroid. Fortunately for the designer, the necessary calculations are done by the manufacturers of the standard structural shapes. However, there are many instances when a built-up section or a special section or shape must be used, in which case it is necessary for the designer to make the appropriate calculations of the centroid and moment of inertia.

EXAMPLE 9-1

The area shown in Fig. 9-3 is about the size of the cross-sectional area of lumber often used for joists in wood-frame construction. Determine I_x and I_y for the area.

SOLUTION

Both I_x and I_y may be obtained by use of the information for the rectangle in Appendix C.

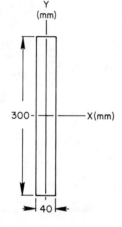

FIGURE 9-3

$$I_x = \frac{bh^3}{12}$$

$$= \frac{40 \times 300^3}{12}$$

$$= 90.0 \times 10^6 \text{ mm}^4$$

$$I_y = \frac{b^3h}{12}$$

$$= \frac{40^3 \times 300}{12}$$

$$= 1.60 \times 10^6 \text{ mm}^4$$

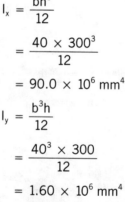

$$I_x = 90.0 \times 10^6 \text{ mm}^4$$
$$I_y = 1.60 \times 10^6 \text{ mm}^4$$

Note that the standard form for expressing the value of the area moment of inertia is in terms of 10^6 mm^4.

If this section is used as a beam so that it bends about the x axis, there is a high moment of inertia and little bending compared to when it is used as a beam so that it bends about the y axis. Then there is a low moment of inertia and much bending. Most people have had experience with the difference in bending of such a beam.

EXAMPLE 9-2

Calculate I_x and I_y for the section shown in Fig. 9-4.

SOLUTION

The section consists of a rectangle with a circular area removed. Since the axes used in Appendix C are common with those in the figure for both shapes, the moment of inertia for the circle can be subtracted from the tabulated moment of inertia of the rectangle to find the resultant moment of inertia for the given section. A summary of the calculations for I, based on Appendix C, is the suggested first step in the solution. The information can then be combined to obtain the required moment of inertia of the section.

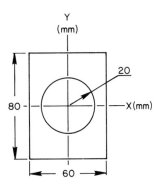

FIGURE 9-4

Rectangle — Part 1

$$(I_x)_1 = \frac{bh^3}{12}$$

$$= \frac{60 \times 80^3}{12}$$

$$= 2.560 \times 10^6 \text{ mm}^4$$

$$(I_y)_1 = \frac{b^3h}{12}$$

$$= \frac{60^3 \times 80}{12}$$

$$= 1.440 \times 10^6 \text{ mm}^4$$

Circle — Part 2

$$(I_x)_2 = \frac{\pi r^4}{4}$$

$$= \frac{\pi \times 20^4}{4}$$

$$= 0.126 \times 10^6 \text{ mm}^4$$

$$(I_y)_2 = \frac{\pi r^4}{4}$$

$$= \frac{\pi \times 20^4}{4}$$

$$= 0.126 \times 10^6 \text{ mm}^4$$

$$I_x = (I_x)_1 - (I_x)_2$$

$$= 2.560 \times 10^6 - 0.126 \times 10^6$$

$$= 2.434 \times 10^6 \text{ mm}^4$$

$$I_y = (I_y)_1 - (I_y)_2$$

$$= 1.440 \times 10^6 - 0.126 \times 10^6$$

$$= 1.314 \times 10^6 \text{ mm}^4$$

$$\boxed{\begin{array}{l} I_x = 2.43 \times 10^6 \text{ mm}^4 \\ I_y = 1.31 \times 10^6 \text{ mm}^4 \end{array}}$$

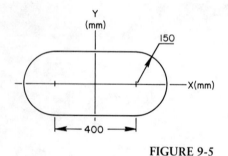

FIGURE 9-5

EXAMPLE   9-3

For the area shown in Fig. 9-5, determine I_x.

SOLUTION

The given area is made up of a rectangle and four quarter circles whose axes coincide with the axes tabulated in Appendix C. *The value for the moment of inertia of each area should be tabulated, and the information then used to find the total moment of inertia for the total area. Note that the value for I_x for the quarter circle does not depend on whether the area is above or below the axis.*

Rectangle — Part 1

$$(I_x)_1 = \frac{bh^3}{12}$$

$$= \frac{400 \times 300^3}{12}$$

$$= 900.0 \times 10^6 \text{ mm}^4$$

Quarter circle — Part 2

$$(I_x)_2 = \frac{\pi r^4}{16}$$

$$= \frac{\pi \times 150^4}{16}$$

$$= 99.4 \times 10^6 \text{ mm}^4$$

Total area:

$$I_x = (I_x)_1 + 4(I_x)_2$$

$$= 900.0 \times 10^6 + 4 \times 99.4 \times 10^6$$

$$= 900.0 \times 10^6 + 397.6 \times 10^6$$

$$= 1297.6 \times 10^6 \text{ mm}^4$$

$$\boxed{I_x = 1300 \times 10^6 \text{ mm}^4}$$

PROBLEMS

9-1 For a square 50 mm on a side, determine I_x for an axis through the centroid, parallel to a side.

9-2 Calculate I_x about an axis through the centroid for a circle with a diameter of 25 mm.

9-3 Determine I_x for the area shown in Fig. P9-3.

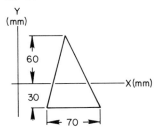

FIGURE P9-3

9-4 Find I_x and I_y for the rectangular area shown in Fig. P9-4.

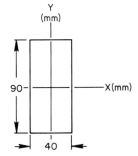

FIGURE P9-4

9-5 Calculate I_x and I_y for the section shown in Fig. P9-5. The wall thickness is 10 mm.

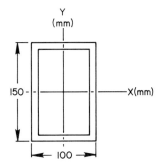

FIGURE P9-5

9-6 The tube shown in Fig. P9-6 has an outside diameter of 120 mm and a wall thickness of 5 mm. Determine the area moment of inertia about any centroidal axis.

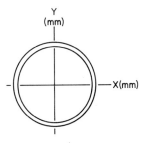

FIGURE P9-6

9-7 Find the moment of inertia about the y axis for the tubing shown in Fig. P9-7. The wall thickness is 2 mm.

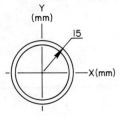

FIGURE P9-7

9-8 Determine I_x and I_y for the rectangular tubing shown in Fig. P9-8. The wall thickness is 4 mm.

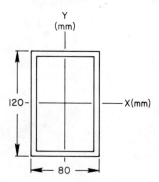

FIGURE P9-8

9-9 Calculate I_x and I_y for the area shown in Fig. P9-9.

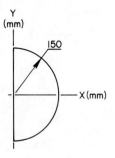

FIGURE P9-9

9-10 Calculate the area moment of inertia with respect to the x axis for the shape shown in Fig. P9-10.

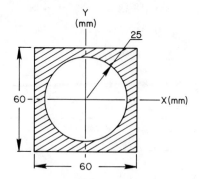

FIGURE P9-10

9-11 Determine I_y for the area shown in Fig. P9-11.

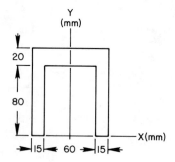

FIGURE P9-11

9-12 Find I_y for the area shown in Fig. P9-12.

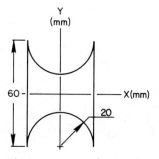

FIGURE P9-12

9-13 Calculate I_x and I_y for the section shown in Fig. P9-13.

9-14 For the area shown in Fig. P9-14, find I_x and I_y.

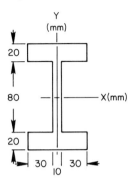

FIGURE P9-13

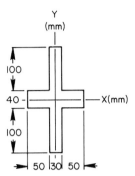

FIGURE P9-14

9-3 PARALLEL-AXIS THEOREM

In many instances, particularly when determining the moment of inertia of composite areas, the reference axis for measuring the moment of inertia does not coincide with the axis given in tables such as Appendix C. It is necessary to develop a procedure for determining the moment of inertia about some other axis that is parallel to and some distance away from the axis used in the tables. The parallel-axis theorem provides a method for determining the moment of inertia of an area about some other axis parallel to the axes shown in Appendix C.

Figure 9-6 shows an area composed of many elements of area A_i. The $\bar{x}$ axis shown is the centroidal axis for the area. Since the distance from the x axis to the element of area A_i is $d + y_i$, the moment of inertia of A_i about the x axis is

$$(d + y_i)^2 A_i$$

and the moment of inertia of the total area about the x axis is the sum of the moments of inertia of each of the elements of area

$$
\begin{aligned}
I_x &= \Sigma\,(d + y_i)^2 A_i \\
&= \Sigma\,(d^2 + 2dy_i + y_i^2)A_i \\
&= \Sigma\,(d^2 A_i + 2dA_iy_i + y_i^2 A_i) \\
&= \Sigma\, d^2 A_i + \Sigma\, 2dA_iy_i + \Sigma\, y_i^2 A_i
\end{aligned}
$$

Since d and 2 are constants, they may be taken outside of the Σ sign, and the equation becomes

$$I_x = d^2 \Sigma\, A_i + 2d \Sigma\, A_iy_i + \Sigma\, y_i^2 A_i$$

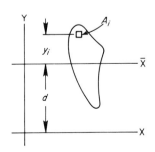

FIGURE 9-6

But $\Sigma \, A_i$ equals the total area A, and $\Sigma \, y_i^2 A_i = \bar{I}_x$ for the total area A, where $\bar{I}_x$ is the moment of inertia with respect to an x axis through the centroid of the area.

From Eq. (8-5), $\bar{Y} = \dfrac{\Sigma \, A_i y_i}{\Sigma \, A_i}$ and since $\bar{Y} = 0$ for the area shown in Fig. 9-6, then it follows that $\Sigma \, A_i y_i = 0$.

The moment of inertia for the total area A with respect to the x axis then becomes

$$I_x = d^2 A + \bar{I}_x$$

$$\text{or } I_x = \bar{I}_x + Ad^2 \tag{9-3}$$

where I_x is the moment of inertia of the area with respect to the x axis,

$\bar{I}_x$ is the moment of inertia of the area with respect to an x axis through the centroid of the area, and

Ad^2 is the product of the area and the square of the distance between the two x axes.

In a similar fashion, it may be shown that the parallel-axis theorem for moments of inertia of areas with respect to a y axis is

$$I_y = \bar{I}_y + Ad^2 \tag{9-4}$$

The application of Eqs. (9-3) and (9-4) involves little more than straight substitution of values in the equations. One should observe from the form of the equations that the moment of inertia of an area about an axis through its centroid is the smallest moment of inertia. The moment of inertia about some other parallel axis must always be larger.

EXAMPLE 9-4

The value of $\bar{I}_x$ for an area of 20 000 mm^2 was found to be 18.0×10^6 mm^4. Determine the moment of inertia of the area about an x axis 25 mm away from the $\bar{x}$ axis.

SOLUTION

The determination of I_x involves a simple substitution of values in Eq. (9-3). The result will be the same whether the second axis is above or below the $\bar{x}$ axis.

$$\begin{aligned}
I_x &= \bar{I}_x + Ad^2 \\
&= 18.0 \times 10^6 + 20\ 000 \times 25^2 \\
&= 18.0 \times 10^6 + 12.50 \times 10^6 \\
&= 30.50 \times 10^6 \text{ mm}^4
\end{aligned}$$

$$I_x = 30.5 \times 10^6 \text{ mm}^4$$

EXAMPLE 9-5

Calculate I_y for a y axis passing through the left side of the rectangle shown in Fig. 9-7.

SOLUTION

Finding I_y with respect to the specified axis involves using Eq. (9-4). *The value for the moment of inertia about the y axis passing through the centroid is found using* Appendix C.

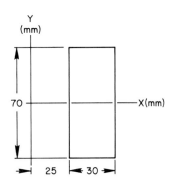

FIGURE 9-7

$$\bar{I}_y = \frac{b^3 h}{12}$$

$$= \frac{30^3 \times 70}{12}$$

$$= 0.1575 \times 10^6 \text{ mm}^4$$

The value for d is 15 mm, which is the distance from the centroidal y axis to a y axis at the left side of the rectangle.
   The above information is now used in Eq. (9-4).

$$I_y = \bar{I}_y + Ad^2$$

$$= 0.1575 \times 10^6 + 30 \times 70 \times 15^2$$

$$= 0.1575 \times 10^6 + 0.4725 \times 10^6$$

$$= 0.6300 \times 10^6 \text{ mm}^4$$

$$I_y = 0.630 \times 10^6 \text{ mm}^4$$

EXAMPLE 9-6

Find I_{x_2} for the 60 000 mm² area shown in Fig. 9-8, if I_{x_1} is 170.0×10^6 mm⁴.

SOLUTION

It would appear that Eq. (9-3) *could be used in the solution of this problem. However, it is noted that $\bar{I}_x$ is not given information. Thus it is necessary to find $\bar{I}_x$ before it is possible to use the parallel-axis theorem to find I_{x_2}.*

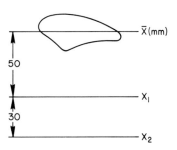

FIGURE 9-8

To find $\bar{I}_x$:

$$I_{x_1} = \bar{I}_x + Ad^2$$

$$170.0 \times 10^6 = \bar{I}_x + 60\ 000 \times 50^2$$

$$\bar{I}_x = 170.0 \times 10^6 - 150.0 \times 10^6$$

$$= 20.0 \times 10^6\ mm^4$$

It is now possible to rewrite Eq. (9-3) *to find* I_{x_2}. *Note that the value for d will be* 80 mm, *the distance between the* x_2 *axis and the* $\bar{x}$ *axis.*

To find I_{x_2}:

$$I_{x_2} = \bar{I}_x + Ad^2$$

$$= 20.0 \times 10^6 + 60\ 000 \times 80^2$$

$$= 20.0 \times 10^6 + 384.0 \times 10^6$$

$$= 404.0 \times 10^6\ mm^4$$

$$\boxed{I_{x_2} = 404 \times 10^6\ mm^4}$$

PROBLEMS

9-15 Determine the area moment of inertia of the square shown in Fig. P9-15 with respect to the *x* axis.

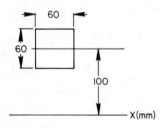

FIGURE P9-15

9-16 For the area shown in Fig. P9-16, calculate I_x.

9-17 Calculate I_y for the area shown in Fig. P9-17.

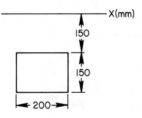

FIGURE P9-16

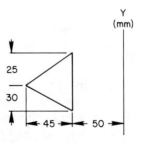

FIGURE P9-17

9-18 Find I_y for the circular area shown in Fig. P9-18.

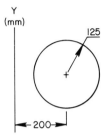

FIGURE P9-18

9-19 Determine I_y for the area shown in Fig. P9-19.

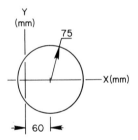

FIGURE P9-19

9-20 For the rectangular area shown in Fig. P9-20, calculate I_x.

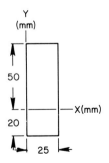

FIGURE P9-20

9-21 Calculate I_x for the area shown in Fig. P9-21.

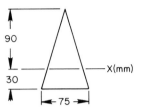

FIGURE P9-21

9-22 Calculate I_y for the triangular area shown in Fig. P9-22.

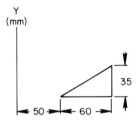

FIGURE P9-22

9-23 Find $\bar{I}_y$ for the area shown in Fig. P9-23.

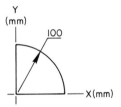

FIGURE P9-23

9-24 For the area shown in Fig. P9-24, calculate $\bar{I}_x$.

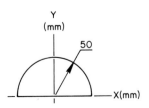

FIGURE P9-24

9-25 The area shown in Fig. P9-25 is 1700 mm², and has a moment of inertia of 40.0 × 10⁶ mm⁴ with respect to the x axis. Calculate $\bar{I}_x$.

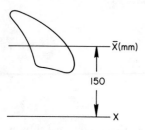

FIGURE P9-25

9-26 The area shown in Fig. P9-26 is 12 000 mm² and has a moment of inertia about the y axis of 35.0 × 10⁶ mm⁴. Find $\bar{I}_y$.

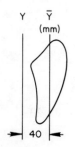

FIGURE P9-26

9-27 For the area shown in Fig. P9-27, I_{y_2} is 4325 × 10⁶ mm⁴. The area is 24 000 mm². Determine I_{y_1}.

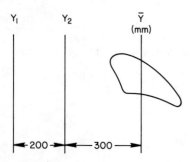

FIGURE P9-27

9-28 In Fig. P9-28, I_{x_1} is 60.0 × 10⁶ mm⁴ and the area is 12 000 mm². Determine I_{x_2}.

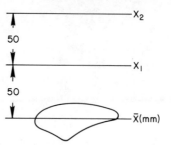

FIGURE P9-28

9-29 Determine the width of a 25 mm thick plate parallel to the reference axis required to provide a moment of inertia of 50.0 × 10⁶ mm⁴ if the centroid of the plate is 100 mm from the reference axis.

9-30 How far apart must the centroidal axes of two 50 by 150 mm plates be placed to provide a total moment of inertia of 1500 × 10⁶ mm⁴ about an axis midway between the 150 mm sides?

9-4 MOMENT OF INERTIA OF COMPOSITE AREAS

Many standard sections used for beams and columns have their moments of inertia tabulated in handbooks. However, the designer often resorts to nonstandard sections for members that carry a very high load or to adapt members for special purposes. Most special sections are made up of a combination of simple shapes, such as those tabulated in Appendix C. However, the designer is limited only by imagination when making special shapes for load-carrying members. Processes such as welding, extrusion and casting make a large variety of cross-sectional shapes possible for load-carrying members.

Moments of inertia of the various areas that make up the composite areas are added. All of the moments of inertia for the parts *must* be measured with respect to the same axis. Hence, the parallel-axis theorem, Eqs. (9-3) and (9-4), will be used extensively in the calculations. In most cases, the reference axis for the calculations will be an axis passing through the centroid of the composite area, since this is the moment of inertia that is usually required for design purposes. In some cases, to simplify problems, a reference axis other than the centroidal axis will be used.

Some composite areas are formed by subtracting one area from another. The moment of inertia of the removed area is subtracted from the moment of inertia of the whole area. Again, all moments of inertia must be measured with respect to the same axis.

There is more than one method for setting up the calculations for moments of inertia of composite areas. The table form, shown in the example problems, is probably the best method.

There is a small problem with symbols. It is necessary to deal with the centroidal axis of the parts making up the composite area as well as with the centroidal axis of the composite area. To differentiate between the two, $\bar{I}_x$ or $\bar{I}_y$ will represent the moment of inertia about a centroidal axis of the part of the area, while $I_{\bar{x}}$ or $I_{\bar{y}}$ will refer to the moment of inertia about a centroidal axis of the total composite area. In some cases, the x or y axis will coincide with the centroidal axis, and the moment of inertia about the axis may simply be shown as I_y or I_x.

EXAMPLE 9-7

Determine I_x for the box section shown in Fig. 9-9.

SOLUTION

The area should be broken up into its components and the pertinent information tabulated with the aid of Appendix C.

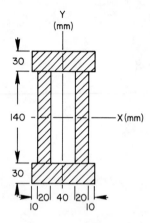

Y
(mm)

30

140 ── X (mm)

30

|20| 40 |20|
10   10

FIGURE 9-9

Upper rectangle — Part 1

$$A_1 = 100 \times 30$$

$$= 3000 \text{ mm}^2$$

$$(\bar{I}_x)_1 = \frac{100 \times 30^3}{12}$$

$$= 0.2250 \times 10^6 \text{ mm}^4$$

$$d_1 = 70 + \frac{30}{2}$$

$$= 70.0 + 15.0$$

$$= 85.0 \text{ mm}$$

$$A_1(d_1)^2 = 3000 \times 85.0^2$$

$$= 21.675 \times 10^6 \text{ mm}^4$$

Lower rectangle — Part 2

Same as part 1

Left vertical rectangle — Part 3

$$A_3 = 20 \times 140$$

$$= 2800 \text{ mm}^2$$

$$(\bar{I}_x)_3 = \frac{20 \times 140^3}{12}$$

$$= 4.5733 \times 10^6 \text{ mm}^4$$

$$d_3 = 0.0 \text{ mm}$$

$$A_3(d_3)^2 = 2800 \times 0.0$$

$$= 0$$

Right vertical rectangle — Part 4

Same as Part 3

Since the centroids for Parts 3 *and 4 are on the x axis, the value for d for them is zero.*

To obtain I_x for Parts 1 *and 2, it is necessary to use the parallel-axis theorem. Usually a table is set up showing $\bar{I}_x$ and Ad^2 for each part, and the values in the table are added (or subtracted, if appropriate) to obtain the total value for I_x.*

The value for I_x can also be obtained from the summation of the moments of inertia of each part using the parallel-axis theorem. This would give $I_x = (\bar{I}_x)_1 + (Ad^2)_1 + (\bar{I}_x)_2 + (Ad^2)_2 + (\bar{I}_x)_3 + (Ad^2)_3 + (\bar{I}_x)_4 + (Ad^2)_4$. Although the expression is satisfactory, it tends to be harder to follow and less tidy than the table, which contains exactly the same information.

Part	$\bar{I}_x$	Ad^2
1	0.2250×10^6	21.675×10^6
2	0.2250×10^6	21.675×10^6
3	4.5733×10^6	0
4	4.5733×10^6	0

$$\Sigma \bar{I}_x = 9.5966 \times 10^6 \quad \Sigma Ad^2 = 43.350 \times 10^6$$

$$\Sigma Ad^2 = \underline{43.350 \times 10^6}$$

$$I_x = 52.9466 \times 10^6$$

$$\boxed{I_x = 52.9 \times 10^6 \text{ mm}^4}$$

EXAMPLE 9-8

Calculate I_y for the area shown in Fig. 9-10.

SOLUTION

The first step is to break the area up into its basic shapes and summarize $\bar{I}_y$, A and d for the parts, with the aid of Appendix C.

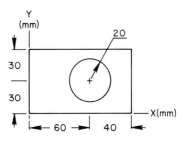

FIGURE 9-10

Rectangle — Part 1

$$A_1 = 100 \times 60$$
$$= 6000 \text{ mm}^2$$

$$(\bar{I}_y)_1 = \frac{60 \times 100^3}{12}$$
$$= 5.000 \times 10^6 \text{ mm}^4$$

$$d_1 = \frac{100}{2}$$
$$= 50.0 \text{ mm}$$

$$A_1(d_1)^2 = 6000 \times 50.0^2$$
$$= 15.000 \times 10^6 \text{ mm}^4$$

Circle — Part 2

$$A_2 = \pi \times 20^2$$

$$= 1257 \text{ mm}^2$$

$$(\bar{I}_y)_2 = \frac{\pi \times 20^4}{4}$$

$$= 0.1257 \times 10^6 \text{ mm}^4$$

$$d_2 = 60.0 \text{ mm}$$

$$A_2(d_2)^2 = 1257 \times 60.0^2$$

$$= 4.524 \times 10^6 \text{ mm}^4$$

Part	$\bar{I}_y$	Ad^2
1	5.000×10^6	15.000×10^6
2	-0.126×10^6	-4.524×10^6

$$\Sigma \bar{I}_y = 4.874 \times 10^6 \qquad \Sigma Ad^2 = 10.476 \times 10^6$$

$$\Sigma Ad^2 = \underline{10.476 \times 10^6}$$

$$I_y = 15.350 \times 10^6$$

$$\boxed{I_y = 15.4 \times 10^6 \text{ mm}^4}$$

The total moment of inertia for the circle is $(\bar{I}_y + Ad^2)$. Thus, the sum of both terms, or in other words, both terms, are subtracted in the table in order to find I_y.

EXAMPLE 9-9

For the T section shown in Fig. 9-11 determine $I_{\bar{x}}$.

SOLUTION

First calculate $\bar{Y}$, which locates the $\bar{x}$ axis. Equation (8-5) is used for this step.

Horizontal rectangle — Part 1

$$A_1 = 115 \times 20$$

$$= 2300 \text{ mm}^2$$

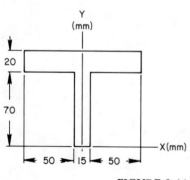

FIGURE 9-11

$$y_1 = 70 + \frac{20}{2}$$

$$= 70.0 + 10.0$$

$$= 80.0 \text{ mm}$$

Vertical rectangle — Part 2

$$A_2 = 15 \times 70$$

$$= 1050 \text{ mm}^2$$

$$y_2 = \frac{70}{2}$$

$$= 35.0 \text{ mm}$$

$$\bar{Y} = \frac{\Sigma A_i y_i}{\Sigma A_i}$$

$$= \frac{2300 \times 80.0 + 1050 \times 35.0}{2300 + 1050}$$

$$= \frac{184\,000 + 36\,750}{3350}$$

$$= \frac{220\,750}{3350}$$

$$= 65.90 \text{ mm}$$

Now the data can be tabulated for the parts, and the parallel-axis theorem (in tabular form) can be used to find $I_{\bar{x}}$. Figure 9-12 will help in establishing the relationships between the various distances.

Horizontal rectangle — Part 1

$$A_1 = 2300 \text{ mm}^2$$

$$(\bar{I}_x)_1 = \frac{115 \times 20^3}{12}$$

$$= 0.0766 \times 10^6 \text{ mm}^4$$

$$d_1 = 80.0 - 65.90$$

$$= 14.10 \text{ mm}$$

$$A_1(d_1)^2 = 2300 \times 14.10^2$$

$$= 0.4573 \times 10^6 \text{ mm}^4$$

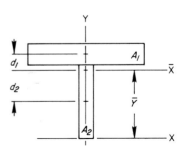

FIGURE 9-12

Vertical rectangle — Part 2

$$A_2 = 1050 \text{ mm}^2$$

$$(\bar{I}_x)_2 = \frac{15 \times 70^3}{12}$$

$$= 0.4288 \times 10^6 \text{ mm}^4$$

$$d_2 = 65.90 - 35.0$$

$$= 30.90 \text{ mm}$$

$$A_2(d_2)^2 = 1050 \times 30.90^2$$

$$= 1.0026 \times 10^6 \text{ mm}^4$$

Part	$\bar{I}_x$	Ad^2
1	0.0766×10^6	0.4573×10^6
2	0.4288×10^6	1.0026×10^6

$$\Sigma \bar{I}_x = 0.5054 \times 10^6 \qquad \Sigma Ad^2 = 1.4599 \times 10^6$$

$$\Sigma Ad^2 = \underline{1.4599 \times 10^6}$$

$$I_{\bar{x}} = 1.9653 \times 10^6 \text{ mm}^4$$

$$\boxed{I_{\bar{x}} = 1.97 \times 10^6 \text{ mm}^4}$$

PROBLEMS

9-31 Calculate I_x and I_y for the I section shown in Fig. P9-31.

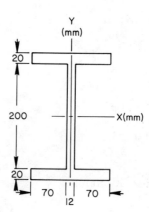

FIGURE P9-31

9-32 For the wide flange shape shown in Fig. P9-32, determine I_x and I_y.

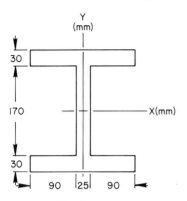

FIGURE P9-32

9-33 Calculate I_y for the area shown in Fig. P9-33.

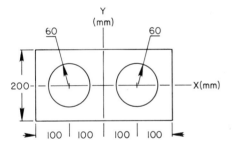

FIGURE P9-33

9-34 For the built-up shape shown in Fig. P9-34, determine I_y.

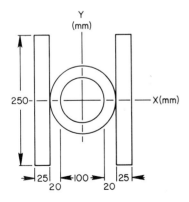

FIGURE P9-34

9-35 For the area shown in Fig. P9-35, find I_y.

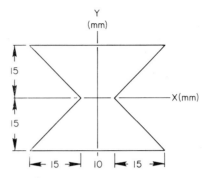

FIGURE P9-35

9-36 Determine I_x for the area shown in Fig. P9-36.

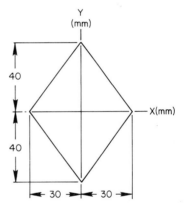

FIGURE P9-36

9-37 Calculate I_x for the area shown in Fig. P9-37.

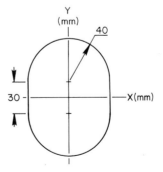

FIGURE P9-37

9-38 Determine I_y for the area shown in Fig. P9-38.

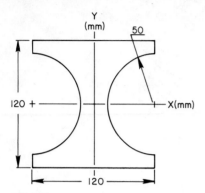

FIGURE P9-38

9-39 Calculate I_x for the area shown in Fig. P9-39.

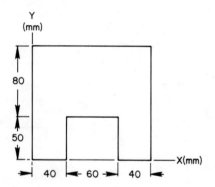

FIGURE P9-39

9-40 For the area shown in Fig. P9-40, calculate I_y.

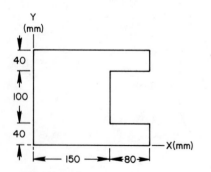

FIGURE P9-40

9-41 Determine I_y for the area shown in Fig. P9-41.

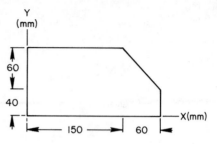

FIGURE P9-41

9-42 Find I_x for the area shown in Fig. P9-42.

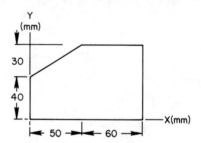

FIGURE P9-42

9-43 Calculate I_x for the area shown in Fig. P9-43.

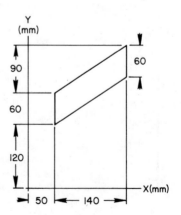

FIGURE P9-43

9-44 Determine I_y for the area shown in Fig. P9-44.

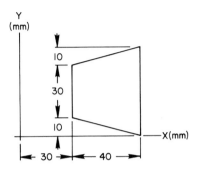

FIGURE P9-44

9-45 Calculate $I_{\bar{x}}$ and $I_{\bar{y}}$ for the Z section shown in Fig. P9-45.

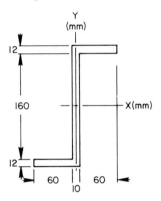

FIGURE P9-45

9-46 For the Z section shown in Fig. P9-46, determine $I_{\bar{x}}$ and $I_{\bar{y}}$.

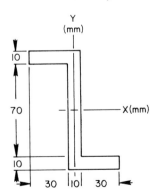

FIGURE P9-46

9-47 Determine $I_{\bar{x}}$ and $I_{\bar{y}}$ for the section shown in Fig. P9-47.

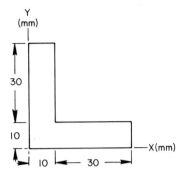

FIGURE P9-47

9-48 Calculate $I_{\bar{x}}$ and $I_{\bar{y}}$ for the angle shown in Fig. P9-48.

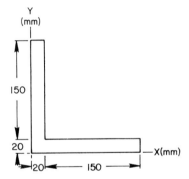

FIGURE P9-48

9-49 For the T section shown in Fig. P9-49, determine $I_{\bar{x}}$ and $I_{\bar{y}}$.

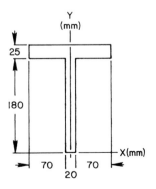

FIGURE P9-49

9-50 Find $I_{\bar{x}}$ and $I_{\bar{y}}$ for the section shown in Fig. P9-50.

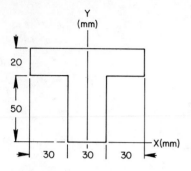

FIGURE P9-50

9-51 For the channel shown in Fig. P9-51, calculate $I_{\bar{x}}$ and $I_{\bar{y}}$.

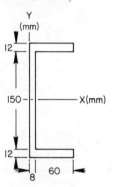

FIGURE P9-51

9-52 Determine $I_{\bar{x}}$ and $I_{\bar{y}}$ for the channel section shown in Fig. P9-52.

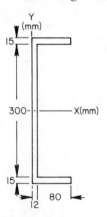

FIGURE P9-52

9-53 Calculate $I_{\bar{x}}$ and $I_{\bar{y}}$ for the angle section shown in Fig. P9-53

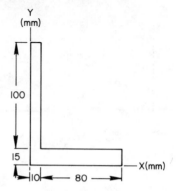

FIGURE P9-53

9-54 Determine $I_{\bar{x}}$ and $I_{\bar{y}}$ for the bulb angle shown in Fig. P9-54.

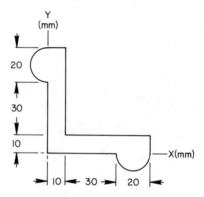

FIGURE P9-54

9-5   RADIUS OF GYRATION

The radius of gyration of an area is another mathematical expression that does not have a defined physical meaning. It is related to the area moment of inertia in the following manner:

$$k_x = \sqrt{\frac{I_x}{A}} \qquad (9\text{-}5)$$

where k_x is the radius of gyration with respect to the x axis,
   I_x is the area moment of inertia with respect to the x axis, and
   A is the area of the shape.

Similarly, the radius of gyration with respect to the y axis is

$$k_y = \sqrt{\frac{I_y}{A}} \qquad (9\text{-}6)$$

If Eq. (9-5) or (9-6) is examined, it is noted that the units of the radius of gyration will be mm. The terms $k_{\bar{x}}$ and $k_{\bar{y}}$ will be used to represent the radii of gyration with respect to the centroidal axes.

   Sometimes the radius of gyration is referred to as the distance from the reference axis to the location at which the area can be assumed to be concentrated, as shown in Fig. 9-13. However, note that the radius of gyration is *not* equal to the distance to the centroid, for the radius of gyration is related to the second moment of area, while the distance to the centroid is related to the first moment of area.

   The radius of gyration of an area is commonly used in the analysis and design of columns, where the resistance of a column to buckling is dependent on the radius of gyration as well as other geometric and physical properties.

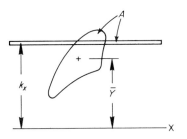

FIGURE 9-13

EXAMPLE   9-10

Calculate the radius of gyration with respect to an x axis passing through the center of a circular area with a radius of 50 mm.

SOLUTION

The area and moment of inertia with respect to a centroidal x axis should be calculated. The values may then be substituted in Eq. 9-5. to solve for k_x.

$$I_x = \frac{\pi \times 50^4}{4}$$

$$= 4.909 \times 10^6 \text{ mm}^4$$

$$A = \pi \times 50^2$$
$$= 7854 \text{ mm}^2$$
$$k_x = \sqrt{\frac{I_x}{A}}$$
$$= \sqrt{\frac{4.909 \times 10^6}{7854}}$$
$$= \sqrt{625.0}$$
$$= 25.00 \text{ mm}$$

$$\boxed{k_x = 25.0 \text{ mm}}$$

EXAMPLE 9-11

Determine k_y for the column section shown in Fig. 9-14.

SOLUTION

The first step is to calculate I_y *and the area of the section. It will then be possible to calculate* k_y *by using* Eq. (9-6).

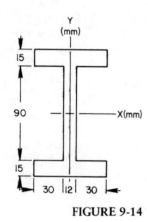

FIGURE 9-14

Upper horizontal rectangle — Part 1

$$A_1 = 72 \times 15$$
$$= 1080 \text{ mm}^2$$
$$(I_y)_1 = \frac{15 \times 72^3}{12}$$
$$= 0.466\ 56 \times 10^6 \text{ mm}^4$$

Lower horizontal rectangle — Part 2

Same as Part 1

Vertical rectangle — Part 3

$$A_3 = 12 \times 90$$
$$= 1080 \text{ mm}^2$$
$$(I_y)_3 = \frac{90 \times 12^3}{12}$$
$$= 0.012\ 96 \times 10^6 \text{ mm}^4$$

Total I_y

$$I_y = 0.466\ 56 \times 10^6 + 0.466\ 56 \times 10^6 + 0.012\ 96 \times 10^6$$
$$= 0.946\ 08 \times 10^6 \text{ mm}^4$$

Total A

$$A = 1080 + 1080 + 1080$$

$$= 3240 \text{ mm}^2$$

$$k_y = \sqrt{\frac{I_y}{A}}$$

$$= \sqrt{\frac{0.946\ 08 \times 10^6}{3240}}$$

$$= \sqrt{292.00}$$

$$= 17.088 \text{ mm}$$

$$\boxed{k_y = 17.1 \text{ mm}}$$

EXAMPLE 9-12

The radius of gyration with respect to the centroidal x axis for the column cross section shown in Fig. 9-15 is 41.9 mm. Determine $I_{\bar{x}}$ for the area.

SOLUTION

Finding $I_{\bar{x}}$ involves simple substitution in Eq. (9-5), as rewritten to solve for $I_{\bar{x}}$, after first finding the area of the section.

$$A = 15 \times 120 + 115 \times 20$$

$$= 1800 + 2300$$

$$= 4100 \text{ mm}^2$$

$$k_{\bar{x}} = \sqrt{\frac{I_{\bar{x}}}{A}}$$

$$I_{\bar{x}} = k_{\bar{x}}^2 A$$

$$= 41.9^2 \times 4100$$

$$= 7.198 \times 10^6 \text{ mm}^4$$

$$\boxed{I_{\bar{x}} = 7.20 \times 10^6 \text{ mm}^4}$$

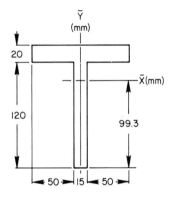

FIGURE 9-15

PROBLEMS

9-55 Determine k_x for the rectangle with a base of 95 mm and a height of 125 mm. The x axis passes through the centroid and is parallel to the base.

9-56 A triangle has a base of 30 mm and a height of 150 mm. Determine k_y if the y axis passes through the centroid parallel to the base.

9-57 Find k_y for the area shown in Fig. P9-57.

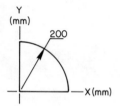

FIGURE P9-57

9-58 Calculate the value of k_x for the section shown in Fig. P9-58. The thickness of the pipe wall is 15 mm.

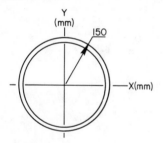

FIGURE P9-58

9-59 Determine the radius of gyration with respect to an axis tangent at the circumference for a circular area with a radius of 25 mm.

9-60 For a rectangle of 120 by 300 mm, determine k_y if the y axis is along a 300 mm side.

9-61 For the triangular area shown in Fig. P9-61, determine the radius of gyration with respect to the $\bar{x}$ and x axes.

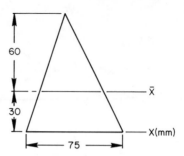

FIGURE P9-61

9-62 Determine $k_{\bar{x}}$ and k_x for the area shown in Fig. P9-62.

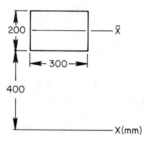

FIGURE P9-62

9-63 Calculate k_y for the area shown in Fig. P9-63.

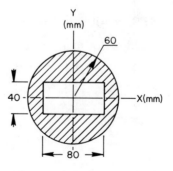

FIGURE P9-63

9-64 Determine k_y for the area shown in Fig. P9-64.

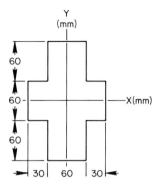

FIGURE P9-64

9-65 For the H section shown in Fig. P9-65, determine k_x.

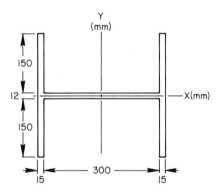

FIGURE P9-65

9-66 Find k_x for the area shown in Fig. P9-66.

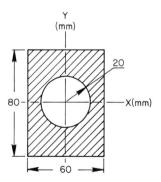

FIGURE P9-66

9-67 For the area shown in Fig. P9-67, k_y was found to be 50.7 mm. Determine I_y.

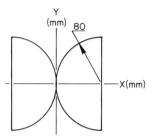

FIGURE P9-67

9-68 Determine I_x for the area shown in Fig. P9-68 if k_x was found to be 24.5 mm.

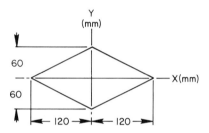

FIGURE P9-68

9-69 If k_x for the area shown in Fig. P9-69 was found to be 127 mm, determine I_x.

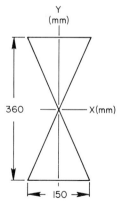

FIGURE P9-69

9-70 For the area shown in Fig. P9-70, k_x was found to be 39.9 mm. Calculate I_x.

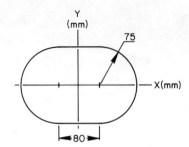

FIGURE P9-70

9-6 POLAR MOMENT OF INERTIA

This is another mathematical expression encountered in stress analysis and related design problems. The polar moment of inertia of an area is required when analyzing the stress or twist in a shaft due to the applied torque, and is thus required information in many aspects of machine design.

The polar moment of inertia of an area is measured with respect to an axis perpendicular to the plane of the area, as shown in Fig. 9-16. The polar moment of inertia with respect to the z axis for each element of area A_i at a distance r_i from the z axis is $A_i r_i^2$. The approximate value for the polar moment of inertia for the total area is the sum of the polar moments of inertia for each of the parts, which is

$$J_z = \Sigma A_i r_i^2 \tag{9-7}$$

Precise values of J_z are best obtained using the calculus, which was the method employed to obtain the values for J_z given in Appendix C. The units of polar moment of inertia will be mm^4, and will usually be written in terms of $10^6 \ mm^4$.

Referring to Fig. 9-16, it will be observed that $r_i^2 = x_i^2 + y_i^2$. Thus, Eq. (9-7) may be written as

$$J_z = \Sigma A_i(x_i^2 + y_i^2)$$
$$= \Sigma (A_i x_i^2 + A_i y_i^2)$$
$$= \Sigma A_i x_i^2 + \Sigma A_i y_i^2$$
$$= I_y + I_x$$

or $$J_z = I_x + I_y \tag{9-8}$$

Equation (9-8) is very useful for calculating the polar moment of inertia for composite areas when the polar moment of inertia has not been tabulated.

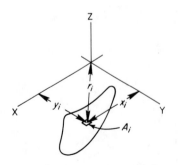

FIGURE 9-16

There is also a parallel-axis theorem for polar moments of inertia. It may be derived in a manner similar to that used for obtaining Eq. (9-3) or (9-4). The parallel-axis theorem for the polar moment of inertia is

$$J_z = \bar{J}_z + Ar^2 \qquad (9\text{-}9)$$

where J_z is the polar moment of inertia with respect to the z axis,

$\bar{J}_z$ is the polar moment of inertia with respect to the $\bar{z}$ axis through the centroid of the area and

Ar^2 is the product of the area and the square of the distance between the z axis and the $\bar{z}$ axis. Note that in this case, r does *not* represent the radius.

EXAMPLE 9-13

Calculate the polar moment of inertia with respect to an axis through the centroid for the cross section of a circular shaft with a diameter of 50 mm.

SOLUTION

In this instance, $\bar{J}_z$ is tabulated in Appendix C, so substitution of values is all that is required. Note that the given information is the diameter, and not the radius.

$$\bar{J}_z = \frac{\pi d^4}{32}$$

$$= \frac{\pi \times 50^4}{32}$$

$$= 0.613\ 59 \times 10^6 \text{ mm}^4$$

$$\boxed{\bar{J}_z = 0.614 \times 10^6 \text{ mm}^4}$$

EXAMPLE 9-14

Determine J_z for the area shown in Fig. 9-17.

SOLUTION

Since J_z for such a shape is not tabulated, it will first be necessary to find I_x and I_y in order to use Eq. (9-8).

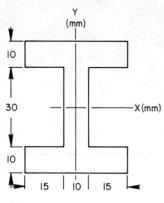

FIGURE 9-17

Upper horizontal rectangle — Part 1

$$A_1 = 40 \times 10$$
$$= 400 \text{ mm}^2$$
$$(\bar{I}_x)_1 = \frac{40 \times 10^3}{12}$$
$$= 0.003\,33 \times 10^6 \text{ mm}^4$$
$$(d_y)_1 = 15 + \frac{10}{2}$$
$$= 15.0 + 5.0$$
$$= 20.0 \text{ mm}$$
$$A_1(d_y)_1^2 = 400 \times 20.0^2$$
$$= 0.160\,00 \times 10^6 \text{ mm}^4$$
$$(\bar{I}_y)_1 = \frac{10 \times 40^3}{12}$$
$$= 0.053\,33 \times 10^6 \text{ mm}^4$$
$$(d_x)_1 = 0.0 \text{ mm}$$

Lower horizontal rectangle — Part 2

Same as Part 1

Vertical rectangle — Part 3

$$A_3 = 10 \times 30$$
$$= 300 \text{ mm}^2$$
$$(\bar{I}_x)_3 = \frac{10 \times 30^3}{12}$$
$$= 0.022\,50 \times 10^6 \text{ mm}^4$$
$$(d_y)_3 = 0.0 \text{ mm}$$
$$A_3(d_y)_3^2 = 300 \times 0^2$$
$$= 0$$
$$(\bar{I}_y)_3 = \frac{30 \times 10^3}{12}$$
$$= 0.002\,50 \times 10^6 \text{ mm}^4$$
$$(d_x)_3 = 0.0 \text{ mm}$$

I_x *may be found by using a table of values for* $\bar{I}_x$ *and* Ad^2.

Part	$\bar{I}_x$	Ad^2
1	$0.003\ 33 \times 10^6$	$0.160\ 00 \times 10^6$
2	$0.003\ 33 \times 10^6$	$0.160\ 00 \times 10^6$
3	$0.022\ 50 \times 10^6$	0.0

$$\Sigma\,\bar{I}_x = 0.029\ 16 \times 10^6 \quad \Sigma\,Ad^2 = 0.320\ 00 \times 10^6$$

$$\Sigma\,Ad^2 = \underline{0.320\ 00 \times 10^6}$$

$$I_x = 0.349\ 16 \times 10^6 \text{ mm}^4$$

I_y *may be found by simple addition, since the parallel-axis theorem is not needed for any of the parts.*

$$I_y = 0.053\ 33 \times 10^6 + 0.053\ 33 \times 10^6 + 0.002\ 50 \times 10^6$$

$$= 0.109\ 16 \times 10^6 \text{ mm}^4$$

Now Eq. (9-8) may be used to determine J_z.

$$J_z = I_x + I_y$$

$$= 0.349\ 16 \times 10^6 + 0.109\ 16 \times 10^6$$

$$= 0.458\ 32 \times 10^6 \text{ mm}^4$$

$$\boxed{J_z = 0.458 \times 10^6 \text{ mm}^4}$$

EXAMPLE 9-15

Find J_z for the rectangular area shown in Fig. 9-18.

SOLUTION

From Appendix C, *it is possible to determine* $\bar{J}_z$. *However, to find* J_z, *the parallel-axis theorem must be used. Thus, it is advisable to first find* $\bar{J}_z$, A *and* r^2.

$$\bar{J}_z = \frac{70 \times 150}{12}\left(70^2 + 150^2\right)$$

$$= 875(4900 + 22\ 500)$$

$$= 875 \times 27\ 400$$

$$= 23.975 \times 10^6 \text{ mm}^4$$

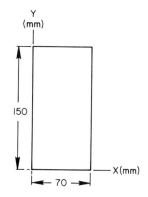

FIGURE 9-18

$$A = 70 \times 150$$
$$= 10\ 500 \text{ mm}^2$$
$$r^2 = \left(\frac{70}{2}\right)^2 + \left(\frac{150}{2}\right)^2$$
$$= 1225 + 5625$$
$$= 6850 \text{ mm}^2$$

Since r^2 is used in Eq. (9-9), *it is not necessary to find the value of r. The values may now be substituted in* Eq. (9-9),

$$J_z = \bar{J}_z + Ar^2$$
$$= 23.975 \times 10^6 + 10\ 500 \times 6\ 850$$
$$= 23.975 \times 10^6 + 71.925 \times 10^6$$
$$= 95.900 \times 10^6 \text{ mm}^4$$

$$\boxed{J_z = 95.9 \times 10^6 \text{ mm}^4}$$

PROBLEMS

9-71 Determine the polar moment of inertia with respect to an axis through the center of a circular area with a radius of 125 mm.

9-72 Calculate the polar moment of inertia for a square 80 by 80 mm with respect to an axis through its center.

9-73 Find the polar moment of inertia with respect to an axis through the centroid for a rectangle 200 by 250 mm.

9-74 Calculate the polar moment of inertia for a circular area with a diameter of 40 mm, with respect to a centroidal axis.

9-75 Calculate J_z for the area shown in Fig. P9-75.

9-76 Determine J_z for the area shown in Fig. P9-76.

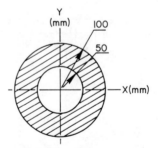

FIGURE P9-75

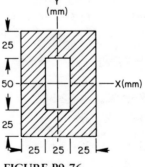

FIGURE P9-76

9-77 For the area shown in Fig. P9-77, calculate J_z.

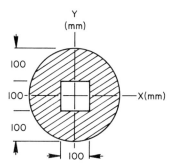

FIGURE P9-77

9-78 Determine J_z for the area shown in Fig. P9-78.

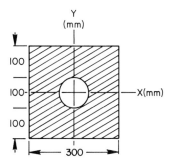

FIGURE P9-78

9-79 Determine J_z for the quarter-circle area shown in Fig. P9-79.

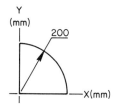

FIGURE P9-79

9-80 Calculate J_z for the triangle shown in Fig. P9-80.

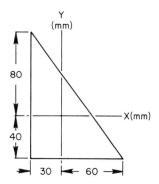

FIGURE P9-80

9-81 For the area shown in Fig. P9-81, determine J_z.

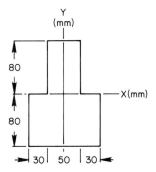

FIGURE P9-81

9-82 Calculate J_z for the area shown in Fig. P9-82.

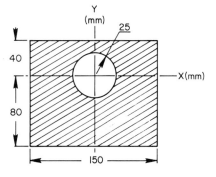

FIGURE P9-82

9-83 Determine the polar moment of inertia of a 250 mm diameter circle with respect to an axis through the circumference.

9-84 Find the polar moment of inertia of a 140 by 140 mm square with respect to an axis through the midpoint of one side.

9-85 Find J_z for the area shown in Fig. P9-85.

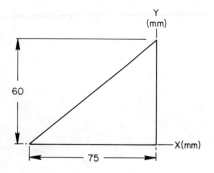

FIGURE P9-85

9-86 For the area shown in Fig. P9-86, determine $\bar{J}_z$.

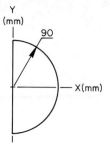

FIGURE P9-86

10 INTRODUCTION — STRESS ANALYSIS

10-1 WHAT IS STRESS ANALYSIS

Stress analysis is the study of the magnitudes and types of internal distributed loads in members and the deformation of the members. Both are caused by the external loads applied to the members. Stress analysis may be compared with statics, where the external forces acting on bodies are studied. In statics the bodies are assumed to be rigid, whereas in stress analysis the deformation of members is a definite and important part of the study. In fact, knowledge of the deformations will sometimes be one of the tools used to determine loads on members. The principles of statics and static equilibrium will continue to be applied in stress analysis, for the deformations encountered usually are sufficiently small that they do not cause any significant error in the calculations, as far as equilibrium equations are concerned.

Stress analysis is often called "strength of materials," which is somewhat incorrect, for the study of strength of materials forms only a small portion of the analysis.

Historically, much of stress analysis is based on mathematical theories that were developed by mathematicians in the past two or three centuries. Advanced topics in stress analysis are still under development today, and stress analysis is still a largely mathematical concern.

The engineering team tends to be most concerned with the application of these mathematical theories, rather than with the theory itself. Since application is the primary emphasis, the theory will be introduced primarily to illustrate the limitations and assumptions that apply to a particular analysis procedure.

Stress analysis may be studied either theoretically, using mathematics, or experimentally. Since theoretical stress analysis is used in most design, that will be the approach emphasized here. Experimental stress analysis, which relies on physical principles to relate experimental observations to actual stress, will be introduced briefly in a later chapter.

10-2 APPLICATIONS OF STRESS ANALYSIS

The analysis of stress in a member is generally not an objective in itself, but is usually a part of the process in the design of the members that make up any frame or machine. Using principles from statics and dynamics, the loads applied to a member are determined, and the principles of stress analysis are used to select the most suitable size, shape and material for the member so that neither the stress nor the deformation will exceed acceptable standards.

Diesel-electric locomotives, as shown in Fig. 10-1, contain literally thousands of components that underwent a stress analysis as part of the design process. In other words, the internal forces, as well as the deformations, were determined for each of the components. The size and shape of the components were determined from this analysis. A frame or machine is similar to a chain in some respects, for each is only as strong as its weakest link. Failure of a single component in a frame or machine may not cause collapse, but it may make the frame or machine inoperative.

Stress analysis is a part of the design of frames for buildings and machines as well as for all load-carrying components in machines. For instance, the piston, connecting rod and crankshaft

FIGURE 10-1 Diesel-electric locomotives under construction. The stress and strain in each of the hundreds of components must be analyzed if the locomotives are to perform in a reliable manner. *Photo courtesy of Diesel Division, General Motors of Canada Ltd.*

of the diesel engine must be analyzed, for they carry very heavy loads. Generally, the application of stress analysis is called *structural design* or *machine design*, and will apply to every type of load-carrying device from a record changer to a skyscraper. Even the rock that forms the workings of a mine can be subjected to stress analysis. (This is usually called rock mechanics.)

Although the primary use of stress analysis is in the design process, components of a completed design are often analyzed as a checking procedure to determine that the design meets the stated criteria, or to determine if the design may be modified to make it more economical.

Sometimes existing machines or buildings are used in a different manner than originally intended, and a stress analysis will be performed on the components to determine whether the machine or building will be safe for its new use. This use of stress analysis occurs most frequently when it is not possible to find the original design calculations.

10-3 NORMAL STRESS

The simplest form of stress is normal stress, which is the stress perpendicular to the surface on which it acts. Figure 10-2(a) shows a member with a load, **P**, applied at the center of the member and collinear with the longitudinal axis of the member. This is called a centric, axial load. A plane, *BCD*, is passed through the member so that it is perpendicular to the long axis, as shown. If a free-body diagram of the lower portion of the member is drawn, as shown in Fig. 10-2(b), there must be some form of load on the cut surface that will keep the part in equilibrium. If the cut surface is some distance from the end, then the

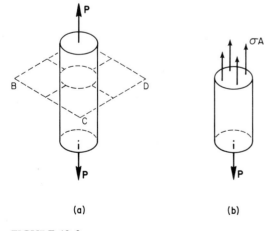

(a)   (b)

FIGURE 10-2

load on this surface will be uniformly distributed over the surface. The normal stress, σ, may be defined as the load per unit area on the cut surface. The total load on the cut surface will be σA. Since equilibrium must be maintained, then:

$$\Sigma F_y = 0$$

$$\sigma A - P = 0$$

$$\sigma = \frac{P}{A} \qquad (10\text{-}1)$$

where σ is the normal stress,
    P is the centric axial load, and
    A is the area of the section.

The normal stress is usually expressed in pascals (Pa), where one pascal is equal to one newton per square metre, that is, 1 Pa = 1 N/m^2. A pascal is a very small unit of stress, so one can usually expect to see stresses expressed in kPa or MPa.

In this section only uniform stress will be dealt with, but in later sections the stress studied will not necessarily be uniform. For nonuniform stress, a more exact definition of the normal stress is:

$$\sigma = \frac{\Delta P}{\Delta A} \qquad (10\text{-}2)$$

where σ is the normal stress,
    ΔP is the load perpendicular to the element of area being considered, and
    ΔA is the element of area on which the load acts.

This definition becomes precise as ΔA becomes very small. However, for the problems of this section, Eq. (10-1) is entirely satisfactory.

The normal stress illustrated in Fig. 10-2(b) is a normal *tensile* stress, but is usually called "tensile stress." It is customary to use the plus sign (+) to indicate a tensile stress, which, of course, occurs in a member with an axial tensile load. If the applied load is axial compression, as shown in Fig. 10-3, then the normal stress will be a *compressive* stress, which is usually signified by a negative sign (–). Although the calculation of compressive stress also uses Eq. (10-1), the equation will only apply if the member is relatively short, since long, slender compression members tend to buckle. A thin plastic ruler loaded in compression will illustrate the buckling failure of a slender compression member.

There is a third type of normal stress that can be calculated using Eq. (10-1). This is the stress that exists where the surfaces

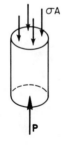

FIGURE 10-3

of two members come in contact. For instance, a column resting on or bearing on a footing for a foundation, as shown in Fig. 10-4(a), would cause a uniform stress on the surface of the footing where the two members meet, as shown in Fig. 10-4(b). This type of stress is called *bearing* stress.

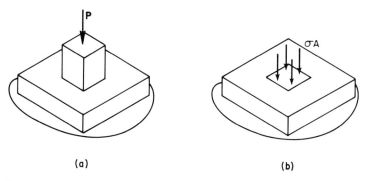

(a)   (b)

FIGURE 10-4

EXAMPLE   10-1

A structural-steel angle with a cross-sectional area of 1400 mm^2 is used as a diagonal in a truss. If the axial load in the member is +75 kN, determine the normal stress in the angle.

SOLUTION

In this case, both the load and area of the cross section are given, so the normal stress may be obtained by substitution in Eq. (10-1). Remember that the units of stress are pascals, which are N/m^2, so the units of area must be converted from mm^2 to m^2 by multiplying the area in mm^2 by 10^{-6}.

$$\sigma = \frac{P}{A}$$

$$= \frac{75\,000}{1400 \times 10^{-6}}$$

$$= 53.571 \times 10^6 \text{ Pa}$$

As usual, the answer should be summarized. In the case of stress, it will usually be expressed in MPa *rather than written in terms of powers of ten. To reduce the possibility of misunderstanding, it is a good idea to include the sign with the stress.*

$$\boxed{\sigma = +53.6 \text{ MPa}}$$

EXAMPLE   10-2

A rod on a machine has a hollow circular cross section with an outside diameter of 100 mm and an inside diameter of 60 mm. If the normal compressive stress in the material must not exceed 75 MPa determine the maximum axial load that may be carried by the machine part.

SOLUTION

Since the stress is known, Eq. (10-1) *should be rewritten so that the value of the load will be obtained. It is probably worthwhile to make a separate calculation for the area, which must be expressed in* m², *for use in* Eq. (10-1).

$$A = \frac{\pi}{4}\left(100^2 - 60^2\right)$$

$$= 5026.55 \text{ mm}^2$$

$$= 5026.55 \times 10^{-6} \text{ m}^2$$

$$\sigma = \frac{P}{A}$$

$$P = \sigma A$$

$$= 75 \times 10^6 \times 5026.55 \times 10^{-6}$$

$$= 376\ 991 \text{ N}$$

$$\boxed{P = 377 \text{ kN}}$$

EXAMPLE   10-3

Tie plates, which lie between the rail and the tie on a railway track, anchor the track to the tie and also reduce the bearing stress on the tie, which is often made of wood. If the load applied to the tie plate from the track is 45 kN, determine the length required for a tie plate with a width of 200 mm if the bearing stress on the tie is not to exceed 1.00 MPa.

SOLUTION

Since the load and stress are known, Eq. (10-1) *should be rewritten to solve for the area.*

$$\sigma = \frac{P}{A}$$

$$A = \frac{P}{\sigma}$$

$$= \frac{45\ 000}{1.0 \times 10^6}$$

$$= 45\ 000 \times 10^{-6}\ m^2$$

$$= 45\ 000 \times mm^2$$

Let length of plate be b:

$$A = 200\ b$$

$$200\ b = 45\ 000$$

$$b = \frac{45\ 000}{200}$$

$$= 225.00\ mm$$

Length = 225 mm

PROBLEMS

10-1 A piece of steel plate 8 mm thick and 12 mm wide is loaded to fracture in tension. If the load on the plate at failure is 48 kN, determine the tensile stress in the plate.

10-2 A steel-trussed floor joist has diagonals made of 10 by 25 mm bar stock. If the tension in a diagonal is 15 kN, determine the stress in the diagonal.

10-3 A nylon fishing line with a diameter of 0.60 mm will just support a fish with a mass of 10 kg. Determine the normal stress in the line.

10-4 A round cast-iron sample with a diameter of 12.5 mm carries an axial tensile load of 20.0 kN when it breaks. What is the tensile stress at failure?

10-5 A link that controls the position of the bucket on a front-end loader has an outside diameter of 40 mm, an inside diameter of 25 mm and a length of 400 mm. In one position of the

bucket, there is an axial tensile force of 12 kN in the link. Determine the normal stress in the link.

10-6 A chandelier in a hotel lobby has a mass of 75 kg and is suspended by a conduit with an outside diameter of 25 mm and a wall thickness of 2 mm. Determine the stress in the conduit.

10-7 Two pieces of steel are joined end to end with epoxy cement. If the cement will fail when the normal tensile stress in the cement is 50 MPa, determine the maximum load that can be carried if the cemented surface is 20 mm in diameter.

10-8 The D-string on a guitar has a normal stress of 1090 MPa in it. Determine the tensile force in the string if it has a diameter of 0.75 mm.

10-9 A tie in a frame is made of square bar stock. If the force to be carried is 85 kN tension, and if the stress is not to exceed 110 MPa, determine the minimum dimensions of the bar.

10-10 The stem of a hydraulic control for a backhoe boom has a load of 500 kN in tension. If the stress in the stem is not to exceed 80 MPa, determine the minimum diameter for the stem.

10-11 A concrete test cylinder has a diameter of 300 mm and it fails under an axial compressive load of 1500 kN. Determine the normal stress at failure.

10-12 A small house with a mass of 20 000 kg is supported on six round timber posts, each with a diameter of 200 mm. Calculate the compressive stress in the timber if each post carries the same load.

10-13 A large desk and its contents have a mass of 110 kg. It is supported on four legs, and each leg carries the same load and is made of 25 mm square tubing with a wall thickness of 1 mm. Determine the stress in each leg.

10-14 The body of a short jack that supports a mass of 5000 kg is made of a pipe with an outside diameter of 100 mm and an inside diameter of 90 mm. Calculate the stress in the body of the jack.

10-15 A short aluminum pipe has an outside diameter of 25 mm and an inside diameter of 20 mm. If the compressive stress in the pipe is not to exceed 15 MPa, determine the maximum axial compressive load that may be carried by the pipe.

10-16 A short hollow square tube whose sides are 100 mm each is formed by welding 15 mm steel plates together. If the safe compressive stress in the steel is 85 MPa, determine the maximum axial load that can be carried by the tube.

10-17 A large masonry smokestack has a mass of 2 000 000 kg and rests on a footing with an outside diameter of 25 m and an inside diameter of 15 m. Determine the bearing stress the footing applies to the soil.

10-18 A wall footing carries a load of 250 kN/m and has a width of 800 mm. Determine the bearing stress on the soil beneath the footing.

10-19 Spike or stiletto heels on shoes have been fashionable at times. They have also caused problems because of the high bearing stress they cause on floors. If the area of the heel is about 10×15 mm, determine the bearing stress caused if the force applied on the heel when walking is 1000 N.

10-20 A drafting table with a mass of 80 kg contacts the floor through four furniture glides. If each glide has a diameter of 20 mm, determine the bearing stress on the floor under the glides.

10-21 A building with a 30 by 40 m raft-type foundation rests on a soil for which the maximum permissible bearing stress is 60 kPa. Determine the maximum permissible mass of the building and contents.

10-22 A steel girder carries a total load of 300 kN. Each end of the girder rests on a steel bearing plate with a width of 200 mm. Determine the minimum length of the bearing plate if the maximum allowable bearing stress under the plate is 7 MPa and if half of the load from the girder is carried by each of the bearing plates.

10-4   SHEAR STRESS

Shear stress is stress parallel to the surface on which it acts. Figure 10-5(a) shows two plates fastened together by a cement on their contact surfaces, and with a force, V, acting on each. They would tend to slide apart under the action of the forces shown. A free-body diagram is made of the right-hand plate, as shown in Fig. 10-5(b). The plate must be in equilibrium, and the shear

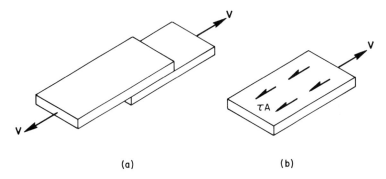

(a)   (b)

FIGURE 10-5

stress is the distributed load that acts on and parallel to the surface in contact with the other plate. If the shear stress is uniform, then from the rules of equilibrium we have

$$\Sigma F_x = 0$$

$$-\tau A + V = 0$$

$$\tau = \frac{V}{A} \qquad (10\text{-}3)$$

where τ is the shear stress acting on the surface,
   V is the force acting parallel to the surface and
   A is the area on which the shear stress acts.

The units for shear stress are also pascals, where 1 Pa = 1 N/m². Because the pascal is a very small unit of stress, shear stress will most frequently be expressed in kPa or MPa. This discussion assumes that the shear stress is uniformly distributed over the surface, which is approximately true for the situation described. However, in the more general case, the shear stress is

$$\tau = \frac{\Delta V}{\Delta A} \qquad (10\text{-}4)$$

where τ is the shear stress,
   ΔV is the force parallel to the element of area being considered, and
   ΔA is the element of area on which the shear stress acts.

This definition of shear stress becomes precise as ΔA approaches zero. However, Eq. (10-3) will be quite adequate for the problems of this section.

The example of shear illustrated in Fig. 10-5 is an example of *single shear*, where only one pair of surfaces is subjected to a shear stress. Figure 10-6(a) shows three plates connected by a single rivet, and Fig. 10-6(b) shows a free-body diagram of a side

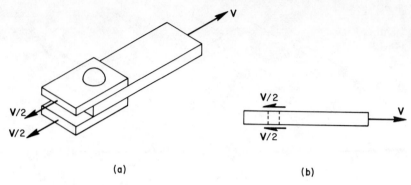

(a)   (b)

FIGURE 10-6

view of the right-hand plate. The force transferred from the right-hand plate to the two left-hand plates is transferred through the rivet in two places, as shown in Fig. 10-6(b). Because two surfaces of the rivet are used to transfer the shear forces from the single plate to the other two plates, the rivet is said to be in *double shear*.

The shear stresses illustrated in Figs. 10-5(b) and 10-6(b) are examples of *direct shear*, in which the longitudinal axis of the member and the applied load are collinear. *Punching shear* is illustrated in Fig. 10-7, where the force from one member is directed across a second member. The material of the second member around the circumference of the first must resist the force applied by the first member. This distributed force, as shown in Fig. 10-7(b), is also parallel to the surface being punched out, and is the punching-shear stress. The magnitude of the punching-shear stress is also

$$\tau = \frac{V}{A} \qquad (10\text{-}3)$$

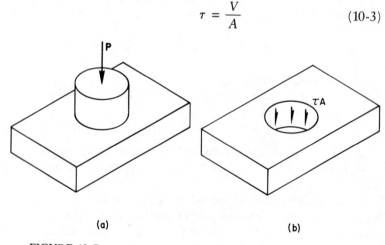

(a)   (b)

FIGURE 10-7

The area on which the shear stress acts is the thickness of the member being punched times the circumference of the member causing the punching stress.

EXAMPLE   10-4

Two pieces of plastic are joined by gluing overlapping areas of 50 by 70 mm, as shown in Fig. 10-8. If a tensile force of 780 N applied parallel to the glued surfaces causes the glue to fail, at what shear stress did the glue fail?

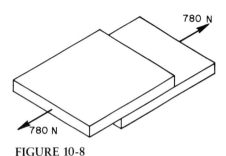

780 N

780 N

FIGURE 10-8

SOLUTION

The shear stress acting on the glued surface may be determined by direct substitution of values in Eq. (10-3). Note that if the stress is to be expressed in Pa, the area must be given in m².

$$\tau = \frac{V}{A}$$

$$= \frac{780}{50 \times 70 \times 10^{-6}}$$

$$= 222\ 860\ \text{Pa}$$

$$= 222.860\ \text{kPa}$$

$$\boxed{\tau = 223\ \text{kPa}}$$

EXAMPLE   10-5

A bolt with a diameter of 25 mm is used to connect two thick steel plates in a lap joint. If the tension in each plate is 20 kN, determine the shear stress in the bolt.

SOLUTION

Since only two plates are being fastened together, only one section of the bolt would be.in shear, as shown in Fig. 10-9. The stress on that cross-sectional area of the bolt may be calculated using Eq. (10-3). The area must be in m².

$$\tau = \frac{V}{A}$$

$$= \frac{20\ 000}{\dfrac{\pi \times 25^2}{4} \times 10^{-6}}$$

20 kN

V

FIGURE 10-9

$$= 40.744 \times 10^6 \text{ Pa}$$

$$= 40.744 \text{ MPa}$$

$$\boxed{\tau = 40.7 \text{ MPa}}$$

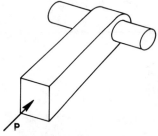

FIGURE 10-10

EXAMPLE 10-6

The connection between a connecting rod and crankshaft is shown in Fig. 10-10. Determine the shear stress in the 50 mm diameter crankshaft due to the 50 kN axial load, **P**, in the connecting rod.

SOLUTION

Two surfaces of the crankshaft, one on each side of the connecting rod, will resist the 50 kN force. Thus, the crankshaft is subjected to double shear. The shear stress may be calculated using Eq. (10-3), keeping in mind that twice the cross-sectional area of the crankshaft resists the shear force.

$$\tau = \frac{V}{A}$$

$$= \frac{50\ 000}{2\left(\dfrac{\pi \times 50^2}{4}\right) \times 10^{-6}}$$

$$= 12.732 \times 10^6 \text{ Pa}$$

$$= 12.732 \text{ MPa}$$

$$\boxed{\tau = 12.7 \text{ MPa}}$$

EXAMPLE 10-7

A square hole 40 by 40 mm is to be punched in a chassis for electronic equipment. If the material is 1.5 mm thick, determine the force that must be applied to the punch. The stress that must be overcome is 375 MPa.

SOLUTION

To determine the force, Eq. (10-3) should be rewritten to find the value of V. The area resisting the shear force should be calculated separately. It is the circumference of the punch times the thickness of the material. The area should be calculated in m².

$$A = 40 \times 4 \times 1.5$$
$$= 240.00 \text{ mm}^2$$
$$= 240.00 \times 10^{-6} \text{ m}^2$$
$$\tau = \frac{V}{A}$$
$$V = \tau A$$
$$= 375 \times 10^6 \times 240.00 \times 10^{-6}$$
$$= 90\ 000 \text{ N}$$

$$\boxed{V = 90.0 \text{ kN}}$$

PROBLEMS

10-23 Two pieces of wood are joined by a 50 by 150 mm lap joint. The tensile force parallel to the joint on each piece of wood is 750 N. Determine the shear stress in the adhesive in the joint.

10-24 Two pieces of plastic are lapped together and joined with epoxy. Calculate the shear stress in the epoxy if the area of the lap is 12 by 25 mm and if the force in each piece of plastic parallel to the joint is 1500 N.

10-25 A single 15 mm diameter bolt connects one end of a diagonal to the chord in a truss-type tower. If the tension in the diagonal is 25 kN, determine the shear stress in the bolt.

10-26 Two aluminum sheets are joined together in a lap joint by a row of eight spot welds. Each spot weld has an effective diameter of 4 mm, and the tension on each sheet is 2500 N. Calculate the shear stress in each of the spot welds.

10-27 In Fig. P10-27, the adhesive holding the two pieces of wood together will fail if the shear stress in it exceeds 10 MPa. Determine the minimum value for *b* if the load, **P**, is 25 kN.

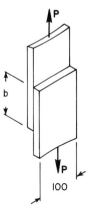

FIGURE P10-27

10-28 A stop used on a workbench to hold parts has a force, **P**, of 500 N applied to it, as shown in Fig. P10-28. If the pin for the stop is made of plastic with an allowable shear stress of 10 MPa, determine the minimum required diameter, *d*, for the pin.

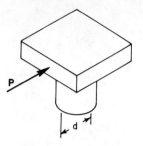

FIGURE P10-28

10-29 Two 5 mm thick plates are riveted to an 8 mm plate by a single 6 mm diameter rivet, as shown in Fig. P10-29. Determine the shear stress in the rivet.

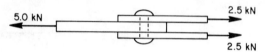

FIGURE P10-29

10-30 Find the shear stress on the clevis pin shown in Fig. P10-30. The diameter of the pin is 50 mm.

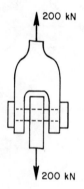

FIGURE P10-30

10-31 The pin supporting one side of one end of a bridge is shown in Fig. P10-31. If the maximum allowable shear stress in the pin is 65 MPa, calculate the minimum required diameter for the pin.

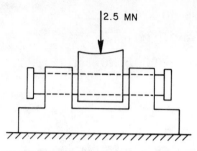

FIGURE P10-31

10-32 Calculate the magnitude of the load, **P**, that may be carried by the left-hand plate shown in Fig. P10-32. The shear stress in the 20 mm diameter bolt is not to exceed 75 MPa.

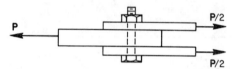

FIGURE P10-32

10-33 To punch a single 7 mm diameter hole in a sheet of paper 0.050 mm thick, a force of 0.80 N is required. Determine the shear stress in the paper when the hole is being punched.

10-34 A rectangular hole 30 by 35 mm is to be punched in a piece of steel sheet 5 mm thick. A gage on the punch shows that a force of 145 kN is applied in punching the hole. What is the shear stress in the sheet caused by the punch?

10-35 A chassis for a piece of electronic equipment is to have a rectangular hole 12 by 18 mm punched in it. If the material of the chassis is 0.65 mm thick, determine the force that must be applied to the punch if the material will be sheared when the stress reaches 230 MPa.

10-36 A press with a capacity of 1000 kN is used for punching holes in steel plate. The stress that must be overcome to punch a hole in a structural steel is 270 MPa. What is the maximum number of 20 mm diameter holes that can be punched at one time in 10 mm thick plate?

10-5 STRESSES ON INCLINED PLANES

In previous articles, the concepts of normal stress and shear stress have been discussed. Normal stress was analyzed on a plane perpendicular to the load, and shear stress was analyzed on a plane parallel to the load. If the plane on which the stress is acting is neither perpendicular to nor parallel to the load, then the stress analysis will be somewhat different. An understanding of the stress on these inclined planes is helpful in determining the behavior of materials — in particular, their forms of failure.

Figure 10-11 shows a side view of a member carrying an axial load, **P**, as well as the normal force, **P$_n$**, and the tangential force, **P$_t$**, which acts on the inclined plane cut through the member. If the cross-sectional area of the member is A, then the area of the inclined plane A' will be $A' = A/\cos \theta$. **P$_n$** and **P$_t$** would be the components of **P**, and their magnitude would be $P_n = P \cos \theta$ and $P_t = P \sin \theta$. From this, the normal stress on the inclined plane can be calculated as

$$\sigma_\theta = \frac{P_n}{A'} = \frac{P \cos \theta}{A/\cos \theta}$$

$$\sigma_\theta = \frac{P}{A} \cos^2 \theta \qquad (10\text{-}5)$$

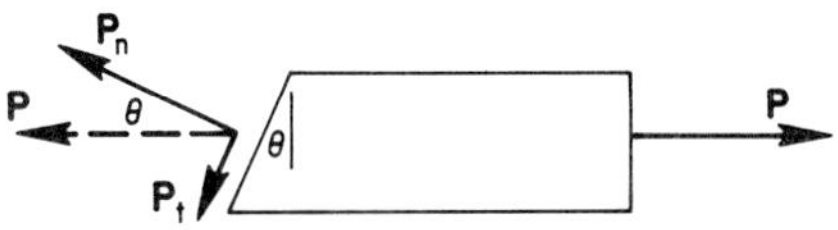

Similarly, the shear stress can be calculated as

$$\tau_\theta = \frac{P_t}{A'} = \frac{P \sin \theta}{A/\cos \theta}$$

$$\tau_\theta = \frac{P}{A} \sin \theta \cos \theta \qquad (10\text{-}6)$$

FIGURE 10-11

where σ_θ is the normal stress acting on the inclined plane,
τ_θ is the shear stress acting on the inclined plane,
P is the magnitude of the axial load,
A is the cross-sectional area, and
θ is the angle between the cross section and the inclined plane on which the stress is being evaluated.

Note how the angle θ is measured in Fig. 10-11. It must be always measured the same way — that is, from the cross section to the inclined plane — when using Eqs. (10-5) and (10-6).

The values for Eqs. (10-5) and (10-6) are plotted in Fig. 10-12. It may be observed that the curve for σ_θ has its maximum value when $\theta = 0°$. In other words, for an axially loaded member, the normal stress has its maximum value on the cross section of the member, and the value is $\sigma_{max} = P/A$. However, the curve for τ_θ

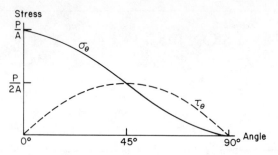

FIGURE 10-12

shows a maximum value at $\theta = 45°$. Thus, the shear stress has its maximum value for an axially loaded member on a plane at $45°$ to the cross section. By substituting $\theta = 45°$ in Eq. (10-6), the maximum value for the shear stress is found to be $\tau_{max} = P/2A$. This observation is important because ductile materials (materials in which there is a large amount of deformation) tend to fail because of the shear stress in them when they are subjected to an axial tensile load. As a result, the failure will occur on a plane approximately at $45°$ to the longitudinal axis. Brittle materials (materials that exhibit very little deformation) tend to fail in tension under an axial tensile load because of the normal stress on them. As a result, the tensile failure is usually on a cross section of the material. In the case of a compressive axial load in a brittle material, the member tends to be weakest in shear; consequently, the failure surface is at approximately $45°$ from the cross section. Ductile materials subjected to an axial compressive load tend to fail by excessive deformation rather than by fracture.

EXAMPLE 10-8

A bronze bar with a 25 by 25 mm cross section has an axial tensile load of 30 kN applied to it. Calculate the normal stress and the shear stress on a plane at $40°$ to the cross section

SOLUTION

The values for the normal stress and shear stress may be calculated by direct substitution in to Eqs. (10-5) and (10-6). Note that the given angle of $40°$ was measured from the cross section, which is the measurement required for the angle in the two equations.

$$\sigma_\theta = \frac{P}{A} \cos^2 \theta$$

$$= \frac{30\,000}{25 \times 25 \times 10^{-6}} \cos^2 40°$$

$$= 28.168 \times 10^6 \text{ Pa}$$

$$= 28.168 \text{ MPa}$$

$$\tau_\theta = \frac{P}{A} \sin \theta \cos \theta$$

$$= \frac{30\,000}{25 \times 25 \times 10^{-6}} \sin 40° \cos 40°$$

$$= 23.635 \times 10^6 \text{ Pa}$$

$$= 23.635 \times \text{MPa}$$

> $\sigma_{40} = 28.2 \text{ MPa}$
> $\tau_{40} = 23.6 \text{ MPa}$

EXAMPLE 10-9

Determine the shear stress and normal stress on a plane at 20° from the longitudinal axis for a member with an axial compressive load of 125 kN and a circular cross section with a diameter of 80 mm.

SOLUTION

The normal stress and shear stress may be calculated by direct substitution in to Eqs. (10-5) and (10-6). Note that the given angle is measured from the longitudinal axis; but, to use the equations, the angle must be measured from the cross section or transverse axis.

$$\theta = 90° - 20°$$

$$= 70°$$

$$\sigma_\theta = \frac{P}{A} \cos^2 \theta$$

$$= -\frac{125\,000}{\frac{\pi \times 80^2}{4} \times 10^{-6}} \cos^2 70°$$

$$= -2.9090 \times 10^6 \text{ Pa}$$

$$= -2.9090 \text{ MPa}$$

$$\tau_\theta = \frac{P}{A} \sin \theta \cos \theta$$

$$= \frac{125\,000}{\dfrac{\pi \times 80^2}{4} \times 10^{-6}} \sin 70° \cos 70°$$

$$= 7.9924 \times 10^6 \text{ Pa}$$

$$= 7.9924 \times \text{MPa}$$

$$\boxed{\begin{aligned} \sigma_{70} &= -2.91 \text{ MPa} \\ \tau_{70} &= 7.99 \text{ MPa} \end{aligned}}$$

EXAMPLE 10-10

For a rectangular member with a 25 by 50 mm cross section carrying an axial tensile load of 360 kN, determine the maximum normal stress and the maximum shear stress in the member.

SOLUTION

From Fig. 10-12, *it can be seen that the maximum normal stress occurs when* $\theta = 0°$, *and the maximum shear stress occurs when* $\theta = 45°$. *Substituting the values for these angles in Eqs.* (10-5) *and* (10-6), *the maximum values for the stresses may be obtained.*

$$\sigma_{max} = \frac{P}{A} \cos^2 0°$$

$$= \frac{P}{A}$$

$$= \frac{360\,000}{25 \times 50 \times 10^{-6}}$$

$$= 288.00 \times 10^6 \text{ Pa}$$

$$= 288.00 \text{ MPa}$$

$$\tau_{max} = \frac{P}{A} \sin 45° \cos 45°$$

$$= \frac{P}{2A}$$

$$= \frac{360\,000}{2 \times 25 \times 50 \times 10^{-6}}$$

$$= 144.00 \times 10^6 \text{ Pa}$$

= 144.00 × MPa

$$\sigma_{max} = 288 \text{ MPa}$$
$$\tau_{max} = 144 \text{ MPa}$$

PROBLEMS

10-37 Calculate the normal stress and shear stress on a plane at 30° to the cross section of a 40 mm diameter tensile member that has an axial load of 150 kN.

10-38 An axial tensile load of 2 MN is applied to a rectangular bar 50 by 75 mm. Find the normal stress and shear stress on a plane at 55° to the cross section.

10-39 For a 20 by 20 mm bar with an axial compressive load of 300 kN, determine the normal stress and the shear stress on a plane at 60° to the cross section

10-40 Find the normal stress and shear stress on a plane at 15° to the cross section for a 125 mm diameter bar carrying an axial compressive load of 3 MN.

10-41 An S310x52 (see S shapes in Appendix F) carries an axial tensile force of 5 MN. Find the normal stress and shear stress on a plane at 25° from the longitudinal axis.

10-42 Find the normal stress and shear stress on a plane at 75° from the longitudinal axis in a W200x46 (see W shapes in Appendix F) that has an axial compressive load of 1.5 MN.

10-43 A short bar with a cross section of 100 by 150 mm carries an axial compressive load of 850 kN. Determine the maximum normal stress and the maximum shear stress in the bar.

10-44 Calculate the maximum normal stress and the maximum shear stress in a 50 mm diameter bar with an axial tensile load of 85 kN.

10-45 A 12 mm diameter aluminum sample fails under an axial tensile load of 60 kN. Determine the maximum normal stress and the maximum shear stress in the sample.

10-46 A concrete cylinder with a diameter of 300 mm fails when the axial compressive load is 800 kN. Calculate the maximum normal stress and the maximum shear stress in the cylinder at failure.

10-6 NORMAL STRAIN

An axially loaded member carrying a tensile load will stretch or deform, as shown in Fig. 10-13. This may come as a surprise, because materials such as steel are thought of as rigid materials. Everyone knows that if a piece of rubber is pulled it will stretch. The same is true of steel and aluminum, and all other materials. The difference is in the amount of stretch. The stretch is usually called *deformation*, and the symbol for deformation is δ. To compare one material to another, or one sample of the same material to another, it is customary to use strain, which is the deformation per unit of length.

FIGURE 10-13

$$\epsilon = \frac{\delta}{L} \qquad (10\text{-}7)$$

where ϵ is the normal strain,

δ is the normal deformation, and

L is the original length of the member before deformation.

Because both δ and L have the same units, either mm or m, ϵ will be unitless although it is customary to express the units for ϵ as m/m.

The normal strain is in the direction of the force. In the case of normal strain associated with a tensile force, the strain will be positive. If an axial compressive force is applied to a member, the member will shorten and the strain will be negative.

For purposes of comparing materials, the strain is sometimes expressed in terms of percent deformation instead of strain. This is calculated from

$$\% \text{ deformation} = \frac{\delta}{L} \times 100 \qquad (10\text{-}8)$$

The strain calculated using Eq. (10-7) is an average strain over the length measured. As long as the member is axially loaded and uniform in cross section, and not carrying a load about to cause failure, the normal strain at any point will be very close to the average value.

EXAMPLE 10-11

A 15 m wire is suspended in a stairwell and a load is applied. If the wire stretches 12 mm, calculate the average normal strain in the wire.

SOLUTION

The average strain may be calculated by direct substitution into Eq. (10-7). Be certain that deformation and original length are expressed in the same units.

$$\epsilon = \frac{\delta}{L}$$

$$= \frac{12 \times 10^{-3}}{15}$$

$$= 0.800\,00 \times 10^{-3} \text{ m/m}$$

$$\boxed{\epsilon = 0.800 \times 10^{-3} \text{ m/m}}$$

EXAMPLE 10-12

By means of a device called a strain gage, the strain in a 75 mm long axially loaded compression member is found to be $-0.000\,125$ m/m. Find the deformation in the member.

SOLUTION

If the strain is known, the deformation in a member can be calculated by rewriting Eq. (10-7). Remember to be careful with units. Note that the strain value is the same whether expressed in m/m or mm/mm. Since the strain is negative, the deformation will also be negative.

$$\epsilon = \frac{\delta}{L}$$

$$\delta = \epsilon L$$

$$= -0.000\,125 \times 75$$

$$= -9.3750 \times 10^{-3} \text{ mm}$$

$$= -0.009\,375 \text{ mm}$$

$$\boxed{\delta = -0.009\,38 \text{ mm}}$$

PROBLEMS

10-47 A 10 m long tie rod stretches 4.7 mm. Calculate the strain in the tie rod.

10-48 Calculate the average strain in a 150 mm long block under a compressive load if the axial deformation is 3 mm.

10-49 A 600 mm long concrete sample has a deformation of 1.70 mm when it fails under an axial compressive load. Determine the average normal strain in the sample at failure.

10-50 A gray cast-iron sample with a test length of 50 mm elongates a total of 0.450 mm at failure. Calculate the average normal strain at failure.

10-51 The strain in a 4 m long steel tension member was found to be 450×10^{-6} m/m. Calculate the total deformation in the member.

10-52 A short aluminum compression member was found to have a strain of 1.0×10^{-3} m/m. If the original length of the member was 50 mm, calculate the deformation in the member.

10-53 A member subjected to an axial load of 25 kN compression has a strain of -0.0025 m/m. If the original length of the member was 0.40 m, determine the deformation of the member.

10-54 Calculate the deformation in a member that is 1500 mm long and has an axial load of 2 kN. The strain in the member is $0.002\,50$ m/m.

10-55 Calculate the percent deformation in a rubber gasket 20 mm thick if it is compressed 7 mm when loaded.

10-56 A 200 mm long sample of aluminum stretches 11.3 mm when an axial load is applied. Determine the percent elongation for the sample.

10-57 A 50 m steel surveyor's chain has a length of 50.0020 m when an axial tensile load is applied. Find the percent deformation in the chain.

10-58 A 100 mm long sample of cast nylon has a length of 52 mm after a compressive load is applied. Calculate the percent deformation of the sample.

10-7 SHEAR STRAIN

If a small square element is cut out of a body where a shear stress acts on one surface, as shown in Fig. 10-14(a), it would be observed that in order to maintain equilibrium in the y direction, there must also be an equal shear stress on the opposite face, as shown in Fig. 10-14(b). The stresses shown in Fig. 10-14(b) would form a couple, and in order to maintain rotational equilibrium, an equal and opposite couple must exist, as shown in Fig. 10-14(c). The combination of forces due to the shear stress on each face would cause the element to deform as shown in somewhat exaggerated form in Fig. 10-14(d).

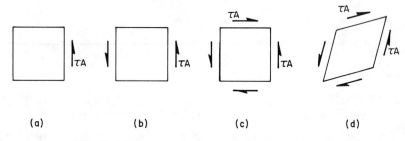

(a)   (b)   (c)   (d)

FIGURE 10-14

In Fig. 10-15, δ_s is the shear deformation, and L is the length of one side of the element. The shearing strain is

$$\frac{\delta_s}{L} = \tan \gamma$$

But for small angles, measured in radians, $\tan \gamma = \gamma$. Thus,

$$\frac{\delta_s}{L} = \gamma \qquad (10\text{-}9)$$

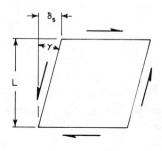

FIGURE 10-15

Note that δ_s/L has no units (although it may be expressed in m/m) and γ also has no units, since radians are a unitless measure.

In many instances shear deformations are measured indirectly, so no shear strain calculations will be illustrated at this time, but they will be illustrated in a later chapter.

10-8   ELASTIC CONSTANTS

The topics of normal stress and normal strain have been discussed in previous articles. For all materials, it has been found that when a normal stress is applied, a normal strain also occurs if the material is not restrained. The values for stress and the strain which exist for a specific stress in a material may be plotted as a stress-strain diagram. Two such diagrams are shown in Fig. 10-16. As noted in the figure, one diagram is for a typical ductile material, and the second is for a typical brittle material. Each material has its own unique stress-strain diagram.

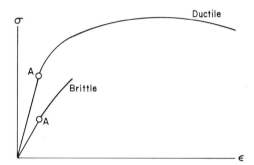

FIGURE 10-16

Many materials behave elastically. This means that when the load or stress is removed, the material will return to its original dimensions. In other words, the deformation or strain will disappear. Point A in each of the diagrams of Fig. 10-16 shows the approximate limit of elastic behavior for the two materials. When a material is strained beyond its elastic limit (*i.e.* to the right of point A on the diagram) it is said to behave plastically. A material which is behaving plastically will not return to its original length after the load is removed, but will have some permanent deformation. Most of our study of stress analysis is based on the elastic behavior of materials. Thus, the emphasis will be on what happens to materials while they are behaving elastically. (A more thorough examination of entire stress-strain diagrams will take place in Chap. 17.)

In the elastic range, the stress-strain diagram is often a straight line, or very nearly a straight line. If the stress-strain diagram is a straight line, then stress is proportional to strain. The slope of

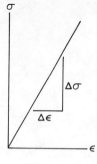

FIGURE 10-17

the stress-strain diagram, as shown in Fig. 10-17, is called the modulus of elasticity. It is also sometimes called Young's modulus

$$E = \frac{\Delta\sigma}{\Delta\epsilon} \qquad (10\text{-}10)$$

where E is the modulus of elasticity,
$\qquad \Delta\sigma$ is the change in normal stress which corresponds to
$\qquad \Delta\epsilon$ the change in normal strain

In the majority of calculations, the modulus of elasticity is simply expressed as

$$E = \frac{\sigma}{\epsilon} \qquad (10\text{-}11)$$

where E is the modulus of elasticity,
$\qquad \sigma$ is the normal stress, and
$\qquad \epsilon$ is the normal strain.

Since the units of stress are Pa, and the strain is unitless, the units for the modulus of elasticity will be Pa. For metallic materials the value for stress is usually very high and the value for strain is usually very low, so the modulus of elasticity will usually be expressed in GPa. For nonmetallic materials, the modulus of elasticity is usually expressed in MPa.

Since the value for E for any given material is a constant if the material is behaving elastically, E is one of the elastic constants. The modulus of elasticity is a measure of a material's resistance to elastic deformation. Materials with a high modulus of elasticity have a high resistance to elastic deformation, and are said to be stiff.

When an axial load is applied to a member, the member deforms, and there is normal strain in the longitudinal direction, as discussed in Article 10-6. When a material has a normal strain under a normal stress, the transverse dimension of the member also changes, as shown in Fig. 10-18, so that there is also a transverse strain. For material behaving elastically, there is a fixed ratio between the longitudinal strain and the transverse strain. This ratio is called Poisson's ratio.

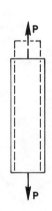

FIGURE 10-18

$$\nu = \frac{\epsilon_t}{\epsilon_l} \qquad (10\text{-}12)$$

where ν is Poisson's ratio,
$\qquad \epsilon_t$ is the transverse normal strain, and
$\qquad \epsilon_l$ is the longitudinal normal strain.

As might be expected with a ratio, ν has no units. Although there are signs associated with strain, and the longitudinal and transverse strains would have opposite signs, Poisson's ratio is simply a ratio, so that its sign is positive. Values for Poisson's ratio vary from about 0.25 to 0.35 for metals, but always fall between 0 and 0.5.

In the case of shear stress, a shearing strain also occurs if the member is not restrained, and a shear stress — shear strain diagram can be drawn relating the shear stress and shear strain, as shown in Fig. 10-19. Typical diagrams for both ductile and brittle materials are shown. Materials can have elastic behavior in shear, just as they can for normal stress and strain. The limit of the elastic behavior in shear is shown at A in Fig. 10-19. The slope of the straight line portion of the shear stress-strain diagram is called the shear modulus of elasticity.

$$G = \frac{\Delta\tau}{\Delta\gamma} \qquad (10\text{-}13)$$

where G is the shear modulus of elasticity,
    $\Delta\tau$ is the change in shear stress which corresponds to
    $\Delta\gamma$ the change in shear strain.

In the majority of calculations, the shear modulus of elasticity is simply expressed as

$$G = \frac{\tau}{\gamma} \qquad (10\text{-}14)$$

where G is the shear modulus of elasticity,
    τ is the shear stress, and
    γ is the shear strain.

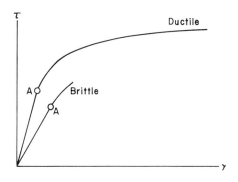

FIGURE 10-19

The units for G will also be Pa, usually a multiple, such as GPa or MPa.

The shear modulus of elasticity is another elastic constant, and it measures the resistance of a material to elastic shearing deformation.

Many tables of properties of materials, unlike the one shown in the Appendix, do not give values for both G and ν. This is not a big problem, since it has been shown that

$$G = \frac{E}{2(1 + \nu)} \qquad (10\text{-}15)$$

which is sometimes rewritten as

$$\nu = \frac{E}{2G} - 1 \qquad (10\text{-}16)$$

where E is the modulus of elasticity,
  G is the shear modulus of elasticity, and
  ν is Poisson's ratio

Thus if either G or ν is known, along with E, the third elastic constant can be calculated.

It must be noted that stress-strain diagrams provide much more information than is discussed in this chapter. The additional information is provided in Article 17-1 through Article 17-3 of Chapter 17.

EXAMPLE 10-13

An aluminum alloy sample is tested in tension. When the stress is 150 MPa the normal strain is 2.1×10^{-3} m/m. Calculate the modulus of elasticity for this alloy.

SOLUTION

The modulus of elasticity may be obtained by direct substitution in to Eq. (10-11).

$$E = \frac{\sigma}{\epsilon}$$

$$= \frac{150 \times 10^6}{2.1 \times 10^{-3}}$$

$$= 71.429 \times 10^9 \text{ Pa}$$

$$= 71.429 \text{ GPa}$$

$$\boxed{E = 71.4 \text{ GPa}}$$

EXAMPLE 10-14

A 2 m long round bar of polystyrene plastic with a diameter of 25 mm carries a 5 kN tensile load. If the modulus of elasticity of the polystyrene is 3.0 GPa, calculate the longitudinal deformation in the bar.

SOLUTION

From Eq. (10-7) we can find that the deformation is

$$\delta = \epsilon L$$

Equation (10-11) *may be rewritten to give*

$$\epsilon = \frac{\sigma}{E}$$

From Eq. (10-1) *we have*

$$\sigma = \frac{P}{A}$$

Rewriting the above, we have

$$\delta = \epsilon L$$

$$= \frac{\sigma}{E} L$$

$$= \frac{PL}{AE}$$

$$= \frac{5000 \times 2}{\dfrac{\pi \times 25^2}{4} \times 10^{-6} \times 3.0 \times 10^9}$$

$$= 6.7906 \times 10^{-3} \text{ m}$$

$$= 6.7906 \text{ mm}$$

$$\boxed{\delta = 6.79 \text{ mm}}$$

EXAMPLE 10-15

Accurate experimental measurements in a compression test of a 200 mm long square sample with a 50 by 50 mm cross section give a longitudinal deformation of –0.100 mm and a transverse deformation of 0.008 00 mm. Determine Poisson's ratio for the material.

SOLUTION

To calculate Poisson's ratio, it is necessary to first determine both the longitudinal and transverse strains using Eq. (10-7).

$$\epsilon_l = \frac{\delta_l}{L_l}$$

$$= \frac{-0.100}{200}$$

$$= -0.000\ 500\ 00 \text{ m/m}$$

$$\epsilon_t = \frac{\delta_t}{L_t}$$

$$= \frac{0.008\ 00}{50}$$

$$= 0.000\ 160\ 00\ \text{m/m}$$

Now Poisson's ratio may be calculated by substitution into Eq. (10-12). *Note that the negative sign is not used in the calculation.*

$$\nu = \frac{\epsilon_t}{\epsilon_l}$$

$$= \frac{0.000\ 160\ 00}{0.000\ 500\ 00}$$

$$= 0.320\ 00$$

$$\boxed{\nu = 0.320}$$

EXAMPLE 10-16

Find the shear strain in a material if the shear modulus of elasticity for the material is 80 GPa and the shear stress is 175 MPa.

SOLUTION

The shear strain may be calculated by rewriting Eq. (10-14) *and substituting values.*

$$G = \frac{\tau}{\gamma}$$

$$\gamma = \frac{\tau}{G}$$

$$= \frac{175 \times 10^6}{80 \times 10^9}$$

$$= 2.1875 \times 10^{-3}\ \text{m/m}$$

$$\boxed{\gamma = 2.19 \times 10^{-3}\ \text{m/m}}$$

EXAMPLE 10-17

Determine the value for G for tin if E is known to be 40 GPa and ν is 0.36.

SOLUTION

The value for G may be obtained by direct substitution of values in Eq. (10-15).

$$G = \frac{E}{2(1 + \nu)}$$

$$= \frac{40 \times 10^9}{2(1 + 0.36)}$$

$$= 14.706 \times 10^9 \text{ Pa}$$

$$= 14.706 \text{ GPa}$$

$$\boxed{G = 14.7 \text{ GPa}}$$

EXAMPLE   10-18

A table of mechanical properties gives $E = 96$ GPa and $G = 36$ GPa for a titanium alloy, but does not give the value for ν. Calculate ν.

SOLUTION

Values of E and G may be substituted directly into Eq. (10-16) to obtain the value for ν.

$$\nu = \frac{E}{2G} - 1$$

$$= \frac{96 \times 10^9}{2 \times 36 \times 10^9} - 1$$

$$= 1.3333 - 1$$

$$= 0.3333$$

$$\boxed{\nu = 0.333}$$

PROBLEMS

Note: For the following problems, assume that the stress in the material is less than the elastic limit. Required values of E, G and v are found in Appendix E.

10-59 Determine the modulus of elasticity for steel piano wire if it has a strain of 2.62×10^{-3} m/m when the stress in it is 550 MPa.

10-60 A dry red-oak sample has a strain of -1.67×10^{-3} m/m when the stress in the wood is −20 MPa. Calculate the modulus of elasticity for this sample.

10-61 If a medium-strength concrete has a modulus of elasticity of 20 GPa, find the strain in the concrete when the stress is −8.0 MPa.

10-62 Determine the strain in a rigid-vinyl sample if the modulus of elasticity is 3.0 GPa, and the stress in the sample is 22 MPa.

10-63 A strip of bronze 5 by 20 mm carries an axial tensile load of 30 kN. In a length of 200 mm, there is a deformation of 0.513 mm. Calculate the modulus of elasticity for the bronze.

10-64 A 300 mm long concrete cylinder with a 150 mm diameter shortens 0.323 mm under an axial load of 400 kN. Calculate the modulus of elasticity.

10-65 A 50 by 75 mm 6061-T6 aluminum-alloy bar is subjected to an axial tensile stress of 175 MPa. Determine the longitudinal deformation, in mm, in the bar if it is 1200 mm long.

10-66 A 2000 mm long structural steel bar with a diameter of 75 mm carries an axial tensile load of 1600 kN. Determine the deformation in the bar under this load.

10-67 A carbon-steel rock bolt with a diameter of 25 mm was instrumented and found to have a strain of 1.50×10^{-3} m/m. Determine the load carried by the rock bolt.

10-68 A 5 m long hard-copper wire with a diameter of 2 mm stretches a total of 6.80 mm under an unknown load. Determine the magnitude of the load.

10-69 A sample of platinum was tested in tension. The longitudinal strain was found to be 0.800×10^{-3} m/m and the transverse strain was -0.300×10^{-3} m/m when the normal stress was 120 MPa. Determine Poisson's ratio for platinum.

10-70 If the longitudinal strain in a concrete cylinder was found to be -0.55×10^{-3} m/m and the transverse strain was 0.11×10^{-3} m/m, determine Poisson's ratio for concrete.

10-71 Using precision measuring equipment, the deformation in a lead bar with a length of 300 mm and a diameter of 60 mm was measured. If the bar shortened by 0.200 mm and its diameter increased by 0.0175 mm, determine Poisson's ratio for lead.

10-72 A sheet of aluminum 2 m long and 1 m wide is loaded along the long dimension and the deformation is found to be 5.00 mm. Determine the deformation in the 1 m dimension.

10-73 When the shear stress in invar was found to be 75 MPa, the corresponding shear strain was 1.33×10^{-3} m/m. Determine the shear modulus of elasticity for invar.

10-74 Calculate the shear modulus of elasticity for a stainless steel that has a shear strain of 2.20×10^{-3} m/m when the shear stress of 190 MPa.

10-75 Determine the shear modulus of elasticity for zinc if $E = 110$ GPa and $v = 0.25$.

10-76 If Poisson's ratio for gold is 0.44 and the modulus of elasticity is 71 GPa, find the shear modulus of elasticity for gold.

10-77 Find Poisson's ratio for extruded magnesium using the tabulated values for E and G found in Appendix E.

10-78 Use the tabulated values of E and G from Appendix E to calculate Poisson's ratio for structural steel.

11 APPLICATIONS OF BASIC PRINCIPLES

11-1 FACTOR OF SAFETY AND ALLOWABLE STRESS

The primary purpose of stress analysis is to provide the analytical skills used in designing various types of structures with efficient use of materials and minimum risk of failure. The storage tank shown in Fig. 11-1 is just one such structure where the material must be used efficiently to minimize cost, and where the tank must be unlikely to fail, to minimize risk to workers and others nearby. Most structures, whether they are buildings, machines, storage tanks or ships, are not designed to be absolutely failure-proof, for the cost of designing for an improbable failure such as an aircraft striking a storage tank or a tornado striking a building would be prohibitive.

FIGURE 11-1 These butane storage Hortonspheres shown under construction at a Canadian oil refinery have a diameter of nearly 20 m, and the normal operating pressure in them will be about 480 kPa. *Photo courtesy of Horton CBI, Limited.*

For our purposes, failure of a structure or of a member of a structure occurs when that structure or member no longer performs its intended function. Physically, a failure may occur because a part deforms excessively or because of fracture or breaking of the part. An engine crankshaft that bends excessively and causes vibration in the engine has failed even though it has not broken. A cable that breaks in a crane while the crane is lifting a load is an example of a failure by fracture.

Whether or not a member has failed depends on the relationship between the actual stress in the member and the yield strength or ultimate strength of the material in the member. Figure 11-2 illustrates two typical stress-strain diagrams. The upper diagram is for a ductile material and the lower one is for a brittle material. Point *A* is the yield strength, and it is at this point that large strains start to occur with little change in stress, at least in ductile materials. In other words, when the stress in a member exceeds the yield strength, large (and usually unacceptable) deformations are likely to occur. Point *B* is the ultimate strength, which is the highest stress carried by the material prior to fracture. If the stress in a member exceeds the ultimate strength, fracture failure will occur.

More detail on stress-strain diagrams and mechanical properties of materials is given in Chap. 17. One may find it useful to read the first three articles of Chap. 17 in conjunction with this article.

Consider a crane lifting a load. It would be foolish to stand under the load if the stress in the cable was 550 MPa and it was known that the ultimate strength of the material in the cable was 550 MPa. The risk of the consequences of failure by fracture of the cable is a bit too high.

There are two methods used for ensuring that the actual stresses in structures are relatively safe. One method is to determine an *allowable stress* for a particular material under a given condition of load. The other is to specify a *factor of safety* for a given type of load.

An allowable stress, which is sometimes called a working stress, is frequently set out in a code that is sometimes incorporated in a law or used as a law. The designer must select members of such a size and shape that the stress in them does not exceed the specified allowable stress. The allowable stress for a given material will vary depending on the type of stress (tension, compression or shear), the type of load (static, impact or repeated) and, in some cases, the dimensions of the member. The designer has little influence over the choice of allowable stresses, but must be governed by the code that applies to the material being used and the type of project being designed. Allowable

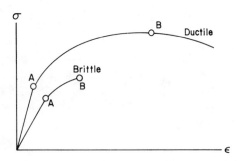

FIGURE 11-2

stresses are usually selected by experts with knowledge of the materials and the structures in which they will be used.

The factor of safety, which is also sometimes called the design factor or the factor of ignorance, may be defined by

$$N = \frac{\text{failure load}}{\text{actual load}} \qquad (11\text{-}1)$$

This may also be expressed as

$$N = \frac{\sigma_y}{\sigma_{all}} \qquad (11\text{-}2)$$

or

$$N = \frac{\sigma_u}{\sigma_{all}} \qquad (11\text{-}3)$$

where N is the factor of safety,
  σ_{all} is the allowable stress,
  σ_y is the yield strength, and
  σ_u is the ultimate strength.

The failure load may be based on either yielding or fracture, and the failure stress may be based on either the yield strength or the ultimate strength, depending on whether excessive deformation or fracture is considered most critical. For brittle materials, the factor of safety is usually based on the ultimate strength.

The magnitude of the factor of safety depends on the type of material, the type of failure, the type of load and the likelihood of the most severe loading condition actually occuring.

In the case of a ductile material, visible excessive deformation frequently precedes fracture, thus giving warning of impending fracture. In the case of a brittle material, there usually is no visible warning, so there is a need for a higher factor of safety for the brittle material.

If failure is based on the yield strength for a ductile material, the factor of safety can often be lower than if failure is based on the ultimate strength, since there is usually a large additional stress that can be carried, without fracture occurring, after the material yields.

Materials behave differently under different loading conditions; this behavior has an influence on the factor of safety. The basic properties of materials are usually based on a single load gradually applied to the material. This approximates a static load, which is a load gradually applied, and which may remain for an extended period of time. The strength characteristics of a material change under an impact load, which is a load applied quickly. The couplings and frames of railway cars are subjected to impact loads as a train starts up. The frame of a press is subjected to impact loads as the material is being formed in the die. Repeated loads are loads that are alternately applied and removed. The piston rod in an internal-combustion engine would be subjected to alternating or repeated loads as the engine operates. Similarly, a diving board at a swimming pool would be loaded and unloaded as a diver bounces on the end of the board in preparation for the dive.

When deciding on the assumed loads to be applied to a structure, if the assumed loads are so extreme as to be very unlikely to occur, then a relatively small factor of safety may be used, and if the assumed loads are the normal, day-to-day types of loads, then a relatively large factor of safety will be used.

Factors of safety are not usually selected by the novice designer, but by experienced personnel knowledgeable in the materials and structures under consideration. Some typical values for the factor of safety are shown in Table 11-1. Note that using the typical factors of safety given in the table will not necessarily give the same values of allowable stresses that may be specified in some codes.

TABLE 11-1
TYPICAL VALUES FOR FACTOR OF SAFETY

MATERIAL	LOAD TYPE		
	Static	Impact	Repeated
Ductile			
based on yield strength	2	4	6
based on ultimate strength	4	8	12
Brittle			
based on ultimate strength	6	10	15

EXAMPLE 11-1

A concrete pier with a square cross section is to be constructed to carry an axial compressive load of 160 kN. Determine the minimum required section for the pier if the specified allowable stress in the concrete is given as 6 MPa.

SOLUTION

Since both the normal stress and the load are known, Eq. (10-1) may be rewritten to determine the area. The length of each side can be b, so that A = b².

$$\sigma = \frac{P}{A} = \frac{P}{b^2} \quad \text{where } A = b^2$$

$$b^2 = \frac{P}{\sigma}$$

$$= \frac{160 \times 10^3}{6 \times 10^6}$$

$$= 26.667 \times 10^{-3}$$

$$b = 0.163\ 30\ \text{m}$$

$$= 163.30\ \text{mm}$$

> 163 by 163 mm

EXAMPLE 11-2

A 15 mm diameter gray cast-iron bar is to carry an axial tensile load. Determine the maximum load that may be carried for (a) static, (b) impact and (c) repeated load conditions.

SOLUTION

Gray cast iron is a brittle material, since it has only 0.5% deformation at failure (see Appendix E). *Its ultimate strength in tension is* 170 MPa. *Values for the factor of safety are obtained from* Table 11-1. *The allowable stress for each type of load may be obtained from* Eq. (11-3). *The allowable stress may then be used in* Eq. (10-1) *to calculate the maximum value of the load for each type of load.*
  Rewriting Eq. (11-3):

$$N = \frac{\sigma_u}{\sigma_{all}}$$

$$\sigma_{all} = \frac{\sigma_u}{N}$$

(a) Static load

$$\sigma_{all} = \frac{\sigma_u}{N}$$

$$= \frac{170 \times 10^6}{6}$$

$$= 28.333 \times 10^6\ \text{Pa}$$

$$P = \sigma A$$

$$= 28.333 \times 10^6 \times \frac{\pi}{4} \times 15^2 \times 10^{-6}$$

$$= 5006.9 \text{ N}$$

(b) Impact load

$$\sigma_{all} = \frac{\sigma_u}{N}$$

$$= \frac{170 \times 10^6}{10}$$

$$= 17.000 \times 10^6 \text{ Pa}$$

$$P = \sigma A$$

$$= 17.000 \times 10^6 \times \frac{\pi}{4} \times 15^2 \times 10^{-6}$$

$$= 3004.1 \text{ N}$$

(c) Repeated load

$$\sigma_{all} = \frac{\sigma_u}{N}$$

$$= \frac{170 \times 10^6}{15}$$

$$= 11.333 \times 10^6 \text{ Pa}$$

$$P = \sigma A$$

$$= 11.333 \times 10^6 \times \frac{\pi}{4} \times 15^2 \times 10^{-6}$$

$$= 2002.7 \text{ N}$$

(a) $P = 5.01$ kN
(b) $P = 3.00$ kN
(c) $P = 2.00$ kN

PROBLEMS

11-1 A short timber post with a cross section of 150 by 150 mm has an allowable stress in compression of 15 MPa. Find the maximum load that may be carried by the post.

11-2 A gray cast iron has an allowable stress in tension of 30 MPa. Determine the maximum load that a 25 mm diameter bar may support.

11-3 Calculate the width of a 2 mm thick aluminum sheet required to support a 5000 N load. The allowable stress in the sheet is 90 MPa.

11-4 Find the minimum diameter required for a round vinyl part in tension if the allowable stress in the vinyl is 12 MPa and the tensile load is 600 kg.

11-5 A steel bolt is to carry a shear force of 35 kN. Determine the minimum diameter of bolt required if the allowable shear stress in the bolt is 125 MPa.

11-6 Determine the maximum shear force that can be applied to a 20 mm diameter pin if the allowable shear stress in the pin is 80 MPa.

11-7 For 18-8 stainless steel, determine the allowable stress based on the yield strength for (a) static (b) impact and (c) repeated loads.

11-8 Calculate the allowable stress for malleable cast iron based on ultimate strength for (a) static (b) impact and (c) repeated loads.

11-9 For a gray cast iron, determine the maximum allowable stress in both (a) tension and (b) compression. The loads are static loads.

11-10 Find the allowable stress for a 0.8% carbon hot-rolled steel subjected to an impact load if the factor of safety is based on (a) yield strength and (b) ultimate strength.

11-11 The tie bar *BD* shown in Fig. P11-11 has a square section and is made of 230G structural steel. Determine the minimum dimensions required if there must be a factor of safety of 2 based on yield strength.

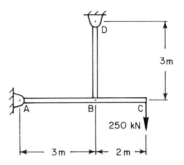

FIGURE P11-11

11-12 The lower chord of the truss shown in Fig. P11-12 is made of two 230G steel equal-leg angles back to back. (See Appendix F for dimensions of angles.) If the loads are static, and the factor of safety is based on yield strength, determine the lightest angles that may be used.

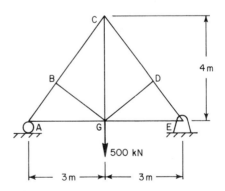

FIGURE P11-12

11-2   STRESS CONCENTRATIONS

In developing the basic equation for normal stress, $\sigma = P/A$, certain conditions were met. The load was applied through the centroid of the section, and the load was parallel to the longitudinal axis of the member. If the cross section of the member changes, the change, sometimes called a discontinuity, causes a change in the stress from that calculated using $\sigma = P/A$. A discontinuity could be a hole, a notch, or a reduction in the size of the member.

A plate with a constant thickness carrying an axial tensile load would have the internal loads ΔP uniformly spread over the section as shown at the right end of Fig. 11-3(a). If there is a hole cut in the plate, the same total amount of force must be carried by the reduced amount of material at the hole. The forces will be crowded together at the vicinity of the hole, as shown in Fig. 11-3(b). With more force per unit of area, the stress will be higher in the vicinity of the hole. The stress distribution at the hole is shown in Fig. 11-3(c). The stress is said to be concentrated at the hole, and thus the hole causes a stress concentration. Since materials tend to fail where the stress is maximum, evaluating the maximum stress is very important.

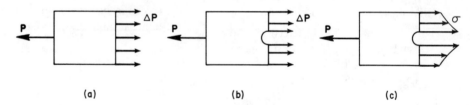

(a)   (b)   (c)

FIGURE 11-3

The magnitude of the maximum stress at a stress concentration is obtained from

$$\sigma_{max} = K_t \sigma_{nom} \tag{11-4}$$

where σ_{max} is the maximum stress at the stress concentration,
K_t is the stress-concentration factor, and
σ_{nom} is the nominal stress at the stress concentration.

The stress-concentration factor varies depending on the shape of the member, the shape of the discontinuity and the proportions of the member and discontinuity. Because there are so many influencing variables, the values for K_t are usually shown in chart or graph form. Figures 11-4, 11-5 and 11-6 show charts for K_t for three different types of tension members. In each figure, part (a) shows the chart for the stress-concentration factor, part (b) shows the shape of the member and part (c) shows the actual stress distribution and the nominal stress distribution. Note that the appropriate equation for the nominal stress for each of the illustrated members is given with the figures.

Since the stress-concentration factor changes for each different shape of member and discontinuity, the stress-concentration factors are appropriate only for the conditions shown. For example, the stress-concentration factors for a circular hole in the center of a flat plate, as shown in Fig. 11-4, are different from the stress-concentration factors that would exist for a circular hole near the edge of a flat plate. Many combinations of shape of member and discontinuity exist, and only three are shown here. Entire books are available with nothing but charts of stress-concentration factors.

The values of the stress-concentration factors shown in the charts are obtained from theoretical mathematical analysis or experimental methods, or from a combination of both. Because localized high compressive stress tends not to lead to fracture types of failure, stress concentrations are of concern primarily when the stress is tension.

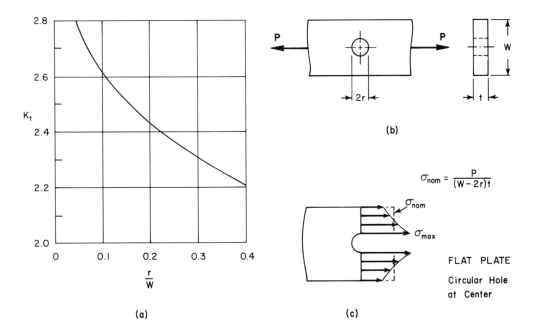

$$\sigma_{nom} = \frac{P}{(W - 2r)t}$$

FLAT PLATE
Circular Hole
at Center

(a)

(b)

(c)

FIGURE 11-4

EXAMPLE 11-3

A 10 mm thick steel plate with a width of 150 mm and a length of 1200 mm has a 30 mm diameter hole at its center. If there is an axial tensile load of 140 kN on the plate, determine the maximum tensile stress in the plate.

SOLUTION

The plate matches the member illustrated in Fig. 11-4, *which is a flat plate with a circular hole at the center. To use the chart in* Fig. 11-4(a), *it is necessary to calculate the ratio r/W to determine the stress-concentration factor.*

$$\frac{r}{W} = \frac{30/2}{150}$$

$$= 0.10$$

To determine the stress-concentration factor, the procedure is to use Fig. 11-4(a) *and start on the r/W axis where r/W = 0.10. Move vertically up the line r/W = 0.10 to where it intercepts the curve shown. At that point, move horizontally to the left to determine the value of the stress-concentration factor on the K_t axis. The value is 2.61. This indicates that the actual stress in the plate at the edge of the hole is actually 2.61 times as great as the nominal stress in the plate.*

Use the nominal-stress equation shown with Fig. 11-4 *and then use* Eq. (11-4) *to calculate the maximum stress.*

$$\sigma_{nom} = \frac{P}{(W - 2r)t}$$

$$= \frac{140 \times 10^3}{(150 - 30)10 \times 10^{-6}}$$

$$= 116.67 \times 10^6 \text{ Pa}$$

$$\sigma_{max} = K_t\sigma_{nom}$$

$$= 2.61 \times 116.67 \times 10^6$$

$$= 304.50 \times 10^6 \text{ Pa}$$

$$= 304.50 \text{ MPa}$$

$$\boxed{\sigma_{max} = 304 \text{ MPa}}$$

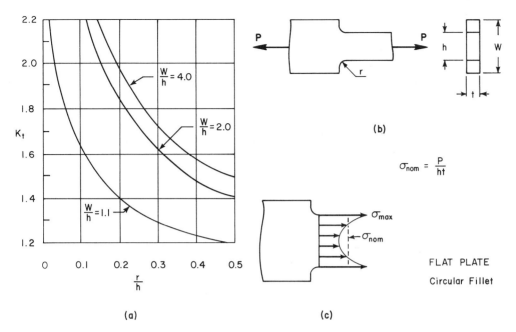

$$\sigma_{nom} = \frac{P}{ht}$$

FLAT PLATE

Circular Fillet

(a)   **(c)**

FIGURE 11-5

EXAMPLE 11-4

Calculate the maximum stress that occurs in a 50 mm diameter bar with an axial tensile load of 75 kN if there is a section in the bar which is reduced to a 25 mm diameter. There is a 4 mm radius fillet between the full sections and the reduced section.

SOLUTION

The member shown in Fig. 11-6(b) *matches the member in the problem. To determine the stress concentration factor, it is necessary to first calculate the ratios r/d and D/d in order to use the chart. Note that in* Fig. 11-6, *D is used for the larger diameter and d refers to the smaller diameter.*

$$\frac{r}{d} = \frac{4}{25}$$

$$= 0.16$$

$$\frac{D}{d} = \frac{50}{25}$$

$$= 2.0$$

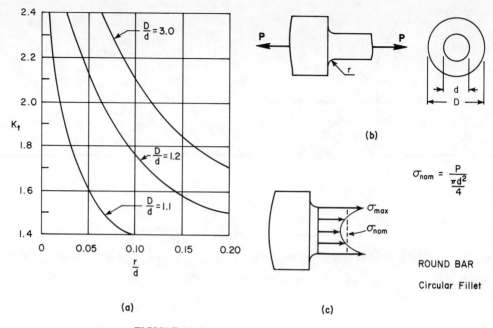

FIGURE 11-6

$\sigma_{nom} = \dfrac{P}{\dfrac{\pi d^2}{4}}$

ROUND BAR

Circular Fillet

To use the chart in Fig. 11-6(a) start on the r/d axis at r/d = 0.16. Go vertically up at r/d = 0.16 to the D/d = 2.0 curve. This curve is not shown, so it is necessary to estimate its position. Note that the spacing between curves is not linear, so D/d = 2.0 will be fairly close to the D/d = 3.0 curve. After estimating the position where r/d = 0.16 intersects the D/d = 2.0 curve, move horizontally from the intercept to the left to the K_t axis and determine the value of K_t. The approximate value of K_t is 1.68.

Calculate σ_{nom} using the equation given with Fig. 11-6, and then use Eq. (11-4) to determine σ_{max}.

$$\sigma_{nom} = \frac{P}{\dfrac{\pi d^2}{4}}$$

$$= \frac{75 \times 10^3}{\dfrac{\pi \times 25^2}{4}} \times 10^{-6}$$

$$= 152.79 \times 10^6 \text{ Pa}$$

$$\sigma_{max} = K_t \sigma_{nom}$$

$$= 1.68 \times 152.79 \times 10^6$$

$$= 256.69 \times 10^6 \text{ Pa}$$

$$= 256.69 \text{ MPa}$$

$$\boxed{\sigma_{max} = 257 \text{ MPa}}$$

Note that because of the estimating of values required in using the charts in this and similar problems, it is normal for two persons to obtain two somewhat different values for σ_{max}.

PROBLEMS

11-13 An aluminum plate 50 mm wide and 8 mm thick has an axial tensile load of 40 kN. Determine the maximum stress in the plate if there is a 5 mm diameter hole in the center of the plate.

11-14 Find the maximum tensile stress in a plate 25 by 200 mm if there is an 80 mm diameter hole in the plate on the center line, and if the tensile force acting on the plate is 175 kN.

11-15 A plate 75 mm wide and 10 mm thick has a 15 mm diameter hole at its center. If the plate carries an axial tensile load, determine the maximum safe load if the allowable stress is 80 MPa.

11-16 Find the maximum allowable tensile load in a 2 mm thick plastic sheet 20 mm wide if it has a 12 mm diameter hole at its center. The allowable stress in the plastic is 7 MPa.

11-17 A vinyl bar 15 mm thick has a width of 50 mm. This is reduced to 35 mm and there are 5 mm radius fillets where the section is reduced. If the axial load on the bar is 2500 N tension, determine the maximum stress in the bar.

11-18 A 75 mm diameter aluminum bar with an axial tensile load of 300 kN has a section reduced to a diameter of 50 mm. If the radius of the fillet at the reduced section is 5 mm, determine the maximum stress in the bar.

11-19 Determine the maximum allowable tensile load on a 5 mm diameter stainless-steel bar if it has a reduced section with a diameter of 4 mm. The sections are joined by circular fillets with 0.5 mm radii. The allowable stress in the steel is 400 MPa.

11-20 A steel tie bar is cut from 50 mm thick plate that has an allowable stress of 220 MPa. If the tie bar is 150 mm wide and has a reduced section with a width of 75 mm, find the maximum load that can be carried by the tie bar if the sections are joined with circular fillets with a radius of 25 mm.

11-3   THIN-WALLED PRESSURE VESSELS

Thin-walled pressure vessels, in the form of spheres or cylinders, are used for storing fluids under pressure. Figure 11-1 shows one example of such a storage tank. To be classed as a thin-walled pressure vessel, the ratio of the radius to the wall thickness, $r{:}t$, must be more than 10:1. If the ratio $r{:}t$ is greater than 10:1 the stress is approximately uniform across the thickness of the material. As the ratio $r{:}t$ decreases from 10:1, the stress distribution in the wall becomes increasingly nonuniform, and then the pressure vessel must be analyzed as a thick-walled pressure vessel, which is a much more complex analysis, and is beyond the scope of this text.

To analyze the stress in a cylindrical thin-walled pressure vessel, consider the tank shown in Fig. 11-7(a). Half of a section, with a length of L, is cut out; the section, with only the circumferential forces shown acting on it, is shown in Fig. 11-7(b). The force on each wall is shown as $\mathbf{P}_c$, and is equal to the product of the stress, σ_c, and the area, tL, on which it acts. The force $\mathbf{P}$ due to the internal pressure p acting in the pressure vessel is the same as if the pressure were acting on a plane surface (rather than a curved surface) with an area of dL. From equilibrium,

$$\Sigma F_y = 0$$

$$P_c + P_c - P = 0$$

$$\sigma_c tL + \sigma_c tL - pdL = 0$$

$$2\sigma_c tL = pdL$$

$$\sigma_c = \frac{pdL}{2tL}$$

$$\sigma_c = \frac{pd}{2t} \tag{11-5}$$

where σ_c is the circumferential stress in the wall of the pressure vessel,

p is the pressure of the contents,

d is the diameter, and

t is the wall thickness.

The circumferential stress is also sometimes called the hoop stress. It is the stress that exists in the direction of the curve in a cylindrical pressure vessel. The diameter used for these calculations is actually the mean of the inside and outside diameters of the pressure vessel. However, in most problems a diameter will be given; it may be assumed to be the mean diameter.

The stress which is parallel to the longitudinal axis of the pressure vessel is called the longitudinal stress, and it may be calculated with the aid of Fig. 11-8. The area on which the longitudinal stress acts may be approximated closely by πdt, where πd is the mean circumference of the vessel. Thus the total

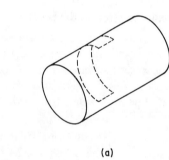

(a)

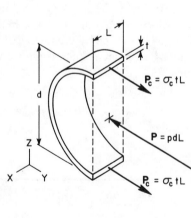

(b)

FIGURE 11-7

force due to the longitudinal stress on the section would be P_l and would be equal to $\pi dt\sigma_l$. For equilibrium, this force must be opposed by the total force due to the internal pressure acting in the longitudinal direction, which is shown as **P** in Fig. 11-8. Its magnitude is $p\pi d^2/4$.

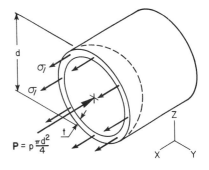

$$\Sigma F_x = 0$$

$$P_l - P = 0$$

$$\pi dt\sigma_l - p\frac{\pi d^2}{4} = 0$$

FIGURE 11-8

$$\sigma_l = \frac{p\pi d^2}{4\pi dt}$$

$$\sigma_l = \frac{pd}{4t} \tag{11-6}$$

where σ_l is the longitudinal stress in the wall of the pressure vessel,

    p is the pressure of the contents,

    d is the diameter, and

    t is the wall thickness.

Note that the longitudinal stress in a pressure vessel is half of the circumferential stress.

In the case of a spherical thin-walled pressure vessel, there are only longitudinal stresses. The maximum stress in a spherical pressure vessel is half the maximum stress in a cylindrical pressure vessel with the same diameter, wall thickness and internal pressure. Refer to Fig. 11-8, and note that the analysis of the longitudinal stress does not depend on the shape of the pressure vessel to the right of the section. In fact, the spherical shape has been shown as a dashed line just to indicate that the same analysis applies to both the cylindrical and spherical pressure vessels.

A pipe containing a fluid under pressure is a long cylindrical pressure vessel, and can be analyzed as a pressure vessel, providing it is not buried.

EXAMPLE 11-5

Determine (a) the circumferential stress and (b) the longitudinal stress in a cylindrical thin-walled pressure vessel with a diameter of 3 m, a length of 8 m and a wall thickness of 6 mm if the pressure of the gas in the vessel is 450 kPa.

SOLUTION

Both parts of the solution may be obtained by direct substitution into Eqs. (11-5) and (11-6) respectively. All dimensions must be expressed in metres.

$$(a) \ \sigma_c = \frac{pd}{2t}$$

$$= \frac{450 \times 10^3 \times 3}{2 \times 6 \times 10^{-3}}$$

$$= 112.50 \times 10^6 \ Pa$$

$$= 112.50 \ MPa$$

$$(b) \ \sigma_l = \frac{pd}{4t}$$

$$= \frac{450 \times 10^3 \times 3}{4 \times 6 \times 10^{-3}}$$

$$= 56.250 \times 10^6 \ Pa$$

$$= 56.250 \ MPa$$

(a) σ_c = 112 MPa
(b) σ_l = 56.2 MPa

EXAMPLE 11-6

For a spherical storage tank with a diameter of 8 m and an internal pressure of 500 kPa, determine the minimum allowable wall thickness if the stress in the wall is not to exceed 75 MPa.

SOLUTION

Since this is a spherical pressure vessel, the only stress to be considered is the longitudinal stress. Equation (11-6) may be re-written to obtain the thickness.

$$\sigma_l = \frac{pd}{4t}$$

$$t = \frac{pd}{4\sigma_l}$$

$$= \frac{500 \times 10^3 \times 8}{4 \times 75 \times 10^6}$$

$$= 13.333 \times 10^{-3}\, m$$

$$= 13.333\, mm$$

$$\boxed{t = 13.3\ mm}$$

If there is any likelihood that r:t is less than 10:1, the ratio should be checked to be certain that the equations for thin-walled pressure vessels may actually be used.

PROBLEMS

11-21 Find (a) the circumferential stress and (b) the longitudinal stress in a cylindrical thin-walled pressure vessel that has a diameter of 6 m, a length of 18 m, a wall thickness of 10 mm and an internal pressure of 450 kPa.

11-22 For a 2 m diameter pressure vessel that has a cylindrical shape, calculate (a) the circumferential stress and (b) the longitudinal stress, if the wall thickness is 3 mm and the internal pressure is 250 kPa.

11-23 Calculate both (a) the circumferential stress and (b) the longitudinal stress in a 300 mm diameter pipe containing natural gas at 800 kPa. The pipe has a thickness of 4 mm.

11-24 A 1 m diameter pipeline operating with an internal pressure of 900 kPa has a wall thickness of 4 mm. Calculate (a) the circumferential stress and (b) the longitudinal stress in the pipe.

11-25 Find the stress in a 12 m diameter spherical tank if the wall thickness is 25 mm and the pressure of the contents is 400 kPa.

11-26 For a 2 m diameter thin-walled spherical pressure vessel with a wall thickness of 20 mm and an internal pressure of 1100 kPa, calculate the stress in the wall.

11-27 A pressure vessel is a cylinder with a diameter of 3 m and a length of 12 m. It is made of 6061-T6 aluminum and has a wall thickness of 4 mm. If the factor of safety, based on yield strength, is 3, determine the allowable pressure in the tank.

11-28 Determine the allowable pressure in a 150 mm diameter pipe with a wall thickness of 3 mm if the pipe is made of 18-8 stainless steel and is to have a factor of safety of 6 based on yield strength.

11-29 Find the wall thickness required for a 25 mm diameter pipe carrying compressed air at 1200 kPa if the pipe is hard copper with an allowable stress of 100 MPa.

11-30 Calculate the wall thickness required for a spherical pressure vessel 4 m in diameter that will hold a gas at 260 kPa if the allowable stress in the material is 95 MPa.

11-4 RIVETED AND BOLTED CONNECTIONS

Riveting and bolting are two methods used for connecting parts in a wide variety of applications. The analysis of connections using both rivets and bolts is similar unless the bolts are high strength and used in a friction connection. The discussion here will generally refer to both rivets and bolts.

The use of rivets is becoming less common, particularly in building structures, where they have been replaced by bolts or welds. One reason for replacing rivets in building structures was the high cost of riveting, for it required skilled personnel to heat the rivets properly and to toss them to the two-person riveting crew. The risks from red-hot rivets flying around, and the high noise level involved, were also detriments.

Most riveted or bolted connections involve multiple rivets or bolts. However, the connections shown in Fig. 11-9 have been kept simple, since the objective is to illustrate the types of connection. The connection in Fig. 11-9(a) is a lap joint. Figure 11-9(b) shows a butt joint with a single cover or splice plate, while the connection in Fig. 11-9(c) is a butt joint that has two cover or splice plates. These three connections, which will be examined in some detail, have axial, centric loads. The plate shown in Fig. 11-9(d) has the load applied eccentrically to the rivet pattern. The rivets in Fig. 11-9(e) act in tension, while those in the other examples all act in shear.

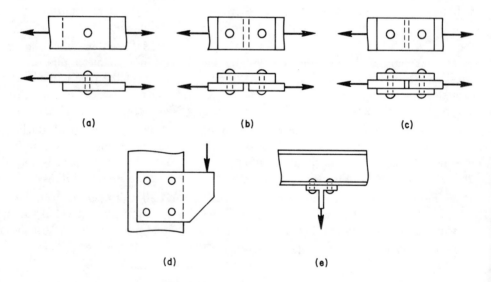

(a)   (b)   (c)

(d)   (e)

FIGURE 11-9

Simple riveted and bolted connections, such as those shown in Figs. 11-9(a), (b) and (c), can fail in any one of several different methods. The failure illustrated in Fig. 11-10(a) is a shear failure in the rivet. This type of failure was discussed in Article 10-4 as an example of direct shear. A tension failure at the net section or minimum section of the plate is shown in Fig. 11-10(b), and Fig. 11-10(c) shows a bearing failure at the edge of the hole where excessive deformation has occurred. The failures shown in Figs. 11-10(d) and 11-10(e) are both edge type failures, and both tend to be complex. In Fig. 11-10(d) the rivet has punched out the material between the hole and the edge of the plate, and in Fig. 11-10(e) there is a combination of bearing failure and tearing of the plate. Punching failure and the combination of bearing and tearing are avoided by following applicable codes and design practice that specify the minimum edge distance from the center of the hole to the edge of the plate based on experience and experimental observations.

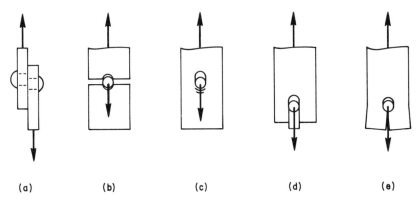

| (a) | (b) | (c) | (d) | (e) |

FIGURE 11-10

Any one of the five causes of failure may exist in any connection. In design, the objective is to prevent all of these failures.

The actual behavior of a riveted or bolted joint is very complex because of distortion in the rivets or bolts and in the plates as the loads are applied, and because of the friction that may exist between the plates.

The approach used in analyzing the stresses in riveted and bolted connections and in determining their load-carrying capacity is based on a combination of simplifying assumptions. Different design codes use somewhat different assumptions; in actual design, one must adhere to the pertinent design code.

Usually, the rivets or bolts are assumed to each carry an equal share of the load, so that if a connection has ten rivets each would be assumed to carry one tenth of the load. This would not apply if the rivets were of different sizes or if the load were applied eccentrically to the connection.

If each rivet in a joint carries the same load, then the shear stress on each rivet is

$$\tau = \frac{P}{nA_r} \qquad (11\text{-}7)$$

where τ is the shear stress in each rivet,

    P is the load on the joint,

    n is the number of rivet sections in shear and

    A_r is the cross-sectional area of each rivet.

If the rivets are in single shear, n will be the number of rivets; if the rivets are in double shear, n will be twice the number of rivets. Note that in a lap joint the rivets transmit the force from one plate to the other, whereas in a butt joint, the rivets transmit the load from the main plate to the splice plate and a second set of rivets transfers the load from the splice plate back to the second main plate. Thus, in analyzing a butt joint, only the part of the joint to one side of the butt is used.

When analyzing the tensile stress in the plate at the holes for the rivets or bolts, normal practice is to ignore stress-concentration factors. In design, the allowable stresses used are low enough that the joint remains safe. The nominal tensile stress in the plates is obtained from

$$\sigma = \frac{P}{A_{net}} \qquad (11\text{-}8)$$

where σ is the tensile stress in the plate at the net section,

    P is the load on the *plate* at the net section and

    A_{net} is the net cross-sectional area of the plate at the section being analyzed.

When using Eq. (11-8), there are a few points to keep in mind. If there is more than one row of rivets, the force on the net section will be the same as the force on the joint only for the outer row of rivets. The force on the inner rows will be reduced by the amount of force transmitted by the rivets or bolts to the other plate.

The area of the net section is

$$A_{net} = t(b - nd) \qquad (11\text{-}9)$$

where A_{net} is the net section,

    t is the thickness of the plate,

    b is the width of the plate,

    n is the number of rivet or bolt holes in the net section, and

    d is the diameter of the rivet or bolt hole.

There is considerable variation in the dimension used for the diameter, d, when calculating the net section, for the effective size of the hole depends on fabricating techniques. For design purposes, the applicable code will indicate whether d will be the diameter of the fastener or some larger diameter that will allow for oversize holes for fitting or damage to the hole edge if the hole is punched rather than drilled. For purposes of illustration in the problems, the hole diameters in the structural materials will be increased by 2 mm for rivets and by 4 mm for bolts. In all other cases, the nominal diameter of the fastener will be used.

Since each rivet or bolt is assumed to carry the same load, the bearing stress on the edge of the hole in any one plate in the connection will be the same. The bearing stress is assumed to be uniform, and the area in bearing is assumed to be the thickness of the plate times the diameter of the rivet or bolt. Thus, the bearing stress at the edge of each hole in a plate is

$$\sigma = \frac{P}{nA_b} \qquad (11\text{-}10)$$

where σ is the bearing stress on the edge of the hole,

P is the load applied to the plate,

n is the number of rivets or bolts resisting the load and

A_b is the area of each surface in bearing.

Table 11-2 gives some typical values for allowable stresses in riveted and bolted connections. These may be used to determine the load-carrying capacity of a joint.

It must be pointed out that the emphasis here is on stress analysis, and not on design. If you are designing actual connections, you *must* refer to the applicable code for rules on allowable stresses, net sections, edge distances and net sections for multiple rows of fasteners. In addition, space limitations have led to the elimination of discussion of eccentrically loaded connections and connections in tension.

TABLE 11-2
TYPICAL ALLOWABLE STRESSES
RIVETED AND BOLTED CONNECTIONS

Material	Tension MPa	Bearing MPa	Shear in Fastener MPa
Pressure Vessels			
Aluminum 6061-T6	70	110	55
Steel 0.2% Carbon	95	150	75
Structures			
Aluminum 6061-T6	130	235	95
Steel 230G	140	310	100
Steel 400G	240	540	175

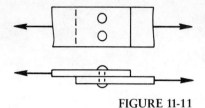

FIGURE 11-11

EXAMPLE 11-7

Two 10 mm thick structural-steel plates with a width of 150 mm are joined by two 20 mm diameter rivets, as shown in Fig. 11-11. If the axial load on the joint is 95 kN, calculate (a) the shear stress in each rivet, (b) the tension stress on the net section of the plate and (c) the bearing stress at the edge of each hole.

SOLUTION

The shear stress in each rivet is calculated using Eq. (11-7). *In this lap joint the rivets are in single shear, so there will be one rivet section resisting the load for each rivet in the joint.*

$$\text{(a) } \tau = \frac{P}{nA_r}$$

$$= \frac{95 \times 10^3}{2 \times \frac{\pi \times 20^2}{4} \times 10^{-6}}$$

$$= 151.20 \times 10^6 \text{ Pa}$$

$$= 151.20 \text{ MPa}$$

The tensile stress in the net section is found by using Eq. (11-8). *The net section will be obtained from* Eq. (11-9). *Since this is a structural steel, the net section will be based on the rivet diameter plus 2 mm.*

$$\text{(b) } A_{net} = t(b - nd)$$

$$= 10\left[150 - 2(20 + 2)\right]10^{-6}$$

$$= 1060.0 \times 10^{-6} \text{ m}^2$$

$$\sigma = \frac{P}{A_{net}}$$

$$= \frac{95 \times 10^3}{1060.0 \times 10^{-6}}$$

$$= 89.623 \times 10^6 \text{ Pa}$$

$$= 89.623 \text{ MPa}$$

To obtain the bearing stress, use Eq. (11-10). *There are two areas in bearing, and each area is equal to the product of the plate thickness and the rivet diameter.*

$$\text{(c) } \sigma = \frac{P}{nA_b}$$

$$= \frac{95 \times 10^3}{2 \times 10 \times 20 \times 10^{-6}}$$

$$= 237.50 \times 10^6 \text{ Pa}$$

$$= 237.50 \text{ MPa}$$

> (a) $\tau = 151$ MPa
> (b) $\sigma = 89.6$ MPa
> (c) $\sigma = 238$ MPa

EXAMPLE 11-8

The bolted connection shown in Fig. 11-12 has 20 by 200 mm main plates and a 25 by 200 mm splice plate connected by 30 mm diameter bolts in closely fitted holes. If the axial load on the connection is 210 kN, determine (a) the shear stress in the bolts, (b) the maximum tensile stress in the main plates, (c) the maximum tensile stress in the splice plate, (d) the bearing stress in the main plates and (e) the bearing stress in the splice plate.

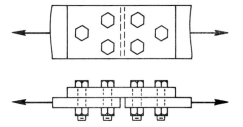

SOLUTION

FIGURE 11-12

This butt joint has a single splice plate, so the bolts are in single shear. There are thus three bolt sections transferring the load from the main plate to the splice plate. This information is substituted into Eq. (11-7) to find the shear stress in each bolt.

$$\text{(a) } \tau = \frac{P}{nA_r}$$

$$= \frac{210 \times 10^3}{3 \times \frac{\pi \times 30^2}{4} \times 10^{-6}}$$

$$= 99.030 \times 10^6 \text{ Pa}$$

$$= 99.030 \text{ MPa}$$

In determining the maximum tensile stress in the main plates, free-body diagrams showing the various forces acting on the left main plate will be useful, as shown in Fig. 11-13. Figure 11-13(a) shows the part of the plate containing the single bolt. Each bolt carries an equal share of the load and there are three bolts, so one third of the load is transmitted from the plate to the bolt, and the remaining two thirds of the load is carried by the section

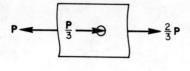

(a)

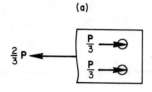

(b)

FIGURE 11-13

*of the plate between the two rows of bolts. The total load **P** acts on the net section at the single bolt hole. Since the holes are closely fitted, the actual diameter of the hole will be assumed to be the same as the bolt diameter when calculating the net section using* Eq. (11-9).

(b) One bolt hole

$$A_{net} = t(b - nd)$$

$$= 20(200 - 1 \times 30)10^{-6}$$

$$= 3400 \times 10^{-6} \, m^2$$

The stress is determined using Eq. (11-8) *and using the fact that the total load acts on the plate at the single bolt hole.*

$$\sigma = \frac{P}{A_{net}}$$

$$= \frac{210 \times 10^3}{3400 \times 10^{-6}}$$

$$= 61.765 \times 10^6 \, Pa$$

$$= 61.765 \, MPa$$

From the free-body diagram shown in Fig. 11-13(b) *it can be seen that the force that would act on the net section where there are two bolt holes would be two thirds of the total load on the joint.*

The net section where there are two bolt holes is obtained from Eq. (11-9).

Two bolt holes

$$A_{net} = t(b - nd)$$

$$= 20(200 - 2 \times 30)10^{-6}$$

$$= 2800 \times 10^{-6} \, m^2$$

The stress at the net section may be calculated using Eq. (11-8) *and using the fact that the load applied to the plate at the section is two thirds of the total load on the joint.*

$$\sigma = \frac{P}{A_{net}}$$

$$= \frac{^2/_3 \times 210 \times 10^3}{2800 \times 10^{-6}}$$

$$= 50.000 \times 10^6 \, Pa$$

$$= 50.000 \, MPa$$

Maximum tensile stress in main plate is 61.765 MPa

In the splice plate, the net section with the two bolt holes will also be the section that will carry the total load. A free-body diagram of the part of the splice plate to the left of the butt line is shown in Fig. 11-14. At the bolts, two thirds of the load will be transferred from the splice plate to the main plate. For this reason, it will be necessary to check the stress at only one section for the splice plate, since the larger section where there is only one hole carries only one third of the load. The net section is calculated using Fig. (11-9).

$$\text{(c) } A_{net} = t(b - nd)$$
$$= 25(200 - 2 \times 30)10^{-6}$$
$$= 3500 \times 10^{-6} \text{ m}^2$$

The stress on the net section is calculated using Eq. (11-8).

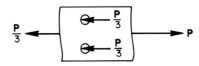

FIGURE 11-14

$$\sigma = \frac{P}{A_{net}}$$
$$= \frac{210 \times 10^3}{3500 \times 10^{-6}}$$
$$= 60.000 \times 10^6 \text{ Pa}$$
$$= 60.000 \text{ MPa}$$

The bearing stress in the main plates can be calculated by substitution into Eq. (11-10).

$$\text{(d) } \sigma = \frac{P}{nA_b}$$
$$= \frac{210 \times 10^3}{3 \times 20 \times 30 \times 10^{-6}}$$
$$= 116.67 \times 10^6 \text{ Pa}$$
$$= 116.67 \text{ MPa}$$

The bearing stress in the splice plate is also calculated by using Eq. (11-10).

$$\text{(e) } \sigma = \frac{P}{nA_b}$$
$$= \frac{210 \times 10^3}{3 \times 25 \times 30 \times 10^{-6}}$$
$$= 93.333 \times 10^6 \text{ Pa}$$
$$= 93.333 \text{ MPa}$$

(a) τ = 99.0 MPa
(b) σ = 61.8 MPa
(c) σ = 60.0 MPa
(d) σ = 117 MPa
(e) σ = 93.3 MPa

EXAMPLE 11-9

The rivet pattern shown in Fig. 11-15 is used for a seam in a 6061-T6 aluminum pressure vessel. Determine the maximum safe load that may be applied to the pattern if the main plates are 12 mm thick, the splice plates are 10 mm thick, and the rivets are 15 mm in diameter. The width of the rivet pattern is 120 mm.

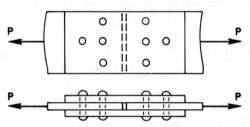

FIGURE 11-15

SOLUTION

The plates in the connections are treated as if they are the same width as the rivet pattern. To determine the maximum safe load for the pattern, it is necessary to determine the load that can be carried under each of the potential failure conditions; rivet shear, tension failure in the plates or bearing failure in the plates. The smallest of the potential failure loads is the maximum safe load that can be carried by the pattern.

The load that can carried by shear in the rivets may be calculated by rewriting Eq. (11-7). The rivets are in double shear, so there are a total of eight rivet sections that resist the load. The allowable stress is taken from Table 11-2.

Rivet Shear

$$\tau = \frac{P}{nA_r}$$

$$P = \tau n A_r$$

$$= 55 \times 10^6 \times 8 \times \frac{\pi \times 15^2}{4} \times 10^{-6}$$

$$= 77\ 754\ \text{N}$$

The plates in the connection could fail at several places. The main plates could fail in either row, while the splice plates would be most likely to fail in the inner row.

In the main plate, the total load acts on the net section where there is only one rivet hole, as shown in Fig 11-16(a), *which shows the left portion of the main plate. The allowable load is calculated by rewriting* Eq. (11-8), *and using* Eq. (11-9) *to determine the net section. For this joint, the size of the rivet hole is assumed to be the same size as the rivet diameter.*

Tension — Main Plate, Outer Row

$$\sigma = \frac{P}{A_{net}}$$

$$P = \sigma A_{net}$$

$$= \sigma t(b - nd)$$

$$= 70 \times 10^6 \times 12(120 - 1 \times 15)10^{-6}$$

$$= 88\ 200\ \text{N}$$

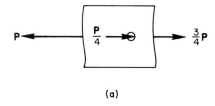

(a)

At the inner row of rivets in the main plate, as shown in Fig. 11-16(b), *the load on the net section will be three quarters of the total load, and the net section has three holes. The rewritten* Eq. (11-8) *is used to calculate the magnitude of the load.*

Tension — Main Plate, Inner Row

Load on net section $= \dfrac{3}{4}P$

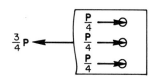

(b)

FIGURE 11-16

$$\frac{3}{4}P = \sigma t(b - nd)$$

$$\frac{3}{4}P = 70 \times 10^6 \times 12(120 - 3 \times 15)10^{-6}$$

$$P = \frac{4}{3} \times 70 \times 10^6 \times 12(120 - 3 \times 15)10^{-6}$$

$$= 84\ 000\ \text{N}$$

Each splice will carry one half of the total load on the joint. At the net section of the splice plate at the inner row of rivets, the total load in the splice plate must be carried, and the section is minimum. A free-body diagram of the part of one splice plate to

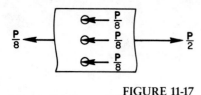

FIGURE 11-17

the left of the butt line is shown in Fig. 11-17. *The rewritten form of* Eq. (11-8) *may be used to calculate the allowable load on this section.*

Tension — Splice Plate, Inner Row

$$\text{Load on net section} = \frac{1}{2}P$$

$$\frac{1}{2}P = \sigma t(b - nd)$$

$$\frac{1}{2}P = 70 \times 10^6 \times 10(120 - 3 \times 15)10^{-6}$$

$$P = 2 \times 70 \times 10^6 \times 10(120 - 3 \times 15)10^{-6}$$

$$= 105\ 000\ \text{N}$$

There is no need to calculate the stress at the net section of the splice plate at the outer rivet row, since the net section is larger and the load is smaller than at the inner row.

The allowable load due to bearing stress on the plates may be determined using Eq. (11-10). *Since the total thickness of the two splice plates is more than twice the thickness of the main plates, the maximum bearing stress will occur in the main plates. Each of the four rivets will carry an equal portion of the load.*

Bearing — Main Plates

$$\sigma = \frac{P}{nA_b}$$

$$P = \sigma n A_b$$

$$= 110 \times 10^6 \times 4 \times 12 \times 15 \times 10^{-6}$$

$$= 79\ 200\ \text{N}$$

The joint would become unsafe at the lowest calculated load, so that load is the maximum safe load for the joint. In this case, the joint would fail due to the shear in the rivets.

$$\boxed{P = 77.8\ \text{kN}}$$

PROBLEMS

11-31 Determine (a) the shear stress in the bolt, (b) the tensile stress in the plate and (c) the bearing stress on the plate for two 5 by 25 mm carbon-steel plates connected by a single 10 mm diameter bolt in a lap joint. The bolt hole is drilled for a close fit, and the axial load on the plates is 18 kN.

11-32 Two 20 by 70 mm plates are joined in a butt joint using a 25 by 70 mm splice plate and a single 25 mm diameter rivet in closely fitted holes on each side of the butt. Find (a) the shear stress in the rivet, (b) the maximum tensile stress in the main plate and (c) the bearing stress in the main plate if the axial load on the connection is 125 kN.

11-33 A butt joint is made with 5 by 15 mm main plates and two 3 by 15 mm splice plates. If there is one 5 mm diameter rivet in closely fitted holes through each main plate, calculate (a) the shear stress on the rivets, (b) the maximum tensile stress in the main plates, (c) the maximum tensile stress in the splice plates and (d) the bearing stress in the main plates if the axial tensile load on the joint is 7.5 kN.

11-34 A structural connection is formed by bolting two plates together in a lap joint. The plates are 15 mm thick and 100 mm wide, and they are fastened together by two 20 mm diameter bolts placed in a row perpendicular to the load. If the load on the splice is 140 kN, calculate (a) the shear stress in the bolts, (b) the maximum tensile stress in the plates and (c) the bearing stress on the plates.

11-35 A 15 by 300 mm steel splice plate is used to join two 12 by 300 mm steel main plates using a single row of 14 rivets in punched holes. The rivets have a diameter of 10 mm. The row of rivets is parallel to the butt line. If the axial load on the connection is 150 kN, determine (a) the shear stress in the rivets, (b) the maximum tensile stress in the main plates, (c) the maximum tensile stress in the splice plate and (d) the bearing stress

in the main plates. The connection is part of a structure.

11-36 Two 18 by 120 mm aluminum 6061-T6 plates are connected in a butt joint by two 10 by 120 mm splice plates. There is one row of three 15 mm diameter bolts parallel to the butt through each main plate. Calculate (a) the shear stress in the bolts, (b) the maximum tensile stress in the main plates, (c) the maximum tensile stress in the splice plates, (d) the bearing stress in the main plate and (e) the bearing stress in the splice plates. The load on the connection is 55 kN. Assume that the holes are closely fitted drilled holes.

11-37 The bolted lap joint shown in Fig. P11-37 carries an axial load of 15 kN and is made of sheets of 4 by 40 mm steel fastened by 5 mm diameter bolts in closely fitted holes. Find (a) the shear stress in the bolts, (b) the maximum tensile stress in the plates, and (c) the bearing stress on the plates.

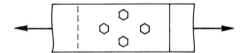

FIGURE P11-37

11-38 An axial load of 225 kN is applied to 15 by 250 mm main plates in the structural connection shown in Fig. P11-38. The rivets have a diameter of 20 mm and are in punched holes. The splice plate is 18 mm thick. Calculate (a) the shear stress in the rivets, (b) the maximum tensile stress in the main plates, (c) the maximum tensile stress in the splice plate and (d) the bearing stress on the main plates.

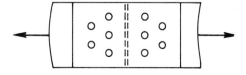

FIGURE P11-38

11-39 For the joint shown in Fig. P11-39, find (a) the shear stress in the rivets, (b) the maximum tensile stress in the main plates, (c) the maximum tensile stress in the splice plates and (d) the bearing stress on the main plates. The load on the joint is 35 kN, the rivets have a diameter of 8 mm and are in closely fitted holes, the main plates are 10 by 50 mm and the two splice plates are 6 by 50 mm.

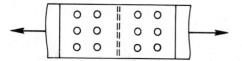

FIGURE P11-39

11-40 Two 4 by 40 mm plates are joined in a lap joint by five 5 mm diameter bolts in closely fitted holes, as shown in Fig. P11-40. If the axial load on the joint is 10 kN, find (a) the shear stress in the bolts, (b) the maximum tensile stress in the plates and (c) the bearing stress on the plates.

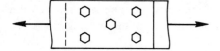

FIGURE P11-40

11-41 Two structural-steel plates 20 by 200 mm are connected by a single 25 by 200 mm splice plate and 30 mm diameter bolts in punched holes, as shown in Fig. P11-41. Determine (a) the shear stress in the bolts, (b) the maximum tensile stress in the main plates, (c) the maximum tensile stress in the splice plate and (d) the bearing stress in the main plate. The axial load on the joint is 600 kN.

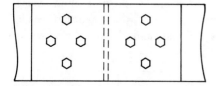

FIGURE P11-41

11-42 If the axial load on the joint shown in Fig. P11-42 is 60 kN, calculate (a) the shear stress in the rivets, (b) the maximum tensile stress in the main plates, (c) the maximum tensile stress in the splice plates and (d) the bearing stress in the main plates. The main plates are 10 by 65 mm and the two splice plates are 6 by 65 mm. The rivets are 8 mm in diameter, and are in closely fitted holes.

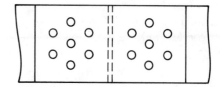

FIGURE P11-42

11-43 A single 20 mm diameter rivet connects two 8 by 50 mm 230G structural-steel plates in a lap joint. Calculate the maximum allowable axial tensile load that can be applied to the connection.

11-44 A butt joint is formed by connecting two 20 by 120 mm plates by a 25 by 120 mm splice plate using a single row of two 30 mm diameter bolts in punched holes. The row of bolts is parallel to the butt line. Calculate the maximum allowable load on the joint if the material is 400G structural steel.

11-45 The bolt pattern shown in Fig. P11-45 repeats along the seam of a pressure vessel. The material is 0.2% carbon steel, the pattern width is 90 mm, the bolts have a diameter of 15 mm, the main plates are 12 mm thick and the splice plates are 7 mm thick. Find the maximum allowable load on the pattern.

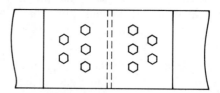

FIGURE P11-45

11-46 Using the allowable stress for 6061-T6 aluminum in pressure vessels, find the maximum safe load on the lap joint shown in Fig. P11-46. The diameter of the rivets is 10 mm and the two plates are 8 by 100 mm.

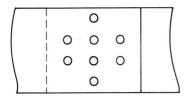

FIGURE P11-46

11-47 Determine the safe load on the joint shown in Fig. P11-47 if it is made of 400G structural steel. The main plates are 18 by 200 mm, the splice plate is 25 by 200 mm, and the rivets are 30 mm in diameter.

11-48 The bolt pattern shown in Fig. P11-48 has a width of 120 mm and is made using 20 mm thick main plates, 12 mm thick splice plates and 15 mm diameter bolts in punched holes. Determine the maximum allowable load if the material is 230G steel.

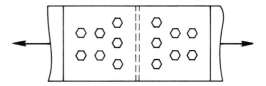

FIGURE P11-48

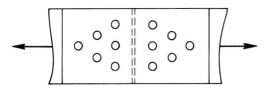

FIGURE P11-47

11-5 WELDED CONNECTIONS

Welding is a process of joining two parts together, and it has become one of the more common methods of making connections. In the arc-welding process molten metal, which is added to the parts being joined, forms the bonding agent between the two parts. Of the many different types of welds, the two most common are shown in Fig. 11-18. The weld shown in Fig. 11-18(a) is one form of butt weld. The edge preparation of the butting parts may vary, but the analysis of the stress in the joint remains the same. With an axial load, the weld section is considered to have the same area as the cross section of the members

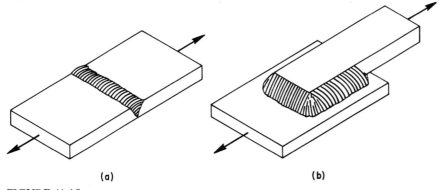

(a)   (b)

FIGURE 11-18

being joined, so the stress in the weld is the same as the stress in the members being analyzed. The stress is found from $\sigma = P/A$, which is Eq. (10-1). In a properly made butt weld, the strength of the weld is as great as or greater than the strength of the members being joined.

A fillet weld is shown in Fig. 11-18(b). The built-up weld metal between the two plates being joined must carry the load between the plates. The weld along the side of the plate and parallel to the load is called a side fillet weld, and the weld at the end of the plate and perpendicular to the load is called an end fillet weld. A section of a fillet weld is shown in Fig. 11-19(a). The length of the leg, t, is usually designated as the size of the weld.

The force transmitted through a side weld from one plate to the other is a force parallel to the side weld. The stress in the weld will be maximum on the least section of the weld. The area with the highest stress is shown in Fig. 11-19(b). The throat of the weld, line a-b in Fig. 11-19(a), is the plane with the least area to resist the force, so that will be the plane with the highest stress. The area of the plane will be $(t \sin 45°)L$. The fact that the weld is built up to a convex form is not taken into account in the calculations.

The maximum shear stress in a fillet weld is found from

$$\tau = \frac{P}{A}$$

$$\tau = \frac{P}{(t \sin 45°)L} \qquad (11\text{-}11)$$

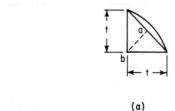

(a)

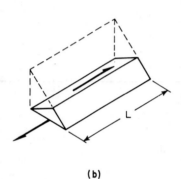

(b)

FIGURE 11-19

where τ is the shear stress on the throat of the weld,
P is the load carried by the weld,
t is the weld size or length of the leg and
L is the length of the weld.

The end fillet weld, which is transverse to the load, is actually stronger than the side fillet weld. However, it is common practice to analyze the stress in an end weld in the same manner as the side fillet weld, and to asume that it has the same load-carrying capacity for the same size of weld and weld material. Welds at an angle are also assumed to have the same load-carrying capacity as a side weld, so Eq. (11-11) is valid for all fillet welds.

When analyzing the load on a fillet weld, it is fairly common to express the load in terms of load per unit length of weld.

$$q = \frac{P}{L}$$

$$= \frac{\tau A}{L}$$

$$= \frac{\tau(t \sin 45°)L}{L}$$

$$q = \tau t \sin 45° \qquad (11\text{-}12)$$

where q is the load on the weld per unit length of weld,
τ is the shear stress in the weld, and
t is the weld size or length of the leg.

Usually, q will be expressed in terms of N/m.

Weld types, as well as the loads on welds, can become quite complex, and the study of them can be extensive. Our discussion is limited to fillet welds with an axially applied load through the centroid of the weld pattern.

EXAMPLE 11-10

Two plates are joined by two 15 mm fillet welds each 120 mm long. If the axial load on the connection is 200 kN, determine the maximum shear stress in the welds.

SOLUTION

The maximum shear stress may be calculated by direct substitution into Eq. (11-11). Since the dimensions t and L are usually give in mm, their values must be changed to m.

$$\tau = \frac{P}{(t \sin 45°)L}$$

$$= \frac{200 \times 10^3}{15 \sin 45° \times 2 \times 120 \times 10^{-6}}$$

$$= 78.567 \times 10^6 \text{ Pa}$$

$$= 78.567 \text{ MPa}$$

$$\boxed{\tau = 78.6 \text{ MPa}}$$

EXAMPLE 11-11

Determine the length d required for the 10 mm fillet weld shown in Fig. 11-20 so that the weld will support an axial load of 800 kN if the allowable stress in the weld is 95 MPa.

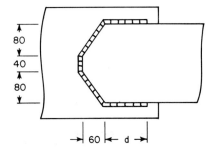

FIGURE 11-20

SOLUTION

The weld strength per unit of length may be obtained by direct substitution into Eq. (11-12). If the units of q are to be N/m, then the units of t must be m.

$$q = \tau t \sin 45°$$

$$= 95 \times 10^6 \times 10 \times 10^{-3} \sin 45°$$

$$= 671.75 \times 10^3 \text{ N/m}$$

The length of the weld required to carry the load may be obtained by dividing the load on the weld by the value of q.

$$L = \frac{P}{q}$$

$$= \frac{800 \times 10^3}{671.75 \times 10^3}$$

$$= 1.190 \; 92 \text{ m}$$

$$= 1190.92 \text{ mm}$$

$$L = 2d + 2(60^2 + 80^2)^{\frac{1}{2}} + 40$$

$$1190.92 = 2d + 2 \times 100 + 40$$

$$2d = 1190.92 - 200 - 40$$

$$d = \frac{950.92}{2}$$

$$= 475.46 \text{ mm}$$

$$\boxed{d = 475 \text{ mm}}$$

EXAMPLE 11-12

Determine the maximum allowable axial load on the connection shown in Fig. 11-21. The wide plate is 20 by 200 mm, the narrow plate is 25 by 150 mm, and the length of each side fillet weld is 175 mm. The allowable stress in the plates is 75 MPa and the allowable stress in the 12 mm fillet welds is also 75 MPa.

SOLUTION

The allowable load in each part of the connection must be calculated separately, and the part that can carry the smallest allowable load is the one that governs the strength of the connection.

The allowable load in the plates may be obtained by direct substitution into Eq. (10-1) after rewriting.

Large Plate:

$$P = \sigma A$$

$$= 75 \times 10^6 \times 20 \times 200 \times 10^{-6}$$

$$= 300 \; 000 \text{ N}$$

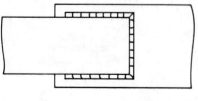

FIGURE 11-21

Small Plate:

$$P = \sigma A$$
$$= 75 \times 10^6 \times 25 \times 150 \times 10^{-6}$$
$$= 281\ 250\ \text{N}$$

The load-carrying capacity of the weld may be obtained by re-writing Eq. (11-11).

Weld:

$$\tau = \frac{P}{(t \sin 45°)L}$$

$$P = \tau(t \sin 45°)L$$
$$= 75 \times 10^6(12 \sin 45°)(175 + 175 + 150)10^{-6}$$
$$= 318\ 198\ \text{N}$$

The small plate will be at its maximum load when the load reaches 281 250 N, so this is the maximum load that can be carried by the connection.

$$\boxed{P = 281\ \text{kN}}$$

PROBLEMS

11-49 Two plates are joined by means of two 8 mm fillet welds parallel to the axis of the 150 kN load. If each weld is 180 mm long, calculate the maximum shear stress in the welds.

11-50 Calculate the maximum shear stress in two 18 mm side fillet welds used to connect two plates if the axial load on the plates is 220 kN and the length of each weld is 140 mm.

11-51 Calculate the maximum shear stress in the 12 mm welds used to connect the two plates shown in Fig. P11-51. The side welds are 150 mm long, and the end weld is 50 mm long. The axial load on the joint is 300 kN.

11-52 The welded connection shown in Fig. P11-52 has 15 mm welds. Calculate the maximum

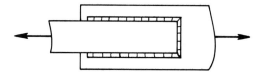

FIGURE P11-51

shear stress in the welds if the side welds are 200 mm long, the end weld is 75 mm long, and the load on the connection is 375 kN.

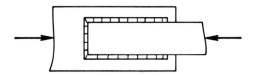

FIGURE P11-52

11-53 Calculate the maximum shear stress in the 15 mm fillet weld shown in Fig. P11-53 if the axial load on the connection is 225 kN.

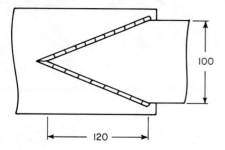

FIGURE P11-53

11-54 For the connection shown in Fig. P11-54, calculate the maximum shear stress in the 12 mm fillet weld if the axial load on the connection is 300 kN.

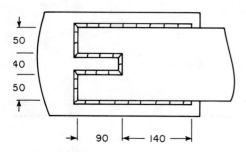

FIGURE P11-54

11-55 Calculate the load per metre of weld length that a 20 mm fillet weld can carry if the allowable stress in the weld is 120 MPa.

11-56 If the allowable stress in a weld is 95 MPa, determine the allowable load per metre of weld length that a 12 mm fillet weld can carry.

11-57 Determine the axial load-carrying capacity of the 10 mm weld shown in Fig. P11-57 if the allowable stress in the weld is 65 MPa.

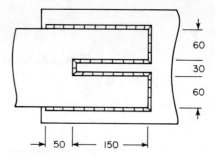

FIGURE P11-57

11-58 The 15 mm fillet welded connection shown in Fig. P11-58 has an allowable stress of 80 MPa. Determine the axial load the weld can carry if the narrower plate has a width of 90 mm.

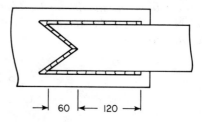

FIGURE P11-58

11-59 Determine the maximum allowable load in the joint shown in Fig. P11-59 if the wide plate is 25 by 100 mm, the narrow plate is 35 by 60 mm and the welds are 15 mm fillet welds. The length of each side weld is 90 mm. The allowable stress in the plates is 125 MPa, and the allowable stress in the welds is 105 MPa.

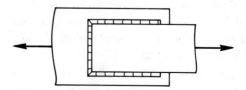

FIGURE P11-59

11-60 If the connection shown in Fig. P11-60 is made using a 40 by 400 mm plate and a 50 by 300 mm plate and 25 mm fillet welds, determine the maximum allowable load on the connection. The allowable stress in the plates is 110 MPa and the allowable stress in the welds is 85 MPa. Each weld is 500 mm long.

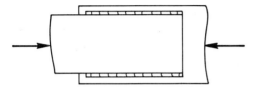

FIGURE P11-60

11-61 Find the length d required for the connection shown in Fig. P11-61 if the weld is to carry the same axial load as the plates in the connection. The plates are 25 by 225 mm and 30 by 190 mm and have an allowable stress of 90 MPa. The fillet weld is 12 mm, and has an allowable shear stress of 80 MPa.

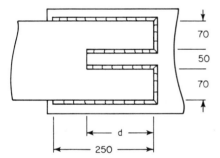

FIGURE P11-61

11-62 In the welded connection shown in Fig. P11-62, the large plate is 25 by 180 mm and the small plate is 35 by 140 mm. The length of each side weld is 200 mm. If the allowable stress in the plates is 120 MPa, and the allowable stress in the welds is 110 MPa, determine (a) the maximum allowable axial load in the connection and (b) the required weld size necessary to carry this load.

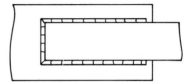

FIGURE P11-62

11-6 THERMAL EXPANSION

Most materials, when subjected to a change in temperature, will change their dimensions. Usually, dimensions increase with increasing temperature. Many rail lines are laid with a gap between the rail ends to allow for the expansion of the rails as temperatures increase. At the ends of many bridges there is a plate across the roadway, which looks like a series of interlocking fingers. This is an expansion joint designed to allow for the changes in the length of the bridge that are caused by changes in temperature. If an automobile engine is not properly cooled, parts will seize because of the expansion that closes the small gaps between moving parts and restricts their movement.

The amount of deformation in a member depends on the material, the length of the member and the change in temperature. It has been found that the rate of linear expansion of most materials is a constant per unit of length for each degree change in temperature over a fairly wide range of temperatures. This constant is called the coefficient of thermal linear expansion. The symbol used is α and typical values are given in Appendix E. The units of α are $m/m/°C$. Since the coefficient of thermal expansion is given as deformation per unit of length, it has the same units as strain, and is sometimes misnamed thermal strain. It is preferable to use the term strain only for unit change in length caused by a force.

If the coefficient of thermal expansion is in terms of $m/m/°C$, then the total linear deformation in a member subjected to a temperature change would be

$$\delta_t = \alpha L(\Delta t) \tag{11-13}$$

where δ_t is the deformation due to the change in temperature,
α is the coefficient of thermal expansion of the material,
L is the original dimension of the member in the direction in which deformation is being measured, and
Δt is the change in temperature.

For most materials, the length increases with an increase in temperature.

If a member is fastened between two rigid supports and is subjected to a change in temperature, the member will attempt to change in length, but will be prevented from doing so by the rigid supports. The supports create a force that prevents the attempted change in length, and the force causes a stress that is sometimes called thermal stress. The process is illustrated in Fig. 11-22. The top part of the figure shows a bar fixed between two rigid supports. If the temperature increases, the bar would try to increase in length by an amount δ_t. However, as shown in the bottom of the figure, the rigid support would create a force on the member large enough to cause deformation δ_p, so that the bar would retain its original length. In the case of a bar that initially just fits between two rigid supports, the stress induced by the temperature change can be determined as follows:

$$\delta_t = \delta_p$$

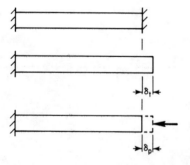

FIGURE 11-22

From Eqs. (11-13) and (10-7)

$$\alpha L(\Delta t) = \epsilon L$$

$$\alpha(\Delta t) = \epsilon$$

From Eq. (10-11)

$$\epsilon = \frac{\sigma}{E}$$

Thus,

$$\alpha(\Delta t) = \frac{\sigma}{E}$$

$$\sigma = \alpha(\Delta t)E \qquad\qquad (11\text{-}14)$$

where σ is the normal stress caused by the change in temperature,

α is the coefficient of thermal expansion of the material,

Δt is the change in temperature, and

E is the modulus of elasticity of the material.

Equation (11-14) applies only if there is no initial or final gap between the member and the supports. If the temperature increases when the member is supported as shown in Fig. 11-22, the stress in the member will be compression. If the temperature decreases, the stress in the member will be tension.

EXAMPLE 11-13

A 120 m long bridge constructed of structural steel is built in a region where the temperature ranges from −48°C to 27°C. Determine the total change in length of the bridge for which allowance must be made.

SOLUTION

The total deformation to be considered is that which would occur if the temperature changed from coldest to hottest or from hottest to coldest. The total temperature change and the value for α from Appendix E are substituted into Eq. (11-13). Note that the value for α in Appendix E has units of 10^{-6} m/m/°C.

$$\delta_t = \alpha L(\Delta t)$$

$$= 11.7 \times 10^{-6} \times 120\left[27 - (-48)\right]$$

$$= 0.105\ 30\ \text{m}$$

$$= 105.30\ \text{mm}$$

$$\boxed{\delta_t = 105\ \text{mm}}$$

EXAMPLE 11-14

A magnesium bar with a diameter of 200 mm and a length of 600 mm just fits between two rigid supports when the temperature is 12°C. If the stress in the magnesium is not to exceed −115 MPa, determine the temperature at which this stress will be reached.

SOLUTION

The stress in the bar due to the change in temperature may be calculated using Eq. (11-14) *and rewriting to solve for* Δt.

$$\sigma = \alpha(\Delta t)E$$

$$\Delta t = \frac{\sigma}{\alpha E}$$

$$= \frac{115 \times 10^6}{25.9 \times 10^{-6} \times 45 \times 10^9}$$

$$= 98.670°C$$

The temperature at which the stress is reached is the initial temperature plus the temperature change.

$$t = t_i + \Delta t$$

$$= 12 + 98.670$$

$$= 110.67°$$

$$\boxed{t = 111°C}$$

EXAMPLE 11-15

Determine the stress that will exist in the two bars between rigid supports shown in Fig. 11-23 if the temperature is increased by 65°C. Bar *ST* is stainless steel and bar *AL* is 2014-T6 aluminum, and both bars have the same cross section.

SOLUTION

As the temperature increases, the 0.3 mm gap will close and the compressive stress will develop in the two bars. Since both bars have the same cross section and both must have the same load, both bars must have the same stress.
The bars will attempt to deform as much as required by the 65°C temperature change.

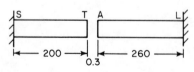

FIGURE 11-23

Attempted thermal deformation:

$\delta_t = \left[\alpha L(\Delta t)\right]_{ST} + \left[\alpha L(\Delta t)\right]_{AL}$

$= 17.3 \times 10^{-6} \times 0.200 \times 65 + 22.5 \times 10^{-6} \times 0.260 \times 65$

$= (224.90 + 380.25)10^{-6}$

$= 605.15 \times 10^{-6} \text{ m}$

After taking up the 0.3 mm gap, the stress caused in the bars must be sufficient to overcome the thermal deformation that remains.

Deformation due to load:

$\delta_p = 605.15 \times 10^{-6} - 300 \times 10^{-6}$

$\quad = 305.15 \times 10^{-6} \text{ m}$

$\delta_p = \delta_{ST} + \delta_{AL}$

$305.15 \times 10^{-6} = \left(\dfrac{PL}{AE}\right)_{ST} + \left(\dfrac{PL}{AE}\right)_{AL}$

$305.15 \times 10^{-6} = \dfrac{\sigma \times 0.200}{190 \times 10^9} + \dfrac{\sigma \times 0.260}{73 \times 10^9}$

Recall that the stress in both the steel and the aluminum is the same.

Multiply each term by 10^9 and simplify.

$305.15 \times 10^3 = 1.0526 \times 10^{-3}\sigma + 3.5616 \times 10^{-3}\sigma$

$305.15 \times 10^3 = 4.6142 \times 10^{-3}\sigma$

$\sigma = \dfrac{305.15 \times 10^3}{4.6142 \times 10^{-3}}$

$\quad = 66.133 \times 10^6 \text{ Pa}$

$\quad = 66.133 \text{ MPa}$

$$\boxed{\sigma = 66.1 \text{ MPa}}$$

PROBLEMS

11-63 If a gray cast-iron piston with a diameter of 120 mm is installed at 18°C, determine the increase in the piston's diameter if the temperature reaches 250°C.

11-64 A steel pipe 30 m long is to carry superheated steam at 300°C. If the pipe is placed at 17°C, determine the change in length of the pipe when it is at operating temperature.

11-65 An aluminum angle 6 m long was left lying in the sun on an asphalt-surfaced shipping area. When measured, it was found to be 9 mm longer than when originally measured at 18°C. Determine the temperature of the heated aluminum.

11-66 The diameter of a malleable iron shaft was measured immediately after machining and found to be 35.627 mm. The diameter was remeasured after the shaft cooled to room temperature, 17°C, and the diameter was found to be 35.591 mm. Determine the temperature of the shaft when its diameter was first measured.

11-67 Determine the increase in temperature required to just close the gap between the aluminum strip AB and the copper strip CD shown in Fig. P11-67.

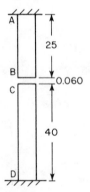

FIGURE P11-67

11-68 In the system shown in Fig. P11-68, hanger MG is magnesium and hanger ST is steel, and each has a length of 800 mm. Determine the

change in temperature required to give the bar GT a slope of 1° if it was horizontal initially. The length of GT is 150 mm.

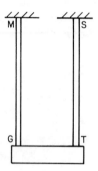

FIGURE P11-68

11-69 Determine the tensile stress developed in a continuous steel rail for a railroad if the temperature drops from 18°C, the temperature at which the rail was laid, to –40°C. Assume that the rail is fully constrained from contraction and that the modulus of elasticity is 200 GPa.

11-70 A 2014-T6 aluminum bar 200 mm long with a cross section of 75 by 100 mm just fits between two rigid supports when the temperature of the aluminum is 20°C. Determine the stress in the aluminum if the temperature is raised to 150°C.

11-71 A 300 mm diameter carbon-steel pipe with an inside diameter of 285 mm spans a length of 3 m between two rigid walls. The pipe is installed at 15°C, and it is designed to carry a fluid at 75°C. Determine the force the pipe would apply to the walls at operating temperature if no provision is made for the expansion.

11-72 Two rigid towers are connected by a horizontal 20 mm diameter 6061-T6 aluminum tie at a temperature of 28°C. Determine the force applied to the towers if the temperature drops to –18°C.

11-73 A carbon-steel bar is 0.75 m long, with a diameter of 0.20 m, is fixed between two rigid supports. If there is an axial stress of 180 MPa compression in the bar, determine the temperature drop required to leave a total gap of 0.20 mm between the ends of the bar and the supports.

11-74 An ABS plastic pipe 6 m long is fastened between two rigid walls. The temperature drops to 2°C so that there is a tensile stress of 7 MPa in the pipe. Find the temperature at which the stress will be –3 MPa.

11-75 Bar *AB* is 6061-T6 aluminum, and bar *BC* is gray cast iron. The bars are between two rigid supports, as shown in Fig. P11-75. Calculate the temperature drop required to just remove the stress from the bars if the initial stress in them is –15 MPa. Both bars have the same cross section.

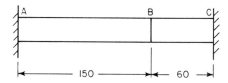

FIGURE P11-75

11-76 Find the increase in temperature that will cause a stress of 85 MPa in the two bars shown in Fig. P11-76. The bars are mounted between rigid supports. Bar *CU* is copper, bar *ST* is carbon steel, and both have the same cross-sectional area.

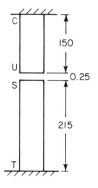

FIGURE P11-76

11-7 STATICALLY INDETERMINATE AXIALLY LOADED SYSTEMS

A statically indeterminate system is one in which the forces acting on the system cannot be determined using only the equations of static equilibrium. In the case of axially loaded members, there is only one equation of equilibrium available, so if there is more than one unknown term in the equation for the forces, some other relationship must be used for developing any additional equations. Usually, the additional equations used are deformation equations that relate the deformation in the member to the applied loads.

A statically indeterminate system with axially loaded members is shown in Fig. 11-24(a). Three bars of two different known materials, *A* and *B*, support a known load, **P**. If the objective is to find the stress in materials *A* and *B*, the loads on each member must be found. The free-body diagram of Fig. 11-24(b) and the equation of equilibrium summing forces in the *y* direc-

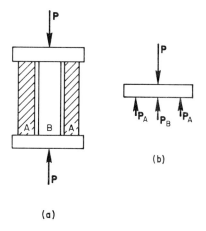

FIGURE 11-24

tion may be used to show that $P = P_A + P_B + P_A$ or $P = 2P_A + P_B$. If P is the only known term, there are two unknown terms in the equation. If the load **P** has been applied through rigid end plates, the deformation in all three bars must be the same. Thus $\delta_A = \delta_B$, which could be rewritten as $(PL/AE)_A = (PL/AE)_B$, which is a second equation relating the two loads. The system of two equations with two unknown terms can then be solved, providing that the values for L, A and E are available.

There is a variety of statically indeterminate axially loaded system problems, so there is no single formula that can be developed. Generally, one equation is an equilibrium equation and the second equation relates the deformations in the members. The deformations may or may not be the same, depending on the geometry of the problem.

EXAMPLE 11-16

A 60 mm diameter stainless-steel pipe with an inside diameter of 50 mm is used as a liner inside a carbon-steel pipe that has an outside diameter of 80 mm. The two pipes fit snugly together, and have an axial tensile load of 250 kN applied to the system of two pipes. Determine the stress in each pipe.

SOLUTION

The total load is carried jointly by both pipes, as shown in Fig. 11-25.

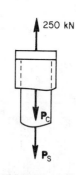

FIGURE 11-25

$$\text{Let } P_S = \text{load in stainless-steel pipe}$$

$$P_C = \text{load in carbon-steel pipe}$$

$$\Sigma\, F_y = 0$$

$$250\,000 - P_S - P_C = 0 \qquad\qquad \text{Eq. (a)}$$

The deformation in each pipe must be the same.

$$\text{Let } \delta_S = \text{deformation in stainless-steel pipe}$$

$$\delta_C = \text{deformation in carbon-steel pipe}$$

$$\delta_S = \delta_C$$

$$\left(\frac{PL}{AE}\right)_S = \left(\frac{PL}{AE}\right)_C$$

Substitute in values of A and E, and note that the length of each pipe is the same.

$$\frac{P_S}{\frac{\pi}{4}\left(60^2 - 50^2\right)10^{-6} \times 190 \times 10^9}$$

$$= \frac{P_C}{\frac{\pi}{4}\left(80^2 - 60^2\right)10^{-6} \times 207 \times 10^9}$$

The equation may be simplified, and P_S may be written in terms of P_C so that it may be substituted into Eq. (a).

$$P_S = \frac{(60^2 - 50^2)\,190}{(80^2 - 60^2)207}\,P_C$$

$$P_S = 0.360\ 59\ P_C \qquad\qquad \text{Eq. (b)}$$

Substituting Eq. (b) in Eq. (a):

$$250\ 000 - 0.360\ 59\ P_C - P_C = 0$$

$$1.360\ 59\ P_C = 250\ 000$$

$$P_C = \frac{250\ 000}{1.360\ 59}$$

$$= 183\ 744\ \text{N}$$

From Eq. (b):

$$P_S = 0.360\ 59 \times 183\ 744$$

$$= 66\ 256\ \text{N}$$

Now that the load in each material has been calculated, the stress in each material may be determined.

$$\sigma_C = \frac{P_C}{A_C}$$

$$= \frac{183\ 744}{\frac{\pi}{4}\left(80^2 - 60^2\right)10^{-6}}$$

$$= 83.554 \times 10^6\ \text{Pa}$$

$$= 83.554\ \text{MPa}$$

$$\sigma_S = \frac{P_S}{A_S}$$

$$= \frac{66\ 256}{\frac{\pi}{4}\left(60^2 - 50^2\right)10^{-6}}$$

$$= 76.691 \times 10^6 \text{ Pa}$$

$$= 76.691 \text{ MPa}$$

Carbon steel
$\sigma = 83.6$ MPa
Stainless steel
$\sigma = 76.7$ MPa

EXAMPLE 11-17

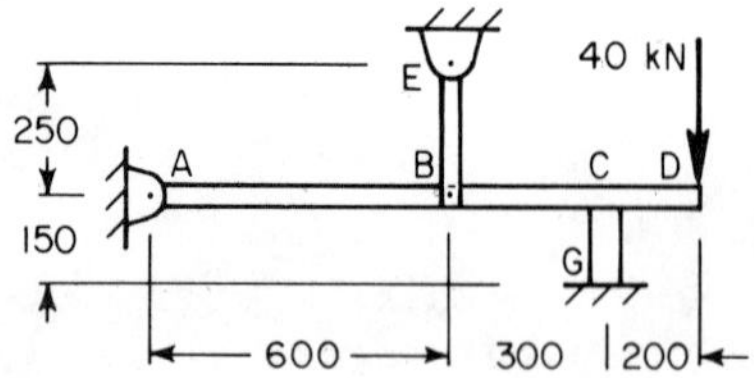

Determine the force in the 6061-T6 aluminum bar, *BE*, and in the gray cast-iron cylinder, *CG*, when the 50 kN load is applied to the system shown in Fig. 11-26. Bar *BE* has a cross section of 240 mm² and cylinder *CG* has a cross section of 800 mm². The beam *AD* is considered to be rigid and to have negligible mass.

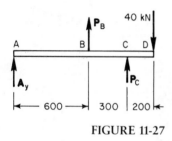

FIGURE 11-26

SOLUTION

A free-body diagram of the beam AD is drawn, as shown in Fig. 11-27. *There are three unknown forces acting on the beam. Since the objective is to find the forces at B and C, moments can be taken about A to obtain one equation with the two required unknown terms.*

$$\Sigma M_A = 0$$

$$P_B \times 0.600 + P_C \times 0.900 - 40\ 000 \times 1.100 = 0$$

$$0.600\ P_B + 0.900\ P_C = 44\ 000 \qquad \text{Eq. (a)}$$

FIGURE 11-27

Since the beam AD is rigid, the deformations in BE and CG must be proportional to the distance from the pin at A. This is shown in Fig. 11-28. *The relationship between the deformations will give a second equation relating the two unknown forces.*

From similar triangles:

$$\frac{\delta_B}{600} = \frac{\delta_C}{900}$$

$$\delta_B = \frac{600}{900}\ \delta_C$$

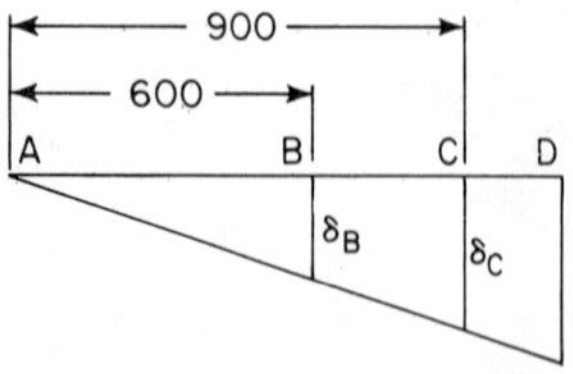

$$\delta_B = 0.666\ 67\ \delta_C \qquad \text{Eq. (b)}$$

FIGURE 11-28

$$\delta_B = \left(\frac{PL}{AE}\right)_B$$

$$\delta_C = \left(\frac{PL}{AE}\right)_C$$

From Eq. (b):

$$\left(\frac{PL}{AE}\right)_B = 0.666\ 67 \left(\frac{PL}{AE}\right)_C \qquad \text{Eq. (c)}$$

Substituting into Eq. (c)

$$\frac{P_B \times 0.250}{240 \times 10^{-6} \times 69 \times 10^9}$$

$$= 0.666\ 67\ \frac{P_C \times 0.150}{800 \times 10^{-6} \times 100 \times 10^9}$$

$$P_B = \frac{0.666\ 67\ P_C \times 0.150 \times 240 \times 69}{0.250 \times 800 \times 100}$$

$$= 0.082\ 800\ P_C$$

Substitute into Eq. (a):

$$0.600(0.082\ 800\ P_C) + 0.900\ P_C = 44\ 000$$

$$0.049\ 680\ P_C + 0.900\ P_C = 44\ 000$$

$$0.949\ 680\ P_C = 44\ 000$$

$$P_C = \frac{44\ 000}{0.949\ 680}$$

$$= 46\ 331\ \text{N}$$

From Eq. (a):

$$0.600\ P_B + 0.900 \times 46\ 331 = 44\ 000$$

$$P_B = \frac{44\ 000 - 41\ 698}{0.600}$$

$$= 3836.7\ \text{N}$$

The original assumption in drawing the free-body diagram in Fig. 11-27 was that BE was in tension and that CG was in compression. Since positive values were obtained for both answers, the assumptions were correct.

$$\boxed{\begin{aligned} F_{BE} &= +3840\ \text{N} \\ F_{CG} &= -46\ 300\ \text{N} \end{aligned}}$$

EXAMPLE 11-18

A round concrete pier has an outside diameter of 300 mm and is reinforced by eight 30 mm diameter structural-steel bars set in the concrete. If the allowable stress in the high-strength concrete is −12 MPa and the allowable stress in the steel is −80 MPa, determine the maximum allowable load on the pier.

SOLUTION

It is unlikely that both the steel and concrete will be stressed to their maximum allowable stress, and it is not possible to determine beforehand which material will reach maximum allowable stress first. Calculations must be based on the information that is known: that the load carried by the concrete plus the load carried by the steel will equal the total load, and that the deformation in the concrete will equal the deformation in the steel.

$$\text{Let } P = \text{maximum total load}$$
$$P_C = \text{load in concrete}$$
$$P_S = \text{load in steel}$$

Figure 11-29 is a free-body diagram showing the forces acting on the pier. The total of the forces in the eight steel bars is shown.

$$\Sigma F_y = 0$$

$$-P + P_C + P_S = 0$$

$$P = P_C + P_S$$

$$= \sigma_C A_C + \sigma_S A_S$$

$$= \sigma_C \frac{\pi}{4}(300^2 - 8 \times 30^2)10^{-6} + \sigma_S(8 \times \frac{\pi}{4} \times 30^2)10^{-6}$$

$$P = 65\ 031 \times 10^{-6}\sigma_C + 5654.9 \times 10^{-6}\sigma_S \qquad \text{Eq. (a)}$$

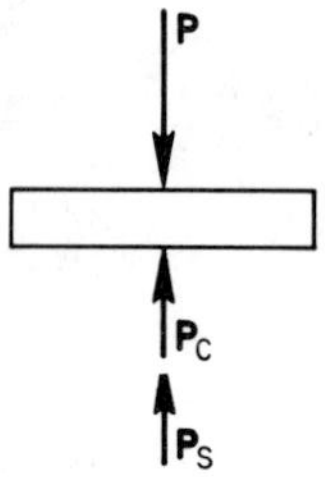

$$\delta_C = \delta_S$$

$$\left(\frac{PL}{AE}\right)_C = \left(\frac{PL}{AE}\right)_S$$

FIGURE 11-29

Both the concrete and steel have the same length. The term P/A may be replaced by σ.

$$\frac{\sigma_C}{34 \times 10^9} = \frac{\sigma_S}{200 \times 10^9}$$

$$\sigma_C = \frac{34}{200}\sigma_S$$

$$\sigma_C = 0.170\ 00\ \sigma_S \qquad \text{Eq. (b)}$$

If the steel is at its maximum allowable stress, then the corresponding value of the stress in the concrete may be calculated.

If σ_S governs:

$$\sigma_C = 0.170\ 00 \times 80 \times 10^6$$

$$= 13.600 \times 10^6 \text{ Pa}$$

The stress in the concrete may not exceed 12 MPa, *so the stress in the concrete must govern. Use* Eq. (b) *to find the actual value of the stress in the steel.*

σ_C governs:

From Eq. (b)

$$\sigma_S = \frac{\sigma_C}{0.170\ 00}$$

$$= \frac{12 \times 10^6}{0.170\ 00}$$

$$= 70.588 \times 10^6 \text{ Pa}$$

Now that the actual stress in both the concrete and steel is known, Eq. (a) *may be used to calculate the total allowable load on the pier.*

From Eq. (a):

$$P = 65\ 031 \times 10^{-6} \times 12 \times 10^6 + 5654.9 \times 10^{-6} \times 70.588 \times 10^6$$

$$= 780\ 372 + 399\ 168$$

$$= 1\ 179\ 540 \text{ N}$$

$$\boxed{P = 1.18 \text{ MN}}$$

PROBLEMS

11-77 A 6061-T6 aluminum tube with a 25 mm outside diameter and a 22 mm inside diameter is filled with glass-filled epoxy. If the assembly is then subjected to an axial tensile load of 5000 N, determine the stress in each member. The modulus of elasticity for the glass-filled epoxy is 21 GPa.

11-78 A pier 500 by 500 mm is made of 25 mm thick structural-steel walls and is filled with high-strength concrete. The pier carries an axial compressive load of 8000 kN, which is applied through rigid end plates. Calculate the stress in the concrete and the steel.

11-79 A 900 mm high concrete pier has a 250 by 250 mm cross section and is reinforced by five 25 mm diameter structural-steel reinforcing bars. If the pier has an axial compressive load of 900 kN applied through rigid end plates, calculate the stress in the concrete and the steel if the concrete is low-strength concrete.

11-80 Two 6061-T6 aluminum bars, *A*, and a structural-steel bar, *S*, are loaded as shown in Fig. P11-80, through two rigid parallel plates. Calculate the stress in the aluminum and steel. Each aluminum bar has a cross section of 100 by 250 mm and the steel bar has a cross section of 200 by 250 mm.

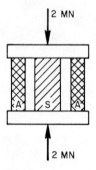

FIGURE P11-80

11-81 Determine the force in each of the two 6061-T6 aluminum members, *A*, and in the malleable cast-iron bar, *C*, shown in Fig. P11-81. The magnitude of **P** is 175 kN, the cross-sectional area of each aluminum member is 140 mm² and the cross-sectional area of the cast iron is 500 mm². The end supports and the plate between the aluminum and cast iron are assumed to be rigid.

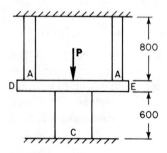

FIGURE P11-81

11-82 In the system shown in Fig. P11-82, the bars *A* are ABS plastic and each has a cross-sectional area of 7000 mm². *C* is vinyl and has a cross-sectional area of 4000 mm². If the magnitude of **P** is 6000 N, determine the stress in each of the materials. The two end plates are rigid, as is the plate between the ABS and the vinyl. Both materials are fastened to the plate.

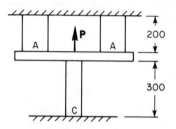

FIGURE P11-82

11-83 A rigid bar, *AD*, is pinned at *A* and suspended by two wires, *CG* and *HS*, as shown in Fig. P11-83. *CG* is copper, has a cross-sectional area of 5 mm² and is 2 m long, and *HS* is carbon steel, has a cross-sectional area of 3 mm², and is 3 m long. Determine the stress in each wire.

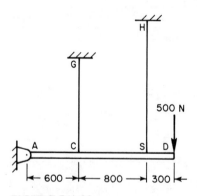

FIGURE P11-83

11-84 For the rigid bar *BS* shown in Fig. P11-84, determine the magnitude of the force **P** if the stress in the 6061-T6 aluminum wire at *A* is 80 MPa and its cross-sectional area is 120 mm². The length of the aluminum wire is 4 m. The wire at *S* is carbon steel, has a length of 3 m and has a cross-sectional area of 75 mm².

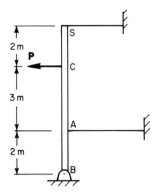

FIGURE P11-84

11-85 In Fig. P11-85, *AB* is 6061-T6 aluminum with a cross section of 120 mm² and *DE* is 2014-T6 aluminum with a cross section of 140 mm². Calculate the distance *x* to locate the load so that the rigid bar *BD* will remain horizontal.

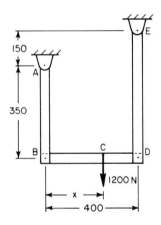

FIGURE P11-85

11-86 Three wires support a rigid, uniform bar with a mass of 120 kg, as shown in Fig. P11-86. Each wire has a length of 900 mm and a cross-sectional area of 4 mm². Determine the force in each wire if the one at *S* is carbon steel, the one at *A* is 2014-T6 aluminum and the one at *C* is hard copper.

11-87 A short 50 mm diameter bronze bar fits snugly inside a hollow carbon-steel tube that has an outside diameter of 75 mm. The two members are axially loaded in compression through a

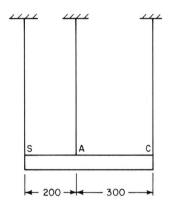

FIGURE P11-86

plate at each end. The allowable stress in the steel is 80 MPa and the allowable stress in the bronze is 20 MPa. Determine the total allowable load carried by the system. The modulus of elasticity for bronze is 117 GPa.

11-88 Calculate the allowable load in a concrete pier with a 200 by 350 mm cross section that is reinforced with 12 structural-steel bars with a diameter of 20 mm. The concrete is low strength and has an allowable stress of 5 MPa and the steel has an allowable stress of 80 MPa.

11-89 The system shown in Fig. P11-89 is made of low-carbon steel welded together at the plate joining *B* and *C*. The stress in *AB* may not exceed 30 MPa and the stress in *CD* may not exceed 75 MPa. Find the maximum value of **P**. The cross-sectional area of *AB* is 22 000 mm² and the cross-sectional area of *CD* is 4000 mm².

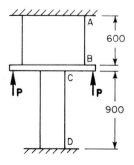

FIGURE P11-89

11-90 For the rigid bar *AD* shown in Fig. P11-90, determine the maximum load, **P**, that may be applied if the maximum allowable stress in the 2 mm diameter copper wire at *C* is 120 MPa and the maximum allowable stress in the 3 mm diameter carbon-steel wire at *S* is 95 MPa. The steel wire has a length of 350 mm and the copper wire has a length of 250 mm.

FIGURE P11-90

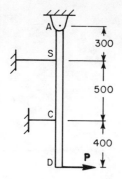

12 TORSION

12-1 SHEAR STRESS IN CIRCULAR SHAFTS

One of the most common methods of transmitting power from one point to another is by means of a circular shaft, which connects the power source, such as an engine, to the point where the power is to be used, such as the propeller of a ship, the transmission of an automobile or the workpiece in a lathe. The large shaft shown in Fig. 12-1 is used to transmit power from an electric motor to a steel mill.

FIGURE 12-1   This drive shaft is used to transmit nearly 6000 kW at 35 r/min to a steel mill. *Photo courtesy of Canadian General Electric Co. Ltd.*

In the examples cited, a torque is applied to a circular shaft to transmit the power. When the torque is applied there is a twisting in the shaft and, as is expected with such a deformation, a corresponding stress is developed. With twisting, the tendency is for the shaft to change shape, which implies that the stress involved is a shear stress. (Normal stress causes a change in length.) If you imagine that the shaft is a series of thin discs stacked together, you can see that, as the shaft is twisted, the discs would tend to rotate or slip relative to each other. This is a way to visualize the existence of shear deformation and shear stress in such a shaft.

It is possible to develop a relationship between the applied torque, the shear stress and the dimensions of a circular shaft. The relationship that can be developed will be valid only if *all* of the following assumptions are correct:

1. The shaft is in equilibrium, either at rest or with a uniform angular velocity.
2. The shaft has a uniform circular transverse section, which may be solid or hollow.
3. The shear proportional limit, which is the maximum shear stress for which shear stress is proportional to shear strain, is not exceeded.
4. The material is homogeneous.
5. A plane transverse section in the unstressed shaft remains a plane transverse section after the shaft is twisted.
6. A diameter of a transverse section of the unstressed shaft remains a straight line after the shaft is twisted.

To determine the shear stress in a circular shaft subjected to a torque, **T**, consider the shaft shown in Fig. 12-2. The line *AB* is twisted to a helix *A'B* due to the torque **T**. The angle subtended by the arc *AA'* is θ. As discussed in Article 10-7, the shear strain γ is the angle of deformation. Both θ and γ are measured in radians. For small angles, as exist in this case, the shear strain at the surface, which is a distance c from the center, is

$$\gamma_c = \tan \theta_c = \frac{AA'}{L} = \frac{c\theta}{L} \tag{12-1}$$

Similarly, the shear strain a distance r_i from the center is

$$\gamma_{r_i} = \tan \gamma_{r_i} = \frac{DD'}{L} = \frac{r_i\theta}{L} \tag{12-2}$$

Thus, we now may obtain the ratio

$$\frac{\gamma_c}{\gamma_{r_i}} = \frac{\dfrac{c\theta}{L}}{\dfrac{r_i\theta}{L}} = \frac{c}{r_i} \tag{12-3}$$

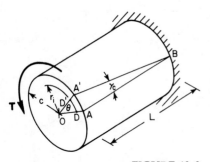

FIGURE 12-2

Since $\tau = G\gamma$, then

$$\frac{\gamma_c}{\gamma_{r_i}} = \frac{\dfrac{\tau_c}{G}}{\dfrac{\tau_{r_i}}{G}} = \frac{\tau_c}{\tau_{r_i}} \qquad (12\text{-}3)$$

But

$$\frac{\gamma_c}{\gamma_{r_i}} = \frac{c}{r_i}$$

thus

$$\frac{\tau_c}{\tau_{r_i}} = \frac{c}{r_i} \qquad (12\text{-}4)$$

From this relationship, it can be seen that the shear stress at a point on the section is directly proportional to the distance to the point from the center of the section.

At all points a distance r_i from the center, the stress in the shaft is τ_{r_i}, as shown in Fig. 12-3. The stress is shown acting on a circular element of area ΔA_i. The total force acting on the element of area is $\tau_{r_i}\Delta A_i$, and the torque resisted by the element of area will be $r_i\tau_{r_i}\Delta A_i$. For equilibrium, the total torque resisted by the section of the shaft must be the torque **T** applied to the shaft, and is equal to the sum of the torques due to each resisting area of the section. Thus

$$T = \Sigma\, r_i \tau_{r_i} \Delta A_i$$

But Eq. (12-4) may be rewritten to give

$$\tau_{r_i} = \frac{\tau_c r_i}{c}$$

Substituting,

$$T = \Sigma\, r_i \left(\frac{\tau_c r_i}{c}\right) \Delta A_i$$

$$= \Sigma\, \frac{\tau_c}{c}\, r_i^2 \Delta A_i$$

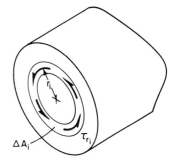

FIGURE 12-3

τ_c/c is a ratio that may be moved outside of the summation sign, giving

$$T = \frac{\tau_c}{c} \Sigma\, r_i^2\, \Delta A_i$$

$\Sigma\, r_i^2 \Delta A_i$ is recognized as the polar moment of inertia J as studied in Article 9-6.
The equation now becomes

$$T = \frac{\tau_c}{c} J$$

which is customarily rewritten as

$$\tau = \frac{Tc}{J} \qquad (12\text{-}5)$$

where τ is the maximum shear stress in the shaft,
 T is the torque applied to the shaft,
 c is the radius of the shaft and
 J is the polar moment of inertia of the cross section of the shaft.

To evaluate the shear stress at some interior point on the cross section of the shaft, the expression $\tau_{r_i}/\tau_c = r_i/c$ is used to rewrite Eq. (12-5) as follows:

$$\tau_{r_i} = \frac{Tr_i}{J}$$

which is usually expressed as

$$\tau_r = \frac{Tr}{J} \qquad (12\text{-}6)$$

where τ_r is the shear stress in the shaft at some distance, r, from the center
 T is the torque applied to the shaft,
 r is the distance measured from the center of the shaft and
 J is the polar moment of inertia of the cross section of the shaft.

From Eq. (12-6) it may be observed that the shear stress in a circular shaft increases linearly from zero, at the center of the shaft, to a maximum at the outside of the shaft, as shown in Fig. 12-4.

In many applications, you will be dealing with circular hollow shafts. Referring to Fig. 12-4, it can be seen that the shear stress near the center of the solid shaft is small. The torque resisted by this stress is small because of the low value for the shear stress combined with the low value of the distance from the center of rotation to the shear stress. Thus, if the center portion of a shaft is removed, the torque-carrying capacity of the shaft is reduced, but the reduction is small compared to the reduction in mass of the shaft. The reduced mass may reduce material costs as well as operating costs. There are limits to how thin the walls of a shaft may be, for if they are too thin they will fail by collapsing or buckling.

When calculating the stress in a hollow shaft, use Eq. (12-5) or (12-6), depending on whether you need to find the maximum

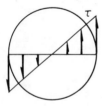

FIGURE 12-4

stress or the stress at some interior point. The stress distribution will be as shown in Fig. 12-5. The value of the polar moment of inertia of the section is obtained by parts, where the polar moment of inertia of the interior circular area is subtracted from the polar moment of inertia of the overall circular area to give the polar moment of inertia of the hollow section.

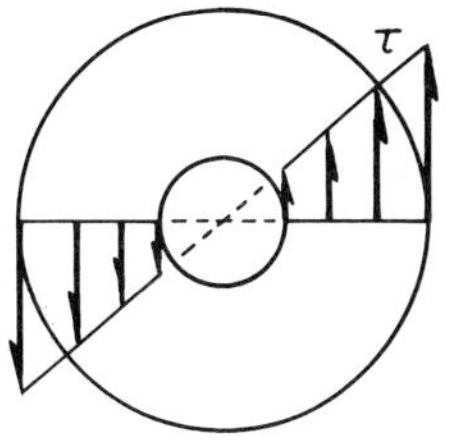

EXAMPLE 12-1

A power boat has a 35 mm diameter shaft, which has a torque of 1500 N·m applied to it. Determine (a) the maximum shear stress in the shaft and (b) the shear stress at a point 10 mm from the center.

FIGURE 12-5

SOLUTION

The maximum shear stress may be obtained by direct substitution of values into Eq. (12-5). This gives the shear stress at the outside which is the maximum shear stress. As usual, care must be taken to use consistent units. The torque must be in N·m, *the distance c must be in* m *and the polar moment of inertia must be in* m^4, *which is obtained by multiplying* mm^4 *by* 10^{-12}. *Note that the polar moment of inertia may be expressed as either* $\pi r^4/2$ *or* $\pi d^4/32$.

$$\text{(a)} \quad \tau = \frac{Tc}{J}$$

$$= \frac{1500 \times 17.5 \times 10^{-3}}{\dfrac{\pi \times 35^4}{32} \times 10^{-12}}$$

$$= 178.18 \times 10^6 \text{ Pa}$$

$$= 178.18 \text{ MPa}$$

The shear stress at any distance from the center of a circular shaft may be calculated by substituting values into Eq. (12-6). Regardless of where the stress is evaluated, the polar moment of inertia used is the value for the total shaft section.

$$\text{(b)} \quad \tau_r = \frac{Tr}{J}$$

$$= \frac{1500 \times 10 \times 10^{-3}}{\dfrac{\pi \times 35^4}{32} \times 10^{-12}}$$

$$= 101.82 \times 10^6 \text{ Pa}$$

$$= 101.82 \text{ MPa}$$

$$(a)\ \tau = 178\ \text{MPa}$$
$$(b)\ \tau = 102\ \text{MPa}$$

The shear stress a distance 10 mm *from the center of the shaft could also be obtained using a ratio, since the stress is proportional to the distance from the center, as noted in Eq. (12-4).*

$$\frac{\tau_c}{\tau_r} = \frac{c}{r}$$

$$\tau_r = \frac{r}{c}\tau_c$$

$$= \frac{10}{17.5} \times 178.18 \times 10^6$$

$$= 101.82 \times 10^6\ \text{Pa}$$

$$= 101.82\ \text{MPa}$$

EXAMPLE 12-2

Calculate the torque that may be transmitted by a hollow circular shaft with an outside diameter of 30 mm and an inside diameter of 25 mm if the stress in the shaft is not to exceed 60 MPa.

SOLUTION

Equation (12-5) may be rewritten to determine the torque that may be transmitted. In the case of a hollow shaft, the maximum shear stress is at the outside of the shaft.

$$\tau = \frac{Tc}{J}$$

$$T = \frac{\tau J}{c}$$

The polar moment of inertia for a hollow shaft may be calculated by subtracting the polar moment of inertia of the area removed from the polar moment of inertia of the solid cross section.

$$J = \frac{\pi d_o^4}{32} - \frac{\pi d_i^4}{32}$$

$$= \frac{\pi}{32}\left(d_o^4 - d_i^4\right)$$

It is now possible to proceed with the calculation of the torque.

$$T = \frac{\tau J}{c}$$

$$= \frac{60 \times 10^6 \times \frac{\pi}{32}\left(30^4 - 25^4\right)10^{-12}}{15 \times 10^{-3}}$$

$$= 164.69 \ \text{N·m}$$

$$\boxed{T = 165 \ \text{N·m}}$$

EXAMPLE 12-3

A solid shaft is to be used to transmit a torque of 21 kN·m. Determine the minimum diameter of shaft required if the shear stress in the shaft is not to exceed 65 MPa.

SOLUTION

Equation (12-5) *may be rewritten to solve for d. Note that c =* *d/2, so c may be eliminated from the equation,*

$$\tau = \frac{Tc}{J}$$

$$= \frac{T \times \dfrac{d}{2}}{\dfrac{\pi d^4}{32}}$$

$$\tau = \frac{16T}{\pi d^3}$$

$$d^3 = \frac{16T}{\pi \tau}$$

$$= \frac{16 \times 21\ 000}{\pi \times 65 \times 10^6}$$

$$= 1645.42 \times 10^{-6}$$

$$d = 11.806 \times 10^{-2} \ \text{m}$$

$$= 118.06 \ \text{mm}$$

$$\boxed{d = 118 \ \text{mm}}$$

Calculations for d had units of m, *since that is the base unit used in Eq. (12-5).*

PROBLEMS

12-1 Calculate the maximum shear stress in a 15 mm diameter shaft if a torque of 75 N·m is applied to it.

12-2 A circular shaft with a diameter of 100 mm is subjected to a torque of 8000 N·m. Determine the maximum shear stress in the shaft.

12-3 The drive shaft for a large tractor engine has a diameter of 40 mm, and it has a torque of 2 kN·m applied to it. Calculate the maximum shear stress in the shaft.

12-4 An extension for a socket wrench has a diameter of 15 mm. Determine the maximum shear stress in the extension if the mechanic applies a torque of 50 N·m.

12-5 A 150 mm diameter rolling-mill shaft has a torque of 16 kN·m applied to it. Determine the shear stress in the shaft (a) 50 mm from the center and (b) at the outside surface.

12-6 Determine the shear stress (a) at 1 mm from the center and (b) at the outside surface for a 3 mm diameter servomotor shaft that has a torque of 0.6 N·m.

12-7 Calculate the maximum shear stress in a 5 mm diameter shaft if the shaft is hollow and has a wall thickness of 1 mm. The torque applied to the shaft is 2 N·m.

12-8 For a 200 mm diameter hollow shaft with an inside diameter of 150 mm and an applied torque of 65 kN·m, determine the maximum shear stress in the shaft.

12-9 For a hollow circular shaft with an outside diameter of 25 mm and an inside diameter of 20 mm, determine the shear stress (a) at the outer surface and (b) at the inner surface, if the shaft is subjected to a torque of 80 N·m.

12-10 Calculate the shear stress (a) at the outer surface and (b) at the inner surface of a 25 mm diameter hollow shaft with an inside diameter of 10 mm. The torque applied to the shaft is 80 N·m.

12-11 A torque of 300 N·m is applied to a bronze shaft that has an outside diameter of 60 mm and a wall thickness of 5 mm. Determine the shear stress on the section at the inside surface of the shaft.

12-12 Determine the minimum shear stress in a circular shaft with an outside diameter of 40 mm and an inside diameter of 25 mm if it is subjected to a torque of 1000 N·m.

12-13 A valve stem on a seized valve has a diameter of 10 mm and will fail if the shear stress in it exceeds 300 MPa. Determine the torque that will cause the valve stem to break, assuming that the shear stress equation is valid for the material.

12-14 Calculate the torque that may be transmitted by a 45 mm diameter motor shaft if the allowable stress in the shaft is 75 MPa.

12-15 Calculate the maximum torque that may be transmitted by a 35 mm diameter shaft (a) that is solid and (b) that is hollow, with a 15 mm inside diameter, if the maximum allowable shear stress is 60 MPa.

12-16 Determine (a) the torque that can be resisted by a solid shaft with a diameter of 40 mm and (b) the torque that can be resisted by the shaft if it is hollow, with an inside diameter of 30 mm. The allowable shear stress is 60 MPa.

12-17 Calculate the diameter of shaft required to transmit a torque of 250 N·m if the shear stress in the shaft is not to exceed 50 MPa.

12-18 A shaft for a motor transmits a torque of 7500 N·m. Determine the minimum diameter for the shaft if the shear stress in it is not to exceed 25 MPa.

12-19 Find the outside diameter required for a hollow shaft if the torque applied to the shaft is 18 kN·m, the maximum allowable stress in the shaft is 75 MPa and the inside diameter of the shaft is to be half of the outside diameter.

12-20 A torque of 300 N·m is applied to a 25 mm diameter shaft in which the shear stress is not to exceed 100 MPa. Since the shaft could be hollow and the stress would not exceed the limit, determine the maximum allowable inside diameter.

12-2 STRESS CONCENTRATIONS IN SHAFTS

One of the conditions imposed on the development and use of the torsional shear stress formula $\tau = Tc/J$ is that the shaft must have a *uniform* circular cross section. If the cross section is reduced, the material that would usually transmit the stress from one section to another is not there. As a result, there is a redistribution of the stress at the section. This redistribution usually causes a higher stress than that which would be obtained using the torsional shear stress formula. This location in the shaft with the higher stress is called a *stress concentration*. The actual or maximum stress at the point may be calculated by multiplying the nominal stress at the point by a stress-concentration factor.

$$\tau_{max} = K_t \tau_{nom} \tag{12-7}$$

where τ_{max} is the maximum shear stress at the stress concentration,

K_t is the stress-concentration factor and

τ_{nom} is the nominal stress on the section where the stress concentration is located.

The stress-concentration factor varies depending on the geometry of the stress concentration. Values of the stress-concentration factor have been determined experimentally and theoretically, and have been tabulated in charts such as those shown in Figs. 12-6, 12-7 and 12-8. There are many other charts available for different types of stress concentrations. Be careful to use the chart that corresponds to the geometry of the member. In the case of the standard key seat shown in Fig. 12-6, the value of K_t would vary if the geometry of the key seat is varied from the standard values of width and depth shown. With each chart is a drawing that shows the approximate actual and nominal stress distribution at the stress concentration. The formula for the nominal shear stress to be used is also shown as part of each chart.

EXAMPLE 12-4

Find the maximum shear stress in an 80 mm diameter shaft if it has a torque of 3 kN·m applied to it and if there is a standard end-milled key seat in the shaft.

SOLUTION

The nominal stress in the shaft is obtained from the equation given in Fig. 12-6, and the value for the stress-concentration factor for a standard key seat is also given in Fig. 12-6. The two values are multiplied together, as indicated by Eq. (12-7). Note that the equation for nominal stress involves the term d^3, so conversion of this term from mm^3 to m^3 involves the factor 10^{-9}.

$$K_t = 1.6$$

$$\tau_{nom} = \frac{16T}{\pi d^3}$$

$$= \frac{16 \times 3000}{\pi \times 80^3 \times 10^{-9}}$$

$$= 29.842 \times 10^6 \text{ Pa}$$

$$\tau_{max} = K_t \tau_{nom}$$

$$= 1.6 \times 29.842 \times 10^6$$

$$= 47.746 \times 10^6 \text{ Pa}$$

$$= 47.746 \text{ MPa}$$

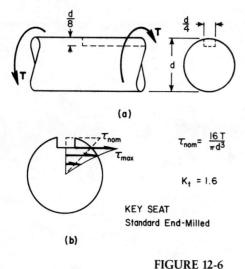

(a)

$$\tau_{nom} = \frac{16T}{\pi d^3}$$

$$K_t = 1.6$$

KEY SEAT
Standard End-Milled

(b)

FIGURE 12-6

$$\boxed{\tau_{max} = 47.7 \text{ MPa}}$$

EXAMPLE 12-5

For a 200 mm diameter shaft that has a reduced section with a diameter of 120 mm, determine the maximum shear stress in the shaft if there is a 15 mm radius fillet joining the sections and if the torque applied to the shaft is 25 kN·m.

SOLUTION

The shaft is the type shown in Fig. 12-7(b). To use the chart in Fig. 12-7(a), it is necessary to determine the values for the ratios r/d and D/d,

$$\frac{r}{d} = \frac{15}{120}$$

$$= 0.125$$

$$\frac{D}{d} = \frac{200}{120}$$

$$= 1.667$$

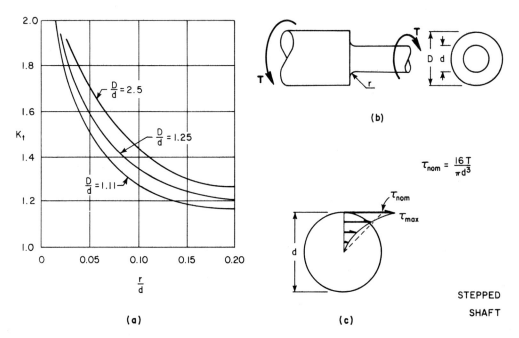

FIGURE 12-7

Now the chart may be used to determine the stress-concentration factor. Start on the r/d axis at r/d = 0.125 and go vertically up until the estimated location of the D/d = 1.67 line is intercepted. The value of K_t is obtained by going horizontally to the left from this intercept and reading the value off the K_t axis.

$$K_t = 1.31$$

The value for the nominal stress in the shaft is calculated using the equation given with Fig. 12-7. *Note that the equation uses the smaller value of the diameter.*

$$\tau_{nom} = \frac{16T}{\pi d^3}$$

$$= \frac{16 \times 25 \times 10^3}{\pi \times 120^3 \times 10^{-9}}$$

$$= 73.683 \times 10^6 \text{ Pa}$$

With both the stress-concentration factor and the nominal shear stress known, the maximum shear stress may be calculated using Eq. (12-7).

$$\tau_{max} = K_t\tau_{nom}$$
$$= 1.31 \times 73.683 \times 10^6$$
$$= 96.525 \times 10^6 \text{ Pa}$$
$$= 96.525 \text{ MPa}$$

$$\boxed{\tau_{max} = 96.5 \text{ MPa}}$$

In cases where the location of the D/d curve has to be estimated, it is normal to find minor differences in answers obtained by different people.

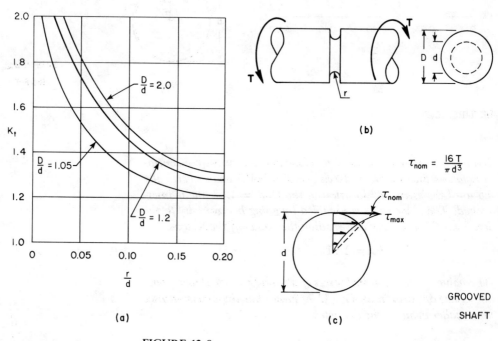

$$\tau_{nom} = \frac{16\,T}{\pi d^3}$$

GROOVED SHAFT

(a)   (c)

FIGURE 12-8

PROBLEMS

12-21 Determine the maximum shear stress in a 40 mm diameter shaft with a standard key seat if the torque applied to the shaft is 1500 N·m.

12-22 For a 150 mm diameter shaft with a standard key seat, calculate the maximum shear stress in the shaft if the torque applied is 75 kN·m.

12-23 Determine the maximum shear stress in a 25 mm diameter shaft if there is a 3 mm deep circular groove cut in the shaft. The radius of the bottom of the groove is 2 mm. The torque applied is 200 N·m.

12-24 A 200 mm diameter shaft is subjected to a torque of 12 kN·m. The shaft has a reduced section with a diameter of 150 mm, and the radius of the fillet at the reduced section is 15 mm. Determine the maximum shear stress in the shaft.

12-25 Find the maximum shear stress in a 60 mm diameter shaft with a torque of 1400 N·m applied to it. The shaft has a reduced section with a diameter of 40 mm and the radius of the fillet connecting the two sections is 6 mm.

12-26 A shaft with a diameter of 150 mm has a groove with a depth of 30 mm. If the radius of the groove is 10 mm and the torque applied to the shaft is 15 kN·m, calculate the maximum shear stress in the shaft.

12-27 Find the maximum torque that may be transmitted by a 150 mm diameter solid shaft with a standard key seat if the stress in the shaft is not to exceed 110 MPa.

12-28 For a 25 mm diameter shaft with a standard key seat, determine the maximum torque that may be transmitted if the shear stress in the shaft is not to exceed 85 MPa.

12-29 Determine the diameter of shaft required to transmit a torque of 12 kN·m if the stress in the shaft is not to exceed 140 MPa and if the shaft has a standard key seat.

12-30 A circular shaft with a standard key seat is to transmit a torque of 800 N·m, and the stress in the shaft is not to exceed 110 MPa. Find the minimum required diameter of the shaft.

12-31 Calculate the maximum torque that may be safely transmitted by a 130 mm diameter shaft with a reduced section having a diameter of 90 mm. The two sections are joined by a fillet with a radius of 15 mm, and the maximum allowable stress in the shaft is 105 MPa.

12-32 A 75 mm diameter plastic shaft has a groove with a 50 mm diameter. The radius of the groove is 2 mm. Determine the maximum torque that may be applied to the shaft if the shear stress in the shaft is not to exceed 8 MPa.

12-3 ANGLE OF TWIST

As discussed in Article 12-1, a shaft subjected to a torque will twist. The amount of twist may need to be limited if the shaft is used for transmitting power or if the shaft is used as a spring. It may be necessary to calculate the angle of twist in the shaft.

To calculate the angle of twist in a circular shaft such as shown in Fig. 12-9, the same assumptions apply as were made about the shaft in Article 12-1 when the shear stress was calculated.

The shear strain at the outside surface is γ_c, and in Article 12-1 was found to be

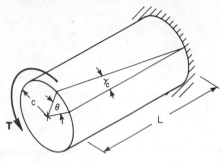

FIGURE 12-9

$$\gamma_c = \frac{c\theta}{L} \tag{12-1}$$

The expression for G, which is the shear modulus of elasticity, can be rewritten as $\gamma_c = \tau_c / G$,

but

$$\tau_c = \frac{Tc}{J}$$

thus

$$\gamma_c = \frac{\tau_c}{G} = \frac{\dfrac{Tc}{J}}{G} = \frac{Tc}{JG} \tag{12-8}$$

Both expressions for γ_c, as given in Eqs. (12-1) and (12-8), must be equal to each other. This gives

$$\frac{c\theta}{L} = \frac{Tc}{JG}$$

which can be rewritten as

$$\theta = \frac{TL}{JG} \tag{12-9}$$

where θ is the angle of twist in the shaft,
     T is the torque applied to the shaft,
     L is the length of the shaft through which the torque acts,
     J is the polar moment of inertia of the cross section of the shaft and
     G is the shear modulus of elasticity of the material in the shaft

It will be recalled that, in the derivation of Eq. (12-1), and thus in Eq. (12-9), the angle of twist θ *must* be expressed in radians.

Equation (12-9) is also valid for a hollow circular shaft using the appropriate value for the polar moment of inertia.

EXAMPLE 12-6

Calculate the angle of twist, in degrees, of a ship's 200 mm diameter steel propeller shaft 6 m long if the torque applied to the shaft is 40 kN·m. The shear modulus of elasticity of the shaft is the same as that of carbon steel.

SOLUTION

Calculation of the angle of twist, in radians, requires direct substitution of values into Eq. (12-9). The value for the shear modulus of elasticity is obtained from Appendix E. All terms must be in N or m, so care must be taken with units.

$$\theta = \frac{TL}{JG}$$

$$= \frac{40 \times 10^3 \times 6}{\dfrac{\pi \times 200^4}{32} \times 10^{-12} \times 80 \times 10^9}$$

$$= 0.019\ 099 \text{ rad}$$

To convert the angle in radians to degrees, the value in radians must be multiplied by $180/\pi$.

$$\theta = 0.019\ 099 \times \frac{180}{\pi}$$

$$= 1.0943°$$

$$\boxed{\theta = 1.09°}$$

EXAMPLE 12-7

The carbon-steel drive shaft for an engine has an outside diameter of 60 mm, an inside diameter of 40 mm and a length of 750 mm. If the angle of twist in the shaft is not to exceed $3°$, calculate the maximum torque the drive shaft may transmit.

SOLUTION

In this case, the maximum angle of twist is known, and it is necessary to calculate the applied torque. Equation (12-9) is rewritten to solve for the torque.

$$\theta = \frac{TL}{JG}$$

$$T = \frac{\theta JG}{L}$$

Values are substituted in the equation. However, the value for θ must be expressed in radians, and care must be taken to ensure that all other terms are expressed in the base units of N and m.

$$T = \frac{3 \times \dfrac{\pi}{180} \times \dfrac{\pi}{32}\left(60^4 - 40^4\right)10^{-12} \times 80 \times 10^9}{750 \times 10^{-3}}$$

$$= 5702.4 \text{ N·m}$$

$$\boxed{T = 5700 \text{ N·m}}$$

EXAMPLE 12-8

A solid magnesium shaft 450 mm long is to be used to transmit a torque of 2.5 kN·m. Determine the minimum shaft diameter required if the shear stress in the shaft is not to exceed 60 MPa and if the angle of twist is not to exceed 4°.

SOLUTION

The size of shaft has two limitations placed on it: the allowable shear stress and the allowable angle of twist. The minimum diameters required to satisfy each of these conditions must be determined, and the larger of the two values will be the minimum diameter that will satisfy both conditions. It makes no difference which limitation is investigated first.

If one starts with the limitation on stress, then Eq. (12-5) should be rewritten to solve for d, keeping in mind that c = d/2.

$$\tau = \frac{Tc}{J}$$

$$= \frac{T \times \dfrac{d}{2}}{\dfrac{\pi d^4}{32}}$$

$$= \frac{16T}{\pi d^3}$$

$$d^3 = \frac{16T}{\pi \tau}$$

$$= \frac{16 \times 2.5 \times 10^3}{\pi \times 60 \times 10^6}$$

$$= 0.212\ 207 \times 10^{-3}$$

$$d = 0.596\ 47 \times 10^{-1}\ \text{m}$$

$$= 59.647\ \text{mm}$$

In the case of the limitation of the angle of twist, Eq. (12-9) is rewritten to solve for d. Keep in mind that θ must be expressed in radians.

$$\theta = \frac{TL}{JG}$$

$$= \frac{TL}{\dfrac{\pi d^4}{32}\ G}$$

$$d^4 = \frac{32TL}{\pi G \theta}$$

$$= \frac{32 \times 2.5 \times 10^3 \times 450 \times 10^{-3}}{\pi \times 17 \times 10^9 \times 4 \times \dfrac{\pi}{180}}$$

$$= 965.53 \times 10^{-8}$$

$$d = 5.5743 \times 10^{-2} \text{ m}$$

$$= 55.743 \text{ mm}$$

If the diameter is only 55.743 mm, the shear stress will exceed 60 MPa. If the diameter is 59.647 mm, the angle of twist will be less than 4°, but the shear stress will not exceed 60 MPa. The larger diameter is the required diameter.

$$\boxed{d = 59.6 \text{ mm}}$$

PROBLEMS

12-33 A 6061-T6 aluminum shaft 150 mm long has a diameter of 15 mm. Calculate the angle of twist in the shaft in degrees if the shaft is subjected to a torque of 80 N·m.

12-34 A bronze shaft with a length of 3 m and a diameter of 100 mm is subjected to a torque of 8000 N·m. Determine the angle of twist of the shaft in degrees if the shear modulus of elasticity of bronze is 38 GPa.

12-35 Calculate the angle of twist in degrees in a carbon-steel shaft if it has a diameter of 90 mm, a length of 4 m and a torque of 5 kN·m applied to it.

12-36 A key used to turn the on-off valve for a residential water supply is attached to a 2.5 m long carbon-steel rod, which has a 20 mm diameter. If a torque of 30 N·m is applied to the rod to loosen an old valve, determine the angle of twist in degrees in the rod.

12-37 For a 2014-T6 aluminum shaft with an outside diameter of 60 mm and an inside diameter of 30 mm, determine the angle of twist in degrees if the length of the shaft is 1.25 m and if the torque applied is 1800 N·m.

12-38 Determine the angle of twist in degrees in a hollow carbon-steel shaft 2 m long if there is a torque of 2000 N·m applied at each end. The shaft has an outside diameter of 40 mm and a wall thickness of 10 mm.

12-39 Calculate the maximum torque that may be applied to a 150 mm diameter monel shaft if the angle of twist in the 2.5 m long shaft is not to exceed 4°. The shear modulus of elasticity for monel is 65 GPa.

12-40 A shaft made of carbon steel is 2 m long and has a diameter of 75 mm. If the maximum allowable angle of twist in the shaft is 3°, determine the maximum allowable torque.

12-41 The shaft for an auger used for drilling holes for utility poles is made of carbon steel. If its length is 5 m, its outside diameter is 80 mm and its inside diameter is 40 mm, determine the angle of twist in the shaft, in degrees, when the maximum shear stress in the shaft is 55 MPa.

12-42 A small titanium-alloy shaft (G = 36 GPa) has a length of 180 mm, an outside diameter of 12 mm and an inside diameter of 8 mm. If it has been designed for a maximum shear stress of 200 MPa, calculate the angle of twist, in degrees, that will occur at this stress.

12-43 Determine the maximum torque that may be transmitted by a 500 mm long 2014-T6 aluminum shaft with an outside diameter of 30 mm and an inside diameter of 20 mm. The shear stress is not to exceed 80 MPa and the angle of twist must not exceed 6°.

12-44 A carbon-steel shaft is 1.5 m long and has an outside diameter of 50 mm and an inside diameter of 30 mm. Determine the maximum allowable torque that may be applied to the shaft if the angle of twist may not exceed 2.4° and the maximum shear stress is 60 MPa.

12-45 Determine the diameter of a 3 m long solid monel shaft required to transmit a torque of 60 kN·m if the shear stress in the shaft is not to exceed 75 MPa and the angle of twist must not exceed 5°. The shear modulus of elasticity for monel is 65 GPa.

12-46 A solid titanium shaft 150 mm long is to be used to transmit a torque of 240 N·m. Determine the minimum diameter required if the shear stress must not exceed 180 MPa and the angle of twist must not exceed 9°. The shear modulus of elasticity for titanium is 36 GPa.

12-4 STATICALLY INDETERMINATE SHAFTS

A statically indeterminate member is one for which it is not possible to determine the reactions at the supports using the equilibrium equations only because there are more unknown terms than there are available equilibrium equations. Both statically determinate and statically indeterminate shafts are shown in Fig. 12-10. If a free-body diagram of the shaft shown in Fig. 12-10(a) is drawn, there will be a torque at the rigid support at A and its magnitude can be determined, assuming $\mathbf{T_B}$ is known, by taking

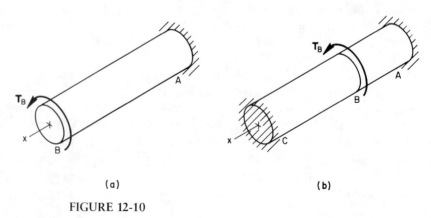

| (a) | (b) |

FIGURE 12-10

moments about the x axis. In the case of the shaft shown in Fig. 12-10(b), which is rigidly supported at both ends, there will be a torque applied by each support, and taking moments about the x axis would give an equation with two unknown terms, assuming that T_B is known. Since no other equilibrium equation is available, some other information is required to calculate the torque at A and C. The additional information usually used relates the torques and the deformation in the member to provide an additional equation. In the shaft shown in Fig. 12-10(b), the angle of twist between A and B must equal the angle of twist between B and C.

In a composite shaft, the inside of the shaft is of one material and the outer portion is of a second material. Both portions of the shaft must have the same angle of twist if the shaft is to meet the condition that the diameter of the unstressed shaft is to remain a straight line in the stressed shaft.

For either type of shaft, equations relating the torque and angle of twist and the equation of equilibrium are available to make it possible to solve for two unknown terms.

EXAMPLE 12-9

Determine the torque resisted by each support of a 1.6 m long shaft that is rigidly supported at each end and has a torque of 2.5 kN·m applied 0.7 m from the left end. The portion of the shaft to the left of the point of application of the torque is carbon steel with a diameter of 120 mm, and the portion to the right is 2014-T6 aluminum with a diameter of 150 mm.

SOLUTION

A free-body diagram of the shaft is shown in Fig. 12-11. *Since there is only one equilibrium equation available for solving for the two unknown torques shown, the shaft is statically indeterminate. However, the equilibrium equation will provide one of the necessary equations.*

$$\Sigma \, M_x = 0$$

$$-T_L + 2500 - T_R = 0 \qquad \text{(a)}$$

The supports are rigid, and the section where the torque is applied is common. Both the left portion and the right portion of the shaft between the supports and the point of application of the torque must have the same angle of twist. This information will provide a second equation.

$$\theta_L = \theta_R$$

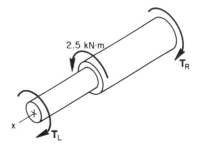

FIGURE 12-11

$$\left(\frac{TL}{JG}\right)_L = \left(\frac{TL}{JG}\right)_R$$

$$\frac{T_L \times 0.7}{\frac{\pi}{32} \times 120^4 \times 10^{-12} \times 80 \times 10^9}$$

$$= \frac{T_R \times 0.9}{\frac{\pi}{32} \times 150^4 \times 10^{-12} \times 28 \times 10^9}$$

$$T_L = \frac{T_R \times 0.9 \times 120^4 \times 80}{0.7 \times 150^4 \times 28}$$

$$T_L = 1.5047\, T_R \tag{b}$$

Equations (a) and (b) can be solved simultaneously to determine the torques.

Substitute Eq. (b) in Eq. (a)

$$-T_L + 2500 - T_R = 0 \tag{a}$$

$$-(1.5047\, T_R) + 2500 - T_R = 0$$

$$2.5047\, T_R = 2500$$

$$T_R = \frac{2500}{2.5047}$$

$$= 998.12\ \text{N·m}$$

From Eq. (b)

$$T_L = 1.5047 \times 998.12$$

$$= 1501.9\ \text{N·m}$$

$$\boxed{\begin{aligned} T_L &= 1500\ \text{N·m} \\ T_R &= 998\ \text{N·m} \end{aligned}}$$

EXAMPLE 12-10

A composite 600 mm long shaft is made of two parts. The outside is magnesium with an outside diameter of 75 mm and an inside diameter of 50 mm; the inside part is solid 2014-T6 aluminum that fits snugly inside the magnesium and does not slip. Determine the maximum stress in each material if the torque applied to each end of the shaft is 1200 N·m.

SOLUTION

To calculate the maximum stress in each material, it is necessary to determine the torque resisted by each material. The total torque applied must equal the sum of the torques resisted by each material, as shown in Fig. 12-12, *if the shaft is in equilibrium. The angle of twist for each part must be the same if the torsional shear stress formula Eq.* (12-5) *is to be valid. These two relationships are used to calculate the torque in each part of the shaft.*

For equilibrium:

$$\Sigma M_y = 0$$

$$1200 - T_A - T_M = 0 \qquad \text{(a)}$$

Angle of twist is the same in each part:

$$\theta_A = \theta_M$$

$$\left(\frac{TL}{JG}\right)_A = \left(\frac{TL}{JG}\right)_M$$

Both parts have the same length, so L is a common factor,

$$\frac{T_A}{\frac{\pi}{32} \times 50^4 \times 10^{-12} \times 28 \times 10^9}$$

$$= \frac{T_M}{\frac{\pi}{32}\left(75^4 - 50^4\right)10^{-12} \times 17 \times 10^9}$$

$$T_A = \frac{50^4 \times 28\ T_M}{(75^4 - 50^4) \times 17}$$

$$T_A = 0.405\ 43\ T_M \qquad \text{(b)}$$

Substitute Eq. (b) in Eq. (a)

$$1200 - T_A - T_M = 0 \qquad \text{(a)}$$

$$1200 - 0.405\ 43\ T_M - T_M = 0$$

$$1.405\ 43\ T_M = 1200$$

$$T_M = \frac{1200}{1.405\ 43}$$

$$= 853.83\ \text{N·m}$$

From Eq. (b)

$$T_A = 0.405\ 43 \times 853.83$$

$$= 346.17\ \text{N·m}$$

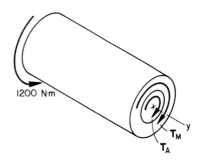

1200 N·m

T_M

T_A

y

FIGURE 12-12

The values for the maximum shear stress may be obtained by substitution of values in the shear stress formula Eq. (12-5).

For magnesium:

$$\tau_M = \left(\frac{Tc}{J}\right)_M$$

$$= \frac{853.83 \times 37.5 \times 10^{-3}}{\frac{\pi}{32}\left(75^4 - 50^4\right)10^{-12}}$$

$$= 12.845 \times 10^6 \text{ Pa}$$

$$= 12.845 \text{ MPa}$$

For aluminum:

$$\tau_A = \left(\frac{TC}{J}\right)_A$$

$$= \frac{346.17 \times 25 \times 10^{-3}}{\frac{\pi}{32} \times 50^4 \times 10^{-12}}$$

$$= 14.104 \times 10^6 \text{ Pa}$$

$$= 14.104 \text{ MPa}$$

It will be noted that the maximum stress in the aluminum is higher than the maximum stress in the magnesium. This is due to the fact that the magnesium has a lower shear modulus of elasticity, and thus has less stress for the same amount of deformation.

$$\boxed{\begin{array}{l} \tau_M = 12.8 \text{ MPa} \\ \tau_A = 14.1 \text{ MPa} \end{array}}$$

PROBLEMS

12-47 A 2014-T6 aluminum shaft 1.8 m long is rigidly supported at each end. The left part of the shaft is solid, with a diameter of 80 mm, and the right part is hollow, with an outside diameter of 100 mm, an inside diameter of 60 mm and a length of 1.1 m. Calculate the torque resisted by each of the left and right supports if there is a torque of 5 kN·m applied at the interface of the two parts.

12-48 Determine the torque applied by the supports at each end of a 900 mm long carbon-steel shaft that is rigidly fastened at the ends if a torque of 800 N·m is applied at the center of the shaft. The left half of the shaft is solid with a diameter of 25 mm and the right half is hollow with an outside diameter of 30 mm and an inside diameter of 20 mm.

12-49 A shaft with a constant diameter of 35 mm is made of two sections: one bronze, 750 mm long, and the other 6061-T6 aluminum, 500 mm long. The two sections are fastened together, and a torque of 600 N·m is applied at the common face. The outer ends of the shaft are rigidly fastened to supports so that they cannot rotate. Determine the torque in the bronze and in the aluminum. The bronze has a shear modulus of elasticity of 41 GPa.

12-50 Determine the torque resisted by the left and right rigid supports for a 2 m long shaft if there is a torque of 12 kN·m applied at a section 0.7 m from the left support. The left part of the shaft is carbon steel, is 0.7 m long and has a diameter of 75 mm. The right part is malleable cast iron and has a diameter of 60 mm. Its shear modulus of elasticity is 65 GPa.

12-51 Calculate the maximum stress in each part of a 200 mm long shaft that is rigidly supported at each end and has a torque of 900 N·m applied at the interface of the two parts, which is 50 mm from the left end. The left part is extruded magnesium and has a diameter of 40 mm. The right part is 2014-T6 aluminum, and has a diameter of 35 mm.

12-52 A shaft 900 mm long is rigidly fixed at both ends. The left portion is 600 mm long, made of 6061-T6 aluminum, and has a diameter of 60 mm. The right portion is made of 2014-T6 aluminum and is hollow, with an outside diameter of 60 mm and an inside diameter of 20 mm. If a torque of 4 kN·m is applied where the two materials are joined, determine the maximum stress in each material.

12-53 A composite shaft is made with an outer section of carbon steel with an outside diameter of 30 mm and an inside diameter of 20 mm. It has a stainless-steel close-fitting liner with an inside diameter of 15 mm. If a torque of 1200 N·m

is applied to the shaft, calculate the torque resisted by each material.

12-54 Calculate the torque carried by each material in a composite shaft if the torque applied to the shaft is 8 kN·m. The outer part of the shaft is stainless steel with an outside diameter of 80 mm and an inside diameter of 70 mm. The center of the shaft is filled with 6061-T6 aluminum

12-55 A 2 m long extruded-magnesium shaft with an outside diameter of 150 mm and an inside diameter of 120 mm is entirely filled by a 6061-T6 aluminum shaft. If the ends of both shafts are fastened together, and if a torque of 25 kN·m is applied at each end, calculate the maximum stress in each material.

12-56 A 400 mm long hollow shaft is made of 2014-T6 aluminum with an outside diameter of 60 mm and an inside diameter of 40 mm. It has an 18-8 stainless-steel liner with an outside diameter of 40 mm and an inside diameter of 30 mm. If the two are rigidly connected, determine the maximum stress in each material if the torque applied to the shaft is 1800 N·m.

12-57 A composite shaft 500 mm long has an outside section of 2014-T6 aluminum with an outside diameter of 60 mm and an inside diameter of 40 mm. This is lined with a tight-fitting hard-copper liner with an inside diameter of 30 mm. Determine the maximum torque that may be applied to the shaft if the shear stress in the aluminum may not exceed 80 MPa and the shear stress in the copper may not exceed 65 MPa.

12-58 Calculate the maximum torque that can be transmitted by a composite magnesium-steel shaft if the maximum allowable stress in the magnesium is 60 MPa and the maximum allowable stress in the stainless steel is 200 MPa. The solid magnesium core has an outside diameter of 50 mm and the stainless-steel cover has an outside diameter of 60 mm.

12-5 POWER TRANSMISSION

The most common use of the circular shaft is the transmission of power, where torque is applied to a rotating shaft at one point and the torque is transmitted by the shaft to some other point.

Power may be defined as the time rate of doing work. It is usually measured in watts (W), where one watt is one joule per second (J/s). Work may be defined as the product of torque and angle of rotation. It is usually measured in joules, where one joule is one newton metre. It may be shown that the power transmitted by a torque applied to a rotating shaft is

$$P = T\omega \qquad (12\text{-}10)$$

where *P* is the power transmitted,
  T is the torque applied to the shaft, and
  ω is the angular speed of the shaft.

The power is measured in watts, the torque in newton metres and the angular speed, as used in Eq. (12-10), must be in radians per second (rad/s), although it will be usual for the information to be given in revolutions per minute (r/min).

The relationship between power and torque is important in the design of shafts, for when the power transmitted and angular speed of the shaft are known, the torque acting on the shaft can be determined. It is then possible to select the material and size of the shaft required to transmit the power.

EXAMPLE 12-11

Determine the maximum shear stress in a 40 mm diameter shaft that transmits 80 kW at 750 r/min.

SOLUTION

It is necessary to find the torque applied to the shaft, using Eq. (12-10), *before the stress can be calculated. The angular speed used in* Eq. (12-10) *must be in* rad/s.

$$P = T\omega$$

$$T = \frac{P}{\omega}$$

$$= \frac{80 \times 10^3}{\dfrac{750 \times 2\pi}{60}}$$

$$= 1018.6 \text{ N·m}$$

The shear stress may now be calculated using Eq. (12-5).

$$\tau = \frac{Tc}{J}$$

$$= \frac{1018.6 \times 20 \times 10^{-3}}{\dfrac{\pi \times 40^4}{32} \times 10^{-12}}$$

$$= 81.057 \times 10^6 \text{ Pa}$$

$$= 81.057 \text{ MPa}$$

$$\boxed{\tau = 81.1 \text{ MPa}}$$

EXAMPLE 12-12

Calculate the amount of power that may be transmitted by a carbon-steel shaft with a diameter of 12 mm if the shear stress in the shaft is not to exceed 85 MPa and if the shaft will rotate at 1760 r/min.

SOLUTION

To calculate the power that may be transmitted, it is first necessary to determine the torque applied to the shaft. Since the dimensions of the shaft and the allowable stress are known, Eq. (12-5) *may be rewritten to calculate the torque.*

$$\tau = \frac{Tc}{J}$$

$$T = \frac{\tau J}{c}$$

$$= \frac{85 \times 10^6 \times \dfrac{\pi}{32} \times 12^4 \times 10^{-12}}{6 \times 10^{-3}}$$

$$= 28.840 \text{ N·m}$$

The power may be determined using Eq. (12-10). *Note that the angular speed must be changed from* r/min *to* rad/s.

$$P = T\omega$$

$$= 28.840 \times 1760 \times \frac{2\pi}{60}$$

$$= 5315.4 \text{ W}$$

$$P = 5.32 \text{ kW}$$

EXAMPLE 12-13

The drive shaft for a large bulldozer transmits 900 kW when rotating at 600 r/min. If the shear stress in the shaft is not to be greater than 65 MPa, determine the minimum size of solid shaft required.

SOLUTION

To select the size of the shaft, the torque acting on the shaft must be calculated first, using Eq. (12-10). *Remember that the angular speed must be expressed in* rad/s.

$$P = T\omega$$

$$T = \frac{P}{\omega}$$

$$= \frac{900 \times 10^3}{\dfrac{600 \times 2\pi}{60}}$$

$$= 14\ 324 \text{ N·m}$$

It is now possible to rewrite Eq. (12-5) *to calculate the diameter. Keep in mind that c = d/2.*

$$\tau = \frac{Tc}{J}$$

$$= \frac{T \times \dfrac{d}{2}}{\dfrac{\pi d^4}{32}}$$

$$= \frac{16T}{\pi d^3}$$

$$d^3 = \frac{16T}{\pi \tau}$$

$$= \frac{16 \times 14\ 324}{\pi \times 65 \times 10^6}$$

$$= 1122.33 \times 10^{-6}$$

$$d = 10.392 \times 10^{-2} \text{ m}$$

$$= 0.103\ 92 \text{ m}$$

$$= 103.92 \text{ mm}$$

$$\boxed{d = 104 \text{ mm}}$$

PROBLEMS

12-59 A 3 kW motor operates at 675 r/min. If the shaft has a 15 mm diameter, calculate the maximum shear stress in the shaft.

12-60 A 200 mm diameter ship's shaft delivers 1200 kW of power to the propeller at 50 r/min. Determine the maximum shear stress in the shaft.

12-61 A hollow shaft with an outside diameter of 3 mm and a wall thickness of 1 mm is used to transmit power from a 25 W motor operating at 900 r/min. Calculate the maximum shear stress in the shaft.

12-62 Calculate the maximum shear stress in a 60 mm diameter hollow shaft with a 40 mm inside diameter used to transmit 20 kW at 300 r/min.

12-63 An 80 mm diameter shaft is to be used to transmit power. If it rotates at 150 r/min, and if the stress in it is not to exceed 45 MPa, calculate the maximum power it may transmit.

12-64 Determine the power that may be transmitted by a 4 mm diameter shaft rotating at

3500 r/min if the shear stress in the shaft is not to exceed 95 MPa.

12-65 A 10 mm diameter shaft with an inside diameter of 7 mm is used to transmit power from a motor operating at 880 r/min. If the allowable shear stress in the shaft is 75 MPa, determine the maximum power that may be transmitted by the shaft.

12-66 If the shear stress in a 120 mm diameter hollow shaft is not to exceed 90 MPa, determine the maximum power it may transmit when rotating at 120 r/min. The wall thickness of the shaft is 25 mm.

12-67 Calculate the minimum diameter of solid shaft required to transmit 50 kW at 200 r/min if the stress in the shaft is not to exceed 85 MPa.

12-68 A motor delivers 1500 W at 1760 r/min. If the motor has a solid shaft, determine the required shaft diameter if the shear stress in the shaft is not to exceed 50 MPa.

12-6 NONCIRCULAR SHAFTS

All the discussions in the preceeding articles in this chapter have related to torque acting on shafts with a circular cross section. If a shaft has a rectangular or other noncircular cross section, the equations developed here will not apply. The analysis of shear stress and deformation in noncircular shafts is very complex, and is beyond the scope of this book.

In general, the circular shaft is the most efficient method of transmitting a torque, in that it uses the least amount of material to transmit a given torque. Thus, the form of shaft which is usually the most practical to use is also the one in which the stress and deformation can be most easily analyzed.

13 FLEXURE

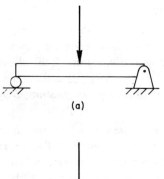

(a)

(b)

FIGURE 13-1

13-1 BEHAVIOR OF BEAMS

A beam is a member in which the load is applied perpendicular to the longitudinal axis of the member, as shown in Fig. 13-1(a). As a result of the transverse load, the beam bends or deforms, as shown in Fig. 13-1(b). In a large proportion of applications, beams are horizontal members, but it is quite possible to have an inclined or vertical load-carrying member that is a beam.

The overhead traveling crane shown in Fig. 13-2 is one example of a beam. In this case, the applied load is quite obvious. Not so obvious is the fact that, if there is too much bending in the crane girder or beam, the crane hoist will roll towards the low point in the girder, which is an undesirable, and possibly danger-ous, condition.

By now, one should realize that if a member deforms, there will be stress in the member (unless the deformation is due to thermal effects only). In the beam shown in Fig. 13-1, the defor-mation is due primarily to internal bending moments. The inter-nal bending moments cause flexural stress, which is a normal stress acting on the cross section of the beam. Flexural stress will be discussed in detail in Article 13-5. There are also internal shear forces acting in the beam shown in Fig. 13-1. Although shear forces generally do not contribute as much to the deforma-tion as the bending moments, the shear stress caused may be significant, and it is discussed in Article 13-7.

The maximum flexural stress usually occurs where the inter-nal bending moment is maximum, and the maximum shear stress usually occurs where the internal shear is maximum, so before investigating the stresses, it is first necessary to analyze the bending moments and shear forces that cause them.

13-2 SHEAR AND MOMENT AT A SECTION

A free-body diagram of a simply supported beam with a single load is shown in Fig. 13-3(a). If a section is cut through the beam

FIGURE 13-2 When designing the beams or girders of this overhead crane for the heavy loads it is to lift, both the stress and deformation must be determined. *Photo courtesy of Richards-Wilcox of Canada Limited.*

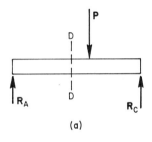

(a)

(b)

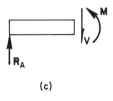

(c)

FIGURE 13-3

at *D-D*, a free-body diagram of the part of the beam to the left of *D-D* can be drawn, as shown in Fig. 13-3(b). To maintain equilibrium in the *y* direction, there must be some vertical force, **V**, on the cut section. This vertical force is called the shear on the section. Its magnitude and direction may be determined through the equilibrium equation $\Sigma F_y = 0$. If Fig. 13-3(b) is examined carefully, it will be observed that the free body is not in equilibrium, for the two forces shown form a couple. The only place that a resisting couple may exist to maintain equilibrium is on the cut section, as shown in Fig. 13-3(c). The couple is labeled

M, and it is called the *internal bending moment*, or just the moment. Strictly speaking it is a couple, but there are many generations of tradition of calling it a moment. The magnitude and direction of **M** may be obtained using the equilibrium equation $\Sigma M = 0$.

The calculation of the internal shear and bending moment at any point in a beam is necessary to determine the shear stress and flexural stress in a beam.

There is a sign convention for the internal shear and moment in a beam. It is based on the deformation caused by the shear and moment. Positive internal shear, as shown in Fig. 13-4(a), occurs when the shear force tends to make the part of the beam to its right move up or the part of the beam to its left move down. Conversely, if the shear force tends to make the part of the beam to its right move down or the part of the beam to its left move up, the shear is negative, as indicated in Fig. 13-4(b). A positive bending moment is one that places the top fibers of the beam in compression and the bottom fibers in tension, so that the beam is concave up, as shown in Fig. 13-4(c). The negative bending moment causes the beam to take the shape shown in Fig. 13-4(d), where the shape of the beam is concave down, since the top fiber is in tension and the bottom is in compression.

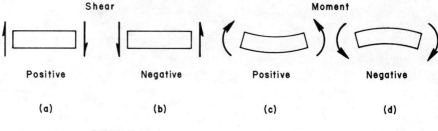

FIGURE 13-4

Note that when writing equilibrium equations in which the internal shear and moment occur, the usual rules of signs for equilibrium apply. That is, up is positive, down is negative, counterclockwise is positive, clockwise is negative. In the free-body diagrams drawn for internal shears and moments, the assumed direction of the internal shear and moment is always shown as positive, according to the internal shear and moment sign convention. The signs obtained when solving the equilibrium equations will always be the appropriate signs for the internal shear and moment, since a negative sign simply indicates that the actual direction is opposite to that assumed.

EXAMPLE 13-1

Find the shear and moment on sections at 2 m and 4 m from the left end for the beam shown in Fig. 13-5.

SOLUTION

To analyze internal forces in the beam, it will first be necessary to calculate the reaction at one support. If the part of the beam to the left of the section is used for calculating the shear and moment, then the left reaction will be required. Figure 13-6 is a free-body diagram of the whole beam used for calculating the reaction.

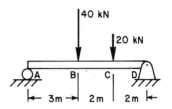

FIGURE 13-5

$$\Sigma M_D = 0$$

$$-(A_y \times 7) + 40 \times 4 + 20 \times 2 = 0$$

$$A_y = \frac{160.00 + 40.00}{7}$$

$$= \frac{200.00}{7}$$

$$= 28.571 \text{ kN}$$

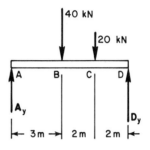

FIGURE 13-6

A free-body diagram of the part of the beam to the left of the section at 2 m is drawn to analyze the shear and moment on the section. The diagram is shown in Fig. 13-7. The assumed directions for V and M in the figure are positive, based on the sign convention for internal shears and moments. The magnitudes of V and M may be calculated using the equilibrium equations. Moments are usually taken about a point on the section, since this eliminates V from the moment equation. Distances to identify the location of the section are usually measured from the left end.

At x = 2m:

$$\Sigma F_y = 0$$

$$28.571 - V = 0$$

$$V = 28.571 \text{ kN}$$

$$\Sigma M_O = 0$$

$$-(28.571 \times 2) + M = 0$$

$$M = 57.142 \text{ kN} \cdot \text{m}$$

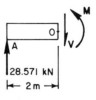

FIGURE 13-7

Both answers have positive values, indicating that the assumed directions for **V** and **M** are correct.

A new free-body diagram, as shown in Fig. 13-8, is drawn to show **V** and **M** on the section 4 m *right of the left end. Again, both* **V** *and* **M** *are drawn in the positive direction for internal shear and moment. The values for V and M can be obtained using the equilibrium equations. The moment is taken about a point on the section to eliminate V from the moment equation.*

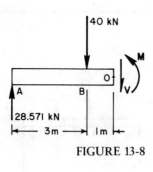

FIGURE 13-8

At x = 4 m:

$$\Sigma F_y = 0$$

$$28.571 - 40 - V = 0$$

$$V = 28.571 - 40.000$$

$$= -11.429 \text{ kN}$$

$$\Sigma M_o = 0$$

$$-(28.571 \times 4) + 40 \times 1 + M = 0$$

$$M = 114.284 - 40.000$$

$$= 74.284 \text{ kN} \cdot \text{m}$$

At x = 2 m
V = 28.6 kN
M = 57.1 kN·m
At x = 4 m
V = −11.4 kN
M = 74.3 kN·m

The negative sign for the shear at x = 4 m *indicates that the shear is opposite to that assumed, so it is actually a negative shear.*

EXAMPLE 13-2

Determine the shear and moment on sections 4 m and 6 m right of point *A* for the beam shown in Fig. 13-9.

SOLUTION

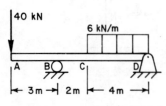

FIGURE 13-9

The reaction at B will be on the free-body diagram if a section is cut at 4 m or 6 m from the left end, and if the part of the beam to the left of the section is used for determining V and M. Thus, the reaction at B must be found. The free-body diagram shown in Fig. 13-10 is used for determining the reaction at B.

$$\Sigma M_D = 0$$

$$40 \times 9 - B_y \times 6 + 6 \times 4 \times 2 = 0$$

$$B_y = \frac{360.00 + 48.00}{6}$$

$$= \frac{408.00}{6}$$

$$= 68.00 \text{ kN}$$

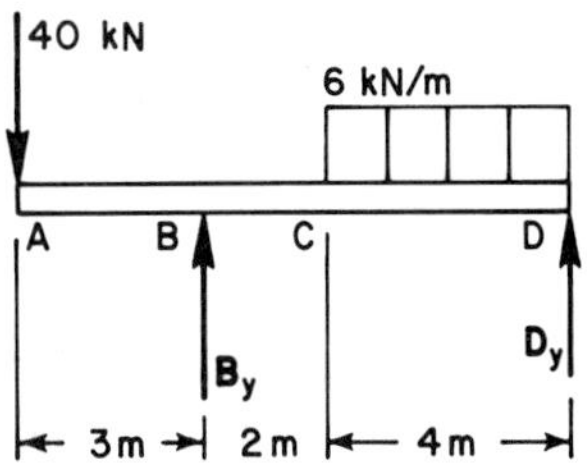

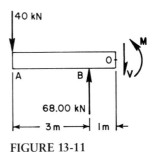

FIGURE 13-10

To find the shear and moment on the section 4 m right of A, a free-body diagram is drawn of the part of the beam to the left of the section, as shown in Fig. 13-11. *Both the shear and moment are assumed to have a positive direction, based on the sign convention for shears and moments. The values for V and M may be calculated using the equilibrium equations. Note that when the moment equation is used, moments are taken about a point on the section to eliminate V from the moment equation.*

At x = 4 m:

$$\Sigma F_y = 0$$

$$-40 + 68.00 - V = 0$$

$$V = -40.00 + 68.00$$

$$= 28.00 \text{ kN}$$

$$\Sigma M_O = 0$$

$$40 \times 4 - 68.00 \times 1 + M = 0$$

$$M = -160.00 + 68.00$$

$$= -92.00 \text{ kN} \cdot \text{m}$$

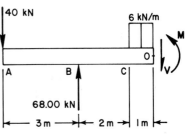

FIGURE 13-11

The negative sign with the value for M indicates that **M** *is opposite to the direction assumed. It is really a negative moment.*

Another free-body diagram, showing the part of the beam to the left of the section at 6 m, is necessary to calculate the shear and moment when x = 6 m. The free-body diagram is shown in Fig. 13-12.

As usual, the shear and moment are assumed to have a positive direction, according to the convention for shears and moments. The magnitude of the shear is calculated by summing forces in the y direction. Note that for the distributed load, only 1 m of load is acting on the free body, so only a 6 kN force will act on this free body due to the distributed load.

FIGURE 13-12

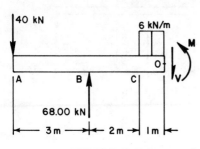

FIGURE 13-12 (*repeated*)

At x = 6 m:

$$\Sigma F_y = 0$$

$$-40 + 68.00 - 6 \times 1 - V = 0$$

$$V = -40.00 + 68.00 - 6.00$$

$$= 22.00 \text{ kN}$$

The bending moment at x = 6 m may be calculated using the moment equilibrium equation. To eliminate the moment due to V, moments are taken about a point on the section. The distributed load acts for only 1 m on the free body, and the distance from the center of gravity of the distributed load on the free body to the section is 0.5 m.

$$\Sigma M_O = 0$$

$$40 \times 6 - 68.00 \times 3 + 6 \times 1 \times 0.5 + M = 0$$

$$M = -240.00 + 204.00 - 3.00$$

$$= -39.00 \text{ kN} \cdot \text{m}$$

The negative value for M indicates that the moment is opposite in direction to the assumed direction; it is actually negative.

At x = 4 m
V = 28.0 kN
M = -92.0 kN·m
At x = 6 m
V = 22.0 kN
M = -39.0 kN·m

EXAMPLE 13-3

Evaluate the shear and moment on the sections just to the right of *B* and 1200 mm to the right of *A* in Fig. 13-13.

SOLUTION

Since this is a cantilever beam, there are no values for reactions that need to be calculated to the left of either of the sections. To find the shear and moment on the section just to the right of B, a free-body diagram is drawn of the part of the beam to the left of the section, as shown in Fig. 13-14. *Since the section is just to the right of B, the 500 N force is shown, but the length of the free body is taken as 400 mm. Both the shear and the moment are*

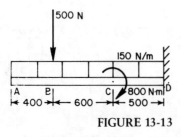

FIGURE 13-13

assumed to be positive, based on the shear and moment sign conventions. The value for V may be calculated by summing forces in the y direction. Note that on the free body, the distributed load is acting over a length of only 400 mm.

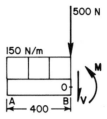

At x = 400+ mm:

$$\Sigma F_y = 0$$

$$-(150 \times 0.400) - 500 - V = 0$$

$$V = -60.00 - 500.00$$

$$= -560.00 \text{ N}$$

FIGURE 13-14

The negative sign for V indicates that the shear is actually opposite in direction to that assumed.

When calculating the moment, the axis of rotation is on the section so that **V** will cause no moment. The distance from the axis of rotation to the center of gravity of the distributed load acting on the free body is 200 mm.

$$\Sigma M_0 = 0$$

$$150 \times 0.400 \times 0.200 + M = 0$$

$$M = -12.00 \text{ N} \cdot \text{m}$$

As usual, the negative value for M indicates that it is opposite in direction to what was assumed.

To calculate the shear and moment on the section at x = 1200 mm, a free-body diagram of the part of the beam to the left of the section is drawn, as shown in Fig. 13-15. Both the shear and moment are assumed to be positive. The total distributed load on the free body acts over a length of 1200 mm. The torque has no effect on the shear. The shear is obtained by summing forces in the y direction.

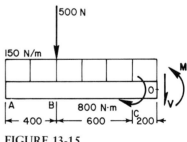

At x = 1200 mm:

$$\Sigma F_y = 0$$

$$-(150 \times 1.200) - 500 - V = 0$$

$$V = -180.00 - 500.00$$

$$= -680.00 \text{ N}$$

FIGURE 13-15

In calculating the value for M, moments are taken about an axis on the section to avoid the use of V. The distance from the center of gravity of the distributed load on the free body to the section is 600 mm. The couple at C is included in the moment calculation. Since the couple itself causes pure rotation, the distance from C to the section is not used.

$$\Sigma M_0 = 0$$

$$150 \times 1.200 \times 0.600 + 500 \times 0.800 - 800 + M = 0$$

$$M = -108.00 - 400.00 + 800.00$$

$$= 292.00 \text{ N} \cdot \text{m}$$

> At $x = 400+$ mm
> $V = -560$ N
> $M = -12.0$ N·m
> At $x = 1200$ mm
> $V = -680$ N
> $M = 292$ N·m

PROBLEMS

13-1 A beam 8 m long has a load of 40 kN applied at a distance of 5 m from the left end. Determine the shear and bending moment at distances of 3 m and 6 m from the left end. The beam is supported by a roller at the left end and a pin at the right end.

13-2 Find the shear and moment at sections 200 mm and 500 mm from the left end for a beam 600 mm long. The beam has a pin support at the left end and a roller support at the right, and it carries a load of 300 N 400 mm from the left end.

13-3 A beam 1300 mm long has a roller support at the left end and a pin at the right. If there is a 450 N load 500 mm from the left end, determine the shear and moment on sections at 400 mm and 800 mm from the left end.

13-4 A beam 5 m long has a 75 kN load 2 m from the left end. Determine the shear and moment at sections 1 m and 4 m from the left end if the beam has a roller support at the left end and a pin support at the right end.

13-5 For the beam shown in Fig. P13-5, determine the shear and moment on sections 4 m and 7 m from the left end.

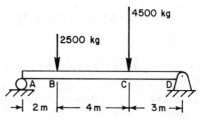

FIGURE P13-5

13-6 Calculate the shear and moment at sections 4 m and 6 m right of *A* for the beam shown in Fig. P13-6.

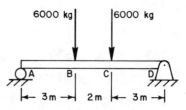

FIGURE P13-6

13-7 A beam 3 m long has a uniformly distributed load of 80 kN/m. Find the shear and moment on the sections 1 m and 2 m from the left end. The left end of the beam is supported by a roller and the right end is supported by a pin.

13-8 Find the shear and moment on sections 300 mm and 500 mm from the left end for a beam 900 mm long that has a uniform load of 400 N/m. A pin supports the left end of the beam and the right end is supported by a roller.

13-9 Calculate the shear and moment on sections just to the left of B and 900 mm right of A for the beam shown in Fig. P13-9.

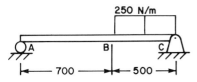

FIGURE P13-9

13-10 For the beam shown in Fig. P13-10, determine the shear and moment 2 m to the right of A and just to the right of B.

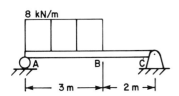

FIGURE P13-10

13-11 For the beam shown in Fig. P13-11, calculate the shear and moment 500 mm right of A and just to the left of C.

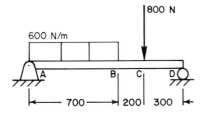

FIGURE P13-11

13-12 Find the shear and moment at a section just to the right of B and at a section 7 m to the right of A for the beam shown in Fig. P13-12.

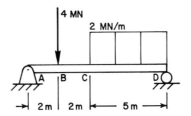

FIGURE P13-12

13-13 Find the shear and moment at sections 1 m and 4 m to the right of A for the beam shown in Fig. P13-13.

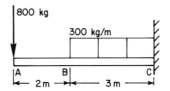

FIGURE P13-13

13-14 For the beam shown in Fig. P13-14, calculate the shear and moment at sections 400 mm and 700 mm to the right of A.

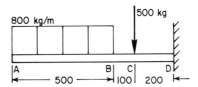

FIGURE P13-14

13-15 Find the shear and moment on sections just to the left of C and 1100 mm right of A for the beam shown in Fig. P13-15.

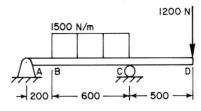

FIGURE P13-15

13-16 Determine the shear and moment on sections just to the left of C and 8 m right of A for the beam shown in Fig. P13-16.

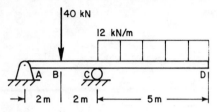

FIGURE P13-16

13-17 Determine the shear and bending moment for the beam shown in Fig. P13-17 at sections 3 m, 5 m and 6 m right of A.

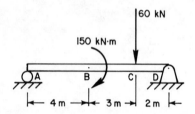

FIGURE P13-17

13-18 For sections 7 m and 9 m right of A, calculate the shear and moment for the beam shown in Fig. P13-18.

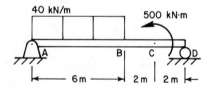

FIGURE P13-18

13-19 For the beam shown in Fig. P13-19, find the shear and moment on sections 100 mm, 1000 mm and 1500 mm right of A.

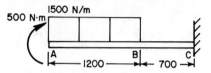

FIGURE P13-19

13-20 Find the shear and moment on sections 100 mm, 400 mm and 800 mm right of A for the beam shown in Fig. P13-20.

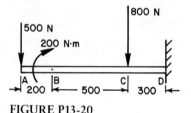

FIGURE P13-20

13-3 SHEAR AND MOMENT EQUATIONS

From the examples and problems of Article 13-2, it appears that the internal shear and moment on sections in a beam will vary depending on the location of the section along the beam. One method of evaluating the shear or moment at any section in a beam is to write the shear and moment equations for the beam. If the equations are plotted, it is then possible to determine the maximum numeric values for *V* and *M*. The maximum values are important, because the shear stress and flexural stress will be maximum when *V* and *M* are maximum in a beam with a uniform cross section.

Writing equations for *V* and *M* differs very little from the process of calculating *V* and *M* at a specific section. The only significant difference is that the distance from the reference point will be *x*, as shown in Fig. 13-16, instead of a specified value. Generally, it will require more than one equation to describe either the shear or moment, because each time there is a loading change on the free body a new equation will be required for the interval from that load change to the next change in load. In Fig. 13-17(a), a free-body diagram of a beam is shown. The free-body diagram shown in Fig. 13-17(b) is correct for any value of *x* between 0 and *a*. Similarly, the free-body diagram shown in Fig. 13-17(c) is correct for any value of *x* between *a* and (*a* + *b*). Thus, one shear equation and one moment equation will be valid for the interval $0 \le x \le a$, and a second shear and moment equation will be required for the interval $a \le x \le (a + b)$.

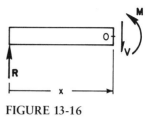

FIGURE 13-16

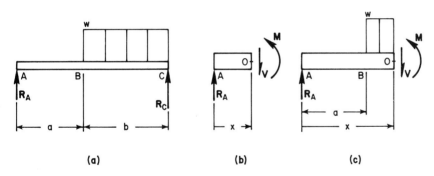

FIGURE 13-17

EXAMPLE 13-4

Write the shear and moment equations for the beam shown in Fig. 13-18. Plot the equations for the shear and moment.

SOLUTION

It will be necessary to calculate the value of the reaction at B for part of the solution, so it may as well be calculated now. The value for the reaction at C will be needed as a check and to complete the plot of the shear and moment equations. The free-body diagram shown in Fig. 13-19 *is used for calculating the reactions.*

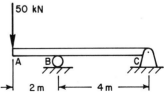

FIGURE 13-18

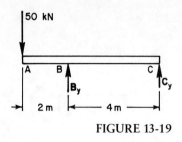

FIGURE 13-19

$$\Sigma \ M_C = 0$$

$$50 \times 6 - B_y \times 4 = 0$$

$$B_y = \frac{50 \times 6}{4}$$

$$= 75.000 \text{ kN}$$

$$\Sigma \ F_y = 0$$

$$-50 + 75.000 + C_y = 0$$

$$C_y = 50.000 - 75.000$$

$$= -25.000 \text{ kN}$$

To write the shear and moment equations, it is necessary to first decide which part of the beam should be shown in the free-body diagram. A section cut between A and B, as shown in Fig. 13-20, would be the same for any section between A and B, so the equations written will be valid between x = 0 m and x = 2 m. Equilibrium equations may then be written for this region to determine V and M. As usual, the moment is taken about an axis on the section.

FIGURE 13-20

For $0 \le x \le 2$ m

$$\Sigma \ F_y = 0$$

$$-50 - V = 0$$

$$V = -50.00 \text{ (kN)}$$

$$\Sigma \ M_O = 0$$

$$50 \times x + M = 0$$

$$M = -50.00x \text{ (kN·m)}$$

For the next region for which one set of equations would be valid, a section is cut between B and C, as shown in Fig. 13-21. The free-body diagram shown in Fig. 13-21 is valid everywhere between B and C, or when x has values between 2 m and 6 m. The equilibrium equations can be used to develop equations for V and M.

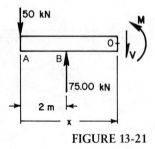

FIGURE 13-21

For $2 \le x \le 6$ m

$$\Sigma \ F_y = 0$$

$$-50 + 75.00 - V = 0$$

$$V = -50.00 + 75.00$$

$$= 25.00 \text{ (kN)}$$

$$\Sigma M_O = 0$$

$$50 \times x - 75.00 (x - 2) + M = 0$$

$$M = -50.00x + 75.00 (x - 2) \ (kN \cdot m)$$

Although it is not normal mathematical practice to leave an equation in the form shown for the moment equation, it is common practice in stress analysis.

For $0 \le x \le 2$ m:
 $V = -50.0$ (kN)
 $M = -50.0x$ (kN·m)
For $2 \le x \le 6$ m:
 $V = 25.0$ (kN)
 $M = -50.0x + 75.0(x - 2)$ (kN·m)

The shear and moment equations may be plotted by evaluating the equations at 1 m intervals, as shown in the table below.

x	0	1	2	2	3	4	5	6
V	-50.0	-50.0	-50.0	25.0	25.0	25.0	25.0	25.0
M	0.0	-50.0	-100.0	-100.0	-75.0	-50.0	-25.0	0.0

$\longleftarrow 0 \le x \le 2 \longrightarrow \! \longleftarrow \qquad 2 \le x \le 6 \longrightarrow$

Two values for V and M are shown when x = 2 m, since there is a change in loading at this point. The shear and moment equations are plotted in Fig. 13-22. Shear and moment diagrams always start and end at zero, although there may be an abrupt change at the ends due to concentrated loads such as those that occur at the supports.

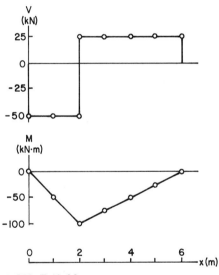

FIGURE 13-22

EXAMPLE 13-5

For the beam shown in Fig. 13-23, write the shear and moment equations and plot the curves for the equations.

SOLUTION

The first step in solving the problem is to calculate the reactions at A and C. The free-body diagram shown in Fig. 13-24 is used for this purpose.

$$\Sigma M_C = 0$$

$$-(A_y \times 8) + 2 \times 8 \times 4 + 6 \times 3 = 0$$

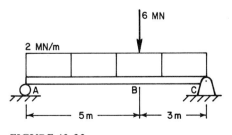

FIGURE 13-23

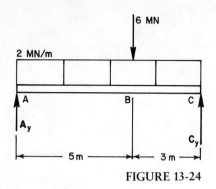

FIGURE 13-24

$$A_y = \frac{64.00 + 18.00}{8}$$

$$= \frac{82.00}{8}$$

$$= 10.25 \text{ MN}$$

$$\Sigma F_y = 0$$

$$10.25 - 2 \times 8 - 6 + C_y = 0$$

$$C_y = -10.25 + 16.00 + 6.00$$

$$= 11.75 \text{ MN}$$

There is no change in loading on the beam between A and B, so the first section is cut between $x = 0$ m and $x = 5$ m, as shown in Fig. 13-25. The equations for V and M may be obtained using the equilibrium equations.

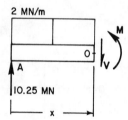

FIGURE 13-25

$$\text{For } 0 \leq x \leq 5 \text{ m:}$$

$$\Sigma F_y = 0$$

$$10.25 - 2 \times x - V = 0$$

$$V = 10.25 - 2x \text{ (MN)}$$

When writing the moment equation, the distance from the center of the distributed load on the free body to the axis of rotation at 0 will be $x/2$.

$$\Sigma M_0 = 0$$

$$-(10.25 \times x) + 2 \times x \times \frac{x}{2} + M = 0$$

$$M = 10.25x - x^2 \text{ (MN·m)}$$

Since there is a change in loading at B due to the 6 MN load, a new free-body diagram is required for the region from $x = 5$ m to $x = 8$ m. This is shown in Fig. 13-26. The equilibrium equations may be used for determining the equations for the shear and moment.

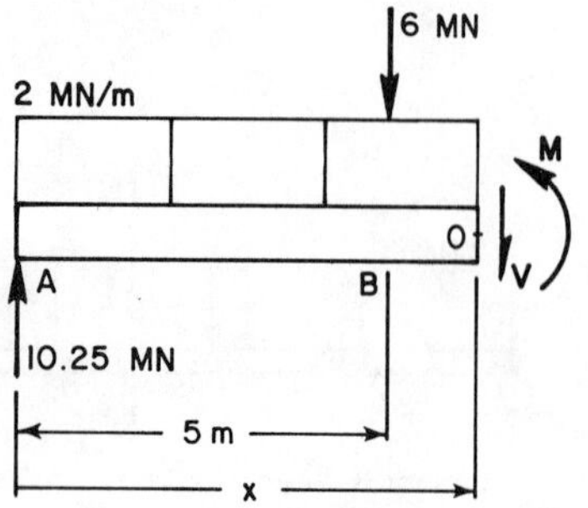

$$\text{For } 5 \leq x \leq 8 \text{ m:}$$

$$\Sigma F_y = 0$$

$$10.25 - 2 \times x - 6 - V = 0$$

$$V = 10.25 - 6 - 2x$$

$$= 4.25 - 2x \text{ (MN)}$$

FIGURE 13-26

$$\Sigma M_O = 0$$

$$-(10.25 \times x) + 2 \times x \times \frac{x}{2} + 6(x - 5) + M = 0$$

$$M = 10.25x - 6(x - 5) - x^2 \text{ (MN·m)}$$

As pointed out previously, it is customary to leave the equations in this form, including the term $(x - 5)$, instead of simplifying it further, as would usually be done in algebra.

For $0 \le x \le 5$ m:
$$V = 10.2 - 2x \text{ (MN)}$$
$$M = 10.2x - x^2 \text{ (MN·m)}$$
For $5 \le x \le 8$ m:
$$V = 4.25 - 2x \text{ (MN)}$$
$$M = 10.2x - 6(x - 5) - x^2 \text{ (MN·m)}$$

To plot the shear and moment equations, values for V and M are calculated at 1 m intervals. Since both sets of equations apply when $x = 5$ m, two values are calculated at this point, one for each equation.

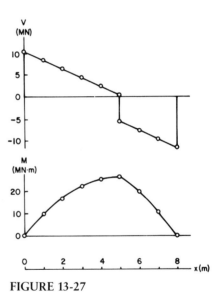

x	0	1	2	3	4	5	5	6	7	8
V	10.2	8.2	6.2	4.2	2.2	0.2	−5.8	−7.8	−9.8	−11.8
M	0.0	9.2	16.5	21.8	25.0	26.2	26.2	19.5	10.8	0.0

|← ———————— $0 \le x \le 5$ ————————→|← ———— $5 \le x \le 8$ ————→|

The equations are plotted, as shown in Fig. 13-27. The maximum values for the shear and bending moment can be readily picked off the plots of the equations shown in Fig. 13-27.

Both the shear and the moment must be zero at the ends of the beam. However, there may be an abrupt change due to a concentrated load, such as is caused by the supports. The concentrated load at B also causes an abrupt change in shear, as shown in the plot of the equations.

FIGURE 13-27

PROBLEMS

13-21 through **13-30**: For Figs. P13-21 through P13-30, (a) write the shear and moment equations and (b) plot the shear and moment equations.

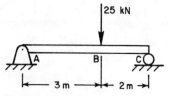

FIGURE P13-21

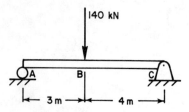

FIGURE P13-22

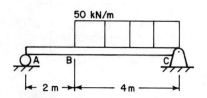

FIGURE P13-23

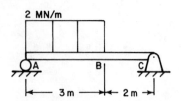

FIGURE P13-24

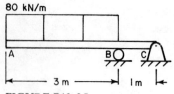

FIGURE P13-25

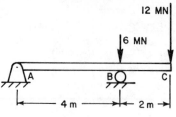

FIGURE P13-26

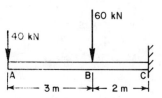

FIGURE P13-27

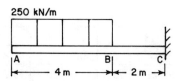

FIGURE P13-28

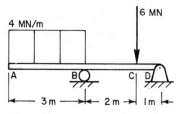

FIGURE P13-29

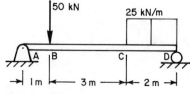

FIGURE P13-30

13-4 SHEAR AND MOMENT DIAGRAMS

When analyzing the stresses in beams, the maximum shear stress and the maximum flexural stress are critical. In general, the maximum shear stress will occur where the internal shear is maximum, and the maximum flexural stress will occur where the bending moment is maximum. Usually, the absolute maximum values for the shear and moment — the largest values without regard to sign — are sought.

The equations for shear and moment may be plotted to find the maximum values. However, another technique permits fairly quick construction of complete, accurate shear and moment diagrams; the technique uses some concepts from basic mathematics.

A beam with a distributed load is shown in Fig. 13-28(a). The forces on a small section of the beam, with a length of Δx, are to be analyzed. The small section is shown to a larger scale in Fig. 13-28(b). Since the shear and moment will vary along the length of the beam, the shear at the right end of the section is shown as $V + \Delta V$ and the moment is shown as $M + \Delta M$, to show that it is different from the shear and moment on the left end. From the section of beam shown in Fig. 13-28(b), the following relationship may be obtained.

$$\Sigma F_y = 0$$

$$V - w(\Delta x) - (V + \Delta V) = 0$$

$$V - w(\Delta x) - V - \Delta V = 0$$

$$-w(\Delta x) - \Delta V = 0$$

$$\Delta V = -w(\Delta x) \qquad (13\text{-}1)$$

$$\frac{\Delta V}{\Delta x} = -w \qquad (13\text{-}2)$$

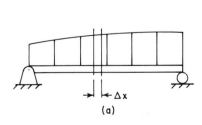

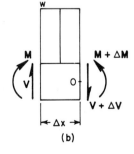

(a)   (b)

FIGURE 13-28

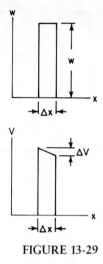

FIGURE 13-29

It is the interpretation of Eqs. (13-1) and (13-2) that is important, rather than just the equations by themselves. From Eq. (13-1) the change in shear ΔV between two points on a beam is equal to the negative of the product of the height of the load diagram w and the distance Δx between the two points on the beam. If Δx is small, the product $w(\Delta x)$ is actually the area of the load diagram between the two points on the beam, as indicated in Fig. 13-29. This leads to the first guideline for drawing shear and moment diagrams.

    1. The change in shear between any two points on a beam is equal to the negative of the area of the load diagram between the same two points on the beam. (Areas above the x axis will cause a negative change in shear.)

The expression $\Delta V/\Delta x$ is the slope of the shear diagram. Thus Eq. (13-2) indicates that the slope of the shear diagram at any point is equal to the negative of the height of the load diagram at the same point. Note that the slope of the shear diagram shown in Fig. 13-29 is negative where the load diagram has a positive value. The second guideline may be expressed as

    2. The slope of the shear diagram at any point on the beam is equal to the negative of the height of the load diagram at that point.

To develop a relationship between shears and moments, refer again to Fig. 13-28(b).

$$\Sigma M_O = 0$$

$$-M - V(\Delta x) + w(\Delta x)\frac{(\Delta x)}{2} + (M + \Delta M) = 0$$

$$-V(\Delta x) + \frac{w(\Delta x)^2}{2} + \Delta M = 0$$

If Δx is a very small number, then as Δx becomes very close to zero, $(\Delta x)^2$ becomes so close to zero that it may be neglected. The equation then becomes

$$-V(\Delta x) + \Delta M = 0$$

$$\Delta M = V(\Delta x) \tag{13-3}$$

$$\frac{\Delta M}{\Delta x} = V \tag{13-4}$$

Equation (13-3) states that the change in moment between any two points on a beam is equal to the product of the height of the shear diagram V times the distance Δx between the two points. This product, as may be observed from Fig. 13-30, is actually the area of the shear diagram between the two points, if Δx is

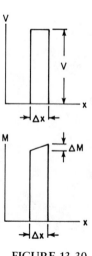

FIGURE 13-30

small. This leads to the third guideline for drawing shear and moment diagrams.

3. The change in moment between any two points on a beam is equal to the area of the shear diagram between the same two points on the beam. (Areas above the x-axis will cause a positive change in moment and areas below will cause a negative change.)

In Eq. (13-4), $\Delta M/\Delta x$ is the slope of the moment diagram. Thus, at any point on the beam the slope of the moment diagram is equal to the height of the shear diagram at the same point on the beam. This leads to a fourth guideline.

4. The slope of the moment diagram at any point on the beam is equal to the height of the shear diagram at the same point.

In load diagrams, there are frequently concentrated loads, and there is sometimes a torque or couple applied at a point. This leads to two more guidelines.

5. A concentrated load on a beam will cause an abrupt change in the shear diagram at the point of application of the load equal to the concentrated load. The change will have the same sign as the shear due to the concentrated load.

6. A torque or couple applied to a point on a beam will cause an abrupt change in the moment at the point of application equal to the torque. The sign of the change will be the same as that of the bending moment due to the applied torque.

The torque or couple (usually called a moment) that exists at the support of a cantilever beam is analyzed as if it were applied at a point on the beam adjacent to the support, and is treated as described in guideline 6.

One other mathematical relationship is very useful when drawing moment diagrams. In many instances, there will be a point on the shear diagram where $V = 0$. It follows that, at this same point, the slope of the moment diagram is zero, since $\Delta M/\Delta x = V$. Whenever a curve has a maximum or minimum value, it has a slope of zero. Thus where the shear diagram has a value of zero, the moment diagram will have a maximum or minimum value.

EXAMPLE 13-6

Draw the shear and moment diagrams for the beam shown in Fig. 13-31. Note the location and maximum value for both the shear and the moment.

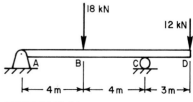

FIGURE 13-31

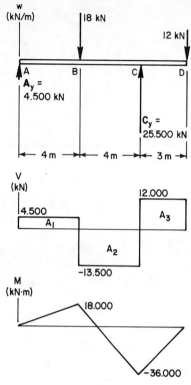

FIGURE 13-32

SOLUTION

It is necessary to start with a free-body diagram of the beam, as shown at the top of Fig. 13-32, to calculate the reactions. The free-body diagram is actually the load diagram; it should be drawn so that there will be space for the shear and moment diagrams underneath. The load, shear and moment diagrams should all be drawn to scale.

$$\Sigma M_A = 0$$

$$-(18 \times 4) + C_y \times 8 - 12 \times 11 = 0$$

$$C_y = \frac{72.000 + 132.000}{8}$$

$$= \frac{204.000}{8}$$

$$= 25.500 \text{ kN}$$

$$\Sigma F_y = 0$$

$$A_y - 18 + 25.500 - 12 = 0$$

$$A_y = 30.000 - 25.500$$

$$= 4.500 \text{ kN}$$

The shear diagram is now constructed underneath the load diagram, as shown in Fig. 13-32. The shear diagram always starts at zero.

At A:

$$V = 0.000 \text{ kN}$$

At the left end of the beam, there is a concentrated load of 4.500 kN due to the reaction at A causing positive shear. This causes an abrupt change in the shear diagram from zero to 4.500 kN at the left end.

At A:

$$V = 4.500 \text{ kN}$$

Between the left end and point B there is no load shown on the load diagram. Thus the area under the load diagram between A and B is zero. Therefore the change in shear between A and B, which is equal to the negative of the area of the load diagram, is equal to zero. Thus the shear is constant from A to B.

At B:

$$V = 4.500 \text{ kN}$$

At B there is another concentrated load causing a negative shear. This will cause a change in shear of –18 kN, which will cause a drop on the shear diagram. The new value of the shear at B will be calculated as follows:

At B:

$$V = 4.500 - 18.000$$

$$= -13.500 \text{ kN}$$

Since there is no area under the load diagram between B and C, there is no change in shear between B and C.

At C:

$$V = -13.500 \text{ kN}$$

At C there is another concentrated load causing a positive shear of 25.500 kN. This will cause an abrupt change in the shear diagram. The new shear at C may then be calculated.

At C:

$$V = -13.500 + 25.500$$

$$= 12.000 \text{ kN}$$

From C to D there is no area under the load diagram, so there is no change in the shear between these two points.

At D:

$$V = 12.000 \text{ kN}$$

At D there is a negative shear of 12.000 kN, which causes an abrupt change in the shear diagram. The new shear at D is then calculated.

At D:

$$V = 12.000 - 12.000$$

$$= 0.000 \text{ kN}$$

The shear diagram should close (return to zero at the right end). This is a check on the calculations.

The moment diagram may now be drawn, as shown at the bottom of Fig. 13-32. *At the left end of the beam there is no moment.*

At A:

$$M = 0.000 \text{ kN} \cdot \text{m}$$

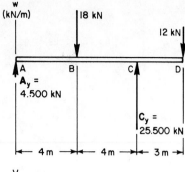

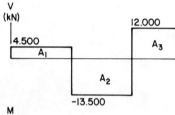

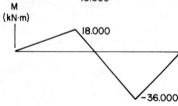

FIGURE 13-32 *(repeated)*

The change in moment between A and B is equal to the area of the shear diagram between A and B, which is A_1.

$$A_1 = 4 \times 4.500$$

$$= 18.000 \text{ kN} \cdot \text{m}$$

The value for the moment at B is now determined.

At B:

$$M = 0.000 + 18.000$$

$$= 18.000 \text{ kN} \cdot \text{m}$$

The height of the shear diagram between A and B has a constant value of 4.500 kN. Thus the slope of the moment diagram must be constant between A and B. Only a straight line has constant slope, so the two points on the moment diagram are joined by a straight line with a slope of 4.500 kN.

The change in moment between B and C is the area of the shear diagram between B and C. Since the area is below the axis, it is a negative area, shown as A_2.

$$A_2 = -(4 \times 13.500)$$

$$= -54.000 \text{ kN} \cdot \text{m}$$

This change in moment between B and C is used to calculate the value for the moment at C.

At C:

$$M = 18.000 - 54.000$$

$$= -36.000 \text{ kN} \cdot \text{m}$$

The height of the shear diagram between B and C is constant (−13.500 kN) so the slope of the moment diagram between B and C will also be constant, which means that there must be a straight line between points B and C on the beam for the moment diagram.

The change in moment between C and D is equal to the area A_3 of the shear diagram between C and D.

$$A_3 = 3 \times 12.000$$

$$= 36.000 \text{ kN} \cdot \text{m}$$

Thus the moment at D will be obtained from

At D:

$$M = -36.000 + 36.000$$

$$= 0.000 \text{ kN} \cdot \text{m}$$

Between C and D, the shear diagram has a constant height of 12.000 kN, so the slope of the moment diagram will also have a constant value of 12.000, and will thus be a straight line.

Generally, the moment diagram should close (except for very small errors that may be due to rounding off). If the moment diagram does not close, this is an indication that there is an error in the procedure. For the shear and moment diagrams to be most useful, values should be noted on the diagram, as shown. The results should be summarized by a statement of maximum values, along with their location.

$$V_{max} = -13.5 \text{ kN}$$
$$\text{at } 4.00 \le x \le 8.00 \text{ m}$$
$$M_{max} = -36.0 \text{ kN} \cdot \text{m}$$
$$\text{at } x = 8.00 \text{ m}$$

EXAMPLE 13-7

For the beam shown in Fig. 13-33, draw the shear and moment diagrams. Note the magnitude and location of the maximum shear and moment.

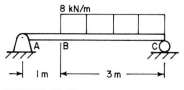

FIGURE 13-33

SOLUTION

The first step in solving the problem is to draw a free-body diagram of the beam, as shown at the top of Fig. 13-34, and to calculate the reactions at the supports for the beam. The free-body diagram is also the load diagram. It should be drawn so that the shear and moment diagrams may be drawn directly underneath. It is advisable to have all these drawings to scale.

$$\Sigma M_A = 0$$

$$-(8 \times 3 \times 2.5) + C_y \times 4 = 0$$

$$C_y = \frac{8 \times 3 \times 2.5}{4}$$

$$= 15.000 \text{ kN}$$

$$\Sigma F_y = 0$$

$$A_y - 8 \times 3 + 15.000 = 0$$

$$A_y = 24.000 - 15.000$$

$$= 9.000 \text{ kN}$$

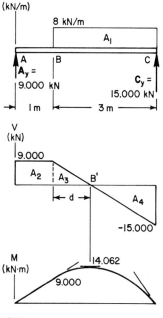

FIGURE 13-34

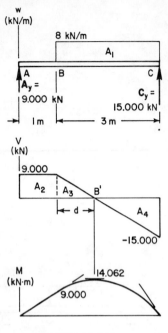

FIGURE 13-34 (*repeated*)

The process continues with the drawing of the shear diagram beneath the load diagram. The shear diagram always starts at zero.

At A:

$$V = 0.000 \text{ kN}$$

Referring to Fig. 13-34, it is seen that at A there is a concentrated load caused by the support. There is an abrupt change in the shear diagram at A due to this concentrated load.

At A:

$$V = 9.000 \text{ kN}$$

Between A and B there is no load, so the area of the load diagram between A and B is equal to zero, and thus the shear has no change between A and B.

At B:

$$V = 9.000 \text{ kN}$$

Between B and C there is a uniform load. The change in shear between B and C is equal to the negative of the area of the load diagram between B and C, and is A_i in the load diagram.

$$A_1 = -(8 \times 3)$$

$$= -24.000 \text{ kN}$$

The value for the shear at C may now be calculated.

At C:

$$V = 9.000 - 24.000$$

$$= -15.000 \text{ kN}$$

The slope of the shear diagram between B and C is the negative of the height of the load diagram, which is −8.00. Since the slope is constant between the two points, there must be a straight line between B and C in the shear diagram.

At C there is also a 15.000 kN concentrated load causing a positive shear. The shear at the end of the beam is now calculated.

At C:

$$V = -15.000 + 15.000$$

$$= 0.000 \text{ kN}$$

Since the shear diagram closes, or returns to zero, calculations up to this point may be correct. If the shear diagram does not close, find and correct the error before proceeding with the moment diagram.

The moment diagram is now drawn under the shear diagram, as shown at the bottom of Fig. 13-34. The moment on the left end of the beam starts at zero.

At A:

$$M = 0.000 \text{ kN·m}$$

The change in moment from A to B is equal to the area of the shear diagram between the same two points, and is shown as A_2.

$$A_2 = 1 \times 9.000$$

$$= 9.000 \text{ kN·m}$$

The value of the moment at B may now be obtained.

At B:

$$M = 0.000 + 9.000$$

$$= 9.000 \text{ kN·m}$$

The height of the shear diagram between A and B is 9.000 kN, which is also the slope of the moment diagram between the same two points. The constant value for the slope of the moment diagram means that the moment diagram must be a straight line between A and B.

To continue with constructing the moment diagram, some observations must be made about the shear diagram. It crosses the axis at a point labelled B'. Since the slope of the moment diagram is equal to the height of the shear diagram at B', the moment diagram at B' has zero slope, and hence must be a maximum or minimum value at this point. Both the location of the point and the value of the moment at the point are important, so the location of B' must be accurately determined. The two triangles between B and C in the shear diagram are similar triangles; this fact may be used to evaluate the distance d.

From similar triangles:

$$\frac{9.000}{15.000} = \frac{d}{3 - d}$$

$$27.000 - 9.000 \text{ d} = 15.000 \text{ d}$$

$$24.000 \text{ d} = 27.000$$

$$d = \frac{27.000}{24.000}$$

$$= 1.125 \text{ m}$$

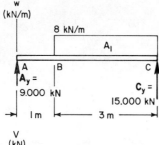

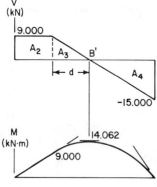

FIGURE 13-34 (*repeated*)

The change in moment between B and B' is equal to the area of the shear diagram A_3 between the same two points.

$$A_3 = \frac{1}{2} \times 1.125 \times 9.000$$

$$= 5.062 \text{ kN} \cdot \text{m}$$

The value for the moment at B' may now be calculated.

At B':

M = 9.000 + 5.062

= 14.062 kN·m

At B, the height of the shear diagram is 9.000 kN, so the slope of the moment diagram at B is 9.000. At B', the height of the shear diagram is zero, so the slope of the moment diagram at B' will also be zero. The only curve that will pass through the two points at B and B' and that will have the correct slopes at the points must be concave up, as shown in the moment diagram of Fig. 13-34.

The change in moment between B' and C is equal to the area of the shear diagram between B' and C. The area is labelled A_4. The length of the base of the triangle is (3 – 1.125) m.

$$A_4 = -\frac{1}{2} \times (3 - 1.125) \times 15.000$$

$$= -14.062 \text{ kN} \cdot \text{m}$$

The moment at C may now be determined.

At C:

M = 14.062 – 14.062

= 0.000 kN·m

The slope of the moment diagram at B' must be zero, and at C it must be –15.000. Only a curve that is concave up will fit the two points and the tangents at the two points. The moment diagram returned to zero, or closed, at C. This is a good indication that the shear and moment diagrams have been correctly calculated and drawn.

$V_{max} = -15.0 \text{ kN}$
at x = 4.00 m
$M_{max} = 14.1 \text{ kN} \cdot \text{m}$
at x = 2.12 m

EXAMPLE 13-8

Construct the shear and moment diagrams and determine the magnitude and location of the maximum shear and moment for the beam shown in Fig. 13-35.

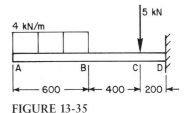

FIGURE 13-35

SOLUTION

The first step for the solution of most shear and moment diagram problems is to draw a free-body diagram of the beam and to calculate the reactions at the supports. The free-body diagram is shown at the top of Fig. 13-36. *It is used as an aid for calculating the reactions. Note that the shear and moment diagrams should be constructed so that they are directly below the free-body or load diagram.*

$$\Sigma F_y = 0$$

$$-(0.600 \times 4) - 5 + D_y = 0$$

$$D_y = 2.400 + 5.000$$

$$= 7.400 \text{ kN}$$

$$\Sigma M_D = 0$$

$$0.600 \times 4 \times 0.900 + 5 \times 0.200 + M_S = 0$$

$$M_S = -2.160 - 1.000$$

$$= -3.160 \text{ kN} \cdot \text{m}$$

The shear diagram, as shown in Fig. 13-36, *starts with zero shear at the left end.*

At A:

$$V = 0.000 \text{ kN}$$

The change in shear between A and B is equal to the negative of the area of the load diagram between A and B. The load diagram is also the free-body diagram. The area is shown as A_1.

$$A_1 = -(0.600 \times 4)$$

$$= -2.400 \text{ kN}$$

The shear at B is now known.

At B:

$$V = 0.000 - 2.400$$

$$= -2.400 \text{ kN}$$

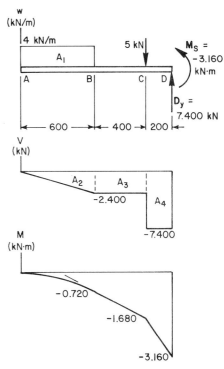

FIGURE 13-36

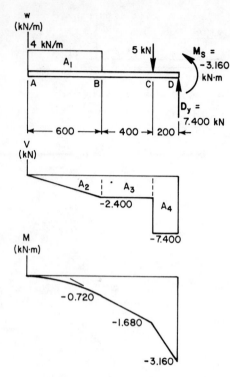

FIGURE 13-36 (*repeated*)

The load diagram has a constant height between A and B, so the shear diagram must have a constant slope between the same points. Thus it is a straight line.

There is no load between B and C, so there is no change in shear between B and C.

At C:

$$V = -2.400 \text{ kN}$$

At C there is a concentrated load of 5 kN, which will cause an abrupt change in shear of –5 kN.

At C:

$$V = -2.400 - 5.000$$
$$= -7.400 \text{ kN}$$

There is no load on the beam between C and D, so there is no change in shear between these two points.

At D:

$$V = -7.400 \text{ kN}$$

At the support at D, there is a concentrated load that was found to be 7.400 kN. Thus the final value for the shear at D may now be found.

At D:

$$V = -7.400 + 7.400$$
$$= 0.000 \text{ kN}$$

Once the shear diagram is complete, the moment diagram may be drawn beneath the load and shear diagrams, as shown in Fig. 13-36. The moment diagram always starts at zero.

At A:

$$M = 0.000 \text{ kN·m}$$

The change in moment between A and B is equal to the area of the shear diagram between A and B, shown as A_2.

$$A_2 = -\left(\frac{1}{2} \times 0.600 \times 2.400\right)$$
$$= -0.720 \text{ kN·m}$$

The value for the moment at B may now be determined.

At B:

$$M = 0.000 - 0.720$$

$$= -0.720 \text{ kN} \cdot \text{m}$$

The height of the shear diagram at A is zero, so the slope of the moment diagram at A must also be zero. At B the height of the shear diagram is −2.400 kN, so the slope of the moment diagram at B is −2.400. The only curve that will fit the two points and slopes is concave up, as shown in **Fig. 13-36.**

The change in moment between B and C is equal to the area A_3 of the shear diagram between B and C.

$$A_3 = -(0.400 \times 2.400)$$

$$= -0.960 \text{ kN} \cdot \text{m}$$

The value of the moment at C may now be determined.

At C:

$$M = -0.720 - 0.960$$

$$= -1.680 \text{ kN} \cdot \text{m}$$

Since the height of the shear diagram is constant between B and C, the slope of the moment diagram between B and C will be constant, or a straight line.

The change in moment between C and D is equal to the area of the shear diagram between C and D, which is A_4.

$$A_4 = -(0.200 \times 7.400)$$

$$= -1.480 \text{ kN} \cdot \text{m}$$

The moment at D may now be calculated.

At D:

$$M = -1.680 - 1.480$$

$$= -3.160 \text{ kN} \cdot \text{m}$$

The height of the shear diagram between C and D is constant, so the slope of the moment diagram between C and D must be constant, which gives a straight line.

The moment due to the support is a clockwise moment of 3.160 kN·m. Such a moment, if applied to the beam immediately to the left of the support, would put the top fiber in compression and the bottom fiber in tension, so it would be a positive bending moment.

The final moment at the right end will be found as follows:

At D:

$$M = -3.160 + 3.160$$

$$= 0.000 \text{ kN} \cdot \text{m}$$

The fact that the moment diagram does end at zero suggests that the moment diagram, along with the shear diagram, is probably correct.

$$V_{max} = 7.40 \text{ kN}$$
$$\text{at } 1.00 \leq x \leq 1.20 \text{ m}$$
$$M_{max} = -3.16 \text{ kN·m}$$
$$\text{at } x = 1.20 \text{ m}$$

EXAMPLE 13-9

For the beam shown in Fig. 13-37, draw the shear and moment diagrams, and note the magnitude and location of the maximum shear and moment.

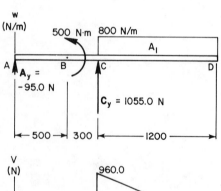

FIGURE 13-37

SOLUTION

Start by drawing a free-body diagram, which is also a load diagram, of the beam. It should be placed so that the shear and moment diagrams may be drawn directly beneath, as shown in Fig. 13-38. The free-body diagram or load diagram is used as an aid in calculating the reactions at the supports.

$$\Sigma M_A = 0$$
$$500 + C_y \times 0.800 - 800 \times 1.200 \times 1.400 = 0$$
$$C_y = \frac{-500.0 + 1344.0}{0.800}$$
$$= 1055.0 \text{ N}$$

$$\Sigma F_y = 0$$
$$A_y + 1055.0 - 800 \times 1.200 = 0$$
$$A_y = -1055.0 + 960.0$$
$$= -95.0 \text{ N}$$

The shear diagram starts at zero.

At A:

$$V = 0.0 \text{ N}$$

The shear diagram immediately has an abrupt change of −95.0 N due to the concentrated load at the left support.

At A:

$$V = -95.0 \text{ N}$$

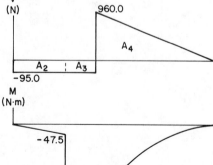

FIGURE 13-38

There is a change in load between A and C, but this is a couple or torque. A couple or torque causes pure rotation, so it has no effect on the shear diagram. Thus, there is no change in the shear between A and C.

At C:

$$V = -95.0 \text{ N}$$

Because of the concentrated load due to the support at C, there is an abrupt change in the shear diagram. The value of the shear at C thus becomes:

At C:

$$V = -95.0 + 1055.0$$
$$= 960.0 \text{ N}$$

The change in shear between C and D is equal to the negative of the area of the load diagram between C and D, which is shown as A_1.

$$A_1 = -(1.200 \times 800)$$
$$= -960.0 \text{ N}$$

The value of the shear at D may now be calculated.

At D:

$$V = 960.0 - 960.0$$
$$= 0.0 \text{ N}$$

As noted previously, the shear diagram should end at zero. The slope of the shear diagram between C and D is constant, since the height of the load diagram is constant between the same two points.

The moment diagram is now drawn beneath the shear diagram, as shown in Fig. 13-38. *The moment diagram starts at zero.*

At A:

$$M = 0.0 \text{ N·m}$$

The change in moment between A and B is equal to the area of the shear diagram between A and B, which is A_2.

$$A_2 = -(0.500 \times 95.0)$$
$$= -47.5 \text{ N·m}$$

The value of the moment at B may now be determined.

At B:

$$M = 0.0 - 47.5$$

$$= -47.5 \ \text{N} \cdot \text{m}$$

Since the shear diagram has constant height between A and B, the moment diagram has constant slope between A and B.

Point B is the point of application of the 500 N·m couple, which will cause an abrupt change in the moment diagram. Based on the bending moment sign convention, the couple would put the top fibers to its right in tension, and would be negative, thus causing an abrupt negative change in the moment diagram.

At B:

$$M = -47.5 - 500.0$$

$$= -547.5 \ \text{N} \cdot \text{m}$$

The change in moment between B and C is equal to the area A_3 in the shear diagram.

$$A_3 = -(0.300 \times 95.0)$$

$$= -28.5 \ \text{N} \cdot \text{m}$$

The value of the moment at C can now be calculated.

At C:

$$M = -547.5 - 28.5$$

$$= -576.0 \ \text{N} \cdot \text{m}$$

The slope of the moment diagram between B and C is constant, since the height of the shear diagram is constant between B and C. Note that the slope of the moment diagram between A and B is the same as between B and C, since the shear diagram has the same height for both regions.

The change in moment between C and D is equal to the area of the shear diagram between C and D, which is A_4.

$$A_4 = \frac{1}{2} \times 1.200 \times 960.0$$

$$= 576.0 \ \text{N} \cdot \text{m}$$

The value for the moment at D can now be determined.

At D:

$$M = -576.0 + 576.0$$

$$= 0.0 \ \text{N} \cdot \text{m}$$

The fact that the moment diagram closes, or returns to zero, indicates that the solution is probably correct.

The shape of the curve between C and D in the moment diagram may be determined in the following manner. At C, the height of the shear diagram for the portion between C and D is 960.0 N, so the slope of the moment diagram at C must be 960.0. At D, the height of the shear diagram is zero, so the slope of the moment diagram is zero. Only a curve that is concave upwards can pass through the points at C and D with the correct slopes.

$$V_{max} = 960 \text{ N}$$
$$\text{at } x = 0.800 \text{ m}$$
$$M_{max} = -576 \text{ N} \cdot \text{m}$$
$$\text{at } x = 0.800 \text{ m}$$

PROBLEMS

13-31 through 13-54: For Figs. P13-31 through P13-54, draw the complete shear and moment diagrams, and note the value and location for the maximum value for both the shear and moment.

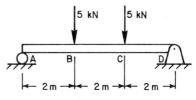

FIGURE P13-33

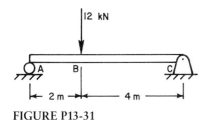

FIGURE P13-31

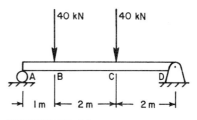

FIGURE P13-34

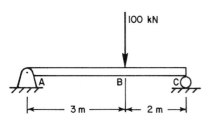

FIGURE P13-32

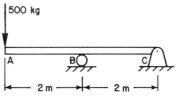

FIGURE P13-35

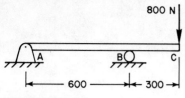

FIGURE P13-36

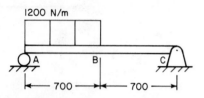

FIGURE P13-37

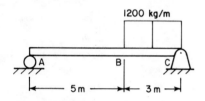

FIGURE P13-38

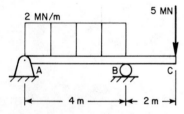

FIGURE P13-39

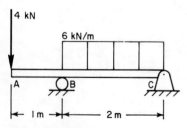

FIGURE P13-40

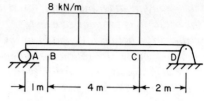

FIGURE P13-41

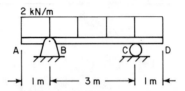

FIGURE P13-42

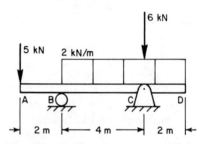

FIGURE P13-43

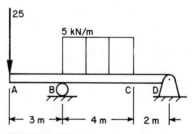

FIGURE P13-44

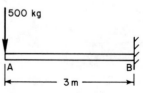

FIGURE P13-45

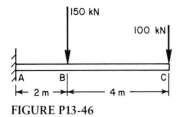

FIGURE P13-46

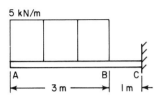

FIGURE P13-47

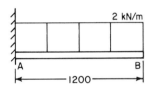

FIGURE P13-48

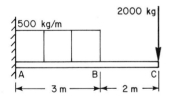

FIGURE P13-49

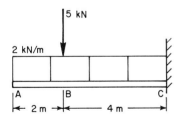

FIGURE P13-50

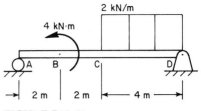

FIGURE P13-51

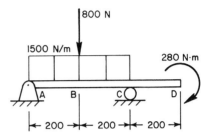

FIGURE P13-52

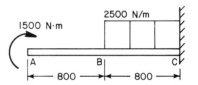

FIGURE P13-53

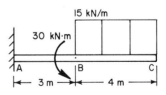

FIGURE P13-54

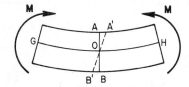

FIGURE 13-39

13-5 FLEXURAL STRESS IN BEAMS

In Article 13-1, it was observed that a beam tends to deform due to the bending moments in the beam, and in the process of deformation, some of the fibers in the beam get longer and others get shorter. If there is deformation there is strain, and if the strain is due to loads on the beam there must also be stress associated with the strain. The normal stress, tension and compression, associated with bending is called *flexural stress*.

To devise a method of calculating the flexural stress, a short segment of initially straight beam with a uniform cross section, as shown in Fig. 13-39, is examined. The segment of beam has a positive bending moment, M, applied at each end, so that the beam has the shape shown. Any initial cross section of the beam AOB remains a plane cross section $A'OB'$ after bending. The fibers above O have shortened in the bending process, and those below O have lengthened. The plane GH that contains point O, and on which there is no change in length of the fibers, is called the neutral plane. The line that the neutral plane forms on the beam cross section is called the neutral axis. The deformations are redrawn to a larger scale in Fig. 13-40(a). Since the original plane section AOB remains a plane section $A'OB'$ after deformation, the deformation at any distance y from the neutral plane is proportional to the distance from the neutral plane.

$$\frac{\delta_y}{\delta_c} = \frac{y}{c}$$

If the original length of the fibers was L, then the strains at y and c are ϵ_y and ϵ_c, and the corresponding deformations would be $\delta_y = \epsilon_y L$ and $\delta_c = \epsilon_c L$. The equation then becomes

$$\frac{\delta_y}{\delta_c} = \frac{\epsilon_y L}{\epsilon_c L} = \frac{\epsilon_y}{\epsilon_c} = \frac{y}{c}$$

Thus, the strain in the beam cross section is proportional to the distance from the neutral plane. From Eq. (10-11) we have

$$\epsilon = \frac{\sigma}{E}$$

so the equation may be rewritten as

$$\frac{\epsilon_y}{\epsilon_c} = \frac{\sigma_y/E}{\sigma_c/E} = \frac{\sigma_y}{\sigma_c} = \frac{y}{c}$$

From this it is observed that the stress at a point on the cross section of the beam is proportional to the distance of the point

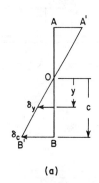

(a)

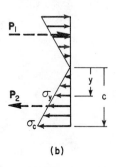

(b)

FIGURE 13-40

from the neutral plane. The distribution of stress is shown in Fig. 13-40(b). It is two triangular distributed loads. This internal load system must be equal to the internal torque (commonly called a bending moment) that exists in the beam.

If the stress σ_y acts on a small element of area ΔA at a distance y from the neutral plane, then the moment about O caused by the stress on the element of area is

$$\Delta M_O = \sigma_y \Delta A y$$

But $\sigma_y = \sigma_c \dfrac{y}{c}$

Thus $\Delta M_O = \dfrac{\sigma_c y}{c} \Delta A y = \dfrac{\sigma_c}{c} \Delta A y^2$

The total moment would be the sum of all of the moments due to the stress on all the elements of area, and is equal to the bending moment M.

$$M = \Sigma \, \Delta M_O = \Sigma \, \frac{\sigma_c}{c} \Delta A y^2$$

But σ_c/c is a ratio, so the equation may be rewritten as

$$M = \frac{\sigma_c}{c} \, \Sigma \, \Delta A y^2$$

The expression $\Sigma \, \Delta A y^2$ has the form of the moment of inertia of the area, which was discussed in Chap. 9. In this case, $\Sigma \, \Delta A y^2$ is measured with respect to the axis through O, the neutral plane or neutral axis. The equation can now be written as

$$M = \frac{\sigma_c}{c} I$$

or $\sigma_c = \dfrac{Mc}{I}$

which is usually written as

$$\sigma = \frac{Mc}{I} \qquad (13\text{-}5)$$

Since $\sigma_y/\sigma_c = y/c$, the equation may also be written as

$$\sigma_y = \frac{My}{I} \qquad (13\text{-}6)$$

where σ_c is the flexural stress at the outside fiber,

c is the distance from the neutral axis to the outside fiber,

σ_y is the flexural stress at a fiber a distance y from the neutral axis,

y is a distance measured from the neutral axis,

M is the bending moment occurring on the section where the flexural stress is being evaluated, and

I is the moment of inertia of the entire cross section with respect to an axis that is also the neutral axis.

When applying Eqs. (13-5) or (13-6) to beams, it must be kept in mind that, if the beam is carrying a positive bending moment, all the flexural stress above the neutral axis will be compression, and all flexural stress below the neutral axis will be tension. Similarly, if there is a negative bending moment acting on the beam section where the stress is being evaluated, the stress above the neutral axis will be tension; the stress below will be compression. The usual sign convention — a plus sign (+) for tensile stress and a minus sign (–) for compressive stress — applies.

Referring back to Fig. 13-40(b), if $\mathbf{P}_1$ and $\mathbf{P}_2$ truly form a couple, then $\Sigma F_x = 0$. The force acting on an element at area ΔA is

$$\Delta P = \sigma_y \Delta A$$

and the total force is

$$\Sigma F_x = 0 = \Sigma \sigma_y \Delta A$$

But $\sigma_y = \sigma_c \dfrac{y}{c}$

so the equation becomes

$$\Sigma F_x = 0 = \Sigma \frac{\sigma_c}{c} y \Delta A$$

Since σ_c/c is a ratio, the equation may be written as

$$0 = \frac{\sigma_c}{c} \Sigma y \Delta A$$

but $\Sigma y \Delta A = \bar{y} A$

Both terms are expressions for the centroid or first moment of area, as discussed in Chap. 8. If $\Sigma y \Delta A = 0$, then since A, the total area, is not zero, $\bar{y}$ must be zero. If this is true, the distance from the neutral plane, which was the reference axis, to the centroid, is zero. Thus, the centroidal axis of the cross section and the neutral axis of the cross section must coincide.

A number of conditions were assumed or implied in the derivation of Eqs. (13-5) and (13-6); those conditions must be observed when applying these equations. They are:

1. The beam must be straight.
2. The cross section of the beam must be uniform.
3. The material in the beam must be homogeneous.
4. The modulus of elasticity in tension and compression must be the same.
5. The stress in the beam must not exceed the proportional limit of the material.
6. The beam must be relatively long compared to its depth.
7. Loads must be applied perpendicular to the long axis.
8. The beam must not twist; nor can it have parts that buckle.

When using Eqs. (13-5) or (13-6) for the determination of flexural stress in beams, a few points should be kept in mind. The maximum flexural stress, which is usually the critical stress, will occur at that point in the beam where the bending moment has its maximum value, and on the fibers that are furthest from the neutral axis. In the case of a beam for which the neutral axis is also an axis of symmetry for the beam cross section, both the maximum tensile and maximum compressive stresses will have the same magnitude. In the case of a beam with a cross section for which the neutral axis is not an axis of symmetry, such as a T-beam, it will be necessary to determine the maximum values for both the positive and negative bending moments as well as the maximum tensile and compressive stresses that occur at these points.

When analyzing the stress in a beam, one of the loads on the beam is the distributed load due to the mass of the beam itself. In some cases, the load due to the mass is very small relative to the other loads applied to the beam and can be neglected. In extreme cases, the load due to the mass of the beam may be the largest load the beam must carry, and the load due to the mass must certainly be taken into account. In the problems that follow, the mass of the beam is to be neglected unless otherwise stated in the problem. It might also be noted that in the problems that follow, it is assumed that the beam cross section is oriented so that the section with the larger moment of inertia resists the applied bending moment. In this manner, the beam material is used most efficiently.

For many standard structural shapes produced by various mills, the values for the moment of inertia, along with other information, have already been calculated and tabulated. Samples of such tables are shown in Appendix F. When selecting a

suitable size of beam to carry a specified load at a given allowable stress, base your decision on the beam's moment of inertia
and the distance to the outside fiber. To reduce the two variables
to one, in many design procedures the ratio I/c is replaced by the
section modulus. The symbol for the section modulus is Z or S.
In the text Z is used; in some tables, such as in Appendix F, S is
used. Thus

$$\sigma = \frac{Mc}{I} \qquad (13\text{-}5)$$

$$\text{becomes } \sigma = \frac{M}{I/c}$$

$$\sigma = \frac{M}{Z} \qquad (13\text{-}7)$$

Values of Z are tabulated in Appendix F for various structural
shapes. The units for Z are usually mm³.

When using tables to select a beam size, usually the lightest
beam with the minimum required section modulus is chosen.
This will usually be the most economical beam.

EXAMPLE 13-10

Using the information from Appendix F to obtain I and c, determine the magnitude of the maximum flexural stress in a steel
W360x196. The maximum bending moment in the beam has
been found to be 250 kN·m.

SOLUTION

*The solution of this problem involves direct substitution of val-
ues into* Eq. (13-5). *The only difficulty is that the values of the
different terms have different units, so care must be taken in
converting all units to the base units of newtons and metres.
Multiply* kN *by* 10^3 *to convert to* N; *multiply* mm *by* 10^{-3} *to
convert to* m; *multiply* mm⁴ *by* 10^{-12} *to convert to* m⁴.

Since I_x *is much greater than* I_y, *it is assumed that the beam
would be used so that bending would occur about the x axis.*

Note that the actual depth of the beam, 372 mm, *is different
from the nominal depth,* 360 mm.

$$\sigma = \frac{Mc}{I}$$

$$= \frac{250 \times 10^3 \times \frac{372}{2} \times 10^{-3}}{636 \times 10^6 \times 10^{-12}}$$

$$= 73.113 \times 10^6 \text{ Pa}$$

$$= 73.113 \text{ MPa}$$

$$\boxed{\sigma = 73.1 \text{ MPa}}$$

EXAMPLE 13-11

A wood beam 3 m long and simply supported at each end has a section of 50 mm by 250 mm and carries a concentrated load of 5 kN at midspan. If the beam is supported on its narrow side, determine the maximum tensile and compressive flexural stress in the beam. Also determine the distance from the neutral axis to the point where the flexural stress will be 5.00 MPa on the section with the maximum bending moment.

SOLUTION

It is necessary to determine the maximum bending moment and the moment of inertia of the cross section about the centroidal axis before the flexural stress can be calculated.

From Appendix C, the moment of inertia of the section, which is shown in Fig. 13-41, *can be calculated. Note that the neutral axis and centroidal axis coincide.*

$$I_x = \frac{bh^3}{12}$$

$$= \frac{50 \times 250^3}{12}$$

$$= 65.104 \times 10^6 \text{ mm}^4$$

To determine the maximum moment, the shear and moment diagrams are drawn, along with the load diagram, as shown in Fig. 13-42.

From the free-body diagram (which is also the load diagram) shown at the top of Fig. 13-42, *the reactions are calculated.*

$$\Sigma M_A = 0$$

$$-(5 \times 1.5) + C_y \times 3 = 0$$

$$C_y = \frac{5 \times 1.5}{3}$$

$$= 2.500 \text{ kN}$$

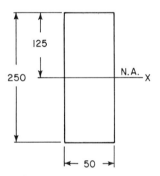

FIGURE 13-41

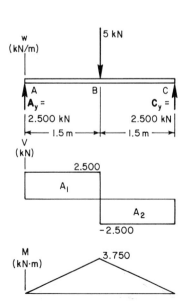

FIGURE 13-42

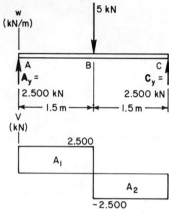

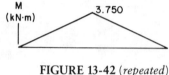

FIGURE 13-42 (*repeated*)

$$\Sigma F_y = 0$$

$$A_y - 5 + 2.500 = 0$$

$$A_y = 5.000 - 2.500$$

$$= 2.500 \text{ kN}$$

The shear diagram is now drawn, as shown in the middle of Fig. 13-42.

At A:

$$V = 0.000 \text{ kN}$$

There is an abrupt change in shear at A of 2.500 kN due to the force at the support.

At A:

$$V = 0.000 + 2.500$$

$$= 2.500 \text{ kN}$$

There is no change in shear from A to B since there is no change in load.

At B:

$$V = 2.500 \text{ kN}$$

At B there is a concentrated load of 5 kN, causing an abrupt negative change in the shear.

At B:

$$V = 2.500 - 5.000$$

$$= -2.500 \text{ kN}$$

From B to C there is no change in loading, and thus no change in shear.

At C:

$$V = -2.500 \text{ kN}$$

At C there is an abrupt change in shear of 2.500 kN due to the support.

At C:

$$V = -2.500 + 2.500$$

$$= 0.000 \text{ kN}$$

The moment diagram, as shown at the bottom of Fig. 13-42, is now drawn. The moment diagram always starts at zero.

At A:

$$M = 0.000 \text{ kN·m}$$

The change in moment from A to B is found, and is equal to area A_1.

$$A_1 = 1.5 \times 2.500$$
$$= 3.750 \text{ kN·m}$$

At B:

$$M = 0.000 + 3.750$$
$$= 3.750 \text{ kN·m}$$

The change in moment from B to C is determined using area A_2.

$$A_2 = -(1.5 \times 2.500)$$
$$= -3.750 \text{ kN·m}$$

The value for the moment at C may now be determined.

At C:

$$M = 3.750 - 3.750$$
$$= 0.000 \text{ kN·m}$$

It can now be observed from the moment diagram that the maximum bending moment in the beam is +3.750 kN·m.

$$M_{max} = +3.750 \text{ kN·m}$$

Now there is enough information available to use Eq. (13-5) to calculate the values for the flexural stress. It can be seen from Fig. 13-41 that the distance from the neutral axis to the most distant fiber is 125 mm. The values are substituted into Eq. (13-5). The values have a variety of units, so care must be taken to convert the kN·m to N·m (multiply by 10^3), the mm to m (multiply by 10^{-3}) and mm^4 to m^4 (multiply by 10^{-12}).

$$\sigma = \frac{Mc}{I}$$

$$= \frac{3.750 \times 10^3 \times 125 \times 10^{-3}}{65.104 \times 10^6 \times 10^{-12}}$$

$$= 7.2000 \times 10^6 \text{ Pa}$$

$$= 7.2000 \text{ MPa}$$

Since the maximum moment is positive, the flexural stress at the top fiber will be compressive; that at the bottom fiber will be tensile.

To obtain the distance to the point where the flexural stress is 5.00 MPa, Eq. (13-6) is solved for y.

$$\sigma = \frac{My}{I}$$

$$5.00 \times 10^6 = \frac{3.750 \times 10^3\, y}{65.104 \times 10^6 \times 10^{-12}}$$

$$y = \frac{5.00 \times 10^6 \times 65.104 \times 10^6 \times 10^{-12}}{3.750 \times 10^3}$$

$$= 86.805 \times 10^{-3}$$

$$= 86.805 \text{ mm}$$

The distance will be below the neutral axis, since the stress is positive.

$\sigma = -7.20$ MPa at top,
at $x = 1.50$ m
$\sigma = +7.20$ MPa at bottom,
at $x = 1.50$ m
$y = 86.8$ mm below N.A.

EXAMPLE 13-12

Find the lightest 3 m long steel W shape that can be used to carry a uniform distributed load of 1200 kg/m. The beam is a cantilever beam with a fixed support at one end, and the stress in it is not to exceed 80 MPa. The mass of the beam may be neglected.

SOLUTION

The maximum allowable stress is known and the maximum moment can be calculated, but neither I nor c are known quantities. Thus, Eq. (13-7), which uses the section modulus, should be used to solve for Z.

Before using Eq. (13-7) it is necessary to determine the maximum bending moment due to the given load on the beam. The load, shear and moment diagrams are constructed, as shown in Fig. 13-43. The load diagram or free-body diagram shown at the top of Fig. 13-43 is used to calculate the reactions.

$$\Sigma F_y = 0$$

$$A_y - 1.200 \times 9.807 \times 3 = 0$$

$$A_y = 35.305 \text{ kN}$$

$$\Sigma M_A = 0$$

$$M_S - 1.200 \times 9.807 \times 3 \times 1.5 = 0$$

$$M_S = 52.958 \text{ kN} \cdot \text{m}$$

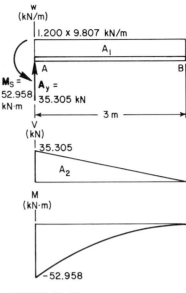

FIGURE 13-43

The shear diagram may now be constructed. The shear diagram always starts at zero.

At A:

$$V = 0.000 \text{ kN}$$

Due to the concentrated load from the support at A, there is an abrupt positive change in shear at A.

At A:

$$V = 0.000 + 35.305$$

$$= 35.305 \text{ kN}$$

The change in shear from A to B is equal to the negative of the area A_1 of the load diagram between A and B.

$$A_1 = -(3 \times 1.200 \times 9.807)$$

$$= -35.305 \text{ kN}$$

At B:

$$V = 35.305 - 35.305$$

$$= 0.000 \text{ kN}$$

The moment diagram, as shown at the bottom of Fig. 13-43, *may now be determined. The moment diagram always starts at zero.*

At A:

$$M = 0.000 \text{ kN} \cdot \text{m}$$

At A there is an abrupt change in moment due to the moment reaction at A. This moment is a negative bending moment.

At A:

$$M = 0.000 - 52.958$$

$$= -52.958 \text{ kN} \cdot \text{m}$$

The change in moment between A and B is equal to the area A_2 of the shear diagram between A and B.

$$A_2 = \frac{1}{2} \times 3 \times 35.305$$

$$= 52.958 \text{ kN} \cdot \text{m}$$

The moment at B may now be calculated.

At B:

$$M = -52.958 + 52.958$$

$$= 0.000 \text{ kN} \cdot \text{m}$$

From the moment diagram in Fig. 13-43, *the maximum moment is now available.*

$$M_{max} = -52.958 \text{ kN} \cdot \text{m}$$

Now Eq. (13-7) *may be rewritten and solved for the section modulus. Caution must be used with the units, which must be compatible.*

$$\sigma = \frac{M}{Z}$$

$$Z = \frac{M}{\sigma}$$

$$= \frac{52.958 \times 10^3}{80 \times 10^6}$$

$$= 0.661\ 97 \times 10^{-3} \text{ m}^3$$

Tables for Z usually use units of 10^3 mm³, *so the value for Z must be converted.*

$$Z = 0.661\ 97 \times 10^{-3} \times 10^9$$

$$= 661.97 \times 10^3 \text{ mm}^3$$

The W tables of Appendix F *are searched to find the lightest W shape that has a section modulus equal to or greater than 661.97 × 10^3 mm³. This is the section to select, since the lightest section will also be the least expensive. The lightest section with a Z_x (S_x in* Appendix F) *greater than 661.97 × 10^3 mm³ is a W360x45, which has a mass of approximately 45 kg/m.*

W360x45

EXAMPLE 13-13

For the beam shown in Fig. 13-44(a), determine the values and locations of the maximum tensile and compressive flexural stresses if the beam has the cross section shown in Fig. 13-44(b).

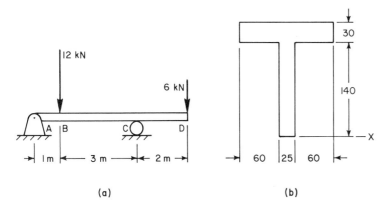

(a)   (b)

FIGURE 13-44

SOLUTION

It is necessary to draw the shear and moment diagrams for the beam to determine the maximum value for the moment. It is also necessary to locate the centroidal x axis for the beam cross section and to determine $I_{\bar{x}}$ to calculate the flexural stress in the beam. It makes no difference which calculations are done first.

The free-body diagram of the beam, which is also the load diagram, is drawn as shown at the top of Fig. 13-45. This is used to obtain the reactions at the supports at A and C,

$$\Sigma M_A = 0$$

$$-(12 \times 1) + C_y \times 4 - 6 \times 6 = 0$$

$$C_y = \frac{12 \times 1 + 6 \times 6}{4}$$

$$= \frac{12 + 36}{4}$$

$$= \frac{48}{4}$$

$$= 12.000 \text{ kN}$$

$$\Sigma F_y = 0$$

$$A_y - 12 + 12.000 - 6 = 0$$

$$A_y = 6.000 \text{ kN}$$

The shear diagram may now be constructed, as shown in the middle of Fig. 13-45. The shear diagram always starts at zero.

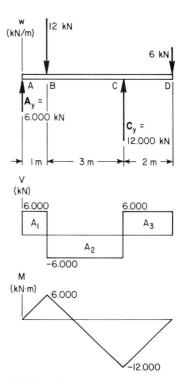

FIGURE 13-45

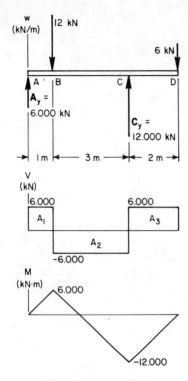

FIGURE 13-45 *(repeated)*

At A:

$$V = 0.000 \text{ kN}$$

Due to the concentrated load at the support, there is an abrupt change in the shear at A of +6.000 kN.

At A:

$$V = 0.000 + 6.000$$

$$= 6.000 \text{ kN}$$

From A to B there is no change in loading on the beam, so there is no change in the shear diagram.

At B:

$$V = 6.000 \text{ kN}$$

At B there is a concentrated load causing an abrupt change in the shear of –12.000 kN.

At B:

$$V = 6.000 - 12.000$$

$$= -6.000 \text{ kN}$$

From B to C there is no change in loading, and thus no change in the shear diagram.

At C:

$$V = -6.000 \text{ kN}$$

The concentrated load at C due to the support causes an abrupt change in shear of +12.000 kN.

At C:

$$V = -6.000 + 12.000$$

$$= 6.000 \text{ kN}$$

Between C and D there is no change in loading, so there is no change in the shear in the beam

At D:

$$V = 6.000 \text{ kN}$$

At D there is a concentrated load of 6 kN, which causes an abrupt change in shear.

At D:

$$V = 6.000 - 6.000$$

$$= 0.000 \text{ kN}$$

Now that the shear diagram is completed, the moment diagram, as shown at the bottom of Fig. 13-45, may be drawn. The moment diagram always starts at zero.

At A:

$$M = 0.000 \text{ kN} \cdot \text{m}$$

The change in moment from A to B is equal to the area of A_1 of the shear diagram between A and B.

$$A_1 = 1 \times 6.000$$
$$= 6.000 \text{ kN} \cdot \text{m}$$

The moment at B may now be determined.

At B:

$$M = 0.000 + 6.000$$
$$= 6.000 \text{ kN} \cdot \text{m}$$

The area A_2 between B and C gives the change in moment between these two points on the beam.

$$A_2 = -(3 \times 6.000)$$
$$= -18.000 \text{ kN} \cdot \text{m}$$

From this, the moment at C may be calculated.

At C:

$$M = 6.000 - 18.000$$
$$= -12.000 \text{ kN} \cdot \text{m}$$

The change in moment between C and D is equal to the area A_3 between C and D.

$$A_3 = 2 \times 6.000$$
$$= 12.000 \text{ kN} \cdot \text{m}$$

Now the moment at D can be calculated.

At D:

$$M = -12.000 + 12.000$$
$$= 0.000 \text{ kN} \cdot \text{m}$$

By inspecting the moment diagram, the maximum values may be obtained.

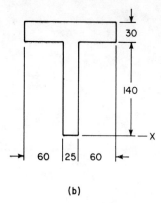

(b)

FIGURE 13-44(b) *(repeated)*

$$M_{max} = +6.000 \text{ kN·m at } x = 1.00 \text{ m}$$

$$\text{and } -12.000 \text{ kN·m at } x = 4.00 \text{ m}$$

The next step in the solution is to locate the y coordinate of the centroid of the cross section so that $I_{\bar{x}}$ may be calculated. The centroid is located using the procedure described in Article 8-5 *and using information from* Appendix C.

Vertical rectangle — Part 1

$$A_1 = 25 \times 140$$

$$= 3500 \text{ mm}^2$$

$$y_1 = \frac{140}{2}$$

$$= 70.0 \text{ mm}$$

Horizontal rectangle — Part 2

$$A_2 = 145 \times 30$$

$$= 4350 \text{ mm}^2$$

$$y_2 = 140 + \frac{30}{2}$$

$$= 140 + 15$$

$$= 155.0 \text{ mm}$$

Use is made of Eq. (8-5) *to find* $\bar{Y}$.

$$\bar{Y} = \frac{\Sigma A_i y_i}{\Sigma A_i}$$

$$= \frac{3500 \times 70.0 + 4350 \times 155.0}{3500 + 4350}$$

$$= \frac{245\ 000 + 674\ 250}{7850}$$

$$= \frac{919\ 250}{7850}$$

$$= 117.10 \text{ m}$$

Now the procedures of Article 9-4 *and information from* Appendix C *are used to calculate* $I_{\bar{x}}$.

Vertical rectangle — Part 1

$$(\bar{I}_x)_1 = \frac{25 \times 140^3}{12}$$

$$= 5.717 \times 10^6 \text{ mm}^4$$

$$d_1 = 117.10 - 70.0$$

$$= 47.10 \text{ mm}$$

$$A_1(d_1)^2 = 3500 \times 47.10^2$$

$$= 7.764 \times 10^6 \text{ mm}^4$$

Horizontal rectangle — Part 2

$$(\bar{I}_x)_2 = \frac{145 \times 30^3}{12}$$

$$= 0.326 \times 10^6 \text{ mm}^4$$

$$d_2 = 155.0 - 117.10$$

$$= 37.90 \text{ mm}$$

$$A_2(d_2)^2 = 4350 \times 37.90^2$$

$$= 6.248 \times 10^6 \text{ mm}^4$$

The values of $\bar{I}_x$, A and d may now be used to calculate $I_{\bar{x}}$.

Part	$\bar{I}_x$	Ad^2
1	5.717×10^6	7.764×10^6
2	0.326×10^6	6.248×10^6

$$\Sigma \bar{I}_x = 6.043 \times 10^6 \qquad \Sigma Ad^2 = 14.012 \times 10^6$$

$$\Sigma Ad^2 = 14.012 \times 10^6$$

$$I_{\bar{x}} = 20.055 \times 10^6 \text{ mm}^4$$

Most of the necessary information has now been calculated so Eq. (13-5) may be used to calculate the flexural stress at the points where the moments are maximum. Note that the value for c differs depending on whether it is measured to the top or bottom fiber. For this reason, both values of stress should be calculated at points where the moment is maximum.

At x = 1.00 m

Tension stress — bottom fiber

$$\sigma = \frac{Mc}{I}$$

$$= \frac{6.000 \times 10^3 \times 117.10 \times 10^{-3}}{20.055 \times 10^6 \times 10^{-12}}$$

$$= 35.034 \times 10^6 \text{ Pa}$$

$$= 35.034 \text{ MPa}$$

Compression stress — top fiber

$$\sigma = \frac{Mc}{I}$$

$$= -\frac{6.000 \times 10^3 \times (170 - 117.10) \times 10^{-3}}{20.055 \times 10^6 \times 10^{-12}}$$

$$= -15.826 \times 10^6 \text{ Pa}$$

$$= -15.826 \text{ MPa}$$

At x = 4.00 m

Tension stress — top fiber

$$\sigma = \frac{Mc}{I}$$

$$= \frac{12.000 \times 10^3 \times (170 - 117.10) \times 10^{-3}}{20.055 \times 10^6 \times 10^{-12}}$$

$$= 31.653 \times 10^6 \text{ Pa}$$

$$= 31.653 \text{ MPa}$$

Compression stress — bottom fiber

$$\sigma = \frac{Mc}{I}$$

$$= -\frac{12.000 \times 10^3 \times 117.10 \times 10^{-3}}{20.055 \times 10^6 \times 10^{-12}}$$

$$= -70.067 \times 10^6 \text{ Pa}$$

$$= -70.067 \text{ MPa}$$

Note that the maximum tensile and compressive stresses do not occur at the same location along the beam. This is due to the combination of the differences in positive and negative bending moments and because of the different distances to the extreme fibers.

$$\sigma_{max} = +35.0 \text{ MPa at bottom fiber}$$
$$\text{at } x = 1.00 \text{ m}$$
$$\sigma_{max} = -70.1 \text{ MPa at bottom fiber}$$
$$\text{at } x = 4.00 \text{ m}$$

PROBLEMS

13-55 Using Appendix F to find I for a W460x106 steel beam, find the magnitude of the maximum stress in the beam if the maximum moment is 125 kN·m.

13-56 Determine the magnitude of the maximum flexural stress in a steel S380x74 beam using Appendix F to find I if the maximum moment in the beam is −95 kN·m.

13-57 For a timber beam 200 mm wide by 300 mm deep, determine the magnitude of the maximum flexural stress in the beam if the maximum moment in the beam is −8 kN·m.

13-58 Find the magnitude of the maximum flexural stress in a beam if the maximum moment in the beam is 1200 N·m, and if the cross section of the beam is 25 by 40 mm.

13-59 A beam with the cross section shown in Fig. P13-59 has a positive moment throughout, with a maximum value of 18 kN·m. Calculate the maximum tensile stress in the beam.

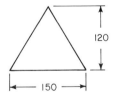

FIGURE P13-59

13-60 For the beam section shown in Fig. P13-60, determine the maximum compressive stress.

The beam has a negative moment throughout with a maximum value of −25 kN·m.

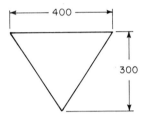

FIGURE P13-60

13-61 Determine the magnitude of the maximum flexural stress in a machine part that acts as a cantilever beam. It is a rectangle 12 mm deep and 5 mm wide, has a length of 75 mm and carries a load of 150 N at its free end.

13-62 A timber beam 5 m long is simply supported at the ends and carries a single concentrated load of 100 kN. The load is 2 m from the left end. Determine the magnitude of the maximum flexural stress in the beam if it has a section of 400 by 600 mm.

13-63 A cantilever beam rigidly supported at one end is 4.5 m long and carries a uniform distributed load of 800 kg/m. If the beam is a square box section 150 by 150 mm made up by welding 20 mm plates, calculate (a) the magnitude of the maximum flexural stress in the beam and (b) the magnitude of the maximum flexural stress at the inside of the section.

13-64 Find (a) the magnitude of the maximum flexural stress in a circular beam 1.30 m long if it carries a uniform load of 200 kg/m and is simply supported at each end and (b) the magnitude of the maximum flexural stress at the inside of the section. The beam has an outside diameter of 50 mm and an inside diameter of 30 mm.

13-65 For the beam shown in Fig. P13-65(a) with the cross section shown in Fig. P13-65(b), determine (a) the magnitude of the maximum flexural stress and (b) the flexural stress 30 mm above the neutral axis at C.

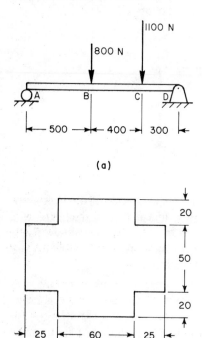

(a)

(b)

FIGURE P13-65

13-66 Determine (a) the magnitude of the maximum flexural stress and (b) the flexural stress 25 mm below the neutral axis at C for the beam shown in Fig. P13-66(a) with the section shown in Fig. P13-66(b).

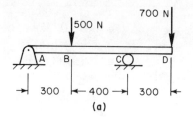

(a)

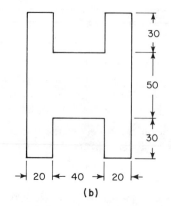

(b)

FIGURE P13-66

13-67 Find the lightest steel W beam 8 m long and simply supported at each end that can carry a load of 60 kN 2 m from each end. The mass of the beam may be neglected. The maximum allowable flexural stress is 50 MPa.

13-68 A 7 m long beam is supported by a pin at the left end and by a roller at a point 4 m from the left end. A load of 25 kN is located 2 m from the left end; there is a load of 60 kN at the right end. If the effect of the mass of the beam may be neglected, and if the maximum flexural stress is not to exceed 60 MPa, find the lightest steel W shape that may be used.

13-69 A steel S beam 6 m long, which is simply supported at each end, is used to carry a uniformly distributed load of 800 kg/m. Determine the size of the lightest suitable beam if the stress in the beam is not to exceed 45 MPa. The mass of the beam may be neglected.

13-70 Find the lightest steel W beam 9 m long that can be used to carry a uniform load of 300 kg/m over the left 5 m of the beam if the beam is simply supported at each end. The maximum flexural stress is not to exceed 60 MPa, and the mass of the beam may be neglected in the calculations.

13-71 A round bar of ABS plastic has a diameter of 40 mm and a length of 250 mm. Calculate the maximum concentrated load it can support at its center if it is simply supported at each end and if the flexural stress in it is not to exceed 16 MPa.

13-72 A 5 m long timber beam simply supported at each end has a section of 150 by 250 mm. If the flexural stress is not to exceed 12 MPa, determine the maximum uniform distributed load, in kg/m, that may be carried by the beam.

13-73 For the beam shown in Fig. P13-73(a), with the section shown in Fig. P13-73(b), determine the magnitude and location of the maximum tensile stress.

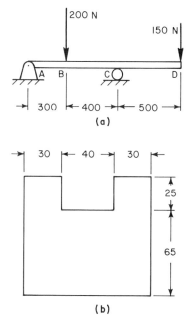

(a)

(b)

FIGURE P13-73

13-74 The beam shown in Fig. P13-74(a) has a T cross section, as shown in Fig. P13-74(b). Determine the maximum compressive stress in the beam and state where this stress occurs.

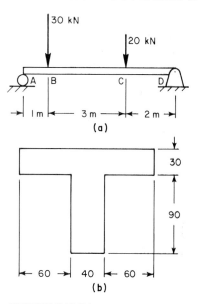

FIGURE P13-74

13-75 Determine the magnitude and location of the maximum compressive stress in the beam shown in Fig. P13-75(a), which has the cross section shown in Fig. P13-75(b).

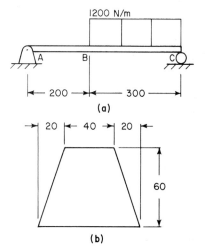

(a)

(b)

FIGURE P13-75

13-76 Find the location and magnitude of the maximum tensile stress for the beam shown in Fig. P13-76(a). The beam has the cross section shown in Fig. P13-76(b).

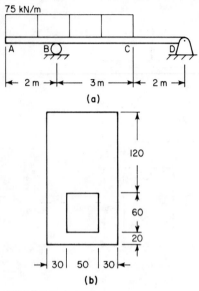

(a)

(b)

FIGURE P13-76

13-77 Determine the maximum tensile and compressive stresses in the beam shown in Fig. P13-77(a) if it has a triangular cross section as shown in Fig. P13-77(b). Indicate where these stresses occur.

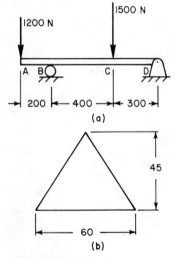

(a)

(b)

FIGURE P13-77

13-78 Find the location and magnitude of the maximum tensile stress for the beam shown in Fig. P13-78(a). The beam has the cross section shown in Fig. P13-78(b).

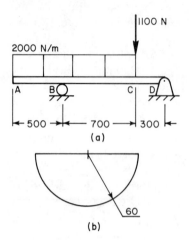

(a)

(b)

FIGURE P13-78

13-79 The beam shown in Fig. P13-79(a) has the cross section shown in Fig. P13-79(b). Determine the maximum tensile and compressive stresses in the beam and indicate where each occurs.

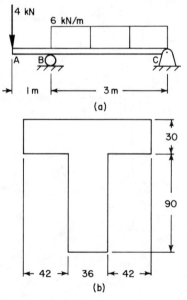

(a)

(b)

FIGURE P13-79

13-80 For the beam shown in Fig. P13-80(a), which has the cross section shown in Fig. P13-80(b), determine the magnitude and location of the maximum tensile and compressive stresses.

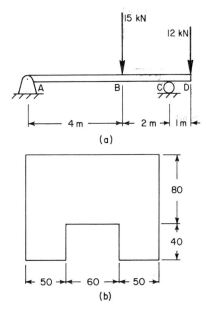

(a)

(b)

FIGURE P13-80

13-6 STRESS CONCENTRATIONS IN BENDING

One of the assumptions that was made in the derivation of the formula for flexural stress, Eq. (13-6), was that the cross section of the beam is uniform. If there is a change in the cross section, such as a hole or change in dimensions, the change in shape causes a stress concentration where the material is removed and the stress is much higher than is calculated using Eq. (13-6). The magnitude of the maximum stress at the concentration may be determined by multiplying the stress calculated from Eq. (13-6), which is the nominal stress, by a stress-concentration factor, K_t.

$$\sigma_{max} = K_t \sigma_{nom} \qquad (13\text{-}8)$$

As will be noted in charts of stress concentrations shown in Figs. 13-46, 13-47 and 13-48, Eq. (13-6) is not actually used directly, for a formula for calculating the nominal stress for each case is shown with the information on the stress concentration. The figures also indicate approximately how the actual stress at the concentration compares with the nominal stress at the section.

Values for the stress-concentration factors for different changes in cross section have been obtained experimentally or theoretically. A different stress-concentration factor chart is required for each different type of change in cross section. Be sure to use the chart that describes the particular change in section that exists. There are specialized books that have a large number of stress-concentration factor charts. Only three of the more common changes of section are illustrated here.

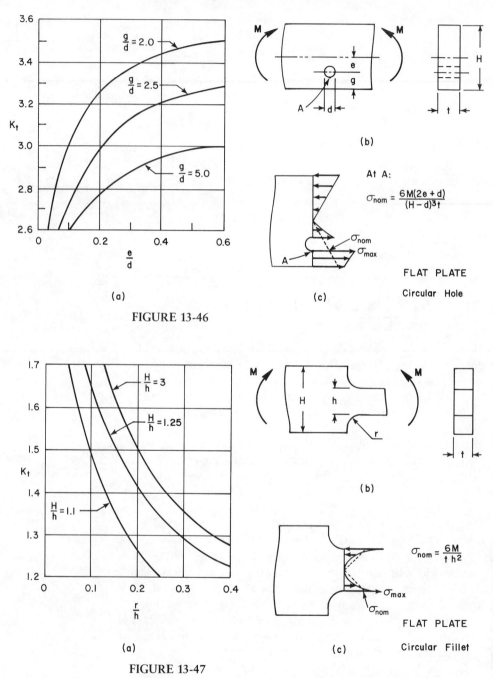

$$\sigma_{nom} = \frac{6M(2e + d)}{(H - d)^3 t}$$

FLAT PLATE

Circular Hole

(a)   (c)

FIGURE 13-46

$$\sigma_{nom} = \frac{6M}{t h^2}$$

FLAT PLATE

Circular Fillet

(a)   (c)

FIGURE 13-47

In the case of bending where there is a stress concentration, the maximum stress will usually occur at the stress concentration, and not necessarily at the fiber furthest from the neutral axis. If the stress concentration does not occur where the moment is maximum, it may be necessary to calculate both the flexural stress at the stress concentration and at the section with the maximum moment to determine the highest value for the flexural stress in the beam.

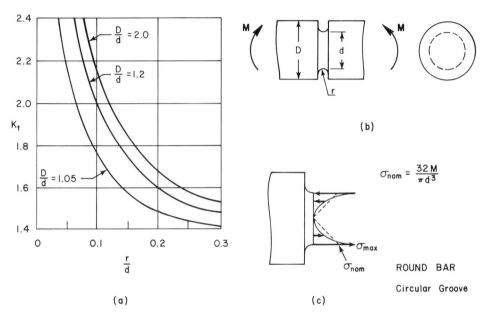

(a) (b) (c)

$$\sigma_{nom} = \frac{32 M}{\pi d^3}$$

ROUND BAR

Circular Groove

FIGURE 13-48

EXAMPLE 13-14

A round bar with a diameter of 125 mm is used as a beam. At a section where the bending moment is 12 kN·m there is a circular groove cut. Determine the maximum flexural stress at the section if the groove has a diameter of 100 mm and if the radius of the groove is 10 mm.

SOLUTION

The stress concentration is of the type shown in the chart in Fig. 13-48. *To use the chart, values for r/d and D/d must be obtained.*

$$\frac{r}{d} = \frac{10}{100}$$

$$= 0.100$$

$$\frac{D}{d} = \frac{125}{100}$$

$$= 1.25$$

To use the chart in Fig. 13-48(a), *start with the value of r/d. Move vertically along the line r/d = 0.1 to where it intercepts the line for D/d = 1.25. There is no such line in the chart but its location can be interpolated between the lines for D/d = 1.2 and D/d = 2.0. Note that the distance between D/d lines is not proportional to their values. From the estimated intercept point, move horizontally left to the K_t axis and determine the value of K_t.*

$$K_t = 2.04$$

The equation given with Fig. 13-48 *may be used to calculate nominal stress.*

$$\sigma_{nom} = \frac{32\,M}{\pi d^3}$$

$$= \frac{32 \times 12 \times 10^3}{\pi \times 100^3 \times 10^{-9}}$$

$$= 122.23 \times 10^6 \text{ Pa}$$

With values for both the stress-concentration factor and the nominal stress now available, the maximum stress on the section may be calculated.

$$\sigma_{max} = K_t \sigma_{nom}$$

$$= 2.04 \times 122.23 \times 10^6$$

$$= 249.35 \times 10^6$$

$$= 249.35 \text{ MPa}$$

$$\boxed{\sigma_{max} = 249 \text{ MPa}}$$

Because some judgment is required in interpolating between curves in the charts, it is normal for individuals to obtain small differences in values for K_t and, consequently, values of σ_{max} will also vary somewhat.

EXAMPLE 13-15

A wood floor joist 50 by 250 mm is 4 m long, simply supported at each end, and carries a uniformly distributed load of 150 kg/m. If there is a 40 mm diameter hole in the joist 1.50 m from the left end, and with its center 105 mm from the bottom of the joist, calculate the maximum tensile stress in the joist.

SOLUTION

To calculate the flexural stress, it is necessary to calculate the maximum moment as well as the moment at the section with the stress concentration.

By now, it is recognized that the maximum bending moment for a simply supported beam with a uniform load will be at the center of the beam. Thus, the moments at the center of the beam and at the section with the stress concentration should be calculated. First the reaction at A must be determined. The free-body diagram of the beam shown in Fig. 13-49 *is used as an aid in calculating the reaction.*

$$\Sigma M_B = 0$$

$$-(A_y \times 4) + 150 \times 9.807 \times 4 \times 2 = 0$$

$$A_y = \frac{150 \times 9.807 \times 4 \times 2}{4}$$

$$= 2942.1 \text{ N}$$

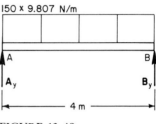

FIGURE 13-49

The free-body diagram shown in Fig. 13-50 *can be used for calculating the moments at x = 1.50 m and x = 2.00 m.*

At x = 1.50 m

$$\Sigma M_0 = 0$$

$$-(2942.1 \times 1.50) + 150 \times 9.807 \times 1.50 \times 0.75 + M = 0$$

$$M = 4413.2 - 1654.9$$

$$= 2758.3 \text{ N} \cdot \text{m}$$

At x = 2.00 m

$$\Sigma M_0 = 0$$

$$-(2942.1 \times 2.00) + 150 \times 9.807 \times 2.00 \times 1.00 + M = 0$$

$$M = 5884.2 - 2942.1$$

$$= 2942.1 \text{ N} \cdot \text{m}$$

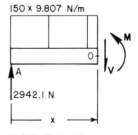

FIGURE 13-50

The maximum stress at each location may now be analyzed. The stress concentration at x = 1.50 m must be taken into account. To select the stress-concentration factor, reference is made to Fig. 13-46. *It will be necessary to first calculate the ratios e/d and g/d.*

$$\frac{e}{d} = \frac{125 - 105}{40}$$

$$= \frac{20}{40}$$

$$= 0.50$$

$$\frac{g}{d} = \frac{105}{40}$$

$$= 2.625$$

To find K_t, start with the value of e/d in Fig. 13-46(a). *Go up the vertical line at $e/d = 0.50$ until just below the curve for $g/d = 2.5$. This would be near the value for $g/d = 2.625$. From that point, go horizontally to the K_t axis, and determine the value.*

$$K_t = 3.23$$

The value for the nominal stress at the outer edge of the hole, which is the location of the maximum stress at the section, is obtained from the equation shown in Fig. 13-46.

$$\sigma_{nom} = \frac{6M(2e + d)}{(H - d)^3 t}$$

$$= \frac{6 \times 2758.3(2 \times 20 + 40)10^{-3}}{(250 - 40)^3 \times 50 \times 10^{-12}}$$

$$= 2.8593 \times 10^6 \text{ Pa}$$

The maximum stress at the hole may now be calculated.

$$\sigma_{max} = K_t \sigma_{nom}$$

$$= 3.23 \times 2.8593 \times 10^6$$

$$= 9.2355 \times 10^6 \text{ Pa}$$

$$= 9.2355 \text{ MPa}$$

The maximum stress at the hole must be compared with the stress at the outside fibers at the midspan of the beam where one would normally expect to find the maximum flexural stress.

At x = 2.00 m

$$\sigma = \frac{Mc}{I}$$

$$= \frac{2942.1 \times 125 \times 10^{-3}}{\dfrac{50 \times 250^3}{12} \times 10^{-12}}$$

$$= 5.6488 \times 10^6 \text{ Pa}$$

$$= 5.6488 \text{ MPa}$$

The maximum stress occurs at the stress concentration, and not where the moment is maximum.

$$\sigma_{max} = 9.24 \text{ MPa}$$

PROBLEMS

13-81 A circular bar with a diameter of 50 mm has a bending moment of 300 N·m at a point where there is a circular groove in the bar. Determine the maximum flexural stress in the bar if the minimum diameter at the groove is 40 mm and if the radius of the groove is 5 mm.

13-82 A rectangular beam with a cross section of 150 by 50 mm is reduced to a section of 100 by 50 mm. Determine the maximum stress at the reduced section if there is a moment of 14.0 kN·m acting on the section and if there is a 25 mm radius fillet at the reduced section.

13-83 A small beam in a machine is 40 mm deep by 15 mm wide. At a section where there is a moment of 450 N·m, there is a 7 mm diameter hole with its center 16 mm from the edge of the beam. Calculate the maximum stress at the edge of the hole.

13-84 A 200 mm diameter bar has a circular groove 15 mm deep. The radius of the groove is 12 mm. If the bar has a bending moment of 25 kN·m at the section with the groove, determine the maximum flexural stress at the section.

13-85 A cast-iron beam 300 mm long is simply supported at the ends and has a concentrated load of 400 N at its midpoint. The beam has a rectangular cross section. The left 200 mm of the beam is 20 by 40 mm deep and the right end is

20 by 30 mm deep. The radius of the fillet joining the two sections is 6 mm. Determine the maximum flexural stress in the beam.

13-86 A cantilever beam 1500 mm long has a single force of 900 N at its free end. Calculate the maximum flexural stress in the beam if it has a cross section 70 mm deep and 20 mm wide. At a distance of 500 mm from the support, there is a 15 mm diameter hole with its center 30 mm from the outside fiber on the tension side.

13-87 A 100 mm diameter bar 2 m long is used as a beam. It is simply supported at each end. One third of the length from one support there is a load of 9 kN, and one third of the length from the other support there is a circular groove with a diameter of 60 mm. The radius of the groove is 7 mm. Determine the maximum flexural stress in the beam.

13-88 A small beam 900 mm long is 20 mm wide throughout its length. The middle third is 70 mm deep, and the end thirds are both 60 mm deep. The change in section has a 10 mm radius. If the beam is simply supported at each end, and carries a single concentrated load of 1500 N at midspan, find the maximum flexural stress in the beam.

13-7 SHEAR STRESS IN BEAMS

At the beginning of this chapter, when the topic of flexure was introduced, it was pointed out that when a load is applied to a beam, deformation takes place in the beam, as was illustrated in Fig. 13-1(b). If a beam was made of layers of material, as shown in Fig. 13-51(a), the surfaces of the layers would tend to slide relative to one another as the beam deformed under load, as shown in Fig. 13-51(b). The horizontal shear stress that exists between the "layers" is what prevents the slipping of surfaces in the beam.

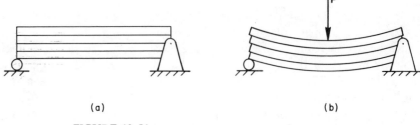

(a) (b)

FIGURE 13-51

In Article 13-2 the transverse shear force on a section of a beam was discussed. It follows that if there is a shear force on a transverse section of a beam there must also be a shear stress on that section.

When the topic of shear strain was first introduced in Article 10-7, the shear stress acting on a small element of the material was discussed. Such a small element taken from some point in a beam is shown in Fig. 13-52(a), and the deformed shape of the element is shown in Fig. 13-52(b). If there is a horizontal shear stress on the lower surface, as exists between "layers" in a beam, there must be an opposing stress on the upper surface. The two horizontal stresses acting on their respective areas would form a couple. This couple must be opposed by an equal and opposite couple if the element is to be in equilibrium. This equal and opposite couple is formed by the shear stresses acting on the areas of the vertical planes. If each plane of the element has the same area, then each shear stress must also be the same. At any point in a beam there is both a longitudinal and transverse shear stress, and both stresses have the same magnitude.

The objective now is to determine the magnitude of these shear stresses. The analysis starts with a section with a length of Δx cut from a beam, as shown in Fig. 13-53(a). The forces acting on a small part of the beam below the cut, *a-a*, are shown in

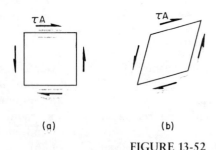

(a) (b)

FIGURE 13-52

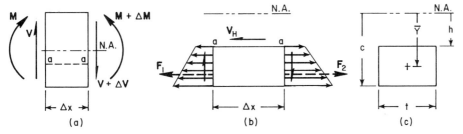

FIGURE 13-53

Fig. 13-53(b), and the end view of the part is shown in Fig. 13-53(c).

The flexural stress on the left end of the part below *a-a* acts as a distributed load.

At *h*:

$$\sigma = \frac{Mh}{I}$$

At *c*:

$$\sigma = \frac{Mc}{I}$$

The resultant force on the left end, which can replace the flexural stress, is $\mathbf{F_1}$. The magnitude can be obtained from the average stress times the area on which it acts.

$$F_1 = \frac{\left(\dfrac{Mh}{I} + \dfrac{Mc}{I}\right)}{2}(c - h)t$$

Similarly, on the right end

At *h*:

$$\sigma = \frac{(M + \Delta M)h}{I}$$

At *c*:

$$\sigma = \frac{(M + \Delta M)c}{I}$$

The resultant force, $\mathbf{F_2}$, on the right end is

$$F_2 = \frac{\left(\dfrac{(M + \Delta M)h}{I} + \dfrac{(M + \Delta M)c}{I}\right)}{2}(c - h)t$$

V_H is the longitudinal shear force acting on the surface at *a-a*. From equilibrium in the horizontal direction

$$\Sigma F_x = 0$$

$$F_2 - F_1 - V_H = 0$$

$$V_H = F_2 - F_1$$

$$= \frac{\left(\dfrac{(M + \Delta M)h}{I} + \dfrac{(M + \Delta M)c}{I}\right)}{2}(c - h)t - \frac{\left(\dfrac{Mh}{I} + \dfrac{Mc}{I}\right)}{2}(c - h)t$$

This simplifies to

$$V_H = \frac{(\Delta Mh + \Delta Mc)}{2I}(c - h)t$$

$$= \frac{\Delta M}{2I}t(c + h)(c - h)$$

The shear stress on the longitudinal plane is

$$\tau = \frac{V_H}{A}$$

$$= \frac{\dfrac{\Delta M}{2I}t(c + h)(c - h)}{\Delta x t}$$

$$= \frac{\dfrac{\Delta M}{\Delta x}t\dfrac{(c + h)(c - h)}{2}}{It}$$

From Article 13-4 it was learned that $\Delta M/\Delta x = V$. If the expression $t(c + h)(c - h)/2$ is replaced by the symbol Q, then the value for the magnitude of the shear stress becomes

$$\tau = \frac{VQ}{It} \tag{13-9}$$

where τ is the shear stress (both longitudinal and transverse) acting at a point in a beam,

V is the transverse shear force on the section where the stress is being evaluated,

Q is the first moment about the neutral axis of the area of the part of the section away from the surface on which the stress is being evaluated,

I is the moment of inertia of the entire cross section, and

t is the width of the section at the point where the stress is being evaluated.

Since the flexure formula was used in the derivation of Eq. (13-9), the same limitations that applied to the flexure formula also apply to Eq. (13-9). In addition, Eq. (13-9) applies only when the sides of the beam are parallel and if the thickness of the section is less than the depth of the section. When the sides of a beam are not parallel and when the thickness is greater than the depth, Eq. (13-9) is used to obtain an *approximate* value for the shear stress at a point in a beam.

The term Q often causes some difficulty. It is the first moment about the neutral axis of the part of the section away from the plane where the stress is being evaluated. In the derivation, Q replaced the expression $t(c + h)(c - h)/2$. Referring to Fig. 13-54, it can be seen that $(c - h)$ is the depth of the shaded area and that t is its thickness or width, so that $(c - h)t$ is the area of the shaded portion. The term $(c + h)/2$ is the average distance to the shaded area or, more correctly it is $\bar{Y}$ for the shaded area. Thus

$$Q = \bar{Y}A \qquad (13\text{-}10)$$

where Q is the first moment about the neutral axis of the part of the section away from the surface on which stress is being evaluated,

$\bar{Y}$ is the distance from the neutral axis to the centroid of the area of the part of the section away from the plane where the stress is being evaluated, and

A is the area of the part of the section away from the plane where the stress is being evaluated.

In the case of a cross section that is a composite area made up of several simple shapes, recall from Chap. 8

$$\bar{Y} = \frac{\Sigma A_i y_i}{\Sigma A_i} \qquad (8\text{-}5)$$

or $\bar{Y} \Sigma A_i = \Sigma A_i y_i$

but $A = \Sigma A_i$

Thus

$$Q = \bar{Y}A = \bar{Y} \Sigma A_i = \Sigma A_i y_i$$
$$Q = \Sigma A_i y_i \qquad (13\text{-}11)$$

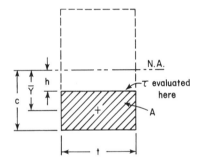

FIGURE 13-54

where Q is the first moment of the area about the neutral axis of the part of the section away from the plane where the stress is being evaluated, and

$\Sigma\, A_i y_i$ is the sum of the products of each component area and the y coordinate of the centroid of each individual component area measured from the neutral axis.

From examining Eq. (13-9), it will be seen that if the cross section is rectangular, the only term that will vary is Q. It will have a value of zero at the outside fibers of the beam, and a maximum value at the neutral axis. If the value of the shear stress across the section for a rectangular cross section is plotted, the stress distribution will appear as shown in Fig. 13-55. The shear stress distributions for a T section and a Greek cross section are shown in Figs. 13-56(a) and 13-56(b).

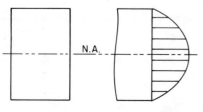

FIGURE 13-55

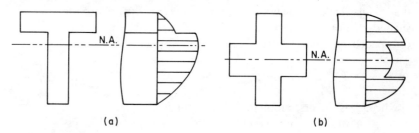

(a)

(b)

FIGURE 13-56

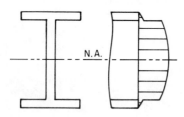

FIGURE 13-57

In the case of standard W or S shapes, most of the shear is carried by the web, as shown in Fig. 13-57. Because of this, an approximate value for the shear is calculated. One of the formulae used for calculating the maximum shear in the web is

$$\tau = \frac{V}{td} \qquad (13\text{-}12)$$

where τ is the maximum shear stress acting on the section,
V is the shear force acting on the section,
t is the thickness of the web and
d is the depth of the beam.

Much of the time, the longitudinal or transverse shear stress is not the critical stress in beams, except in the case of short, deep beams. In most situations, the flexural stress will be the critical stress. However, it is still necessary to check both stresses.

The shear stress formula of Eq. (13-9) is sometimes modified to obtain the shear flow, which is the shear force per unit of length acting on a plane in a beam. This information is useful when designing connections, such as nails or welds, if a member with a section like the T of Fig. 13-56(a) is built up in timber or steel. The shear flow is obtained from

$$q = \frac{VQ}{I} \qquad (13\text{-}13)$$

where q is the shear flow,

V is the transverse shear force acting on the section where the shear flow is being evaluated,

Q is the first moment about the neutral axis of the area of the part of the section away from the plane where the shear flow is being evaluated and

I is the moment of inertia of the area of the entire cross section.

The shear flow will have units of N/m or kN/m. Once it has been evaluated, then the number of connections or the size of connections required to resist the shear force on each unit of length can be determined.

EXAMPLE 13-16

If the maximum transverse shear force in a beam with a section 40 by 90 mm deep is 18 kN, determine the value for the maximum longitudinal and transverse shear stresses in the beam.

SOLUTION

Both the longitudinal and transverse shear stresses have the same value at any point in the beam. For a beam with a rectangular section, the maximum value occurs at the neutral axis. The magnitude is obtained from Eq. (13-9). It is probably a good idea to calculate I and Q separately, using Fig. 13-58 as an aid

$$I = \frac{bh^3}{12}$$

$$= \frac{40 \times 90^3}{12}$$

$$= 2.430 \times 10^6 \text{ mm}^4$$

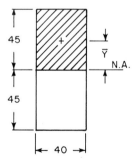

FIGURE 13-58

Q is the first moment about the neutral axis of the area from the plane where the stress is evaluated to the outside fibers, and is shown shaded in Fig. 13-58.

$$Q = \bar{Y}A$$

$$= \frac{45}{2} \times 40 \times 45$$

= 40 500 mm³

The values for I and Q are substituted into Eq. (13-9). V must be expressed in N, Q in m³, I in m⁴ and t in m, so terms must be converted where necessary.

$$\tau = \frac{VQ}{It}$$

$$= \frac{18\ 000 \times 40\ 500 \times 10^{-9}}{2.430 \times 10^6 \times 10^{-12} \times 40 \times 10^{-3}}$$

$$= 7.5000 \times 10^6 \text{ Pa}$$

$$= 7.5000 \text{ MPa}$$

$$\boxed{\tau_{max} = 7.50 \text{ MPa}}$$

EXAMPLE 13-17

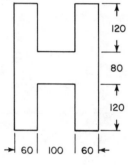

120

80

120

60 | 100 | 60

FIGURE 13-59

A timber H beam has the section shown in Fig. 13-59. If the maximum shear force on the section is 175 kN, calculate the shear stress (a) on the neutral axis and (b) at a point 42 mm above the neutral axis.

SOLUTION

Determining the required shear stress is simply a matter of substitution of values into Eq. (13-9). Values for I, Q and t must be obtained. The value required for I is for the entire cross section, so it is common for both parts of the problem. If the section is broken up as shown in Fig. 13-60, where each component has its centroid coincide with the centroidal axis of the entire section, the simplest calculation for I will be obtained.

Part (1):

$$(I_x)_1 = \frac{bh^3}{12}$$

$$= \frac{60 \times 320^3}{12}$$

$$= 163.84 \times 10^6 \text{ mm}^4$$

Part (2)

$$(I_x)_2 = \frac{bh^3}{12}$$

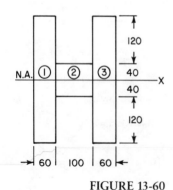

120

N.A. ① ② ③ 40

40

X

120

60 | 100 | 60

FIGURE 13-60

$$= \frac{100 \times 80^3}{12}$$

$$= 4.267 \times 10^6 \text{ mm}^4$$

Part (3):

Same as Part (1)

$$(I_x)_3 = 163.84 \times 10^6 \text{ mm}^4$$

Total:

$$I_x = (I_x)_1 + (I_x)_2 + (I_x)_3$$

$$= (163.84 + 4.267 + 163.84)10^6$$

$$= 331.95 \times 10^6 \text{ mm}^4$$

Part (a)

The first moment of the area of the section away from the neutral axis must be calculated. From Eq. (13-11) it will be recalled that Q equals Σ $A_i y_i$. Thus, Q may be obtained by breaking the section above the neutral axis into the parts shown in Fig. 13-61.

Part (4):

$$A_4 = 60(40 + 120)$$

$$= 9600 \text{ mm}^2$$

$$y_4 = \frac{40 + 120}{2}$$

$$= \frac{160}{2}$$

$$= 80.0 \text{ mm}$$

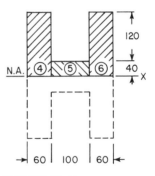

FIGURE 13-61

Part (5):

$$A_5 = 100 \times 40$$

$$= 4000 \text{ mm}^2$$

$$y_5 = \frac{40}{2}$$

$$= 20.0 \text{ mm}$$

Part (6):

Same as Part (4)

$$Q = \Sigma\, A_i y_i$$

$$= 9600 \times 80.0 + 4000 \times 20.0 + 9600 \times 80.0$$

$$= 768\,000 + 80\,000 + 768\,000$$

$$= 1\,616\,000 \text{ mm}^3$$

The value for t is the total width at the neutral axis, which is 220 mm. Values may now be substituted into Eq. (13-9). *Remember to convert units so that V is expressed in* N, *Q in* m^3, *I in* m^4 *and t in* m.

$$\tau = \frac{VQ}{It}$$

$$= \frac{175 \times 10^3 \times 1\,616\,000 \times 10^{-9}}{331.95 \times 10^6 \times 10^{-12} \times 220 \times 10^{-3}}$$

$$= 3872.4 \times 10^3 \text{ Pa}$$

$$= 3.8724 \text{ kPa}$$

Part (b)

To calculate the shear stress 42 mm above the neutral axis requires calculating Q for the part of the section away from the 42 mm cutting plane. The areas involved are shown in Fig. 13-62.

Part (7):

$$A_7 = 60 \times 118$$

$$= 7080 \text{ mm}^2$$

$$y_7 = 42 + \frac{118}{2}$$

$$= 42.0 + 59.0$$

$$= 101.0 \text{ mm}$$

Part (8):

Same as Part (7)

$$Q = \Sigma\, A_i y_i$$

$$= 7080 \times 101.0 + 7080 \times 101.0$$

$$= 715\,080 + 715\,080$$

$$= 1\,430\,160 \text{ mm}^3$$

The value for t is the total thickness where the stress is being evaluated, which is 120 mm. Values may now be substituted into Eq. (13-9) *to calculate the shear stress. Be sure to make the*

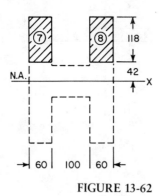

FIGURE 13-62

necessary conversions so that all terms are expressed in metres and newtons.

$$\tau = \frac{VQ}{It}$$

$$= \frac{175 \times 10^3 \times 1\,430\,160 \times 10^{-9}}{331.95 \times 10^6 \times 10^{-12} \times 120 \times 10^{-3}}$$

$$= 6283.0 \times 10^3 \text{ Pa}$$

$$= 6.2830 \text{ kPa}$$

(a) $\tau = 3.87$ kPa
(b) $\tau = 6.28$ kPa

Due to the shape of the section and to the sudden decrease in t which occurs, the shear stress is actually lower at the neutral axis than it is further out from the neutral axis.

EXAMPLE 13-18

An S250x38 steel beam is used to carry the loads shown in Fig. 13-63. Determine the location and value of the maximum shear stress in the beam.

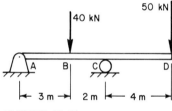

FIGURE 13-63

SOLUTION

The maximum shear stress will occur at the neutral axis where the shear force is maximum. It is necessary to draw a shear diagram to find the value and location of the maximum shear force. A free-body diagram, as shown at the top of Fig. 13-64, *is used as an aid in calculating the forces at the supports.*

$$\Sigma M_A = 0$$

$$-(40 \times 3) + C_y \times 5 - 50 \times 9 = 0$$

$$C_y = \frac{120.00 + 450.00}{5}$$

$$= \frac{570.00}{5}$$

$$= 114.00 \text{ kN}$$

$$\Sigma F_y = 0$$

$$A_y - 40 + 114.00 - 50 = 0$$

$$A_y = 90.00 - 114.00$$

$$= -24.00 \text{ kN}$$

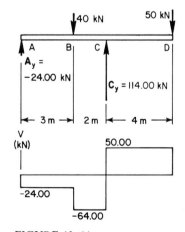

FIGURE 13-64

The shear diagram is drawn beneath the free-body diagram, as shown in the lower part of Fig. 13-64. *The shear starts at zero and has an abrupt change at the left end of −24.00 kN due to the force from the support.*

At A:

$$V = 0.00 \text{ kN}$$

At A:

$$V = 0.00 - 24.00$$
$$= -24.00 \text{ kN}$$

The shear is constant from A to B

At B:

$$V = -24.00 \text{ kN}$$

The next change in the shear diagram is at B, where there is an applied load.

At B:

$$V = -24.00 - 40.00$$
$$= -64.00 \text{ kN}$$

The shear is constant from B to C,

At C:

$$V = -64.00 \text{ kN}$$

At C, the force from the support causes a change of + 114.00 kN.

At C:

$$V = -64.00 + 114.00$$
$$= 50.00 \text{ kN}$$

The shear is constant from C to D.

At D:

$$V = 50.00 \text{ kN}$$

The shear diagram has a change at D due to the applied load.

At D:

$$V = 50.00 - 50.00$$
$$= 0.00 \text{ kN}$$

The complete shear diagram is plotted, as shown in the lower part of Fig. 13-64, and the location and maximum value for V is determined.

$$V_{max} = -64.00 \text{ kN}$$

$$\text{at } 3.00 \leq x \leq 5.00 \text{ m}$$

The values for t and d for the beam section are obtained from the tables of Appendix F and substituted into Eq. (13-12). Note that in the tables of Appendix F, the symbol for web thickness is w. As usual, care must be taken with units, since dimensions must be expressed in terms of metres.

$$\tau = \frac{V}{td}$$

$$= \frac{64 \times 10^3}{7.9 \times 10^{-3} \times 254 \times 10^{-3}}$$

$$= 31.895 \times 10^6 \text{ Pa}$$

$$= 31.895 \text{ MPa}$$

$$\boxed{\begin{array}{c} \tau_{max} = 31.9 \text{ MPa} \\ \text{at } 3.00 \leq x \leq 5.00 \text{ m} \end{array}}$$

EXAMPLE 13-19

A steel beam is built up by riveting together a W310x74 and a C250x30, as shown in Fig. 13-65. If the maximum transverse shear force in the beam is 150 kN, determine the maximum spacing allowed along the beam for 20 mm diameter rivets. The maximum allowable shear stress in the rivets is 60 MPa.

SOLUTION

To calculate the shear flow, which is required to determine the rivet spacing, the values for I and Q are needed. To determine I and Q, the centroid of the entire section must be determined. The information necessary for calculating the location of the centroid can be found in Appendix F.

For a W310x74:

$$A_1 = 9490 \text{ mm}^2$$

$$y_1 = \frac{310}{2}$$

$$= 155.0 \text{ mm}$$

FIGURE 13-65

The distance to the centroid for the channel is the distance from the base of the wide flange to its top, plus the thickness of the web of the channel, less the distance from the back of the channel to the centroid of the channel. The last measurement is the value for x shown in Appendix F.

For a C250x30:

$$A_2 = 3780 \text{ mm}^2$$

$$y_2 = 310 + 9.6 - 15.3$$

$$= 304.3 \text{ mm}$$

$$\bar{Y} = \frac{\Sigma A_i y_i}{\Sigma A_i}$$

$$= \frac{9490 \times 155.0 + 3780 \times 304.3}{9490 + 3780}$$

$$= \frac{1\ 470\ 950 + 1\ 150\ 254}{13\ 270}$$

$$= \frac{2\ 621\ 204}{13\ 270}$$

$$= 197.53 \text{ mm}$$

Now that the centroidal and neutral axes have been located, the moment of inertia of the area of the section about the centroidal axis must be calculated.

For a W310x74:

$$(\bar{I}_x)_1 = 165 \times 10^6 \text{ mm}^4$$

$$A_1 = 9490 \text{ mm}^2$$

$$d_1 = 197.53 - \frac{310}{2}$$

$$= 197.53 - 155.0$$

$$= 42.53 \text{ mm}$$

For a C250x30:

$$(\bar{I}_x)_2 = 1.16 \times 10^6 \text{ mm}^4$$

$$A_2 = 3780 \text{ mm}^2$$

$$d_2 = 304.3 - 197.53$$

$$= 106.77 \text{ mm}$$

Part	$\bar{I}_x$	Ad^2
W310x74	165.000×10^6	17.166×10^6
C250x30	1.160×10^6	43.091×10^6

$$\Sigma\, \bar{I}_x = 166.160 \times 10^6 \quad \Sigma\, Ad^2 = 60.257 \times 10^6$$

$$\Sigma\, Ad^2 = \underline{ 60.257 \times 10^6}$$

$$I_{\bar{x}} = 226.417 \times 10^6$$

Finally, the value for Q must be determined before the shear flow is calculated. The rivets connect the top of the flange of the wide flange shape with the inside of the web of the channel. All the shear force transmitted to the channel must be carried through the rivets on this plane. For this reason, use the total area of the channel when calculating Q. The value for $\bar{Y}$ is the distance from the centroid of the entire section to the centroid of the channel, which is the same as d_2.

$$Q = \bar{Y}A$$

$$= 106.77 \times 3780$$

$$= 403\ 591\ \text{mm}^3$$

The shear flow is obtained using Eq. (13-13). As usual, distance units must be metres and forces must be newtons.

$$q = \frac{VQ}{I}$$

$$= \frac{150 \times 10^3 \times 403\ 591 \times 10^{-9}}{226.42 \times 10^6 \times 10^{-12}}$$

$$= 267\ 373\ \text{N/m}$$

The shear force each rivet can resist may be obtained from Eq. (10-3). Call this force V' to distinguish it from the transverse shear.

$$\tau = \frac{V'}{A}$$

$$V' = \tau A$$

$$= 60 \times 10^6 \times \frac{\pi \times 20^2}{4} \times 10^{-6}$$

$$= 18\ 850\ \text{N}$$

The rivets are in pairs, with one on each side of the flange, so the total shear force that each pair of rivets can resist is

Force per pair of rivets:

$$2V' = 2 \times 18\,850$$

$$= 37\,700 \text{ N}$$

The necessary rivet spacing can be calculated by dividing the force each pair of rivets may carry by the shear flow.

Rivet spacing:

$$s = \frac{2V'}{q}$$

$$= \frac{37\,700}{267\,373}$$

$$= 0.141\,00 \text{ m}$$

$$\boxed{s = 141 \text{ mm}}$$

PROBLEMS

13-89 Calculate the maximum shear stress on the section of a beam that is 80 by 150 mm deep if the shear force on the section is 50 kN.

13-90 Determine the maximum shear stress in a beam with a rectangular cross section 40 mm wide by 80 mm high if the maximum shear force on the section is 250 kN.

13-91 For a beam cross section 50 by 80 mm deep, calculate the horizontal shear stress at a point 20 mm from the top surface if the transverse shear force at the section is 60 kN.

13-92 Find the shear stress on a surface 15 mm from the bottom of a 25 by 70 mm deep cross section in a beam if the transverse shear on the section is 135 kN.

13-93 Determine the maximum shear stress on the box cross section shown in Fig. P13-93 if the shear force on the section is 30 kN.

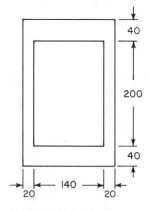

FIGURE P13-93

13-94 The section shown in Fig. P13-94 is used for a beam that has a maximum transverse shear force of 50 kN. Determine the maximum shear stress on the section.

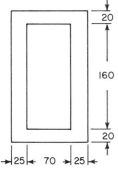

FIGURE P13-94

13-95 A beam with the section shown in Fig. P13-95 has a maximum transverse shear of 7500 N. Determine the shear stress at (a) the neutral axis and (b) on a plane 21 mm from the neutral axis, on the section where the shear is maximum.

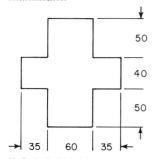

FIGURE P13-95

13-96 A small beam with the cross section shown in Fig. P13-96 has a maximum shear of 3 kN applied to it. Calculate the shear stress at (a) the neutral axis and (b) 16 mm below the neutral axis, for the section with maximum shear.

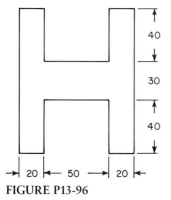

FIGURE P13-96

13-97 Calculate the shear stress at (a) the neutral axis and at (b) a plane 76 mm above the neutral axis for a beam with the section shown in Fig. P13-97. The maximum shear force on the section is 250 kN.

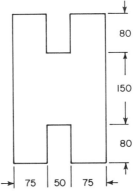

FIGURE P13-97

13-98 If the maximum shear force acting on the section shown in Fig. P13-98 is 3 MN, find the shear stress at (a) the neutral axis and (b) 62 mm above the neutral axis.

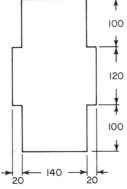

FIGURE P13-98

13-99 The timber beam shown in Fig. P13-99 has a cross section of 150 by 250 mm deep. Determine the location and magnitude of the maximum shear stress in the beam.

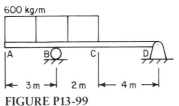

FIGURE P13-99

13-100 A small beam 30 by 70 mm deep carries the loads shown in Fig. P13-100. Find the location and magnitude of the maximum shear stress in the beam.

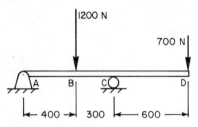

FIGURE P13-100

13-101 For the beam shown in Fig. P13-101, which is a steel W310x39, determine the magnitude and location of both the maximum flexural stress and the maximum shear stress.

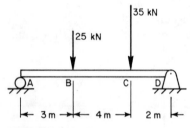

FIGURE P13-101

13-102 Find the magnitude and location of the maximum flexural stress and the maximum shear stress for the steel S200x27 beam shown in Fig. P13-102.

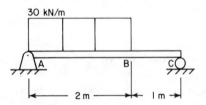

FIGURE P13-102

13-103 Determine the minimum size of steel W beam required to support a load of 450 kN 0.75 m from the right end. The beam is simply supported at each end and has an overall length of 2.5 m. The flexural stress is not to exceed 70 MPa, and the maximum allowable shear stress is 30 MPa. (Select the section based on flexural stress requirements, then check the shear stress.)

13-104 Find the lightest steel W shape that can be used for a cantilever beam 1.8 m long. The beam carries a concentrated load of 60 kN at its free end and is rigidly supported at the other end. The maximum allowable flexural stress is 125 MPa and the maximum allowable shear stress is 70 MPa. (Select the section based on the flexural stress requirements, then check the shear stress.)

13-105 A timber beam is fabricated by gluing pieces together, as shown in Fig. P13-105. Calculate the maximum shear stress between the web and the flange that must be resisted by the adhesive. The beam is 3 m long, simply supported at each end, and has a uniformly distributed load of 110 kg/m. Also calculate the maximum shear flow between the web and the flange.

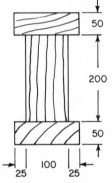

FIGURE P13-105

13-106 A 3 m long beam simply supported at each end and carrying a 140 kN load 1.2 m from the left end is made up by welding steel plates together, as shown in Fig. P13-106. Determine the maximum stress that occurs where the web and flange join, and calculate the maximum shear flow at the same location.

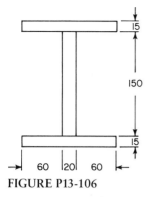

FIGURE P13-106

13-107 A beam is made by welding two 25 by 150 mm plates to a steel W360x39, as shown in Fig. P13-107. If the maximum shear force on the beam is 100 kN, calculate the maximum force in kN/m each weld must resist.

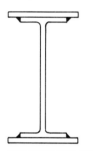

FIGURE P13-107

13-108 The timber-beam cross section shown in Fig. P13-108 has a maximum transverse shear force of 20 kN acting on it. If each nail can resist a shear force of 1400 N, find the maximum allowable spacing for the nails.

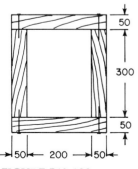

FIGURE P13-108

13-109 An aluminum extrusion with 5 mm thick walls is spot welded to a thin aluminum plate by a single row of welds, as shown in Fig. P13-109. If the maximum transverse shear force in the beam is 15 kN, and if the maximum shear force that can be resisted by each spot weld is 5 kN, calculate the maximum allowable spacing between welds.

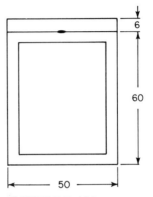

FIGURE P13-109

13-110 A beam is made by bolting two steel L125x75x8 to a plate 20 by 150 mm, as shown in Fig. P13-110. The maximum shear force on the section is 70 kN, and the maximum allowable shear force in each bolt is 18 kN. Determine the maximum bolt spacing.

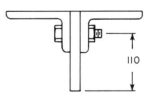

FIGURE P13-110

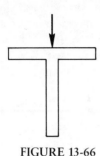

FIGURE 13-66

13-8 SHEAR CENTER

When the flexural formula, Eq. (13-5) or (13-6), was developed in Article 13-5, one of the conditions or assumptions made was that the beam does not twist. One method of preventing twisting is to apply the load so that it is along the axis of symmetry of the cross section, as illustrated for the T section shown in Fig. 13-66. It has thus been implied that the loads in the flexure and shear stress problems in the previous articles have all been applied along an axis of symmetry.

For some sections, such as channels and angles, it is not practical to apply the load along the axis of symmetry; this loading might not make efficient use of the section, or it might create problems with connections. One might consider loading a channel as shown in Fig. 13-67(a), but under such a loading, the channel would twist, as shown in Fig. 13-67(b). However, there is a point called the shear center where the load may be applied without causing twisting. This is shown in Fig. 13-67(c). The shear center is located on the axis of symmetry (if there is one) and at such a point so that the section will not twist.

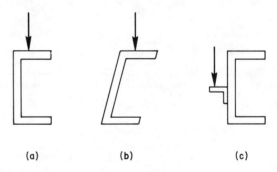

(a)   (b)   (c)

FIGURE 13-67

The calculations involved in locating the shear center are beyond the scope of this text, and one should refer to advanced texts on strength of materials or stress analysis for the necessary background if one finds it necessary to locate the shear center when the load will not be applied along an axis of symmetry. In the case of standard steel channels, the location of the shear center, measured from the center of the web, is given in the tables in Appendix F.

14 BEAM DEFLECTIONS

14-1 ELASTIC CURVE

In the discussion of beams in Chap. 13 it was pointed out that a beam with a load on it will deform. The amount of deformation can be of considerable importance. The brittle plaster in a ceiling will crack if the beams supporting it have large deformations. Any objects on wheels would tend to roll on a floor supported by beams with large deformations, and walking on a sloping or

FIGURE 14-1 The arbor of this milling machine is a rotating beam in which the deflection must be minimal if accurate machining is to be achieved. *Photo courtesy of Cincinnati Milacron Canada Limited.*

bouncing floor would be somewhat disconcerting. Excessive deformation in most machines would interfere with the operation of the machines. Large deformations in the bed of a lathe would prohibit accurate machining. The arbor supporting the cutter in the milling machine shown in Fig. 14-1 behaves as a rotating beam, and excessive deformation in the arbor would make it difficult to control the depth of the cut.

The actual deflection in a beam depends on a number of factors, including the loads and the types of supports. In addition, the higher the modulus of elasticity of the material in the beam, the smaller the deflection will be. Similarly, increasing the area moment of inertia of the cross section of the beam decreases the deflection. The moment of inertia used for determining beam deflections is the moment of inertia of the cross-sectional area with respect to the neutral axis for bending, which is the same moment of inertia that is used when calculating flexural stress.

The deformation or deflection of a beam is described in terms of its elastic curve. Figure 14-2(a) shows a beam that has deformed due to the load on it. The elastic curve is a side view of the neutral plane of the deformed beam, and is shown as a dashed line in Fig. 14-2(a). The elastic curve only of the same beam is shown in Fig. 14-2(b). The elastic curve is usually plotted on an x-y axis system; the axis is not always shown, but is sometimes imaginary. The deflection at D is the deviation from a straight line of the elastic curve at D, and is shown as δ, and the slope of the curve at the same point is shown as θ.

There are a number of methods available for determining the values of the deflection or slope at any point in a beam. Any of these methods may be used to develop a set of tables of slopes and deflections similar to the one shown in Fig. 14-3, and discussed in Article 14-2. The area-moment method, as discussed in Article 14-4, is one method that can be used for determining values of slopes and deflections in a beam, or for developing the tables shown in Fig. 14-3.

Regardless of the method, the list of beam conditions or assumptions imposed on the derivation of the flexural-stress formula in Article 13-5 also applies to the beams for which deflections are calculated.

In most cases, it will be the maximum deflection that is required. In many situations, the maximum deflection will *not* occur under a load, and the location of the maximum deflection must be determined before the value of the maximum deflection may be calculated. In a simple beam, the maximum deflection will occur where the slope of the elastic curve is zero.

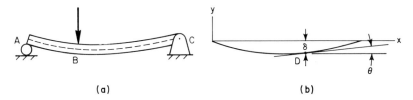

FIGURE 14-2

CASE	LOAD	MAXIMUM DEFLECTION	DEFLECTION EQUATION	SLOPE AT ENDS
1	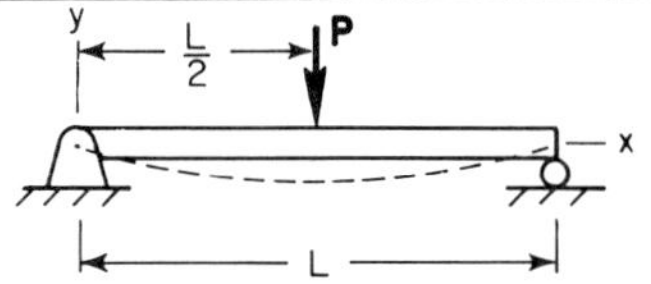	$\delta = -\dfrac{PL^3}{48EI}$ AT $x = \dfrac{L}{2}$	$\delta = -\dfrac{Px}{12EI}\left[\dfrac{3}{4}L^2 - x^2\right]$ FOR $0 \le x \le \dfrac{L}{2}$	$\theta_L = -\dfrac{PL^2}{16EI}$ $\theta_R = \dfrac{PL^2}{16EI}$
2	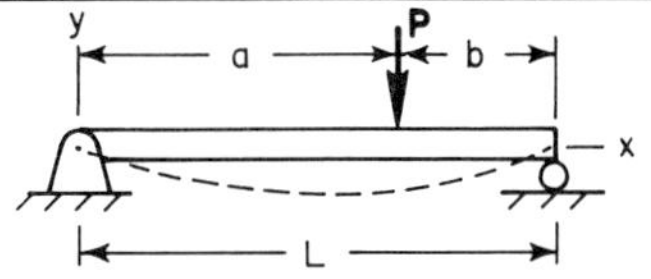	$\delta = -\dfrac{Pb(L^2 - b^2)^{3/2}}{9\sqrt{3}\,EIL}$ AT $x = \sqrt{\dfrac{L^2 - b^2}{3}}$	$\delta = -\dfrac{Pbx}{6EIL}(L^2 - x^2 - b^2)$ FOR $0 \le x \le a$ $\delta = -\dfrac{Pb}{6EIL}\left[\dfrac{L}{b}(x-a)^3 + (L^2 - b^2)x - x^3\right]$ FOR $a \le x \le L$	$\theta_L = -\dfrac{Pb(L^2 - b^2)}{6EIL}$ $\theta_R = \dfrac{Pa(L^2 - a^2)}{6EIL}$
3	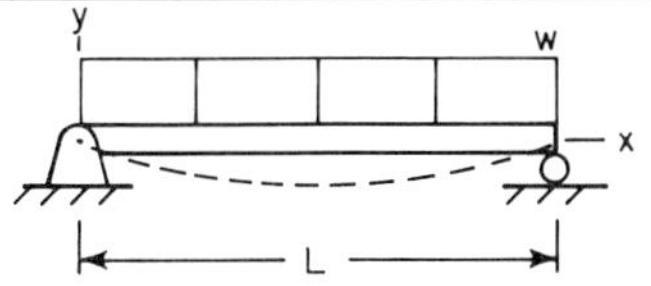	$\delta = -\dfrac{5wL^4}{384EI}$ AT $x = \dfrac{L}{2}$	$\delta = -\dfrac{wx}{24EI}(L^3 - 2Lx^2 + x^3)$	$\theta_L = -\dfrac{wL^3}{24EI}$ $\theta_R = \dfrac{wL^3}{24EI}$
4	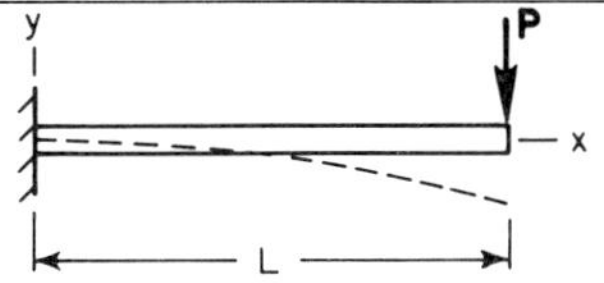	$\delta = -\dfrac{PL^3}{3EI}$ AT $x = L$	$\delta = -\dfrac{Px^2}{6EI}(3L - x)$	$\theta_L = 0$ $\theta_R = -\dfrac{PL^2}{2EI}$
5	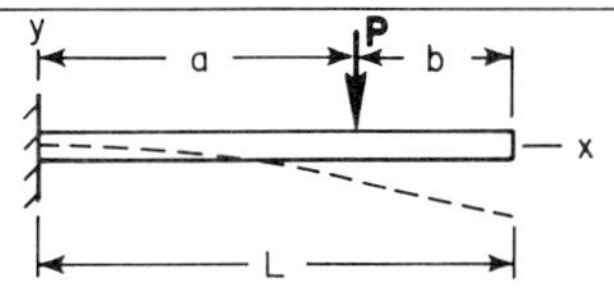	$\delta = -\dfrac{Pa^2}{6EI}(3L - a)$ AT $x = L$	$\delta = -\dfrac{Px^2}{6EI}(3a - x)$ FOR $0 \le x \le a$ $\delta = -\dfrac{Pa^2}{6EI}(3x - a)$ FOR $a \le x \le L$	$\theta_L = 0$ $\theta_R = -\dfrac{Pa^2}{2EI}$
6	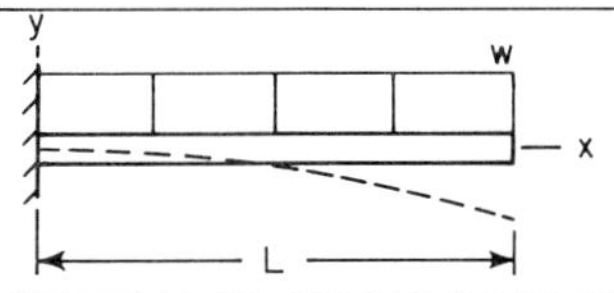	$\delta = -\dfrac{wL^4}{8EI}$ AT $x = L$	$\delta = -\dfrac{wx^2}{24EI}(6L^2 - 4Lx + x^2)$	$\theta_L = 0$ $\theta_R = -\dfrac{wL^3}{6EI}$

FIGURE 14-3

14-2   BEAM-DEFLECTION TABLES

The easiest method for determining the maximum deflection in a beam is to use beam-deflection tables, such as those shown in Fig. 14-3. Equations have been developed so that the relationship between the load, dimensions, moment of inertia and modulus of elasticity with the deflection can be expressed for a variety of loaded beams. These equations are given in the beam-deflection tables. Using these tables, all that is required is to select the beam in the table that matches the support and loading conditions given, substitute values in the equation given for the deflection, and evaluate the deflection.

If the support and loading system of the given beam does not match exactly the one in the table, the problem becomes more complex, and will be dealt with in following articles. The load due to the mass of the beam will usually be neglected when calculating the deflection in the initial set of problems.

Note from the tables in Fig. 14-3 that in some cases the maximum deflection is not at the point of application of the load or at the center of the beam. In some cases, a deflection other than the maximum may be required; the deflection equation is also given, so that the deflection at any point in the beam may be calculated.

EXAMPLE 14-1

A 3 m long W200x86 structural-steel beam is used to support a hoist in a small shop. It is simply supported at each end and carries a concentrated load of 80 kN due to the hoist at mid-span. Calculate the maximum deflection in the beam if the effect of the mass of the beam is neglected.

SOLUTION

The beam described in the problem matches Case 1 *in* Fig. 14-3, *so the maximum deflection can be calculated using the maximum deflection equation given in the table. As usual, care must be taken with units. The force must be in newtons, the length in metres, the modulus of elasticity in pascals, and the moment of inertia in metres to the fourth power. The value obtained for the deflection will be in metres, but it is usually expressed in millimetres in the final answer. The values for E and I are obtained from* Appendix E *and* Appendix F.

$$\delta = -\frac{PL^3}{48EI}$$

$$= -\frac{80 \times 10^3 \times 3^3}{48 \times 200 \times 10^9 \times 94.7 \times 10^6 \times 10^{-12}}$$

$$= -2.3759 \times 10^{-3} \text{ m}$$

$$= -2.3759 \text{ mm}$$

$$\boxed{\delta = -2.38 \text{ mm}}$$

EXAMPLE 14-2

A Douglas fir timber beam with a cross section of 150 by 250 mm deep is simply supported at each end, has a length of 5 m, and has a concentrated load of 15 kN 2 m from the right end. Determine (a) the maximum deflection and (b) the deflection at the midspan for the beam.

SOLUTION

The beam described matches Case 2 *in* Fig. 14-3. *The maximum deflection may be calculated using the equation given. Make certain that all units used in the calculations are in the base units of newtons and metres. Note that when working with* Case 2 *the distance labelled as a is always the larger distance, and not necessarily the distance from the left support to the load.*

Since it will be necessary to use the moment of inertia in both parts of the problem, it may be more efficient to calculate it separately.

$$I = \frac{bh^3}{12}$$

$$= \frac{150 \times 250^3}{12}$$

$$= 195.31 \times 10^6 \text{ mm}^4$$

(a) $$\delta = -\frac{Pb(L^2 - b^2)^{3/2}}{9\sqrt{3} \, EIL}$$

$$= -\frac{15 \times 10^3 \times 2(5^2 - 2^2)^{3/2}}{9\sqrt{3} \times 13 \times 10^9 \times 195.31 \times 10^6 \times 10^{-12} \times 5}$$

$$= -0.014\ 588 \text{ m}$$

$$= -14.588 \text{ mm}$$

To find the deflection at midspan for the beam, it will be necessary to use the deflection equation for the region $0 \le x \le a$ *for the beam given in* Fig. 14-3, *and to set* $x = 2.50$ m *for midspan.*

(b) $\delta = -\dfrac{Pbx}{6EIL}\left(L^2 - x^2 - b^2\right)$

$= -\dfrac{15 \times 10^3 \times 2 \times 2.50(5^2 - 2.50^2 - 2^2)}{6 \times 13 \times 10^9 \times 195.31 \times 10^6 \times 10^{-12} \times 5}$

$= -0.014\ 523$ m

$= -14.523$ mm

Note that the midspan deflection is only slightly less than the maximum deflection. This is due to the fact that the point of application of the load is relatively close to midspan.

> (a) $\delta = -14.6$ mm
> (b) $\delta = -14.5$ mm

EXAMPLE 14-3

A carbon-steel tool post on a lathe is fixed at its base and has a height of 90 mm. The maximum force applied by the tool holder at the free end of the tool post is 14 kN perpendicular to the axis of the post. Calculate the minimum diameter of tool post if the maximum allowable deflection is 0.500 mm.

SOLUTION

The tool post is a cantilever beam with the applied force at its end, as shown in Case 4 *in* Fig. 14-3. *In this situation, the deflection is known, but the moment of inertia, which is* $\pi d^4/64$, *is unknown. The deflection equation will be set up in the usual manner, but will be solved for the unknown term, d. Note that both sides of the equation will have the same sign, either positive or negative. A positive deflection is assumed. All terms must be in the base units of newtons and metres.*

$\delta = \dfrac{PL^3}{3EI}$

$0.500 \times 10^{-3} = \dfrac{14 \times 10^3(90 \times 10^{-3})^3}{3 \times 207 \times 10^9 \times \dfrac{\pi d^4}{64}}$

$d^4 = \dfrac{14 \times 10^3(90 \times 10^{-3})^3 \times 64}{3 \times 207 \times 10^9 \times \pi \times 0.500 \times 10^{-3}}$

$$= 669\ 613 \times 10^{-12}$$
$$d = 28.606 \times 10^{-3}\ m$$
$$= 28.606\ mm$$

$$\boxed{d = 28.6\ mm}$$

PROBLEMS

14-1 A structural-steel W310x129 beam is 3 m long and rigidly supported at one end. A concentrated load of 85 kN is applied perpendicular to the axis at the free end. Determine the maximum deflection in the beam. Ignore the deflection due to the mass of the beam.

14-2 Calculate the deflection at the midspan of a 2 m long beam simply supported at each end if it has a concentrated load of 65 kN at midspan and a cross section with a moment of inertia of 7.5×10^6 mm^4. The material has a modulus of elasticity of 110 GPa.

14-3 A 2 m long 6061-T6 aluminum beam with a moment of inertia of 45×10^6 mm^4 is simply supported at each end and carries, 0.400 m from its right end, a concentrated load of 30 kN. Find the maximum deflection in the beam.

14-4 Calculate the maximum deflection in a 1.5 m long red oak cantilever beam rigidly supported at one end if there is an 8 kN load that is 0.5 m from the free end. The moment of inertia of the cross section of the beam is 6×10^6 mm^4.

14-5 For a 1.5 m long S380x64 structural-steel cantilever beam that is rigidly supported at one end, determine the deflection at the free end for (a) a concentrated load of 900 kN at 0.75 m from the free end and (b) a uniform load of 600 kN/m over the length of the beam. Ignore the deflection due to the mass of the beam.

14-6 Calculate the midspan deflection for a 3 m long W250x58 structural-steel beam simply supported at each end with (a) a 75 kN concentrated load at midspan and (b) a uniform load of 25 kN/m over the length of the beam. Ignore the deflection due to the mass of the beam.

14-7 Calculate the deflection at midspan for a Douglas fir floor joist 3 m long with a cross section of 40 by 240 mm deep. It is simply supported at each end and it supports a uniform load of 160 kg/m over its length.

14-8 A small cantilever beam made of ABS plastic is rigidly supported at one end and supports a uniform load of 20 kg/m along its 600 mm length. Calculate the maximum deflection in the beam if its cross section is 20 by 35 mm deep.

14-9 A round vinyl cantilever beam with a diameter of 20 mm is rigidly supported at one end, and supports a 25 kg load 120 mm from the single support. If the total length of the beam is 200 mm, determine the deflection of the beam at the point of application of the load.

14-10 An arbor for a milling machine has a diameter of 30 mm and a length of 350 mm. It is simply supported at each end and a load of 1800 N is applied through the cutter which is 100 mm from one end. Determine the deflection at the cutter if the arbor is made of carbon steel.

14-11 Calculate the deflection 2.5 m from the left end of a W410x132 structural-steel beam 7 m long and simply supported at each end if it carries a uniform load of 125 kN/m over its length. The mass of the beam is part of the load.

14-12 A 3 m long structural-steel W310x202 beam is a cantilever, rigidly supported at one end and free at the other. It carries a load of 80 kN/m over its length. Determine its deflection at a point 0.90 m from the free end. Ignore the deflection due to the mass of the beam.

14-13 A 5 m long beam simply supported at each end carries a uniform distributed load of 40 kN/m over its entire length. Determine the lightest structural steel W beam that may be used to support this load. (Assume the given load includes the load due to the mass of the beam.) The beam deflection is not to exceed $L/360$.

14-14 Determine the lightest structural steel S shape that may be used as a cantilever beam 2.5 m long, fixed at one end, with a 50 kN load at the free end. The maximum deflection in the

beam is not to exceed 6 mm. The deflection due to the mass of the beam may be neglected.

14-15 A circular malleable cast-iron shaft 450 mm long is used as a cantilever beam, with a rigid support at one end, and free at the other, to carry a uniform distributed load of 1.5 kN/m over its length. If the maximum deflection is not to exceed 2.0 mm, determine the minimum allowable diameter for the shaft.

14-16 Determine the minimum dimensions required for an ABS plastic beam with a square cross section, which is simply supported at both ends and carries a load of 350 N 60 mm from the left end. The total length of the beam is 130 mm, and the maximum allowable deflection is 0.75 mm.

14-3 PRINCIPLE OF SUPERPOSITION

The principle of superposition provides a technique for solving more complex problems by breaking them up into two or more simple problems. According to the principle of superposition, the deflection at any point in a beam is equal to the algebraic sum of the deflections at that point due to each of the loads acting on the beam. For the principle of superposition to be valid, the stress must be proportional to the strain for the material, and the total deformation must be small enough that the material has not started to yield.

The application of the principle of superposition is illustrated in Fig. 14-4. Figure 14-4(a) shows a beam with a distributed load plus a concentrated load at midspan. The deflection of the beam is also shown by the dashed line. Figures 14-4(b) and 14-4(c) show the same beam with the distributed load and with the concentrated load, and their respective deflections. The deflection at any point in the beam shown in Fig. 14-4(a) is simply

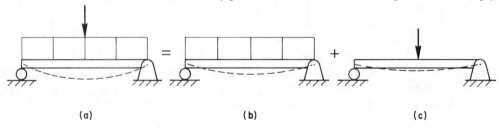

(a)   (b)   (c)

FIGURE 14-4

equal to the sum of the two deflections at the same point for the loads of Figs. 14-4(b) and 14-4(c). In this case, both loads cause maximum deflection at midspan, so the maximum deflection in the beam can be readily calculated.

In the case of a beam such as shown in Fig. 14-5, where the load consists of a uniformly distributed load and a concentrated load not at the center, the maximum deflection would be located somewhere between the point of maximum deflection for each of the separate loadings. Calculating the deflection at a point midway between the two maximum deflections would give an *approximation* of the magnitude of the maximum deflection.

In general, a simple beam that is loaded symmetrically with respect to the center will have its maximum deflection at the center. If the loading is not symmetrical, the maximum deflection will tend to be between the center of the beam and the resultant of the applied loads. In the case of a cantilever beam, the maximum deflection will be at the free end, if all the loads are in the same direction.

The deflection due to the mass of the beam is usually small relative to the deflection due to the other loads on the beam. Thus, in the following problems, the mass of the beam will be neglected when calculating the deflection.

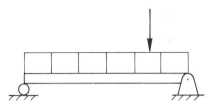

FIGURE 14-5

EXAMPLE 14-4

A small plastic cantilever beam with a length of 250 mm has a uniform distributed load of 300 N/m over its length and a concentrated load of 150 N at its free end. Determine the maximum deflection in the beam if the plastic has a modulus of elasticity of 1.5 GPa and if the moment of inertia of the cross section is 0.150×10^6 mm^4.

SOLUTION

To use the information from Fig. 14-3 *and the principle of superposition, a drawing, as shown in* Fig. 14-6, *should be made. The given beam is shown in* Fig. 14-6(a). *Figures 14-6(b) and 14-6(c) show the two loadings, which, when added together, give the original load. The elastic curve for each loading is also shown, and one can infer that the maximum deflection for the combined loading will be at the free end, since each loading by itself also causes a maximum deflection at the free end.*

The loadings shown in Fig. 14-6(b) *and* 14-6(c) *match* Case 6 *and* Case 4 *respectively in* Fig. 14-3. *Thus, the maximum deflections for those two cases may be added algebraically to give the total maximum deflection for the given beam.*

The subscripts with the deflections refer to the case from Fig. 14-3.

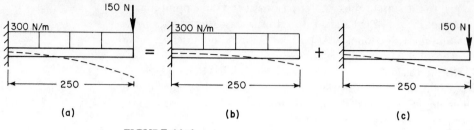

FIGURE 14-6

At free end:

$$\delta = \delta_6 + \delta_4$$

$$= -\frac{wL^4}{8EI} - \frac{PL^3}{3EI}$$

$$= -\frac{300 \times 0.250^4}{8 \times 1.5 \times 10^9 \times 0.150 \times 10^6 \times 10^{-12}}$$

$$-\frac{150 \times 0.250^3}{3 \times 1.5 \times 10^9 \times 0.150 \times 10^6 \times 10^{-12}}$$

$$= -0.651\ 04 \times 10^{-3} - 3.4722 \times 10^{-3}$$

$$= -4.1232 \times 10^{-3}\ \text{m}$$

$$= -4.1232\ \text{mm}$$

$$\boxed{\delta = -4.12\ \text{mm}}$$

EXAMPLE 14-5

The beam shown in Fig. 14-7 is 6061-T6 aluminum and its cross section has a moment of inertia of 35×10^6 mm^4. Calculate the deflection at the center of the beam.

SOLUTION

A drawing, as shown in Fig. 14-8, is made showing the separate loadings that make up the load in the given problem, and the deflections they cause. The loading shown in Fig. 14-8(b) matches that of Case 3 in Fig. 14-3, and the loading in Fig. 14-8(c) is the same as in Case 2 of Fig. 14-3, with two significant exceptions. In the problem, the concentrated load and its deflection are upwards. Also, for the concentrated load the distance from the left support to the load is smaller than the distance from the load to the right support.

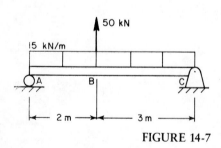

FIGURE 14-7

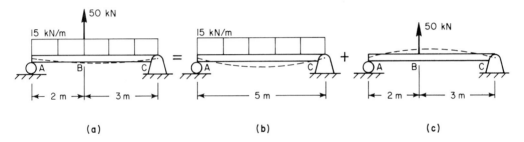

FIGURE 14-8

The total deflection at the center of the beam will be the algebraic sum of the deflections at the center of the beam caused by each of the two loads.

The deflection at the center due to the distributed load is the maximum deflection as given for Case 3 *in* Fig. 14-3.

To obtain the deflection due to the concentrated load, the diagram is reversed, as shown in Fig. 14-9, *so that distances match* Case 2. *The deflection when x* = 2.50 m *will be the midspan deflection due to the 50 kN load. This must be calculated using the deflection equation with* Case 2 *for the region* $0 \leq x \leq a$ *and setting x* = 2.50 m.

The subscripts with the deflections refer to the Case *used.*

$$\delta = \delta_3 + \delta_2$$

$$= -\frac{5wL^4}{384EI} + \frac{Pbx}{6EIL}\left(L^2 - x^2 - b^2\right)$$

$$= -\frac{5 \times 15 \times 10^3 \times 5^4}{384 \times 69 \times 10^9 \times 35 \times 10^6 \times 10^{-12}}$$

$$+ \frac{50 \times 10^3 \times 2 \times 2.50(5^2 - 2.50^2 - 2^2)}{6 \times 69 \times 10^9 \times 35 \times 10^6 \times 10^{-12} \times 5}$$

$$= -0.050\ 5467 + 0.050\ 8971$$

$$= 0.000\ 3504\ \text{m}$$

$$= 0.3504\ \text{mm}$$

$$\boxed{\delta = 0.350\ \text{mm}}$$

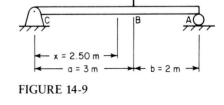

FIGURE 14-9

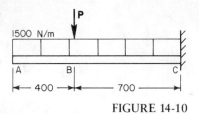

FIGURE 14-10

EXAMPLE 14-6

The extruded-magnesium beam shown in Fig. 14-10 has a cross section with a moment of inertia of 5×10^6 mm^4. Determine the magnitude of the maximum load, **P**, which may be applied if the maximum deflection is not to exceed 2.50 mm.

SOLUTION

The given beam is redrawn in Fig. 14-11(a), *and the two separate loadings that make up the original loading are shown in* Figs. 14-11(b) *and* 14-11(c). *These loadings match those in* Case 6 *and* Case 5 *respectively of* Fig. 14-3.

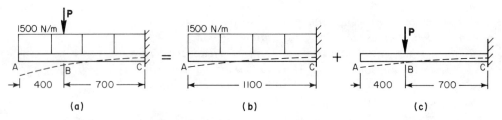

FIGURE 14-11

In this situation, the maximum deflection is known and one load is unknown. The maximum deflection is at the free end and is equal to the algebraic sum of the deflections due to each load. The deflection equation is set up as usual, but this time the equation is solved for P rather than δ.

Note that the dimension, a, in Case 5 is always the dimension from the support to the load.

The numbers in the equation may be slightly more convenient if all terms in the equation are multiplied by EI.

$$\delta = \delta_6 + \delta_5$$

$$\delta = -\frac{wL^4}{8EI} - \frac{Pa^2}{6EI}\left(3L - a\right)$$

$$\delta EI = -\frac{wL^4}{8} - \frac{Pa^2}{6}\left(3L - a\right)$$

$$-2.50 \times 10^{-3} \times 45 \times 10^9 \times 5 \times 10^6 \times 10^{-12}$$

$$= -\frac{1500 \times 1.100^4}{8} - \frac{P \times 0.700^2}{6}\left(3 \times 1.100 - 0.700\right)$$

$$-562.50 = -274.52 - 0.212\,33\,P$$

$$P = \frac{562.50 - 274.52}{0.212\,33}$$

$$= \frac{287.98}{0.212\ 33}$$

$$= 1356.3 \text{ N}$$

$$\boxed{P = 1360 \text{ N}}$$

PROBLEMS

14-17 For the malleable cast-iron beam shown in Fig. P14-17, which has a cross section with a moment of inertia of 65×10^6 mm^4, determine the deflection at the free end.

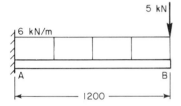

FIGURE P14-17

14-18 Calculate the deflection at midspan for the 2014-T6 aluminum beam shown in Fig. P14-18 if the moment of inertia of its cross section is 225×10^6 mm^4.

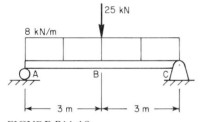

FIGURE P14-18

14-19 The beam shown in Fig. P14-19 is made of structural steel and the moment of inertia of its cross section is 85×10^6 mm^4. Find the deflection at midspan.

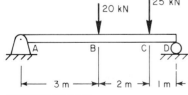

FIGURE P14-19

14-20 Determine the deflection at the left end for the 6061-T6 aluminum beam shown in Fig. P14-20. The moment of inertia of its cross section is 260×10^6 mm^4.

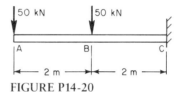

FIGURE P14-20

14-21 Calculate the deflection at midspan for the rigid vinyl beam shown in Fig. P14-21 if its cross section is 30 by 50 mm deep.

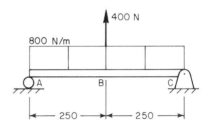

FIGURE P14-21

14-22 The red oak beam shown in Fig. P14-22 has a cross section 40 by 80 mm deep. Determine the deflection at the free end of the beam.

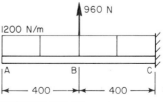

FIGURE P14-22

14-23 Determine the maximum deflection for the beam shown in Fig. P14-23 if it is made of malleable cast iron and if its cross section is 35 by 50 mm deep.

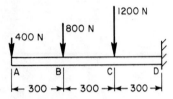

FIGURE P14-23

14-24 For the structural-steel W310x86 beam shown in Fig. P14-24, calculate the deflection at the free end.

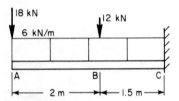

FIGURE P14-24

14-25 Calculate the deflection at midspan for the W460x113 structural-steel beam shown in Fig. P14-25.

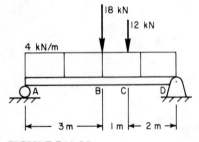

FIGURE P14-25

14-26 The red oak beam shown in Fig. P14-26 has a 50 by 60 mm deep cross section. Determine the deflection at midspan.

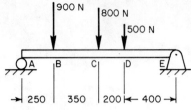

FIGURE P14-26

14-27 The carbon-steel beam shown in Fig. P14-27 has a cross section with a moment of inertia of 110×10^6 mm^4. Calculate the magnitude of the force, **P**, so that the deflection at the free end will be zero.

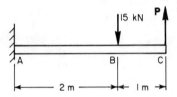

FIGURE P14-27

14-28 Determine the magnitude of the force, **P**, so that the midspan deflection of the beam shown in Fig. P14-28 will be zero.

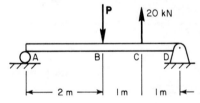

FIGURE P14-28

14-29 The beam shown in Fig. P14-29 is red oak and its cross section has a moment of inertia of 4×10^6 mm^4. If the maximum allowable deflection in the beam is 5.0 mm, determine the maximum allowable value for the distributed load.

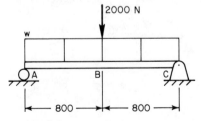

FIGURE P14-29

14-30 Determine the magnitude of the force, **P**, required to cause a deflection of 2 mm at the free end of the rigid vinyl beam shown in Fig. P14-30. The moment of inertia of the cross section of the beam is 0.40×10^6 mm^4.

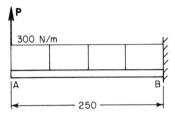

FIGURE P14-30

14-31 If the allowable deflection at midspan for the beam shown in Fig. P14-31 is 2 mm, determine the lightest structural-steel W shape that may be used.

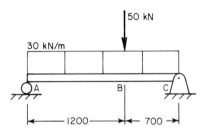

FIGURE P14-31

14-32 Find the lightest structural-steel S shape that may be used for the beam shown in Fig. P14-32 if the maximum deflection is not to exceed $L/240$.

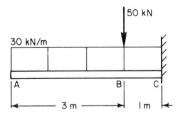

FIGURE P14-32

14-33 The extruded-magnesium beam shown in Fig. P14-33 has a rectangular cross section with a width of 40 mm. Determine the required depth of the cross section if the maximum deflection is $L/300$.

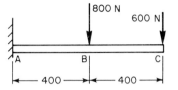

FIGURE P14-33

14-34 The midspan deflection of the malleable cast-iron beam shown in Fig. P14-34 is not to exceed 2 mm. Determine the diameter required if the beam has a circular cross section.

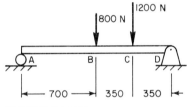

FIGURE P14-34

14-4 AREA-MOMENT METHOD

This is one of several methods that may be used to calculate the deflection at any point in a beam for any loading. Since it is a general method, it is useful when deflection tables do not provide the required information. The area-moment method involves the use of two theorems that relate the moment diagram, slope of the elastic curve, and tangential deviation.

Before developing the area-moment theorems, it is first necessary to develop the general equation for the elastic curve of a beam.

If a beam that is behaving elastically has only bending moments applied to it, as shown in Fig. 14-12, the elastic curve, shown as a dashed line, is an arc of a circle with radius ρ. The length of the elastic curve is L and, from geometry,

$$L = \rho\theta$$

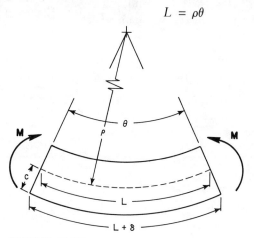

FIGURE 14-12

This may be rewritten as

$$\theta = \frac{L}{\rho}$$

Similarly,

$$L + \delta = (\rho + c)\theta$$

or

$$\theta = \frac{L + \delta}{\rho + c}$$

Since the two expressions for θ must equal each other

$$\frac{L}{\rho} = \frac{L + \delta}{\rho + c}$$

By cross multiplying,

$$L\rho + Lc = L\rho + \delta\rho$$

Hence,

$$Lc = \delta\rho$$

Dividing both sides by L and ρ gives

$$\frac{c}{\rho} = \frac{\delta}{L}$$

However, $\delta/L = \epsilon$, $\epsilon = \sigma/E$, and in flexure, $\sigma = Mc/I$.

The equation becomes

$$\frac{c}{\rho} = \frac{\delta}{L} = \epsilon = \frac{\sigma}{E} = \frac{Mc}{EI}$$

This reduces to

$$\frac{1}{\rho} = \frac{M}{EI} \tag{14-1}$$

where ρ is the radius of curvature of the elastic curve of the beam,

M is the bending moment acting on the beam,

E is the modulus of elasticity of the material, and

I is the moment of inertia of the cross section of the beam.

Since the flexure-stress formula, Eq. (13-5), was used in developing Eq. (14-1), all the limitations that apply to the flexure-stress formula also apply to Eq. (14-1).

Equation (14-1) is the basic equation for the elastic curve of a beam. Procedures for calculating slopes and deflections in a beam are based on this formula. The area-moment method is one of these procedures.

The first theorem of the area-moment method is developed using Fig. 14-13, which shows the elastic curve of a portion of a beam in Fig. 14-13(a) and the corresponding moment diagram in Fig. 14-13(b). Two points, m and n, are picked a short distance apart on the elastic curve, and tangents are drawn at these points. The angle between the tangents is $\Delta\theta$. The angle subtended by the arc mn is also $\Delta\theta$, and the length of the arc for a large radius of curvature is approximately Δx.

From geometry

$$\Delta x = \rho\Delta\theta$$

or

$$\Delta\theta = \frac{\Delta x}{\rho}$$

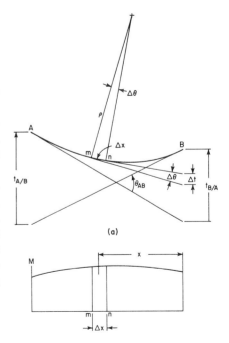

FIGURE 14-13

From Eq (14-1), $1/\rho = M/EI$.

Thus

$$\Delta\theta = \frac{M\Delta x}{EI}$$

The total angle subtended by the arc between A and B is θ_{AB}, and is the sum of all the angles subtended by the short lengths of arc between A and B.

$$\theta_{AB} = \Sigma\,\Delta\theta = \Sigma\,\frac{M\Delta x}{EI}$$

The expression $M\Delta x$ is the area under the moment diagram between m and n, and the expression $\Sigma\,M\Delta x$ is the total area under the moment diagram between A and B.

The mathematical statement of the first area-moment theorem is

$$\theta_{AB} = \Sigma\,\frac{M\Delta x}{EI} \qquad (14\text{-}2)$$

where θ_{AB} is the angle measured from the tangent at A to the tangent at B,

$\Sigma\,M\Delta x$ is the area under the moment diagram between A and B, and

EI is the product of the modulus of elasticity of the material and the moment of inertia of the cross section of the beam.

Theorem 1: The angle between the tangents to the elastic curve of a loaded beam at any two points, A and B, along the elastic curve is equal to the area under the moment diagram of the beam between A and B divided by EI.

As might be expected from the development of Eqs. (14-1) and (14-2), units of the angle θ will be radians. The area under a positive moment is treated as positive and indicates that the angle measured from the tangent at the point on the left to the tangent at the point on the right is a positive or counterclockwise angle. The negative area under the moment diagram indicates a negative or clockwise angle in measuring from the tangent to the point on the left to the tangent to the point on the right.

In the case where one of the tangents is horizontal, the angle obtained using Theorem 1 will be the slope of the elastic curve at the other tangent point. This is true because, for the small angles involved, $\tan\theta = \theta$ where $\tan\theta$ is the slope of the tangent line and θ is measured in radians.

The second area-moment theorem provides the tangential deviation, which is the vertical distance between tangents to two points on the elastic curve of a beam. Referring to Fig. 14-13(a), $t_{B/A}$ is the tangential deviation measuring the distance to B from the tangent drawn through A, and $t_{A/B}$ is the tangential deviation measuring the distance to A from the tangent drawn through B. Note that in many cases, $t_{B/A} \neq t_{A/B}$.

To develop the second theorem, refer to Fig. 14-13. Since the actual angles are very small, $\Delta t \cong x\Delta\theta$, where x is the distance from the midpoint between m and n and the vertical reference line at B. From Fig. 14-13(a) it can be seen that the tangential deviation of B from the tangent drawn through A is equal to the sum of all the tangential deviations Δt between A and B.

$$t_{B/A} = \Sigma \, \Delta t = \Sigma \, x\Delta\theta$$

but $\Delta\theta = M\Delta x/EI$

Thus

$$t_{B/A} = \frac{\Sigma \, (M\Delta x)x}{EI} \tag{14-3}$$

where $t_{B/A}$ is the tangential deviation of point B measured from a tangent drawn through point A,

$\Sigma \, (M\Delta x)x$ is the first moment of the area under the moment diagram between A and B about a vertical axis through B, and

EI is the product of the modulus of elasticity of the material and the moment of inertia of the cross section of the beam.

Theorem 2: The tangential deviation of point B on the elastic curve of a loaded beam measured from the tangent drawn through A is equal to the first moment of the area of the bending-moment diagram between A and B about an axis through B, divided by EI.

When applying Theorem 2, a positive area under the moment diagram will give a positive first moment and a positive value for the tangential deviation, and a negative area will give a negative first moment and a negative value for the tangential deviation, where the positive value means that the point is above the reference tangent and the negative value means that the point is below the reference tangent. This is illustrated in Fig. 14-14.

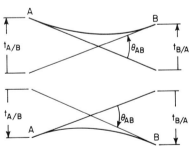

FIGURE 14-14

Using the area-moment method to calculate beam deflections usually requires drawing a free-body diagram, a moment diagram, and an elastic curve for the beam. The desired tangents, angles and tangential deviations are drawn on the elastic curve, and the necessary calculations are performed. Some ingenuity is often required to relate tangential deviations to deflections, and this is best illustrated by means of the example problems that follow.

Construction of moment diagrams will not follow procedures discussed in Article 13-4, which were most useful for determining the maximum moment. Instead, moment diagrams will be drawn by parts, where a separate moment diagram is drawn for each individual load. This method gives simpler solutions when using the area-moment method. The process is illustrated in Figs. 14-15 and 14-16. After the free-body diagram of the beam is drawn and the reactions are calculated, a moment diagram is drawn for each individual load, including reactions, starting at either the left end or the right end of the beam. It will be recalled that a single concentrated load causes a triangular-shaped moment diagram, a uniform distributed load causes a parabolic-shaped moment diagram *under the load*, and a torque or moment causes a rectangular-shaped moment diagram. In Figs.

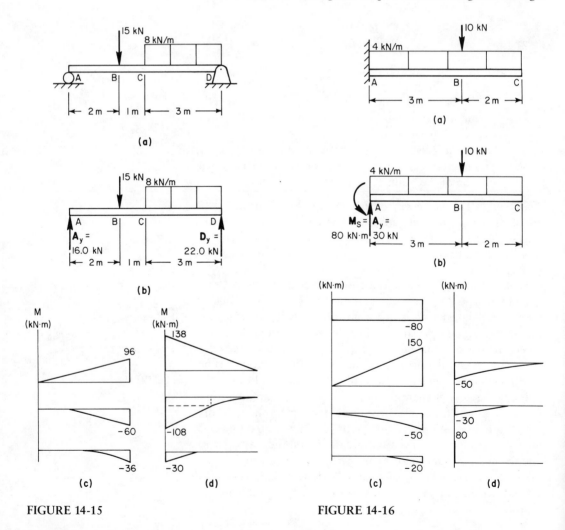

FIGURE 14-15

FIGURE 14-16

14-15(c) and 14-16(c), the moment diagrams are drawn from left to right, and in Figs. 14-15(d) and 14-16(d), the moment diagrams are drawn from right to left.

It is a good idea to draw the moment diagrams in a logical sequence. When drawing the moment diagrams from left to right, the top diagram should be the moment diagram for the first load on the left end of the beam, and the bottom moment diagram should be that for the load furthest to the right. If the moment diagrams are drawn from right to left, the top moment diagram should be for the first load on the right end of the beam and the bottom moment diagram should be for the load furthest to the left.

One might visualize the process of drawing moment diagrams by parts by assuming that the beam is a cantilever rigidly supported at the end opposite to the starting point. Then, each moment diagram is the same as would be drawn for the cantilever beam with that single load applied to it.

Usually, the simpler solution using the area-moment method involves the simpler moment diagram. It can be seen that the simpler figure may require drawing the moment diagram from either the left or the right. A quick and easy check on the accuracy of the moment diagram can be made by summing the moments at the end opposite the starting point. The sum of the moments, including any moments applied at that point, must be zero.

The basic geometric shapes for moment diagrams, their areas, and the location of their centroids are shown in Fig. 14-17.

SHAPE	AREA	CENTROID ($\bar{x}$)
Rectangle	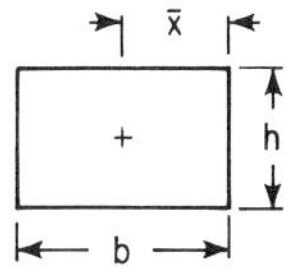 bh	$\dfrac{b}{2}$
Triangle	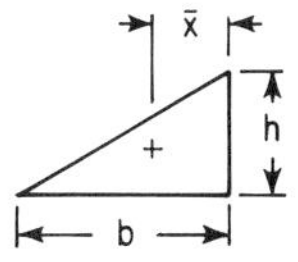 $\dfrac{1}{2}bh$	$\dfrac{b}{3}$
Spandrel of a Parabola	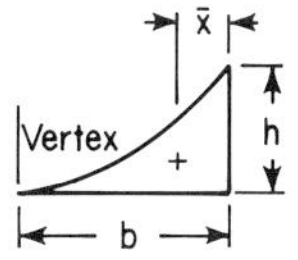 $\dfrac{1}{3}bh$	$\dfrac{b}{4}$

FIGURE 14-17

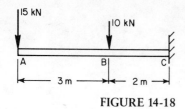

FIGURE 14-18

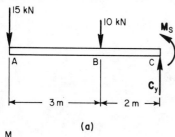

(a)

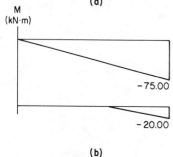

(b)

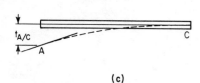

(c)

FIGURE 14-19

EXAMPLE 14-7

Determine the deflection at the free end of the cantilever beam shown in Fig. 14-18 if the beam is made of 6061-T6 aluminum, and if its cross section has a moment of inertia of 375×10^6 mm^4.

SOLUTION

Start by drawing a free-body diagram of the beam, as shown in Fig. 14-19(a). The magnitude of the moment at the support will be used as a check on the moment diagram, so it should be calculated.

$$\Sigma M_C = 0$$
$$15 \times 5 + 10 \times 2 + M_S = 0$$
$$M_S = -75.00 - 20.00$$
$$= -95.00 \text{ kN} \cdot \text{m}$$

Generally, when drawing a moment diagram by parts for a cantilever beam, it is best to start with the free end. The moment diagram, drawn by parts, is shown in Fig. 14-19(b). The top portion is the moment diagram due to the 15 kN load at the left end. The magnitude of the moment increases linearly to the support, and the value at the support can be calculated. The sign convention will be the same as that already established for bending moments.

For 15 kN load:

At right end,

$$M = -(15 \times 5)$$
$$= -75.00 \text{ kN} \cdot \text{m}$$

There is no moment caused by the 10 kN load until the load is actually encountered on the beam. The load causes a moment whose magnitude increases linearly to the support, and its maximum value at the support may also be calculated.

For 10 kN load:

At right end,

$$M = -(10 \times 2)$$
$$= -20.00 \text{ kN} \cdot \text{m}$$

The moment at the support must act as though it is applied to the beam immediately before the end of the beam, and hence is a positive bending moment. The moments may be checked to determine if their sum is zero.

Moment check:

$$\Sigma M = -75.00 - 20.00 + 95.00$$

$$= 0.00 \qquad \text{Check}$$

The values for the moment diagrams are probably (but not guaranteed) correct.

Figure 14-19(c) *shows the elastic curve of the beam. The tangential deviation,* $t_{A/C}$, *which measures the distance from the tangent through C to point A on the elastic curve, is shown. This coincides with the deflection of A, since the slope of a cantilever beam at the support, and thus the tangent at that point, is horizontal.*

The value for $t_{A/C}$ *may be calculated using* Theorem 2. *The first moment of the area under the moment diagram between A and C is taken about A, where the tangential deviation is being determined, so the distance to the centroid for each triangular area must be measured from A, and not from the base of the triangle.*

It simplifies the numbers if E and I are used as symbols until near the end of the calculations. Since the load was given in kN, the common factor 10^3 *has been taken outside of the brackets.*

$$\delta_A = t_{A/C}$$

$$= \frac{1}{EI}\left[-\frac{1}{2}(5 \times 75.00)\left(\frac{2}{3} \times 5\right) - \frac{1}{2}(2 \times 20.00)\left(3 + \frac{2}{3} \times 2\right)\right]10^3$$

$$= \frac{(-625.00 - 86.67)10^3}{EI}$$

$$= \frac{-711.67 \times 10^3}{69 \times 10^9 \times 375 \times 10^6 \times 10^{-12}}$$

$$= -0.027\ 504 \text{ m}$$

$$= -27.504 \text{ mm}$$

The negative sign indicates that point A is below the tangent drawn through C.

$$\boxed{\delta = -27.5 \text{ mm}}$$

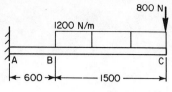

FIGURE 14-20

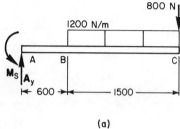

(a)

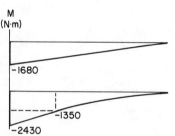

(b)

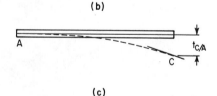

(c)

FIGURE 14-21

EXAMPLE 14-8

The red oak beam shown in Fig. 14-20 has a cross section with a moment of inertia of 30×10^6 mm^4. Calculate the deflection at the free end.

SOLUTION

The first step is to draw a free-body diagram of the beam, as shown in Fig. 14-21(a). *Then use the diagram as an aid in calculating the moment at the support, which will be used when checking the moment diagrams.*

$$\Sigma M_A = 0$$

$$M_S - 1200 \times 1.500 \times \left(0.600 + \frac{1.500}{2}\right)$$

$$- 800 \times 2.100 = 0$$

$$M_S = 2430.0 + 1680.0$$

$$= 4110.0 \text{ N}\cdot\text{m}$$

In this case, moments will be drawn starting at the free end of the beam. They are shown in Fig. 14-21(b). *The magnitude of the moment due to the 800 N concentrated load increases linearly from right to left, and its value at the support can be calculated. When working from right to left the sign convention for bending moments does not change.*

For 800 N load:

At left end,

$$M = -(800 \times 2.100)$$

$$= -1680.0 \text{ N}\cdot\text{m}$$

The shape of the moment diagram under a uniform distributed load is parabolic. However, from the left end of the load to the support the change in moment will be linear. Due to this change in shape, the value of the moment at the change in the diagram, as well as at the left end, must be calculated.

For 1200 N/m load:

At left end of load,

$$M = -\left(1200 \times 1.500 \times \frac{1.500}{2}\right)$$

$$= -1350.0 \text{ N}\cdot\text{m}$$

At left end of beam,

$$M = -(1200 \times 1.500)\left(0.600 + \frac{1.500}{2}\right)$$

$$= -2430.0 \text{ N} \cdot \text{m}$$

The moment at the support must be treated as if applied immediately before the end of the beam as it is approached from the right, giving it a positive sign.

Moment check:

$$\Sigma M = -1680.0 - 2430.0 + 4110.0$$

$$= 0.00 \qquad \qquad \text{Check}$$

The elastic curve for the beam is shown in **Fig. 14-21(c)**. *The tangent through point A at the support is horizontal, so the tangential deviation, $t_{C/A}$, will also equal the deflection at C.*

Theorem 2 is used to calculate $t_{C/A}$. The first moment of the areas between A and C is taken about an axis through C, where the tangential deviation is measured, so measurements to the centroids must be from C. The moment diagram for the distributed load is broken into three simple areas, as shown by the dashed lines.

It will be more convenient to use the symbols for E and I, and to substitute values at the end of the calculations.

$$\delta_C = t_{C/A}$$

$$= \frac{1}{EI}\left[-\frac{1}{2} \times 2.100 \times 1680 \times \frac{2}{3} \times 2.100 \right.$$

$$-\frac{1}{3} \times 1.500 \times 1350 \times \frac{3}{4} \times 1.500$$

$$-0.600 \times 1350\left(1.500 + \frac{0.600}{2}\right)$$

$$\left. -\frac{1}{2} \times 0.600(2430 - 1350)\left(1.500 + \frac{2}{3} \times 0.600\right)\right]$$

$$= \frac{-2469.6 - 759.4 - 1458.0 - 615.6}{EI}$$

$$= \frac{-5302.6}{12 \times 10^9 \times 30 \times 10^6 \times 10^{-12}}$$

$$= -14.729 \times 10^{-3} \text{ m}$$

$$= -14.729 \text{ mm}$$

$$\boxed{\delta = -14.7 \text{ mm}}$$

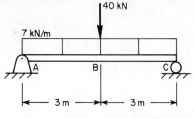

FIGURE 14-22

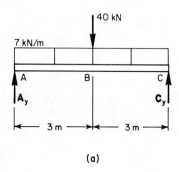

(a)

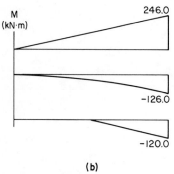

(b)

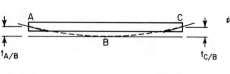

(c)

FIGURE 14-23

EXAMPLE 14-9

If the beam shown in Fig. 14-22 is a structural-steel W360x101 beam, calculate the maximum deflection in the beam.

SOLUTION

The usual first step is to draw the free-body diagram, as shown in Fig. 14-23(a), and to solve for the reactions at the supports.

$$\Sigma M_C = 0$$

$$-(A_y \times 6) + 7 \times 6 \times 3 + 40 \times 3 = 0$$

$$A_y = \frac{126.00 + 120.00}{6}$$

$$= \frac{246.00}{6}$$

$$= 41.00 \text{ kN}$$

$$\Sigma F_y = 0$$

$$41.00 - 7 \times 6 - 40 + C_y = 0$$

$$C_y = 42.00 + 40.00 - 41.00$$

$$= 41.00 \text{ kN}$$

The next step is to draw the moment diagram by parts. Since the beam and its loads are symmetrical about the midpoint, it makes no difference whether the moment diagrams are drawn from left to right or from right to left. They have been drawn from left to right in this case. The top moment diagram shown in Fig. 14-23(b) is that due to the reaction at A. It causes a triangular moment diagram.

For A_y = 41.00 kN load:

At right end,

$$M = 41.00 \times 6$$

$$= 246.00 \text{ kN} \cdot \text{m}$$

The moment diagram due to the distributed load will have a parabolic shape.

For 7 kN/m load:

At right end,

$$M = -(7 \times 6 \times 3)$$

$$= -126.00 \text{ kN} \cdot \text{m}$$

The 40 kN load will not cause any moment in the left half of the beam when drawing the moment diagram by parts from left to right. The moment diagram will be triangular between the midpoint and the right end.

For 40 kN load:

At right end,

$$M = -(40 \times 3)$$

$$= -120.00 \text{ kN·m}$$

If the moment diagrams are correct, the sum of the moments at the right end of the beam must be zero.

Moment check:

$$\Sigma M = 246.00 - 126.00 - 120.00$$

$$= 0.00 \qquad \text{Check}$$

The elastic curve of the beam is shown in Fig. 14-23(c). *Since the beam and its loads are symmetrical about the midpoint of the beam, the midpoint, point B, will also be the point of maximum deflection. The tangent through B will be horizontal. Thus, both $t_{A/B}$ and $t_{C/B}$ will have the same magnitude as the maximum deflection. Theorem 2 may be used to calculate either $t_{A/B}$ or $t_{C/B}$. However, it is much simpler mathematically to calculate the first moment of the areas between A and B than the one between B and C.*

In either case, it is necessary to have the height of the moment diagram at B.

For $A_y = 41.00$ kN load:

At B,

$$M = 41.00 \times 3$$

$$= 123.00 \text{ kN·m}$$

For 7 kN/m load:

At B,

$$M = -\left(7 \times 3 \times \frac{1}{2} \times 3\right)$$

$$= -31.50 \text{ kN·m}$$

When calculating $t_{A/B}$, substitute values of E and I near the end of the solution to avoid unnecessary numbers. Moments of the area between A and B must be taken with respect to an axis through A.

$$t_{A/B} = \frac{1}{EI}\left(\frac{1}{2} \times 3 \times 123.00 \times \frac{2}{3} \times 3\right.$$

$$\left. - \frac{1}{3} \times 3 \times 31.50 \times \frac{3}{4} \times 3\right)10^3$$

$$= \frac{(369.00 - 70.88)\,10^3}{EI}$$

$$= \frac{298.12 \times 10^3}{200 \times 10^9 \times 302 \times 10^6 \times 10^{-12}}$$

$$= 4.9358 \times 10^{-3}\ \text{m}$$

$$= 4.9358\ \text{mm}$$

Point A is above the tangent drawn through B, so the sign of $t_{A/B}$ is opposite to that of the deflection at B.

$$\delta_B = -t_{A/B}$$

$$= -4.9358\ \text{mm}$$

$$\boxed{\delta = -4.94\ \text{mm}}$$

EXAMPLE 14-10

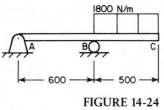

1800 N/m

A B C

|← 600 →|← 500 →|

FIGURE 14-24

If the extruded-magnesium beam shown in Fig. 14-24 has a cross section with a moment of inertia of $1.2 \times 10^6\ \text{mm}^4$, calculate (a) the maximum deflection between supports, and (b) the deflection at the free end.

SOLUTION

The location of the maximum deflection between supports is not known, but it will occur where the slope of the elastic curve is zero. Once the usual free-body diagram, moment diagram, and elastic curve are drawn, it will be possible to develop a technique for locating the point of maximum deflection and calculating its value.

Start with the free-body diagram of the beam, as shown in Fig. 14-25(a), and use it as an aid to calculate the reactions at the supports.

$$\Sigma\ M_A = 0$$

$$B_y \times 0.600 - 1800 \times 0.500 \times 0.850 = 0$$

$$B_y = \frac{765.00}{0.600}$$

$$= 1275.0 \text{ N}$$

$$\Sigma F_y = 0$$

$$A_y + 1275.0 - 1800 \times 0.500 = 0$$

$$A_y = -1275.0 + 900.0$$

$$= -375.0 \text{ N}$$

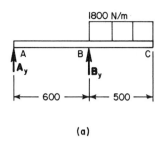

(a)

The moment diagram may now be drawn by parts, as shown in Fig. 14-25(b). *Since the distributed load is on the right end of the beam, the diagrams will be simpler if drawn from left to right.*

For $A_y = -375.0$ N load:

At right end,

$$M = -(375.0 \times 1.100)$$

$$= -412.50 \text{ N·m}$$

For $B_y = 1275.0$ N load:

At right end,

$$M = 1275.0 \times 0.500$$

$$= 637.50 \text{ N·m}$$

For 1800 N/m load:

At right end,

$$M = -(1800 \times 0.500 \times 0.250)$$

$$= -225.00 \text{ N·m}$$

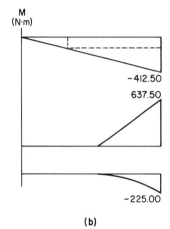

(b)

The moment calculations may be checked by determining if the sum of the moments is zero at the right end.

Moment check:

$$\Sigma M = -412.50 + 637.50 - 225.00$$

$$= 0.00 \qquad \text{Check}$$

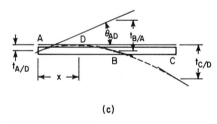

(c)

FIGURE 14-25

The assumed elastic curve is shown in Fig. 14-25(c). *Since there is no load between A and B, it is expected that all of the elastic curve between the two points will be above the horizontal line.*

The point of maximum deflection between A and B is assumed to be at D, and a horizontal tangent is drawn through D.

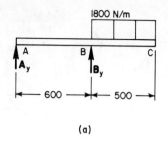

(a)

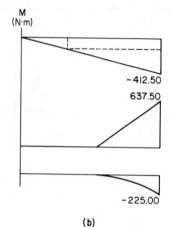

(b)

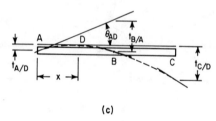

(c)

FIGURE 14-25 (*repeated*)

A tangent through A is also drawn, and it intersects the tangent through D to form the angle θ_{AD}. This angle is a negative or clockwise angle. The tangential deviation, $t_{B/A}$, is shown, and $t_{B/A}$ divided by 0.600 is the slope of the tangent through A. Note from Fig. *14-25(c) that θ_{AD} is equal to the angle between the horizontal and the tangent drawn through A. For the small angles that exist here, the tangent of the angle is equal to the angle in radians, so*

$$\theta_{AD} = \frac{t_{B/A}}{0.600}$$

The angle θ_{AD} may be calculated using Theorem 1, and $t_{B/A}$ may be calculated using Theorem 2. The distance x, which locates D, is unknown, and it must be determined by solving the equation $\theta_{AD} = t_{B/A}/0.600$. The values of the moment diagrams at D and B will be required to set up the equation. Since EI will be a common factor, symbols only are used.

(a) For $A_y = -375.0$ load:

At D,

$$M = -(375.0 \times x) \text{ N·m}$$

At B,

$$M = -(375.0 \times 0.600)$$
$$= -225.00 \text{ N·m}$$

$$\theta_{AD}EI = -\left(\frac{1}{2} \times x \times 375.0\,x\right)$$

$$= -187.50\,x^2$$

$$t_{B/A}EI = -\left(\frac{1}{2} \times 0.600 \times 225.00 \times \frac{1}{3} \times 0.600\right)$$

$$= -13.50$$

$$\theta_{AD}EI = \frac{t_{B/A}EI}{0.600}$$

$$-187.50\,x^2 = \frac{-13.50}{0.600}$$

$$x^2 = \frac{13.50}{187.50 \times 0.600}$$

$$= 0.120\ 00$$

$$x = 0.346\ 41 \text{ m}$$

(In some problems, it may be necessary to solve for x using the quadradic equation, or by trial and error.)

Now that the location of the maximum deflection is known, its value may be calculated using Theorem 2. From Fig. 14-25(c) it can be seen that δ_D will be positive and $t_{A/D}$ will be negative, but will have the same magnitude as δ_D.

$$\delta_D = -t_{A/D}$$

$$= -\frac{1}{EI}\left(-\frac{1}{2} \times 0.346\ 41 \times (375.00 \times 0.346\ 41) \times \frac{2}{3} \times 0.346\ 41\right)$$

$$= \frac{5.1961}{45 \times 10^9 \times 1.2 \times 10^6 \times 10^{-12}}$$

$$= 0.096\ 225 \times 10^{-3}\ \text{m}$$

$$= 0.096\ 225\ \text{mm}$$

(b) *The deflection at the free end cannot be calculated directly. However, it can be seen from Fig. 14-25(c) that* $\delta_C = t_{C/D} + \delta_D$. *The value for $t_{C/D}$ can be found using* Theorem 2. *Since it is the area between D and C that is used, the top moment diagram is broken up into a rectangle and a triangle, as shown by the dashed lines.*

(b) For moment diagram due to $A_y = -375.0$ N load:

Base of rectangle and triangle,

$$b = 1.100 - 0.346\ 41$$

$$= 0.753\ 59\ \text{m}$$

Height of rectangle,

$$h_1 = -(0.346\ 41 \times 375.00)$$

$$= -129.90\ \text{N·m}$$

Height of triangle,

$$h_2 = (-412.50 + 129.90)$$

$$= -282.60\ \text{N·m}$$

$$t_{C/D} = \frac{1}{EI}\left[-\left(0.753\ 59 \times 129.90 \times \frac{1}{2} \times 0.753\ 59\right)\right.$$

$$-\frac{1}{2} \times 0.753\ 59 \times 282.60 \times \frac{1}{3} \times 0.753\ 59$$

$$+\frac{1}{2} \times 0.500 \times 637.50 \times \frac{1}{3} \times 0.500$$

$$\left.-\frac{1}{3} \times 0.500 \times 225.00 \times \frac{1}{4} \times 0.500\right]$$

$$= \frac{1}{EI}(-36.885 - 26.748 + 26.563 - 4.688)$$

$$= \frac{-41.758}{45 \times 10^9 \times 1.2 \times 10^6 \times 10^{-12}}$$

$$= -0.773\ 30 \times 10^{-3}\ m$$

$$= -0.773\ 30\ mm$$

$$\delta_C = t_{C/D} + \delta_D$$

$$= -0.773\ 30 + 0.096\ 22$$

$$= -0.677\ 08\ mm$$

> (a) = +0.0962 mm
> (b) = −0.677 mm

ALTERNATE SOLUTION — PART (b)

If it had been necessary to calculate only the deflection at the free end, the following method could be used, since it does not depend on the maximum deflection between supports.

Figure 14-26 shows the elastic curve. In this figure the tangential deviations $t_{B/A}$ and $t_{C/A}$ are shown. It can be seen that

$$\delta_C = t_{C/A} - gh$$

From similar triangles

$$\frac{gh}{t_{B/A}} = \frac{1.100}{0.600}$$

$$gh = 1.8333\ t_{B/A}$$

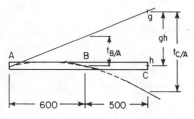

FIGURE 14-26 *Theorem 2 may be used to calculate both $t_{C/A}$ and $t_{B/A}$. The value of the moment diagram at B will be required.*

For $A_y = -375.0$ N load:

At B,

$$M = -(375.0 \times 0.600)$$

$$= -225.00 \text{ N·m}$$

$$t_{B/A} = \frac{1}{EI}\left(-\frac{1}{2} \times 0.600 \times 225.00 \times \frac{1}{3} \times 0.600\right)$$

$$= \frac{-13.500}{45 \times 10^9 \times 1.2 \times 10^6 \times 10^{-12}}$$

$$= -0.250\ 00 \times 10^{-3} \text{ m}$$

$$= -0.250\ 00 \text{ mm}$$

$$t_{C/A} = \frac{1}{EI}\left(-\frac{1}{2} \times 1.100 \times 412.50 \times \frac{1}{3} \times 1.100\right.$$

$$+ \frac{1}{2} \times 0.500 \times 637.50 \times \frac{1}{3} \times 0.500$$

$$\left.- \frac{1}{3} \times 0.500 \times 225.00 \times \frac{1}{4} \times 0.500\right)$$

$$= \frac{(-83.188 + 26.562 - 4.688)}{EI}$$

$$= \frac{-61.312}{45 \times 10^9 \times 1.2 \times 10^6 \times 10^{-12}}$$

$$= -1.135\ 42 \times 10^{-3} \text{ m}$$

$$= -1.135\ 42 \text{ mm}$$

$$\delta_C = t_{C/A} - 1.8333\, t_{B/A}$$

$$= -1.135\ 42 - 1.8333(-0.250\ 00)$$

$$= -1.135\ 42 + 0.458\ 32$$

$$= -0.677\ 09 \text{ mm}$$

$$\boxed{\text{(b) } \delta = -0.677 \text{ mm}}$$

PROBLEMS

14-35 Calculate the deflection at the free end for the structural-steel S310x74 beam shown in Fig. P14-35.

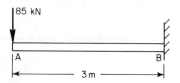

FIGURE P14-35

14-36 For the structural-steel S510x143 beam shown in Fig. P14-36, calculate the deflection at the free end.

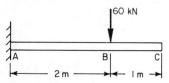

FIGURE P14-36

14-37 The beam shown in Fig. P14-37 is made of extruded magnesium and its cross section has a moment of inertia of 8×10^6 mm^4. Determine the maximum deflection.

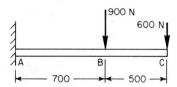

FIGURE P14-37

14-38 Calculate the deflection at the free end of the Douglas fir beam shown in Fig. P14-38. The cross section has a moment of inertia of 1.2×10^6 mm^4.

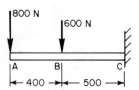

FIGURE P14-38

14-39 Determine the maximum deflection in the W410x85 structural-steel beam shown in Fig. P14-39.

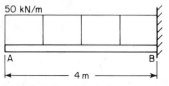

FIGURE P14-39

14-40 The 6061-T6 aluminum beam shown in Fig. P14-40 has a cross section with a moment of inertia of 5×10^6 mm^4. Find the maximum deflection.

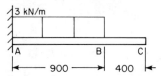

FIGURE P14-40

14-41 Calculate the maximum deflection in the carbon-steel beam shown in Fig. P14-41. Its cross section has a moment of inertia of 1.5×10^6 mm^4.

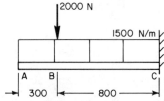

FIGURE P14-41

14-42 For the Douglas fir timber beam shown in Fig. P14-42, determine its maximum deflection if the moment of inertia of its cross section is 1250×10^6 mm^4.

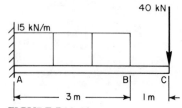

FIGURE P14-42

14-43 If the 6061-T6 aluminum beam shown in Fig. P14-43 has a cross section with a moment of inertia of 12×10^6 mm^4, calculate the maximum deflection.

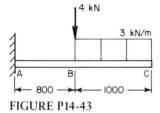

FIGURE P14-43

14-44 Find the deflection at the free end of the W310x179 structural-steel beam shown in Fig. P14-44.

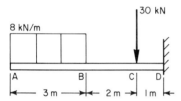

FIGURE P14-44

14-45 Determine the midspan deflection for the rigid vinyl beam shown in Fig. P14-45 if it has a cross section of 30 by 50 mm deep.

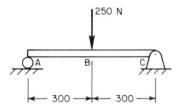

FIGURE P14-45

14-46 The Douglas fir beam shown in Fig. P14-46 has a cross section 150 by 200 mm deep. Calculate its maximum deflection.

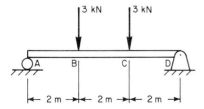

FIGURE P14-46

14-47 The 6061-T6 aluminum beam shown in Fig. P14-47 has a cross section with a moment of inertia of 375×10^6 mm^4. Calculate the maximum deflection in the beam.

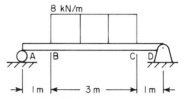

FIGURE P14-47

14-48 Find the maximum deflection in the ABS plastic beam shown in Fig. P14-48 if its cross section has a moment of inertia of 0.75×10^6 mm^4.

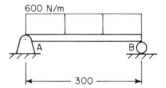

FIGURE P14-48

14-49 Calculate the maximum deflection for the structural-steel W310x149 beam shown in Fig. P14-49.

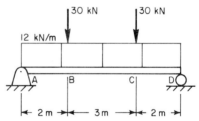

FIGURE P14-49

14-50 If the rigid vinyl beam shown in Fig. P14-50 has a cross section with a moment of inertia of 0.45×10^6 mm^4, calculate the maximum deflection.

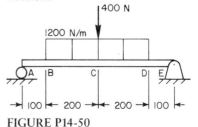

FIGURE P14-50

14-51 The 2014-T6 aluminum beam shown in Fig. P14-51 has a cross section with a moment of inertia of 85×10^6 mm^4. Calculate the deflection at (a) midspan and (b) the free end.

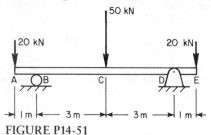

FIGURE P14-51

14-52 Determine the deflection at (a) midspan and (b) the free end for the structural-steel S510x112 beam shown in Fig. P14-52.

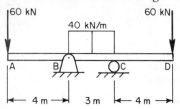

FIGURE P14-52

14-53 If the carbon-steel beam shown in Fig. P14-53 has a cross section with a moment of inertia of 0.75×10^6 mm^4, find the maximum deflection.

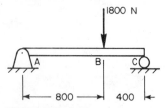

FIGURE P14-53

14-54 Determine the maximum deflection for the structural-steel W530x182 beam shown in Fig. P14-54.

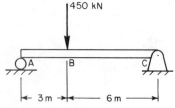

FIGURE P14-54

14-55 Find the maximum deflection for the beam shown in Fig. P14-55 if it is made of malleable cast iron, and if its cross section has a moment of inertia of 0.25×10^6 mm^4.

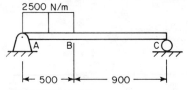

FIGURE P14-55

14-56 The 6061-T6 aluminum beam shown in Fig. P14-56 has a cross section with a moment of inertia of 225×10^6 mm^4. Determine its maximum deflection.

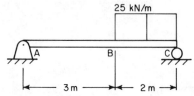

FIGURE P14-56

14-57 If the beam shown in Fig. P14-57 is Douglas fir, and its cross section has a moment of inertia of 30×10^6 mm^4, calculate the deflection at the free end.

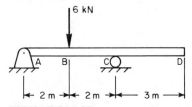

FIGURE P14-57

14-58 Determine the deflection at the free end of the red oak beam shown in Fig. P14-58 if its cross section has a moment of inertia of 5×10^6 mm^4.

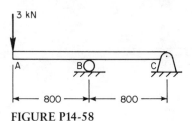

FIGURE P14-58

14-59 Figure P14-59 shows a structural-steel W410x74 beam. Calculate the maximum deflection.

14-60 If the beam shown in Fig. P14-60 is malleable cast iron, determine the maximum deflec-

tion. The cross section has a moment of inertia of 0.80×10^6 min^4. (Hint: The cubic equation used to locate the point of maximum deflection may be solved by trial and error.)

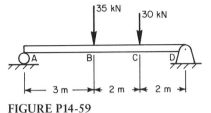

FIGURE P14-59

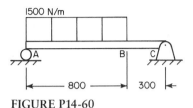

FIGURE P14-60

14-5 STATICALLY INDETERMINATE BEAMS

A statically indeterminate beam is one for which it is not possible to calculate the reactions at the supports using only the static-equilibrium equations. For a statically indeterminate beam, there are more unknown reaction forces or moments than there are equilibrium equations available. To provide the additional equations required, it is necessary to consider the deflection or slope of some point on the elastic curve of the beam.

Statically indeterminate beams are shown in Figs. 14-27(a) and 14-28(a). Their respective free-body diagrams are shown in Figs. 14-27(b) and 14-28(b). In each case, there are two equilibrium equations available for solving for the reactions, $\Sigma F_y = 0$ and $\Sigma M_O = 0$. For the beam in Fig. 14-27, there are three unknown reactions, A_y, B_y and M_S, and for the beam in Fig. 14-28 there are also three unknown reactions, A_y, C_y and E_y. The third equation used for solving for the reactions for the beam shown in Fig. 14-27 is the deflection equation for the cantilever beam. The force A_y must be just the right magnitude so that the deflection it causes plus the deflection due to the distributed load is zero at point A. Similarly, for the beam in Fig. 14-28, the force at C must be just large enough so that the deflection it causes at C plus the deflection at C due to the other loads equals zero.

If there is more than one reaction making the beam statically indeterminate, then additional slope or deflection equations will be required. The beam in Fig. 14-29 would require two additional equations besides the equilibrium equations, since there are four unknown reactions, A_y, C_y, M_{S_A} and M_{S_C}. In this case, the deflection at each end of the beam is zero, and the slope at each end is also zero. Thus, the forces at A and C must have the right magnitude to cause zero deflection at these points, and the

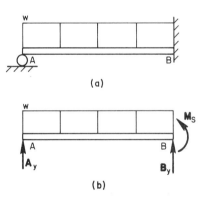

FIGURE 14-27

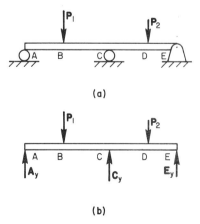

FIGURE 14-28

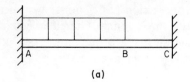

(a)

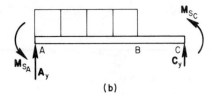

(b)

FIGURE 14-29

moments at A and C must be the correct magnitude so that the slope of the elastic curve at A and at C will be zero.

Beam-deflection tables and the principle of superposition may be used together for solving statically indeterminate beam problems, or the area-moment method may be used. The problems may be solved using one method and checked using the other, in many cases.

When using beam-deflection tables and the principle of superposition, the deflections at the extra support due to each of the loads, including the load from the extra support, are added algebraically. The deflection is now the known quantity (usually zero) and the force at the support is the unknown quantity for which one must solve.

Solutions of statically indeterminate beam problems using the area-moment method follow the usual procedure for the area-moment method. However, for indeterminate beams, one or more of the moment diagrams will be drawn using an unknown force or moment, but the slope or tangential deviation at a specified point on the elastic curve will be a known quantity, usually zero.

The procedures for both types of solution are illustrated in the example problems. In some of the problems at the end of the section, the method of solution to be used is specified. For the other problems, either the deflection tables or the area-moment method may be used.

EXAMPLE 14-11

Calculate the reactions at the supports for the beam shown in Fig. 14-30.

SOLUTION – DEFLECTION TABLES

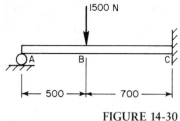

FIGURE 14-30

A free-body diagram of the beam, as shown in Fig. 14-31(a), *is a good starting point. It can be seen that there are three unknown reactions. The two loads shown in* Fig. 14-31(b), *when superimposed, will be the equivalent loading to that shown in* Fig. 14-31(a). *Because of the support at A, there will be no deflection at A in the beam. Thus, the sum of the deflections at A for beams 1 and 2 in* Fig. 14-31(b) *must be zero. The beam-deflection table of* Fig. 14-3 *is used to calculate the deflection due to each of the two loads. Beam 1 of* Fig. 14-31(b) *coincides with* Case 5 *and Beam 2 of* Fig 14-31(b) *coincides with* Case 4 *of* Fig. 14-3. *Note that E and I are common factors, so it is not necessary to know the material in the beam or its cross section.*

$$-\delta_1 + \delta_2 = 0$$

$$-\frac{P_1 a^2(3L - a)}{6EI} + \frac{P_2 L^3}{3EI} = 0$$

$$-\frac{1500 \times 0.700^2(3 \times 1.200 - 0.700)}{6EI} + \frac{A_y \times 1.200^3}{3EI} = 0$$

$$A_y = \frac{1500 \times 0.700^2(3 \times 1.200 - 0.700) \times 3}{6 \times 1.200^3}$$

$$= 616.75 \text{ N}$$

This is the force that, when applied to A, will cause the loaded beam to have zero deflection at A. Now that A_y is known, the free-body diagram of Fig. 14-31(a) *may be used as an aid in calculating the force and moment at C.*

$$\Sigma F_y = 0$$

$$616.75 - 1500 + C_y = 0$$

$$C_y = 1500.00 - 616.75$$

$$= 883.25 \text{ N}$$

$$\Sigma M_C = 0$$

$$-(616.75 \times 1.200) + 1500 \times 0.700 + M_S = 0$$

$$M_S = 740.10 - 1050.00$$

$$= -309.90 \text{ N·m}$$

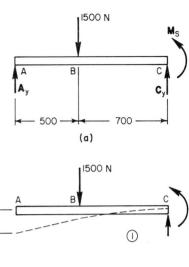

(a)

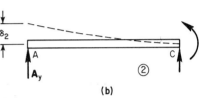

(b)

FIGURE 14-31

$$\boxed{\begin{array}{l} \vec{R}_A = 617 \text{ N at } 90.00° \\ \vec{R}_C = 883 \text{ N at } 90.00° \\ M_S = -310 \text{ N·m} \end{array}}$$

SOLUTION — AREA MOMENT

A free-body diagram of the beam is drawn, as shown in Fig. 14-32(a). *There are three unknown reactions shown. The moment diagram is drawn by parts, as shown in* Fig. 14-32(b), *and the values at the right end are calculated. Since A_y is unknown, the value of the moment due to this load will be expressed in terms of A_y.*

For A_y load:

At right end,

$$M = A_y \times 1.200$$

$$= 1.200 \, A_y \ \text{N·m}$$

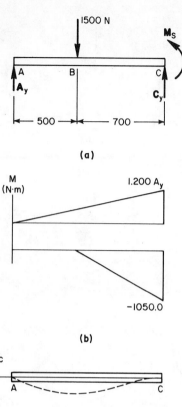

(a)

(b)

(c)

FIGURE 14-32

For 1500 N load:

At right end,

$$M = -(1500 \times 0.700)$$

$$= -1050.0 \ N \cdot m$$

The elastic curve for the beam is drawn as shown in Fig. 14-32(c). *At A there will be zero deflection, and since there is a rigid support at C the slope of the elastic curve at C will be zero, and a tangent through C will be horizontal. Thus,* $t_{A/C}$ *will be zero, as shown in* Fig. 14-32(c). *This fact provides a method for solving for* A_y. *Theorem 2 is used to calculate* $t_{A/C}$, *and the resulting equation can be solved for* A_y. *E and I are common factors, so it is not necessary to know the material used or the cross-sectional dimensions of the beam.*

$$t_{A/C} = 0$$

$$= \frac{1}{EI}\Big(\frac{1}{2} \times 1.200 \times 1.200 \ A_y \times \frac{2}{3} \times 1.200$$

$$-\frac{1}{2} \times 0.700 \times 1050.0 \times (0.500 + \frac{2}{3} \times 0.700)\Big)$$

$$0 = 0.576 \ 00 \ A_y - 355.25$$

$$A_y = \frac{355.25}{0.576 \ 00}$$

$$= 616.75 \ N$$

Now the free-body diagram shown in Fig. 14-32(a) *may be used as an aid in determining the remaining two reactions.*

$$\Sigma \ F_y = 0$$

$$616.75 - 1500 + C_y = 0$$

$$C_y = 1500.00 - 616.75$$

$$= 883.25 \ N$$

$$\Sigma \ M_C = 0$$

$$-(616.75 \times 1.200) + 1500 \times 0.700 + M_S = 0$$

$$M_S = 740.10 - 1050.00$$

$$= -309.90 \ N \cdot m$$

$$\vec{R}_A = 617 \ N \ at \ 90.00°$$
$$\vec{R}_C = 883 \ N \ at \ 90.00°$$
$$M_S = -310 \ N \cdot m$$

EXAMPLE 14-12

For the beam shown in Fig. 14-33, find the reactions at each support.

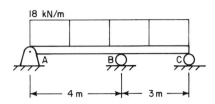

FIGURE 14-33

SOLUTION — AREA MOMENT

Start with a free-body diagram of the beam, as shown in Fig. 14-34(a). *Three unknown reactions are shown on the free-body diagram. The assumed elastic curve for the beam shown is in* Fig. 14-34(b). *It must have zero deflection at points A, B and C. If a tangent is drawn through B, as shown, it will provide a geometric construction that can be used for solving the problem, for two similar triangles are formed within the tangent line and* $t_{A/B}$ *and* $t_{C/B}$. *The value for* $t_{C/B}$ *is negative, so the distance, which is required when using similar triangles, must be* $-t_{C/B}$.

From similar triangles:

$$\frac{t_{A/B}}{4} = \frac{-t_{C/B}}{3}$$

$$3\,t_{A/B} = -4\,t_{C/B}$$

Both $t_{A/B}$ *and* $t_{C/B}$ *can be calculated using* Theorem 2 *of the area-moment method.* Figure 14-34(c) *shows the moment diagram drawn by parts starting at the left end. It is fairly simple to use this to calculate* $t_{A/B}$, *but calculating* $t_{C/B}$ *will be awkward. It is much simpler to calculate* $t_{C/B}$ *using the moment diagram by parts starting from the right end, as shown in* Fig. 14-34(d).

The values for the critical points on the moment diagram are obtained as follows:

Moments — Left to right:

For A_y load:

At right end,

$$M = A_y \times 7.00$$

$$= 7.00\,A_y \text{ kN} \cdot \text{m}$$

At B,

$$M = A_y \times 4.00$$

$$= 4.00\,A_y \text{ kN} \cdot \text{m}$$

For 18 kN/m load:

At right end,

$$M = -(18 \times 7 \times 3.5)$$

$$= -441.00 \text{ kN} \cdot \text{m}$$

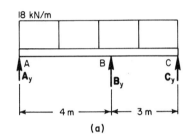

(a)

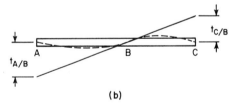

(b)

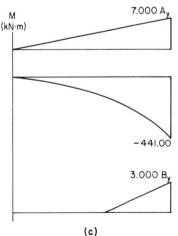

(c)

FIGURE 14-34

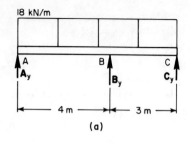

(a)

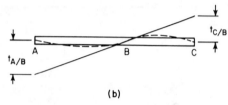

(b)

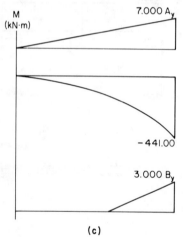

(c)

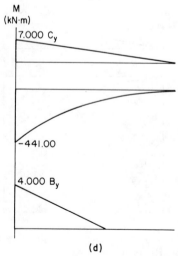

(d)

FIGURE 14-34 (*repeated*)

At B,

$$M = -(18 \times 4 \times 2)$$

$$= -144.00 \text{ kN} \cdot \text{m}$$

For B_y load:

At right end,

$$M = B_y \times 3.00$$

$$= 3.00 \ B_y \ \text{kN} \cdot \text{m}$$

Moments — Right to left:

For C_y load:

At left end,

$$M = C_y \times 7.00$$

$$= 7.00 \ C_y \ \text{kN} \cdot \text{m}$$

At B,

$$M = C_y \times 3.00$$

$$= 3.00 \ C_y \ \text{kN} \cdot \text{m}$$

For 18 kN/m load:

At left end,

$$M = -(18 \times 7 \times 3)$$

$$= -441.00 \text{ kN} \cdot \text{m}$$

At B,

$$M = -(18 \times 3 \times 1.5)$$

$$= -81.00 \text{ kN} \cdot \text{m}$$

For B_y load:

At left end,

$$M = B_y \times 4.00$$

$$= 4.00 \ B_y \ \text{kN} \cdot \text{m}$$

With the complete moment diagrams, the equation relating $t_{A/B}$ and $t_{C/B}$ can be set up. The equation will contain two unknown terms, A_y and C_y. Note that E and I will be common factors, so their values will not be required.

$$3 \ t_{A/B} = -4 \ t_{C/B}$$

$$3\frac{1}{EI}\left(\frac{1}{2} \times 4 \times 4.00\ A_y \times \frac{2}{3} \times 4\right.$$

$$\left. -\frac{1}{3} \times 4 \times 144.00 \times \frac{3}{4} \times 4\right)10^3$$

$$= -4\frac{1}{EI}\left(\frac{1}{2} \times 3 \times 3.00\ C_y \times \frac{2}{3} \times 3\right.$$

$$\left. -\frac{1}{3} \times 3 \times 81.00 \times \frac{3}{4} \times 3\right)10^3$$

$$3(21.333\ A_y - 576.00) = -4(9.00\ C_y - 182.25)$$

$$64.00\ A_y - 1728.00 = -36.00\ C_y + 729.00$$

$$64.00\ A_y + 36.00\ C_y - 2457.00 = 0 \qquad\qquad \text{(a)}$$

Using the free-body diagram of Fig. 14-34(a), *moments may be taken about B, which would give a second equation in terms of A_y and C_y.*

$$\Sigma\ M_B = 0$$

$$-(A_y \times 4) + 18 \times 7 \times 0.500 + C_y \times 3 = 0$$

$$-4.00\ A_y + 63.00 + 3.00\ C_y = 0$$

$$A_y = \frac{3.00\ C_y + 63.00}{4}$$

$$A_y = 0.750\ C_y + 15.75 \qquad\qquad \text{(b)}$$

Substitute Eq. (b) in Eq. (a):

$$64.00\ A_y + 36.00\ C_y - 2457.00 = 0 \qquad\qquad \text{(a)}$$

$$64.00(0.750\ C_y + 15.75) + 36.00\ C_y - 2457.00 = 0$$

$$48.00\ C_y + 1008.00 + 36.00\ C_y - 2457.00 = 0$$

$$84.00\ C_y = 1449.00$$

$$C_y = \frac{1449.00}{84.00}$$

$$= 17.250\ \text{kN}$$

Substitute for C_y in Eq. (b):

$$A_y = 0.750\ C_y + 15.75 \qquad\qquad \text{(b)}$$

$$= 0.750 \times 17.250 + 15.75$$

$$= 12.94 + 15.75$$

$$= 28.69\ \text{kN}$$

The reaction at B may be calculated by summing forces in the y direction.

$$\Sigma F_y = 0$$

$$28.69 - 18 \times 7 + B_y + 17.25 = 0$$

$$B_y = 126.00 - 28.69 - 17.25$$

$$= 80.06 \text{ kN}$$

$$\boxed{\begin{aligned} \vec{R}_A &= 28.7 \text{ kN at } 90.00° \\ \vec{R}_B &= 80.1 \text{ kN at } 90.00° \\ \vec{R}_C &= 17.2 \text{ kN at } 90.00° \end{aligned}}$$

SOLUTION — DEFLECTION TABLES

The free-body diagram of the beam is drawn, as shown in Fig. 14-35(a). *Three unknown reaction forces are shown on it. The two load systems that will be superimposed on each other to make up the given system of loads are shown in* Fig. 14-35(b). *The sum of the deflections at B due to each loading must be zero if there is a support at B. The loading shown on Beam 1 coincides with* Case 3 *in* Fig. 14-3. *The deflection equation must be used, since point B is not where the deflection is maximum. Beam 2 is the same type of loading as that shown in* Case 2 *of* Fig. 14-3. *Since E and I are common factors, their values are unnecessary.*

$$-\delta_1 + \delta_2 = 0$$

$$-\frac{wx}{24EI}\left(L^3 - 2Lx^2 + x^3\right) + \frac{Pbx}{6EIL}\left(L^2 - x^2 - b^2\right) = 0$$

In this equation, P = B_y, and there is a common factor of x. The value for x is the distance from the left support to B, since the deflection is being evaluated at B.

$$\frac{w}{24}\left(L^3 - 2Lx^2 + x^3\right) = \frac{B_y b}{6L}\left(L^2 - x^2 - b^2\right)$$

$$\frac{18}{24}\left(7^3 - 2 \times 7 \times 4^2 + 4^3\right) = \frac{B_y \times 3}{6 \times 7}\left(7^2 - 4^2 - 3^2\right)$$

$$137.25 = 1.714\ 28\ B_y$$

$$B_y = \frac{137.25}{1.714\ 28}$$

$$= 80.063 \text{ kN}$$

The reactions at A and C may now be calculated using the equilibrium equations.

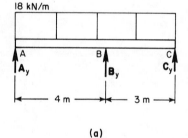

(a)

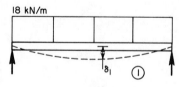

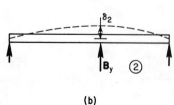

(b)

FIGURE 14-35

$\Sigma M_C = 0$

$\quad -(A_y \times 7) + 18 \times 7 \times 3.5 - 80.063 \times 3 = 0$

$\quad A_y = \dfrac{441.00 - 240.19}{7}$

$\qquad = \dfrac{200.81}{7}$

$\qquad = 28.687 \text{ kN}$

$\Sigma F_y = 0$

$\quad 28.687 + 80.063 + C_y - 18 \times 7 = 0$

$\quad C_y = 126.000 - 28.687 - 80.063$

$\qquad = 17.250 \text{ kN}$

$$\boxed{\begin{array}{l} \vec{R}_A = 28.7 \text{ kN at } 90.00° \\ \vec{R}_B = 80.1 \text{ kN at } 90.00° \\ \vec{R}_C = 17.2 \text{ kN at } 90.00° \end{array}}$$

EXAMPLE 14-13

Use the area-moment method along with the equilibrium equations to calculate the reactions at the supports for the beam shown in Fig. 14-36.

SOLUTION

The free-body diagram for the beam is shown in Fig. 14-37(a). At each end, there will be a vertical force and a moment. The deflection at each end and the slope of the elastic curve at each end will be zero. The elastic curve for the beam is shown in Fig. 14-37(b). If tangents are drawn through A and D, the two tangents lie on top of each other. Thus, the angle between the two tangents, θ_{AD}, is zero, and the tangential deviation, $t_{D/A}$, is also zero. These known values give information that provides a method of solution for the problem.

The moment diagram is drawn by parts, as shown in Fig. 14-37(c). It can be drawn either from left to right or from right to left.

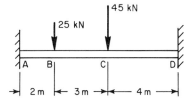

FIGURE 14-36

$\qquad$ For A_y load:

$\qquad\qquad$ At right end,

$\qquad\qquad\qquad M = A_y \times 9.00$

$\qquad\qquad\qquad\quad = 9.00 \, A_y \text{ kN·m}$

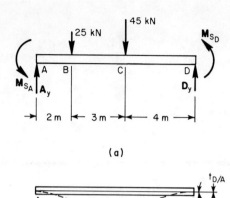

(a)

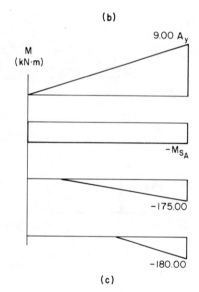

(b)

(c)

FIGURE 14-37

For M_{S_A} moment:

At right end,

$$M = -M_{S_A} \text{ kN} \cdot \text{m}$$

For 25 kN load:

At right end,

$$M = -(25 \times 7)$$
$$= -175.00 \text{ kN} \cdot \text{m}$$

For 45 kN load:

At right end,

$$M = -(45 \times 4)$$
$$= -180.00 \text{ kN} \cdot \text{m}$$

With the moment diagram completed, the equations for θ_{AD} and $t_{D/A}$ may be written, using Theorems 1 *and* 2.

$$\theta_{AD} = 0$$

$$0 = \frac{1}{EI}\left(\frac{1}{2} \times 9 \times 9.00 \, A_y - 9 \, M_{S_A} - \frac{1}{2} \times 7 \times 175.00\right.$$

$$\left. - \frac{1}{2} \times 4 \times 180.00\right)10^3$$

$$0 = 40.50 \, A_y - 9.00 \, M_{S_A} - 612.50 - 360.00$$

$$40.50 \, A_y - 9.00 \, M_{S_A} - 972.50 = 0 \qquad \text{(a)}$$

$$t_{D/A} = 0$$

$$0 = \frac{1}{EI}\left(\frac{1}{2} \times 9 \times 9.00 \, A_y \times \frac{1}{3} \times 9 - 9 \times M_{S_A} \times \frac{1}{2} \times 9\right.$$

$$- \frac{1}{2} \times 7 \times 175.00 \times \frac{1}{3} \times 7$$

$$\left. - \frac{1}{2} \times 4 \times 180.00 \times \frac{1}{3} \times 4\right)10^3$$

$$0 = 121.50 \, A_y - 40.50 \, M_{S_A} - 1429.17 - 480.00$$

$$121.50 \, A_y - 40.50 \, M_{S_A} - 1909.17 = 0 \qquad \text{(b)}$$

Equations (a) *and* (b) *may be solved simultaneously to determine the values of A_y and M_{S_A}.*

Divide Eq. (b) by 3, and subtract Eq. (a):

$$40.50 \, A_y - 13.50 \, M_{S_A} - 636.39 = 0$$

$$40.50 \, A_y - 9.00 \, M_{S_A} - 972.50 = 0$$

$$\overline{-4.50 \, M_{S_A} + 336.11 = 0}$$

$$M_{S_A} = \frac{336.11}{4.50}$$

$$= 74.691 \text{ kN·m}$$

Substitute for M_{S_A} in Eq. (a):

$$40.50 \, A_y - 9.00 \times 74.691 - 972.50 = 0$$

$$A_y = \frac{672.22 + 972.50}{40.50}$$

$$= \frac{1644.72}{40.50}$$

$$= 40.610 \text{ kN}$$

The remaining reactions may be calculated by using the free-body diagram and the equilibrium equations.

$$\Sigma \, F_y = 0$$

$$40.610 - 25 - 45 + D_y = 0$$

$$D_y = 70.000 - 40.610$$

$$= 29.390 \text{ kN}$$

$$\Sigma \, M_D = 0$$

$$-(40.610 \times 9) + 74.691 + 25 \times 7 + 45 \times 4 + M_{S_D} = 0$$

$$M_{S_D} = 365.490 - 74.691 - 175.000 - 180.000$$

$$= -64.201 \text{ kN·m}$$

$$\boxed{\begin{array}{l} \vec{R}_A = 40.6 \text{ kN at } 90.00° \\ \vec{R}_D = 29.4 \text{ kN at } 90.00° \\ M_{S_A} = +74.7 \text{ kN·m} \\ M_{S_D} = -64.2 \text{ kN·m} \end{array}}$$

PROBLEMS

14-61 Determine the reactions at the supports for the beam shown in Fig. P14-61.

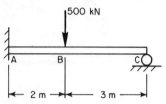

FIGURE P14-61

14-62 For the beam shown in Fig. P14-62, calculate the reactions at the supports.

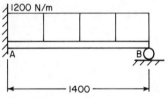

FIGURE P14-62

14-63 For the beam shown in Fig. P14-63, find the reactions at the supports.

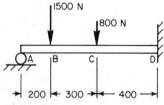

FIGURE P14-63

14-64 Determine the reactions at the roller and wall for the beam shown in Fig. P14-64.

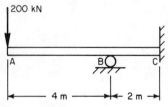

FIGURE P14-64

14-65 Calculate the reaction at each of the three supports for the beam shown in Fig. P14-65.

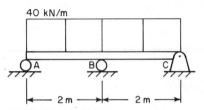

FIGURE P14-65

14-66 Find all of the reactions for the beam shown in Fig. P14-66.

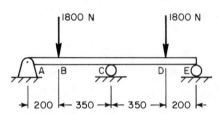

FIGURE P14-66

14-67 For the beam shown in Fig. P14-67, determine the reactions at the supports.

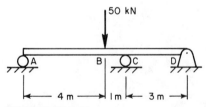

FIGURE P14-67

14-68 For the beam shown in Fig. P14-68, calculate the reactions at the supports.

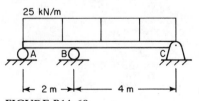

FIGURE P14-68

14-69 Determine the reactions at the supports for the beam shown in Fig. P14-69, using the area-moment method to solve for one of the reactions.

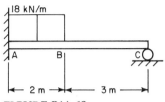

FIGURE P14-69

14-70 For the beam shown in Fig. P14-70, calculate the reactions at the supports, using the area-moment method for one of the calculations.

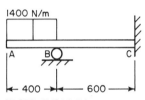

FIGURE P14-70

14-71 Use the area-moment method and the equilibrium equations to find the reactions for the beam shown in Fig. P14-71.

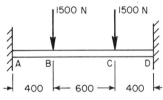

FIGURE P14-71

14-72 Find the reactions at the supports for the beam shown in Fig. P14-72 using the equilibrium equations and the area-moment method.

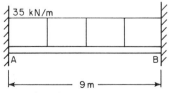

FIGURE P14-72

14-73 For the beam shown in Fig. P14-73, calculate the reactions at the supports using the area-moment method and equilibrium equations.

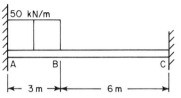

FIGURE P14-73

14-74 Find the reactions at the supports for the beam shown in Fig. P14-74 using the area-moment method for two of the calculations.

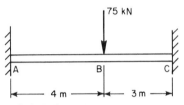

FIGURE P14-74

14-75 Determine the reactions at the supports for the beam shown in Fig. P14-75 using the beam-deflection tables.

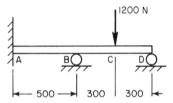

FIGURE P14-75

14-76 For the beam shown in Fig. P14-76, calculate the reactions at the supports using the beam-deflection tables.

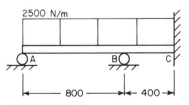

FIGURE P14-76

15 COLUMNS

15-1 COLUMN TERMINOLOGY

A simple column is a slender compression member on which the load is applied along the long axis of the member. One often thinks of columns as the vertical members in buildings framed with steel, reinforced concrete or timber. However, many structural components that behave as columns are not vertical. Cords or diagonals of a truss may be horizontal, inclined or vertical, and any of these members may meet the criteria for a column. Any machine part, such as the connecting rod in a gasoline or diesel engine, provided it is slender and supports an axial compressive load, is a column.

Figure 15-1 shows structural steel and reinforced concrete columns in a shopping center under construction. The design of these columns is based on some of the discussion in this chapter.

FIGURE 15-1 Both structural steel and reinforced concrete columns are shown in this construction scene. The steel columns at the center and left are probably classified as long columns. *Photo courtesy of Rene T. Dionne Photography Limited.*

The analysis and design of columns is really an analysis of the stability of columns, for their behavior is different from that of other structural components that have been analyzed. If an axial compressive load is applied to a column that is pinned at both ends, as shown in Fig. 15-2(a), the load can be increased up to some maximum load called the *critical load, P_{cr},* at which load the column will deform excessively, or buckle, as shown in Fig. 15-2(b). The column has failed at this point, and cannot carry any additional load.

The load-carrying capacity of columns has been the subject of a great deal of research, both theoretical and experimental. The *critical stress*, which is P_{cr}/A, has been found to increase as the modulus of elasticity of the material in the column increases, and to decrease as the slenderness ratio of the column increases. The critical stress is the average stress on the section at failure, since the bending at failure causes the stress to be nonuniform.

The change in critical stress with change in slenderness ratio is shown in Fig. 15-3, and it can be seen that the slenderness ratio of a column will be of major significance in analyzing or designing columns. There is no generally accepted symbol for slenderness ratio, so usually all three terms are used.

$$\text{Slenderness ratio} = \frac{kL}{r} \qquad (15\text{-}1)$$

where k is the effective length factor for the column,
    L is the column length between loading points, and
    r is the radius of gyration measured with respect to a
    centroidal axis.

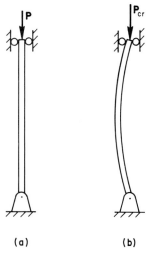

(a)   (b)

FIGURE 15-2

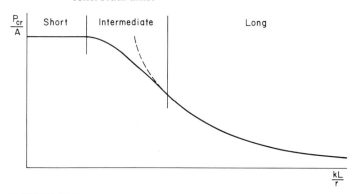

FIGURE 15-3

The shape a column takes when the load approaches the critical load depends on whether the column ends are pinned, fixed or free, as shown in Fig. 15-4. In Fig. 15-4, the actual length of each column is L, and the effective length is as shown on the

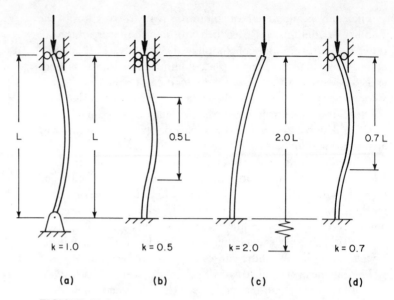

FIGURE 15-4

figure. The end conditions illustrated are: pinned at both ends, in Fig. 15-4(a); fixed at both ends, in Fig. 15-4(b); fixed at one end and free at the other, in Fig. 15-4(c); and fixed at one end and pinned at the other, in Fig. 15-4(d).

The radius of gyration used when calculating the slenderness ratio is measured with respect to the centroidal axis about which buckling is being investigated. In general, a column will tend to fail about the axis for which it would have the larger slenderness ratio. In most cases, this will be the axis giving the smaller moment of inertia and thus the smaller radius of gyration. But if the ends are not supported in the same manner for both axes, then the two values for slenderness ratio will have to be compared to determine the larger value. When dealing with columns, the use of the symbol r for radius of gyration is much more common than the use of the symbol k, which is commonly used in mechanics.

For column cross sections for which the centroidal x or y axis is an axis of symmetry, the smaller of the two radii of gyration, r_x or r_y, will be the smallest radius of gyration of the cross section. However, if neither the x nor the y axis is an axis of symmetry, as is the case for the angles shown in Appendix F, some other centroidal axis will give the smallest radius of gyration. This axis is shown as the Z-Z axis in Appendix F. Depending on end conditions with respect to the various axes, the radius of gyration with respect to the Z-Z axis may yield the largest slenderness ratio.

Figure 15-3 shows that the relationship between critical stress and slenderness ratio is described by three distinct curves. The end of each curve marks the boundary between what are called *short columns* (sometimes called *compression blocks*), *intermediate columns*, and *long columns*. The exact value of the slenderness ratio at the boundaries varies from material to material. The short columns were discussed in Articles 10-3 and 11-1, for in the case of a short column, failure occurs by simple yielding, and not buckling, so the critical stress is the yield strength. The long and intermediate columns will be discussed in the following articles.

EXAMPLE 15-1

Calculate the maximum slenderness ratio for a 3 m long wood column with a cross section of 150 × 250 mm if each end is pinned with respect to both axes.

SOLUTION

Appropriate values are substituted into the definition of slenderness ratio in Eq. (15-1). *The value for the effective length factor is obtained from* Fig. 15-4. *Since both ends are pinned, k = 1.0.*

To obtain the larger slenderness ratio, the smaller value of I, and hence of r, must be calculated. This will be obtained if r is measured with respect to the centroidal axis parallel to the 250 mm side. It may be quicker because of the common terms to calculate r in symbol form first.

$$r = \sqrt{\frac{I}{A}}$$

$$= \sqrt{\frac{\frac{bh^3}{12}}{bh}}$$

$$= \sqrt{\frac{h^2}{12}}$$

$$= \sqrt{\frac{150^2}{12}}$$

$$= \sqrt{1875.0}$$

$$= 43.301 \text{ mm}$$

Values may now be substituted into Eq. (15-1). *Both r and L must be expressed in the same units, which may be either* mm *or* m.

$$\text{Slenderness ratio} = \frac{kL}{r}$$

$$= \frac{1.0 \times 3}{43.301 \times 10^{-3}}$$

$$= 69.282$$

Since a ratio is unitless, there are no units associated with the answer.

$$\boxed{\frac{kL}{r} = 69.3}$$

EXAMPLE 15-2

A structural-steel column 4 m long is made up by welding two C75x9 shapes back to back, as shown in Fig. 15-5. For buckling about the x axis, the column is pinned at both ends, and for buckling about the y axis, the column is fixed at both ends. Calculate the maximum slenderness ratio for the column.

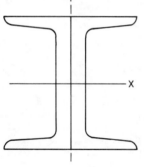

FIGURE 15-5

SOLUTION

Since the end conditions are not the same for both axes, it will be necessary to calculate the slenderness ratio with respect to both axes to determine the maximum value.

For x axis:

For buckling about the x axis, both ends are pinned, so from Fig. 15-4 it can be seen that k = 1.0. The moment of inertia and radius of gyration for one channel can be obtained from Appendix F. Since $r_x = \sqrt{I_x/A}$ for one channel, for two channels back to back, $r_x = \sqrt{2I_x/2A} = \sqrt{I_x/A}$, so the value of r_x will be as given in the tables. The slenderness ratio is calculated from Eq. (15-1). Both L and r must be given in the same units.

$$\text{Slenderness ratio} = \frac{kL}{r}$$

$$= \frac{1.0 \times 4}{27.5 \times 10^{-3}}$$

$$= 145.45$$

For y axis:

For buckling with respect to the y axis, the column is fixed at both ends, so from Fig. 15-4, it is seen that k = 0.5.

To calculate the moment of inertia with respect to the y axis, it is necessary to use the values from Appendix F *and the parallel-axis theorem. The distance from the centroidal y axis for one channel to its back is given as* 11.4 mm. *The moment of inertia for two channels with respect to an axis through the back will be twice that of one channel.*

$$I_y = 2(\bar{I}_y + Ad^2)$$
$$= 2(0.123 \times 10^6 + 1120 \times 11.4^2)$$
$$= 2(0.123 \times 10^6 + 0.1456 \times 10^6)$$
$$= 2 \times 0.2686 \times 10^6$$
$$= 0.5372 \times 10^6 \text{ mm}^4$$

$$r_y = \sqrt{\frac{I_y}{A}}$$
$$= \sqrt{\frac{0.5372 \times 10^6}{2 \times 1120}}$$
$$= \sqrt{239.82}$$
$$= 15.486 \text{ mm}$$

The slenderness ratio can be calculated using Eq. (15-1). *The same units must be used for L and r.*

$$\text{Slenderness ratio} = \frac{kL}{r}$$
$$= \frac{0.5 \times 4}{15.486 \times 10^{-3}}$$
$$= 129.15$$

The maximum slenderness ratio is selected by comparing the two values.

$$\boxed{\frac{kL}{r} = 145}$$

PROBLEMS

15-1 A structural-steel W460x113 section with a length of 8 m is used as a column. Calculate its slenderness ratio for failure about the y axis if it is pinned at both ends.

15-2 Calculate the slenderness ratio for failure about the y axis for a structural-steel S510x112 column 5 m long if it is fixed at both ends.

15-3 Determine the slenderness ratio for a vinyl column 150 mm long. The column is fixed at one end, free at the other, and has a circular cross section with a diameter of 12 mm.

15-4 A timber column 4 m long has a cross section of 150 by 150 mm. If it is fixed at both ends, calculate its slenderness ratio.

15-5 An aluminum extrusion 600 mm long is used as a column that is fixed at both ends. Determine the slenderness ratio if it has a 20 by 20 mm hollow section with a wall thickness of 3 mm.

15-6 Calculate the slenderness ratio for a round plastic tube with an outside diameter of 50 mm, a wall thickness of 5 mm and a length of 2.5 m. The tube is fixed at one end and pinned at the other.

15-7 A column is made by lacing together two structural-steel C200x28 channels, as shown in Fig. P15-7. If the column is 7 m long, fixed at one end and pinned at the other in both planes, calculate the maximum slenderness ratio. The lacing joining the two channels does not affect the moment of inertia, but does make the channels act as one member.

15-8 Two structural-steel 125x75x10 angles are fastened back to back, as shown in Fig. P15-8, to form a column 3 m long. If the ends are fixed in both planes, find the maximum slenderness ratio.

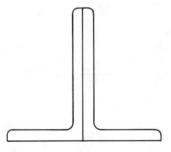

FIGURE P15-8

15-9 Four 90x65x10 structural-steel angles are welded back to back to form a 4 m long brace, which will act in compression. If both ends are fixed with respect to buckling about the x axis shown in Fig. P15-9, and if both ends are pinned with respect to the y axis, calculate the maximum slenderness ratio.

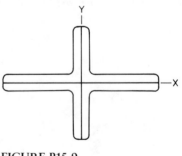

FIGURE P15-9

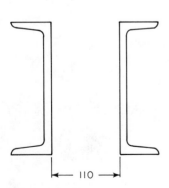

FIGURE P15-7

15-10 Calculate the maximum slenderness ratio for the 5 m timber column cross section shown in Fig. P15-10. It is pinned at both ends with respect to buckling about the x axis; it is pinned at one end and fixed at the other for buckling about the y axis.

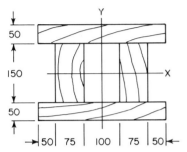

FIGURE P15-10

15-11 Determine the maximum slenderness ratio for a structural-steel 200x200x10 angle 6 m long

used as a column if the ends have ball-and-socket connections that have the effect of making the ends pinned about any axis.

15-12 A 150x100x16 structural-steel angle 3.5 m long and fixed at both ends with respect to all axes is used as a column. Calculate the maximum slenderness ratio.

15-13 A 90x75x10 structural-steel angle 2 m long is fixed at both ends with respect to rotation about the z axis and pinned at both ends with respect to rotation about the x and y axes. Determine its maximum slenderness ratio.

15-14 Find the maximum slenderness ratio for a 65x65x10 structural-steel angle 1.8 m long. It is fixed at one end and free at the other with respect to the x and y axes, and it is fixed at one end and pinned at the other with respect to the z axis.

15-2 LONG COLUMNS

A long column is one with a relatively large slenderness ratio. The exact value depends on the material. One of the methods commonly used to determine whether a column is long is the use of the expression

$$\frac{kL}{r} > \sqrt{\frac{2\pi^2 E}{\sigma_y}} \qquad (15\text{-}2)$$

where $\dfrac{kL}{r}$ is the slenderness ratio,

E is the modulus of elasticity of the column material, and

σ_y is the yield strength of the column material.

Whenever the slenderness ratio exceeds that given by Eq. (15-2) the column is considered to be long. Although Eq. (15-2) was developed for use with structural steel, it gives a reasonable approximation for the lower limit for the slenderness ratio for long columns for many materials, and will be used here. In design practice, if the design is governed by a code, the design code will specify the limiting value for the slenderness ratio for long columns, and the value may differ from that obtained using Eq.

(15-2). The slenderness ratio for long columns has no upper limit, but it can be seen from Fig. 15-3 that there is a practical upper limit because of the load-carrying capacity of very long columns. It is at about $kL/r = 200$.

The load-carrying capacity of ideal long columns was analyzed mathematically by the Swiss mathematician Leonard Euler in the mid-eighteenth century. The columns he analyzed were long, straight, axially loaded, and had pinned ends. With the use of differential equations, he developed what is now known as the Euler equation for columns,

$$P_{cr} = \frac{\pi^2 EI}{L^2} \tag{15-3}$$

where P_{cr} is the critical load on the column that causes buckling,

E is the modulus of elasticity of the column material,

I is the moment of inertia about the centroidal axis about which buckling occurs, and

L is the length of the column between points of application of the load.

Since only some columns have pinned ends, the effect of end conditions is taken in to account by rewriting the Euler equation as

$$P_{cr} = \frac{\pi^2 EI}{(kL)^2} \tag{15-4}$$

where P_{cr} is the critical load on the column that causes buckling,

E is the modulus of elasticity of the column material,

I is the moment of inertia about the centroidal axis about which buckling occurs,

k is the effective length factor for the column, as given in Fig. 15-4, and

L is the length of the column between points of application of the load.

The Euler equation is also written in a third form to give critical stress, by using the fact that $I = Ar^2$.

$$\frac{P_{cr}}{A} = \frac{\pi^2 E}{\left(\dfrac{kL}{r}\right)^2} \tag{15-5}$$

where $\dfrac{P_{cr}}{A}$ is the critical stress at which the column buckles,

E is the modulus of elasticity of the column material,

and

$\dfrac{kL}{r}$ is the largest slenderness ratio for the column.

As a practical matter, in most instances, it will be the critical load rather than the critical stress that is sought. Equation (15-5) may be simply rewritten to solve for the critical load.

In design, columns are never designed to carry the critical load because of the risk of failure. Some factor of safety is always used. The value of the factor of safety will be similar to that shown in Table 11-1 based on yield strength. For design purposes, the Euler equation will not be written in terms of the critical load, but rather in terms of the allowable load, and the equation can be expressed as

$$P_{all} = \frac{\pi^2 EI}{N(kL)^2} \qquad (15\text{-}6)$$

where P_{all} is the allowable load on the column,

E is the modulus of elasticity of the column material,

I is the moment of inertia about the centroidal axis about which buckling occurs,

N is the factor of safety, and

kL is the effective length of the column between points of application of the load.

For column design, usually the material, load, end conditions and length will be known, so it will be necessary to determine the moment of inertia of the cross section. Calculating the cross-section dimensions from the moment of inertia is a simple matter if the cross section is round or square. Tables such as Appendix F may be used to find sections with a suitable moment of inertia for standard structural shapes.

A critical part of the design process is to determine whether the selected column cross section is of such size that the column really is a long column, for if the slenderness ratio for the column is less than that given by Eq. (15-2), the Euler equation may not be used for analysis or design, and the column must be designed using the methods for intermediate-length columns.

EXAMPLE 15-3

Calculate the critical stress in a 230G structural-steel W200x46 column 7 m long if it is pinned at both ends with respect to buckling about all axes.

SOLUTION

There is a bit more involved in the solution than just substituting into Eq. (15-5). First the slenderness ratio must be calculated and then checked to determine if it is high enough to use the Euler equation for long columns, as given in Eq. (15-5).

Since both ends are pinned, k = 1.0, and the smaller radius of gyration given in Appendix F *will be used.*

$$\frac{kL}{r} = \frac{1.0 \times 7}{51.1 \times 10^{-3}}$$

$$= 136.99$$

Use Eq. (15-2) *to determine if the column is a long column.*

$$\sqrt{\frac{2\pi^2 E}{\sigma_y}} = \sqrt{\frac{2\pi^2 \times 200 \times 10^9}{230 \times 10^6}}$$

$$= 131.01$$

$$136.99 > 131.01 \qquad \text{Column is long}$$

Since the column is a long column, Eq. (15-5) *may be used to calculate the critical stress.*

$$\frac{P_{cr}}{A} = \frac{\pi^2 E}{\left(\dfrac{kL}{r}\right)^2}$$

$$= \frac{\pi^2 \times 200 \times 10^9}{136.99^2}$$

$$= 105.18 \times 10^6 \text{ Pa}$$

$$= 105.18 \text{ MPa}$$

Note that for a column with this slenderness ratio, failure will occur when the critical stress is less than half the yield strength of the material.

$$\boxed{\dfrac{P_{cr}}{A} = 105 \text{ MPa}}$$

EXAMPLE 15-4

A malleable cast-iron column 5.5 m long has the section shown in Fig. 15-6. Calculate the critical load in the column if it is fixed at one end and pinned at the other with respect to both axes.

SOLUTION

It is not readily apparent which axis will provide the smaller moment of inertia and hence the smaller radius of gyration, so both I_x and I_y must be calculated.

The area will be required for both calculations, so it is calculated first.

$$A = 25 \times 110 \times 2 + 35 \times 30$$

$$= 5500 + 1050$$

$$= 6550 \text{ mm}^2$$

The moment of inertia about the x axis is calculated most easily if the area is broken up as shown in Fig. 15-7.

$$I_x = 2(I_x)_1 + (I_x)_2$$

$$= 2 \times \frac{25 \times 110^3}{12} + \frac{35 \times 30^3}{12}$$

$$= (5.5458 + 0.0787)10^6$$

$$= 5.6245 \times 10^6 \text{ mm}^4$$

The easy method to calculate the moment of inertia about the y axis is to treat the section as a rectangle with two small rectangles removed, as shown in Fig. 15-8.

$$I_y = (I_y)_1 - 2(I_y)_2$$

$$= \frac{110 \times 85^3}{12} - 2 \times \frac{40 \times 35^3}{12}$$

$$= (5.6295 - 0.2858)10^6$$

$$= 5.3437 \times 10^6 \text{ mm}^4$$

The smaller moment of inertia will give the smaller radius of gyration.

$$r_y = \sqrt{\frac{I_y}{A}}$$

$$= \sqrt{\frac{5.3437 \times 10^6}{6550}}$$

$$= 28.563 \text{ mm}$$

The effective-length factor is found from Fig. 15-4, *and is found to be 0.7. The slenderness ratio can now be found.*

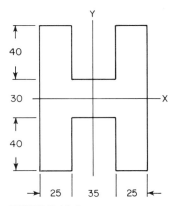

FIGURE 15-6

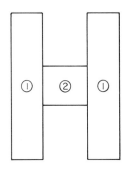

FIGURE 15-7

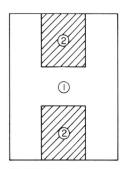

FIGURE 15-8

$$\frac{kL}{r} = \frac{0.7 \times 5.5}{28.563 \times 10^{-3}}$$

$$= 134.79$$

Next, Eq. (15-2) *is used to determine whether the column is long.*

$$\sqrt{\frac{2\pi^2 E}{\sigma_y}} = \sqrt{\frac{2\pi^2 \times 170 \times 10^9}{220 \times 10^6}}$$

$$= 123.50$$

$$134.79 > 123.50 \qquad \text{Column is long}$$

The critical load for the column may be calculated using Eq. (15-5). *Remember to convert the area from* mm^2 *to* m^2.

$$P_{cr} = \frac{\pi^2 EA}{\left(\dfrac{kL}{r}\right)^2}$$

$$= \frac{\pi^2 \times 170 \times 10^9 \times 6550 \times 10^{-6}}{134.79^2}$$

$$= 604.89 \times 10^3 \text{ N}$$

$$= 604.89 \text{ kN}$$

$$\boxed{P_{cr} = 605 \text{ kN}}$$

EXAMPLE 15-5

Determine the minimum diameter of 2014-T6 round aluminum bar required to support an axial compressive load of 40 kN. The bar is 2 m long; it is fixed at one end and free at the other; and there is a factor of safety of 2.5.

SOLUTION

If the form of the Euler equation given in Eq. (15-6) *is used, the required moment of inertia of the cross section can be calculated, and from this the diameter may be determined.*

$$P_{all} = \frac{\pi^2 EI}{N(kL)^2}$$

$$I = \frac{P_{all}N(kL)^2}{\pi^2 E}$$

$$= \frac{40 \times 10^3 \times 2.5(2 \times 2)^2}{\pi^2 \times 73 \times 10^9}$$

$$= 2.220\,74 \times 10^{-6}\,\text{m}^4$$

The moment of inertia may be expressed as I = πd⁴/64, and the expression may be solved for d.

$$\frac{\pi d^4}{64} = 2.220\,74 \times 10^{-6}$$

$$d^4 = \frac{64 \times 2.220\,74 \times 10^{-6}}{\pi}$$

$$= 45.241 \times 10^{-6}$$

$$d = 0.082\,013\,\text{m}$$

$$= 82.013\,\text{mm}$$

Equation (15-6) is valid for long columns. Use Eq. (15-2) to determine the minimum slenderness ratio required for a long column for 2014-T6

$$\sqrt{\frac{2\pi^2 E}{\sigma_y}} = \sqrt{\frac{2\pi^2 \times 73 \times 10^9}{365 \times 10^6}}$$

$$= 62.832$$

The actual slenderness ratio must be compared with the minimum allowable slenderness ratio for the column.

$$r = \sqrt{\frac{I}{A}}$$

$$= \sqrt{\frac{\dfrac{\pi \times 82.013^4}{64}}{\dfrac{\pi \times 82.013^2}{4}}}$$

$$= \frac{82.013}{4}$$

$$= 20.503\,\text{mm}$$

$$\frac{kL}{r} = \frac{2 \times 2}{20.503 \times 10^{-3}}$$

$$= 195.09$$

$$195.09 > 62.832 \qquad \text{Column is long}$$

Since the column is long, it is correct to use the Euler equation to design the column.

$$\boxed{d = 82.0\,\text{mm}}$$

PROBLEMS

15-15 Find the critical stress for a 6061-T6 aluminum bar 1.5 m long acting as a column if its cross section is 25 by 25 mm and it is pinned at both ends.

15-16 A round red oak dowel with a diameter of 30 mm has a length of 2 m. Calculate the critical stress if it is a column fixed at both ends.

15-17 Determine the critical load for a 400G structural-steel W200x36 column with a length of 5 m if the ends of the column are pinned with respect to buckling about both axes.

15-18 A 400G structural-steel W360x91 column with a length of 8 m is pinned at both ends for buckling about both axes. Calculate the critical load.

15-19 A 2 m magnesium strut is used as a wing support in a light aircraft. The strut has an outside diameter of 30 mm and a wall thickness of 3 mm. Determine the critical load on the strut if it is fixed at both ends.

15-20 A 25 m flagpole that is not guyed is made of 6061-T6 aluminum with an outside diameter of 100 mm and an inside diameter of 80 mm. Assuming that a person at the top of the pole may apply the force due to his mass axially, what is the maximum mass of person that may be supported at the top of the pole?

15-21 The cross section for a 230G structural-steel column 8 m long is shown in Fig. P15-21. Compute the critical load for the column if it is

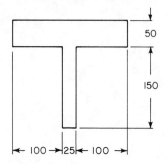

FIGURE P15-21

loaded through the centroidal axis and if it is pinned at both ends with respect to both axes.

15-22 A 6061-T6 aluminum extrusion with the section shown in Fig. P15-22 is to be loaded in compression. If the column is 2000 mm long, and fixed at both ends, determine the critical load for the column.

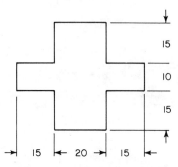

FIGURE P15-22

15-23 Select the lightest 400G structural-steel W shape that may be used as a 5 m long column with pinned ends with respect to both axes to support a load of 125 kN. Use a factor of safety of 2.

15-24 Find the lightest 230G structural-steel W shape that can be used as a 6 m long column, fixed at one end and free at the other, to support a load of 300 kN with a factor of safety of 2.5.

15-25 Determine the minimum square cross section required for a Douglas fir column 5 m long if it is to carry an axial load of 90 kN, and if both ends are fixed. Use a factor of safety of 3.

15-26 A round, hollow magnesium bar 750 mm long is to be used to support an axial compressive load of 42 kN. If both ends are fixed, calculate the minimum diameter d required if the inside diameter is $d/2$. Use a factor of safety of 3.

15-3 INTERMEDIATE COLUMNS

Columns that are neither long nor short are intermediate. The division point between intermediate and long columns used here was defined by Eq. (15-2). The line between short and intermediate columns also varies with material, and in practice the range for slenderness ratios varies from about 10 to about 30. For our purposes, a short column will arbitrarily be defined as one with a slenderness ratio of less than 15. In design practice, the appropriate design code will specify the limiting value. Thus, the range of slenderness ratios for intermediate columns in the following problems will be

$$15 < \frac{kL}{r} < \sqrt{\frac{2\pi^2 E}{\sigma_y}} \qquad (15\text{-}7)$$

The Euler equation still gives values for intermediate-length columns, and it is shown, plotted as a dashed line, in Fig. 15-3. It can be seen that the actual critical stress for intermediate columns is less than that obtained using the Euler equation.

Many attempts have been made to write equations that accurately fit the curve in the intermediate-column range, as shown in Fig. 15-3. The most popular equations are:

Straight line

$$\frac{P_{cr}}{A} = \sigma_o - C_1\left(\frac{kL}{r}\right) \qquad (15\text{-}8)$$

Parabolic

$$\frac{P_{cr}}{A} = \sigma_o - C_2\left(\frac{kL}{r}\right)^2 \qquad (15\text{-}9)$$

Gordon-Rankine

$$\frac{P_{cr}}{A} = \frac{\sigma_o}{1 + C_3\left(\frac{kL}{r}\right)^2} \qquad (15\text{-}10)$$

where $\frac{P_{cr}}{A}$ is the critical stress on the column that causes buckling,

σ_o is an experimentally determined stress, based on the column material,

C_1, C_2 and C_3 are experimentally determined constants that depend on the column material, and

$\frac{kL}{r}$ is the maximum slenderness ratio for the column.

Most design codes use some form of these three equations although the parabolic equation used for timber design is a fourth-order parabola, using the term $(kL/r)^4$. The design codes usually incorporate a factor of safety in the values of σ_o and C_1, C_2 or C_3. The values are given as part of the code.

A widely accepted expression for the critical stress for intermediate columns, which will be used in the examples and problems that follow, is the J.B. Johnson formula

$$\frac{P_{cr}}{A} = \sigma_y \left(1 - \frac{\sigma_y \left(\frac{kL}{r} \right)^2}{4\pi^2 E} \right) \tag{15-11}$$

where $\dfrac{P_{cr}}{A}$ is the critical stress on the column that causes buckling,

σ_y is the yield strength of the column material,

$\dfrac{kL}{r}$ is the largest slenderness ratio for the column, and

E is the modulus of elasticity of the column material.

As is the case with long columns, a factor of safety is used in column design because of the risk of failure if the column is loaded up to its critical load. For design purposes, the J.B. Johnson formula may be rewritten as

$$P_{all} = \frac{\sigma_y A}{N} \left(1 - \frac{\sigma_y \left(\frac{kL}{r} \right)^2}{4\pi^2 E} \right) \tag{15-12}$$

where P_{all} is the allowable load on the column,

σ_y is the yield strength of the column material,

A is the area of the column cross section,

N is the factor of safety,

$\dfrac{kL}{r}$ is the largest slenderness ratio, and

E is the modulus of elasticity of the column material.

If the column cross section is relatively simple, such as circular or square, so that A and r may be expressed in terms of one unknown dimension, design using the J.B. Johnson formula is not too complex. However, if the shape is not simple, the design may become more complex and may require trial-and-error procedures.

The column formula used must correspond with the column size range. The problems that follow will include short, intermediate and long columns.

EXAMPLE 15-6

Calculate the critical stress in a 400G structural-steel S200x34 column 1.5 m long if it is pinned at both ends with respect to both axes.

SOLUTION

The slenderness ratio should be calculated and compared with the limits for intermediate columns. From Appendix F it can be seen that the smaller radius of gyration is r_y.

$$\frac{kL}{r} = \frac{1.0 \times 1.5}{20.4 \times 10^{-3}}$$

$$= 73.529$$

The maximum value of the slenderness ratio for an intermediate column is obtained from Eq. (15-7).

$$\sqrt{\frac{2\pi^2 E}{\sigma_y}} = \sqrt{\frac{2\pi^2 \times 200 \times 10^9}{400 \times 10^6}}$$

$$= \sqrt{9869.6}$$

$$= 99.346 > 73.529$$

Column is intermediate

Since the column is intermediate, the J.B. Johnson formula, Eq. (15-11), will be used to determine the critical stress.

$$\frac{P_{cr}}{A} = \sigma_y\left(1 - \frac{\sigma_y\left(\frac{kL}{r}\right)^2}{4\pi^2 E}\right)$$

$$= 400 \times 10^6\left(1 - \frac{400 \times 10^6 \times 73.529^2}{4\pi^2 \times 200 \times 10^9}\right)$$

$$= 400 \times 10^6(1 - 0.273\ 90)$$

$$= 400 \times 10^6 \times 0.726\ 10$$

$$= 290.44 \times 10^6 \text{ Pa}$$

$$= 290.44 \text{ MPa}$$

$$\boxed{\frac{P_{cr}}{A} = 290 \text{ MPa}}$$

EXAMPLE 15-7

A round red oak column with a length of 2.4 m is to be used to carry a load of 2.5 MN with a factor of safety of 2.8. Calculate the required diameter of the column if it is fixed at one end and free at the other.

SOLUTION

If it is assumed that the column is an intermediate column (a good first assumption), it will be necessary to have values of A and r to use the J.B. Johnson formula, Eq. (15-12). They will be expressed in terms of the diameter, d.

$$A = \frac{\pi d^2}{4}$$

$$I = \frac{\pi d^4}{64}$$

$$r = \sqrt{\frac{I}{A}}$$

$$= \sqrt{\frac{\frac{\pi d^4}{64}}{\frac{\pi d^2}{4}}}$$

$$= \sqrt{\frac{d^2}{16}}$$

$$= \frac{d}{4}$$

Equation (15-12) *may be written and known values substituted in it. The diameter, d, is expressed in* m.

$$P_{all} = \frac{\sigma_y A}{N}\left(1 - \frac{\sigma_y\left(\frac{kL}{r}\right)^2}{4\pi^2 E}\right)$$

$$2.5 \times 10^6 = \frac{32 \times 10^6 \times \frac{\pi d^2}{4}}{2.8}\left(1 - \frac{32 \times 10^6\left(\frac{2 \times 2.4}{d/4}\right)^2}{4\pi^2 \times 12 \times 10^9}\right)$$

$$2.5 \times 10^6 = 8.9760 \times 10^6 d^2\left(1 - \frac{32 \times 10^6\left(\frac{368.64}{d^2}\right)}{4\pi^2 \times 12 \times 10^9}\right)$$

$$2.5 \times 10^6 = 8.9760 \times 10^6 d^2 \left(1 - \frac{24.901 \times 10^{-3}}{d^2}\right)$$

$$2.5 \times 10^6 = 8.9760 \times 10^6 \, (d^2 - 24.901 \times 10^{-3})$$

$$2.5 \times 10^6 = 8.9760 \times 10^6 d^2 - 0.233\,51 \times 10^6$$

$$d^2 = \frac{(2.500\,00 + 0.233\,51)\,10^6}{8.9760 \times 10^6}$$

$$= \frac{2.733\,51}{8.9760}$$

$$= 0.304\,54$$

$$d = 0.551\,85 \text{ m}$$

$$= 551.85 \text{ mm}$$

It is now necessary to check the actual slenderness ratio to determine if the column really is intermediate in length.

$$r = \frac{d}{4}$$

$$= \frac{551.85}{4}$$

$$= 137.96 \text{ mm}$$

$$\frac{kL}{r} = \frac{2 \times 2.4}{137.96 \times 10^{-3}}$$

$$= 34.792$$

The slenderness ratio is larger than the minimum value for intermediate columns, but it must also be compared with the maximum value, as given in Eq. (15-7).

$$\sqrt{\frac{2\pi^2 E}{\sigma_y}} = \sqrt{\frac{2\pi^2 \times 12 \times 10^9}{32 \times 10^6}}$$

$$= 86.036 > 34.792 \qquad \text{Column is intermediate}$$

The J.B. Johnson formula was the correct formula to use for the design. If the slenderness ratio had been greater than 86.036, it would have been necessary to recalculate the diameter using the Euler equation. If the slenderness ratio was less than 15, then the column would be designed as a short compression member.

$$\boxed{d = 552 \text{ mm}}$$

EXAMPLE 15-8

230G structural-steel equal-leg angles are to be used as diagonals in a truss. The ends of the diagonals will be fixed with respect to the x axis and pinned with respect to the y and z axes. Determine the lightest angle that may be used if the length is 1.8 m, the maximum compressive load is 150 kN and the factor of safety is 2.

SOLUTION

The diagonals are probably intermediate-length columns, so the J.B. Johnson formula will be used. Since both A and r are unknown terms, it will be necessary to use a trial-and-error solution.

For a first trial, pick an angle with a large enough cross section so that the stress in it is 75% of the allowable stress on a short compression member.

$$\text{Use } \sigma = 0.75 \times \frac{\sigma_y}{N}$$

$$= 0.75 \times \frac{230 \times 10^6}{2}$$

$$= 86.250 \times 10^6 \text{ Pa}$$

Area of section required:

$$\sigma = \frac{P}{A}$$

$$A = \frac{P}{\sigma}$$

$$= \frac{150\ 000}{86.250 \times 10^6}$$

$$= 1739.1 \times 10^{-6} \text{ m}^2$$

$$= 1739.1 \text{ mm}^2$$

Since the objective is to find the lightest equal-legged angle that will carry the load, use a 90x90x10 as a first trial. The 75x75x13 has a slightly larger cross section but is heavier and has a significantly smaller value for r_z. It is r_z that will give the largest slenderness ratio for the given end conditions. Equation (15-12) is used to determine the allowable load on the trial section.

Before checking the suitability of the section, the slenderness ratio for the trial section must be calculated and compared with the maximum value for an intermediate column.

First trial:

Try $90 \times 90 \times 10$

$$\frac{kL}{r} = \frac{1 \times 1.8}{17.6 \times 10^{-3}}$$

$$= 102.27$$

$$\sqrt{\frac{2\pi^2 E}{\sigma_y}} = \sqrt{\frac{2\pi^2 \times 200 \times 10^9}{230 \times 10^6}}$$

$$= 131.01 > 102.27$$

Column is intermediate

$$P_{all} = \frac{\sigma_y A}{N}\left(1 - \frac{\sigma_y\left(\frac{kL}{r}\right)^2}{4\pi^2 E}\right)$$

$$= \frac{230 \times 10^6 \times 1700 \times 10^{-6}}{2}\left(1 - \frac{230 \times 10^6 (102.27)^2}{4\pi^2 \times 200 \times 10^9}\right)$$

$$= 195\,500(1 - 0.304\,67)$$

$$= 195\,500 \times 0.695\,33$$

$$= 135\,940\text{ N} \qquad\qquad\qquad \text{Inadequate}$$

The trial section will not carry the required load. A 90x90x13 angle has enough additional area that it might carry the required load. A 100x100x10 has more area than a 90x90x10, but is lighter and has a higher r_z than a 90x90x13, so it might be preferable. Determine the slenderness ratio and allowable load for the 100x100x10.

Second trial:

Try $100 \times 100 \times 10$

$$\frac{kL}{r} = \frac{1 \times 1.8}{19.7 \times 10^{-3}}$$

$$= 91.371 < 131.01$$

Column is intermediate

$$P_{all} = \frac{\sigma_y A}{N}\left(1 - \frac{\sigma_y\left(\frac{kL}{r}\right)^2}{4\pi^2 E}\right)$$

$$= \frac{230 \times 10^6 \times 1900 \times 10^{-6}}{2} \left(1 - \frac{230 \times 10^6 (91.371)^2}{4\pi^2 \times 200 \times 10^9}\right)$$

$$= 218\ 500(1 - 0.243\ 20)$$

$$= 218\ 500 \times 0.756\ 80$$

$$= 165\ 360\ \text{N} \qquad\qquad\qquad \text{Adequate}$$

$$\boxed{\text{L}100 \times 100 \times 10}$$

It may be necessary to make several trials before finding the lightest section.

If the first trial gives a slenderness ratio in the long-column range, a new trial section should be selected so that the stress is 50% of the allowable on a short column, and trials should be started from the new section selected. In some cases, it will be necessary to use the Euler equation, for the column will actually be a long column, and not intermediate.

PROBLEMS

15-27 Find the critical stress for a 230G structural-steel column 4 m long if the column section is a W360x79 and is fixed at both ends.

15-28 A W610x113 made of 400G structural steel is used as a 4 m long column. If the column is pinned at both ends for both axes, determine the critical stress.

15-29 Calculate the critical load for a square Douglas fir timber column 300 mm long if it has a cross section of 150 by 150 mm. The column is fixed at one end and free at the other.

15-30 A round magnesium bar with a diameter of 8 mm and a length of 750 mm is used as a column. Calculate the critical load if both ends are fixed.

15-31 A 6061-T6 round aluminum tube with a length of 1.2 m, an outside diameter of 30 mm and a wall thickness of 5 mm is used as a column

that is fixed at both ends. Determine the allowable load on the column if there is a factor of safety of 2.5.

15-32 Find the allowable load on a red oak column with a cross section of 200 by 250 mm. It has a length of 3 m, is pinned at both ends with respect to both axes, and the factor of safety is 3.

15-33 For a 400G structural-steel L150x150x20 that is 2.5 m long, determine the allowable compressive load if there is a factor of safety of 2. Both ends are pinned with respect to buckling about the x and y axes, and both ends are fixed with respect to buckling about the z axis.

15-34 Determine the allowable compression load on a 230G structural-steel L100x75x8 used as a diagonal in a truss. It is 2.4 m long, fixed at both ends with respect to buckling about the y axis, and pinned at both ends with respect to buckling about all other axes. The factor of safety is 2.5.

15-35 A 6061-T6 aluminum column 1200 mm long has the cross section shown in Fig. P15-35. If one end is fixed and the other is free with respect to both axes, determine the critical load.

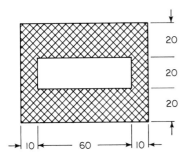

FIGURE P15-35

15-36 Calculate the critical load for the Douglas fir column with the cross section shown in Fig. P15-36. Both ends are fixed, and the column has a length of 3 m.

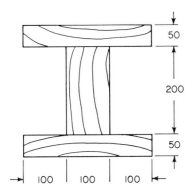

FIGURE P15-36

15-37 Find the minimum dimensions required for a square stainless-steel column 350 mm long if it is to carry a load of 85 kN with a factor of safety of 2.5. Both ends are fixed with respect to all axes.

15-38 A solid round 6061 T-6 aluminum bar 2 m long is to be used as a column pinned at both ends. The column is to support a load of 3 MN with a factor of safety of 2.5. Calculate the diameter of the bar.

15-39 A hollow, round column 1 m long is to be designed to carry a load of 900 kN with a factor of safety of 2.5. The column is made of 230G structural steel, is fixed at both ends, and has an outside diameter of d and an inside diameter of $0.75d$. Calculate d.

15-40 Determine the required dimensions for a rectangular malleable cast-iron column 600 mm long that is to carry a load of 45 kN with a factor of safety of 3. The column dimensions are b and $\frac{2}{3}b$. Both ends are fixed with respect to both axes.

15-41 Find the lightest 400G structural-steel unequal-leg angle 3 m long that may be used as a brace to carry a compressive load of 400 kN with a factor of safety of 2. Both ends are fixed with respect to buckling about the y axis, and both ends are pinned with respect to buckling about all other axes.

15-42 Select the lightest 230G structural-steel equal-leg angle 1.8 m long to be used as a compression diagonal in a truss. The load on the diagonal is 140 kN, the factor of safety is 2.5, and the angle is fixed at both ends for buckling with respect to the x and y axes, and pinned at both ends with respect to the z axis.

15-43 A 230G structural-steel W shape is to be used as a column 4 m long to carry a load of 425 kN using a factor of safety of 2. If the column is pinned at both ends with respect to all axes, determine the lightest W shape that may be used.

15-44 Select the lightest 400G structural-steel column 7 m long that will carry a load of 1.5 MN with a factor of safety of 2.5. Both ends are fixed with respect to all axes.

15-4 LOCALIZED BUCKLING

In addition to the column behavior already discussed, where the entire member fails by buckling, there are situations where there may be localized buckling failures in a part of a member. Some examples of such localized buckling are shown in Fig. 15-9. The analysis of localized buckling is quite complex, since the area of failure behaves much like a small column with support at the ends and along one or both sides. For design purposes, the approach used is to impose limitations on the ratios of certain dimensions. If these restrictions are adhered to, the localized buckling can be avoided.

If a beam section has a web that is thin relative to its depth, so that the ratio of depth to thickness is large, the web may buckle under the point of application of load, as shown in Fig. 15-9(a). A compression member with thin walls, such as shown in Fig. 15-9(b), may have localized buckling if the ratio of the major cross-sectional dimension to the wall thickness is large. The

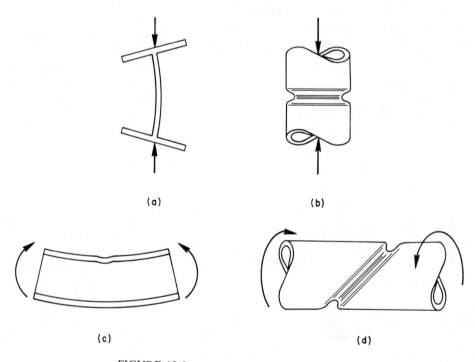

(a)

(b)

(c)

(d)

FIGURE 15-9

compression flange of a beam may have localized buckling, as shown in Fig. 15-9(c), if the ratio of the flange width to thickness is high. A thin-walled tube that is subjected to a torque may have localized buckling, as shown in Fig. 15-9(d). The compressive stress that causes the buckling in the tube shown in Fig. 15-9(d) will be explained in the discussions in Chap. 16. This type of buckling can be avoided if the ratio of the diameter to the thickness is limited.

In general, the limitations on the ratios of the dimensions for members will vary with the material and the application, and they will be specified in the pertinent design code.

16 COMBINED LOADING

16-1 STRESS ON AN ELEMENT

The stresses due to axial, torsional and flexural loads have been discussed in preceding chapters. In each case, it has been the stress on a section transverse or parallel to the longitudinal axis that has been analyzed. For axial loads, stress on inclined planes was discussed in Article 10-5. It was observed that on a plane inclined from the transverse section there was both a normal and a shear stress. For other types of loads, it will also be observed that there will usually be some combination of normal and shear stress on any inclined plane through a point.

A member with an axial load is shown in Fig. 16-1(a), one with a torsional load is shown in Fig. 16-2(a), and one with a transverse load causing bending is shown in Fig. 16-3(a). In each case a very small element, E, is shown on the member, and the element is shown enlarged in Figs. 16-1(b), 16-2(b) and 16-3(b). The stresses acting on the longitudinal and transverse planes of each of the elements are also shown. These are all stresses that can be calculated using the procedures discussed in preceding chapters. If an inclined plane is drawn through the element, and the stresses on the inclined plane are analyzed, they will be as shown in Figs. 16-1(c) and (d), 16-2(c) and (d) and 16-3(c) and (d). The stresses on the inclined plane for the axially loaded member have already been discussed. It might come as a bit of a surprise to find that tensile and compressive stresses exist in a shaft subjected to a torque, but an analysis of the stresses on the elements in Figs. 16-2(c) and 16-2(d) would show that the tensile and compressive stresses must exist if equilibrium is to be maintained. In the beam shown in Fig. 16-3(a), by equilibrium it can be shown that there will generally be some combination of normal and shear stresses on inclined planes, as shown in Figs. 16-3(c) and 16-3(d).

The stresses on the inclined planes will vary with the angle, and may be significant. They may be the cause for failure of a member. For this reason, a relatively simple technique for determining stresses on any plane is required. The technique developed is known as Mohr's circle for stress.

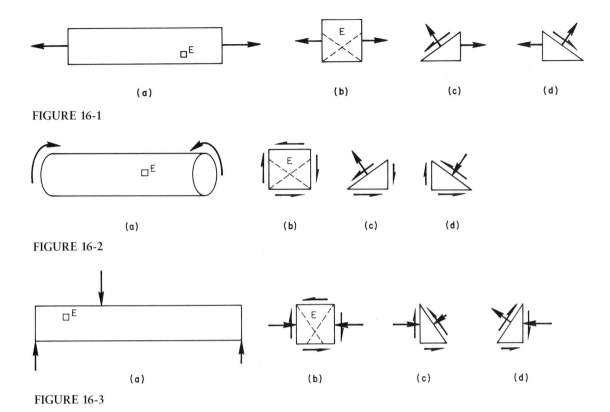

FIGURE 16-1

FIGURE 16-2

FIGURE 16-3

16-2 MOHR'S CIRCLE FOR PLANE STRESS

It is possible to calculate the stress on any inclined plane through any point in a plane member under load using principles of equilibrium. The process can be tedious, and may not yield the maximum values of stress, which are usually the critical values.

In the late nineteenth century, a German engineer, Otto Mohr, developed a method for calculating the stresses on any plane through an element of a member once the stresses on any two orthogonal (perpendicular) planes have been calculated.

Figure 16-4(a) shows an element from some member, and the stresses acting on that element. The normal stresses are labelled σ_x and σ_y, indicating stresses parallel to the x and y axes respectively, and the shear stress is labelled τ_{xy}, indicating that the stress is on the plane perpendicular to the x axis and pointing in the y direction, or τ_{yx}, indicating that the stress is on the plane perpendicular to the y axis and pointing in the x direction. For the element to be in equilibrium, the magnitudes of τ_{xy} and τ_{yx} must be the same.

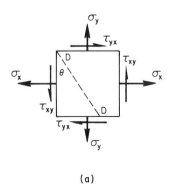

(a)

FIGURE 16-4

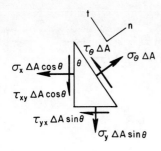

(b)

FIGURE 16-4 *(cont'd)*

A plane, *D-D*, is passed through the element at some angle θ, and the portion of the cut element, with the forces due to the stresses acting on it, is shown in Fig. 16-4(b). The area of the inclined plane cut by *D-D* has been assumed to be ΔA, so the area of the vertical plane is $\Delta A \cos \theta$, and the area of the horizontal plane is $\Delta A \sin \theta$.

The relationship between the stresses on the inclined plane, σ_θ and τ_θ, θ, and the stresses on the *x* and *y* planes, σ_x, σ_y, τ_{xy}, and τ_{yx}, can be determined using the equilibrium equations.

$$\Sigma F_n = 0$$

$$\sigma_\theta \, \Delta A - \sigma_x(\Delta A \cos \theta) \cos \theta - \sigma_y(\Delta A \sin \theta) \sin \theta$$
$$- \tau_{xy}(\Delta A \cos \theta) \sin \theta - \tau_{yx}(\Delta A \sin \theta) \cos \theta = 0$$

Since ΔA is a common factor, and $\tau_{xy} = \tau_{yx}$, the equation becomes

$$\sigma_\theta - \sigma_x \cos^2\theta - \sigma_y \sin^2\theta - 2 \, \tau_{xy} \sin \theta \cos \theta = 0$$

From trigonometry, $\cos^2 \theta = \dfrac{1 + \cos 2\theta}{2}$, $\sin^2 \theta = \dfrac{1 - \cos 2\theta}{2}$

and $\sin \theta \cos \theta = \dfrac{\sin 2\theta}{2}$. The equation may be rewritten as

$$\sigma_\theta - \sigma_x\left(\frac{1 + \cos 2\theta}{2}\right) - \sigma_y\left(\frac{1 - \cos 2\theta}{2}\right) - 2 \, \tau_{xy}\frac{\sin 2\theta}{2} = 0$$

which may be expressed in the following form:

$$\sigma_\theta - \frac{\sigma_x + \sigma_y}{2} = \left(\frac{\sigma_x - \sigma_y}{2}\right)\cos 2\theta + \tau_{xy} \sin 2\theta \quad (16\text{-}1)$$

$$\Sigma F_t = 0$$

$$\tau_\theta \, \Delta A + \sigma_x(\Delta A \cos \theta)\sin \theta - \sigma_y(\Delta A \sin \theta)\cos \theta$$
$$- \tau_{xy}(\Delta A \cos \theta)\cos \theta + \tau_{yx}(\Delta A \sin \theta)\sin \theta = 0$$

But ΔA is a common factor, and $\tau_{xy} = \tau_{yx}$, so the equation becomes

$$\tau_\theta + \sigma_x \sin \theta \cos \theta - \sigma_y \sin \theta \cos \theta - \tau_{xy} \cos^2\theta + \tau_{xy} \sin^2\theta = 0$$

Using the trigonometric relationships noted above, the equation becomes

$$\tau_\theta + \sigma_x \frac{\sin 2\theta}{2} - \sigma_y \frac{\sin 2\theta}{2} - \tau_{xy}\left(\frac{1 + \cos 2\theta}{2}\right)$$

$$+ \tau_{xy}\left(\frac{1 - \cos 2\theta}{2}\right) = 0$$

This may be simplified to

$$\tau_\theta = -\left(\frac{\sigma_x - \sigma_y}{2}\right)\sin 2\theta + \tau_{xy}\cos 2\theta \qquad (16\text{-}2)$$

If Eqs. (16-1) and (16-2) are both squared we get

$$\left[\sigma_\theta - \frac{\sigma_x + \sigma_y}{2}\right]^2 = \left[\left(\frac{\sigma_x - \sigma_y}{2}\right)\cos 2\theta + \tau_{xy}\sin 2\theta\right]^2$$

and

$$[\tau_\theta]^2 = \left[-\left(\frac{\sigma_x - \sigma_y}{2}\right)\sin 2\theta + \tau_{xy}\cos 2\theta\right]^2$$

and if the two equations are added together, after simplifying, we obtain

$$\left(\sigma_\theta - \frac{\sigma_x + \sigma_y}{2}\right)^2 + \left(\tau_\theta\right)^2 = \left(\frac{\sigma_x - \sigma_y}{2}\right)^2 + \left(\tau_{xy}\right)^2 \qquad (16\text{-}3)$$

It will be recalled that one of the standard forms of the equation of a circle is $(x - c)^2 + y^2 = r^2$, which is a circle with its center on the x axis at c, and having a radius of r. With a little imagination, it can be seen that Eq. (16-3) is an equation of similar form where the coordinate axes are σ_θ and τ_θ. The common practice, which will be followed here, is to label the axes as σ and τ.

The coordinate of the center is

$$c = \frac{\sigma_x + \sigma_y}{2} \qquad (16\text{-}4)$$

and the radius is

$$r = \left[\left(\frac{\sigma_x - \sigma_y}{2}\right)^2 + \left(\tau_{xy}\right)^2\right]^{1/2} \qquad (16\text{-}5)$$

where c is the coordinate of the center of the circle located on the σ axis,
r is the radius of the circle,
σ_x is the normal stress on the x plane,
σ_y is the normal stress on the y plane, and
τ_{xy} is the shear stress on the x plane.

The circle, known as Mohr's circle, is plotted in Fig. 16-5, where σ is the horizontal axis, τ is the vertical axis, point V represents the stresses on the vertical, or x plane, and point H represents the stresses on the horizontal, or y plane. Note that because of the use of the double-angle trigonometric identities, an angle of $90°$ in the element will be $180°$ in the circle. Thus, points V and H are the ends of a diameter of the circle.

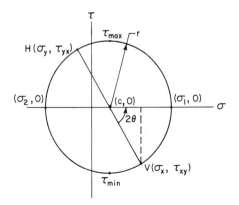

FIGURE 16-5

When plotting Mohr's circle, the sign conventions used are as follows: tensile stress is positive, compressive stress is negative, a shear stress that is part of a clockwise couple is positive, and a shear stress that is part of a counterclockwise couple is negative. It is recognized that the sign convention for couples due to shear stress is opposite to that normally used for torques and couples. However, the sign convention used for shear stress in Mohr's circle is well established, and will be followed.

From an inspection of Mohr's circle in Fig. 16-5, it can be seen that the maximum and minimum values of normal stress, and maximum shear stress, may be obtained from the plot of Mohr's circle. The maximum and minimum normal stresses are called the principal stresses. The highest algebraic value of normal stress is always labelled σ_1 and the lowest algebraic value is always labelled σ_2. From Mohr's circle the following expressions may be obtained:

$$\sigma_1 = \sigma_{max} = c + r \tag{16-6}$$

$$\sigma_1 = \frac{\sigma_x + \sigma_y}{2} + \left[\left(\frac{\sigma_x - \sigma_y}{2}\right)^2 + \left(\tau_{xy}\right)^2\right]^{1/2} \tag{16-7}$$

$$\sigma_2 = \sigma_{min} = c - r \tag{16-8}$$

$$\sigma_2 = \frac{\sigma_x + \sigma_y}{2} - \left[\left(\frac{\sigma_x - \sigma_y}{2}\right)^2 + \left(\tau_{xy}\right)^2\right]^{1/2} \tag{16-9}$$

$$\tau_{max} = r \tag{16-10}$$

$$\tau_{max} = \left[\left(\frac{\sigma_x - \sigma_y}{2}\right)^2 + \left(\tau_{xy}\right)^2\right]^{1/2} \tag{16-11}$$

Since σ_1 and σ_2 are at the ends of a diameter, they are 180° apart in the circle. Because of the double angle, the planes on which they act are 90° apart in the element. Similarly, τ_{max} is 90° from both σ_1 and σ_2 in the circle, so the planes on which τ_{max} acts are 45° from the planes on which σ_1 and σ_2 act in the element. The planes on which σ_1 and σ_2 act are called principal planes. It can be seen from Mohr's circle that the shear stress is zero on the principal planes.

Since failure in members tends to be due to one of the principal stresses or the maximum shear stress, these are the stresses usually required. In addition, the orientation of the planes on which the principal stresses act is usually required. Again from Fig. 16-5, it can be seen that

$$\tan 2\theta = \left| \frac{\tau_{xy}}{\sigma_x - \left(\dfrac{\sigma_x + \sigma_y}{2}\right)} \right|$$

$$\tan 2\theta = \left| \frac{2\tau_{xy}}{\sigma_x - \sigma_y} \right| \qquad (16\text{-}12)$$

where 2θ is the angle in Mohr's circle between the diameter formed by the given stress and the σ axis.

From the geometry, 2θ will be $90°$ or less, so the absolute value of $\tan 2\theta$ will be used to calculate 2θ and θ.

Figure 16-6 shows the element that corresponds with Mohr's circle as drawn in Fig. 16-5. A counterclockwise angle of 2θ in the circle from point V to σ_1 corresponds with the counterclockwise angle of θ from the plane on which σ_x acts to the plane on which σ_1 acts in the element. The minimum normal stress, σ_2, acts on a plane at $90°$ to the plane on which σ_1 acts, and the maximum shear stress acts on a plane at $45°$ to both principal planes in the element. A positive shear stress would tend to cause clockwise rotation about point A, which is the intersection of the two principal planes in the element.

The angle θ as obtained from Eq. (16-12) measures the angle from the x plane (the vertical plane) in the element to the plane on which one of the principal stresses acts. It may be either a positive (counterclockwise) or negative (clockwise) angle, and will always be less than $45°$. For convenient reference for answers, it is suggested that the angle given should be the positive (counterclockwise) angle from the vertical plane to the plane on which the maximum principal stress, σ_1, acts. This angle will be called ϕ.

Mohr's circle can be used to obtain the stress on any plane passing through a point with biaxial stresses acting on it. Biaxial stresses are those that exist when dealing with a plane or two-dimensional stress system. Stresses acting on all three orthogonal planes form a triaxial system, which is beyond the scope of this book.

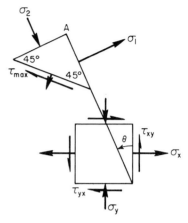

FIGURE 16-6

EXAMPLE 16-1

The stresses on an element at a point in a member were found to be $\sigma_x = +75$ MPa, $\sigma_y = +25$ MPa and $\tau_{xy} = -40$ MPa. Calculate the principal stresses and the maximum shear stress, and determine the orientation of the plane on which the maximum normal stress acts.

SOLUTION

A sketch of the element with the stresses acting on it should be drawn, as shown in Fig. 16-7. *This will make the solution easier to follow. When making the sketch, recall that the negative shear stress, τ_{xy}, acting on the vertical plane forms part of a couple*

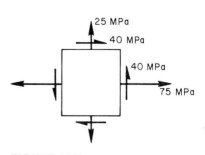

FIGURE 16-7

642 *Combined Loading*

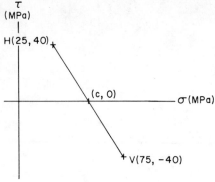

FIGURE 16-8

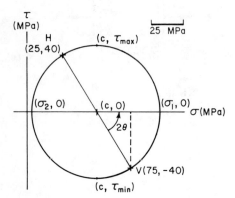

FIGURE 16-9

causing counterclockwise rotation, and that the same shear stress, but opposite in rotation, must also act on the y or horizontal plane. The stresses on the x and y planes are plotted as coordinates of the two points V and H on the σ-τ axis system, as shown in Fig. 16-8. *It is recommended that the drawing be to scale so that it serves as a graphical check.*

The two points are joined, and the line joining V and H is the diameter of Mohr's circle. The center of the circle is at (c, 0). Using the center point and the radius, Mohr's circle is completed as shown in Fig. 16-9. *From Eqs.* (16-4) *and* (16-5), *the values for c and r are determined.*

$$c = \frac{\sigma_x + \sigma_y}{2}$$

$$= \frac{75 + 25}{2}$$

$$= \frac{100}{2}$$

$$= 50.000 \text{ MPa}$$

$$r = \left[\left(\frac{\sigma_x - \sigma_y}{2}\right)^2 + \left(\tau_{xy}\right)^2\right]^{1/2}$$

$$= \left[\left(\frac{75 - 25}{2}\right)^2 + \left(-40\right)^2\right]^{1/2}$$

$$= [25^2 + (-40)^2]^{1/2}$$

$$= (625 + 1600)^{1/2}$$

$$= 2225^{1/2}$$

$$= 47.170 \text{ MPa}$$

As shown by Eqs. (16-6), (16-8) *and* (16-10), *the values of c and r are used to obtain* σ_1, σ_2 *and* τ_{max}.

$$\sigma_1 = c + r$$
$$= 50.000 + 47.170$$
$$= 97.170 \text{ MPa}$$

$$\sigma_2 = c - r$$
$$= 50.000 - 47.170$$
$$= 2.830 \text{ MPa}$$

$$\tau_{max} = r$$
$$= 47.170 \text{ MPa}$$

The value of θ may be obtained using Eq. (16-12). The absolute or positive value of tan 2θ is used, and the direction is obtained by inspection of Mohr's circle.

$$\tan 2\theta = \left| \frac{2\tau_{xy}}{\sigma_x - \sigma_y} \right|$$

$$= \left| \frac{2(-40)}{75 - 25} \right|$$

$$= \frac{80}{50}$$

$$= 1.6000$$

$$2\theta = 57.99°$$

$$\theta = 29.00°$$

Note also that the dimensions required to calculate the value for tan 2θ may be picked off the triangle shown in Fig. 16-9.

It can be seen from Fig. 16-9 *that the angle from the x plane (the vertical plane) to the plane on which σ_1 acts is a counterclockwise or positive angle. The angle from the plane on which σ_x acts to the plane on which σ_1 acts is obtained directly.*

$$\phi = \theta$$

$$= 29.00°$$

Since the type of stress (tensile or compressive) is important, it is recommended that the signs always be shown with the normal stress in the final answer.

$$\sigma_1 = +97.2 \text{ MPa}$$
$$\sigma_2 = +2.83 \text{ MPa}$$
$$\tau_{max} = 47.2 \text{ MPa}$$
$$\phi = 29.00°$$

It is also helpful to show the results on a sketch, as shown in Fig. 16-10. *The element as shown in* Fig. 16-7 *is drawn and the principal stresses are added on the appropriate planes as shown in* Fig. 16-10. *The plane on which the maximum shearing stress acts is shown at 45° to the principal planes. On the plane on which τ_{max} acts there is a normal stress equal in magnitude to c, the location of the center.*

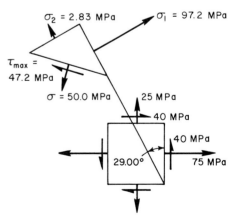

FIGURE 16-10

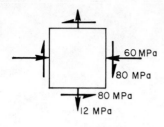

FIGURE 16-11

EXAMPLE 16-2

Calculate σ_1, σ_2 and τ_{max} and determine the orientation of σ_1 for an element with the stresses on it as shown in Fig. 16-11.

SOLUTION

The stress values on the vertical and horizontal faces of the element are used to plot the points V and H on the σ-τ coordinate system for Mohr's circle, as shown in Fig. 16-12. *The couple on the x planes (vertical planes) is clockwise, which is positive when plotting Mohr's circle. The line connecting V and H is the diameter of Mohr's circle. The location of the center and the magnitude of the radius can be found from Eqs.* (16-4) *and* (16-5).

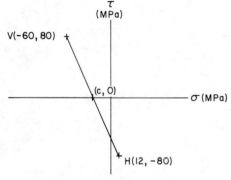

FIGURE 16-12

$$c = \frac{\sigma_x + \sigma_y}{2}$$

$$= \frac{-60 + 12}{2}$$

$$= \frac{-48}{2}$$

$$= -24.000 \text{ MPa}$$

$$r = \left[\left(\frac{\sigma_x - \sigma_y}{2} \right)^2 + \left(\tau_{xy} \right)^2 \right]^{1/2}$$

$$= \left[\left(\frac{-60 - 12}{2} \right)^2 + 80^2 \right]^{1/2}$$

$$= \left[\left(\frac{-72}{2} \right)^2 + 80^2 \right]^{1/2}$$

$$= [(-36)^2 + 80^2]^{1/2}$$

$$= (1296 + 6400)^{1/2}$$

$$= 7696^{1/2}$$

$$= 87.727 \text{ MPa}$$

The Mohr's circle may now be completed, as shown in Fig. 16-13. *If the circle is drawn to scale, the values of r, c, σ_1, σ_2, τ_{max} and θ may be checked graphically. Now that r and c have been obtained, the values for σ_1, σ_2 and τ_{max} may be obtained using* Eqs. (16-6), (16-8) *and* (16-10).

$$\sigma_1 = c + r$$

$$= -24.000 + 87.727$$

$$= 63.727 \text{ MPa}$$

$$\sigma_2 = c - r$$

$$= -24.000 - 87.727$$

$$= -111.727 \text{ MPa}$$

$$\tau_{max} = r$$

$$= 87.727 \text{ MPa}$$

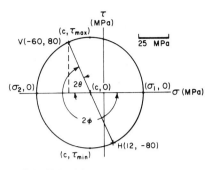

FIGURE 16-13

The angle θ may be obtained from Eq. (16-12), keeping in mind that the absolute value of tan 2θ is used. (In reality, it is just as easy to pick values from the triangle shown in Fig. 16-13 to find tan 2θ.)

$$\tan 2\theta = \left| \frac{2\tau_{xy}}{\sigma_x - \sigma_y} \right|$$

$$= \left| \frac{2 \times 80}{-60 - 12} \right|$$

$$= \frac{160}{72}$$

$$= 2.2222$$

$$2\theta = 65.77°$$

From Fig. 16-13, it can be seen that in Mohr's circle the angle 2φ is the counterclockwise angle from V to σ_1 on the σ axis.

$$2\phi = 180.00° + 2\theta$$

$$= 180.00° + 65.77°$$

$$= 245.77°$$

$$\phi = \frac{245.77°}{2}$$

$$= 122.88°$$

All required information is now available. Although not specifically requested, there is merit in showing the principal stresses and maximum (which has the same magnitude as the minimum) shear stress on a sketch, as shown in Fig. 16-14.

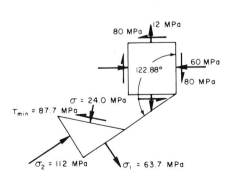

$$\sigma_1 = +63.7 \text{ MPa}$$
$$\sigma_2 = -112 \text{ MPa}$$
$$\tau_{max} = 87.7 \text{ MPa}$$
$$\phi = 122.88°$$

FIGURE 16-14

PROBLEMS

16-1 The stress on an element was found to be σ_x = +60 MPa, σ_y = +60 MPa and τ_{xy} = +110 MPa. Determine the principal stresses, the maximum shear stress and the orientation of σ_1.

16-2 Find the principal stresses, the maximum shear stress and the orientation of σ_1 for an element on which σ_x = +90 MPa, σ_y = +90 MPa and τ_{xy} = −40MPa.

16-3 Determine the principal stresses and maximum shear stress acting on an element if σ_x = +25 MPa, σ_y = +85 MPa and τ_{xy} = −40 MPa. Also determine the orientation of σ_1.

16-4 If the stress on an element has been found to be σ_x = +300 MPa, σ_y = +60 MPa and τ_{xy} = +50 MPa, calculate σ_1, σ_2, τ_{max} and determine the orientation of σ_1.

16-5 For the element shown in Fig. P16-5, determine σ_1, σ_2 and τ_{max}, and find the orientation of σ_1.

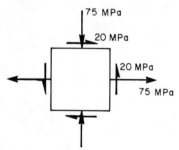

FIGURE P16-5

16-6 Calculate σ_1, σ_2 and τ_{max} for the element with the stresses shown in Fig. P16-6, and determine the orientation of σ_1.

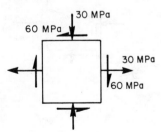

FIGURE P16-6

16-7 Calculate the principal stresses, maximum shear stress and the orientation of the maximum normal stress for an element on which σ_x = −50 MPa, σ_y = −90 MPa and τ_{xy} = +40 MPa.

16-8 Calculate σ_1, σ_2 and τ_{max} for an element if the stresses on the element were found to be σ_x = −60 MPa, σ_y = −10 MPa and τ_{xy} = −30 MPa. Determine the orientation of the plane on which σ_1 acts.

16-9 Determine the principal stresses and the maximum shear stress acting on the element shown in Fig. P16-9 and find the orientation of the maximum principal stress.

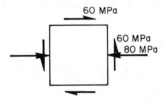

FIGURE P16-9

16-10 If the stresses at some point in a member are found to be as shown in Fig. P16-10, determine the principal stresses, the maximum shear stress at the point and the orientation of the plane on which σ_1 acts.

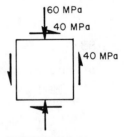

FIGURE P16-10

16-11 The stresses at a point in a member were found to be σ_x = +80 MPa, σ_y = −20 MPa and τ_{xy} = −30 MPa. Determine the principal stresses, the maximum shear stress and the orientation of the maximum normal stress.

16-12 Determine the principal stresses and the maximum shear stress for an element on which the stresses are $\sigma_x = -80$ MPa, $\sigma_y = +60$ MPa and $\tau_{xy} = -40$ MPa. Determine the orientation of the plane on which the maximum principal stress acts.

16-13 Draw Mohr's circle for the stresses on the element shown in Fig. P16-13. Determine σ_1, σ_2 and τ_{max} and determine the orientation of σ_1.

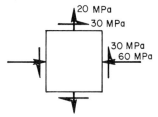

20 MPa
30 MPa
30 MPa
60 MPa

FIGURE P16-13

16-14 For the stresses on the element shown in Fig. P16-14, draw Mohr's circle and calculate the principal stresses and the maximum shear stress and the orientation of the maximum principal stress.

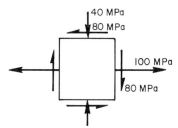

40 MPa
80 MPa
100 MPa
80 MPa

FIGURE P16-14

16-15 A steel bar with a cross-section of 15 by 60 mm supports an axial tensile load of 135 kN. Use Mohr's circle to calculate the maximum shear stress in the member.

16-16 Use Mohr's circle to determine the maximum shear stress in a 150 mm diameter concrete cylinder if the axial compressive load on the cylinder is 350 kN.

16-17 With the aid of Mohr's circle, determine the maximum tensile and compressive stresses in a 75 mm diameter shaft if a torque of 6 kN·m is applied to the shaft.

16-18 For a hollow shaft with an outside diameter of 50 mm and an inside diameter of 45 mm, use Mohr's circle to determine the maximum tensile stress and maximum compressive stress. The torque applied to the shaft is 800 N·m.

16-19 If the beam shown in Fig. P16-19 has a rectangular cross-section of 50 by 180 mm deep, calculate the maximum normal stress and the maximum shear stress at a point just to the right of A and 40 mm above the neutral axis.

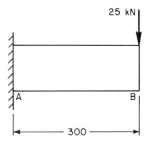

25 kN
A
B
300

FIGURE P16-19

16-20 Determine the maximum normal stress and maximum shear stress at a point just to the left of B and 40 mm above the neutral axis for the beam shown in Fig. P16-20. The rectangular cross-section is 45 by 120 mm deep.

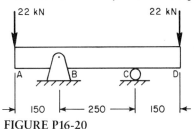

22 kN
22 kN
A
B
C
D
150
250
150

FIGURE P16-20

16-21 If the beam shown in Fig. P16-21 has a cross-section of 50 by 110 mm deep, calculate the principal stresses and maximum shear stress 20 mm below the neutral axis and just to the left of B.

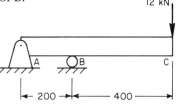

12 kN
A
B
C
200
400

FIGURE P16-21

16-22 Determine the principal stresses and the maximum shear stress at a point just to the left of the support and 5 mm below the neutral axis in the beam shown in Fig. P16-22. The cross-section of the beam is 30 by 70 mm deep.

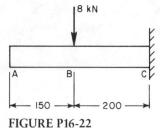

FIGURE P16-22

16-23 A cylindrical thin-walled pressure vessel with a length of 3 m, a diameter of 1.2 m and a wall thickness of 15 mm has an internal pressure of 600 kPa. Determine the principal stresses and the maximum shear stress in the cylindrical wall of the pressure vessel.

16-24 Find the principal stresses and the maximum shear stress in a spherical thin-walled pressure vessel if it has a diameter of 0.8 m, a wall thickness of 20 mm and an internal pressure of 1200 kPa.

16-3   STRESS DUE TO COMBINED LOADING

In earlier chapters the stresses caused by simple loading conditions were discussed. This included the normal stress due to a centric, axial load, the shear stress caused by a torque applied to a circular shaft, the flexural or normal stress caused by a bending moment in a beam, and the shear stress in a beam due to the transverse shear force. A high proportion of members used in frames and machines support such relatively simple load systems. In some cases, however, the loading will be some combination of axial, torsion, bending and transverse shear.

The different possible load combinations are shown in Fig. 16-15. Because shear stress due to a torque can be readily analyzed only if the member has a circular cross section, the three members that have a torque applied as part of the load are shown with a circular cross-section.

The stress on a member with a constant cross section caused by various load combinations may be evaluated using the techniques for simple loading conditions and the principle of superposition, provided that the stress in the member does not exceed the proportional limit. According to the principle of superposition, parallel stresses of the same type (normal or shear) acting at the same point on the same plane may be added algebraically to give the total stress of that type at that point on the plane.

The stress due to simple loading systems evaluated in previous chapters has usually been the stress on a cross-section of the member. An exception to this has been the shear stress caused by a transverse shear force, where the stress evaluated was the stress occurring on both the transverse cross-section and the longitudinal section of the member.

STRESS ON A CROSS SECTION

Case	Loading	Normal Stress Calculation	Shear Stress Calculation	Location of Maximum Normal Stress	Location of Maximum Shear Stress
1	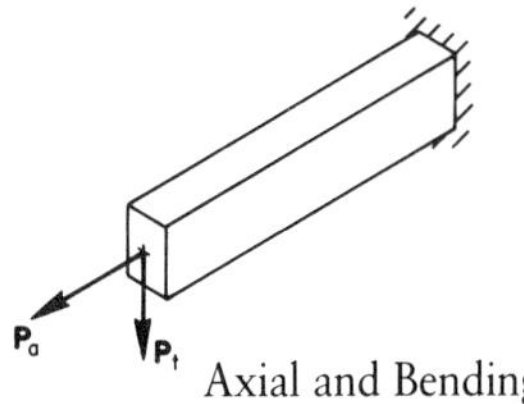 Axial and Bending	$\dfrac{P}{A}\quad \dfrac{My}{I}$	$\dfrac{VQ}{It}$	At extreme fiber for bending where M is maximum and P/A has same sign as My/I.	At neutral axis for bending.
2	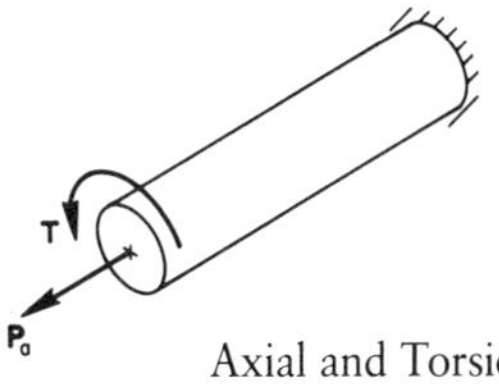 Axial and Torsion	$\dfrac{P}{A}$	$\dfrac{Tr}{J}$	Maximum throughout member.	At outside of section where T is maximum.
3	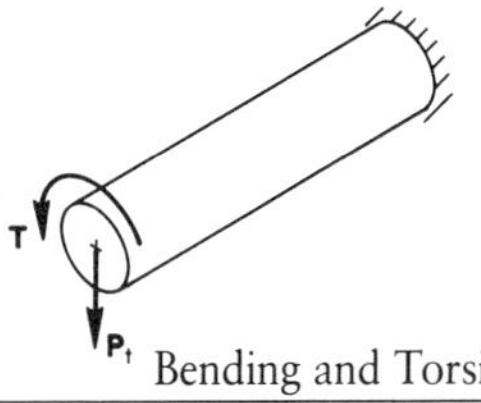 Bending and Torsion	$\dfrac{My}{I}$	$\dfrac{Tr}{J}\quad \dfrac{VQ}{It}$	At extreme fiber for bending where M is maximum.	At outside of section at neutral axis for bending where both T and V are maximum and have same sign.
4	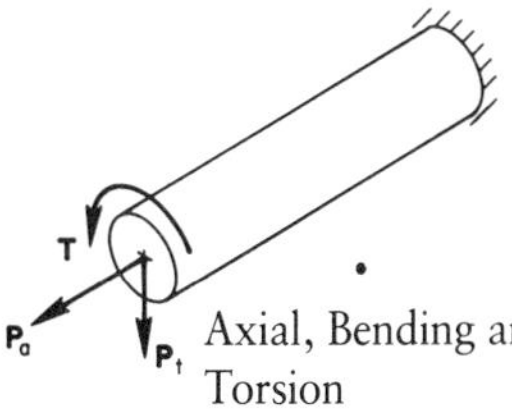 Axial, Bending and Torsion	$\dfrac{P}{A}\quad \dfrac{My}{I}$	$\dfrac{Tr}{J}\quad \dfrac{VQ}{It}$	At extreme fiber for bending where M is maximum and P/A has same sign as My/I.	At outside of section at neutral axis for bending where both T and V are maximum and have same sign.

FIGURE 16-15

The principle of superposition may be used to determine the total normal stress or total shear stress at some point on the cross-section of a member with combined loading. Although the maximum normal stress or maximum shear stress on a cross-section of a member will provide useful information on the order of magnitude of the maximum normal and maximum shear stress in a member, it would be necessary, in many cases, to use Mohr's circle to calculate the maximum principal stresses or the maximum shear stress in a member. Thus, finding the maximum value of normal stress or shear stress anywhere in a member can be very complex.

Where there is a combination of axial and bending loads (Cases 1 and 4 in Fig. 16-15), the normal stress on any section may be determined by calculating the algebraic sum of the normal stresses due to the axial load and due to bending.

$$\sigma = \frac{P}{A} + \frac{My}{I} \qquad (16\text{-}13)$$

The maximum normal stress on a cross section will occur where both P/A and My/I have their maximum values and the same sign. The normal stress due to the axial load will have a constant value if there is no change in the axial load, and the normal stress due to bending will occur at the extreme fiber from the neutral axis for bending where the moment is maximum.

The distribution of normal stress on a cross-section due to the two loads is shown in Fig. 16-16. The stress caused by the axial load is shown in Fig. 16-16(a); the stress caused by the bending is shown in Fig. 16-16(b); and the combined stress, obtained using the principle of superposition, is shown in Fig. 16-16(c). Depending on the relative magnitudes of the two stresses, it is possible that the combined stress might be either tension or compression at all points on the section.

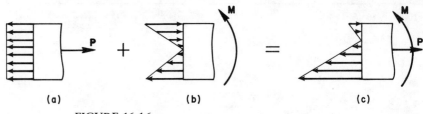

(a)   (b)   (c)

FIGURE 16-16

If the axial load on a member is compression, Eq. (16-13) will be valid for short members only. In the case of slender compression members, the bending caused by an axial compressive load would tend to create an additional bending moment that would further complicate the analysis.

When both a torque and a transverse shear force are applied to a member, as happens with Cases 3 and 4 in Fig. 16-15, each load will cause a shear stress on the cross section. The two shear stresses will be parallel only on the diameter of the cross-section that is perpendicular to the transverse shear force. The directions of the shear stresses on a cross-section due to a torque are shown in Fig. 16-17(a), and the direction of the shear stresses due to a transverse shear are shown in Fig. 16-17(b).

The shear stress at a point on the neutral axis may be calculated from

$$\tau = \frac{Tr}{J} + \frac{VQ}{It} \qquad (16\text{-}14)$$

The maximum shear stress caused by the torque will be at the outside of the section, as shown in Fig. 16-18(a). The maximum shear stress caused by a transverse shear force occurs at the neutral axis for bending, which is a diameter in the case of a beam with a circular cross-section. This is shown in Fig. 16-18(b). The shear-stress distribution along the neutral axis due to the combination of loads is shown in Fig. 16-18(c). Whether the combined shear stress has the same direction at all points on the diameter will depend on the relative magnitudes of the shear stresses caused by the two loads.

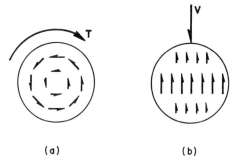

(a)   (b)

FIGURE 16-17

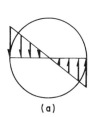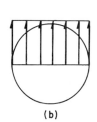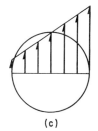

(a)   (b)   (c)

FIGURE 16-18

Since it is possible to add only parallel normal stresses or parallel shear stresses, there are no other loading combinations that give such relatively simple stress-analysis solutions.

Mohr's circle may be used to calculate the principal stresses and maximum shear stress at many points in a member with combined loads if the normal and shear stresses on two orthogonal planes at that point are first calculated.

EXAMPLE 16-3

One of the four supports for a large machine has a load applied as shown in Fig. 16-19. Calculate the maximum and minimum normal stresses on a section.

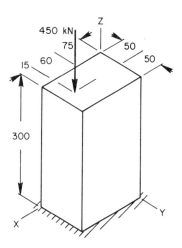

FIGURE 16-19

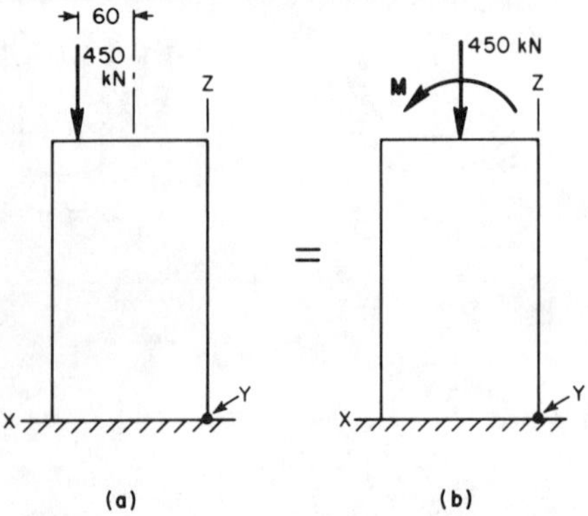

SOLUTION

The given load is not a centric axial load. To analyze the stress in the member, the given load is replaced by a single load at the centroid of the section and a couple, as shown in the side view in Fig. 16-20.

The member shown in Fig. 16-20(b) *now has a centric axial load that causes a compressive stress, and a couple that will cause the same bending moment at any section in the member. The maximum values for both the tensile stress and the compressive stress on a section may be calculated using Eq. (16-13). First the couple (or moment) causing the flexure in the beam must be calculated.*

$$T = Fd = M$$
$$= 450 \times 0.060$$
$$= 27.000 \text{ kN} \cdot \text{m}$$

The bending will be about a centroidal axis parallel to the y axis. The centroidal moment of inertia will be required to calculate the flexural stress.

$$\bar{I}_y = \frac{bh^3}{12}$$
$$= \frac{100 \times 150^3}{12}$$
$$= 28.125 \times 10^6 \text{ mm}^4$$

The maximum compressive stress will occur at the left outside fiber in Fig. 16-20(b), *where both the axial stress and the compressive stresses are negative.*

$$\sigma = \frac{P}{A} + \frac{My}{I}$$
$$= -\frac{450 \times 10^3}{100 \times 150 \times 10^{-6}} - \frac{27.000 \times 10^3 \times 75 \times 10^{-3}}{28.125 \times 10^6 \times 10^{-12}}$$
$$= -30.000 \times 10^6 - 72.000 \times 10^6$$
$$= -102.000 \times 10^6 \text{ Pa}$$
$$= -102.000 \text{ MPa}$$

If there is a tensile stress, the maximum value will occur at the right outside fiber in Fig. 16-20(b), *where the two stresses have the opposite signs. Note that the numeric values for P/A and My/I will be the same as previously calculated.*

FIGURE 16-20

$$\sigma = \frac{P}{A} + \frac{My}{I}$$

$$= -\frac{450 \times 10^3}{100 \times 150 \times 10^{-6}} + \frac{27.000 \times 10^3 \times 75 \times 10^{-3}}{28.125 \times 10^6 \times 10^{-12}}$$

$$= -30.000 \times 10^6 + 72.000 \times 10^6$$

$$= 42.000 \times 10^6 \text{ Pa}$$

$$= 42.000 \text{ MPa}$$

$$\boxed{\begin{aligned} \sigma_{max} &= +42.0 \text{ MPa} \\ \sigma_{min} &= -102 \text{ MPa} \end{aligned}}$$

EXAMPLE 16-4

Figure 16-21 shows a motor, A, which applies a torque of 12 N·m to the 20 mm diameter shaft, AC. The bearing at C is assumed to be frictionless and the supports at both A and C are flexible so that the shaft is not restrained. Calculate (a) the magnitude of the maximum bending stress in the shaft, and (b) the magnitude of the maximum shear stress on a cross-section of the shaft.

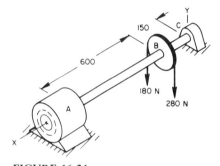

FIGURE 16-21

SOLUTION

It will be necessary to obtain both the transverse shear and the bending moment in the shaft to determine the two stresses required. A free-body diagram of the shaft, as shown in Fig. 16-22, *will be required to draw the shear and moment diagrams. The free-body diagram is used as an aid in determining the reactions at the supports at A and C.*

$$\Sigma M_A = 0$$

$$-(180 \times 0.600) - 280 \times 0.600 + C_y \times 0.750 = 0$$

$$C_y = \frac{108.00 + 168.00}{0.750}$$

$$= \frac{276.00}{0.750}$$

$$= 368.00 \text{ N}$$

$$\Sigma F_y = 0$$

$$A_y - 180 - 280 + 368.00 = 0$$

$$A_y = 180.00 + 280.00 - 368.00$$

$$= 92.00 \text{ N}$$

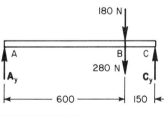

FIGURE 16-22

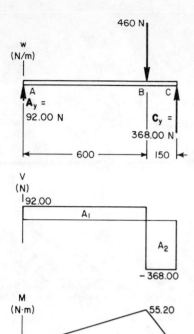

FIGURE 16-23

The shear and moment diagrams can now be drawn, as shown in Fig. 16-23. *The shear starts at zero at A.*

At A:

$$V = 0.00 \text{ N}$$

At A, there is a positive shear due to the reaction at A.

At A:

$$V = 0.00 + 92.00$$

$$= 92.00 \text{ N}$$

Since there are no loads applied between A and B there is no change in shear between A and B.

At B:

$$V = 92.00 \text{ N}$$

There is a concentrated load of 460 N at B, so the shear will decrease by that amount at B.

At B:

$$V = 92.00 - 460.00$$

$$= -368.00 \text{ N}$$

There are no loads applied between B and C, so there is no change in shear between these points.

At C:

$$V = -368.00 \text{ N}$$

At C there is a positive change in shear due to the reaction at the support.

At C:

$$V = -368.00 + 368.00$$

$$= 0.00 \text{ N}$$

The moment diagram will start at zero at the left end, and the change in moment from A to B will be equal to the area A_1, of the shear diagram between A and B.

At A:

$$M = 0.00 \text{ N·m}$$

$$A_1 = \frac{1}{2} \times 0.600 \times 92.00$$

$$= 55.20 \text{ N·m}$$

At B:

$$M = 0.00 + 55.20$$

$$= 55.20 \text{ N} \cdot \text{m}$$

The change in moment from B to C will equal A_2, the area of the shear diagram between B and C.

$$A_2 = -\frac{1}{2} \times 0.150 \times 368.00$$

$$= -55.20 \text{ N} \cdot \text{m}$$

At C:

$$M = 55.20 - 55.20$$

$$= 0.00 \text{ N} \cdot \text{m}$$

The maximum bending stress will occur at the top and bottom of the shaft at B where M has its maximum value. The stress may be calculated using Eq. (13-5).

(a)
$$\sigma = \frac{Mc}{I}$$

$$= \frac{55.20 \times 10 \times 10^{-3}}{\dfrac{\pi \times 20^4}{64} \times 10^{-12}}$$

$$= 70.283 \times 10^6 \text{ Pa}$$

$$= 70.283 \text{ MPa}$$

Between A and B there is both a torque of 12 N·m and a transverse shear force of 92.00 N. Between B and C there is no torque, since the bearing at C is frictionless, but there is a higher transverse shear of 368.00 N. It will be necessary to calculate the maximum shear stress between A and B, and between B and C, to determine the higher value. Use Eq. (16-14) to calculate the maximum shear stress between A and B. It is advisable to calculate Q separately.

(b)
$$Q = \bar{Y}A$$

$$= \frac{4r}{3\pi} \times \frac{\pi d^2}{8}$$

$$= \frac{4 \times 10 \times 20^2}{3 \times 8}$$

$$= 666.67 \text{ mm}^3$$

A to B:

$$\tau = \frac{Tr}{J} + \frac{VQ}{It}$$

$$= \frac{12 \times 10 \times 10^{-3}}{\dfrac{\pi \times 20^4}{32} \times 10^{-12}} + \frac{92 \times 666.67 \times 10^{-9}}{\dfrac{\pi \times 20^4}{64} \times 10^{-12} \times 20 \times 10^{-3}}$$

$$= 7.6394 \times 10^6 + 0.3905 \times 10^6$$

$$= 8.0299 \times 10^6 \text{ Pa}$$

$$= 8.0299 \text{ MPa}$$

B to C:

$$\tau = \frac{VQ}{It}$$

$$= \frac{368 \times 666.67 \times 10^{-9}}{\dfrac{\pi \times 20^4}{64} \times 10^{-12} \times 20 \times 10^{-3}}$$

$$= 1.5618 \times 10^6 \text{ Pa}$$

$$= 1.5618 \text{ MPa}$$

$$\tau_{max} = 8.0299 \text{ MPa}$$

> (a) $\sigma = 70.3$ MPa
> (b) $\tau = 8.03$ MPa

EXAMPLE 16-5

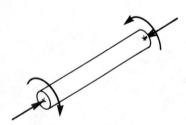

FIGURE 16-24

The forces on the shaft shown in Fig. 16-24 represent the forces acting on a ship's propeller shaft. Determine the principal stresses and maximum shear stress at a point at the surface of the shaft if the torque applied is 700 N·m, the axial load is 45 kN and the diameter of the shaft is 40 mm. Assume that the shaft is supported so that it will not behave as a slender column.

SOLUTION

The normal stress on any cross-section due to the axial load will be constant, and may be calculated using Eq. (10-1).

$$\sigma = \frac{P}{A}$$

$$= -\frac{45 \times 10^3}{\dfrac{\pi \times 40^2}{4}} \times 10^{-6}$$

$$= -35.810 \times 10^6 \text{ Pa}$$

$$= -35.810 \text{ MPa}$$

The shear stress at the outside of any section caused by the torque is determined by using Eq. (12-5).

$$\tau = \frac{Tc}{J}$$

$$= \frac{700 \times 20 \times 10^{-3}}{\dfrac{\pi \times 40^4}{32}} \times 10^{-12}$$

$$= 55.704 \times 10^6 \text{ Pa}$$

$$= 55.704 \text{ MPa}$$

The normal and shear stresses are drawn on a small element of the shaft, as shown in Fig. 16-25. The vertical planes in the element are on the cross-section in the member. If there are shear stresses on the vertical planes, to maintain equilibrium there must be corresponding shear stresses on the other two planes. The stresses on the element are used to draw Mohr's circle, as shown in Fig. 16-26.

The information from Mohr's circle is used, along with Eqs. (16-4) *and* (16-5), *to calculate c and r.*

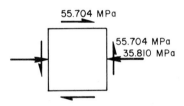

FIGURE 16-25

$$c = \frac{\sigma_x + \sigma_y}{2}$$

$$= \frac{-35.810 + 0}{2}$$

$$= -17.905 \text{ MPa}$$

$$r = \left[\left(\frac{\sigma_x - \sigma_y}{2}\right)^2 + \left(\tau_{xy}\right)^2\right]^{1/2}$$

$$= \left[\left(\frac{-35.810 - 0}{2}\right)^2 + (-55.704)^2\right]^{1/2}$$

$$= (320.59 + 3102.94)^{1/2}$$

$$= 3423.53^{1/2}$$

$$= 58.511 \text{ MPa}$$

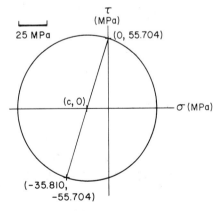

FIGURE 16-26

Now that c and r have been calculated, the information can be used in Eqs. (16-6), (16-8) and (16-10) to calculate σ_1, σ_2 and τ_{max}.

$$\sigma_1 = c + r$$
$$= -17.905 + 58.511$$
$$= +40.606 \text{ MPa}$$

$$\sigma_2 = c - r$$
$$= -17.905 - 58.511$$
$$= -76.416 \text{ MPa}$$

$$\tau_{max} = r$$
$$= 58.511 \text{ MPa}$$

$\sigma_1 = +40.6 \text{ MPa}$
$\sigma_2 = -76.4 \text{ MPa}$
$\tau_{max} = 58.5 \text{ MPa}$

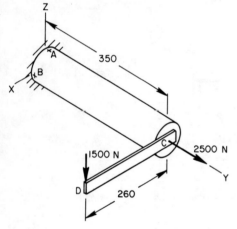

FIGURE 16-27

EXAMPLE 16-6

A machine part with axial, transverse and torsional loads is shown in Fig. 16-27. The part has a diameter of 60 mm. Determine the principal stresses and maximum shear stress at A (at the top near the wall) and at B (at the end of a horizontal diameter near the wall).

SOLUTION

Before analyzing any stresses in the member, it is first necessary to determine the torque, axial load, transverse shear and bending moment that will cause the stresses.

The force at D may be replaced by a force at C and a couple, as shown in Fig. 16-28.

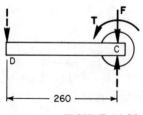

FIGURE 16-28

$$F = -1500 \text{ N}$$
$$T = Fd$$
$$= 1500 \times 0.260$$
$$= 390.00 \text{ N·m}$$

Since the member is a cantilever beam with a force at the free end, the transverse shear force will be constant throughout the length of the member. The bending moment will be maximum at the support, where both A and B are located.

At A and B:

$$V = -1500 \text{ N}$$

$$M = Fd$$

$$= -(1500 \times 0.350)$$

$$= -525.00 \text{ N·m}$$

$$T = 390.00 \text{ N·m}$$

$$P = 2500 \text{ N}$$

At A the stresses occurring on the section will be the normal stress caused by the axial load, the shear stress caused by the torque, and the normal stress caused by the bending. The shear stress due to the transverse shear force will be zero at A, since A is at the extreme fiber from the neutral axis. The shear stress due to the torque is calculated using Eq. (12-5) and the total normal stress is calculated using Eq. (16-13). Both normal-stress terms have the same sign at A.

$$\tau = \frac{Tc}{J}$$

$$= \frac{390.00 \times 30 \times 10^{-3}}{\dfrac{\pi \times 60^4}{32} \times 10^{-12}}$$

$$= 9.1956 \times 10^6 \text{ Pa}$$

$$= 9.1956 \text{ MPa}$$

$$\sigma = \frac{P}{A} + \frac{My}{I}$$

$$= \frac{2500}{\dfrac{\pi \times 60^2}{4} \times 10^{-6}} + \frac{525.00 \times 30 \times 10^{-3}}{\dfrac{\pi \times 60^4}{64} \times 10^{-12}}$$

$$= 0.8842 \times 10^6 + 24.7574 \times 10^6$$

$$= 25.642 \times 10^6 \text{ Pa}$$

$$= 25.642 \text{ MPa}$$

The values for σ and τ should be drawn on an element, as shown in Fig. 16-29. *The total normal stress and the shear stress are shown on the y plane. If the element is to be in equilibrium, a corresponding shear stress must also act on the x plane. The element shown in* Fig. 16-29 *is used to draw Mohr's circle, as shown in* Fig. 16-30.

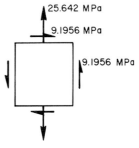

25.642 MPa

9.1956 MPa

9.1956 MPa

FIGURE 16-29

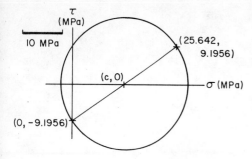

τ
(MPa)

10 MPa

(25.642, 9.1956)

(c, 0)

σ (MPa)

(0, -9.1956)

FIGURE 16-30

The principal stresses and maximum shear stress may be calculated by first determining c and r using Eqs. (16-4) and (16-5).

$$c = \frac{\sigma_x + \sigma_y}{2}$$

$$= \frac{0 + 25.642}{2}$$

$$= 12.821 \text{ MPa}$$

$$r = \left[\left(\frac{\sigma_x - \sigma_y}{2} \right)^2 + \left(\tau_{xy} \right)^2 \right]^{1/2}$$

$$= \left[\left(\frac{0 - 25.642}{2} \right)^2 + (-9.1956)^2 \right]^{1/2}$$

$$= (164.38 + 84.56)^{1/2}$$

$$= 248.94^{1/2}$$

$$= 15.778 \text{ MPa}$$

Equations (16-6), (16-8) and (16-10) may now be used to determine σ_1, σ_2 and τ_{max}.

$$\sigma_1 = c + r$$

$$= 12.821 + 15.778$$

$$= +28.599 \text{ MPa}$$

$$\sigma_2 = c - r$$

$$= 12.821 - 15.778$$

$$= -2.957 \text{ MPa}$$

$$\tau_{max} = r$$

$$= 15.778 \text{ MPa}$$

At B there will be a normal stress due to the axial load, but since B is on the neutral axis, there will be no normal stress due to bending. There will be a shear stress due to the torque as well as a shear stress caused by the transverse shear force, since B is on the neutral axis. Both shear stresses will have the same direction. The normal stress at B can be calculated using Eq. (10-1).

$$\sigma = \frac{P}{A}$$

$$= \frac{2500}{\dfrac{\pi \times 60^2}{4} \times 10^{-6}}$$

$$= 0.8842 \times 10^6 \text{ Pa}$$

$$= 0.8842 \text{ MPa}$$

The shear stress on the section at B is calculated using Eq. (16-14). Calculate the value for Q before using Eq. (16-14).

$$Q = \bar{Y}A$$

$$= \frac{4r}{3\pi} \times \frac{\pi d^2}{8}$$

$$= \frac{4 \times 30}{3\pi} \times \frac{\pi \times 60^2}{8}$$

$$= 18\ 000 \text{ mm}^3$$

$$\tau = \frac{Tr}{J} + \frac{VQ}{It}$$

$$= \frac{390.00 \times 30 \times 10^{-3}}{\dfrac{\pi \times 60^4}{32} \times 10^{-12}}$$

$$+ \frac{1500 \times 18\ 000 \times 10^{-9}}{\dfrac{\pi \times 60^4}{64} \times 10^{-12} \times 60 \times 10^{-3}}$$

$$= 9.1956 \times 10^6 + 0.7074 \times 10^6$$

$$= 9.9030 \times 10^6 \text{ Pa}$$

$$= 9.9030 \text{ MPa}$$

The stresses on an element at B may now be drawn as shown in Fig. 16-31. Because of the orientation of point B on the member, the horizontal planes in Fig. 16-31 are perpendicular to the z axis, and would thus be called z planes. If equilibrium is to be maintained, the shear stress on the z planes must be the same as the shear stress on the y planes, which are vertical in the figure.

The principal stresses and maximum shear stress at point B may be obtained by using the information from Fig. 16-31 to draw Mohr's circle, as shown in Fig. 16-32. Values for c and r are obtained using Eqs. (16-4) and (16-5).

$$c = \frac{\sigma_y + \sigma_z}{2}$$

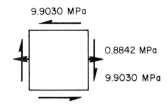

9.9030 MPa

0.8842 MPa

9.9030 MPa

FIGURE 16-31

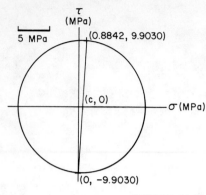

FIGURE 16-32

$$= \frac{0.8842 + 0}{2}$$

$$= 0.4421 \text{ MPa}$$

$$r = \left[\left(\frac{\sigma_y - \sigma_z}{2} \right)^2 + \left(\tau_{yz} \right)^2 \right]^{1/2}$$

$$= \left[\left(\frac{0.8842 - 0}{2} \right)^2 + (9.9030)^2 \right]^{1/2}$$

$$= (0.1955 + 98.0694)^{1/2}$$

$$= 98.2649^{1/2}$$

$$= 9.9129 \text{ MPa}$$

The values for σ_1, σ_2 and τ_{max} at B are calculated using Eqs. (16-6), (16-8) and (16-10).

$$\sigma_1 = c + r$$

$$= 0.4421 + 9.9129$$

$$= +10.3550 \text{ MPa}$$

$$\sigma_2 = c - r$$

$$= 0.4421 - 9.9129$$

$$= -9.4708 \text{ MPa}$$

$$\tau_{max} = r$$

$$= 9.9129 \text{ MPa}$$

At A:
$\sigma_1 = +28.6 \text{ MPa}$
$\sigma_2 = -2.96 \text{ MPa}$
$\tau_{max} = 15.8 \text{ MPa}$
At B:
$\sigma_1 = +10.4 \text{ MPa}$
$\sigma_2 = -9.47 \text{ MPa}$
$\tau_{max} = 9.91 \text{ MPa}$

PROBLEMS

16-25 For the member shown in Fig. P16-25, calculate the normal stress on a section at *A* at the base.

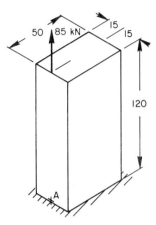

FIGURE P16-25

16-26 Determine the normal stress on the section at point *A* for the member shown in Fig. P16-26.

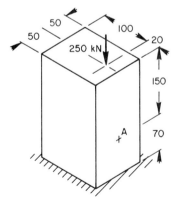

FIGURE P16-26

16-27 Find the normal stress on the section at *A* for the member shown in Fig. P16-27. The member has a cross-section of 75 by 90 mm deep.

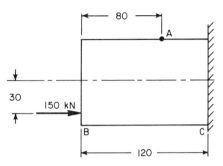

FIGURE P16-27

16-28 The member shown in Fig. P16-28 has a rectangular cross-section 115 by 140 mm deep. Calculate the normal stress on the section at point *A*.

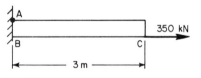

FIGURE P16-28

16-29 The member shown in Fig. P16-29 is a W250x89 structural-steel shape. Determine the normal stress at the top and bottom fibers on the section at the wall.

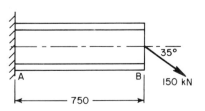

FIGURE P16-29

16-30 Determine the normal stress on the top and bottom fibers on the section at the wall for the W360x216 steel shape shown in Fig. P16-30.

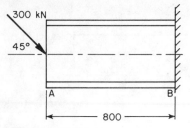

FIGURE P16-30

16-31 If the member shown in Fig. P16-31 has a rectangular hollow cross-section of 150 by 400 mm deep, with a wall thickness of 8 mm, determine the maximum tensile, compressive and shear stresses on any cross-section, and state where these stresses are located.

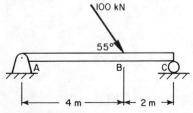

FIGURE P16-31

16-32 The member shown in Fig. P16-32 is a fabricated I-shape made up of 20 mm thick plate. The web is 120 mm high and the flanges are 80 mm wide. Determine the maximum tensile, compressive and shear stresses that occur on a cross-section. Indicate where these stresses occur.

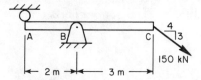

FIGURE P16-32

16-33 The 160 mm diameter shaft shown in Fig. P16-33 has a length of 1.2 m. Determine the magnitude of the maximum flexural stress on a section and the maximum shear stress on a section.

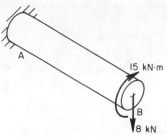

FIGURE P16-33

16-34 For the 15 mm diameter bar shown in Fig. P16-34, find the magnitude of the maximum flexural stress on a section and the magnitude of the maximum shear stress on a section. The bar has a length of 225 mm.

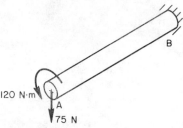

FIGURE P16-34

16-35 The shaft shown in Fig. P16-35 has an outside diameter of 65 mm and an inside diameter of 55 mm. Calculate the magnitude of the flexural stress at the top and bottom of the shaft at A and the shear stress on the section at each end of the neutral axis for bending at A.

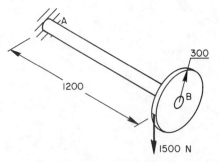

FIGURE P16-35

16-36 For the member shown in Fig. P16-36, calculate the magnitude of the maximum flexural stress on a section at A and the magnitudes of the shear stresses at each end of the neutral axis for bending at *A*. The shaft is a 50 mm diameter tube with a 4 mm wall thickness.

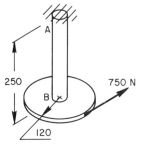

FIGURE P16-36

16-37 The motor at *C* transmits a torque of 3 N·m to the 15 mm diameter shaft shown in Fig. P16-37. Determine the maximum shear stress on a cross-section of the shaft if the bearing at *B* and the connection to the motor are flexible.

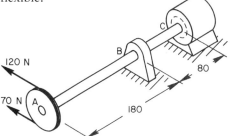

FIGURE P16-37

16-38 The 40 mm diameter shaft shown in Fig. P16-38 is supported by flexible frictionless bearings at *A* and *D*. If the pulley at *B* has a diameter of 180 mm, calculate the magnitude and location of the maximum shear stress on a cross-section in the shaft.

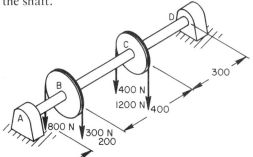

FIGURE P16-38

16-39 For the 75 mm diameter shaft shown in Fig. P16-39, find the principal stresses and the maximum shear stress for a point near the surface of the shaft.

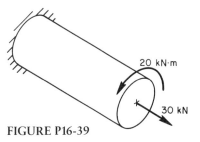

FIGURE P16-39

16-40 The shaft shown in Fig. P16-40 represents the shaft of a small drill bit. Calculate the principal stresses and the maximum shear stress in the shaft for a point near the surface. The diameter of the shaft is 4 mm.

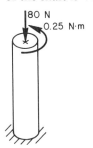

FIGURE P16-40

16-41 Determine the principal stresses and the maximum shear stress at a point near the surface of the hollow drill rod shown in Fig. P16-41. The outside diameter of the rod is 150 mm and the inside diameter is 120 mm.

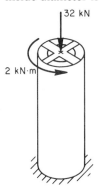

FIGURE P16-41

16-42 Calculate the principal stresses and the maximum shear stress for a point near the surface of the shaft shown in Fig. P16-42. The shaft has an outside diameter of 30 mm and an inside diameter of 20 mm.

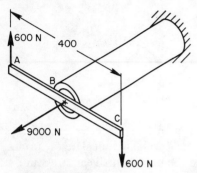

FIGURE P16-42

16-43 For the 80 mm diameter shaft shown in Fig. P16-43, determine the principal stresses for point A, which is at the end of the neutral axis for bending near the support.

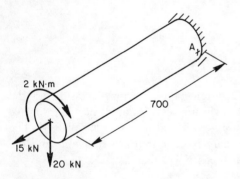

FIGURE P16-43

16-44 For the 30 mm diameter shaft shown in Fig. P16-44, calculate the principal stresses and the maximum shearing stress at A, which is at the extreme fiber from the neutral axis for bending.

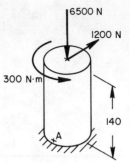

FIGURE P16-44

16-45 Calculate the principal stresses and the maximum shear stress at point A, which is at the top, near the support, of the 18 mm diameter shaft shown in Fig. P16-45.

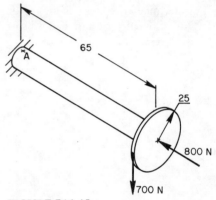

FIGURE P16-45

16-46 Find the principal stresses and the maximum shear stress at point A for the 150 mm diameter shaft shown in Fig. P16-46. Point A is on the end of the neutral axis for bending, at the support.

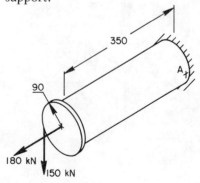

FIGURE P16-46

16-47 The shaft shown in Fig. P16-47 has an outside diameter of 35 mm and an inside diameter of 25 mm. Calculate the principal stresses and maximum shear stress at A, which is at the end of the neutral axis for bending and near the support.

16-48 Calculate the principal stresses and maximum shear stress at A for the shaft shown in Fig. P16-48. Point A is at the extreme fiber from the neutral axis for bending at the support. The shaft has an outside diameter of 75 mm and an inside diameter of 50 mm.

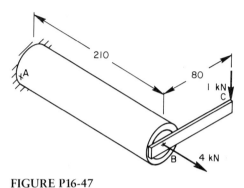

FIGURE P16-47

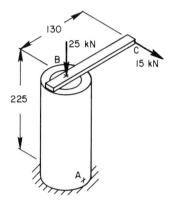

FIGURE P16-48

17 PROPERTIES AND TESTING OF MATERIALS

17-1 MECHANICAL PROPERTIES OF MATERIALS

The selection of a material for a member that supports a load depends very much on the mechanical properties of the materials that might be used. Mechanical properties are those properties that involve the relationship between stress and strain. These properties include the modulus of elasticity, yield strength, ultimate strength, ductility and hardness. Other properties may also be important in the selection process. These include physical properties, such as density and electrical and thermal conductivity; chemical properties, such as corrosion resistance; and optical properties, such as color and luster. Cost of the material is also a very important consideration. Although all of these factors are important to the selection process, it is only the mechanical properties that will be examined here.

Mechanical properties are usually obtained by performing tests on samples of the material for which the mechanical properties are required. The actual test procedures and definitions of terms are usually specified by a national standards organization. However, the basic procedures and definitions are reasonably common throughout the technical world. In the following articles the most common tests and the mechanical properties obtained from the tests will be described.

17-2 TENSION AND COMPRESSION TESTS

The two most common tests performed on materials to determine mechanical properties are the tension test and the compression test. In these tests, a sample of the material, usually a round or rectangular bar, is inserted into a testing machine that applies an axial load to the sample. The dimensions of the sample are measured prior to testing, and during the actual test a record is

FIGURE 17-1 An extensometer is being attached to a tensile test sample in a universal testing machine. The loads applied to the sample will be shown on the large dial on the right. The extensometer shown is an electronic model designed to read strain directly, rather than deformation. *Photo courtesy of Tinius Olsen Testing Machine Co., Inc.*

made of the loads applied and the corresponding deformations until the sample fractures. Figure 17-1 shows a sample about to be tested in tension in a universal testing machine. The deformation is measured by a device called an extensometer, which is attached to the sample, and the load applied is read from the large scale on the machine. Many modern universal testing machines are loading devices connected to computerized electronic devices; all the necessary calculations can be done by the machine once sample dimensions are entered into the machine's computer.

To ensure the reproducibility of tests, sample size and shape are usually specified, along with the gage length, which is the length of sample over which the deformation is measured.

The characteristics of the material to be tested govern whether a tension or compression test will be performed. Most metallic materials are usually tested in tension, but some are tested in both tension and compression since there is a difference in their properties under the different types of load. Materials that are very weak in tension are usually tested in compression, since in actual use they are usually designed to carry compressive loads only. Concrete and stone are examples of such materials.

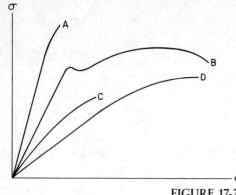

FIGURE 17-2

The information obtained from the tension or compression test is used to calculate the stress and corresponding strain in the material where

$$\sigma = \frac{P}{A} \qquad (10\text{-}1)$$

and

$$\epsilon = \frac{\delta}{L} \qquad (10\text{-}7)$$

The stress and strain are then used to plot a stress-strain diagram, in which stress is usually plotted on the vertical axis and the corresponding strain is plotted on the horizontal axis. Some typical stress-strain diagrams are shown in Fig. 17-2. The end point of the diagram represents the stress and corresponding strain when the material fractures or when testing is stopped because of excessive deformation.

Each material has its own stress-strain diagram with its own characteristics. From these stress-strain diagrams many of the mechanical properties are determined. One of the most important mechanical properties is the determination of the stress at which a material starts to yield, since the allowable stress for design is often based on this stress. A material yields when there is noticeable deformation without significant increase in load. Of the four stress-strain diagrams shown in Fig. 17-2, only in diagram *B* is the point of the start of yielding well defined. The first part of diagram *B* is redrawn as Fig. 17-3(a). In such a diagram there is a well-defined point where the slope of the diagram is zero. This point is just beyond the straight-line portion of the stress-strain diagram, and it is called the *yield point*. Low-carbon steels exhibit this characteristic in their stress-strain diagrams. For other materials, the onset of yielding is determined using other methods, as illustrated in Figs. 17-3(b) and (c), which show the initial portions of stress-strain diagrams for two other materials. Since there is not a well-defined yield point in these two cases, the value determined is called the *yield strength*. For the material with the stress-strain diagram shown in Fig. 17-3(b), the yield strength is specified as the stress when the strain in the sample reaches some specified value, usually 0.5% or 0.005 m/m. Smaller values of strain are usually used for brittle materials. In the stress-strain diagram shown in Fig. 17-3(c), the yield strength is determined by drawing a tangent line parallel to the initial slope of the stress-strain diagram. This tangent is offset a specified distance, usually 0.2% or 0.002 m/m, from the initial tangent. Again, smaller values of offset are used for materials with low ductility. The stress at which the offset line intersects the stress-strain diagram is called the *offset yield strength*.

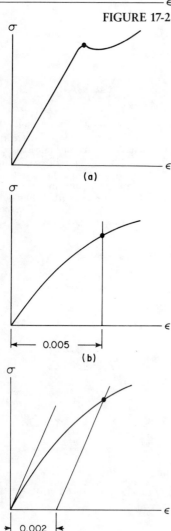

(a)

(b)

0.005

(c)

0.002

FIGURE 17-3

The *ultimate strength* of a material may be determined directly from the stress-strain diagrams such as those shown in Fig. 17-2. It is the maximum stress developed in the sample and is thus the highest value of stress on the stress-strain diagram. For some materials, fracture does not occur at the ultimate strength; instead, the load and stress decrease as the material yields, as indicated by diagram *B* in Fig. 17-2.

Another very important mechanical property that may be obtained from the stress-strain diagram is the *modulus of elasticity*, sometimes called *Young's modulus*. It is a measure of the stiffness of the material. For materials with a straight-line portion at the beginning of the stress-strain diagram, as shown in Fig. 17-4, the modulus of elasticity is determined from

$$E = \frac{\Delta\sigma}{\Delta\epsilon} \qquad (10\text{-}10)$$

In the case of a stress-strain diagram that does not have an initial straight-line portion, the slopes of other lines, as illustrated in Fig. 17-5, are used for determining the modulus of elasticity. One method is to determine the slope of the tangent to the initial part of the diagram, as indicated by the line *OA* in Fig. 17-5. This is called the *initial tangent modulus*. Another method is to calculate the slope of a line such as *OB*, drawn from the origin to some specified point on the stress-strain diagram. The most common methods for locating point *B* are in terms of a specified offset or specified strain, as used in determining the yield strength. The modulus determined using the slope of a line such as *OB* is called the *secant modulus*. Since the different methods used for calculating the modulus of elasticity will give different values for the modulus, the method used must be stated.

If the initial portion of the stress-strain diagram is a straight line, so that stress is proportional to strain, the material is said to obey *Hooke's law*. The *proportional limit* is the largest stress for which stress is proportional to strain.

Referring again to Fig. 17-2, it can be seen that some materials fracture at relatively low values of strain, and others have relatively high values of strain at fracture. The strain at fracture is used as a relative measure of the ductility of materials. Usually the percent deformation at fracture is used, where

$$\% \text{ deformation} = \frac{\delta}{L} \times 100 \qquad (10\text{-}8)$$

Deformations in the direction of load are usually accompanied by deformations transverse to the load. As a consequence, there is usually a large change in the area of the cross-section at the fracture for ductile materials in tension. The percent change in

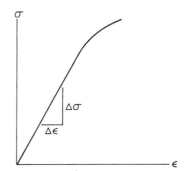

FIGURE 17-4

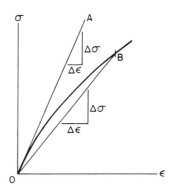

FIGURE 17-5

area is also used as a relative measure of ductility, where

$$\% \text{ change in area} = \left(\frac{A_1 - A_2}{A_1}\right) 100 \qquad (17\text{-}1)$$

where A_1 is the initial area of the cross section, and
A_2 is the final area of the cross section.

The area of the cross-section at fracture is sometimes used to calculate a quantity called *fracture stress*, which is the load at failure divided by the cross-sectional area at fracture. It is also sometimes called the true stress at fracture, and in tension it will be higher than the nominal stress based on the original cross-sectional area used in plotting the stress-strain diagram.

The reduction in area at fracture in a tension test of a ductile material tends to be localized, and this process in change in area and shape is called *necking*. Figure 17-6 shows two tensile samples before and after fracture. The one with little deformation has a brittle failure, and the one with large deformation is a ductile material, which exhibits necking. Figure 17-7 shows before and after photographs of two samples that have been tested

FIGURE 17-6 Before and after photos of standard tensile test samples are shown. The sample to the left is a ductile steel. The fractured sample shows a large amount of deformation and a cup-and-cone shape at the fracture. The brittle cast iron to the right shows very little deformation and a fracture surface which is perpendicular to the applied load. *Photo courtesy of Cambrian College.*

FIGURE 17-7 Before and after photos of short compression samples are shown. The sample on the left is a ductile steel, which shows a large amount of deformation after loading, but no fracture. The brittle cast iron on the right has much less deformation and has fractured on a plane at about 45° to the loading axis. *Photo courtesy of Cambrain College.*

in compression. The one with little deformation has fractured. It is a brittle material. The ductile material has not fractured, but shows a very large deformation.

There is no specified deformation or change in area that forms a boundary between brittle and ductile materials. *Ductility* is the ability of a material to deform plastically before fracturing. A material that is *plastic* is one that deforms continuously and permanently after yielding. Figure 17-8 will help to illustrate why there is no boundary expressed as a percent deformation between ductile and brittle materials. Both hypothetical stress-strain diagrams show the same amount of strain at fracture, yet the material for diagram *B* is a straight line up to fracture, and may not yield until fracture, and thus does not behave plastically. In other words, it is a brittle material. The material for diagram *A* yields at a relatively low strain, and thus has a large amount of plastic deformation before fracture. It would be considered to be a ductile material.

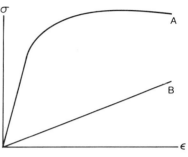

FIGURE 17-8

Two additional material characteristics may be determined from the stress-strain diagram. They are the *modulus of resilience* and the *modulus of toughness*. The modulus of resilience, sometimes simply called resilience, is the amount of energy per unit volume released when the load is released from a sample loaded to its elastic limit. The *elastic limit* is the maximum stress a material may have and still return to its original dimensions after unloading. The elastic limit is somewhat less than the yield strength, and corresponds approximately to the proportional limit. The modulus of resilience is the area under the stress-strain diagram up to the elastic limit.

$$\mu_R = \frac{1}{2} \sigma_e \epsilon_e \qquad (17\text{-}2)$$

where μ_R is the modulus of resilience,
$\quad \sigma_e$ is the normal stress at the elastic limit, and
$\quad \epsilon_e$ is the normal strain at the elastic limit.

The units of the area under the stress-strain diagram are Pa $\times$ m/m. But 1 Pa = 1 N/m^2, so the units become N/m^2 $\times$ m/m which can be rewritten as N·m/m^3. One newton metre is a joule, which is the basic unit for work. Thus, the modulus of resilience is usually expressed in joules per cubic metre or J/m^3.

The toughness of a material is a measure of its ability to absorb energy before fracture. The total area under the stress-strain diagram gives the modulus of toughness, μ_T, for a material.

$$\mu_T = \text{area under } \sigma\text{–}\epsilon \text{ diagram} \qquad (17\text{-}3)$$

As was the case for the modulus of resilience, the modulus of toughness will also have units of J/m^3. The actual calculation of the area may be performed using any of the methods for calculating irregular areas, which include approximations, counting squares, or using the planimeter.

EXAMPLE 17-1

Using the initial portion of the stress-strain diagram shown in Fig. 17-9, determine the modulus of elasticity, the yield point and the modulus of resilience for the material.

SOLUTION

There is a straight-line portion of the stress-strain diagram. The slope of the line will give the modulus of elasticity, as indicated by Eq. (10-10). Two convenient points on the line to use for calculating the modulus of elasticity are where the stress is 200 MPa and where it is zero. In experimental work the line may not always pass through the origin; if it does not, the origin may not be used for calculating the slope.

$$E = \frac{\Delta\sigma}{\Delta\epsilon}$$

$$= \frac{200 \times 10^6 - 0}{0.001 - 0}$$

$$= 200.00 \times 10^9 \text{ Pa}$$

$$= 200.00 \text{ GPa}$$

In the stress-strain diagram there is a well-defined point or maximum stress that occurs prior to yielding. Its value may be obtained by inspection of the stress-strain diagram.

$$\sigma_y = 250 \times 10^6 \text{ Pa}$$

The modulus of resilience is calculated by determining the area under the stress-strain diagram up to the proportional limit, since the proportional limit approximates the elastic limit. Both the stress and strain at the proportional limit are estimated for purposes of the calculation using Eq. (17-2).

$$\sigma_e = 225 \times 10^6 \text{ Pa}$$

$$\epsilon_e = 0.0012 \text{ m/m}$$

$$\mu_R = \frac{1}{2} \sigma_e \epsilon_e$$

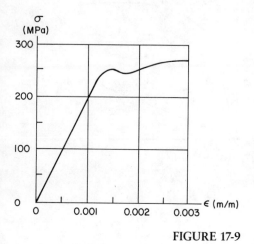

FIGURE 17-9

$$= \frac{1}{2} \times 225 \times 10^6 \times 0.0012$$

$$= 135\ 000\ \text{J/m}^3$$

$$\boxed{\begin{aligned} E &= 200\ \text{GPa} \\ \sigma_y &= 250\ \text{MPa} \\ \mu_R &= 135\ \text{kJ/m}^3 \end{aligned}}$$

EXAMPLE 17-2

Use the initial portion of the stress-strain diagram shown in Fig. 17-10 to determine values for yield strength using (a) a 0.5% strain and (b) a 0.2% offset. Also calculate the modulus of elasticity using (c) the initial slope and (d) the slope of the secant line to the 0.2% offset point on the diagram.

SOLUTION

The value for the yield strength at a 0.5% strain may be determined by reading the value for stress from the stress-strain diagram where the strain is $0.5/100 = 0.005$ m/m, as marked in Fig. 17-11.

(a) $$\sigma_y = 262\ \text{MPa}$$

To determine the yield strength using the 0.2% offset, a tangent must be drawn to the initial part of the stress-strain diagram, as shown in Fig. 17-11. A second line is drawn parallel to this first line, starting on the strain axis where the strain is 0.2% or 0.002 m/m. The value of the stress where this 0.2% offset line crosses the stress-strain diagram is the 0.2% offset yield strength.

(b) $$\sigma_y = 225\ \text{MPa}$$

Calculation of the modulus of elasticity using the initial slope requires that the slope of the tangent that was drawn at the start of the diagram be determined. Values for stress and strain for two points on the line are used for determining the slope. One convenient point on the line is the origin, and a second convenient point is where the line crosses $\sigma = 200$ MPa.

(c) $$E = \frac{\Delta \sigma}{\Delta \epsilon}$$

$$= \frac{200 \times 10^6 - 0}{0.0015 - 0}$$

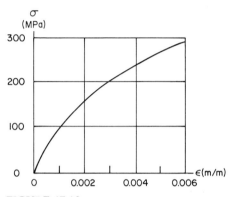

FIGURE 17-10

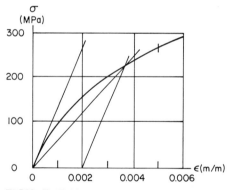

FIGURE 17-11

$$= 133.33 \times 10^9 \text{ Pa}$$

$$= 133.33 \text{ GPa}$$

The secant modulus is obtained by calculating the slope of the line from the origin to the 0.2% yield strength on the stress-strain diagram. The value for the stress at the 0.2% offset yield was determined in Part (b), *and the corresponding value for the strain may be obtained by inspection of the stress-strain diagram.*

(d)
$$E = \frac{\Delta\sigma}{\Delta\epsilon}$$

$$= \frac{225 \times 10^6 - 0}{0.0036 - 0}$$

$$= 62.500 \times 10^9 \text{ Pa}$$

$$= 62.500 \text{ GPa}$$

Note the significant difference in the two values for σ_y and for the two values of E. The need to specify the method used to determine the values should now be apparent.

(a) $\sigma_y = 262$ MPa
(b) $\sigma_y = 225$ MPa
(c) E = 133 GPa
(d) E = 62.5 GPa

EXAMPLE 17-3

Use the data shown below to plot a stress-strain diagram for the material that was tested in tension. From the stress-strain diagram determine (a) modulus of elasticity, (b) proportional limit, (c) 0.2% offset yield strength, (d) ultimate strength, (e) true stress at fracture, (f) percent elongation, (g) percent reduction in area, (h) modulus of resilience and (i) modulus of toughness.

Sample diameter: 12.76 mm

Gage length: 50.00 mm

P (kN)	δ (mm)
0.0	0.000
4.0	0.023
8.0	0.045
12.0	0.068

16.0	0.091
20.0	0.113
24.0	0.150
26.0	0.249
28.0	0.378
29.1	0.500
31.9	1.000
34.9	2.000
36.2	3.000
36.3	4.000
35.8	5.000
34.8	6.000
33.9 Fracture	6.900

Maximum load = 36.4 kN

Final diameter = 9.83 mm

SOLUTION

Use the given data to calculate the values for σ and the corresponding values for ε using Eqs. (10-1) and (10-7). It is best to set this up in a table format alongside the original data.

$$A = \frac{\pi d^2}{4}$$

$$= \frac{\pi \times 12.76^2}{4}$$

$$= 127.88 \text{ mm}^2$$

P (kN)	δ (mm)	$\sigma = \frac{P}{A}$ (MPa)	$\epsilon = \frac{\delta}{L}$ (m/m)
0.0	0.000	0.00	0.000 00
4.0	0.023	31.28	0.000 46
8.0	0.045	62.56	0.000 90
12.0	0.068	93.84	0.001 36
16.0	0.091	125.12	0.001 82
20.0	0.113	156.40	0.002 26

P (kN)	δ (mm)	$\sigma = \dfrac{P}{A}$ (MPa)	$\epsilon = \dfrac{\delta}{L}$ (m/m)
24.0	0.150	187.68	0.003 00
26.0	0.249	203.32	0.004 98
28.0	0.378	218.96	0.007 56
29.1	0.500	227.56	0.010 00
31.9	1.000	249.45	0.020 00
34.9	2.000	272.91	0.040 00
36.2	3.000	283.08	0.060 00
36.3	4.000	283.86	0.080 00
35.8	5.000	279.95	0.100 00
34.8	6.000	272.13	0.120 00
33.9	6.900	265.09	0.138 00

The data from the table are used to plot a stress-strain diagram, as shown in Fig. 17-12. Normal practice is to plot strain along the horizontal axis and stress on the vertical axis. Each experimental value is shown as a small circle, and the diagram is drawn by joining the points by the best fitting curve. In this case, the initial portion of the diagram is a straight line and the balance of the diagram is a smooth curve.

When the diagram is initially drawn, as shown in the upper diagram of Fig. 17-12, the straight-line portion of the diagram is very close to the vertical axis, so that determining strain values in this region will not be very accurate. For this reason, the initial portion of the stress-strain diagram has been redrawn, using an expanded strain scale. This is the lower diagram, and the lower strain scale is the one used for plotting this diagram. The expanded diagram will make it easier to perform calculations in this portion of the stress-strain diagram.

The points give a straight line for the initial portion of the stress-strain diagram. The slope of the straight line is used to determine E. Use the values of stress and strain at the highest point on the straight line and at the origin to calculate the slope of the diagram, using Eq. (10-10).

(a)
$$E = \frac{\Delta\sigma}{\Delta\epsilon}$$

$$= \frac{156.40 \times 10^6 - 0}{0.002\ 26 - 0}$$

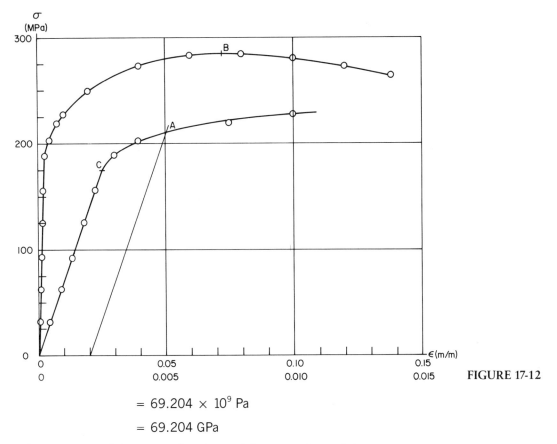

FIGURE 17-12

$$= 69.204 \times 10^9 \text{ Pa}$$

$$= 69.204 \text{ GPa}$$

The proportional limit may be obtained by inspection of the initial portion of the stress-strain diagram drawn using the expanded strain scale. The value is marked as point C in Fig. 17-12.

(b) $\sigma_{pl} = 175$ MPa

The 0.2% offset yield strength is found by drawing a line parallel to the straight-line portion of the diagram at the 0.2% offset or 0.002 m/m strain point on the strain axis, as shown in Fig. 17-12. Again, the expanded diagram is used for clarity and accuracy. The 0.2% offset line intersects the stress-strain diagram at A, and the value of the stress at A is the 0.2% yield strength.

(c) $\sigma_y = 210$ MPa

The ultimate strength is determined by inspecting the stress-strain diagram and locating the highest value of stress on the diagram. This is marked as point B in Fig. 17-12. Most testing machines are able to indicate the maximum load attained in a test, so this value could also be used to determine the ultimate strength.

(d) From diagram:

$$\sigma_u = 285 \text{ MPa}$$

From test:

$$\sigma_u = \frac{P_{max}}{A}$$

$$= \frac{36.4 \times 10^3}{127.88 \times 10^{-6}}$$

$$= 284.64 \times 10^6 \text{ Pa}$$

$$= 284.64 \text{ MPa}$$

Considering the limitations on reading values from the stress-strain diagram, and the precision of the value for the load, the two values for the ultimate strength are remarkably close.

The true stress at fracture is calculated using the load at fracture and the area of the cross-section at fracture, as determined from the final diameter.

(e) $$\sigma_t = \frac{P}{A_{final}}$$

$$= \frac{33.9 \times 10^3}{\dfrac{\pi \times 9.83^2}{4} \times 10^{-6}}$$

$$= 446.69 \times 10^6 \text{ Pa}$$

$$= 446.69 \text{ MPa}$$

The percent elongation is the strain at fracture converted to a percent or the percent deformation at fracture, as calculated from Eq. (10-8).

(f) $$\% \text{ deformation} = \frac{\delta}{L} \times 100$$

$$= \frac{6.900}{50.00} \times 100$$

$$= 13.80 \%$$

The percent reduction in area is determined using the initial and final cross-sectional areas in Eq. (17-1).

(g)

$$\% \text{ change in area} = \left(\frac{A_1 - A_2}{A_1}\right) \times 100$$

$$= \left(\dfrac{\dfrac{\pi}{4} \times 12.76^2 - \dfrac{\pi}{4} \times 9.83^2}{\dfrac{\pi}{4} \times 12.76^2} \right) \times 100$$

$$= \left(\dfrac{12.76^2 - 9.83^2}{12.76^2} \right) \times 100$$

$$= \left(\dfrac{162.82 - 96.63}{162.82} \right) \times 100$$

$$= \dfrac{66.19}{162.82} \times 100$$

$$= 40.653\%$$

The modulus of resilience is calculated by taking the area under the stress-strain diagram up to the elastic limit, as indicated by Eq. (17-2). Since the elastic limit is not specifically known, the proportional limit is taken as a close approximation. The value for the strain at the proportional limit can be determined from the stress-strain diagram, or from the fact that, when stress is proportional to strain, $\epsilon = \sigma/E$.

(h)
$$\mu_R = \dfrac{1}{2} \sigma_e \epsilon_e$$

$$= \dfrac{1}{2} \sigma_e \left(\dfrac{\sigma_e}{E} \right)$$

$$= \dfrac{\sigma_e^2}{2E}$$

$$= \dfrac{1}{2} \times \dfrac{(175 \times 10^6)^2}{69.204 \times 10^9}$$

$$= 221\ 270\ \text{J/m}^3$$

$$= 221.27\ \text{kJ/m}^3$$

To calculate the modulus of toughness requires determining the total area under the stress-strain diagram. In the diagram shown, the area could be approximated by three trapezoids: one under the stress-strain diagram for strains from zero to 0.05 m/m; one for strains between 0.05 and 0.10 m/m; and the third for strains from 0.10 to 0.138 m/m. The area between the σ axis and the straight-line portion of the diagram will be approximately equal to the area above a line from $\sigma = 200$ MPa and $\epsilon = 0$ to $\sigma = 280$ MPa and $\epsilon = 0.05$ m/m.

(i) μ_T = area

$$= \frac{1}{2}\left(200 \times 10^6 + 280 \times 10^6\right)0.05$$

$$+ \frac{1}{2}\left(280 \times 10^6 + 282 \times 10^6\right)0.05$$

$$+ \frac{1}{2}\left(282 \times 10^6 + 265 \times 10^6\right)0.038$$

$$= 12.000 \times 10^6 + 14.050 \times 10^6 + 10.393 \times 10^6$$

$$= 36.443 \times 10^6 \text{ J/m}^3$$

$$= 36.443 \text{ MJ/m}^3$$

(a) E = 69.2 GPa
(b) σ_{pl} = 175 MPa
(c) σ_y = 210 MPa
(d) σ_u = 285 MPa
(e) σ_t = 447 MPa
(f) % deformation = 13.8%
(g) % change in area = 40.7%
(h) μ_R = 221 kJ/m^3
(i) μ_T = 36.4 MJ/m^3

PROBLEMS

17-1 A square bar, 10 by 10 mm, is tested in tension. At a load of 5 kN the deformation in a 50 mm length is 0.024 mm, and at a load of 25 kN the deformation is 0.117 mm. If the stress-strain diagram is a straight line between these two points, calculate the modulus of elasticity for this material.

17-2 A concrete cylinder with a diameter of 150 mm is tested in compression. At a load of 88.0 kN the deformation in 200 mm is 0.030 mm, and at a load of 400.0 kN the deformation is 0.135 mm. Calculate the modulus of elasticity if the stress-strain diagram is assumed to be straight between these two points.

17-3 Calculate the modulus of elasticity and determine the yield point for the material that has the partial stress-strain diagram shown in Fig. P17-3.

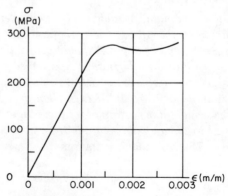

FIGURE P17-3

17-4 Using the partial stress-strain diagram shown in Fig. P17-4, determine the modulus of elasticity and the yield point for the material.

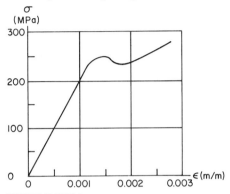

FIGURE P17-4

17-5 For the stress-strain diagram shown in Fig. P17-5, determine (a) the proportional limit, (b) 0.2% offset yield strength, (c) modulus of elasticity, (d) ultimate strength, (e) percent elongation, (f) modulus of resilience and (g) modulus of toughness.

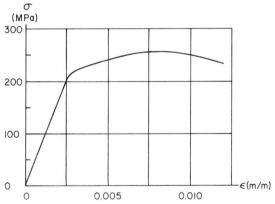

FIGURE P17-5

17-6 Using the stress-strain diagram shown in Fig. P17-6, find (a) the modulus of elasticity, (b) 0.05% offset yield strength, (c) ultimate strength, (d) modulus of resilience and (e) modulus of toughness.

17-7 A round copper bar is tested in tension. Using the test results given, plot the stress-strain diagram and determine the following: (a) 0.2% offset yield strength, (b) ultimate strength, (c) modulus of elasticity, (d) percent elongation, (e)

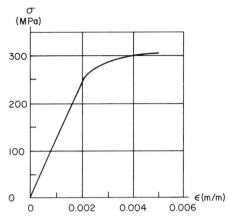

FIGURE P17-6

percent reduction in area, (f) true stress at fracture, (g) modulus of resilience and (h) modulus of toughness.

Sample diameter: 13.00 mm

Gage length: 50.0 mm

P (kN)	δ (µm)
0.0	0
5.0	17
10.0	34
15.0	51
20.0	68
25.0	85
30.0	102
35.0	119
40.0	400
41.0	650
42.0	1040
43.0	1640
43.5	3210
43.5	5600
41.8	8000 (fracture)

Final diameter: 11.62 mm

Maximum load: 43.9 kN

17-8 A magnesium bar with a rectangular cross-section is tested in tension; the test information is reproduced here. Determine (a) modulus of elasticity, (b) proportional limit, (c) 0.2% offset yield strength, (d) ultimate strength, (e) percent elongation, (f) modulus of resilience and (g) modulus of toughness.

Cross section: 25.04 by 10.11 mm

Gage length: 49.8 mm

P (kN)	δ (mm)
0.0	0.000
6.0	0.026
12.0	0.053
18.0	0.079
24.0	0.105
30.0	0.131
36.0	0.157
42.0	0.184
48.0	0.241
54.0	0.373
55.2	0.500
61.3	1.000
67.1	2.000
69.1	3.000
68.4	4.000
65.6	5.000
62.0	6.000
57.7	7.000
56.5	7.120 (fracture)

17-9 A round core of granite was tested in compression. Using the tabulated test results, determine (a) 0.05% offset yield strength, (b) secant modulus of elasticity using the 0.05% offset yield strength, (c) ultimate strength, (d) percent deformation and (e) modulus of toughness.

Sample diameter: 50.13 mm

Gage length: 98.7 mm

P (kN)	δ (mm)
0	0.000
40	0.052
80	0.107
120	0.165
160	0.232
200	0.304
240	0.393
280	0.526
294	0.661 (fracture)

17-10 A cast-iron sample with a diameter of 12.70 mm in the test section and a gage length of 50.0 mm was tested in tension, and the results were tabulated. Plot the stress-strain diagram and find: (a) ultimate tensile strength, (b) 0.05% offset yield strength, (c) percent elongation, (d) secant modulus of elasticity based on the 0.05% offset yield strength, (e) modulus of toughness, (f) percent reduction in area and (g) true stress at fracture. The diameter of the section at fracture was 12.39 mm.

P (kN)	δ (μm)
0.0	0
4.0	12
8.0	29
12.0	50
16.0	74
20.0	103
24.0	140
28.0	208
28.4	224 (fracture)

FIGURE 17-13 This is one type of system used for testing samples in torsion. The test specimen is the round piece between the face plates. In this system the machine is computer controlled, and the test data is collected by the computer. *Photo courtesy of MTS Systems Corporation.*

17-3 TORSION TEST

Materials that are likely to be used where the load will be a torque can be tested in torsion, as shown in Fig. 17-13. In a torsion test a torque is applied to a circular sample of known diameter. Values of torque applied and the corresponding angle of twist in a measured length of sample are recorded as the torque is increased until a predetermined maximum angle of twist is reached or until fracture occurs. The information is used to determine shear stress and shear strain where

$$\tau = \frac{Tc}{J} \qquad (12\text{-}5)$$

and

$$\gamma = \frac{c\theta}{L} \qquad (12\text{-}1)$$

This information is used to plot a shear stress-strain diagram in which the shear stress is plotted on the vertical axis and the corresponding shear strain is plotted along the horizontal axis. Two typical shear-stress diagrams are shown in Fig. 17-14.

In developing the expression for shear stress, Eq. (12-5), it was assumed that the stress in the material did not exceed the shear proportional limit. Thus, once shear stress is no longer proportional to shear strain, Eq. (12-5) is no longer valid as an accurate method of calculating shear stress. However, the equation continues to be used for the calculations for the shear stress-strain diagram beyond the proportional limit, since it will provide a means of comparing properties in shear, even though the values obtained are not actual values of the shear stress in the

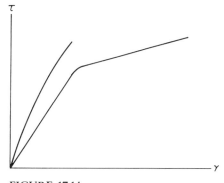

FIGURE 17-14

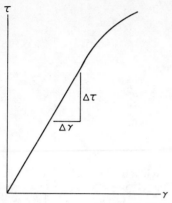

FIGURE 17-15

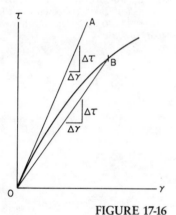

FIGURE 17-16

member. It should also be noted that Eqs. (12-1) and (12-5) give values of shear strain and shear stress on the cross-section at the outer surface of the shaft, and do not give the interior strains and stresses. In spite of this, the shear stress-strain diagram is useful for comparisons between materials.

If the initial portion of the shear stress-strain diagram is a straight line, as shown in Fig. 17-15, the slope of the line is a measure of the stiffness of the material in shear and is called the *shear modulus of elasticity* or *modulus of rigidity*, where

$$G = \frac{\Delta\tau}{\Delta\gamma} \qquad (10\text{-}13)$$

In cases where the material has a shear stress-strain diagram with a curved initial portion, as shown in Fig. 17-16, the shear modulus of elasticity may be expressed in terms of the tangent modulus, which is the slope of the initial tangent to the diagram *OA*, or in terms of the slope of a line from the origin to some point *B*, which is specified in terms of an offset or strain using the same procedures explained in Article 17-2. The slope of line *OB* would give the secant shear modulus of elasticity.

The torsion test is not as frequently used as the tension or compression tests. As well, the shear stress-strain diagram is not an accurate reflection of the stress and strain beyond the proportional limit. The diagram is not used extensively except for the determination of the shear modulus of elasticity. Methods for determining the shear yield strength usually are not specified in standards, probably because Eq. (12-5) gives only an approximation of the magnitude of the shear stress beyond the proportional limit. One could approximate the shear yield strength by use of a specified strain or strain offset to determine the point on the shear stress-strain diagram where yielding begins.

Two additional pieces of information obtained from the shear stress-strain diagram are sometimes used for comparative purposes. The maximum value for shear stress on the shear stress-strain diagram is not a true value of the maximum shear stress in the sample because the shear-stress equation $\tau = Tc/J$ is not valid beyond the proportional limit. In spite of this, the equation is used to calculate a maximum shear-stress value, but it is given the name of *modulus of rupture in shear*, which is

$$\tau_{ru} = \frac{T_{max}c}{J} \qquad (17\text{-}4)$$

where τ_{ru} is the modulus of rupture in shear,

T_{max} is the torque applied at fracture,

c is the radius of the sample, and

J is the polar moment of inertia of the sample section.

The resilience of materials in shear can be compared by use of the *shear modulus of resilience*, which is equal to the area under the shear stress-strain diagram up to the elastic limit in shear. Since the elastic limit is not easily identified on the shear stress-strain diagram, the proportional limit, which is the maximum shear stress for which shear stress is proportional to shear strain, is used in its place. The shear modulus of resilience is

$$\mu_R = \frac{1}{2}\,\tau_e\gamma_e \qquad (17\text{-}5)$$

where μ_R is the shear modulus of resilience,
τ_e is the shear stress at the elastic limit, and
γ_e is the shear strain at the elastic limit.

The units for the shear modulus of resilience will be J/m^3, just as they were for the modulus of resilience calculated for normal stress. However in the case of a torsion test, the shear modulus of resilience does not measure the total-energy-per-unit volume in the sample, because only the outside of the section is stressed to the elastic limit. In spite of this, it is still a useful measure of the relative ability of materials to absorb elastic energy in shear.

Figure 17-17 shows three samples of materials before and after failure caused by the application of a torque. In the one sample, which is a ductile material, the failure has occurred on a transverse cross-section. From the discussion of Mohr's circle in Article 16-2, it can be seen that this is the surface on which the shear stress has the maximum value. The second sample, which is a brittle material, has a more complex fracture, which forms a helical surface. Analysis of the stress on the surface using Mohr's circle would show that this is the surface on which the maximum tensile stress acts, and that there is no shear stress acting on this surface. The third sample is a hollow tube, and the failure in it is caused by buckling due to compressive stresses. Again, Mohr's circle may be used to verify the presence of the compressive stress.

FIGURE 17-17 Before and after photos of three torsion test samples are shown. The sample to the left is a ductile aluminum, the middle sample is a brittle cast iron, and the right sample is a ductile aluminum tube. Each original sample shows a light line on its surface parallel to its long axis, and the twisted line, indicating the amount of deformation, is visible on each failed sample. The aluminum failed on a plane with maximum shear stress, the cast iron failed on a surface with maximum tensile stress, and the aluminum tube failed where the compression stress was maximum. *Photo courtesy of Cambrian College.*

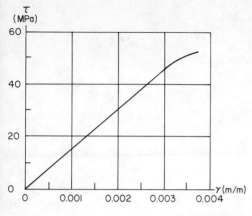

FIGURE 17-18

EXAMPLE 17-4

Use the shear stress-strain diagram shown in Fig. 17-18 to determine the shear modulus of elasticity and the shear modulus of resilience for the material.

SOLUTION

Since the initial portion of the shear stress-strain diagram is a straight line, the shear modulus of elasticity may be determined by calculating the slope of the initial portion of the diagram, as indicated by Eq. (10-13). The proportional limit is well-defined, so the slope of the line from the origin to the proportional limit will be used.

$$G = \frac{\Delta\tau}{\Delta\gamma}$$

$$= \frac{45 \times 10^6 - 0}{0.003 - 0}$$

$$= 15.000 \times 10^9 \text{ Pa}$$

$$= 15.000 \text{ GPa}$$

The shear modulus of resilience is calculated using Eq. (17-5), and using the proportional limit as an approximation of the shear elastic limit.

$$\mu_R = \frac{1}{2} \tau_e \gamma_e$$

$$= \frac{1}{2} \times 45 \times 10^6 \times 0.003$$

$$= 67\ 500 \text{ J/m}^3$$

$$= 67.500 \text{ kJ/m}^3$$

$$\boxed{\begin{array}{l} G = 15.0 \text{ GPa} \\ \mu_R = 67.5 \text{ kJ/m}^3 \end{array}}$$

EXAMPLE 17-5

A circular steel sample was tested in torsion, and the results were tabulated. Use the data to plot a shear stress-strain diagram, and use the diagram to determine (a) shear modulus of elasticity using a 0.1% offset and (b) modulus of rupture for the material.

Sample diameter: 29.16 mm

Test length: 207.5 mm

T (N·m)	θ (°)
0	0.0
100	0.2
200	0.4
300	0.5
400	0.8
500	1.0
600	1.2
700	1.6
800	1.9
900	2.4
1000	3.1
1100	4.2
1160 (fracture)	5.7

SOLUTION

Start by calculating the values of τ and corresponding values of γ, so that a shear stress-strain diagram may be drawn. The shear stress is calculated using Eq. (12-5) *and the shear strain is calculated using* Eq. (12-1). *To speed up the calculation process, these equations may be rewritten so that c/J and c/L become coefficients of T and θ. Since θ is measured in degrees, the conversion to radians is also included in the coefficient.*

$$\tau = \frac{Tc}{J}$$

$$= \frac{\dfrac{29.16}{2} \times 10^{-3}}{\dfrac{\pi \times 29.16^4}{32} \times 10^{-12}} \times T$$

$$= 205\ 403\ T\ (\text{Pa})$$

$$\gamma = \frac{c\theta}{L}$$

$$= \frac{\dfrac{29.16}{2}}{207.5} \times \frac{\pi}{180} \times \theta$$

$$= 0.001\ 226\ \theta\ (\text{m/m})$$

The values of τ and γ are listed in a table alongside the corresponding values of T and θ.

T (N·m)	θ (°)	τ (MPa)	γ (m/m)
0	0.0	0.00	0.000 00
100	0.2	20.54	0.000 25
200	0.4	41.08	0.000 49
300	0.5	61.62	0.000 61
400	0.8	82.16	0.000 98
500	1.0	102.70	0.001 23
600	1.2	123.24	0.001 47
700	1.6	143.78	0.001 96
800	1.9	164.32	0.002 33
900	2.4	184.86	0.002 94
1000	3.1	205.40	0.003 80
1100	4.2	225.94	0.005 15
1160 (fracture)	5.7	238.27	0.006 99

The values for τ and γ are used to plot a shear stress-strain diagram, where strain values are plotted on the horizontal axis and stress values are plotted on the vertical axis. The plotted values are shown as small circles in Fig. 17-19. *The best-fitting curve has been drawn.*

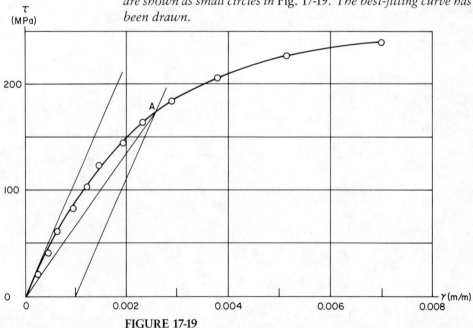

FIGURE 17-19

A tangent to the initial part of the diagram is drawn, and a parallel line is drawn through the 0.1% or 0.001 m/m strain on the strain axis to intersect the shear stress-strain diagram. The point of intersection, A, on the diagram is the value used for the shear stress and shear strain when calculating the shear modulus of elasticity using Eq. (10-13). This will be a secant shear modulus of elasticity.

(a)
$$G = \frac{\Delta\tau}{\Delta\gamma}$$

$$= \frac{172 \times 10^6 - 0}{0.002\ 66 - 0}$$

$$= 64.662 \times 10^9 \text{ Pa}$$

$$= 64.662 \text{ GPa}$$

The modulus of rupture is the shear stress at fracture, which is calculated using either Eq. (12-5) or Eq. (17-4), since both give the same value. Thus, it may also be obtained directly from the table of stresses.

(b)
$$\tau_{ru} = \frac{T_{max}c}{J}$$

$$= \frac{1160 \times \dfrac{29.16}{2} \times 10^{-3}}{\dfrac{\pi \times 29.16^4}{32} \times 10^{-12}}$$

$$= 238.27 \times 10^6 \text{ Pa}$$

$$= 238.27 \text{ MPa}$$

$$\boxed{\begin{array}{l} G = 64.7 \text{ GPa} \\ \tau_{ru} = 238 \text{ MPa} \end{array}}$$

PROBLEMS

17-11 Determine the shear modulus of elasticity for the material with the partial shear stress-strain diagram shown in Fig. P17-11.

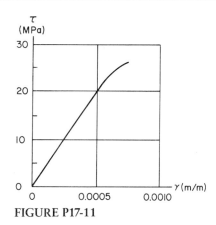

FIGURE P17-11

17-12 Calculate the shear modulus of elasticity for the material whose initial shear stress-strain diagram is shown in Fig. P17-12.

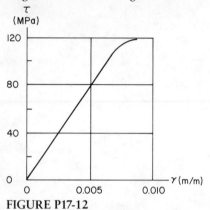

FIGURE P17-12

17-13 A circular sample with a diameter of 18.46 mm is tested in torsion. If the angle of twist in a length of 100.3 mm is 0.5° when a torque of 18 N·m is applied, and the angle of twist is 2.5° when the torque is 90 N·m, calculate the shear modulus of elasticity for the material. The shear stress-strain diagram is a straight line between the two points obtained from the test data.

17-14 Calculate the shear modulus of elasticity for a sample with a diameter of 32.27 mm if, when the applied torque is 160 N·m, the angle of twist in a length of 201 mm is 0.2°; and when the applied torque is 1440 N·m, the angle of twist is 1.8°. The shear stress-strain diagram is a straight line between the two given points.

17-15 A plastic sample is tested in torsion, and the results shown were obtained. Plot a shear stress-strain diagram for the material and use the diagram to determine (a) shear modulus of elasticity based on a secant modulus using a 0.2% offset and (b) modulus of rupture.

Sample diameter: 20.27 mm

Gage length: 150 mm

T (N·m)	θ (°)
0.0	0.0
2.0	1.3
4.0	2.7
6.0	4.4
8.0	6.0
10.0	7.9
12.0	9.9
14.0	12.4
15.7 (fracture)	15.6

17-16 Use the test results to plot a shear stress-strain diagram for the cast-iron sample tested in torsion. From the diagram determine (a) secant shear modulus of elasticity based on a 0.1% deformation and (b) modulus of rupture.

Sample diameter: 25.47 mm

Test length: 302.6 mm

T (N·m)	θ (°)
0	0.0
25	0.2
50	0.4
75	0.7
100	1.0
125	1.3
150	1.6
175	1.9
200	2.3
225	2.7
250	3.2
272 (fracture)	3.7

17-17 Results were obtained from a torsion test on a steel sample. Plot the shear stress-strain diagram to obtain (a) shear modulus of elasticity, (b) proportional limit, (c) shear modulus of resilience and (d) modulus of rupture.

Sample diameter: 19.08 mm		Sample diameter: 25.22 mm	
Test length: 150.3 mm		Test length: 200.8 mm	
T (N·m)	θ (°)	T (N·m)	θ (°)
0	0.0	0	0.0
40	0.3	60	0.6
80	0.7	120	1.3
120	1.0	180	1.9
160	1.3	240	2.6
200	1.7	300	3.2
240	5.8	360	3.9
256	10.0	420	4.5
287	20.0	480	5.1
309	30.0	508	20.0
328	40.0	524	40.0
344	50.0	539	60.0
357	60.0	552	80.0
369	70.0	563	100.0
379	80.0	584	150.0
381 (fracture)	83.9	597	200.0
		606	250.0
		614	300.0
		614 (fracture)	337.0

17-18 An aluminum sample was tested in torsion and results were obtained. Plot the shear stress-strain diagram for the aluminum, and use the diagram to find (a) shear modulus of elasticity, (b) proportional limit, (c) shear modulus of resilience and (d) modulus of rupture.

17-4 FLEXURAL TESTS

Some materials, such as timber, cast-iron and stone, behave differently in tension from the way they behave in compression. Thus, neither the tension test not the compression test is an accurate predictor of behavior in flexure, which involves both tension and compression stresses on transverse cross-sections as well as shear on both transverse and longitudinal planes. Such

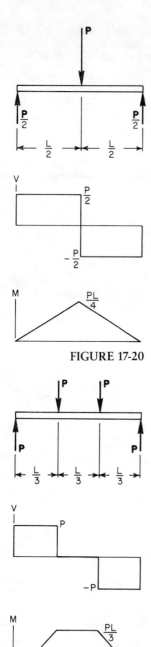

FIGURE 17-20

FIGURE 17-21

materials are sometimes teste   in flexure to better predict their behavior under flexural loads.

The test beam is usually loaded with either a concentrated load at midspan, as shown at the top of Fig. 17-20, or two equal, concentrated loads at the beam's third points, as shown at the top of Fig. 17-21. The shear and moment diagrams have been shown along with the free-body of the loading, since they illustrate the reason for using the third-point loading in some tests. When the deformation in a beam was analyzed to determine the flexural stress and the deflection, the deformations due to the shear forces were neglected. Except for short, deep beams, this omission introduces only a small error. The advantage of using the third-point loading shown in Fig. 17-21 is that in the middle third of the beam there is no transverse shear, and thus there is no deformation caused by the shear. In this region of the beam, the moment also has a constant value rather than a peak value at one point, as occurs in most other loadings.

The information most frequently obtained from a flexural test of a beam is the *modulus of rupture in flexure,* which is

$$\sigma_{ru} = \frac{M_{max}c}{I} \tag{17-6}$$

where σ_{ru} is the modulus of rupture in flexure,

M_{max} is the maximum bending moment acting on a section of the beam,

c is the distance from the neutral axis to the outside fiber, and

I is the moment of inertia of the entire cross section with respect to an axis which is also the neutral axis.

Although the equation for modulus of rupture in flexure looks similar to the equation for maximum flexural stress, Eq. (13-5), it does not actually give the maximum flexural stress in the beam. The flexural-stress equation is valid only when the stress is below the proportional limit. However, the modulus of rupture does provide a method for comparing the flexural strength of materials, and for determining allowable flexural stress in materials for members to be used in flexure.

The flexural test may also be used as a method for determining or checking the value of the modulus of elasticity of a material, since the deflection of a beam depends in part on the modulus of elasticity of the material. If a load is applied to a beam, and the deflection is measured, the equations from Fig. 14-3 may be used to solve for E, the modulus of elasticity, provided the load and the dimensions of the beam are known. Since the equations given in Fig. 14-3 were developed neglecting the deformations due to the shear stresses, some small error will be introduced into the calculations, particularly for short, deep beams.

Note that this article refers to flexural tests and not bend tests. Generally, tests which are called bend tests are performed on relatively small samples of materials, and are used to determine the ductility of a material by measuring the angle through which a bar can be bent in a die of a specified radius. A similar bend test is also used as one method of checking the quality of welds.

17-5 HARDNESS TESTS

The hardness of a material is a measure of its resistance to scratching and indentation. Hardness is usually a relative measure, so no hardness units are used. Several methods are used for measuring hardness; each tends to be used with a different class of materials. The scratch test used for minerals and ceramics rates hardness by noting what materials can and cannot cause a scratch on the tested surface. The Mohs scratch test assigns hardness numbers to ten materials, ranging from one for talc to ten for diamond. If the standard material scratches the test material, the test material is softer than the standard, and a hardness number is assigned. The Mohs hardness scale is not extensively used for metals, because most metals have Mohs hardness values of around four to five, which does not give much range for comparison.

Another method for testing hardness is the rebound test, where a plunger strikes a surface with a fixed force, and the height of rebound is measured as a measure of hardness. This is one of the methods used for testing the quality of concrete.

For metallic materials, the most widely used method of testing is the penetration test. A hardened steel ball or diamond cone is pushed, by a fixed load, into the material, and the diameter of the impression or the depth of the impression is a measure of the hardness of the material. Because each type of test gives a different hardness number, it is imperative that the type of test be included with the number. Some of the more common test types and methods, as well as application, are listed in Table 17-1.

TABLE 17-1
HARDNESS TESTS

Test	Penetrator	Load	Measurement	Application
Brinell	10 mm ball	3000 kg	diameter	soft steels and other metals
Rockwell B	1/16 in. ball	100 kg	depth	soft steels and other metals
Rockwell C	diamond cone	150 kg	depth	hardened metals
Shore	needle	spring	depth	plastics

Figure 17-22 gives an approximate comparison of hardness numbers for some of the tests.

The penetration hardness test is very useful because there is good correlation between the hardness and the ultimate tensile strength for some materials, such as steels. Since the hardness test can be quickly and inexpensively performed, the hardness of a material is often specified instead of a mechanical property such as ultimate strength.

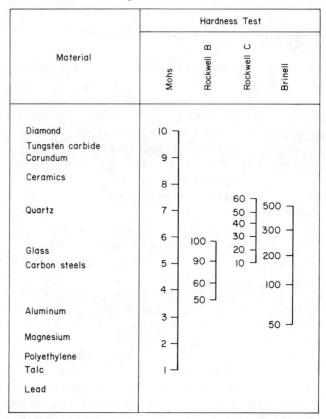

FIGURE 17-22

17-6   FATIGUE

In most machines and in many structures, loads are applied and removed, or change in magnitude; the stresses in the members of the machine or structure change with the changes in load. For instance, a bridge will carry only the load due to its own mass at times, and at other times it must support its own mass plus the mass of stalled bumper-to-bumper traffic. The arbor of the milling machine shown in Fig. 14-1 is a rotating beam, and as a point near the surface rotates, the normal stress due to flexure changes from tension to compression and back to tension for each revolution.

This repeated load or repeated change in stress can cause *metal fatigue*, usually referred to simply as *fatigue*, which is the progressive localized damage in a material due to fluctuating stress. This damage starts as a minute crack, which can suddenly lengthen rapidly and lead to fracture. Fatigue fractures are of great concern because they usually occur in a frame or machine that has been functioning satisfactorily for some period of time, and there is usually little or no warning that the fracture is about to occur. Ductile materials such as steels and aluminum usually exhibit sufficient plastic deformation before fracture under a direct static overload that the high deformation warns of impending failure or fracture. In the case of impending fatigue failure in the same materials, there is no readily apparent excessive deformation, and the initial crack may be virtually invisible to the naked eye.

Most people have had some experience with fatigue failures. If a stiff wire is bent back and forth a number of times it will usually break. This is an example of low-cycle fatigue, since the loading-unloading cycle was repeated only a few times. Fatigue failures may occur after a few cycles, 100 000 cycles or even after more than 1 000 000 cycles.

There are a number of factors involved in fatigue failures, and different materials will behave differently. The stress cycle influences the behavior of the material. The cycle may alternate between equal values of tension and compression, differing values of tension or compression, or some very random stress pattern. The shape of the member is significant, for smooth members with well-rounded corners are less subject to fatigue damage than are members with stress concentrations such as holes, abrupt changes in section, or even tool marks. Whether a fatigue failure will occur depends also on the number of cycles of loading or stressing applied to the member.

So that designers may design to avoid fatigue failures, several tests have been developed to obtain data on fatigue behavior. The tests require that a standard sample be repeatedly loaded through a known stress cycle until the sample fails. The number of cycles to failure is recorded. Although there are limitless variations on possible stress cycles, the most common tests apply a loading that causes alternating equal values of tension and compression. The actual test usually consists of one of three procedures: applying and removing an axial load; rotating a round specimen under load so that it is acting as a cantilever beam; or flexing a plate back and forth.

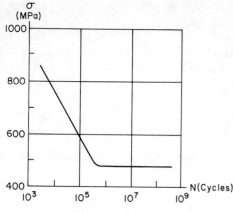

FIGURE 17-23

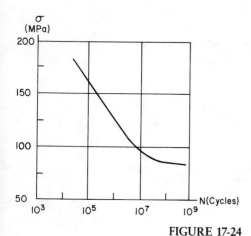

FIGURE 17-24

Test results show maximum stress and number of cycles to failure, and are plotted on a semi-log graph as shown in Figs. 17-23 and 17-24. In fatigue testing there is a great deal of variation in results. The variation is called *scatter*. Many tests must be performed, and the results must be statistically analyzed as part of the process of producing the graphs shown in Fig. 17-23 and 17-24. The graphs are often called *S-N* diagrams, since they show stress (at one time *S* was the symbol for stress) and number of cycles to failure, *N*.

The two *S-N* diagrams shown are significantly different. The diagram in Fig. 17-23 shows a horizontal line after a very large number of cycles, and the corresponding portion of the diagram in Fig. 17-24 continues to slope downward as the number of cycles increases. Figure 17-23 is typical of the shape of diagrams for most steels. For materials with such an *S-N* diagram, there is a stress, called the *fatigue limit*, sometimes called the *endurance limit*, below which fatigue failure will not occur regardless of the number of stress cycles. The *S-N* diagram in Fig. 17-24 has a shape typical of aluminums. For materials that do not have a horizontal portion in the *S-N* diagram, the fatigue limit is sometimes defined in terms of the stress at which the material survives for 500×10^6 cycles. The *fatigue strength* is the stress below which fatigue failure will not occur for a specified number of cycles. When stating the fatigue strength, the number of cycles that the material would survive at that stress must also be stated.

The fatigue strength is widely used, since it is not necessary, nor is it economical, to design all machines or frames to survive for many millions of loading cycles if the machine or frame will not actually be required to withstand that number of load repetitions.

17-7 IMPACT

Most tests of materials discussed up to this point have been "static" tests, in which the load has been applied at a relatively slow rate so that the rate of straining the material, or *strain rate*, has been low. Material properties, such as those given in Appendix E, are usually obtained by static tests. If loads are applied rapidly so that there is a high strain rate, some of the mechanical properties are changed. As the strain rate increases the ductility of the material tends to decrease and the yield strength tends to increase. There is also a lesser increase in the ultimate strength with increasing strain rate.

There are different techniques for testing at high strain rates. These may involve a variable-speed rotating flywheel with a hammer that strikes the specimen grip; a mass dropped from a

FIGURE 17-25   This pendulum type impact tester applies an impact force when the pendulum is released to strike a sample clamped on the base of the machine. The dial face at the top of the machine gives the energy required to cause fracture in a standard sample. *Photo courtesy of Tinius Olsen Testing Machine Co., Inc.*

variable height onto the sample; or a swinging pendulum that strikes the sample.

The most common impact test is not a true measure of impact resistance, because test results are influenced by the presence of a notch in the specimen. These are the Charpy and Izod impact tests, performed using a pendulum-type machine similar to that shown in Fig. 17-25. The Charpy specimen is shown in Fig. 17-26(a) and the Izod specimen is shown in Fig. 17-26(b). Both standard specimens have a cross-section of 10 by 10 mm.

In these tests, the pendulum is released from a known height, strikes and fractures the standard test specimen, and continues with its swing. The height reached by the pendulum after striking the sample is a measure of the energy remaining in the pendulum after applying sufficient energy to the sample to fracture it. The test machine is calibrated to read directly the energy causing fracture. Since the dimensions of the sample are standardized, test results are usually reported in terms of the number of

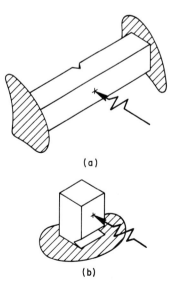

FIGURE 17-26

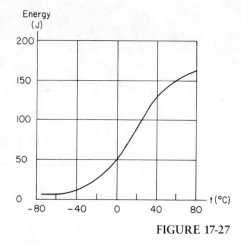

Energy
(J)

FIGURE 17-27

joules of energy required to cause fracture, rather than in terms of energy-per-unit volume.

The energy-absorbing capacity of notched impact specimens is temperature-dependent, as illustrated in Fig. 17-27, which shows the relationship between temperature and energy absorbed in fracturing a low-carbon steel. The energy-absorbing capacity drops sharply in the temperature range that is a normal working temperature for many frames and machines. Associated with this drop is a change from ductile to brittle behavior of the material. The temperature where the change occurs is the *transition temperature* or the *nil-ductility temperature*. There are several ways to determine the transition temperature. For steel, the transition temperature is usually considered to occur when it takes less than about 15 J to cause fracture.

For many materials the transition temperature occurs in normal operating temperature ranges. It is important to select materials where the transition temperature is lower than the operating temperature for the frame or machine if the frame or machine is likely to have impact loads applied to it.

17-8 CREEP

The mechanical properties of a material tend to vary with temperature. Generally, the strength decreases and the ductility increases with increasing temperature. Another temperature-dependent material characteristic is *creep*, which is time-dependent deformation in a material. Usually, creep is considered to be a high-temperature phenomenon, but some common structural materials, such as wood and concrete, have noticeable creep at room temperature.

A typical creep diagram is shown in Fig. 17-28, in which strain and time are the ordinates. The initial strain is the elastic or combination of elastic and plastic strain that takes place when the load is initially applied. The primary creep occurs immediately after the initial application of load and, as can be seen from the diagram, the creep rate, or change in strain with time, decreases until a steady rate is reached. The creep occurring at a steady rate is called *secondary creep*, and it may continue until the member fails. Ductile materials that neck, or have a reduction in cross section prior to fracture, show an acceleration of the creep rate because of the reduced section. This is called *tertiary creep*.

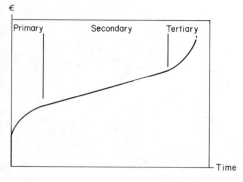

FIGURE 17-28

Quantitatively, the effects of creep vary considerably, depending on the initial stress, the material and the operating temperature. The amount of creep in a steel bridge during the life of the bridge, which may be a hundred years, may not be perceptible.

Conversely, turbine blades operating at high temperature and high stress may fail within hours if adequate care was not taken in material selection. Normal design practice for timber requires that creep be taken into account by lowering the allowable stress for high loads of long duration.

Associated with creep is another phenomenon called *stress relaxation*, in which the stress in a member is reduced with time. This will occur in bolts that have been tightened so that there is a specified stress in them. Due to the creep in the bolt material, less and less tension is required to maintain the same length between the nut and the bolt head; consequently, there is a reduced tension in the bolt over a period of time.

17-9 EXPERIMENTAL STRESS ANALYSIS

Chapters 10 through 13 have discussed the theoretical analysis of stress in simple members. The applications of the formulae developed have been limited. These limitations have included conditions on the mechanical properties of the materials, the shape of the members, and on the way loads were applied.

To analyze stresses in more complex members or structures, and to confirm the validity of the formulae derived for simple loading conditions, experimental stress analysis has been developed. The early experimental techniques involved loading the member or structure with the anticipated maximum load plus some overload as a safety factor. If the structure survived, it was safe, and if it did not, the designer probably did not survive either.

In the last half century, methods have been developed for determining the stress at various points both in and on structures. If used with care, the methods help to confirm, or contradict, assumptions made in the design process, and pinpoint areas of maximum or critical stress so that the design may be modified to make it safer or to use materials more efficiently.

The techniques used in experimental stress analysis use various methods of determining the strains at a point in a member and then correlate the strains with the stresses at that point. Recall that for a simple axial load that there is a strain transverse to the loading direction as well as parallel to it. It can be expected that with more complex loadings, the strain will be more complex. It follows that the relationship between stress and strain under these circumstances will also be complex. For this reason, only the most basic concepts of experimental stress analysis techniques will be discussed here.

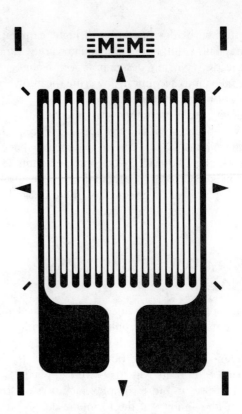

FIGURE 17-29   The majority of electric resistance strain gages have an actual length of about 2 to 5 mm. The large tabs are for soldering connections to the instrumentation for reading the gage. *Courtesy of Measurements Group, Inc., Raleigh, North Carolina, USA.*

Perhaps the most common method used for experimental stress analysis is the electric resistance strain gage, usually called a *strain gage*. As a wire changes in length, the resistance in the wire changes, and the change is proportional to the change in length. The actual gage is made of either several loops of fine wire or a foil grid on a backing, as shown in Fig. 17-29. Gage lengths vary, but a typical gage has a length of 4 or 5 mm. The gage is bonded to the member where strain is to be measured so that it changes length with the member. It is connected to a form of Wheatstone bridge, which measures the change in resistance. The system is usually calibrated to read strain directly. In most tests, readings are obtained at zero load and at increments of load. In many cases the strain at a point in three directions must be measured to determine the stress at that point. A rosette type of gage, as shown in Fig. 17-30, is used for this purpose. The strains at the point may be analyzed to determine the stresses at the point.

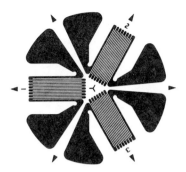

FIGURE 17-30 This foil rosette electric resistance strain gage is three gages precisely positioned on one backing. Most such gages are smaller than shown in the photo. *Courtesy of Measurements Group, Inc., Raleigh, North Carolina, USA.*

Strain-gage installations may consist of only a couple of gages on a simple member supporting a simple load, or there may be several hundred gages used on a structure with many members in it.

Photoelasticity is probably the second most common method of experimental stress analysis. Certain materials develop colored fringe patterns when stressed and viewed in polarized light. A black-and-white photograph of a pattern is shown in Fig. 17-31. Methods have been developed to relate the patterns to the stresses in the member. There are some significant advantages in the use of photoelasticity compared with the use of strain gages. Strain gages measure strain at a point. In photoelasticity the stress distribution over the entire surface may be analyzed. Originally, a two-dimensional model of the member in which the

FIGURE 17-31 The light pattern at the point of contact between parts indicates the concentration of stress in this photoelastic sample. The actual patterns are multicolored. *Courtesy of Measurements Group, Inc., Raleigh, North Carolina, USA.*

stress was to be analyzed was made of photoelastic material, and the stress was analyzed in the model. Now techniques have been developed for applying a photoelastic coating to the actual member, and the stress may be analyzed using the fringe pattern developed in the coating. Another significant advantage of photoelastic stress analysis is that methods have been found for analyzing the stresses in members as well as at the surface, as is the case with strain gage or two-dimensional models. Internal stresses can be very important in castings, dams and tunnel walls.

Brittle coatings provide another method for investigating the stress over an entire surface. A brittle lacquer is sprayed on the surface of the member to be tested. When a load is applied to the member the lacquer will crack where it has a tensile strain greater than some specific value, depending on the lacquer and atmospheric conditions. The density of the cracks is proportional to the maximum tensile strain, and the direction of the cracks is perpendicular to the direction of the maximum tensile strain. Figure 17-32 shows a member that has been tested using a brittle coating. One of the primary advantages of brittle coatings is that they provide a fairly rapid and inexpensive method of doing a preliminary investigation of the stress distribution. This information can be used to select the location of strain gages so that they are placed at points of critical stress.

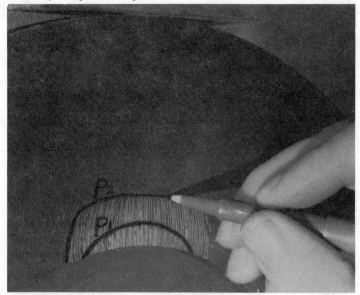

FIGURE 17-32 The test sample has been coated with a brittle coating and a load has been applied. The length and frequency of the cracks (the white lines) in the coating are related to the stress in the sample. *Courtesy of Measurements Group, Inc., Raleigh, North Carolina, USA.*

FIGURE 17-33 This specimen has a fine grid applied to its surface, and is viewed through a second fine grid. When the specimen is loaded the fringe pattern, known as moiré fringes, is formed by the two grids. The pattern can be related to the stress in the specimen. *Courtesy of Measurements Group, Inc., Raleigh, North Carolina, USA.*

The *moiré method* of stress analysis is not widely used. It is most useful when large strains are involved. Two closely spaced grids of parallel lines are used. One is applied to the test specimen, and the specimen is viewed through the second grid as the specimen is loaded. During loading, moiré fringes will appear; these fringes are related to the strains in the specimen. Figure 17-33 shows a moiré fringe pattern. The concept developed from observations of the patterns found in the overlap of curtains made with a fine, open weave.

The field of experimental stress analysis is changing rapidly and is really beyond the scope of basic stress analysis. This discussion has served only to introduce some of the basic terminology of an interesting and rather complex subject.

APPENDIX A

SYMBOLS

a	Coefficient of rolling resistance
$\mathbf{a}$, a	Acceleration, magnitude of acceleration
A	Area
A_i	Element of area
b	Base
c	Distance to extreme fiber
d	Perpendicular distance
d	Diameter
e	Napierian constant 2.718 28
E	Young's modulus of elasticity
$\mathbf{F}$, F	Force, magnitude of force
$\mathbf{F_r}$, F_r	Friction force, magnitude of friction force
g	Acceleration due to gravity 9.807 m/s^2
G	Shear modulus of elasticity
h	Height
I, I_x, I_y	Moment of inertia of area
$\bar{I}$, $\bar{I}_x$, $\bar{I}_y$	Moment of inertia of area with respect to axis through centroid of part
$I_{\bar{x}}$, $I_{\bar{y}}$	Moment of inertia of area with respect to axis through centroid of entire area
J, J_z	Polar moment of inertia of area
$\bar{J}_z$	Polar moment of inertia of area with respect to centroid
k	Effective length factor
k, k_x, k_y	Radius of gyration (used in statics)
$k_{\bar{x}}$, $k_{\bar{y}}$	Radius of gyration with respect to centroidal axis (used in statics)
K_t	Stress concentration factor
L	Length
L_i	Element of length
m	Mass
$\mathbf{M}$, M	Moment, magnitude of moment
$\mathbf{N}$, N	Normal force, magnitude of normal force
N	Factor of safety
$\mathbf{P}$, P	Force, magnitude of force
P	Power
P	Pressure
Q	First moment of area
q	Load per unit length, shear flow

r		Radius
r		Radius of gyration (used in stress analysis)
$\mathbf{R}, R$		Resultant, magnitude of resultant
$\mathbf{s}, s$		Displacement, distance
t		Temperature
$\mathbf{T}, T$		Torque or couple, magnitude of torque or couple
V		Magnitude of shear force
V		Volume
V_i		Element of volume
$\mathbf{v}, v$		Velocity, speed
w		Magnitude of distributed load
$\mathbf{W}, W$		Gravitational force, magnitude of gravitational force
$\bar{x}, \bar{y}, \bar{z}$		Perpendicular distance in x, y and z directions from origin to location of resultant force
$\bar{X}, \bar{Y}, \bar{Z}$		Coordinates of location of centroid or center of gravity
Z		Section modulus

α	(alpha)	Coefficient of thermal expansion
β	(beta)	
γ	(gamma)	Shear strain
δ	(delta)	Deformation or deflection
Δ	(delta)	Element, change
ϵ	(epsilon)	Normal strain
θ	(theta)	Angle of twist
$\theta_x, \theta_y, \theta_z$		Direction angles
μ	(mu)	Coefficient of friction
μ_k, μ_s		Kinetic and static coefficients of friction
μ_R		Modulus or resilience
μ_T		Modulus of toughness
ν	(nu)	Poisson's ratio
π	(pi)	3.1416
ρ	(rho)	Density
σ	(sigma)	Normal stress
σ_{ru}		Modulus of rupture in flexure
Σ	(sigma)	Summation
τ	(tau)	Shear stress
τ_{ru}		Modulus of rupture in shear
ϕ	(phi)	
ω	(omega)	Angular speed

$\alpha, \beta, \gamma, \theta$ and ϕ are also used to designate angles

APPENDIX B

Volumes, Centers of Gravity, and Centroids – Solids

Solid	Volume	Center of Gravity or Centroid
Rectangular Prism	$V = lwh$	$\bar{x} = \dfrac{l}{2}$ $\bar{y} = \dfrac{w}{2}$ $\bar{z} = \dfrac{h}{2}$
Right Circular Cylinder	$V = \pi r^2 h$	$\bar{x} = 0$ $\bar{y} = 0$ $\bar{z} = \dfrac{h}{2}$
Quarter Right Circular Cylinder	$V = \dfrac{\pi r^2 h}{4}$	$\bar{x} = \dfrac{4r}{3\pi}$ $\bar{y} = \dfrac{4r}{3\pi}$ $\bar{z} = \dfrac{h}{2}$

Surface of spherical cap =
$2\pi rh$

APPENDIX B (cont'd)

Sphere		
	$V = \frac{4}{3}\pi r^3$	$\bar{x} = 0$ $\bar{y} = 0$ $\bar{z} = 0$
Hemisphere		
	$V = \frac{2}{3}\pi r^3$	$\bar{x} = 0$ $\bar{y} = 0$ $\bar{z} = \frac{3}{8}r$
Triangular Prism		
	$V = \frac{1}{2}bht$	$\bar{x} = \frac{h}{3}$ $\bar{y}$ – Not Defined $\bar{z} = \frac{t}{2}$
Right Circular Cone		
	$V = \frac{1}{3}\pi r^2 h$	$\bar{x} = 0$ $\bar{y} = 0$ $\bar{z} = \frac{h}{4}$

APPENDIX C

Areas, Centroids and Moments of Inertia – Planes

Plane	Area	Centroid	Moment of Inertia
Rectangle	$A = bh$	$\bar{x} = 0$ $\bar{y} = 0$	$I_x = \dfrac{bh^3}{12}$ $I_y = \dfrac{b^3h}{12}$ $J_z = \dfrac{bh}{12}(b^2+h^2)$
Circle	$A = \pi r^2 = \dfrac{\pi d^2}{4}$	$\bar{x} = 0$ $\bar{y} = 0$	$I_x = \dfrac{\pi r^4}{4} = \dfrac{\pi d^4}{64}$ $I_y = \dfrac{\pi r^4}{4} = \dfrac{\pi d^4}{64}$ $J_z = \dfrac{\pi r^4}{2} = \dfrac{\pi d^4}{32}$
Quarter Circle	$A = \dfrac{\pi r^2}{4}$	$\bar{x} = \dfrac{4r}{3\pi}$ $\bar{y} = \dfrac{4r}{3\pi}$	$I_x = \dfrac{\pi r^4}{16}$ $I_y = \dfrac{\pi r^4}{16}$
Triangle	$A = \dfrac{bh}{2}$	$\bar{x}$ – Not Defined $\bar{y} = 0$	$I_x = \dfrac{bh^3}{36}$

APPENDIX D

Lengths and Centroids – Lines

Line	Length	Centroid
Straight Line 	$L = (a^2 + b^2)^{1/2}$	$\bar{x} = \dfrac{b}{2}$ $\bar{y} = \dfrac{a}{2}$
Circle 	$L = 2\pi r$	$\bar{x} = 0$ $\bar{y} = 0$
Quarter Circle Arc 	$L = \dfrac{\pi r}{2}$	$\bar{x} = \dfrac{2r}{\pi}$ $\bar{y} = \dfrac{2r}{\pi}$

APPENDIX E

TYPICAL* MECHANICAL PROPERTIES OF SELECTED MATERIALS

Material	Yield Strength MPa	Ultimate Strength MPa	Young's Modulus GPa	Shear Modulus GPa	Poisson's Ratio	Density kg/m^3	% Deformation	Thermal Expansion 10^{-6} m/m/°C
METALLIC MATERIALS								
Aluminum								
2014-T6	365	415	73	28	0.34	2770	7	22.5
6061-T6	240	260	69	26	0.34	2770	8	22.5
Copper – Hard	300	330	110	40	0.35	8940	8	16.8
Cast Iron								
Gray	50	170 –690	100	40	0.25	7200	0.5	12.1
Malleable	220	340	170			7370	20	11.9
Magnesium – Extruded	240	340	45	17	0.32	1740	12	25.9
Steels								
0.2% Carbon – Hot-rolled	240	410	207	80	0.29	7850	35	11.7
0.8% Carbon – Hot-rolled	480	830	207	80	0.29	7850	10	11.7
Stainless 18-8	1140	1300	190	86		7920	8	17.3
Structural – 230G	230	400	200	77	0.30	7870	23	11.7
Structural – 400G	400	600	200	77	0.30	7870	22	11.7
NONMETALLIC MATERIALS								
ABS Plastic		41	2.1					95
Concrete								
Low Strength	–8	–21	21		0.20	2400	5	12.0
High Strength		–45	34		0.20	2400		12.0
Vinyl – Rigid		48	3.0			1700	15	63
Wood – Parallel to Grain								
Douglas Fir – Dry	56 –44	–51	13 13			550		5.5
Red Oak – Dry	58 –32	–48	12 12			690		

*Values should not be used for design. Actual values should be obtained from the material supplier.

APPENDIX F

PROPERTIES FOR DESIGNING –
STANDARD STRUCTURAL STEEL SHAPES

W SHAPES
W610 - W530

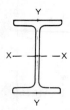

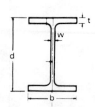

Designation ‡	Dead Load	Total Area	Axis X-X			Axis Y-Y			Depth d	Flange			Web Thickness w
			I_x	S_x	r_x	I_y	S_y	r_y		Width b	Mean Thickness t		
	kN/m	mm²	10^6 mm⁴	10^3 mm³	mm	10^6 mm⁴	10^3 mm³	mm	mm	mm	mm		mm
W610													
X241	2.37	30 800	2 150	6 780	264	184	1 120	77.3	635	329	31.0		17.9
X217	2.13	27 800	1 910	6 070	262	163	995	76.6	628	328	27.7		16.5
X195	1.91	24 900	1 680	5 400	260	142	871	75.5	622	327	24.4		15.4
X174	1.70	22 200	1 470	4 780	257	124	761	74.7	616	325	21.6		14.0
X155	1.51	19 700	1 290	4 220	256	108	666	74.0	611	324	19.0		12.7
W610													
X140	1.37	17 900	1 120	3 630	250	45.1	392	50.2	617	230	22.2		13.1
X125	1.22	15 900	985	3 220	249	39.3	343	49.7	612	229	19.6		11.9
X113	1.11	14 400	875	2 880	247	34.3	300	48.8	608	228	17.3		11.2
X101	0.997	13 000	764	2 530	242	29.5	259	47.6	603	228	14.9		10.5
W610													
X92 *	0.905	11 800	646	2 140	234	14.4	161	34.9	603	179	15.0		10.9
X82 *	0.803	10 400	560	1 870	232	12.1	136	34.1	599	178	12.8		10.0
W530													
X219 *	2.14	27 900	1 510	5 390	233	157	986	75.0	560	318	29.2		18.3
X196 *	1.92	25 000	1 340	4 840	232	139	877	74.6	554	316	26.3		16.5
X182 *	1.78	23 100	1 240	4 480	232	127	808	74.1	551	315	24.4		15.2
X165 *	1.62	21 100	1 110	4 060	229	114	726	73.5	546	313	22.2		14.0
X150 *	1.47	19 200	1 010	3 710	229	103	659	73.2	543	312	20.3		12.7
W530													
X138	1.35	17 600	861	3 140	221	38.7	362	46.9	549	214	23.6		14.7
X123	1.20	15 700	761	2 800	220	33.8	319	46.4	544	212	21.2		13.1
X109	1.06	13 900	667	2 480	219	29.5	280	46.1	539	211	18.8		11.6
X101	0.995	12 900	617	2 300	219	26.9	256	45.7	537	210	17.4		10.9
X92	0.907	11 800	552	2 070	216	23.8	228	44.9	533	209	15.6		10.2
X82	0.808	10 500	479	1 810	214	20.3	194	44.0	528	209	13.3		9.5
W530													
X85 *	0.830	10 800	485	1 810	212	12.6	152	34.2	535	166	16.5		10.3
X74 *	0.733	9 520	411	1 550	208	10.4	125	33.1	529	166	13.6		9.7
X66 *	0.644	8 370	351	1 340	205	8.57	104	32.0	525	165	11.4		8.9

‡Nominal depth in millimetres and mass in kilograms per metre.
Reprinted from the Canadian Institute of Steel Construction's Handbook of Steel Construction, 3rd Edition, with permission.

W SHAPES
W460 - W410

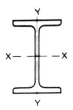 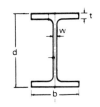

Designation ‡	Dead Load	Total Area	Axis X-X			Axis Y-Y			Depth d	Width b	Flange Mean Thickness t	Web Thickness w
			I_x	S_x	r_x	I_y	S_y	r_y				
	kN/m	mm²	10^6mm⁴	10^3mm³	mm	10^6mm⁴	10^3mm³	mm	mm	mm	mm	mm
W460												
X177*	1.73	22 600	910	3 780	201	105	735	68.2	482	286	26.9	16.6
X158*	1.54	20 100	796	3 350	199	91.4	643	67.4	476	284	23.9	15.0
X144*	1.41	18 400	726	3 080	199	83.6	591	67.4	472	283	22.1	13.6
X128*	1.26	16 400	637	2 730	197	73.3	520	66.9	467	282	19.6	12.2
X113*	1.10	14 400	556	2 400	196	63.3	452	66.3	463	280	17.3	10.8
W460												
X106	1.03	13 500	488	2 080	190	25.1	259	43.1	469	194	20.6	12.6
X97	0.947	12 300	445	1 910	190	22.8	237	43.1	466	193	19.0	11.4
X89	0.876	11 400	410	1 770	190	20.9	218	42.8	463	192	17.7	10.5
X82	0.804	10 400	370	1 610	189	18.6	195	42.3	460	191	16.0	9.9
X74	0.728	9 450	333	1 460	188	16.6	175	41.9	457	190	14.5	9.0
X67	0.668	8 680	300	1 320	186	14.6	153	41.0	454	190	12.7	8.5
X61	0.598	7 760	259	1 150	183	12.2	129	39.7	450	189	10.8	8.1
W460												
X68*	0.672	8 730	297	1 290	184	9.41	122	32.8	459	154	15.4	9.1
X60*	0.584	7 590	255	1 120	183	7.96	104	32.4	455	153	13.3	8.0
X52*	0.510	6 630	212	943	179	6.34	83.4	30.9	450	152	10.8	7.6
W410												
X149*	1.46	19 000	619	2 870	180	77.7	586	63.9	431	265	25.0	14.9
X132*	1.29	16 800	538	2 530	179	67.4	512	63.3	425	263	22.2	13.3
X114*	1.12	14 600	462	2 200	178	57.2	439	62.6	420	261	19.3	11.6
X100*	0.977	12 700	398	1 920	177	49.5	381	62.4	415	260	16.9	10.0
W410												
X85	0.833	10 800	315	1 510	171	18.0	199	40.8	417	181	18.2	10.9
X74	0.735	9 550	275	1 330	170	15.6	173	40.4	413	180	16.0	9.7
X67	0.662	8 600	246	1 200	169	13.8	154	40.1	410	179	14.4	8.8
X60	0.584	7 580	216	1 060	169	12.0	135	39.8	407	178	12.8	7.7
X54	0.524	6 810	186	924	165	10.1	114	38.5	403	177	10.9	7.5
W410												
X46	0.453	5 890	156	773	163	5.14	73.4	29.5	403	140	11.2	7.0
X39	0.384	4 990	127	634	160	4.04	57.7	28.5	399	140	8.8	6.4

‡Nominal depth in millimetres and mass in kilograms per metre.

W SHAPES
W360

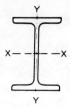
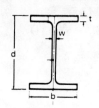

Designation‡	Dead Load	Total Area	Axis X-X			Axis Y-Y				Flange			Web Thickness
			I_x	S_x	r_x	I_y	S_y	r_y	Depth d	Width b	Mean Thickness t		
	kN/m	mm²	10⁶mm⁴	10³mm³	mm	10⁶mm⁴	10³mm³	mm	mm	mm	mm		w mm
W360													
X1086*	10.6	139 000	5 960	20 900	207	1 960	8 650	119	569	454	125		78.0
X990*	9.71	126 000	5 190	18 900	203	1 730	7 740	117	550	448	115		71.9
X900*	8.84	115 000	4 500	17 000	198	1 530	6 940	115	531	442	106		65.9
X818*	8.03	104 000	3 920	15 300	194	1 360	6 200	114	514	437	97.0		60.5
X744*	7.29	94 800	3 420	13 700	190	1 200	5 550	113	498	432	88.9		55.6
X677*	6.64	86 300	2 990	12 400	186	1 070	4 990	111	483	428	81.5		51.2
W360													
X634*	6.22	80 800	2 740	11 600	184	983	4 630	110	474	424	77.1		47.6
X592*	5.81	75 500	2 500	10 800	182	902	4 280	109	465	421	72.3		45.0
X551*	5.40	70 100	2 260	9 940	180	825	3 950	108	455	418	67.6		42.0
X509*	4.99	64 900	2 050	9 170	178	754	3 630	108	446	416	62.7		39.1
X463*	4.53	59 000	1 800	8 280	175	670	3 250	107	435	412	57.4		35.8
X421*	4.13	53 700	1 600	7 510	173	601	2 940	106	425	409	52.6		32.8
X382*	3.75	48 700	1 410	6 790	170	536	2 640	105	416	406	48.0		29.8
X347*	3.40	44 200	1 250	6 140	168	481	2 380	104	407	404	43.7		27.2
X314*	3.07	39 900	1 100	5 530	166	426	2 120	103	399	401	39.6		24.9
X287*	2.82	36 600	997	5 070	165	388	1 940	103	393	399	36.6		22.6
X262*	2.57	33 500	894	4 620	163	350	1 760	102	387	398	33.3		21.1
X237*	2.31	30 100	788	4 150	162	310	1 570	101	380	395	30.2		18.9
X216*	2.12	27 600	712	3 790	161	283	1 430	101	375	394	27.7		17.3
W360													
X196*	1.92	25 000	636	3 420	159	229	1 220	95.7	372	374	26.2		16.4
X179*	1.75	22 800	575	3 120	159	207	1 110	95.3	368	373	23.9		15.0
X162*	1.58	20 600	516	2 830	158	186	1 000	95.0	364	371	21.8		13.3
X147*	1.44	18 800	463	2 570	157	167	904	94.2	360	370	19.8		12.3
X134*	1.31	17 100	415	2 330	156	151	817	94.0	356	369	18.0		11.2
W360													
X122*	1.19	15 500	365	2 010	153	61.5	478	63.0	363	257	21.7		13.0
X110*	1.08	14 000	331	1 840	154	55.7	435	63.1	360	256	19.9,		11.4
X101*	0.993	12 900	302	1 690	153	50.6	397	62.6	357	255	18.3		10.5
X91*	0.891	11 600	267	1 510	152	44.8	353	62.1	353	254	16.4		9.5
W360													
X79	0.777	10 100	227	1 280	150	24.2	236	48.9	354	205	16.8		9.4
X72	0.701	9 110	201	1 150	149	21.4	210	48.5	350	204	15.1		8.6
X64	0.627	8 140	178	1 030	148	18.8	186	48.1	347	203	13.5		7.7
W360													
X57	0.556	7 220	161	897	149	11.1	129	39.2	358	172	13.1		7.9
X51	0.496	6 450	141	796	148	9.68	113	38.7	355	171	11.6		7.2
X45	0.441	5 730	122	691	146	8.18	95.7	37.8	352	171	9.8		6.9
W360													
X39	0.384	4 980	102	580	143	3.75	58.6	27.4	353	128	10.7		6.5
X33	0.321	4 170	82.7	474	141	2.91	45.8	26.4	349	127	8.5		5.8

‡Nominal depth in millimetres and mass in kilograms per metre.

W SHAPES
W310

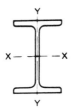
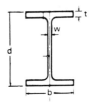

Designation‡	Dead Load	Total Area	Axis X-X			Axis Y-Y			Depth d	Width b	Flange Mean Thickness t	Web Thickness w
			I_x	S_x	r_x	I_y	S_y	r_y				
	kN/m	mm²	10⁶mm⁴	10³mm³	mm	10⁶mm⁴	10³mm³	mm	mm	mm	mm	mm
W310												
X500*	4.90	63 700	1 690	7 910	163	494	2 910	88.1	427	340	75.1	45.1
X454*	4.45	57 800	1 480	7 130	160	436	2 600	86.9	415	336	68.7	41.3
X415*	4.07	52 900	1 300	6 450	157	391	2 340	86.0	403	334	62.7	38.9
X375*	3.67	47 700	1 130	5 760	154	343	2 080	84.8	391	330	57.1	35.4
X342*	3.36	43 700	1 010	5 260	152	310	1 890	84.2	382	328	52.6	32.6
X313*	3.07	39 900	896	4 790	150	277	1 700	83.3	374	325	48.3	30.0
W310												
X283	2.77	36 000	787	4 310	148	246	1 530	82.7	365	322	44.1	26.9
X253	2.48	32 200	682	3 830	146	215	1 350	81.7	356	319	39.6	24.4
X226	2.22	28 900	596	3 420	144	189	1 190	80.9	348	317	35.6	22.1
X202	1.98	25 800	520	3 050	142	166	1 050	80.2	341	315	31.8	20.1
X179	1.75	22 800	445	2 680	140	144	919	79.5	333	313	28.1	18.0
X158	1.54	20 100	386	2 360	139	125	805	78.9	327	310	25.1	15.5
X143	1.40	18 200	348	2 150	138	113	729	78.8	323	309	22.9	14.0
X129	1.27	16 500	308	1 940	137	100	652	77.8	318	308	20.6	13.1
X118	1.15	15 000	275	1 750	135	90.2	588	77.5	314	307	18.7	11.9
X107	1.04	13 600	248	1 590	135	81.2	531	77.3	311	306	17.0	10.9
X97	0.950	12 300	222	1 440	134	72.9	478	77.0	308	305	15.4	9.9
W310												
X86	0.847	11 000	199	1 280	135	44.5	351	63.6	310	254	16.3	9.1
X79	0.774	10 100	177	1 160	132	39.9	314	62.9	306	254	14.6	8.8
W310												
X74	0.730	9 490	165	1 060	132	23.4	229	49.7	310	205	16.3	9.4
X67	0.655	8 510	145	949	131	20.7	203	49.3	306	204	14.6	8.5
X60	0.585	7 590	129	849	130	18.3	180	49.1	303	203	13.1	7.5
W310												
X52	0.513	6 670	118	747	133	10.3	123	39.3	317	167	13.2	7.6
X45	0.438	5 690	99.2	634	132	8.55	103	38.8	313	166	11.2	6.6
X39	0.380	4 940	85.1	549	131	7.27	88.1	38.4	310	165	9.7	5.8
W310												
X33*	0.321	4 180	65.0	415	125	1.92	37.6	21.4	313	102	10.8	6.6
X28*	0.278	3 610	54.3	351	123	1.58	31.0	20.9	309	102	8.9	6.0
X24*	0.234	3 040	42.7	280	119	1.16	22.9	19.5	305	101	6.7	5.6
X21*	0.207	2 690	37.0	244	117	0.983	19.5	19.1	303	101	5.7	5.1

‡Nominal depth in millimetres and mass in kilograms per metre.

W SHAPES
W250 - W200

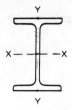 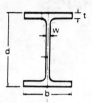

Designation‡	Dead Load	Total Area	Axis X-X I_x	S_x	r_x	Axis Y-Y I_y	S_y	r_y	Depth d	Width b	Flange Mean Thickness t	Web Thickness w
	kN/m	mm²	10^6mm⁴	10^3mm³	mm	10^6mm⁴	10^3mm³	mm	mm	mm	mm	mm
W250												
X167	1.64	21 300	300	2 080	119	98.8	746	68.1	289	265	31.8	19.2
X149	1.46	19 000	259	1 840	117	86.2	656	67.4	282	263	28.4	17.3
X131	1.28	16 700	221	1 610	115	74.5	571	66.8	275	261	25.1	15.4
X115	1.12	14 600	189	1 410	114	64.1	495	66.3	269	259	22.1	13.5
X101	0.992	12 900	164	1 240	113	55.5	432	65.6	264	257	19.6	11.9
X89	0.878	11 400	143	1 100	112	48.4	378	65.2	260	256	17.3	10.7
X80	0.786	10 200	126	982	111	43.1	338	65.0	256	255	15.6	9.4
X73	0.715	9 280	113	891	110	38.8	306	64.7	253	254	14.2	8.6
W250												
X67	0.658	8 550	104	806	110	22.2	218	51.0	257	204	16.7	8.9
X58	0.571	7 420	87.3	693	108	18.8	186	50.3	252	203	13.5	8.0
X49	0.481	6 250	70.6	572	106	15.1	150	49.2	247	202	11.0	7.4
W250												
X45	0.440	5 720	71.1	534	111	7.03	95.1	35.1	266	148	13.0	7.6
X39	0.379	4 920	60.1	459	111	5.94	80.8	34.7	262	147	11.2	6.6
X33	0.321	4 170	48.9	379	108	4.73	64.7	33.7	258	146	9.1	6.1
W250												
X28*	0.279	3 630	40.0	307	105	1.78	34.8	22.1	260	102	10.0	6.4
X25*	0.249	3 230	34.2	266	103	1.49	29.2	21.5	257	102	8.4	6.1
X22*	0.219	2 850	28.9	227	101	1.23	24.0	20.8	254	102	6.9	5.8
X18*	0.175	2 270	22.4	179	99.3	0.913	18.1	20.1	251	101	5.3	4.8
W200												
X100	0.976	12 700	113	989	94.3	36.6	349	53.7	229	210	23.7	14.5
X86	0.851	11 100	94.7	853	92.4	31.4	300	53.2	222	209	20.6	13.0
X71	0.701	9 110	76.6	709	91.7	25.4	246	52.8	216	206	17.4	10.2
X59	0.582	7 560	61.1	582	89.9	20.4	199	51.9	210	205	14.2	9.1
X52	0.513	6 660	52.7	512	89.0	17.8	175	51.7	206	204	12.6	7.9
X46	0.451	5 860	45.5	448	88.1	15.3	151	51.1	203	203	11.0	7.2
W200												
X42	0.409	5 310	40.9	399	87.8	9.00	108	41.2	205	166	11.8	7.2
X36	0.352	4 580	34.4	342	86.7	7.64	92.6	40.8	201	165	10.2	6.2
W200												
X31	0.308	4 000	31.4	299	88.6	4.10	61.1	32.0	210	134	10.2	6.4
X27	0.261	3 390	25.8	249	87.2	3.30	49.6	31.2	207	133	8.4	5.8
W200												
X22*	0.220	2 860	20.0	194	83.6	1.42	27.8	22.3	206	102	8.0	6.2
X19*	0.191	2 480	16.6	163	81.8	1.15	22.6	21.5	203	102	6.5	5.8
X15*	0.147	1 900	12.7	127	81.8	0.869	17.4	21.4	200	100	5.2	4.3

‡Nominal depth in millimetres and mass in kilograms per metre.

S SHAPES
S610 - S180

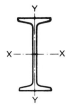
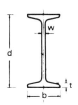

Designation ‡	Dead Load	Total Area	Axis X-X			Axis Y-Y			Depth d	Flange Width b	Mean Thickness t	Web Thickness w
			I_x	S_x	r_x	I_y	S_y	r_y				
	kN/m	mm²	10^6mm⁴	10^3mm³	mm	10^6mm⁴	10^3mm³	mm	mm	mm	mm	mm
S610												
X180*	1.76	22 900	1 310	4 220	239	34.7	340	38.9	622	204	27.7	20.3
X158*	1.54	20 100	1 220	3 940	246	32.4	324	40.1	622	200	27.7	15.7
S610												
X149*	1.45	18 900	996	3 270	230	20.1	218	32.6	610	184	22.1	18.9
X134*	1.31	17 100	939	3 080	234	18.9	209	33.2	610	181	22.1	15.9
X119*	1.16	15 200	879	2 880	240	17.9	201	34.3	610	178	22.1	12.7
S510												
X143*	1.40	18 300	702	2 720	196	21.1	231	34.0	516	183	23.4	20.3
X128*	1.26	16 400	660	2 560	201	19.6	219	34.6	516	179	23.4	16.8
S510												
X112*	1.09	14 200	532	2 090	194	12.5	155	29.7	508	162	20.2	16.1
X98.2*	0.965	12 500	497	1 960	199	11.7	148	30.6	508	159	20.2	12.8
S460												
X104*	1.02	13 300	387	1 690	171	10.3	129	27.8	457	159	17.6	18.1
X81.4*	0.800	10 400	335	1 470	179	8.77	115	29.0	457	152	17.6	11.7
S380												
X74*	0.731	9 500	203	1 060	146	6.60	92.3	26.4	381	143	15.8	14.0
X64*	0.627	8 150	187	980	151	6.11	87.3	27.4	381	140	15.8	10.4
S310												
X74*	0.729	9 470	127	833	116	6.60	94.9	26.4	305	139	16.7	17.4
X60.7*	0.595	7 730	113	744	121	5.67	85.3	27.1	305	133	16.7	11.7
S310												
X52	0.512	6 650	95.8	629	120	4.16	64.5	25.0	305	129	13.8	10.9
X47	0.465	6 040	91.1	597	123	3.94	62.1	25.5	305	127	13.8	8.9
S250												
X52	0.513	6 660	61.6	485	96.2	3.56	56.5	23.1	254	126	12.5	15.1
X38	0.371	4 820	51.4	405	103	2.84	48.2	24.3	254	118	12.5	7.9
S200												
X34	0.336	4 370	27.0	266	78.6	1.81	34.2	20.4	203	106	10.8	11.2
X27	0.270	3 500	24.0	237	82.8	1.59	31.1	21.3	203	102	10.8	6.9
S180												
X30*	0.293	3 800	17.8	200	68.4	1.34	27.3	18.8	178	98	10.0	11.4
X22.8*	0.224	2 910	15.4	173	72.7	1.12	24.0	19.6	178	93	10.0	6.4

‡Nominal depth in millimetres and mass in kilograms per metre.

STANDARD CHANNELS (C SHAPES)

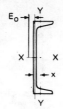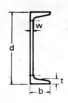

Designation#	Dead Load	Total Area	Axis X-X			Axis Y-Y				Shear Centre	Depth d	Flange			Web Thickness w
			I_x	S_x	r_x	I_y	S_y	r_y	x	E_o		Width b	Mean Thickness t		
	kN/m	mm²	10^6 mm⁴	10^3 mm³	mm	10^6 mm⁴	10^3 mm³	mm	mm	mm	mm	mm	mm	mm
C380															
X74	0.730	9 480	168	881	133	4.60	62.4	22.0	20.3	23.7	381	94	16.5	18.2
X60	0.583	7 570	145	760	138	3.84	55.5	22.5	19.7	25.9	381	89	16.5	13.2
X50	0.495	6 430	131	687	143	3.39	51.4	23.0	20.0	27.6	381	86	16.5	10.2
C310															
X45	0.438	5 690	67.3	442	109	2.12	33.6	19.3	17.0	21.9	305	80	12.7	13.0
X37	0.363	4 720	59.9	393	113	1.85	30.9	19.8	17.1	23.7	305	77	12.7	9.8
X31	0.302	3 920	53.5	351	117	1.59	28.2	20.1	17.5	25.3	305	74	12.7	7.2
C250															
X45*	0.437	5 670	42.8	337	86.9	1.60	26.8	16.8	16.3	17.5	254	76	11.1	17.1
X37	0.365	4 750	37.9	299	89.3	1.40	24.3	17.2	15.7	19.1	254	73	11.1	13.4
X30	0.291	3 780	32.7	257	93.0	1.16	21.5	17.5	15.3	20.8	254	69	11.1	9.6
X23	0.221	2 880	27.8	219	98.2	0.922	18.8	17.9	15.9	22.8	254	65	11.1	6.1
C230															
X30	0.292	3 800	25.5	222	81.9	1.01	19.3	16.3	14.8	18.6	229	67	10.5	11.4
X22	0.219	2 840	21.3	186	86.6	0.806	16.8	16.8	14.9	20.9	229	63	10.5	7.2
X20	0.195	2 530	19.8	173	88.5	0.716	15.6	16.8	15.1	21.5	229	61	10.5	5.9
C200															
X28	0.274	3 560	18.2	180	71.5	0.825	16.6	15.2	14.4	17.0	203	64	9.9	12.4
X21	0.200	2 600	14.9	147	75.7	0.627	13.9	15.5	14.0	19.0	203	59	9.9	7.7
X17	0.167	2 170	13.5	133	78.9	0.544	12.8	15.8	14.5	20.3	203	57	9.9	5.6
C180															
X22*	0.214	2 780	11.3	127	63.8	0.568	12.8	14.3	13.5	16.4	178	58	9.3	10.6
X18	0.178	2 310	10.0	113	65.8	0.476	11.4	14.4	13.2	17.3	178	55	9.3	8.0
X15	0.142	1 850	8.86	99.6	69.2	0.405	10.3	14.8	13.8	19.1	178	53	9.3	5.3
C150															
X19	0.189	2 450	7.12	93.7	53.9	0.425	10.3	13.2	12.9	14.9	152	54	8.7	11.1
X16	0.152	1 980	6.22	81.9	56.0	0.351	9.13	13.3	12.6	16.0	152	51	8.7	8.0
X12	0.118	1 540	5.36	70.6	59.0	0.279	7.93	13.5	12.8	17.4	152	48	8.7	5.1
C130															
X17	0.168	2 190	4.36	68.7	44.6	0.346	8.85	12.6	12.9	14.0	127	52	8.1	12.0
X13	0.131	1 700	3.66	57.6	46.4	0.252	7.20	12.2	11.9	14.5	127	47	8.1	8.3
X10	0.097	1 260	3.09	48.6	49.5	0.195	6.14	12.4	12.2	16.2	127	44	8.1	4.8
C100															
X11	0.106	1 370	1.91	37.4	37.3	0.174	5.52	11.3	11.5	13.5	102	43	7.5	8.2
X9	0.092	1 190	1.77	34.6	38.6	0.158	5.18	11.5	11.6	14.5	102	42	7.5	6.3
X8	0.079	1 020	1.61	31.6	39.7	0.132	4.65	11.4	11.6	14.9	102	40	7.5	4.7
C75															
X9	0.087	1 120	0.85	22.3	27.5	0.123	4.31	10.5	11.4	12.5	76	40	6.9	9.0
X7	0.072	933	0.75	19.7	28.3	0.096	3.67	10.1	10.8	12.7	76	37	6.9	6.6
X6	0.059	763	0.67	17.6	29.6	0.077	3.21	10.1	10.9	13.5	76	35	6.9	4.3

‡Nominal depth in millimetres and mass in kilograms per metre.

ANGLES
Equal Legs

PROPERTIES AND DIMENSIONS

Size	Thickness t	Mass	Dead Load	Area	Axis X-X and Axis Y-Y				Axis Z-Z
					I	S	r	x or y	r
mmxmm	mm	kg/m	kN/m	mm^2	10^{6}mm^4	10^{3}mm^3	mm	mm	mm
200X200									
	30	87.1	0.855	11 100	40.3	290	60.3	60.9	39.0
	25	73.6	0.722	9 380	34.8	247	60.9	59.2	39.1
	20	59.7	0.585	7 600	28.8	202	61.6	57.4	39.3
	16	48.2	0.473	6 140	23.7	165	62.1	55.9	39.5
	13	39.5	0.387	5 030	19.7	136	62.6	54.8	39.7
	10	30.6	0.300	3 900	15.5	106	63.0	53.7	39.9
150X150									
	20	44.0	0.431	5 600	11.6	110	45.5	44.8	29.3
	16	35.7	0.350	4 540	9.63	90.3	46.0	43.4	29.4
	13	29.3	0.287	3 730	8.05	74.7	46.4	42.3	29.6
	10	22.8	0.223	2 900	6.37	58.6	46.9	41.2	29.8
125X125									
	16	29.4	0.288	3 740	5.41	61.5	38.0	37.1	24.4
	13	24.2	0.237	3 080	4.54	51.1	38.4	36.0	24.5
	10	18.8	0.185	2 400	3.62	40.2	38.8	34.9	24.7
	8	15.2	0.149	1 940	2.96	32.6	39.1	34.2	24.8
100X100									
	16	23.1	0.227	2 940	2.65	38.3	30.0	30.8	19.5
	13	19.1	0.187	2 430	2.24	31.9	30.4	29.8	19.5
	10	14.9	0.146	1 900	1.80	25.2	30.8	28.7	19.7
	8	12.1	0.118	1 540	1.48	20.6	31.1	28.0	19.8
	6	9.14	0.090	1 160	1.14	15.7	31.3	27.2	19.9
90X90									
	13	17.0	0.167	2 170	1.60	25.6	27.2	27.2	17.6
	10	13.3	0.131	1 700	1.29	20.2	27.6	26.2	17.6
	8	10.8	0.106	1 380	1.07	16.5	27.8	25.5	17.7
	6	8.20	0.080	1 040	0.826	12.7	28.1	24.7	17.9
75X75									
	13	14.0	0.137	1 780	0.892	17.3	22.4	23.5	14.6
	10	11.0	0.108	1 400	0.725	13.8	22.8	22.4	14.6
	8	8.92	0.087	1 140	0.602	11.3	23.0	21.7	14.7
	6	6.78	0.066	864	0.469	8.68	23.3	21.0	14.8
	5	5.69	0.056	725	0.398	7.32	23.4	20.6	14.9
65X65									
	10	9.42	0.092	1 200	0.459	10.2	19.6	19.9	12.7
	8	7.66	0.075	976	0.383	8.36	19.8	19.2	12.7
	6	5.84	0.057	744	0.300	6.44	20.1	18.5	12.8
	5	4.91	0.048	625	0.255	5.45	20.2	18.1	12.9
55X55									
	10	7.85	0.077	1 000	0.268	7.11	16.4	17.4	10.7
	8	6.41	0.063	816	0.225	5.87	16.6	16.7	10.7
	6	4.90	0.048	624	0.177	4.54	16.9	16.0	10.8
	5	4.12	0.040	525	0.152	3.85	17.0	15.6	10.8
	4	3.33	0.033	424	0.125	3.13	17.1	15.2	10.9
	3	2.52	0.025	321	0.096	2.39	17.3	14.9	11.0

ANGLES
Unequal Legs

PROPERTIES AND DIMENSIONS

Size	Thick-ness t	Mass	Dead Load	Area	Axis X-X				Axis Y-Y				Axis Z-Z	
					I_x	S_x	r_x	y	I_y	S_y	r_y	x	r_z	Tan α
mmxmm	mm	kg/m	kN/m	mm²	10^6mm⁴	10^3mm³	mm	mm	10^6mm⁴	10^3mm³	mm	mm	mm	
200X150*	25	63.8	0.625	8 120	31.6	236	62.3	66.3	15.1	139	43.2	41.3	32.0	0.543
	20	51.8	0.508	6 600	26.2	193	63.0	64.5	12.7	115	43.8	39.5	32.1	0.549
	16	42.0	0.411	5 340	21.6	158	63.5	63.1	10.5	93.8	44.3	38.1	32.3	0.554
	13	34.4	0.337	4 380	17.9	130	64.0	62.0	8.77	77.6	44.7	37.0	32.5	0.557
200X100*	20	44.0	0.431	5 600	22.6	180	63.6	74.3	3.84	50.8	26.2	24.3	21.3	0.256
	16	35.7	0.350	4 540	18.7	147	64.2	72.8	3.22	41.8	26.6	22.8	21.4	0.262
	13	29.3	0.287	3 730	15.6	121	64.6	71.7	2.72	34.7	27.0	21.7	21.6	0.266
	10	22.8	0.223	2 900	12.3	94.8	65.1	70.5	2.18	27.4	27.4	20.5	21.8	0.271
150X100	16	29.4	0.288	3 740	8.40	84.8	47.4	50.9	3.00	40.4	28.3	25.9	21.6	0.434
	13	24.2	0.237	3 080	7.03	70.2	47.8	49.9	2.53	33.7	28.7	24.9	21.7	0.440
	10	18.8	0.185	2 400	5.58	55.1	48.2	48.8	2.03	26.6	29.1	23.8	21.9	0.445
	8	15.2	0.149	1 940	4.55	44.6	48.5	48.0	1.67	21.6	29.3	23.0	22.0	0.448
125X90	16	25.0	0.245	3 180	4.84	58.5	39.0	42.2	2.09	32.0	25.6	24.7	19.2	0.499
	13	20.6	0.202	2 630	4.07	48.6	39.4	41.2	1.77	26.7	26.0	23.7	19.3	0.505
	10	16.1	0.158	2 050	3.25	38.2	39.8	40.1	1.42	21.1	26.4	22.6	19.5	0.511
	8	13.0	0.127	1 660	2.66	31.1	40.1	39.3	1.18	17.2	26.6	21.8	19.6	0.515
125X75	13	19.1	0.187	2 430	3.82	47.1	39.6	43.9	1.04	18.5	20.7	18.9	16.2	0.356
	10	14.9	0.146	1 900	3.05	37.1	40.0	42.8	0.841	14.7	21.0	17.8	16.3	0.363
	8	12.1	0.118	1 540	2.50	30.1	40.3	42.1	0.697	12.0	21.3	17.1	16.4	0.367
	6	9.14	0.090	1 160	1.92	23.0	40.6	41.3	0.542	9.23	21.6	16.3	16.6	0.372
100X90	13	18.1	0.177	2 300	2.17	31.4	30.7	31.1	1.66	25.9	26.8	26.1	18.4	0.796
	10	14.1	0.139	1 800	1.74	24.9	31.1	30.0	1.33	20.5	27.2	25.0	18.5	0.800
	8	11.4	0.112	1 460	1.43	20.3	31.4	29.3	1.10	16.8	27.5	24.3	18.6	0.802
	6	8.67	0.085	1 100	1.11	15.5	31.7	28.5	0.853	12.8	27.8	23.5	18.7	0.805
100X75	13	16.5	0.162	2 110	2.04	30.6	31.1	33.4	0.976	18.0	21.5	20.9	16.0	0.541
	10	13.0	0.127	1 650	1.64	24.2	31.5	32.3	0.791	14.3	21.9	19.8	16.1	0.549
	8	10.5	0.103	1 340	1.35	19.7	31.8	31.5	0.656	11.7	22.2	19.0	16.2	0.554
	6	7.96	0.078	1 010	1.04	15.1	32.1	30.8	0.511	9.01	22.4	18.3	16.3	0.559
90X75	13	15.5	0.152	1 980	1.51	24.8	27.6	29.3	0.946	17.8	21.9	21.8	15.6	0.672
	10	12.2	0.119	1 550	1.22	19.7	28.0	28.2	0.767	14.1	22.2	20.7	15.7	0.679
	8	9.86	0.097	1 260	1.01	16.1	28.3	27.5	0.636	11.6	22.5	20.0	15.8	0.683
	6	7.49	0.073	954	0.779	12.3	28.6	26.8	0.495	8.89	22.8	19.3	15.9	0.687
	5	6.28	0.062	800	0.660	10.4	28.7	26.4	0.421	7.50	22.9	18.9	16.0	0.689
90X65	10	11.4	0.112	1 450	1.16	19.2	28.3	29.8	0.507	10.6	18.7	17.3	13.9	0.506
	8	9.23	0.090	1 180	0.958	15.7	28.5	29.1	0.422	8.72	18.9	16.6	14.0	0.512
	6	7.02	0.069	894	0.743	12.1	28.8	28.4	0.330	6.72	19.2	15.9	14.2	0.518
	5	5.89	0.058	750	0.629	10.2	29.0	28.0	0.281	5.68	19.4	15.5	14.2	0.520

ANSWERS

ODD-NUMBERED PROBLEMS

There may be a minor discrepancy in the third significant figure of numeric values, or in the second decimal place of angles, depending on the number of significant figures used for intermediate steps.

Chapter 1

1-1 $\sin 30° = 0.500$
     $\cos 30° = 0.866$
     $\tan 30° = 0.577$
1-3 $\sin 75.3° = 0.967$
     $\cos 75.3° = 0.254$
     $\tan 75.3° = 3.81$
1-5 $\sin 98° = 0.990$
     $\cos 98° = -0.139$
     $\tan 98° = -7.12$
1-7 $\sin 171.4° = 0.150$
     $\cos 171.4° = -0.989$
     $\tan 171.4° = -0.151$
1-9 $\sin \theta = 0.496$
     $\cos \theta = 0.868$
     $\tan \theta = 0.571$
1-11 $r = 52.0$ mm
     $\theta = 22.62°$
     $\phi = 67.38°$
1-13 $r = 100$ m
     $\theta = 36.87°$
     $\phi = 53.13°$
1-15 $L = 4.47$ m
     $\theta = 26.57°$
1-17 $AB = 2.92$ m
     $\theta = 30.96°$
1-19 $B = 9.01$ m
     $C = 10.0$ m
1-21 $\beta = 78.56°$
     $\gamma = 38.44°$
     $\beta' = 101.44°$
     $\gamma' = 15.56°$
1-23 $AB = 344$ m
1-25 $h = 9.92$ km
1-27 $CD = 3.16$ m
     $DG = 4.24$ m
     $\angle GCD = 71.59°$
     $\angle CDG = 63.41°$
     $\angle CGD = 45.00°$
1-29 $C = 59.5$ mm

1-31 $BC = 96.2$ m
1-33 $BC = 471$ mm
1-35 $\alpha = 36.15°$
1-37 $\alpha = 33.56°$
     $\beta = 50.70°$
     $\gamma = 95.74°$
1-39 $\alpha = 14.36°$
     $\beta = 41.41°$
     $\gamma = 124.23°$

Chapter 2

2-1 $\vec{R} = 125$ N at $53.13°$
2-3 $\vec{R} = 130$ m at $22.62°$
2-5 $\vec{R} = 55.9$ m/s at $153.43°$
2-7 $\vec{a} = 164$ m/s^2 at $328.91°$
2-9 $\vec{R} = 71.7$ m at $77.37°$
2-11 $\vec{R} = 195$ N at $101.21°$
2-13 $\vec{R} = 125$ m at $323.13°$
2-15 $\vec{R} = 130$ N·s at $332.62°$
2-17 $\vec{R} = 90.2$ N·m at $119.50°$
2-19 $\vec{a} = 75.2$ m/s^2 at $30.42°$
2-21 $\vec{R} = 165$ m/s at $176.59°$
2-23 $\vec{v} = 56.3$ m/s at $275.07°$
2-25 $d_x = 16.4$ m
     $d_y = 11.5$ m
2-27 $F_x = 80.0$ N
     $F_y = 60.0$ N
2-29 $s_x = -43.0$ m
     $s_y = 61.4$ m
2-31 $F_x = -360$ N
     $F_y = 150$ N
2-33 $M_x = -17.4$ kN·m
     $M_y = -199$ kN·m
2-35 $S_N = 453$ m
     $S_W = 211$ m
2-37 $v_{180} = 231$ km/h
     $v_{300} = 462$ km/h
2-39 $\vec{A} = 344$ kN at $75°$
     $\vec{B} = 94.8$ kN at $200°$
2-41 $s_{20} = 977$ mm
     $s_{250} = 760$ mm
2-43(1) $\vec{s_1} = 81.1$ m at $90.00°$
     $\vec{s_2} = 60.0$ m at $207.89°$
 (2) $\vec{s_1} = 25.0$ m at $90.00°$
     $\vec{s_2} = 60.0$ m at $152.11°$
2-45(1) $\vec{v_1} = 600$ m/s at $18.81°$
     $\vec{v_2} = 200$ m/s at $147.49°$

 (2) $\vec{v_1} = 600$ m/s at $286.51°$
     $\vec{v_2} = 200$ m/s at $55.19°$
2-47 $\vec{s} = 25.5$ m at $53.96°$
2-49 $\vec{R} = 24.2$ MN at $119.16°$
2-51 $\vec{R} = 97.3$ m/s at $185.23°$
2-53 $\vec{R} = 55.5$ kN at $297.10°$
2-55 $\vec{v} = 76.2$ m/s at $64.72°$
2-57 $\vec{a} = 115$ m/s^2 at $97.36°$
2-59 $\vec{R} = 141$ N at $248.88°$
2-61 $\vec{R} = 284$ kg·m/s at $292.77°$
2-63 $M_O = 300$ N·m
2-65 $M_A = -60.0$ kN·m
2-67 $M_B = 300$ N·m
2-69 $F = 83.3$ N
2-71 $M_A = -272$ kN·m
2-73 $M_A = -195$ kN·m
2-75 $F = 62.1$ N
2-77 $M_A = -300$ N·m
2-79 $M_A = 0$ MN·m
2-81 $M_A = -1650$ kN·m
2-83 $M_A = 1060$ N·m
2-85 $M_O = 480$ kN·m
2-87 $M_O = 720$ N·m
2-89 $M_B = 24.5$ MN·m
2-91 $M_B = -721$ N·m
2-93 $M_A = -1540$ N·m
2-95 $M_A = -2440$ N·m
2-97 $M_A = 40.2$ kN·m
2-99 $M_A = -9.68$ MN·m
2-101 $T = 40.0$ kN·m
2-103 $T = 1200$ N·m
2-105 $T = -5.00$ N·m
2-107 $T = 800$ N·m
2-109 $d = 5.00$ m
2-111 $F = 500$ N
2-113 $F = 250$ kN
2-115 $T = 3.10$ N·m
2-117 $d = 3.33$ m
2-119 $T = -168$ kN·m
2-121 $T = -780$ N·m

Chapter 3

3-1 $\vec{R} = 25.0$ kN at $53.13°$
3-3 $\vec{R} = 3.61$ MN at $123.69°$
3-5 $\vec{R} = 336$ kN at $311.99°$
3-7 $\vec{R} = 257$ N at $48.56°$
3-9 $\vec{R} = 57.9$ kN at $8.02°$
3-11 $\vec{R} = 1190$ N at $252.50°$

3-13 $\vec{R}$ = 8.92 kN at 58.34°
3-15 $\vec{R}$ = 17.5 N at 121.60°
3-17 $\vec{R}$ = 130 kN at 358.91°
3-19 $\vec{R} \cong 0$
3-21 $\vec{R}$ = 114 kN at 124.63°
3-23 $\vec{R}$ = 700 kN at 270.00°
5.71 m right of A
3-25 $\vec{R}$ = 490 N at 90.00°
10.0 m right of A
3-27 $\vec{R}$ = 400 kN at 90.00°
2.25 m left of A
3-29 $\vec{R}$ = 140 N at 0.00°
0.571 m below A
3-31 $\vec{R}$ = 300 kN at 270.00°
2.00 m right of A
3-33 $\vec{R}$ = 7.00 kN at 0.00°
14.6 m below A
3-35 $\vec{R}$ = 22.0 kN at 270.00°
1.68 m right of A
3-37 $\vec{R}$ = 1500 kN at 270.00°
2.50 m right of A
3-39 $\vec{R}$ = 13.7 kN at 270.00°
2.00 m right of A
3-41 $\vec{R}$ = 2400 kN at
270.00°
2.00 m right of A
3-43 $\vec{R}$ = 4900 N at 270.00°
3.33 m right of A
3-45 $\vec{R}$ = 2250 kN at
270.00°
3.83 m right of A
3-47 $\vec{R}$ = 475 kN at 270.00°
7.87 m right of A
3-49 $\vec{R}$ = 5100 N at 270.00°
5.88 m right of A
3-51 $\vec{R}$ = 3000 N at 270.00°
4.67 m right of A
3-53 $\vec{R}$ = 5150 N at 270.00°
3.14 m right of A
3-55 $\vec{R}$ = 1350 kN at 270.00°
4.67 m right of A
3-57 $\vec{R}$ = 1160 N at 257.56°
1.24 m right of A
3-59 $\vec{R}$ = 126 kN at 305.96°
3.05 m right of A
3-61 $\vec{R}$ = 4790 N at 260.04°
4.64 m right of A
3-63 $\vec{R}$ = 5060 N at 217.41°
3.66 m left of A
3-65 $\vec{R}$ = 18.9 kN at 271.61°
6.73 m right of A
3-67 $\vec{R}$ = 337 N at 354.07°
280 mm above of A
3-69 $\vec{R}$ = 11.5 N at 249.49°
6.58 mm left of A

3-71 $\vec{R}$ = 296 N at 248.20°
4.36 m right of A
3-73 $\vec{R}$ = 85.5 kN at 8.69°
0.471 m below A
3-75 $\vec{R}$ = 3240 N at 88.41°
through (0.00, 190)
3-77 $\vec{R}$ = 1020 N at 100.20°
through (7.50, 0.00)
3-79 $\vec{F}$ = 50.0 kN at 90.00°
T = 150 kN·m
3-81 $\vec{F}$ = 250 N at 0.00°
T = −1250 N·m
3-83 $\vec{F}$ = 390 kN at 22.62°
T = −1770 kN·m
3-85 $\vec{F}$ = 750 N at 30.00°
T = 2800 N·m
3-87 $\vec{F}$ = 125 N at 180.00°
T = 0 N·m
3-89 $\vec{F}$ = 32.0 kN at 270.00°
T = −4.14 kN·m
3-91 $\vec{F}$ = 12.9 kN at 270.00°
T = −83.2 kN·m
3-93 $\vec{F}$ = 286 kN at 294.78°
T = −1240 kN·m
3-95 $\vec{F}$ = 584 N at 62.46°
T = 1350 N·m

Chapter 4
4-1 F_{AB} = 250 N
F_{BC} = 150 N
4-3 P = 596 kN
4-5 F_{AB} = 170 kN
θ = 61.93°
4-7 $\vec{F}_A$ = 7850 N at 0.00°
$\vec{F}_B$ = 11 100 N at
135.00°
4-9 F_{AB} = 476 N
F_{BC} = 310 N
4-11 $\vec{F}_A$ = 346 N at 20.00°
$\vec{F}_B$ = 1870 N at 100.00°
4-13 P = 2.25 kN
4-15 F_{AB} = 266 kN
F_{BC} = 342 kN
4-17 $\vec{R}_A$ = 86.0 kN at 90.00°
$\vec{R}_C$ = 260 kN at 160.70°
4-19 $\vec{R}_A$ = 591 N at 56.31°
$\vec{R}_B$ = 262 N at 270.00°
4-21 $\vec{R}_A$ = 2.62 kN at 90.00°
$\vec{R}_C$ = 4.38 kN at 90.00°
4-23 $\vec{R}_A$ = 600 N at 90.00°
$\vec{R}_C$ = 400 N at 90.00°
4-25 $\vec{R}_A$ = 45.0 kN at 90.00°
$\vec{R}_D$ = 55.0 kN at 90.00°
4-27 $\vec{R}_A$ = 644 N at 180.00°
$\vec{R}_D$ = 656 N at 180.00°

4-29 $\vec{R}_A$ = 586 kN at 90.00°
$\vec{R}_D$ = 714 kN at 90.00°
4-31 $\vec{R}_B$ = 1030 N at 90.00°
$\vec{R}_D$ = 371 N at 90.00°
4-33 $\vec{R}_B$ = 20.5 kN at
180.00°
$\vec{R}_D$ = 3.54 kN at 0.00°
4-35 $\vec{R}_C$ = 1330 N at 90.00°
$\vec{R}_D$ = 533 N at 270.00°
4-37 $\vec{R}_A$ = 52.2 kN at 90.00°
$\vec{R}_E$ = 37.8 kN at 90.00°
4-39 $\vec{R}_A$ = 25.0 kN at 90.00°
M_S = 75.0 kN·m
4-41 $\vec{R}_B$ = 500 N at 90.00°
M_S = −150 N·m
4-43 $\vec{R}_C$ = 28.0 kN at 90.00°
M_S = −182 kN·m
4-45 $\vec{R}_A$ = 70.0 kN at 90.00°
M_S = 195 kN·m
4-47 $\vec{R}_A$ = 13.3 kN at 90.00°
$\vec{R}_B$ = 13.3 kN at
270.00°
4-49 $\vec{R}_A$ = 273 N at 270.00°
$\vec{R}_D$ = 273 N at 90.00°
4-51 $\vec{R}_B$ = 51.4 kN at 90.00°
$\vec{R}_D$ = 1.43 kN at
270.00°
4-53 $\vec{R}_A$ = 29.0 kN at 90.00°
$\vec{R}_D$ = 9.00 kN at
270.00°
4-55 $\vec{R}_A$ = 109 kN at 23.42°
$\vec{R}_C$ = 130 kN at 90.00°
4-57 $\vec{R}_A$ = 2.40 MN at 90.00°
$\vec{R}_C$ = 3.40 MN at
151.93°
4-59 $\vec{R}_A$ = 622 kN at 325.75°
$\vec{R}_B$ = 963 kN at 90.00°
4-61 $\vec{R}_A$ = 7.04 kN at 64.79°
$\vec{R}_D$ = 6.82 kN at 90.00°
4-63 $\vec{R}_B$ = 25.1 kN at 90.00°
$\vec{R}_D$ = 7.92 kN at 160.37°
4-65 $\vec{R}_A$ = 1740 N at 106.71°
M_S = 573 N·m
4-67 $\vec{R}_D$ = 13.8 kN at 101.44°
M_S = −34.5 kN·m
4-69 $\vec{R}_A$ = 532 kN at 223.94°
$\vec{R}_D$ = 2490 kN at 90.00°
4-71 $\vec{R}_A$ = 2380 N at 73.90°
$\vec{R}_C$ = 1320 N at 120.00°
4-73 $\vec{R}_A$ = 1.35 MN at 68.33°
$\vec{R}_C$ = 1.96 MN at
320.00°
4-75 $\vec{R}_A$ = 8.00 MN at 90.00°
$\vec{R}_D$ = 6.00 MN at 0.00°
4-77 $\vec{R}_A$ = 31.9 MN at 257.47°
$\vec{R}_B$ = 35.2 MN at 90.00°

Chapter 5

5-1 $\bar{R}_A = 181$ N at $67.49°$

5-3 $\bar{R}_A = 492$ N at $100.00°$

5-5 $m = 92.4$ kg

5-7 $\bar{F}_{AB} = 554$ N at $172.50°$

5-9 $\bar{F} = 392$ N at $270.00°$

5-11 $\bar{P} = 1630$ N at $330.00°$

5-13 $F_{AB} = +83.3$ kN

5-15 $F = 26.7$ N

5-17 $\bar{F}_{AB} = 59.6$ kN at $90.00°$

5-19 $\bar{F} = 112$ kN at $180.00°$

5-21 $T = 736$ N·m

5-23 $T = -3600$ N·m

5-25 $T = 1880$ N·m

5-27 $T = 1.05$ kN·m

5-29 $T = -197$ N·m

5-31 $\bar{P} = 298$ N at $120.00°$

5-33 $F_{AB} = -318$ kN

5-35 $m = 18\ 900$ kg

5-37 $F_{AB} = 8100$ N

5-39 $F_{DE} = 4090$ N

5-41 $F_B = 169$ N

5-43 $\bar{R}_A = 20.0$ kN at $90.00°$
     $\bar{R}_D = 20.0$ kN at $90.00°$

5-45 $\bar{R}_A = 84.9$ kN at
     $135.00°$
     $\bar{R}_D = 60.0$ kN at $0.00°$

5-47 $F_{BC} = -8.86$ MN
     $\bar{R}_A = 3.69$ MN at
     $319.38°$

5-49 $\bar{R}_A = 2560$ N at $339.44°$
     $\bar{R}_G = 3390$ N at $135.00°$

5-51 $\bar{R}_A = 3090$ kN at
     $165.96°$
     $F_{BD} = -3750$ kN

5-53 $\bar{R}_A = 3300$ N at $127.30°$
     $\bar{R}_B = 1790$ N at $90.00°$

5-55 $x = 3.73$ m

5-57 $F_{AB} = +80.0$ kN
     $F_{BC} = -100$ kN

5-59 $F_{AB} = +40.0$ kN
     $F_{AC} = -50.0$ kN
     $F_{BC} = -50.0$ kN

5-61 $F_{AC} = -3100$ N
     $F_{BC} = -15\ 000$ N

5-63 $R_C = 981$ N
     $R_E = 1770$ N
     $R_F = 1530$ N

5-65 $\bar{R}_A = 33.3$ kN at
     $270.00°$
     $\bar{R}_C = 233$ kN at $90.00°$

5-67 $\bar{R}_A = 256$ kN at $102.00°$

5-69 $F_{BC} = 6610$ N

5-71 $\bar{R}_A = 576$ kN at $69.68°$
     $\bar{R}_C = 204$ kN at $191.31°$

5-73 $\bar{R}_C = 4.06$ MN at
     $340.52°$
     $\bar{R}_E = 12.0$ MN at
     $108.62°$

5-75 $R_C = 177$ N
     $R_D = 451$ N

5-77 $\bar{R}_A = 46.2$ kN at $210.00°$
     $\bar{R}_C = 23.1$ kN at $90.00°$
     $F_{AB} = +23.1$ kN
     $F_{BC} = -46.2$ kN
     $F_{AC} = +40.0$ kN

5-79 $F_{AB} = +250$ N
     $F_{BC} = -250$ N
     $F_{CD} = +150$ N
     $F_{AD} = +150$ N
     $F_{BD} = 0.00$ N

5-81 $F_{AB} = -19.2$ kN
     $F_{BC} = -9.63$ kN
     $F_{CD} = -9.63$ kN
     $F_{DE} = +4.81$ kN
     $F_{EG} = +4.81$ kN
     $F_{AG} = +9.63$ kN
     $F_{BG} = -8.33$ kN
     $F_{CG} = +9.63$ kN
     $F_{CE} = 0.00$ kN

5-83 $F_{AB} = -53.3$ kN
     $F_{BC} = -53.3$ kN
     $F_{CD} = -26.7$ kN
     $F_{DE} = +33.3$ kN
     $F_{EG} = -53.3$ kN
     $F_{AG} = -33.3$ kN
     $F_{BG} = 0.00$ kN
     $F_{CG} = +33.3$ kN
     $F_{CE} = -20.0$ kN

5-85 $F_{AB} = -70.8$ kN
     $F_{BC} = -37.5$ kN
     $F_{CD} = +22.5$ kN
     $F_{DE} = +56.7$ kN
     $F_{AE} = +56.7$ kN
     $F_{BE} = +40.0$ kN
     $F_{BD} = -33.3$ kN

5-87 $F_{AB} = -22.5$ kN
     $F_{BC} = -7.50$ kN
     $F_{CD} = -7.50$ kN
     $F_{DE} = -7.50$ kN
     $F_{EG} = +6.50$ kN
     $F_{GH} = +6.50$ kN
     $F_{HJ} = +19.5$ kN
     $F_{AJ} = +19.5$ kN
     $F_{BJ} = 0.00$ kN
     $F_{BH} = -15.0$ kN
     $F_{CH} = +7.50$ kN
     $F_{DH} = 0.00$ kN
     $F_{DG} = 0.00$ kN

5-89 $F_{AB} = -8.20$ kN

$F_{BC} = -6.34$ kN
$F_{CD} = -6.67$ kN
$F_{DE} = -7.45$ kN
$F_{EG} = +4.33$ kN
$F_{GH} = +7.00$ kN
$F_{AH} = +3.67$ kN
$F_{BH} = +5.96$ kN
$F_{CH} = -1.49$ kN
$F_{CG} = -0.746$ kN
$F_{DG} = +5.22$ kN

5-91 $F_{AB} = -475$ kN
     $F_{BC} = -133$ kN
     $F_{CD} = -133$ kN
     $F_{DE} = +167$ kN
     $F_{EG} = +229$ kN
     $F_{GH} = +331$ kN
     $F_{AH} = 0.00$ kN
     $F_{CE} = +50.0$ kN
     $F_{BE} = -62.5$ kN
     $F_{BG} = -438$ kN
     $F_{BH} = -183$ kN

5-93 $F_{AB} = -0.514$ kN
     $F_{BC} = -0.514$ kN
     $F_{CD} = -1.54$ kN
     $F_{DE} = -4.15$ kN
     $F_{EG} = +3.18$ kN
     $F_{GH} = +2.39$ kN
     $F_{HJ} = +2.39$ kN
     $F_{AJ} = +2.39$ kN
     $F_{BJ} = 0.00$ kN
     $F_{CJ} = 0.00$ kN
     $F_{CH} = 0.00$ kN
     $F_{CG} = +1.54$ kN
     $F_{DG} = +1.68$ kN

5-95 $F_{AB} = 0.00$ kN
     $F_{BC} = 0.00$ kN
     $F_{CD} = -6.00$ kN
     $F_{DE} = -9.00$ kN
     $F_{EG} = +5.20$ kN
     $F_{AG} = +10.4$ kN
     $F_{BG} = 0.00$ kN
     $F_{CG} = +5.20$ kN
     $F_{DG} = +5.20$ kN

5-97 $F_{CD} = -1580$ kN
     $F_{DE} = -1660$ kN
     $F_{EG} = -1840$ kN
     $F_{GH} = +1300$ kN
     $F_{HJ} = +1300$ kN
     $F_{JK} = +1580$ kN
     $F_{CJ} = 0.00$ kN
     $F_{DJ} = +525$ kN
     $F_{EJ} = +389$ kN
     $F_{EH} = +500$ kN

5-99 $F_{BC} = -125$ kN
     $F_{BE} = -208$ kN

5-101
F_{EG} = +250 kN
F_{CD} = +2.89 kN
F_{CE} = 0.00 kN
F_{EG} = −2.89 kN

5-103
F_{BC} = −825 kN
F_{CH} = −188 kN
F_{GH} = +938 kN

5-105
F_{BC} = −1500 kN
F_{CG} = +500 kN
F_{EG} = +866 kN

5-107
F_{CD} = −19.4 kN
F_{DH} = −38.9 kN
F_{GH} = +44.7 kN

5-109
F_{AB} = −6.00 kN
F_{BE} = −4.00 kN
F_{DE} = +5.00 kN

5-111
F_{BC} = −5.08 kN
F_{CE} = +6.00 kN
F_{DE} = +4.16 kN

5-113 P = 7.50 kN
5-115 P = 200 kN
5-117 F_{EB} = −961 kN
5-119 F_{GM} = +345 kN

Chapter 6

6-1 d = 11.0 m
6-3 d = 543 mm
6-5 d = 10.8 m

6-7
F_x = 195 kN
F_y = 487 kN
F_z = 292 kN

6-9
F_x = −2.10 kN
F_y = 2.51 kN
F_z = −5.03 kN
$\cos \theta_x$ = −0.349
$\cos \theta_y$ = 0.419
$\cos \theta_z$ = −0.838

6-11
a_x = −373 m/s^2
a_y = 149 m/s^2
a_z = 298 m/s^2

6-13
F_x = −18.9 MN
F_y = −13.5 MN
F_z = 18.9 MN

6-15 M_x = −1480 kN·m
6-17 M_x = 20.3 MN·m
6-19 M_z = −0.849 MN·m
6-21 M_{AA} = −615 kN·m
6-23 M_y = 255 N·m
6-25 M_x = −1.47 MN·m
6-27 M_{AA} = −4.41 kN·m

6-29
R = 85.4 kN
$\cos \theta_x$ = 0.134
$\cos \theta_y$ = −0.134
$\cos \theta_z$ = 0.982

6-31
R = 11.4 kN
$\cos \theta_x$ = 0.453

$\cos \theta_y$ = 0.718
$\cos \theta_z$ = 0.529

6-33
R = 32.8 kN
$\cos \theta_x$ = −0.122
$\cos \theta_y$ = −0.899
$\cos \theta_z$ = 0.421

6-35
R = 11.7 kN
$\cos \theta_x$ = −0.0110
$\cos \theta_y$ = −0.200
$\cos \theta_z$ = 0.980

6-37
R = 120 kN
$\cos \theta_x$ = −0.222
$\cos \theta_y$ = −0.189
$\cos \theta_z$ = 0.956

6-39
R = 109 kN
$\cos \theta_x$ = 0.000
$\cos \theta_y$ = 0.325
$\cos \theta_z$ = −0.946

6-41
Tension = 54.2 kN
Shear = 94.2 kN

6-43
$\bar{R}$ = 120 kN down
at (3.25, 3.58, 0.00)

6-45
$\bar{R}$ = 1250 N down
at (281, 79.0, 0.00)

6-47
$\bar{R}$ = 20.0 kN up
at (0.500, 12.5, 0.00)

6-49
$\bar{R}$ = 80.0 kN down
at (−1.62, −1.25, 0.00)

6-51 D (−9.60, 0.905, 0.00)
6-53 F_{AB} = −488 kN

6-55
F_{AB} = −100 kN
F_{AC} = 88.4 kN
F_{AD} = 88.4 kN

6-57 P = 1520 N

6-59
F_{AB} = −6080 N
F_{AC} = +3090 N
F_{AD} = +3990 N

6-61
F_{AB} = −6.09 kN
F_{AC} = −4.77 kN
F_{AD} = −5.05 kN

6-63 P = 10.4 kN

6-65
F_A = 30.0 kN
F_B = 5.00 kN
F_C = 40.0 kN

6-67
F_B = 981 N
F_D = 654 N
F_E = 327 N

6-69
F_A = 14.4 kN
F_B = 4.38 kN
F_D = 71.2 kN

6-71
F_B = 188 N up
F_D = 125 N down
F_G = 438 N up

6-73
F_{CD} = 9.67 kN
F_{CE} = 9.67 kN
A_x = +7.20 kN

A_z = +12.0 kN

6-75
A_x = +2.00 kN
A_y = −3.00 kN
A_z = +32.0 kN
F_{BE} = 10.0 kN
F_{BG} = 15.0 kN

6-77
F_{CH} = 91.9 N
E_y = −11.0 N
E_z = +88.3 N
G_y = +66.2 N
G_z = −14.7 N

6-79
F_{DE} = 11.5 kN
A_y = 0.00 kN
A_z = 0.00 kN
B_x = +6.62 kN
B_y = +3.31 kN
B_z = +8.83 kN

6-81
F_2 = 1500 N
A_y = −1690 N
A_z = +562 N
C_y = −2810 N
C_z = +938 N

Chapter 7

7-1 F_r = 8.24 N
7-3 P = 172 N
7-5 F_r = 175 N
7-7 F_r = 5.17 kN
7-9 θ = 33.02°
7-11 μ_s = 0.466
7-13 F = 711 N
7-15 F_r = 160 N
7-17 F_r = 376 N
7-19 P = 211 N
7-21 P = 397 N
7-23 F = 185 N
7-25 F_r = 99.4 N
down the plane.
Block is at rest
7-27 μ_s = 0.339
7-29 P = 1750 N
7-31 P = 1810 N
7-33 N = 533 N
7-35 P = 126 N
7-37 P = 4040 N
7-39 m = 262 kg
7-41 P = 6.89 kN
7-43 F = 349 N
7-45 μ_s = 0.994
7-47 μ_s = 0.0326
7-49 θ = 90.04°
7-51 ϕ = 43.47°
7-53 P = 81.5 N
7-55 a = 25.5 mm
7-57 P = 16.7 N
7-59 P = 113 N

Chapter 8

8-1	(4.86, 2.57, 0.00)
8-3	(4.17, 3.03, 0.00)
8-5	(4.12, 2.88, 0.00)
8-7	(1.50, −1.80, 0.00)
8-9	(−0.508, −1.71, 0.00)
8-11	(3.43, 4.29, 3.29)
8-13	(1.43, −1.00, 0.857)
8-15	(2.53, 1.60, 5.13)
8-17	(0.583, 0.250, −0.500)
8-19	(4.46, 5.26, 3.74)
8-21	(0.729, 0.400, 0.250)
8-23	(−5.97, 0.00, 94.3)
8-25	(0.900, 0.400, 0.926)
8-27	(144, 125, 75.0)
8-29	(1.57, 0.911, 0.450)
8-31	(37.5, 0.00, 72.0)
8-33	(0.00, 0.00, 0.818)
8-35	(35.4, 30.0, 34.0)
8-37	(32.5, 58.1)
8-39	(21.3, 82.0)
8-41	(26.2, 44.7)
8-43	(7.50, 82.0)
8-45	(0.00, 171)
8-47	(215, 150)
8-49	(−15.0, 30.0)
8-51	(60.0, 47.4)
8-53	(52.9, −67.6)
8-55	(66.1, 35.5)
8-57	(150, 160)
8-59	(6.83, 14.0)
8-61	(210, 160)
8-63	(64.3, 5.71)
8-65	(10.5, 2.00)
8-67	(158, 44.2)
8-69	(0.00, 256)
8-71	(64.8, 12.8)
8-73	(0.00, −0.420)
8-75	(8.33, 75.0, 33.3)
8-77	(0.0833, −1.25, 0.333)
8-79	(0.143, 0.714, 0.536)
8-81	(57.6, 20.7, 90.5)
8-83	(0.00, 1.00, 0.00)
8-85	(0.553, 0.00, 0.983)
8-87	(49.6, 40.0, 18.5)
8-89	(2.00, 1.00, 2.04)
8-91	(171, 70.0, 50.0)
8-93	(0.00, 0.00, 17.2)
8-95	(0.00, 0.00, 2.62)
8-97	(14.1, 20.0, 49.7)
8-99	(60.0, 29.8, 82.2)

Chapter 9

9-1	$I_x = 0.521 \times 10^6$ mm^4
9-3	$I_x = 1.42 \times 10^6$ mm^4
9-5	$I_x = 13.5 \times 10^6$ mm^4
9-7	$I_y = 6.95 \times 10^6$ mm^4
	$I_y = 0.0173 \times 10^6$ mm^4
9-9	$I_x = 199 \times 10^6$ mm^4
	$I_y = 199 \times 10^6$ mm^4
9-11	$I_y = 4.64 \times 10^6$ mm^4
9-13	$I_x = 7.52 \times 10^6$ mm^4
	$I_y = 1.15 \times 10^6$ mm^4
9-15	$I_x = 37.1 \times 10^6$ mm^4
9-17	$I_y = 5.37 \times 10^6$ mm^4
9-19	$I_y = 88.5 \times 10^6$ mm^4
9-21	$I_x = 4.05 \times 10^6$ mm^4
9-23	$I_y = 5.49 \times 10^6$ mm^4
9-25	$I_x = 1.75 \times 10^6$ mm^4
9-27	$I_{y1} = 8160 \times 10^6$ mm^4
9-29	$b = 199$ mm
9-31	$I_x = 81.8 \times 10^6$ mm^4
	$I_y = 11.7 \times 10^6$ mm^4
9-33	$I_y = 820 \times 10^6$ mm^4
9-35	$I_y = 0.0531 \times 10^6$ mm^4
9-37	$I_x = 5.88 \times 10^6$ mm^4
9-39	$I_x = 100 \times 10^6$ mm^4
9-41	$I_y = 243 \times 10^6$ mm^4
9-43	$I_x = 328 \times 10^6$ mm^4
9-45	$I_{\bar{x}} = 15.9 \times 10^6$ mm^4
	$I_{\bar{y}} = 2.21 \times 10^6$ mm^4
9-47	$I_{\bar{x}} = 0.0944 \times 10^6$ mm^4
	$I_{\bar{y}} = 0.0944 \times 10^6$ mm^4
9-49	$I_{\bar{x}} = 29.8 \times 10^6$ mm^4
	$I_{\bar{y}} = 8.65 \times 10^6$ mm^4
9-51	$I_{\bar{x}} = 13.0 \times 10^6$ mm^4
	$I_{\bar{y}} = 1.26 \times 10^6$ mm^4
9-53	$I_{\bar{x}} = 2.76 \times 10^6$ mm^4
	$I_{\bar{y}} = 1.84 \times 10^6$ mm^4
9-55	$k_x = 36.1$ mm
9-57	$k_y = 100$ mm
9-59	$k = 28.0$ mm
9-61	$k_{\bar{x}} = 21.2$ mm
	$k_x = 36.7$ mm
9-63	$k_y = 32.3$ mm
9-65	$k_x = 76.6$ mm
9-67	$I_y = 51.7 \times 10^6$ mm^4
9-69	$I_x = 435 \times 10^6$ mm^4
9-71	$J_z = 383 \times 10^6$ mm^4
9-73	$J_z = 427 \times 10^6$ mm^4
9-75	$J_z = 147 \times 10^6$ mm^4
9-77	$J_z = 779 \times 10^6$ mm^4
9-79	$J_z = 628 \times 10^6$ mm^4
9-81	$J_z = 37.0 \times 10^6$ mm^4
9-83	$J_z = 1150 \times 10^6$ mm^4
9-85	$J_z = 3.46 \times 10^6$ mm^4

Chapter 10

10-1	$\sigma = 500$ MPa
10-3	$\sigma = 347$ MPa
10-5	$\sigma = 15.7$ MPa
10-7	$P = 15.7$ kN
10-9	27.8 by 27.8 mm
10-11	$\sigma = -21.2$ MPa
10-13	$\sigma = -2.81$ MPa
10-15	$P = 2.65$ kN
10-17	$\sigma = -62.4$ kPa
10-19	$\sigma = -6.67$ MPa
10-21	$m = 7.34 \times 10^6$ kg
10-23	$\tau = 100$ kPa
10-25	$\tau = 141$ MPa
10-27	$b = 25.0$ mm
10-29	$\tau = 88.4$ MPa
10-31	$d = 156$ mm
10-33	$\tau = 728$ kPa
10-35	$V = 8.97$ kN
10-37	$\sigma_{30} = 89.5$ MPa
	$\tau_{30} = 51.7$ MPa
10-39	$\sigma_{60} = -188$ MPa
	$\tau_{60} = 325$ MPa
10-41	$\sigma_{65} = 134$ MPa
	$\tau_{65} = 288$ MPa
10-43	$\sigma_{max} = -56.7$ MPa
	$\tau_{max} = 28.3$ MPa
10-45	$\sigma_{max} = 531$ MPa
	$\tau_{max} = 265$ MPa
10-47	$\epsilon = 0.470 \times 10^{-3}$ m/m
10-49	$\epsilon = -0.002\ 83$ m/m
10-51	$\delta = 1.80$ mm
10-53	$\delta = -1.00$ mm
10-55	% deformation = 35.0%
10-57	% deformation = 0.004 00%
10-59	$E = 210$ GPa
10-61	$\epsilon = -0.400 \times 10^{-3}$ m/m
10-63	$E = 117$ GPa
10-65	$\delta = 3.04$ mm
10-67	$P = 152$ kN
10-69	$\nu = 0.375$
10-71	$\nu = 0.438$
10-73	$G = 56.4$ GPa
10-75	$G = 44.0$ GPa
10-77	$\nu = 0.324$

Chapter 11

11-1	$P = 338$ kN
11-3	$b = 27.8$ mm
11-5	$d = 18.9$ mm
11-7(a)	$\sigma_{all} = 570$ MPa
(b)	$\sigma_{all} = 285$ MPa
(c)	$\sigma_{all} = 190$ MPa
11-9 (a)	$\sigma_{all} = 28.3$ MPa
(b)	$\sigma_{all} = -115$ MPa
11-11	$b = 60.2$ mm
11-13	$\sigma_{max} = 311$ MPa

11-15   P = 18.3 kN
11-17 σ_{max} = 8.95 MPa
11-19   P = 2870 N
11-21(a) σ_c = 135 MPa
   (b) σ_l = 67.5 MPa
11-23(a) σ_c = 30.0 MPa
   (b) σ_l = 15.0 MPa
11-25 σ = 48.0 MPa
11-27   p = 213 kPa
11-29   t = 0.150 mm
11-31 (a) τ = 229 MPa
   (b) σ = 240 MPa
   (c) σ = 360 MPa
11-33 (a) τ = 191 MPa
   (b) σ = 150 MPa
   (c) σ = 125 MPa
   (d) σ = 300 MPa
11-35 (a) τ = 136 MPa
   (b) σ = 94.7 MPa
   (c) σ = 75.8 MPa
   (d) σ = 89.3 MPa
11-37 (a) τ = 191 MPa
   (b) σ = 107 MPa
   (c) σ = 188 MPa
11-39 (a) τ = 58.0 MPa
   (b) σ = 135 MPa
   (c) σ = 112 MPa
   (d) σ = 72.9 MPa
11-41 (a) τ = 212 MPa
   (b) σ = 181 MPa
   (c) σ = 145 MPa
   (d) σ = 250 MPa
11-43   P = 31.4 kN
11-45   P = 59.8 kN
11-47   P = 624 kN
11-49 τ = 73.7 MPa
11-51 τ = 101 MPa
11-53 τ = 81.6 MPa
11-55   q = 1700 kN/m
11-57   P = 391 kN
11-59   P = 262 kN
11-61   d = 52.9 mm
11-63 δ_t = 0.337 mm
11-65   t = 84.7°C
11-67 Δt = 48.6°C
11-69 σ = 136 MPa
11-71   P = 1.00 MN
11-73 Δt = 97.1°C
11-75 Δt = 10.1°C
11-77 σ_A = 22.1 MPa
         σ_E = 6.72 MPa
11-79 σ_C = −10.8 MPa
         σ_S = −103 MPa
11-81 P_A = 12.7 kN
         P_C = −150 kN

11-83 σ_C = 55.6 MPa
         σ_S = 163 MPa
11-85   x = 185 mm
11-87   P = 126 kN
11-89   P = 370 kN

Chapter 12
12-1 τ = 113 MPa
12-3 τ = 159 MPa
12-5(a) τ = 16.1 MPa
   (b) τ = 24.1 MPa
12-7 τ = 93.6 MPa
12-9(a) τ = 44.2 MPa
   (b) τ = 35.3 MPa
12-11 τ = 11.4 MPa
12-13   T = 58.9 N·m
12-15(a) T = 505 N·m
   (b)   T = 488 N·m
12-17   d = 29.4 mm
12-19   d = 109 mm
12-21 τ_{max} = 191 MPa
12-23 τ_{max} = 220 MPa
12-25 τ_{max} = 141 MPa
12-27   T = 45.6 kN·m
12-29   d = 88.7 mm
12-31   T = 11.9 kN·m
12-33 θ = 5.32°
12-35 θ = 2.22°
12-37 θ = 3.86°
12-39   T = 90.2 kN·m
12-41 θ = 4.92°
12-43   T = 340 N·m
12-45   d = 160 mm
12-47 T_L = 2130 N·m
         T_R = 2870 N·m
12-49 T_A = 292 N·m
         T_B = 308 N·m
12-51 τ_A = 26.0 MPa
         τ_M = 54.2 MPa
12-53 T_C = 1020 N·m
         T_S = 184 N·m
12-55 τ_A = 37.9 MPa
         τ_M = 31.0 MPa
12-57   T = 2880 N·m
12-59 τ = 64.0 MPa
12-61 τ = 50.7 MPa
12-63   P = 71.1 kW
12-65   P = 1030 W
12-67   d = 52.3 mm

Chapter 13
13-1   At x = 3 m
         V = 15.0 kN
         M = 45.0 kN·m
         At x = 6 m
         V = −25.0 kN
         M = 50.0 kN·m

13-3   At x = 400 mm
         V = 277 N
         M = 111 N·m
         At x = 800 mm
         V = −173 N
         M = 86.5 N·m
13-5   At x = 4 m
         V = 9.26 kN
         M = 86.1 kN·m
         At x = 7 m
         V = −34.9 kN
         M = 69.7 kN·m
13-7   At x = 1 m
         V = 40.0 kN
         M = 80.0 kN·m
         At x = 2 m
         V = −40.0 kN
         M = 80.0 kN·m
13-9   At x = 700− mm
         V = 26.0 N
         M = 18.2 N·m
         At x = 900 mm
         V = −24.0 N
         M = 18.4 N·m
13-11   At x = 500 mm
         V = 198 N
         M = 174 N·m
         At x = 900− mm
         V = 77.5 N
         M = 217 N·m
13-13   At x = 1 m
         V = −7.85 kN
         M = −7.85 kN·m
         At x = 4 m
         V = −13.7 kN
         M = −37.3 kN·m
13-15   At x = 800− mm
         V = −1310 N
         M = −600 N·m
         At x = 1100 mm
         V = 1200 N
         M = −240 N·m
13-17   At x = 3 m
         V = −3.33 kN
         M = −10.0 kN·m
         At x = 5 m
         V = −3.33 kN
         M = 133 kN·m
         At x = 6 m
         V = −3.33 kN
         M = 130 kN·m
13-19   At x = 100 mm
         V = −150 N
         M = 492 N·m
         At x = 1000 mm

V = −1500 N
M = −250 N·m
At x = 1500 mm
V = −1800 N
M = −1120 N·m

13-21 0 ≤ x ≤ 3
V = 10.0 (kN)
M = 10.0x (kN·m)
3 ≤ x ≤ 5
V = −15.0 (kN)
M = 10.0x − 25.0(x − 3)
(kN·m)

13-23 0 ≤ x ≤ 2
V = 66.7 (kN)
M = 66.7x (kN·m)
2 ≤ x ≤ 6
V = 66.7 −
50.0(x − 2) (kN)
M = 66.7x −
50.0(x − 2)^2/2 (kN·m)

13-25 0 ≤ x ≤ 3
V = −80.0x (kN)
M = −40.0x^2 (kN·m)
3 ≤ x ≤ 4
V = 360 (kN)
M = −240(x − 1.5)
+ 600(x − 3) (kN·m)

13-27 0 ≤ x ≤ 3
V = −40.0 (kN)
M = −40.0x (kN·m)
3 ≤ x ≤ 5
V = −100 (kN)
M = −40.0x −
60.0(x − 3) (kN·m)

13-29 0 ≤ x ≤ 3
V = −4.00x (MN)
M = −2.00x^2 (MN·m)
3 ≤ x ≤ 5
V = 8.00 (MN)
M = −12.0(x − 1.5) +
20.0(x − 3) (MN·m)
5 ≤ x ≤ 6
V = 2.00 (MN)
M = −12.0(x − 1.5)
+ 20.0(x − 3) − 6(x − 5)
(MN·m)

13-31 V_{max} = +8.00 kN
at 0.00 ≤ x ≤ 2.00 m
M_{max} = +16.0 kN·m
at x = 2.00 m

13-33 V_{max} = +5.00 kN
at 0.00 ≤ x ≤ 2.00 m
and V_{max} = −5.00 kN
at 4.00 ≤ x ≤ 6.00 m
M_{max} = +10.0 kN·m
at 2.00 ≤ x ≤ 4.00 m

13-35 V_{max} = +4900 N
at 2.00 ≤ x ≤ 4.00 m
and V_{max} = −4900 N
at 0.00 ≤ x ≤ 2.00 m
M_{max} = −9810 N·m
at x = 2.00 m

13-37 V_{max} = +630 N
at x = 0.00 m
M_{max} = +165 N·m
at x = 525 mm

13-39 V_{max} = −6.50 MN
at x = 4.00 m
M_{max} = −10.0 MN·m
at x = 4.00 m

13-41 V_{max} = +18.3 kN
at 0.00 ≤ x ≤ 1.00 m
M_{max} = +39.2 kN·m
at x = 3.29 m

13-43 V_{max} = +5.50 kN
at x = 2.00 m
M_{max} = −10.0 kN·m
at x = 2.00 m

13-45 V_{max} = −4900 N
at 0.00 ≤ x ≤ 3.00 m
M_{max} = −14 700 N·m
at x = 3.00 m

13-47 V_{max} = −15.0 kN
at 3.00 ≤ x ≤ 4.00 m
M_{max} = −37.5 kN·m
at x = 4.00 m

13-49 V_{max} = +34.3 kN
at x = 0.00 m
M_{max} = −120 kN·m
at x = 0.00 m

13-51 V_{max} = −5.50 kN
at x = 8.00 m
M_{max} = +7.56 kN·m
at x = 5.25 m

13-53 V_{max} = −2000 N
at x = 1.60 m
M_{max} = +1500 N·m
at 0.00 ≤ x ≤
0.800 m

13-55 σ = 60.1 MPa
13-57 σ = 2.67 MPa
13-59 σ = 100 MPa
13-61 σ = 93.8 MPa
13-63(a) σ = 199 MPa
(b) σ = 146 MPa
13-65(a) σ = 4.01 MPa
(b) σ = −2.50 MPa
13-67 W610x101
13-69 S380x64
13-71 P = 1610 N
13-73 σ = 761 kPa
at top fiber

at x = 0.700 m
13-75 σ = −848 kPa
at top fiber
at x = 290 mm
13-77 σ = +47.4 MPa
at top fiber
at x = 200 mm
σ = −30.5 MPa
at top fiber
at x = 600 mm
13-79 σ = +43.6 MPa
at bottom fiber
at x = 2.72 m
σ = −35.6 MPa
at bottom fiber
at x = 1.00 m
13-81 $σ_{max}$ = 90.2 MPa
13-83 $σ_{max}$ = 253 MPa
13-85 $σ_{max}$ = 9.67 MPa
13-87 $σ_{max}$ = 187 MPa
13-89 τ = 6.25 MPa
13-91 τ = 16.9 MPa
13-93 τ = 3.38 MPa
13-95(a) τ = 659 kPa
(b) τ = 1190 kPa
13-97(a) τ = 6.28 MPa
(b) τ = 5.90 MPa
13-99 τ = 706 kPa
at neutral axis
at x = 3.00 m
13-101 σ = 134 MPa
at extreme fibers
at x = 3.00 m
τ = 19.8 MPa
at neutral axis
at 7.00 ≤ x ≤ 9.00 m
13-103 W610x241
13-105 τ = 49.9 kPa
q = 4.99 kN/m
13-107 q = 95.7 kN/m
13-109 s = 32.2 mm

Chapter 14
14-1 δ = −12.4 mm
14-3 δ = −0.933 mm
14-5(a) δ = −8.46 mm
(b) δ = −10.2 mm
14-7 δ = −2.76 mm
14-9 δ = −5.99 mm
14-11 δ = −32.8 mm
14-13 W410x39
14-15 d = 26.1 mm
14-17 δ = −0.401 mm
14-19 δ = −8.48 mm
14-21 δ = +0.417 mm
14-23 δ = −3.89 mm
14-25 δ = −1.75 mm

14-27   P = 7.78 kN
14-29   w = 812 N/m
14-31   W310x21
14-33   h = 71.3 mm
14-35 δ = −30.1 mm
14-37 δ = −1.55 mm
14-39 δ = −25.4 mm
14-41 δ = −2.60 mm
14-43 δ = −6.63 mm
14-45 δ = −1.20 mm
14-47 δ = −2.05 mm
14-49 δ = −5.68 mm
14-51 (a) δ = −21.8 mm
     (b) δ = +7.39 mm
14-53 δ = −0.359 mm
14-55 δ = −0.838 mm
14-57 δ = +46.2 mm
14-59 δ = −7.39 mm
14-61 $\bar{R}_A$ = 396 kN at
         90.00°
         M_S = +480 kN·m
         $\bar{R}_C$ = 104 kN at
         90.00°
14-63 $\bar{R}_A$ = 1210 N at
         90.00°
         $\bar{R}_D$ = 1090 N at
         90.00°
         M_S = −281 N·m
14-65 $\bar{R}_A$ = 30.0 kN at
         90.00°
         $\bar{R}_B$ = 100 kN at
         90.00°
         $\bar{R}_C$ = 30.0 kN at
         90.00°
14-67 $\bar{R}_A$ = 5.50 kN at
         90.00°
         $\bar{R}_C$ = 52.0 kN at
         90.00°
         $\bar{R}_D$ = 7.50 kN at
         270.00°
14-69 $\bar{R}_A$ = 33.4 kN at
         90.00°
         M_S = +23.0 kN·m
         $\bar{R}_C$ = 2.59 kN at
         90.00°
14-71 $\bar{R}_A$ = 1500 N at
         90.00°
         M_{S_A} = +429 N·m
         $\bar{R}_D$ = 1500 N at
         90.00°
         M_{S_D} = −429 N·m
14-73 $\bar{R}_A$ = 136 kN at
         90.00°
         M_{S_A} = +138 kN·m
         $\bar{R}_C$ = 13.9 kN at
         90.00°

         M_{S_C} = −37.5 kN·m
14-75 $\bar{R}_A$ = 249 N at
         270.00°
         M_S = −41.6 N·m
         $\bar{R}_B$ = 988 N at 90.00°
         $\bar{R}_D$ = 461 N at 90.00°

Chapter 15
15-1   kL/r = 121
15-3   kL/r = 100
15-5   kL/r = 42.6
15-7   kL/r = 69.0
15-9   kL/r = 97.4
15-11   kL/r = 150
15-13   kL/r = 90.1
15-15 P_{cr}/A = 15.8 MPa
15-17 P_{cr} = 602 kN
15-19 P_{cr} = 10.4 kN
15-21 P_{cr} = 1160 kN
15-23   W200x27
15-25   112 by 112 mm
15-27 P_{cr}/A = 219 MPa
15-29 P_{cr} = 990 kN
15-31 P_{all} = 23.0 kN
15-33 P_{all} = 949 kN
15-35 P_{cr} = 166 kN
15-37   15.6 by 15.6 mm
15-39   d = 169 mm
15-41   L200x150x13
15-43   W200x42

Chapter 16
16-1 σ_1 = +170 MPa
         σ_2 = −50.0 MPa
         τ_{max} = 110 MPa
         ϕ = 135.00°
16-3 σ_1 = +105 MPa
         σ_2 = +5.00 MPa
         τ_{max} = 50.0 MPa
         ϕ = 63.43°
16-5 σ_1 = +77.6 MPa
         σ_2 = −77.6 MPa
         τ_{max} = 77.6 MPa
         ϕ = 7.47°
16-7 σ_1 = −25.3 MPa
         σ_2 = −115 MPa
         τ_{max} = 44.7 MPa
         ϕ = 148.28°
16-9 σ_1 = +32.1 MPa
         σ_2 = −112 MPa
         τ_{max} = 72.1 MPa
         ϕ = 61.85°
16-11 σ_1 = +88.3 MPa
         σ_2 = −28.3 MPa
         τ_{max} = 58.3 MPa
         ϕ = 15.48°

16-13 σ_1 = +30.0 MPa
         σ_2 = −70.0 MPa
         τ_{max} = 50.0 MPa
         ϕ = 71.57°
16-15 τ_{max} = 75.0 MPa
16-17 σ_1 = +72.4 MPa
         σ_2 = −72.4 MPa
16-19 σ_{max} = +19.0 MPa
         τ_{max} = 12.8 MPa
16-21 σ_1 = +1.70 MPa
         σ_2 = −19.0 MPa
         τ_{max} = 10.4 MPa
16-23 σ_1 = +24.0 MPa
         σ_2 = +12.0 MPa
         τ_{max} = 6.00 MPa
16-25 σ = +227 MPa
16-27 σ = +22.2 MPa
16-29   Top σ = +69.4 MPa
         Bottom σ = −47.9 MPa
16-31 σ = +137 MPa
         at bottom fiber
         immediately left of B
         σ = −130 MPa
         at top fiber
         immediately right of B
         τ = 10.8 MPa
         on neutral plane
         between B and C
16-33 σ = +23.9 MPa
         τ = 19.2 MPa
16-35 σ = 137 MPa
         τ_{left} = 20.3 MPa
         τ_{right} = 14.0 MPa
16-37 τ = 7.75 MPa
16-39 σ_1 = +245 MPa
         σ_2 = −228 MPa
         τ_{max} = 241 MPa
16-41 σ_1 = +3.18 MPa
         σ_2 = −8.21 MPa
         τ_{max} = 5.70 MPa
16-43 σ_1 = +22.0 MPa
         σ_2 = −19.0 MPa
         τ_{max} = 20.5 MPa
16-45 σ_1 = +79.3 MPa
         σ_2 = −2.95 MPa
         τ_{max} = 41.1 MPa
16-47 σ_1 = +13.9 MPa
         σ_2 = −5.42 MPa
         τ_{max} = 9.66 MPa

Chapter 17
17-1   E = 108 GPa
17-3   E = 220 GPa
         σ_y = 280 MPa
17-5 (a) σ_{pl} = 200 MPa
     (b) σ_y = 240 MPa

(c) $E = 80.0$ GPa
(d) $\sigma_u = 255$ MPa
(e) % elongation = 1.20%
(f) $\mu_R = 250$ kJ/m^3
(g) $\mu_T = 244$ MJ/m^3
17-7 (a) $\sigma_y = 290$ MPa
(b) $\sigma_u = 331$ MPa
(c) $E = 111$ GPa
(d) % elongation = 16.0%
(e) % reduction = 20.1%

(f) $\sigma_t = 394$ MPa
(g) $\mu_R = 313$ kJ/m^3
(h) $\mu_T = 52.0$ MJ/m^3
17-9 (a) $\sigma_y = -100$ MPa
(b) $E = 33.1$ GPa
(c) $\sigma_u = -149$ MPa
(d) % deformation = 0.670%
(e) $\sigma_T = 665$ kJ/m^3
17-11 $G = 40.0$ GPa

17-13 $G = 18.1$ GPa
17-15 (a) $G = 0.650$ GPa
(b) $\tau_{ru} = 9.60$ MPa
17-17 (a) $G = 77.9$ GPa
(b) $\tau_{pl} = 150$ MPa
(c) $\mu_R = 144$ kJ/m^3
(d) $\tau_{ru} = 279$ MPa

INDEX

NOTES

NOTES

NOTES

NOTES

NOTES

NOTES